T0350122

ELEMENTS
OF NETWORK
PROTOCOL DESIGN

ELEMENTS OF NETWORK PROTOCOL DESIGN

MOHAMED G. GOUDA

A Wiley-Interscience Publication
JOHN WILEY & SONS, INC.

This text is printed on acid-free paper ⊗.

Copyright © 1998 by John Wiley & Sons, Inc.

No part of this publication may be reproduced, stored in a retrieval system or transmitted in any form or by any means, electronic, mechanical, photocopying, recording, scanning or otherwise, except as permitted under Sections 107 or 108 of the 1976 United States Copyright Act, without either the prior written permission of the Publisher, or authorization through payment of the appropriate per-copy fee to the Copyright Clearance Center, 222 Rosewood Drive, Danvers, MA 01923, (508) 750-8400, fax (508) 750-4744. Requests to the Publisher for permission should be addressed to the Permissions Department, John Wiley & Sons, Inc., 605 Third Avenue, New York, NY 10158-0012, (212) 850-6011, fax (212) 850-6008, E-Mail: PERMREQ @ WILEY.COM.

Library of Congress Cataloging in Publication Data:

Gouda, Mohamed G., 1947–
    Elements of Network protocol design / Mohamed G. Gouda.
        p.   cm.
    Includes bibliographical references and index.
    ISBN 978-0-471-19744-7
    ISBN 0-471-19744-0 (alk. paper)
    1. Computer network protocols.   2. Computer networks.   I. Title.
  TK5105.55.G68   1998
                                                    97-31750
                                                       CIP

10 9 8 7 6 5 4

To
Amal, Nora, and Yehya
with love

CONTENTS

23 RING NETWORKS   425

24 BROADCAST NETWORKS   445

25 PROTOCOL LAYERS AND HIERARCHIES   465

INTRODUCTION

This is a textbook on computer networks and network protocols. As a textbook, it thrives on two ingredients that are absent from many books on the same subject: abstraction and formality. Of particular note, the book introduces an abstract and formal notation for specifying network protocols. This notation is called the Abstract Protocol notation, or the AP notation for short. The AP notation is used in specifying the many networks and many protocols that are covered throughout the book.

BOOK OUTLINE

In some sense, this book tells a "story." It is the story of how messages are transferred from a source computer to a distant destination computer in a computer network. This is a long story, and it is convenient to divide it into seven parts. We outline these seven parts next.

In the first part of our presentation, the syntax and semantics of the AP notation are presented in Chapters 1 through 5. The topics of these chapters are as follows.

i. In Chapter 1, we explain why network protocols need to be specified using an abstract and formal notation.

ii. In Chapter 2, we discuss a number of simple protocols specified using the AP notation.

iii. In Chapter 3, we present the main features of the AP notation.

iv. In Chapter 4, we present some additional features of the AP notation.

v. The semantics of the AP notation, presented in Chapters 2 through 4, is based on the assumption that sent messages are received in the same condition and in the same order in which they were sent. In Chapter 5, we discuss a second semantics of the AP notation that is based on the assumption that sent messages can be corrupted, lost, or reordered before they are received. Both types of semantics are used in this book.

In the second part of our presentation, we discuss how messages are transferred from a computer to a neighboring computer in a network. This part consists of Chapters 6 through 12. The topics of these chapters are as follows.

i. In Chapter 6, we discuss protocols for establishing connections from a computer to a neighboring computer prior to transferring data messages from the former to the later.

ii. In Chapter 7, we discuss protocols for transferring data messages, that belong to different logical streams, as one physical stream.

iii. In Chapter 8, we discuss protocols for detecting message corruption, loss, and reorder when they occur.

iv. In Chapter 9, we discuss protocols by which neighboring computers that exchange messages can recover from message corruption, loss, and reorder when they occur.

v. In Chapter 10, we discuss protocols for controlling the flow of data messages from a computer to a neighboring computer. These protocols ensure that no computer sends data messages at a rate higher than the receiving computer can handle.

vi. In Chapter 11, we discuss protocols that can be used by any computer to check the state, up or down, of any communication line in the computer network.

vii. In Chapter 12, we observe that the protocols in Chapters 8 through 11 can detect and recover from transmission errors, over-flow, and line failures. Then, any protocol that takes full advantage of these protocols can be designed under the assumption that the communication lines between computers are perfect, i.e., they are always up and they never cause message corruption, loss, or reorder.

In the third part of our presentation, we discuss how message transfer between neighboring computers, as discussed in Chapters 6 through 12, can be used to effect message transfer between distant computers. This part consists of Chapters 13 through 16. The topics of these chapters are as follows.

i. In Chapter 13, we discuss protocols for routing each message from one computer to the next, as the message is transferred from its source computer to its destination computer.

ii. In Chapter 14, we discuss protocols for allocating and releasing the needed resources, i.e., computers and communication lines, for transferring messages. Such protocols are called switching protocols.

iii. In Chapter 15, we discuss protocols for controlling congestions that may

arise in a computer network when there are many messages being transferred through the network at the same time.

iv. In Chapter 16, we observe that the protocols in Chapters 13 through 15 can
be used in routing and switching of messages, and in controlling congestions. Thus, any protocol that takes full advantage of these protocols, can be
designed under the assumption that all computers in a network are virtual
neighbors.

In the fourth part of our presentation, we discuss a number of high level issues
concerning the transfer of messages in a computer network. This part consists of
Chapters 17 through 20. The topics of these chapters are as follows.

i. In Chapter 17, we discuss how computers can be named so that it is easier
for human users to remember their names. We also discuss resolution protocols that can be used to deduce from the given name of any computer the address of that computer.

ii. In Chapter 18, we discuss techniques for ensuring that the communication
between any two computers is secure. In particular, we discuss protocols for
providing authentication, privacy, integrity, non-repudiation, and authorization.

iii. In Chapter 19, we discuss data compression protocols whose function is to
reduce the total number of bits that need to be exchanged between any two
computers.

iv. In Chapter 20, we discuss protocols for broadcasting data messages from
one computer to all the computers or to a subset of the computers in a network.

In the fifth part of our presentation, we discuss several issues concerning application programs that can be executed on top of the network protocols discussed earlier. This part consists of two chapters: Chapters 21 and 22. The topics of these
chapters are as follows.

i. In Chapter 21, we discuss common features of application programs. In particular, we discuss the classification of application programs into clients and
servers. We also discuss how clients and servers communicate via sockets
and via remote procedures.

ii. In Chapter 22, we discuss three examples of application programs: one program performs echo, a second program performs file transfer, and a third
program performs remote login.

In the sixth part of our presentation, we discuss protocols for transferring data
messages in two special classes of networks: ring networks (such as token rings) in
Chapter 23, and broadcast networks (such as Ethernets) in Chapter 24.

In the seventh (and last) part of our presentation, we discuss the issue of combining several protocol layers, that perform different functions, into one protocol hier-

archy that performs all these functions. Protocol layers and hierarchies are discussed in Chapter 25.

CASE STUDY

The Internet is used as a running case study throughout the book. Specifically, each chapter in the book ends with a section that relates the formal and abstract concepts discussed in the chapter with the corresponding designs in the Internet. For example in Chapter 13, we formally discuss several routing protocols that include hierarchical routing, default routing, random routing, hot potato routing, distributed routing, backward learning routing, source routing, and mobile routing. We then end the chapter with a discussion on how routing is achieved, using some of these protocols, in the Internet.

EXERCISES

The book has more than 500 exercises. The exercises at the end of each chapter is an integral part of the discussion in that chapter. Most exercises in a chapter ask the student to modify some of the protocols discussed in the chapter, or design new protocols that perform similar functions to those discussed in the chapter.

INTENDED STUDENTS

This book can be covered in a sequence of two one-semester courses. Both courses can be taught to undergraduate seniors or first-year graduate students. Such courses have already been conducted at the University of Texas at Austin, the University of Houston, the University of Nevada at Las Vegas, and the Ohio-State University.

At the University of Texas at Austin, the sequence of two courses is conducted as follows. The first course is offered mainly to undergraduate seniors, and it covers Chapters 1 through 13. The second course is offered mainly to first year graduate students, and it covers Chapters 2 through 4 and Chapters 14 through 25.

ACKNOWLEDGMENTS

To some degree, the scientific vision expressed in this book was made possible, and ultimately inevitable, by the education I received in three universities: Cairo University, University of Waterloo, and the University of Texas at Austin. I will always be grateful for this education.

Two of my former Ph.D. students, Anish Arora and Jorge A. Cobb, carefully read and critiqued earlier versions of this book. Their extensive comments improved the book a great deal, and I am grateful for their contributions.

Other former and current Ph.D. students of mine have greatly influenced the writing of this book, and I am grateful for their influence. They are (alphabetically) James H. Anderson, Chung K. Chang, Sarah Chodrow, Ching H. Chow, Amal El-Nahas, Furman Haddix, Ted Herman, Tommy M. McGuire, Nicholas J. Multari, Marco Schneider, Ambuj K. Singh, Douglas H. Steves, and Phoebe Weidmann.

My friend Hussien Abdel-Wahab at Old Dominion University spent many hours discussing with me the Internet protocols. I cannot thank him enough for his efforts. During the writing of this book, I received ample encouragement and support from my colleagues in the Department of Computer Sciences at The University of Texas at Austin. In particular, I thank Simon S. Lam and Chris Edmonson-Yurkanan, and their colleagues and students for their support.

The Austin Tuesday Afternoon Club, its founder Edsger W. Dijkstra, and its frequence visitors K. Mani Chandy, W. H. J. Feijen, A. J. M. van Gasteren, David Gries, C. A. R. Hoare, Amir Pnueli, and Niklaus Wirth, had great (though indirect) influence on the writing of this book, and I am thankful for their influence.

I am also thankful to the Kuwait Foundation for the Advancement of Science for awarding me the 1993 Kuwait Award in Basic Sciences. The award came at a critical moment while this book was being written and so ensured that the book maintained its original vision and unique style.

During the writing of this book, I spent one summer at Bell Labs at Murray Hill, one summer at the Microelectronics and Computer Technology Corporation at Austin, and one winter at the Eindhoven University of Technology at the Netherlands. I am thankful to these institutions for their generous hospitality and their stimulating environments. I am also thankful to my friends at Bell Labs, Gerard Holzmann, David Lee, Nicholas F. Maxemchuck, and Krishnan Sabnani, for many valuable discussions on network protocols.

Over the past five years, I used earlier versions of this book as a textbook for my classes on Computer Networks at The University of Texas at Austin. These classes were attended by several hundred students, and many of them made helpful comments that improved the presentation. Although I cannot name these students, I am thankful to each one of them.

Earlier versions of this book have also been used in some graduate classes at other institutions. For that, I am thankful to Raymond E. Miller at the University of Maryland at College Park, Jorge A. Cobb at the University of Houston, Ajoy Datta at the University of Nevada at Las Vegas, and to Mike (Ming) T. Liu and Anish Arora at the Ohio-State University.

The two Andrews, Andrew Smith and Andrew Prince, at John Wiley & Sons made the task of publishing this book seem easy and almost enjoyable. I am thankful to both of them.

This book is dedicated to my wife Amal Shaheen and our children Nora and Yehya. In more ways than one, this book was written with them in mind.

This being the last sentence that I write in this book, I can now put down my pen, close my eyes, and savor the moment.

MOHAMED G. GOUDA
Austin, Texas

CHAPTER 1

HOW TO SPECIFY
NETWORK PROTOCOLS

In this chapter, we argue two important points. First, we argue that network protocols should be specified using an abstract and formal notation so that they can be explained clearly and firmly. Second, we argue that the notations, which are commonly used for specifying network protocols, namely the English language, time charts, and the C programming language, are not appropriate for this task. Any reader who already agrees with these two points can skip the current chapter and proceed directly to Chapter 2. For other readers, we start our argument by recalling the "struture" of scientific subjects.

Every scientific (or engineering) subject has a set of concepts and a notation that uniquely define the subject and distinguish it from other subjects. The concepts of a scientific subject define the main objects of the subject, and its notation is used to state relations between different instances of these objects.

An example of a scientific subject is Euclidean geometry. The concepts of this geometry are points, lines, and circles. The notation of this geometry is first order predicate formulas that can be used in stating the relations between a given set of points, lines, and circles.

A second example of a scientific subject is Newtonian mechanics. The concepts of this subject are point objects, forces that act on point objects, and the traveled distances, velocities, and accelerations of point objects. The notation of this subject is time-differential equations (of order 0, 1, and 2) that can be used in stating the relations between the forces acting on a set of point objects and the travelled distances, velocities, and accelerations of these objects.

Choosing the appropriate set of concepts for a scientific subject is a tricky business. It requires achieving a tight balance between two sometimes contradicting concerns, namely our perceptions of nature and mathematical elegance. On one hand, our choice of concepts should be inspired by our perceptions of nature and

1

real-life situations so that relations that can be proven correct between different in-stances of the chosen concepts are valid in real-life situations. On the other hand, our choice of concepts should also simplify the task of proving the correctness be-tween different instances of these concepts.

In order to achieve this later goal, our chosen concepts do not need to closely match our perceptions of nature. They merely need to be appropriate "idealizations" or "abstractions" of these perceptions.

To illustrate this important point, let us return to the Euclidean geometry men-tioned above. One of the main concepts in this geometry is that of a point that has no length and no width. It is easy to argue that such an object cannot exist in nature. Indeed, our perceptions of nature tell us that the mere existence of an object necessi-tates that the object occupies a nonzero area. This implies that an (existing) point should have a nonzero length and a nonzero width. Clearly, Euclid could have cho-sen points with nonzero (but very small) dimensions to match our perceptions of nature. However, the resulting geometry would have been more cumbersome and harder to prove. Luckily for humanity (not to mention millions of high school stu-dents), Euclid had the good sense and great foresight to realize that a simple geom-etry that abstracts nature is far more useful and practical than a complex one that closely matches nature.

There are many other examples of concepts that abstract, rather closely match, our perceptions of nature. One such concept is a line (in Euclidean geometry) that is perfectly straight and has zero width. Another such concept is a point object (in Newtonian mechanics) that has a positive weight but zero dimensions. A third such concept is a wire (in digital networks) whose voltage at any instant is either low or high but never any value in between.

In summary, the concepts of a scientific subject need to be somewhat consistent with our perceptions of nature but do not necessarily need to closely match these perceptions. However, these concepts do need to support mathematical simplicity and effectiveness so that relations between different instances of these concepts can be stated and verified easily.

The scientific subject of this book is network protocols. Network protocols are the hardware and software systems that facilitate the exchange of messages between different computers in a computer network. Like other scientific subjects, network protocols need to have their own concepts and their own notation. The concepts of network protocols are network processes, connecting channels between processes, sending of a message by a process to an outgoing channel, receiving of a message by a process from an incoming channel, and so on. The notation of network proto-cols are needed in order to state the relations between a set of network processes that are connected by a set of channels.

Henceforth, we refer to a statement of the relations between a set of processes that are connected by a set of channels as a protocol specification. We refer to the concepts that underline such a specification as the semantics of the specification and refer to the notation in which the specification is written as the syntax of the specification.

The rest of this chapter is organized as follows. In Sections 1.1 and 1.2, we discuss the traditional semantics and syntax of network protocol specifications and highlight their shortcomings. Then, in Section 1.3, we argue that in order to avoid these shortcomings, we adopt in this book a new syntax and a new semantics for specifying network protocols.

1.1 SEMANTICS OF TRADITIONAL PROTOCOL SPECIFICATIONS

As mentioned above, the semantics of protocol specifications is based on the concepts of network processes, connecting channels between processes, and so on. Unfortunately, the definitions of these concepts are traditionally chosen to closely match our perceptions of nature without any regard to the mathematical elegance that these definitions can provide. The net result is that most existing protocol specifications are hard to prove correct and are hard to appreciate or understand in a formal setting.

We illustrate this point using two examples. In the first example, we compare two possible definitions for the concept of concurrent execution of two actions in different processes. Then in the second example, we compare two possible definitions for the concept of message transmission from a process to another process.

Consider the concept of a process p executing an action C.p while another process q executing another action C.q. How can this concept be defined? The traditional definition of this concept is as follows. Let S.p and S.q denote the time instants when processes p and q start executing actions C.p and C.q, respectively. Also, let F.p and F.q be the time instants when processes p and q finish executing actions C.p and C.q, respectively. In this case, executions of actions C.p and C.q are concurrent if and only if (iff) the two time intervals [S.p, F.p] and [S.q, S.q] overlap.

This definition of concurrent action execution is both good and bad. On one hand, this definition is good because it closely matches our perceptions of nature where concurrent events (in this case, action executions) overlap in time. On the other hand, this definition is bad because it requires many cases to be taken into account when proving some relation in a scenario where actions C.p and C.q are executed concurrently. For example, six of the cases that need to be taken into account are as follows:

i. S.p < S.q < F.p < F.q.
ii. S.p < S.q < F.p = F.q.
iii. S.p < S.q < F.q < F.p.
iv. S.p < S.q = F.p < F.q.
v. S.p < S.q = F.p = F.q.
vi. S.p < S.q = F.q < F.p.

The fact that many cases need to be taken into account when proving such a relation makes the proof long and tedious. Clearly, mathematical elegance is lost.

To regain mathematical elegance, we need to replace the above definition of concurrent execution with another one that abstracts, rather than closely matches, our perceptions of nature. The new definition is as follows. Each action is executed in a single instant. Let T.p and T.q denote the time instants when actions C.p and C.q are executed, respectively. Then, executions of actions C.p and C.q are concurrent iff T.p ≠ T.q along every scenario, T.p < T.q along some scenarios, and T.p > T.q along some other scenarios. (Note that this new definition excludes the possibility of T.p and T.q being equal.)

According to this definition, in order to prove some relation in a scenario, where actions C.p and C.q are executed concurrently, only the following two cases need to be taken into account:

   i. T.p < T.q.
  ii. T.p > T.q.

Clearly, this new definition of concurrent execution is more elegant than the previous one. Therefore, we adopt it in this book.

We now proceed to the second example. Consider the concept of a message m being transmitted from a process p to another process q. How can this concept be defined? The traditional definition of this concept is as follows. Process q has an incoming channel where each message arriving from process p is stored until it is later received by process q. Let S.m be the time instant at which process p sends message m, A.m be the time instant at which message m arrives at an incoming channel of process q, and R.m denote the instant at which process q receives message m from the incoming channel. Then the following inequality holds:

$$S.m < A.m < R.m$$

It follows from this definition that the transmission of message m from process p to process q consists of the following three concepts:

   i. the sending of m by p,
  ii. the arriving of m at an incoming channel of q, and
 iii. the reception of m by q.

Of these three events, only two are important (because they are directly related to the activities of processes p and q): the sending of m by p and the receiving of m by q. Therefore, it would be nice if the definition of message transmission is abstracted to reflect only these two events. This can be accomplished by replacing the above inequality by the following:

$$S.m = A.m < R.m$$

In other words, the transmission of message m from process p to process q is now defined to consist of only two events:

i.   the sending of m by p, causing m to appear in the incoming channel of q, and

ii.   the reception of m by q.

Note that the first event does not closely match our perceptions of nature that there is a nonzero propagation delay for any message when the message is transmitted from a process to an incoming channel of another process. However, by making the propagation delay of every message zero, we simplify the definition of message transmission and make protocol specifications easier to prove correct and easier to understand. In this book, we adopt this new definition of message transmission.

The above discussion concerning the definitions of concurrent execution and message transmission applies to many other concepts of network protocols. Examples of such concepts are occurrence of transmission errors, recovery from transmission errors, timeout actions, and so on. The definitions that we adopt in this book for these (and other) concepts deviate from their traditional definitions, but we end up with a mathematically elegant semantics for protocol specifications. Thus, the resulting protocol specifications are easier to prove correct and easier to understand.

1.2   SYNTAX OF TRADITIONAL PROTOCOL SPECIFICATIONS

So far, we have discussed the semantics of traditional protocol specifications. Now we turn our attention to the syntax of these specifications. Traditionally, the most common forms of syntax for specifying network protocols are the following:

i.   the English language,

ii.   time charts, and

iii.   the C programming language.

Next, we discuss the shortcomings of these forms of syntax and their implied semantics.

The problem of the English language (or any other natural language for that matter) as a specification syntax is its inherent ambiguity: Different words can have similar meanings and the same word can have different meanings. As an example, consider the following five English statements:

Process p sends message m to process q.

Process p transmits message m to process q.

Process p propagates message m to process q.

Process p forwards message m to process q.

Process p delivers message m to process q.

Do these statements have the same meaning? Or do they have different meanings?

Clearly, these questions can never have final answers. As another example, consider the following two English statements:

Process p sends message m to process q.
Process p sends file f to process q.

Should the word send in the second statement be understood in the same way as in the first statement, implying that file f is sent as one message? Or should it be understood differently, implying, for example, that file f can be sent as a sequence of several messages? Again, these questions can never have final answers.

The real problem is not that the ambiguity of the English language cannot be avoided, but that it is usually exploited. Knowing that English specifications are inherently unclear, cannot be proven incorrect, and are expected to be incomplete, one can refer to any English write-up of some network protocol as a specification for that protocol. Indeed, the popular literature of network protocols is full of mostly unclear, incorrect, and incomplete English specifications.

The computing science has matured to the point where it is no longer acceptable to specify a sorting algorithm using the English language. Yet, the network protocol community still finds it acceptable to specify network protocols, which can be more complex than many sorting algorithms, using the English language. This is a sad situation that needs to be corrected. Hence, this book.

The second common syntax for specifying network protocols is time charts. Time charts avoid the ambiguity of the English language by providing exactly one syntax for stating that process p sends message m to process q. This notation is as shown in Figure 1.1.

The problem of time charts, however, is that they are not scalable: time charts that specify simple protocols are quite simple, but those that specify complex protocols are very complex. As an example, consider a simple protocol where process p sends a request message to process q, which replies by sending back a reply message to process p. A simple time chart for specifying this protocol is as shown in Figure 1.2. Now, assume that this protocol is extended slightly to allow process p to send up to three request messages before it receives a reply message for any of

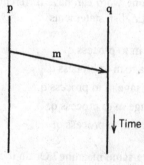

FIG. 1.1

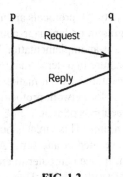

FIG. 1.2

them. Process q still sends a reply message to process p for each request message it receives from p. This extended protocol can be specified using four time charts as shown in Figure 1.3.

If the integer 3 in this extended protocol is replaced by any positive integer n, then the resulting protocol can be specified using $2^{(n-1)}$ time charts! This exponential explosion in the number of needed time charts illustrates that time charts do not provide scalable syntax for specifying network protocols.

The C programming language has also been used extensively in specifying net-

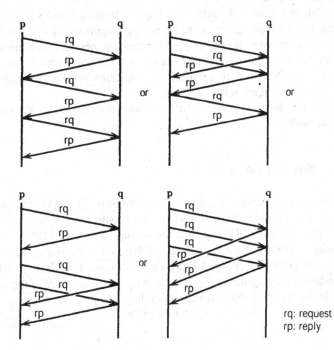

rq: request
rp: reply

FIG. 1.3

work protocols, after all many network protocols are ultimately implemented in this language. However, the C programming language comes with its own well-defined semantics. Moreover, because C is an implementation language, its semantics closely matches our perceptions of nature in order to maximize the execution speed of C programs. This makes the semantics lack the mathematical elegance that we seek and violate our chosen semantics for network protocol specifications.

For example, concurrent executions of actions in C programs that execute in different computers can overlap in time. This violates our chosen semantics where no more than one action can be executed at any time. As another example, message transmission from a C program in one computer to another C program in a second computer takes a nonzero propagation delay. This violates our chosen semantics where message transmission takes zero propagation delay.

From the discussion in this section, we conclude that none of the common syntax for specifying network protocols satisfies our needs.

1.3 NEW PROTOCOL SPECIFICATIONS

In this book, we present a new syntax and semantics for specifying network protocols. Most protocols that we discuss in this book are specified using this syntax and semantics. We refer to this syntax and semantics as the abstract protocol notation, or the AP notation for short.

The AP notation is formal (unlike the English language) and scalable (unlike time charts). Its semantics satisfies two important requirements. First, it is somewhat consistent with but does not necessarily match our perceptions of nature. Second, it provides mathematical elegance (unlike the C programming language) so that proving the correctness of protocol specifications and understanding these specifications in general are relatively easy.

The syntax and semantics of the AP notation are discussed in great detail in Chapters 2 through 5.

1.4 BIBLIOGRAPHICAL NOTES

The idea that network protocols need to be specified formally and their formal specifications need to be analyzed is discussed and promoted in Bochmann [1975], Gouda [1977], Holzmann [1978], Bochmann and Sunshine [1980], Danthine [1980], Hailpern [1980], Zafiropulo et al. [1980], Vissers and Logrippo [1985], Ural and Probert [1986], Brinksma [1988], Liu [1989], and Holzmann [1991].

A method for verifying network protocols that are specified using the AP notation, is outlined in Gouda [1993]. A method for implementing, prototyping and executing these protocols is described in McGuire [1994].

CHAPTER 2

FIRST PROTOCOL EXAMPLES

Informally, a network protocol is a set of rules that govern the exchange of messages between two or more processes in a network (of processes). This characterization of network protocols is rather loose; after all what do the terms *rules, govern, exchange, messages, processes,* and *network* mean? To give some intuitive meaning to these terms, we discuss in this chapter three protocol examples. The first protocol, in Section 2.1, governs the message exchange between a customer process and a vending machine process. The second protocol, in Section 2.2, governs the exchange of request and reply messages between two identical processes. The third protocol, in Section 2.3, governs the transmission of data bits from a sender process to a receiver process.

We start each example by describing some protocol in English, then show how the same protocol can be specified in the AP notation. The AP notation is not introduced formally until the next chapter. Thus, we advise the keen reader to gloss over the current chapter in a hurry and not try to follow it in great detail until after reading the next chapter.

2.1 A VENDING MACHINE PROTOCOL

Consider a network that consists of two processes: process c and process v. Process c represents a customer, and process v represents a vending machine. The rules of communication for process c are as follows:

Rule 1   At every instant, process c is either ready or not ready.

Rule 2   When process c is ready, it can send money and selection messages to process v and become not ready.

9

Rule 3 When process c receives back an item message from process v, it becomes ready.

Based on these three rules, process c can be defined as follows:

```
process c

var     readyc          :         boolean

begin
        readyc                    ->    send money to v;
                                        send selection to v;
                                        readyc := false
[]      rcv item from v   ->    readyc := true
end
```

Rule 1 is represented as a declaration of variable readyc in process c. Variable readyc is of type boolean and so its value at any instant is either true or false.

Rule 2 is represented as the following action in process c.

```
readyc        ->    send money to v;
                    send selection to v;
                    readyc := false
```

This action is enabled for execution when variable readyc is true. When this happens, the action can be executed by first sending a money message to process v, then sending a selection message to process v, then assigning readyc the value false.

The sent messages "reside" in the channel from process c to process v until they are received, one by one, by process v. Messages that reside simultaneously in a channel form a sequence <m.1; m.2; ... ; m.r> in accordance with the order in which they have been sent. The head message in the sequence m.1 is the earliest sent, and the tail message in the sequence m.r is the latest sent. The order of messages in the sequence is important because it is the same order in which the messages are to be received. The head message m.1 is received first, then message m.2 is received second, and so on. Thus if the above action is executed starting from a state where the channel from process c to process v is empty, then the action execution ends in a state where this channel has the message sequence <money; selection>. Starting from this state, process v can first receive the money message, then receive the selection message.

Rule 3 is represented as the following action in process c:

```
rcv item from v     ->    readyc := true
```

This action is enabled for execution when an item message becomes the head message in the message sequence in the channel from process v to process c. When this happens, the action can be executed by first removing the head item message from the channel, then assigning variable readyc the value true.

When only one action of process c is enabled for execution, then only that action can be executed. When neither action of process c is enabled for execution, then neither action is executed. When both actions of process c are enabled for execution, then only one of them, selected arbitrarily, can be executed.

The execution of an action is atomic. This means that actions in a protocol are executed one at a time, and once the execution of an action starts, it continues without interruption until it is finished. Thus, one action execution cannot start while another action execution is in progress.

The rules of communication for process v are as follows:

Rule 4   At every instant, process v is either ready or not ready.

Rule 5   When process v receives a money message from process c, it becomes ready.

Rule 6   When process v receives a selection message from process c, it checks whether or not it is ready. If it is ready, process v sends an item message to process c and becomes not ready. Otherwise, process v does nothing.

Based on these rules, process v can be defined as follows:

```
process v

var     readyv        :        boolean

begin
        rcv money from c        —>    readyv := true

□       rcv selection from c  —>
                                 if readyv  —> send item to c
                                 □ ~readyv  —> skip
                                 fi; readyv := false
end
```

Rule 4 is represented as a declaration of variable readyv in process v. Each of the other two rules is represented as one action in process v.

According to this protocol, if an "unaware" customer, one that is defined by a process other than the earlier process c, sends five successive money messages followed by five successive selection messages, process v sends back only one item message and still keeps all five money messages. This feature is somewhat unfair to the unaware customer and should be modified. The modification consists of replacing Rule 5 by the following rule:

Rule 5a   When process v receives a money message, it checks whether or not it is ready. If it is ready, it sends back the money message. Otherwise, it becomes ready.

This modification can be accommodated in the definition of process v by modifying the first action of v to become as follows:

```
rcv money from c  ->
                    if readyv   -> send money to c
                    [] ~readyv  -> readyv := true
                    fi
```

2.2 A REQUEST–REPLY PROTOCOL

Consider a protocol that governs the exchange of request and reply messages between two identical processes in a network. The protocol consists of two simple rules:

Rule 1   Each process can send request messages to the other process.

Rule 2   When a process receives a request message from the other process, it sends back a reply message.

These two rules may seem acceptable at first, but careful examination of Rule 1 uncovers a problem. Rule 1 allows a process to send any number of successive request messages without ever having to receive or reply to any of the request messages from the other process. Thus, the number of request messages in the two channels can grow beyond any bound. This possibility can be avoided by replacing Rule 1 by two rules, Rules 1a and 1b, as follows:

Rule 1a   At every instant, each process is either ready or not ready.

Rule 1b   A ready process can send one request message to the other process and become not ready.

Rule 2   When a process receives a request message from the other process, it sends back a reply message.

This modification guarantees that, once a process sends one request message, it cannot send a second request message until it receives a reply for the first message. Unfortunately, this modification prevents each process from sending more than one request message in its entire lifetime. This is because the modified protocol does not specify how to make a process ready once it has become not ready. The situation can be corrected by adding one more rule to the protocol. The protocol now has the following four rules.

Rule 1a   At every instant, each process is either ready or not ready.

Rule 1b A ready process can send one request message to the other process and then becomes not ready.

Rule 2 When a process receives a request message from the other process, it sends back a reply message.

Rule 3 When a process receives a reply message, it becomes ready.

From these rules, one of the two processes, p, can be defined as follows (the other process, q, is identical to p except for replacing each occurrence of p by q and replacing each occurrence of readyp by readyq, and vice versa):

process p

var readyp   :   **boolean**

begin
          readyp   —>   **send** request **to** q;
                                              readyp := **false**
☐   **rcv** request **from** q   —>   **send** reply **to** q
☐   **rcv** reply **from** q —> readyp := **true**
end

Note that, in accordance with Rule 1a, process p has one boolean variable readyp. Each of the remaining three rules is represented as an action in process p. For example, Rule 3 is represented as the action

rcv reply **from** q   —>   readyp := **true**

This action is enabled for execution when the head message in the channel from process q to process p is a reply message. When this happens, the action can be executed by first removing the head reply message from the channel from q to p, then assigning variable readyp the value true.

At each instant, each process in this protocol has at most one outstanding request message, that is, a request message that has been sent by the process and for which no reply message has been received by the process. This feature can be generalized by allowing each process to have at most n outstanding request messages. The generalization can be achieved by making the values of variable readyp range over the domain $0..n$ instead of the mere boolean domain. The generalized process p can be defined as follows:

process p

const   n

var   readyp   :   0..n   {comment: readyp = n, initially}

```
begin
        readyp > 0                    -> send request to q;
                                         readyp := readyp - 1
  []    rcv request from q    ->          send reply to q
  []    rcv reply from q  ->   readyp := readyp + 1
end
```

Note that n is declared as a constant in both process p and process q. As discussed later, this means that n is of type positive integer and that its value in process p is the same as its value in process q.

2.3 A MANCHESTER ENCODING PROTOCOL

Consider a protocol that governs the sending of bits from one process s (for sender) to another process r (for receiver). The rules of communication for process s are as follows:

Rule 1   Process s has an infinite array, called data, of 0 and 1 bits.

Rule 2   Process s sends the bits of array data, one by one, to process r.

Rule 3   If the next bit to send is 0, process s sends a message one followed by a message zero. If the next bit to send is 1, process s sends a message zero followed by a message one.

According to Rule 3, each 0 bit is encoded as a sequence of two messages, one followed by zero, and each 1 bit by a sequence of two messages, message zero followed by message one. This encoding is called a Manchester encoding.

From these three rules, process s can be defined as follows:

```
process s

inp    data  :  array [integer] of 0..1

var    x     :  integer

begin
        true  -> if data[x] = 0 -> send one to r;
                                    send zero to r
                 [] data[x] = 1 -> send zero to r;
                                    send one to r
                 fi; x := x + 1
end
```

Process s has one input, namely the infinite array data. This array is declared as an input of process s because its elements are read, but never written, by the statements of process s. Process s also has one variable x. Variable x is read and written by the statements of process s. This variable serves as a pointer to the next element to send in array data.

Process s has only one action. In this action, the value of the x-th element of array data is checked. If this value is 0, process s sends a message one followed by a message zero to process r. If this value is 1, process s sends a message zero followed by a message one to process r. In either case, the value of x is incremented by 1 so that the next element in array data becomes the current element in the array before the action is executed one more time.

The rules of communication for process r are as follows:

Rule 4   Process r has an infinite array, called rcvd, of 0 and 1 bits. Process r uses this array to store the received bits from process s.

Rule 5   The value of each element in array rcvd eventually becomes equal to the value of the corresponding element in array data in process s.

Based on these rules, process r can be defined as follows:

process r

```
var    rcvd  :      array [integer] of 0..1,
       y     :      integer,
       str   :      boolean      {initially, str = false}

begin
       rcv zero from s --> if str --> rcvd[y], y := 0, y+1
                           [] ~str --> skip
                           fi; str := ~str
  []       rcv one from s --> if str --> rcvd[y], y := 1, y+1
                           [] ~str --> skip
                           fi; str := ~str
end
```

Process r has an integer variable y that serves as a pointer to the next element in array rcvd. Process r also has a boolean variable named str. When r receives a message, the value of str is checked. If this value is true, the value of the message is assigned to the current element of array rcvd. If this value is false, the message is discarded. In either case, the value of str is changed (from true to false or from false to true).

Note that the receiver process r does not make full use of the Manchester encoding. In particular, process r discards all even messages without checking that the Manchester encoding has been followed. In Section 5.3, we discuss another receiver process for this protocol that makes a better use of the Manchester encoding to recover from transmission errors, when they occur.

It is clear from the three protocol examples in this chapter that protocols can be defined as networks of communicating processes. In the next two chapters, we present the syntax and semantics of a formal notation for defining network processes.

2.4 THE CURRENT INTERNET

The Internet is the computer network that spans the globe, and we use it as a running case study throughout this book. We start the case study in this section by giving an overview of the architecture of the Internet.

The Internet consists of a large number of connected networks. Each network consists of a large number of subnetworks, with two or more computers attached to each subnetwork.

The computers attached to a subnetwork are of two types: hosts and routers. A host is usually attached to one subnetwork, while a router is attached to two or more subnetworks. The function of a host is to host and execute the application programs of its users. Executing an application program in a host sometimes causes the host to exchange messages with other hosts. The exchanged messages between hosts travel over the subnetworks to which the hosts are attached. The function of a router is to route the exchanged messages between hosts by transferring them between the different subnetworks to which the router is attached.

Figure 2.1 shows an example of a network in the Internet. This network consists of 10 subnetworks, s.0 to s.9, 15 hosts, H.0 to H.14, and 5 routers, R.0 to R.4. Attached to each subnetwork are several computers. For example, attached to subnetwork s.0 are 2 hosts, H.0 and H.1, and 1 router, R.0. Attached to subnetwork s.2 are 3 routers, R.0, R.1, and R.3. The function of router R.0 is to transfer messages between the 3 subnetworks s.0, s.1, and s.2 to which R.0 is attached.

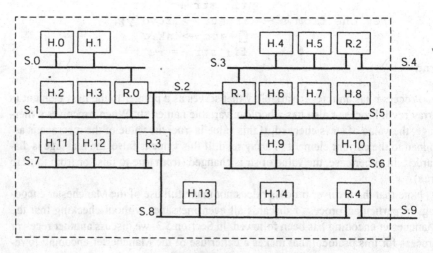

FIG. 2.1

The network in Figure 2.1 is connected to the rest of the Internet by the two routers R.2 and R.4. Thus, each of these two routers, R.2 and R.4, is called a gateway for the network. If host H.0 sends a message intended for a host outside the network in, the message needs to travel from host H.0 either to gateway R.2 (where it leaves the network via subnetwork s.4) or to gateway R.4 (where it leaves the network via subnetwork s.9). A possible route for a message to travel from host H.0 to gateway R.4 consists of three hops: from H.0 to R.0 via s.0, from R.0 to R.3 via s.2, and from R.3 to R.4 via s.8.

A subnetwork is a medium for transmitting data messages between different computers attached to the subnetwork. Examples of subnetworks are local area networks (e.g., Ethernets or token rings), telephone lines, and satellite links. A subnetwork provides three modes for transmitting messages: unicast (or one to one), multicast (or one to some), and broadcast (or one to all). In a unicast mode, a message is transmitted to a specified computer attached to the subnetwork. In a multicast mode, a message is transmitted to one or more specified computers attached to the subnetwork. In a broadcast mode, a message is transmitted to every computer attached to the subnetwork (other than the computer that sent the message). Note that if a subnetwork is a wire connecting two computers, then transmitting a message over the subnetwork in a unicast mode has the same effect as transmitting the message in a multicast or broadcast mode.

Each computer in the Internet has one Internet protocol process, also called IP process, and one interface process for each subnetwork to which the computer is attached. Thus, a host has one IP process and one interface process (because it is attached to one subnetwork), whereas a router has one IP process and two or more interface processes (one for each subnetwork to which the router is attached). The IP process in a computer is placed on top of the interface process(es) in that computer. We delay discussing the IP processes until Section 3.4 and discuss the Interface processes next.

The function of an interface process in a computer is to receive messages from the IP process in that computer and forward them over a subnetwork to which the computer is attached. The interface process also receives messages from the subnetwork and forwards them to the IP process in the computer. In other words, an interface process acts as an "interface" between the IP process in that computer and a subnetwork to which the computer is attached.

When the interface process in a computer receives a message from the IP process in its computer, it adds a header and a tail to the message before forwarding the message over the subnetwork. The added header defines the hardware address of the computer (or computers) that should receive the message. The added tail has a checksum for detecting whether the message has been corrupted during transmission over the subnetwork.

As a message is transmitted over a subnetwork, the interface process of each computer attached to the subnetwork examines the message header and determines whether or not it should receive a copy of the message. If the interface process in a computer does receive a copy of the message, it examines the message tail to check whether or not the message has been corrupted during transmission. If the message

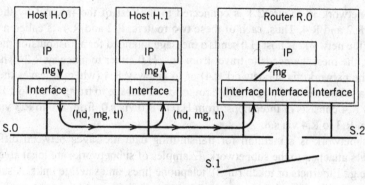

FIG. 2.2

has been corrupted, the interface process discards the received message. Otherwise, the interface process removes the header and tail from the message and forwards the resulting message to the IP process in its computer.

Figure 2.2 illustrates the transmission of a message from host H.0 in a broadcast mode to both host H.1 and router R.0 over subnetwork s.0. The IP message mg is first sent from the IP process to the interface process in host H.0. The interface process in H.0 attaches a header hd to message mg to specify that the message is transmitted in a broadcast mode. It also attaches a tail tl to message mg, then forwards the message over subnetwork s.0. Because the message is transmitted in a broadcast mode, the interface process of each computer attached to s.0 receives a copy of the (hd, mg, tl) message, removes the attached header and tail, then forwards the resulting IP message mg to the IP process in its computer.

2.5   BIBLIOGRAPHICAL NOTES

Formal specifications of network protocols can be used in establishing the correctness of protocols as discussed in Karp and Miller [1969], Owicki and Gries [1976], Bochmann and Gecsei [1977], Gouda [1977, 1993], Hailpern [1980], Milner [1980], Holzmann [1982], Owicki and Lamport [1982], Hoare [1984], Clarke et al. [1986], Maxemchuck and Sabnani [1987], Chandy and Misra [1988], Lundy and Miller [1991], and Liu and Miller [1996].

Moreover, formal specifications of network protocols can be used in generating test sequences for these protocols as discussed in Sabnani and Dahbura [1988], Aho et al. [1988], Chan et al. [1989], Sidhu and Leung [1989], Lee and Yannakakis [1994, 1996], and Miller and Paul [1994].

Formal specifications of network protocols can also be part of any formal method for designing these protocols, as discussed in Bochmann and Sunshine [1980], Merlin and Bochmann [1983], and Holzmann [1984].

EXERCISES

1   (Vending Machine). Modify the vending machine protocol in Section 2.1 to allow process c to send two types of money messages to process v: smoney (for small money) and lmoney (for large money). The value of an lmoney is twice that of an smoney. The cost of each item in the vending machine is smoney. Therefore, if process c sends an lmoney message followed by a selection message to process v, then process v returns back an item message followed by either an smoney message (if process v has smoney) or a sorry message (if process v does not have smoney).

2   (Vending Machine). Modify the protocol in exercise 1 to allow process v to send two types of item messages to process c: sitem (for small item) and litem (for large item). The cost of each sitem is smoney and the cost of each litem is lmoney. Process c can send two types of selection messages: ssel (for selecting a small item) and lsel (for selecting a large item). If process c sends an lmoney message followed by an ssel message, then process v returns back an sitem message followed by either an smoney message (if process v has smoney) or a sorry message (if process v does not have smoney). If process c sends an smoney message followed by an lsel message, then process v returns back a sorry message.

3   (Vending Machine). Modify the protocol in exercise 2 to allow process v to keep track of the number of items it has. If process c selects a small (or large) item when v has no small (or large, respectively) items, then process v returns the money it received from process c.

4   (Half-Duplex Communication). It is required to design a protocol between two processes p and q that exchange data messages such that at each instant no more than one process can send data messages to the other process. This requirement is achieved by the two processes taking turns in sending data messages. When the turn of a process is up, the process sends an arbitrary number (possibly zero) of data messages, then sends a return message to inform the other process that its turn is up, and so on. Design processes p and q.

5   (Memory System). Consider a network that consists of three processes c, h, and m. Process c represents a cpu, process h represents a cache memory, and process m represents a memory. The processes communicate according to the following three rules:

  a Process c sends a request message to process h, requesting a word from the cache memory, then waits to receive the (requested) word message from process h before sending the next request message to process h, and so on.

  b When process h receives a request message from process c, it decides nondeterministically either to send a word message to c or to send a fault message to m. In case h sends a fault message to m, h waits to receive a page message from m before sending a word message to c.

c When process m receives a fault message from process h, it sends a page
message to h.

Design the three processes c, h, and m.

6 (Multiplexing). Consider a network of six processes s_0, s_1, p, q, r_0, and r_1.
Processes s_0 and s_1 send data messages to process p. Process p receives each
data message from process s_0 and forwards it as a message zero to process q.
Similarly, process p receives each data message from process s_1 and forwards
it as a message one to process q. Process q forwards each message zero as a
data message to process r_0 and forwards each message one as a data message
to process r_1. Design processes s_0, p, q, and r_0. (Processes s_1 and r_1 are symmetric to processes s_0 and r_0, respectively.)

7 (Traffic Light System). Two processes p and q represent two traffic lights at an
intersection of two streets. Each of the processes has a variable, named st,
whose value is one of the following: 0 (for red), 1 (for green), and 2 (for yellow). As expected, these values are assigned to each st variable in a cyclic
fashion, from 0 to 1, from 1 to 2, and from 2 to 0. It is required to design a
protocol for the communication between p and q to ensure that the two st variables never have value 1 at the same time. Design p and q.

8 (Encoding/Decoding Protocol). A process s has an infinite array, named data,
where the value of each element is 0, 1, or 2. Process s encodes the values of
these elements, one by one, and sends them to a process r using zero and one
messages as follows.

a. A value 0 is sent as a message zero.

b. A value 1 is sent as a message one followed by a message zero.

c. A value 2 is sent as a sequence of two messages, each is a message one.

Process r receives the zero and one messages and decodes them into 0, 1, and
2 values before storing them in an infinite array, named rcvd. Design processes s and r.

9 (Broadcast). A process p sends two identical streams of blocks of data messages to two processes q and r. Each sent block consists of an arbitrary number
of data messages followed by a mark message that signals the end of the
block. Process p does not send the messages of a block until it is sure that the
messages of the previous block have been received by both q and r. Design
processes p and q. (Process r is identical to process q.)

10 (Telephone System). Two identical processes p and q represent two phones.
Each process can send a dialup message to the other process, then wait to receive a leftup message from the other process. After receiving the leftup message, the process sends a hangup message, then waits to receive a hangup
message before it can send the next dialup message and the cycle repeats. It is
possible that after a process sends a dialup message, the process receives a dialup message (indicating that the two phones are trying to call one another at
the same time). When this happens, each process sends a busy message to the

other process. After a process receives a busy message, the process can send the next dialup message and the cycle repeats. Design process p.

11 (Telephone System). Modify the protocol in exercise 10 to allow each process to send talk messages after that process has sent or received a leftup message and before that process has sent or received a hangup message.

CHAPTER 3

NETWORK PROCESSES

A protocol is defined as a network of processes. The processes in a network communicate with one another by sending and receiving messages over unbounded channels that connect the processes. The processes in a network do not communicate with any agent outside the network. In other words, networks are closed.

In general, a process in a network is of the following form:

```
process   <process name>

const <const name>, ... , <const name>
inp   <inp name> : <inp type>, ... , <inp name> : <inp type>
var   <var name> : <var type>, ... , <var name> : <var type>

begin
      <action> [] ... [] <action>
end
```

The definition of a process consists of two parts. In the first part, constants, inputs, and variables of the process are declared. In the second part, actions of the process are defined. Note that successive declarations of constants, inputs, or variables are separated by commas, whereas successive definitions of actions are separated by boxes. Comments can appear anywhere in a process definition between curly brackets.

The rest of this chapter is organized as follows. Declarations of constants, inputs, and variables are discussed in Section 3.1. Action definitions are presented in Section 3.2. Then network execution is discussed in Section 3.3. Finally, we discuss how protocols in the Internet can be viewed as networks of processes in Section 3.4.

3.1   CONSTANTS, INPUTS, AND VARIABLES

Constants are declared in a process as follows:

```
const <const name>, ... , <const name>
```

A constant can be read, but not written, by the actions of its process. Names of constants are global: If two constants in different processes have the same name, then they also have the same value. Each constant is of type positive integer.

Inputs are declared in a process as follows:

```
inp <inp name> : <inp type>, ... , <inp name> : <inp type>
```

An input can be read, but not written, by the actions of its process. Names of inputs are local: if two inputs in different processes have the same name, then they may have different values and may even be of different types. Inputs are of six types: boolean, range, integer, set, enumerated, and array. We discuss each of these types in order.

An input of type boolean is declared as follows.

```
<inp name> : boolean
```

The value of a boolean input is either true or false.

An input of type range is declared as follows:

```
<inp name> : <lower bound> .. <upper bound>
```

Both the lower and upper bounds are nonnegative integers, and the lower bound is less than or equal to the upper bound. The value of a range input is an integer in the closed interval defined by the two bounds of the input.

An input of type integer is declared as follows:

```
<inp name> : integer
```

The value of an integer input is a nonnegative integer.

An input of type set is declared as follows:

```
<inp name> : set {<member>|<condition involving member>}
```

The value of a set input is the set of all nonnegative integers that satisfy the condition in the set declaration. We require that the specified set be nonempty and finite.

An input of type enumerated is declared as follows:

```
<inp name> : <name of an input of type set>
```

The value of an enumerated input is an integer in the set in its declaration.

An input of type array is declared as follows:

```
<inp name> : array [<index type list>] of <element type>
```

The index type list consists of one or more index types separated by commas. Each index type is one of the following: boolean, range, integer, or enumerated. The element type is also one of the following: boolean, range, integer, or enumerated.

Variables are declared in a process as follows:

```
var <var name> : <var type>, ... ,<var name> : <var type>
```

Variables declared in a process can be read and written by the actions of that process. Variables are of the following five types: boolean, range, integer, enumerated, and array. A variable of some type is declared in the same way as an input of the same type.

3.2   ACTIONS

An action of process p is of the form.

```
<guard of p> —> <statement of p>
```

Next, we describe the three forms of a guard and the six forms of a statement. We also describe the execution of each statement form.

A guard of process p is one of the following: a local guard of p, a receiving guard of p, or a timeout guard. We discuss each of these in turn.

A local guard of process p is a boolean expression that involves equality relations, logical operations, arithmetic operations, and the constants, inputs, and variables of process p:

   i. There are six equality relations:

      = (for equal) $\neq$ (for not equal)
      < (for less than) $\leq$ (for at most)
      > (for greater than) $\geq$ (for at least)

  ii. There are three logical operations:

      $\lor$ (for or) $\land$ (for and)   ~ (for not)

 iii. There are seven arithmetic operations:

      + (for integer addition)
      – (for integer subtraction)
      * (for integer multiplication)
      $+_n$ (for addition modulo n)

$-_n$ (for subtraction modulo n)
min (for computing integer minimum)
max (for computing integer maximum)

A receiving guard of process p is of the form

```
rcv <message of p> from <process name q>
```

A message of process p is a noninterpreted symbol. Process q is different from process p; thus a process cannot receive a message from or send a message to, itself.

A timeout guard is of the form

```
timeout <protocol predicate>
```

A protocol predicate is a boolean expression that involves equality relations, logical operations, arithmetic operations, the constants, inputs, and variables of every process in the protocol, and the content of every channel in the protocol. The content of a channel in a protocol is defined next.

We adopt the notation ch.p.q to denote the content of the channel from process p to process q. In particular, the value of ch.p.q is a sequence of messages taken from those messages that can be sent from p to q. In a protocol predicate, ch.p.q can appear in two forms of boolean expressions. A boolean expression of the form (#ch.p.q $\leq$ k) is true when the channel from p to q has at least k messages. A boolean expression of the form (m#ch.p.q $\leq$ k) is true when the channel from p to q has at least k messages of type m.

Statements of a process p are of six forms: skip, assignment, sending, sequence, selection, and iteration. Next, we describe these different forms of statements and how to execute each statement.

A skip statement of process p is of the form

```
skip
```

This statement is executed by doing nothing.

An assignment statement of process p is of the form

```
x.0, ... , x.k := E.0, ... , E.k
```

Each x.i is a distinct variable of p, and each E.i is an expression of the same type as the corresponding variable x.i and involves only constants, inputs, and variables of p. The assignment statement is executed in two steps. First, compute the current values of all the E.i expressions on the right-hand side. Second, assign the computed value of each E.i to the corresponding variable x.i.

A sending statement of process p is of the form

```
send <message of p> to <process name q>
```

As mentioned earlier, a message of p is a noninterpreted symbol, and process q is different from process p. This statement is executed by placing a copy of the message at the tail (i.e., the end) of the message sequence ch.p.q.

A sequence statement of process p is of the form

```
<statement of p> ; <statement of p>
```

This statement is executed by first executing the first statement of p and then executing the second statement of p.

A selection statement of process p is of the form

```
if lg.0 —> sm.0 ☐ .... ☐ lg.k —> sm.k fi
```

Each lg.i is a local guard of p such that the disjunction of these guards is true for every assignment of values to the variables of p. Each sm.i is a statement of p. The selection statement is executed by first computing the current boolean values of all the local guards and then selecting arbitrarily one local guard lg.i whose value is true and executing its corresponding statement sm.i.

An iteration statement of process p is of the form

```
do lg —> sm od
```

In this statement, lg is a local guard of p and sm is a statement of p. The iteration statement is executed by repeatedly computing the current value of the local guard lg and then executing statement sm when lg is true. Execution of the iteration statement terminates when lg is false. We require that each iteration statement be terminating in the following sense. There is an integer k such that whenever the statement is executed, the statement is guaranteed to terminate within k iterations.

3.3 PROTOCOL EXECUTION

In this section, we describe how a network of processes is executed. We start our presentation by introducing the concept of a network state.

A state of a network is defined by one value for each constant, input, and variable in each process in the network and by one sequence of messages in each channel in the network.

An action gd → sm in a process p in a network is enabled at a network state S iff one of the following two conditions holds at S: gd is a local or timeout guard whose value is true at state S, or gd is of the form **rcv** m **from** q and the head (i.e., first) message in ch.q.p is m at state S.

Let gd → sm be an action in a process p in a network. If this action is enabled at a network state S, then this action can be executed when the network is in state S. Executing this action proceeds as follows. If gd is a local or timeout guard, then executing the action consists of executing statement sm. If gd is of the form **rcv** m

from q, then executing this action consists of first removing the head message (which is of type m) from ch.p.q and then executing statement sm.

If one or more actions in the same process or in different processes in a network are enabled at a network state S, then exactly one of the enabled actions is executed, yielding a next state S' of the network. Likewise, if one or more actions are enabled at state S', then exactly one of those actions is executed, yielding a next state S'', and so on. An execution of the network terminates when the network reaches a "deadlock state," where no action is enabled.

The action to be executed at a network state is selected arbitrarily from the set of all enabled actions at that state, except for the following fairness requirement: If an action continues to be enabled during any execution of the protocol, then eventually that action is executed.

In summary, a network execution satisfies the following three conditions:

i. *Nondeterministic Selection:* Any action that is enabled at a network state can be selected for execution at that state.

ii. *Action Atomicity:* Enabled actions in the same process or in different processes in a network are executed one at a time.

iii. *Fair Execution:* If an action is continuously enabled during a network execution, then that action is eventually executed.

As an example, consider the vending machine protocol discussed in Section 2.1. Assume that this network starts at a state defined by the following protocol predicate R.0:

$$R.0 = readyc \wedge \sim readyv \wedge ch.c.v = <\,> \wedge ch.v.c = <\,>$$

The first conjunct in R.0 asserts that variable readyc in process c has the value true, the second conjunct asserts that readyv in process v has the value false, and the last two conjuncts assert that the two channels between processes c and v are empty.

At state R.0, exactly one action, namely the first action in process c, is enabled. Executing this action at state R.0 leads the network to the following state R.1:

$$R.1 = \sim readyc \wedge \sim readyv \wedge ch.c.v = <money; selection> \wedge ch.v.c = <\,>$$

At state R.1, only the first action in process v is enabled. Executing this action at state R.1 leads the network to the following state R.2:

$$R.2 = \sim readyc \wedge readyv \wedge ch.c.v = <selection> \wedge ch.v.c = <\,>$$

At state R.2, only the second action in process v is enabled. Executing this action at R.2 leads the network to the following state R.3:

$$R.3 = \sim readyc \wedge \sim readyv \wedge ch.c.v = <\,> \wedge ch.v.c = <item>$$

At state R.3, only the second action in process c is enabled. Executing this action at state R.3 leads the network back to the starting state R.0.

Thus, if the network starts at state R.0, the network will indefinitely cycle through the states R.0 to R.3. The network states and the transitions between them can be represented by the state-transition diagram in Figure 3.1*a*. In this diagram, each node represents one network state, and each edge from a node R.i to a node R.j represents an action execution that leads the network from state R.i to R.j.

In general, a network has many state-transition diagrams. For example Figure 3.1*b* shows a second state-transition diagram for the same vending machine protocol. This diagram consists of only one node representing the following network state X.0:

$$X.0 = \sim readyc \wedge \sim readyv \wedge ch.c.v = <> \wedge ch.v.c = <>$$

Because no action in process c or process v is enabled at state X.0, this state-transition diagram has no edges.

As another example, Figure 3.1c shows a third state-transition diagram for the vending machine protocol. This diagram has two nodes representing the following network states Y.0 and Y.1:

$$Y.0 = \sim readyc \wedge \sim readyv \wedge ch.c.v = <money> \wedge ch.v.c = <>$$

$$Y.1 = \sim readyc \wedge readyv \wedge ch.c.v = <> \wedge ch.v.c = <>$$

Only one action, the first action in process v, is enabled at state Y.0. Executing this action at state Y.0 leads the network to state Y.1. State Y.1 is a deadlock state, and no action is enabled at it.

A state-transition diagram for the request–reply protocol in Section 2.2 is shown in Figure 3.2. This diagram has 11 nodes representing the following network states S.0 to S.10:

$$S.0 = readyp \wedge readyq \wedge ch.p.q = <> \wedge ch.q.p = <>$$

$$S.1 = \sim readyp \wedge readyq \wedge ch.p.q = <request> \wedge ch.q.p = <>$$

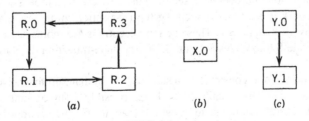

(a)   *(b)*   *(c)*

FIG. 3.1

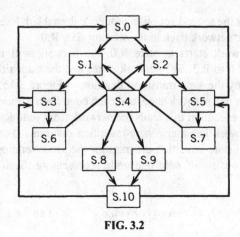

FIG. 3.2

S.2 = S.1 except for replacing each p by q and vice versa

S.3 = ~readyp $\wedge$ readyq $\wedge$ ch.p.q = < > $\wedge$ ch.q.p = <reply>

S.4 = ~readyp $\wedge$ ~readyq $\wedge$ ch.p.q = <request> $\wedge$ ch.q.p = <request>

S.5 = S.3 except for replacing each p by q and vice versa

S.6 = ~readyp $\wedge$ ~readyq $\wedge$ ch.p.q = < > $\wedge$ ch.q.p = <reply;request>

S.7 = S.6 except for replacing each p by q and vice versa

S.8 = ~readyp $\wedge$ ~readyq $\wedge$ ch.p.q = < > $\wedge$ ch.q.p = <request;reply>

S.9 = S.8 except for replacing each p by q and vice versa

S.10 = ~readyp $\wedge$ ~readyq $\wedge$ ch.p.q = <reply> $\wedge$ ch.q.p = <reply>

At state S.0, exactly two actions are enabled. These are the first action in process p and the first action in process q. Executing the first action in process p at state S.0 leads the network to state S.1. Executing the first action in process q at state S.0 leads the network to state S.2. These action executions are represented by the two edges from node S.0 to nodes S.1 and S.2 in the state-transition diagram in Figure 3.2.

The main problem in constructing a state-transition diagram for a given network is that the given network usually has a large, possibly infinite number of states. Therefore, the corresponding state-transition diagram for the network is also very large, possibly infinite, and thus hard or impossible to draw in full.

To solve this problem, the definition of a state-transition diagram for a network can be generalized as follows. Instead of each node in the diagram representing only one state of the network, each node in the diagram represents a nonempty subset of the network states. With this generalization, a state-transition diagram for a network can have a small number of nodes even if the network has an infinite number of states.

As an example, consider the Manchester encoding protocol in Section 2.3. This network has an infinite number of states. In particular, the network can reach a state where there are k messages in the channel from process s to process r for any non-negative integer k. Nevertheless, it is possible to construct a small state-transition diagram for this network. One such diagram is shown in Figure 3.3. This diagram has two nodes T.0 and T.1, defined as follows:

$$T.0 = \sim str \wedge x \geq y \wedge \#ch.s.r = 2(x - y)$$

$$T.1 = str \wedge x > y \wedge \#ch.s.r = 2(x - y) - 1$$

Node T.0 in the diagram represents the set of every network state where the value of variable str is false, the value of variable x is at least the value of variable y, and the channel from process s to process r has k messages, where k is twice the value of variable x minus the value of variable y. Because there are an infinite number of network states that satisfy this condition, node T.0 in the diagram represents an infinite set of network states. Similarly, node T.1 in the diagram represents an infinite set of network states.

In the state-transition diagram in Figure 3.3, executing the action of process s is represented by two edges: One edge is from node T.0 to itself, and the other edge is from node T.1 to itself. Similarly, executing each action of process r is represented by two edges: One edge is from node T.0 to node T.1, and the other edge is from node T.1 to node T.0.

Because each node in a state-transition diagram represents a set of network states, each state-transition diagram can be transformed into a normal form. A normal state-transition diagram has exactly one node and a number of edges from that node to itself. The number of edges in a normal state-transition diagram equals the number of actions in its network. Figure 3.4a shows the normal form of the state-

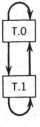

FIG. 3.3

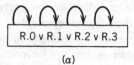 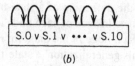

| (a) | (b) | (c) |

FIG. 3.4

transition diagram in Figure 3.1a for the vending machine protocol. Figure 3.4b shows the normal form of the state-transition diagram in Figure 3.2 for the request–reply protocol. Figure 3.4c shows the normal form of the state-transition diagram in Figure 3.3 for the Manchester encoding protocol.

3.4 PROCESSES IN THE INTERNET

Each protocol of the Internet consists of one process in every computer in the Internet. For example, the Internet Protocol, or IP for short, consists of an IP process in every computer in the Internet. Similarly, the transition control protocal (TCP) consists of a TCP process in every computer in the Internet, and the user datagram protocal (UDP) consists of a UDP process in every computer in the Internet, and so on.

In the Internet, if a process that belongs to some protocol sends a message, then the ultimate destination of that message is another process that belongs to the same protocol. Thus, if the IP process in a computer sends a message, then the ultimate destination of that message is the IP process in another computer in the Internet.

In this section, we discuss how IP processes in different computers exchange messages. We start the discussion by explaining IP addresses of computers in the Internet.

Recall from Section 2.4 that the Internet consists of networks, and each network consists of subnetworks with attached computers. All networks in the Internet are assigned distinct identifiers by a worldwide central authority called the Network Information Center, or NIC for short. The subnetworks in each network are assigned distinct identifiers by the local network administrator. (Thus, two subnetworks in different networks may be assigned identical identifiers by the administrators of their networks.) Moreover, computers that are attached to the same subnetwork are assigned distinct identifiers by the administrator of their subnetwork.

Thus, each computer in the Internet has a unique address, called its IP address, that consists of three identifiers: (n, s, c) defined as follows:

n Unique identifier of the network to which the computer belongs

s Unique identifier of the subnetwork, in network n, to which the computer is attached

c Unique identifier of the computer in subnetwork s in network n

Subnetwork s in network n can be referred to as subnetwork (n, s).

Note that a host, being attached to one subnetwork, has exactly one IP address. On the other hand, a router, that is attached to x subnetworks, has x IP addresses: one address for each subnetwork to which it is attached.

Figure 3.5 shows an example of two networks in the Internet. The two networks have distinct identifiers n.0 and n.1 assigned by the NIC. Network n.0 has four subnetworks that are assigned the distinct identifiers s.0 to s.3 by the administrator of n.0. Network n.1 has three subnetworks that are assigned the distinct identifiers s.0 to s.2 by the administrator of n.1. The computers in networks n.0 and n.1 are assigned the identifiers c.0 to c.2 such that any two computers that are attached to the same subnetwork are assigned distinct identifiers.

Network n.0 has four hosts that have the following IP addresses:

$$(n.0, s.0, c.0), (n.0, s.0, c.1), (n.0, s.1, c.1), (n.0, s.2, c.1)$$

Network n.0 also has two routers. One router is attached to three subnetworks, and so it has three IP addresses: (n.0, s.0, c.2), (n.0, s.1, c.2), and (n.0, s.3, c.2). The other router in network n.0 is attached to two subnetworks, and so it has two IP addresses: (n.0, s.1, c.0) and (n.0, s.2, c.0).

In the Internet, each IP address occupies four bytes, or 32 bits. Therefore, it is customary to represent an IP address as a sequence of four integers w. x. y. z, where each of w, x, y, or z is an integer in the range 0, . . . , 255.

IP addresses are of three classes: A, B, and C. (A fourth class, D, is discussed in Chapter 20.) In a class A address, only 7 bits in the address are reserved for the network identifier. In a class B address, 14 bits are reserved for the network identifier. In a class C address, 21 bits are reserved for the network identifier. Figure 3.6 shows the three classes of IP addresses.

Note that the class of an IP address (n, s, c) determines the bits allocated for specifying n but does not determine the bits allocated for specifying s (or those allocated for specifying c). This is intended to allow networks with different sizes to al-

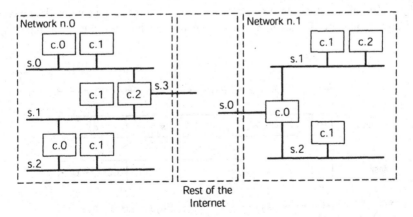

Rest of the
Internet

FIG. 3.5

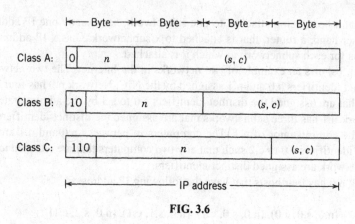

FIG. 3.6

locate different numbers of bits for specifying their subnetworks. In fact, the number of bits allocated for specifying subnetworks in the IP addresses in a network is decided by the local administrator of that network.

The bits allocated for specifying subnetworks in the IP addresses in a network are usually defined by 32 bits, called the subnetwork mask of the network. The 32 bits of a subnetwork mask are partitioned into an interval of 1 bits followed by an interval of 0 bits such that the following condition holds. If some bit in the mask of a network is 1, then the corresponding bit in every IP address (n, s, c) in that network is either part of n or part of s. On the other hand, if some bit in the mask of a network is 0, then the corresponding bit in every IP address (n, s, c) in that network is part of c.

For example, consider a network whose IP addresses are of class B. In this network, the lowest order 16 bits in each IP address (n, s, c) are allocated for specifying s and c. If the administrator of this network decides to divide these 16 bits equally between s and c, then the subnetwork mask of this network consists of twenty four 1 bits followed by eight 0 bits, as shown in Figure 3.7.

Each computer in the Internet stores the subnetwork mask of its network and can use it to compute the IP address of the subnetwork to which it is attached. In partic-

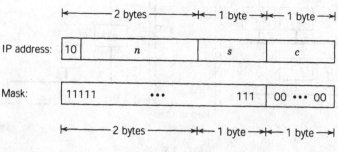

FIG. 3.7

ular, a computer (n, s, c) can perform a bit wise AND operation on two operands of 32 bits each: its IP address (n, s, c) and the subnetwork mask of its network. The resulting 32 bits (n, s, 0) constitute the IP address of the subnetwork to which computer (n, s, c) is attached.

Next, we describe how IP addresses are used to allow IP processes in different computers to exchange messages. For the IP process in a computer (n, s, c) to send a message mg to the IP process in a computer (n', s', c'), the following steps are executed.

i. The IP process in computer (n, s, c) compares its own IP address (n, s, c) with the destination IP address (n', s', c'), which is written in message mg, to determine whether or not n = n' and s = s'. The IP process in computer (n, s, c) performs this comparison in three steps. First, it performs a bit wise AND operation on its own IP address (n, s, c) and its subnetwork mask M. Second, it performs a bit wise AND operation on the destination IP address (n', s', c') and the subnetwork mask M. Third, if the results of these two AND operations are equal, then n = n' and s = s'. Otherwise, n ≠ n' or s ≠ s'.

ii. If n = n' and s = s' (indicating that both the source and destination of message mg are adjacent, i.e. they are attached to the same subnetwork (n, s)), then the IP process in computer (n, s, c) sends mg directly to the IP process in computer (n', s', c') over subnetwork (n, s). (As discussed in Section 2.4, message mg travels from the IP process in computer (n, s, c) to the Interface process in the same computer and then over subnetwork (n, s) to the Interface process in computer (n', s,' c'), and ends up in the IP process in (n', s', c').)

iii. If n ≠ n' or s ≠ s', then the IP process in computer (n, s, c) sends message mg to the IP process in the adjacent router (n.0, s.0, c.0). The IP process in router (n.0, s.0, c.0) extracts the destination IP address (n', s', c') from message mg, computes from its routing table the best adjacent router (n.1, s.1, c.1) for reaching the destination (n', s', c'), and sends message mg to the IP process in router (n.1, s.1, c.1). This is repeated a number of times causing message mg to travel several times from the IP process in a router to the IP process in an adjacent router until mg reaches the IP process of a router (n.k, s.k, c.k) that is adjacent to the destination computer (n', s', c'). When this happens, the IP process in router (n.k, s.k, c.k) sends message mg directly to the IP process in computer (n', s', c').

Referring to Figure 3.5, if the IP process in host (n.0, s.2, c.1) sends a message to the IP process in host (n.1, s.1, c.2), then the route for this message is the IP processes in the following sequence of computers:

$$< (n.0, s.2, c.1), (n.0, s.2, c.0), (n.0, s.1, c.2),$$

$$\ldots \text{ routers in the rest of the Internet} \ldots,$$

$$(n.1, s.0, c.0), (n.1, s.1, c.2) >$$

Note that in this computer sequence only the first and last computers are hosts; all other computers are routers.

In step iii of the above procedure, we suggested that the IP process in each router has a routing table for computing the best adjacent router for reaching any given destination. The details for constructing and maintaining these routing tables is discussed in Chapter 13.

Each message sent by an IP process is called an IP message. An IP message consists of 15 fields: The first 14 fields constitute the message header and the last field is the message text. The 14 fields in the message header are as follows:

1. IP version of the message source   4 bits
2. Length of the header   4 bits
3. Quality of service   8 bits
4. Total length of the message   16 bits
5. Unique identifier of the message   16 bits
6. Not last/last fragment   4 bits
7. Fragment offset   12 bits
8. Remaining hop count of the message   8 bits
9. Transport protocol of the message   8 bits
10. Checksum for the header   16 bits
11. IP address of the message source   32 bits
12. IP address of the message destination   32 bits
13. Other options   x bits
14. Padding   y bits

Field 1 defines the version of the IP process that originated the message. The current version of IP processes is 4. If an IP process receives the message and detects that its own version is different from the source version in field 1, it discards the message. Field 2 defines the length of the message header measured as the number of bits in the header divided by 32. Field 3 defines some objectives that need to be met, if possible, while the message is being transmitted between its original source computer and its ultimate destination computer. Some of these objectives are high precedence (over other transmitted messages), small delay, large throughput, and high reliability. Field 4 defines the total length of the message measured as the number of bits in the message divided by 8.

Fields 5, 6, and 7 are used only when the message is divided into fragments. This happens when the message is too long to be sent over some subnetwork as the message travels from its source to its destination. When this happens, the message is divided into shorter fragments that travel as separate messages until they arrive at the destination, where they are assembled back into one message. Each fragment of a message has the same IP header as the original message except that fields 4, 6, 7, and 10 are modified as follows. Field 4 in a fragment defines the total length of the fragment. Field 6 in a fragment indicates whether this fragment is the last one in the message or there are more fragments to follow. Field 7 in a fragment defines the position of the fragment in the original message. Field 10 in a fragment defines the checksum for the header of the fragment. Field 5 contains a unique identifier of the message. This identifier is copied into the header of each fragment of the message, and it is used to identify which fragment belongs to which message.

Field 8 contains the remaining hop count of the message. The hop count for a message is assigned by the IP process in the source computer that originated the message. When the message arrives at the IP process of an intermediate router, the hop count in the message is reduced by 1. If the hop count of a message becomes zero and the message still has not arrived at the IP process of its destination, the message is discarded. Field 9 defines the transport protocol process, for example the TCP or UDP process, to which the IP process in the destination computer delivers the message text. This is explained further in Section 4.6.

Field 10 has a checksum that is used in detecting corruption that may occur in the message header while the message is transmitted. In Section 8.4, we discuss how this checksum is used in detecting corruption. Fields 11 and 12 contain the IP addresses of the source and destination computers. Field 13 is of variable length and field 14 is added to ensure that the length of the header is a multiple of 32.

The IP performs two functions: message transmission from the source computer to the destination computer and message encapsulation. Message transmission is discussed in this section, and message encapsulation is discussed in Section 4.6. Note that in performing message transmission, IP makes use of some routing tables. The protocols for maintaining these routing tables are discussed in Section 13.8.

3.5 BIBLIOGRAPHICAL NOTES

Defining a network protocol as a set of processes that communicate over unbounded channels is discussed in Bochmann [1975] and Gouda [1977]. The data structure of a process is similar to the data structure in the Pascal programming language defined in Wirth [1971]. The guarded actions of a process are similar to the guarded commands in Dijkstra [1973]. Action execution is similar to statement execution in Chandy and Misra [1988]. The concept of fair execution is discussed in Francez [1986]. Multiple assignment statements are discussed in Gries [1981]. Send and receive statements are discussed in Gouda [1977]. Timeout actions are discussed in Gouda [1993].

IP is discussed in Postel [1980a, 1981a]. An important feature of IP, namely message fragmentation, is discussed in Brachman and Chanson [1988].

EXERCISES

1   (Action Fairness). Consider a network that consists of two processes p and q. Process p is defined as follows.

```
process p
begin
            true --> send data to q
      []    rcv data from q --> skip
end
```

Process q is symmetric to process p. Is each of the four actions in this network guaranteed to be executed infinitely often along any infinite execution of the network? Explain your answer.

2   (Fairness to Receiving). Modify the network in exercise 1 such that each of the two processes is guaranteed to receive at least one data message after sending k successive data messages.

3   (Fairness to Sending). Modify the network in exercise 1 such that each of the two processes is guaranteed to send at least one data message after receiving k successive data messages.

4   (Reset). Two processes p and q exchange data messages. Process p has two integer counters sp and rp that count the number of data messages sent and received by p, respectively. Similarly, process q has two integer counters sq and rq that count the number of data messages sent and received by q, respectively:

   a   Design processes p and q.

   b   Prove that the relation sp $\geq$ rq holds at each reachable state of the protocol?

   c   Augment processes p and q to allow p to initiate a reset operation by which the values of both sp and rq are reset to 0 while the relation sp $\geq$ rq still holds at each reachable state of the protocol.

   d   Augment the two processes that result from part c to allow process q to initiate a reset operation by which the values of both sq and rp are reset to 0 while the relation sq $\geq$ rp still holds at each reachable state of the protocol.

5   (Reset). Consider the two processes p and q in exercise 4 before augmentation. Augment both p and q to allow process p to initiate a reset operation where the values of variables sp, rp, sq, and rq are all reset to 0.

6   (Reset). Consider the two processes p and q in exercise 4 before the augmentation. Augment both p and q to allow each of the two processes to initiate a reset operation where the values of all four variables sp, rp, sq, and rq are reset to 0.

7   (Multiplexing). Consider a network of six processes s_0, s_1, p, q, r_0, and r_1. Processes s_0 and s_1 send data messages to process p. Process p waits to receive a data message from s_0 then forwards it as a message zero to q. If there is no data message for p to receive from s_0, p forwards an idleness message to process q. In either case, process p waits to receive a data message from process s_1 and then forwards it as a message one to process q. If there is no data message for p to receive from s_1, p forwards an idleness message to process q. In either case, process p waits to receive a data message from

process s_0, and the cycle repeats. Process q forwards each message zero as a data message to process r_0, forwards each message one as a data message to process r_1, and discards each idleness message. Design processes s_0, p, q, and r_0. Processes s_1 and r_1 are symmetric to processes s_0 and r_0, respectively.

8   (Computing min and max). A process p has an input array u and a variable array x. Arrays u and x are both infinite, and the value of each element in either array is in the range $0 . . 1$. Similarly, a process r has an input array w and a variable array z. Arrays w and z are both infinite, and the value of each element in either array is in the range $0 . . 1$. Design processes p and r such that each process computes the value of its variable array as follows. For every i,

$$x[i] = \min\{u[i], w[i]\}$$

$$z[i] = \max\{u[i], w[i]\},$$

9   (Computing min, mid, and max). Add a process q between processes p and r in exercise 8. Process q has an input array v and a variable array y. Arrays v and y are both infinite, and the value of each element in either array is in the range $0 . . 1$. Design processes p, q, and r such that each process computes the value of its variable array as follows. For every i,

$$x[i] = \min\{u[i], v[i], w[i]\},$$

$$y[i] = \text{mid}\{u[i], v[i], w[i]\},$$

$$z[i] = \max\{u[i], v[i], w[i]\},$$

Function mid returns the middle value from a set of three values.

10   (Commitment). The communication in a network of three processes p, q, and r goes through an infinite sequence of rounds. In each round, each of the processes p and q decides nondeterministically to send either a commit message or an abort message to process r. When process r receives one message from p and one message from q, r sends a message to p and a message to q according to the following rule. If at least one of the messages received by r is an abort message, then r sends abort messages to both p and q; otherwise, r sends commit messages to both p and q. The round terminates when each of the processes p and q receives a message from process r. After a round terminates, the next round starts, and so on. Design processes p and r. Process q is symmetric to process p.

11   (Virtual Clocks). Two symmetric processes p and q exchange messages according to the following three rules.
a Each process has an integer variable clk whose initial value is 0.

b The processes exchange messages of the form msg(s), where s is an integer
   sequence number.

c At each instant, each process can either send one message to or receive one
   message from the other process.

d To send a msg(s) message, a process increments its clk variable by 1 and
   then makes s the new value of clk.

e On receiving a msg(s) message, a process assigns its clk variable the value
   max(clk, s) + 1.

Design processes p and q.

CHAPTER 4

MORE ON PROCESSES

We discuss in this chapter four new features of our AP notation. In Section 4.1, the definition of a message is extended to allow messages to have fields that store control information and data. In Section 4.2, the definition of an assignment statement is extended such that variables can be assigned arbitrary or random values. In Section 4.3, process arrays are introduced so that an array of identical processes can be defined by defining only one representative process. In Section 4.4, parameters are introduced into action definitions so that a finite set of actions can be defined as a single parameterized action. In Section 4.5, we discuss a resource allocation protocol in which these four new features are illustrated. Finally in Section 4.6, we discuss process communication in the Internet.

4.1 MESSAGES WITH FIELDS

So far messages have been defined as noninterpreted symbols. This definition is now generalized to allow a message to have a noninterpreted name and zero or more fields. In particular, a message of process p, which occurs in the sending or receiving statements of p, can be in either of two forms:

```
<message name>
<message name> ( <field.0> , ... , <field.k> )
```

The message name is a noninterpreted symbol, and each field.i is one of the following: true, false, a nonnegative integer, a constant of process p, an input of process p (other than a set or an infinite array), or a variable of process p (other than an infinite array).

In order to discuss the execution of sending and receiving statements in the case where messages have fields, we need to introduce the concept of a message instance and redefine the concept of a channel content.

A message instance of a protocol is in either of two forms:

```
<message name>
<message name> ( <const.0> , ... , <const.k> )
```

The message name is a noninterpreted symbol, and each const.i is true, false, or a nonnegative integer.

The content of a channel in a protocol is not a sequence of messages, as stated earlier, but in fact a sequence of message instances. Because there is no distinction between messages and message instances when messages have no fields, our earlier statement that the content of a channel is a sequence of messages was valid as long as messages are without fields.

Consider the following sending statement in process p.

```
send m(x.0 , ... ,x.k) to q
```

In this statement, m is a message name and each x.i is true, false, a nonnegative integer, or a constant, an input, or a variable of process p. The execution of this statement consists of first constructing a message instance m(v.0, . . . , v.k) where each v.i is the current value of x.i and then appending this message instance at the tail of the sequence ch.p.q.

Consider the following action in process p.

```
rcv m(x.0 , ... ,x.k) from q --> sm
```

In this action, m is a message name and each x.i is true, false, a nonnegative integer, or a constant, an input, or a variable of process p. This action is enabled for execution when the head message instance in ch.q.p is of the form m(v.0, . . . , v.k) where each v.i is a possible value of x.i. This requirement implies that if some x.i is a value (e.g., true, false, or a nonnegative integer), then the corresponding v.i is the same value. The execution of this action consists of three steps. First, remove the head message instance m(v.0, ... , v.k) from ch.q.p. Second, assign to each x.i the corresponding value v.i. Third, execute statement sm in the action.

4.2 NONDETERMINISTIC ASSIGNMENT

Recall that an assignment statement is of the form

```
x.0, ... , x.k := E.0, ... , E.k
```

where each E.i is an expression of the same type as the corresponding variable x.i.

We now extend this definition as follows. If an x.i is of type boolean, range, or enumerated, then the corresponding E.i can also be the reserved word **any,** or the reserved word **random.**

Executing an assignment statement where some E.i is the reserved word **any** consists of assigning the corresponding x.i an arbitrary value from its domain of values.

Executing an assignment statement where some E.i is the reserved word **random** consists of assigning the corresponding x.i a value, selected using a uniform distribution, from its domain of values.

Note that if the statement x := **any** is executed an infinite number of times, then x can be assigned the same value each time. On the other hand, if the statement x := **random** is executed an infinite number of times, then x is assigned each of its possible values an infinite number of times. Note also that the statement x := **any,** where x is a boolean variable, is equivalent to the following statement:

```
if true -> x := true
[] true -> x := false
fi
```

On the other hand, x := **random** is not equivalent to this statement.

4.3 PROCESS ARRAYS

Protocol definitions are allowed to include process arrays. A process array is a finite set of processes: Each of them has the same set of constants, the same set of inputs, and the same set of variables. Thus, all processes in a process array can be defined by merely defining one representative process in the array.

The concept of a representative process of a process array is better explained by an example. Let p be an array of three processes named p[0], p[1], and p[2]. A representative process of this array can be p[i], where i is an index whose value is 0, 1, or 2. Index i is called the index of array p.

A representative process of a process array is defined as a regular process with two exceptions. First, the process statement in the representative process is defined as follows:

```
process <process array> [<index> : <type>, ... ,
                         <index> : <type>]
```

Each index of a process array is of type range whose lower and upper bounds are treated as constants in the representative process. Second, each index of a process array is treated as an input in the representative process. Therefore, the range bounds and indices of a process array can be read, but not written, by the actions of the representative process.

As an example, consider the following process statement:

process p[i : 0..n-1]

In defining the actions of the representative process p[i], i can be used as an input, while n can be used as a constant.

A process q can send a message mg to some process in a process array p[i : 0 .. n − 1] by executing the statement

send mg **to** p[x]

where x is a nonnegative integer, or a constant, input, or variable of process q.

Process q can also receive a message mg from some process in a process array p[i : 0 .. n − 1] by executing the statement

rcv mg **from** p[x]

where x is a nonnegative integer, or a constant, input, or variable of process q.

4.4 PARAMETERIZED ACTIONS

Parameters can be declared in a process and used in the definition of process actions. If parameters are declared in a process, their declaration follows the declaration of variables and precedes the definition of actions as follows:

```
process     <process name>

const       <constant list>
inp         <input declaration list>
var         <variable declaration list>
par         <parameter declaration list>

begin
            <action definition list>
end
```

The parameter declaration list is of the form.

```
<par name> : <par type>, ... , <par name> : <par type>
```

Each parameter type is one of the following: boolean, range, or enumerated. This implies that each parameter has a finite number of values.

The parameters of a process p occur in the actions of p in the same way as inputs of p occur in the actions of p. Thus, parameters of p can be read but not written by the actions of process p.

An action that refers to one or more parameters is called a parameterized action.

A parameterized action is a shorthand notation for a finite set of actions: Each of them can be obtained from the parameterized action by first selecting for each parameter i in the parameterized action a value v.i from the domain of i, then replacing every occurrence of i in the parameterized action by the selected value v.i.

As an example, let j be a parameter of type 0 . . 2, and r be a parameter of type 0 . . 1, and consider the following parameterized action:

```
rqstd[j,r]—> rqstd[j,r] := false ; send grant(r) to p[j]
```

This parameterized action is a shorthand notation for the following six actions:

```
  rqstd[0,0] —> rqstd[0,0] := false ; send grant(0) to p[0]
□ rqstd[1,0] —> rqstd[1,0] := false ; send grant(0) to p[1]
□ rqstd[2,0] —> rqstd[2,0] := false ; send grant(0) to p[2]
□ rqstd[0,1] —> rqstd[0,1] := false ; send grant(1) to p[0]
□ rqstd[1,1] —> rqstd[1,1] := false ; send grant(1) to p[1]
□ rqstd[2,1] —> rqstd[2,1] := false ; send grant(1) to p[2]
```

The restriction that each parameter has a finite number of values guarantees that each parameterized action defines a finite, rather than infinite, set of actions.

4.5 A RESOURCE ALLOCATION PROTOCOL

In this section, we discuss a resource allocation protocol. The definition of this protocol illustrates the four features in this chapter: messages with fields, nondeterministic assignments, process arrays, and parameterized actions.

Consider a network that has an array u of n user processes. Each user process u[i] in array u can request and be granted any one of s resources on a one-at-a-time basis. The resources are requested from, granted by, and later released to a controller process c. When a user u[i] needs a resource r, it sends a message rqst(r) to process c. When later u[i] receives a message grant(r) from c, it accesses resource r and then sends a message rls(r) to process c. User u[i] can now request another resource and the cycle repeats. Process u[i] can be defined as follows:

```
process u[i: 0 .. n-1]

const s      {s is the number of resources}

var   wait :    boolean,
      r    :    0..s-1

begin
      ~ wait              —> wait, r := true, any;
                             send rqst(r) to c
```

```
[]      rcv grant(r) from c -->  wait := false;
                                 send rls(r) to c
end
```

Note that the first action in process u[i] has a nondeterministic assignment r :=
any. This assignment indicates that user u[i] can request the resources in any order
and with any frequency.

The controller process c has two boolean arrays avail and rqstd. An element
avail[r] of the first array is true when resource r is available, that is, when resource r
is not currently granted to a user. An element rqstd[j, r] of the second array is true
when resource r has been requested by but not yet granted to user u[j]. Process c is
defined as follows:

```
process c

const n, s

var     avail :      array [0..s-1] of boolean,
        rqstd :      array [0..n-1, 0..s-1] of boolean

par     j     :      0..n-1,
        r     :      0..s-1

begin
    rcv rqst(r) from u[j]  -->  rqstd[j,r] := true

[]  rcv rls(r) from u[j]   -->  avail[r] := true

[]  avail[r] /\ rqstd[j,r] -->  avail[r], rqstd[j,r] :=
                                false, false;
                                send grant(r) to u[j]
end
```

Each action in process c is a parameterized action that represents a set of n × s
actions: one action for each combination of values for the pair (j, r). For example,
the third parameterized action in process c has the following meaning. Whenever a
resource r is available and has been requested by a user u[j], the corresponding action in the parameterized action can be executed.

This controller process c is unfair as follows. After process c receives a rqst(r)
message from some user, there is no guarantee that c will ever grant resource r to
that particular user because it may keep on granting r to other users.

This unfairness is caused by the nondeterminism: controller c nondeterministically chooses to which user it grants resources. There are two methods to overcome
this unfairness. Replace the nondeterminism with fair determinism or replace it
with randomization. We discuss these two methods in order.

The first method for overcoming unfairness is to replace the nondeterminism with fair determinism. In particular, process c can be modified as follows. When c receives a rqst(r) message from a user u[j], it checks whether resource r is available. If r is available, c sends a grant(r) message to u[j]. Otherwise, c assigns rqstd[j, r] the value true. When c receives a rls(r) message from u[j], it searches for the next user u[k] after u[j] such that rqstd[k, r] is true and then sends a grant(r) message to u[k] and makes rqstd[k, r] false. The modified process c is as follows:

```
process c

const n, s

var     avail :     array [0..s-1] of boolean,
        rqstd :     array [0..n-1, 0..s-1] of boolean,
        k     :     0..n-1

par   j    :     0..n-1,
      r    :     0.. s-1

begin
      rcv rqst(r) from u[j] ─>
          if avail[r] ─> avail[r] := false;
                          send grant(r) to u[j]
          ▯ ~avail[r] ─> rqstd[j,r] := true
          fi

▯     rcv rls(r) from u[j]  ─>
          k := j +n 1;
          do k≠j ∧ ~rqstd[k,r] ─> k := k +n 1 od;
          if rqstd[k,r] ─> rqstd[k,r] := false;
                            send grant(r) to u[k]
          ▯ ~rqstd[k,r] ─> avail[r] := true
          fi
end
```

Note that if r is declared in process c as a variable instead of a parameter, then the execution of process c remains unchanged.

The second method for overcoming unfairness is to replace the nondeterminism with randomization. In particular, process c can be modified as follows. When c receives a rqst(r) message from a user u[j], it checks whether resource r is available. If r is available, c sends a grant(r) message to u[j]; otherwise it assigns rqstd[j, r] the value true. When c receives a rls(r) message from u[j], it assigns a new variable x a random value and searches for the next user u[k] after u[x] such that rqstd[k, r] is true. Process c then sends a grant(r) message to user u[k] and assigns rqstd[k, r] the value false:

```
process c

const n, s

var     avail :      array [0..s-1] of boolean,
        rqstd :      array [0..n-1, 0..s-1] of boolean,
        k     :      0..n-1,
        x     :      0..n-1              {random user}

par     j     :      0..n-1,
        r     :      0.. s-1

begin
        rcv rqst(r) from u[j] ->
             if avail[r] -> avail[r] := false;
                                 send grant(r) to u[j]
             [] ~avail[r] -> rqstd[j, r] := true
             fi

[]      rcv rls(r) from u[j]->
             x := random;
             k := x +_n 1;
             do k≠x /\ ~rqstd[k,r] -> k := k +_n. 1 od;
             if rqstd[k,r] -> rqstd[k,r] := false;
                                 send grant(r) to u[k]
             [] ~rqstd[k,r] -> avail[r] := true
             fi
end
```

4.6 MORE ON PROCESSES IN THE INTERNET

Protocols in the Internet are stacked as layers on top of one another, forming a hierarchy. There are four protocol layers in the Internet. They are, from bottom to top, as follows:

  i. subnetwork layer,
 ii. network layer,
iii. transport layer, and
 iv. application layer.

The function of the subnetwork layer is to transfer any message one hop between any two computers on the same subnetwork. The function of the network layer is to transfer any message from the original source of the message to the ultimate destination of the message. This usually requires transferring the message several hops across several subnetworks. The function of the transport layer is to transfer messages between corresponding application processes in different computers. The function of the application layer is to perform tasks required by the Internet users, such as file transfer and electronic mail. Performing these tasks usually requires transferring messages between application processes in different computers in the Internet.

Each computer in the Internet has processes in each of the four protocol layers. In particular, as shown in Figure 4.1, each computer has the following processes:

1. an interface process in the subnetwork layer (subnetwork protocols are discussed in Chapters 23 and 24),
2. an IP process in the network layer,
3. TCP and UDP processes in the transport layer (transport protocols are discussed in Chapters 6, 8, 9, and 10), and
4. application processes in the application layer (application protocols are discussed in Chapters 21 and 22).

For an application process p in a computer c to send a text segment to an application process q in a computer d via the TCP, the following steps are executed:

i. The application process p in computer c sends the text segment to the TCP process in c.

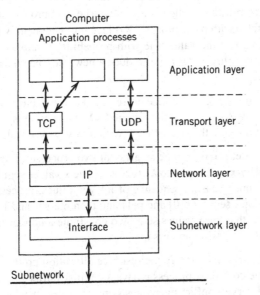

FIG. 4.1

ii.   The TCP process in c adds a TCP header thd to the received text and forwards the resulting TCP message (thd, text) to the IP process in c.

iii. The IP process in c adds an IP header ihd to message (thd, text) forming an IP message of the form (ihd, (thd, text)).

iv.   As discussed in Section 3.4, the IP message (ihd, (thd, text)) is transmitted repeatedly from the IP process in one computer to the IP process in an adjacent computer, until it finally arrives at the IP process in computer d.

v.   The IP process in d removes the IP header from message (ihd, (thd, text)) and sends the resulting TCP message (thd, text) to the TCP process in d.

vi.   The TCP process in d removes the TCP header from message (thd, text) and sends the remaining text segment to the application process q in d.

vii. The application process q in computer d receives the text segment.

4.7 BIBLIOGRAPHICAL NOTES

Nondeterministic assignment statements are discussed in Francez [1986]. Process arrays are discussed in Hoare [1984].

EXERCISES

1 (Biased Randomness). Let x be a boolean variable in some process. The statement x := **random** assigns x the value true with probability $\frac{1}{2}$ and assigns x the value false with probability $\frac{1}{2}$. Replace this statement with another statement that assigns x the value true with probability $\frac{2}{3}$ and assigns x the value false with probability $\frac{1}{3}$. (*Hint:* Introduce a new variable whose value is in the range 0 . . 2.)

2 (Biased Randomness). Generalize exercise 1 for a variable x whose value is in the range u . . w. Assume that the required statement assigns x a value v with a probability P.v, where the sum of P.v's, with u ≤ v ≤ w, equals 1.

3 (Merge Sort). Let p[i: 0 . . 1] be an array of two processes. Each process sends a stream of data(x) messages to a process q. The x values sent by each process constitute a nondecreasing sequence of integer values. Process q receives the data(x) messages sent by p[0] and p[1] and then merges and forwards them to process r such that the x values sent by q constitute a nondecreasing sequence of integer values. Design process q.

4 (Resource Allocation). Modify the resource allocation protocol in Section 4.5 by making the controller process c have a circular buffer to store the received requests and serve conflicting requests in the order in which they were received. This circular buffer is declared as follows:

```
var   usr    : array [0..n] of 0..n-1,
      rsr    : array [0..n] of 0..s-1,
      ns, nr : 0..n
```

The circular buffer consists of two arrays: usr (to store the requesting user) and rsr (to store the requested resource). It also has two indices: ns (to store the location of the next-to-serve request) and nr (to store the location of the next-to-receive request). Design the controller process c.

5   (Resource Allocation). Is your solution of exercise 4 fair? Explain your answer.

6   (Resource Allocation). Modify the resource allocation protocol in Section 4.5 to allow some resources to be shared by more than one user. Ensure fairness using fair determinism. (*Hint:* Replace the boolean avail array with the following array

```
var   avail : array [0..s-1] of 0..n
```

If the initial value of avail[r] = k, then resource r can be shared by k users concurrently.)

7   Resource Allocation). Same as exercise 6 except that fairness is ensured using randomization.

8   (Resource Allocation). Consider a network with two process arrays u[i: 0 .. m − 1] and c[j: 0 .. n − 1]. Each process c[j] has a single resource that can be requested by, granted to, and then released by any process u[i]. Each process c[j] is defined as follows:

```
process c[j : 0..n-1]
var       i   :     0..m-1,
          wait :    boolean
begin
      rcv rqst from u[i] --> send grant to u[i];
                            wait := true
   [] rcv rls from u[i]  --> i, wait := i +m 1, false
   [] timeout ~wait /\
                (#ch.c[j].u[i] + #ch.u[i].c[j] = 0)
                      --> i := i +m 1
end
```

Define process u[i: 0 .. m − 1]. Is the resulting network fair? Explain your answer.

9   (Fault-Tolerant Resource Allocation). Modify the resource allocation protocol in Section 4.5 as follows:

a The s resources are identical.

b Some of the s resources may fail. The failed resources are specified in controller c by the following input array.

inp failed : **array** [0..s-1] **of boolean**

c When a user requests a resource, controller c can grant any of the resources that is available and not failed.

10 (Process Allocation). Consider a linear process array p[i : 0 . . n − 1] where each process p[i], $0 < i < n − 1$, can exchange messages with processes p[i − 1] and p[i + 1]. Before a process p[i] can send data messages to a neighboring process p[j], p[i] sends a rqst message to p[j] and then waits to receive a grant message from p[j] before sending a sequence of data messages followed by a rls message to p[j]. Thus, process p[i] allocates process p[j] before it can send data messages to it and releases p[j] after sending the data messages to it. Design process p[i] in this array under the following three assumptions:

a A process cannot allocate more than one process at a time.

b A process cannot be allocated to more than one process at a time.

c A process cannot allocate and be allocated at the same time.

Ensure fairness using fair determinism.

11 (Process Allocation). Same as exercise 10 except that system fairness is ensured using randomization.

12 (Process Allocation). Same as exercise 10 except that if a process p[i] sends a rqst message to a process p[j] while p[j] is allocating or being allocated to another process, then process p[j] sends a rjct message to p[i], and p[i] may try later to allocate p[j].

13 (Mail System). Consider a network that consists of a process array p[i: 0 . . n − 1] and one process mailer. Each process p[i] can send data messages of the form data(j, t) to process mailer, where j is in the range 0, . . . , n − 1 and t is in the range 0 . . r − 1. Each data message sent to the process mailer has two fields: field j is the index of process p[j] to which the message is eventually forwarded by mailer, and field t is the message text. When process mailer receives a data(j, t) message from process p[i], process mailer stores the message along with index i of the sending process p[i]. Later, when the process mailer receives a nxtmsg message from process p[j] requesting to receive a data message, the process mailer sends the data(j, t) message to p[j] as data(i, t). If the process mailer receives a nxtmsg message from p[j] and it has no data messages intended for p[j], the process mailer sends back a nomsg message to p[j]. Design process p[i] and process mailer.

14 (Mail System). Is your solution of exercise 13 fair? Explain your answer.

15 (Database System). Process p has the following input and variables:

```
process p
inp       n
var       x, y :      array [0..n-1] of integer,
          i    :      0..n,
          v, w :      integer
```

Design the actions of process p according to the following two rules:

    a When p receives a message find(v) from process q, p searches array x. For every element x[i] whose value equals v, p sends a data(y[i]) message to q. At the end, p sends a done message to q.

    b When p receives a message add(v, w) from process q, p searches array x. For every element x[i] whose value equals v, p assigns element y[i] the value w. At the end, p sends a done message to q.

16 (Bit Transmission). Consider a protocol that consists of two processes p and q. Process p has an input infinite array named data. Process p sends the bits in array data to process q as follows. Process p sends each 1 data bit as one message bit(1). It sends each 0 data bit as a sequence of two messages: bit(0); bit(0). It also sends a sequence of n 0 data bits, where n is a constant declared in both p and q, as a sequence of two messages: bit(0); bit(1). Process q receives the bit messages from p and stores the data bits in an infinite array, named rcvd. Design processes p and q.

17 (A Ring with Two Circulating Tokens). Consider a process array p[i: 0 .. n − 1] where each process p[i] has two neighbors p[i $-_n$ 1] and p[i $+_n$ 1]. The processes circulate two tokens in opposite directions. Process p[i] in this protocol can be defined as follows.

```
process p[i : 0..n-1]
begin
      rcv token from p[i -n 1] ->
                          send token to p[i +n 1]
[]    rcv token from p[i +n 1] ->
                          send token to p[i -n 1]
end
```

Modify this protocol to ensure that one of the two tokens travels faster than the other token.

18 (A Ring with Two Circulating Tokens). Consider a process array p[i: 0 .. 2] where each process p[i] has two neighbors p[i $-_3$ 1] and p[i $+_3$ 1]. The processes circulate two tokens in opposite directions. Process p[i] in this protocol can be defined as follows:

```
process p[i : 0..2]
inp       N    :      set { i -3 1, i +3 1 }
```

```
var         g     :      N
begin
      rcv token from p[g] ->
            if g = i -₃ 1 -> g := i +₃ 1
            [] g = i +₃ 1 -> g := i -₃ 1
            fi; send token to p[g]
end
```

Consider the protocol state satisfying the following predicate R:

$$R = (g.0 = 1 \land g.1 = 2 \land g.2 = 1 \land token.1.0 \land token.2.0)$$

where $g.j = k$ states that variable g in process $p[j]$ has the value k, and $token.j.k$ states that there is a token message in the channel from process $p[j]$ to process $p[k]$. Use a state transition diagram to show that starting from state R, the protocol will reach a deadlock state (i.e., a state where no action is enabled for execution). Add a timeout action to each process to ensure that no deadlock state can be reached starting from state R.

19 (Consistent Local States). Consider a process array $p[i: 0 .. 1]$. Each of the two processes has an input array named data and a variable array named rslt. The computation of the process array proceeds in rounds, where in each round one of the following happens:

a Process $p[0]$ sends its current $data[j]$ element to $p[1]$ which replies by sending back an ack message. In this case, each of $p[0]$ and $p[1]$ stores $data[j]$ in its current $rslt[k]$ element and increments each of its j and k by 1.

b Process $p[1]$ sends its current $data[j']$ element to $p[0]$, which replies by sending back an ack message. In this case, each of $p[0]$ and $p[1]$ stores $data[j']$ in its current $rslt[k]$ element and increments each of its j' and k by 1.

c Process $p[0]$ sends its current $data[j]$ element to $p[1]$ and process $p[1]$ sends its current $data[j']$ element to $p[0]$. In this case, each of $p[0]$ and $p[1]$ stores $data[j]$ in its current $rslt[k]$ element and then stores $data[j']$ in $rslt[k+1]$, increments its j or j' by one, and increments its k by 2.

Process $p[i]$ in this protocol can be defined as follows:

```
process p[i : 0..1]
inp  data : array [integer] of integer
var  rslt : array [integer] of integer,
     ready : boolean,        {initially true}
     j     : integer,        {index of data}
     k     : integer,        {index of rslt}
     d     : integer
begin
```

```
ready      --> send nxt(data[j]) to p[i +2 1];
               ready := false
[]    rcv ack from p[i +2 1] -->
               rslt[k], k := data[j], k+1;
               ready, j := true, j+1
[]    rcv nxt(d) from p[i +2 1] -->        S
end
```

Define statement S.

20 (Consistent Local States). Solve exercise 19 for a process array p[i: 0 .. n − 1] rather than for a process array p[i: 0 .. 1].

21 (Biased Resource Allocation). Consider the resource allocation protocol in Section 4.5, where fairness is achieved by randomization. Modify process c such that the chance of user u[0] being granted a resource is four times the chance of any other user being granted the same resource.

22 (Voting in a Network). Consider a network that consists of a process array p[i: 0 .. n − 1] and a single process q. This network executes an infinite sequence of rounds. In each round, each process p[i] sends a vote(b) message to process q, where b is an arbitrary value in the range 0 .. 1. When q receives a vote(b) message from every p[i], q sends the same rslt(c) message to every process p[i], where c is 0 if at least one p[i] has sent vote(0) and c is 1 if every p[i] has sent vote(1). After each p[i] receives a rslt(c) message from q, it starts the next round by sending a vote(b) message to q, and the cycle repeats. Design the processes in this network.

23 (Token Ring). Design a unidirectional ring network p[i: 0 .. n − 1], where there is one channel from each process p[i] to process p[i +n 1]. Around this ring network, a token message circulates. When a process p[i] receives the token message from process p[i −n 1], process p[i] either forwards the token message to process p[i +n 1], or sends a data(d) message, where d is in the range 0 .. n − 1 and d ≠ i, to process p[i +n 1]. In the latter case, the sent data(d) message makes a complete cycle around the ring so that process p[d] can get the data(d) message and copy its data. When the data(d) message returns to its original source p[i], process p[i] sends the token message to process p[i +n 1]. Each process p[i] in this network has two variables: a boolean variable hastkn whose initial value is false and a variable d whose value is in the range 0 .. n − 1. Assume that at the initial state of the network, one channel has exactly one token message and every other channel is empty. Also assume that the communications in the network are error free.

24 (Syntactical Errors). The following definition of process p has several syntax errors. Identify all the syntax errors in process p. Make use of the line numbers on the right-hand side in identifying each syntax error.

```
process p                                                        {1}
inp  n                                                           {2}
var  y        :    array [0..n-1] of integer,                   {3}
     x, z     :    integer,                                      {4}
     j        :    0..n-1                                        {5}
begin                                                            {6}
     rcv data(x) from q ->
               if x ≠ y[j] ∧ j = 0 -> skip                      {7}
               [] x = y[j] ∧ j = 0 -> j := 1                    {8}
               [] rcv data(z) from q ->                          {9}
                      y[j], j = x+z, j +_n 3                     {10}
               fi                                                {11}
     []  timeout x = z           ->
               y[j], j := any, 0;                                {12}
               do y[j] = 0 -> j := j +_n 1 od                   {13}
end                                                             {14}
```

25 (Sending Data Blocks). In a network, processes p and q[i: 0 .. n − 1] are defined as follows:

```
process p
var st                         : 0..2,  {initially 0}
    d                          : 0..n-1
begin
    st = 0                     -> st, d := 1, any;
                                  send first to q[d]
    []  st = 1                 -> send data to q[d]
    []  st = 1                 -> st := 2; send last to q[d]
    []  rcv done from q[d] -> st := 0
end

process q[i : 0..n-1]
var ready                      : boolean  {initially false}
begin
    rcv first from p  -> S.0
    []  rcv data from p   -> S.1
    []  rcv last from p   -> S.2
    []  ready             -> ready := false;
                             send done to p
end
```

Define statements S.0, S.1, and S.2 in process q[i].

26 (Using Variables and Parameters to Receive Messages). Consider a network that consists of the following processes: p[i : 0 .. n − 1], q, and r[i: 0 .. n − 1].

a ·Design an action in process q by which q can receive a signal message from any p[i] process and then send a response message to any r[j] process.

b Design an action in process q by which q can receive n signal messages, one from every p[i] process, and then send n response messages, one to every r[j] process.

Make sure to declare any inputs, variables, or parameters that you use in your actions.

CHAPTER 5

TRANSMISSION ERRORS

In the last two chapters, we discussed protocol executions under the assumption that messages sent from a process p to a process q are received by q in exactly the same condition and the same order in which they were sent by p. In other words, transmission errors cannot occur during protocol execution. Indeed, many protocols that we discuss in this book are based on the assumption that transmission errors cannot occur during protocol executions.

Still, some protocols in this book are based on the opposite assumption that transmission errors may occur during protocol executions. These protocols are designed to perform their functions in spite of the occurrence of transmission errors. In other words, they are error tolerant. In order to be able to explain error-tolerant protocols, we first need to discuss protocol executions in which transmission errors may occur. This is done in this chapter.

By the end of this chapter, we will have defined two types of protocol executions: executions where transmission errors cannot occur and executions where transmission errors can occur. Therefore, it is important, from that point on, to explicitly state the type of executions assumed for any given protocol. Looking ahead, most protocols in Chapters 6 to 12 are designed under the assumption that transmission errors can occur during protocol execution, whereas most protocols in Chapters 13 to 22 are designed under the assumption that transmission errors cannot occur during protocol execution. The reason for this discontinuity will become clear in Chapter 12.

The rest of this chapter is organized as follows. In Section 5.1, the three types of transmission errors, namely message corruption, message loss, and message reorder are presented. In Section 5.2, we discuss protocol execution under the assumption that these three types of errors can occur during the execution. In Section 5.3, we examine the three protocol examples in Chapter 2 and discuss how to make each of them error tolerant. An important mechanism for making protocols error tolerant is timeout actions. A class of timeout actions that are easy to implement using real-time clocks is presented in Section 5.4. These timeout actions are called normal, and implementation of normal timeout actions using real-time clocks is discussed in Section 5.5. Finally in Section 5.6, we discuss transmission errors in the Internet.

5.1 TYPES OF TRANSMISSION ERRORS

It is mentioned in Section 3.3 that the state of a protocol is defined by a value for each constant, input, and variable in each process in the protocol and by a sequence of message instances for each channel in the protocol. It is also mentioned in Section 3.3 that the current state of a protocol is changed as a result of executing one of the enabled actions in the protocol. This last fact is now generalized as follows. The current state of a protocol is changed as a result of either executing one of the enabled protocol actions or executing one of the enabled error actions (assuming that transmission errors can occur during protocol execution). There are three types of error actions: message corruption, message loss, and message reorder. Next, we describe each of these actions in turn.

A message corruption action is enabled for execution at a protocol state iff there is a message instance, other than the reserved message instance **error**, in a channel at that state. A message corruption action that is enabled at a state can be executed at that state by replacing one message instance other than **error** by the message instance **error** in one of the channels yielding a next state of the protocol.

For example, consider the following protocol state R.1 in the vending machine protocol discussed in Section 2.1.

$$R.1 \ = \ \sim readyc \ \wedge \ \sim readyv \ \wedge \ ch.c.v=<money;\ selection> \ \wedge \ ch.v.c=< \ >$$

A message corruption action is enabled for execution at state R.1 because the channel from process c to process v has message instances other than error at that state. Executing a message corruption action starting at state R.1 yields either of the following two states R.4 or R.5:

$$R.4 \ = \ \sim readyc \ \wedge \ \sim readyv \ \wedge \ ch.c.v=<\textbf{error};\ selection> \ \wedge \ ch.v.c=< \ >$$

$$R.5 \ = \ \sim readyc \ \wedge \ \sim readyv \ \wedge \ ch.c.v=<money;\ \textbf{error}> \ \wedge \ ch.v.c=< \ >$$

Message corruption actions are also enabled at states R.4 and R.5. Executing a message corruption action at R.4 or at R.5 yields the following state R.6:

$$R.6 \ = \ \sim readyc \ \wedge \ \sim readyv \ \wedge \ ch.c.v=<\textbf{error};\ \textbf{error}> \ \wedge \ ch.v.c=< \ >$$

No message corruption action is enabled for execution at state R.6 because all message instances in the channels are **error** at that state.

A message loss action is enabled for execution at a protocol state iff there is a message instance in a channel at that state. A message loss action that is enabled at a state can be executed at that state by removing one message instance from one of the channels yielding a next state.

For example, a message loss action is enabled for execution at state R.1 above because the channel from process c to process v has message instances at that state. Executing a message loss action starting at state R.1 yields either of the following two states R.7 or R.8:

$$R.7 = \sim readyc \wedge \sim readyv \wedge ch.c.v=<selection> \wedge ch.v.c=<\,>$$

$$R.8 = \sim readyc \wedge \sim readyv \wedge ch.c.v=<money> \wedge ch.v.c=<\,>$$

Message loss actions are also enabled at states R.7 and R.8. Executing a message loss action at state R.7 or at R.8 yields the following state R.9:

$$R.9 = \sim readyc \wedge \sim readyv \wedge ch.c.v=<\,> \wedge ch.v.c=<\,>$$

No message loss action is enabled for execution at state R.9 because both channels are empty at that state.

A message reorder action is enabled for execution at a protocol state iff there are two distinct message instances in the same channel at that state. A message reorder action that is enabled at a state can be executed at that state by interchanging the orders of two adjacent distinct message instances in the same channel, yielding a next state.

For example, a message reorder action is enabled for execution at state R.1 above because the channel from process c to process v has two distinct message instances at that state. If a message reorder action is executed at state R.1, the resulting state R.10 is as follows:

$$R.10 = \sim readyc \wedge \sim readyv \wedge ch.c.v=<selection; money> \wedge ch.v.c=<\,>$$

A message reorder action is also enabled at state R.10, and executing this action at state R.10 yields state R.1.

5.2   PROTOCOL EXECUTION UNDER ERROR OCCURRENCE

At a protocol state, one of the enabled protocol actions or one of the enabled error actions is executed, yielding a next protocol state, and the cycle repeats generating a protocol execution. Protocol executions satisfy the following two restrictions.

i. *Error Atomicity:* Protocol and error actions are executed one at a time. In other words, the execution of a protocol or error action cannot start while another execution of a protocol or error action is in progress.

ii. *Rare Occurrence of Errors:* Only a finite number of error actions can be executed along any, possibly infinite, protocol execution.

As an example of a protocol execution, consider the state-transition diagram in Figure 5.1 for the vending machine protocol in Section 2.1. In this diagram, transitions represent executions of protocol actions, and the four protocol states R.0 to R.3 are as defined in Section 3.3. This diagram describes an infinite execution of the vending machine protocol when transmission errors cannot occur.

If message corruption can occur during protocol execution, then the state-transition diagram for the vending machine protocol becomes as shown in Figure 5.2. In this diagram, the six transitions labeled C represent executions of message corruption actions, while all other transitions represent executions of protocol actions. States R.4, R.5, and R.6 in this diagram are defined in section 5.1, while states R.11 and R.12 are defined as follows:

$$R.11 = \sim readyc \wedge readyv \wedge ch.c.v = <error> \wedge ch.v.c = < >$$

$$R.12 = \sim readyc \wedge \sim readyv \wedge ch.c.v = < > \wedge ch.v.c = <error>$$

States R.6, R.11, and R.12 are deadlock states because no protocol actions and no corruption actions are enabled at any of them. From this diagram, if message corruption actions are executed in a protocol execution, then this execution terminates at one of the deadlock states R.6, R.11, or R.12.

If message loss can occur during protocol execution, then the state-transition diagram for the vending machine protocol becomes as shown in Figure 5.3. In this diagram, the six transitions labeled L represent executions of message loss actions, while all other transitions represent executions of protocol actions. States R.7, R.8, and R.9 in this diagram are defined in Section 5.1, while state R.13 is defined as follows:

$$R.13 = \sim readyc \wedge readyv \wedge ch.c.v = < > \wedge ch.v.c = < >$$

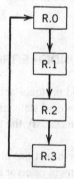

FIG. 5.1

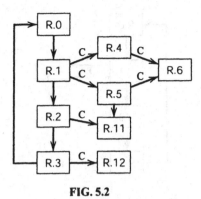

FIG. 5.2

From this diagram, if message loss actions are executed in a protocol execution, then this execution terminates at one of the deadlock states R.9 or R.13.

If message reorder can occur during protocol execution, then the state-transition diagram for the vending machine protocol becomes as shown in Figure 5.4. In this diagram, the two transitions labeled R represent executions of message reorder actions, while all other transitions represent executions of protocol actions. States R.8 and R.10 in this diagram are defined in Section 5.1, while state R.13 is defined above. From this diagram, if message reorder actions are executed an odd number of times in a protocol execution, then this execution terminates at the deadlock state R.13.

The above discussion indicates that the occurrence of transmission errors causes the execution of the vending machine protocol to terminate in a deadlock state. In the next section, we discuss how to make this protocol recover from error occurrence.

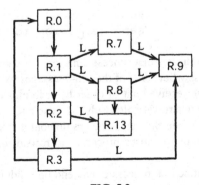

FIG. 5.3

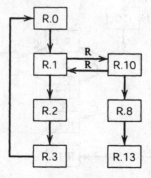

FIG. 5.4

5.3 PROTOCOLS THAT TOLERATE ERROR OCCURRENCE

In this section, we discuss how to modify the three protocols in Chapter 2 to make them error tolerant. These three protocols are the vending machine protocol in Section 2.1, the request–reply protocol in Section 2.2, and the Manchester encoding protocol in Section 2.3.

To make the vending machine protocol in Section 2.1 error tolerant, both processes in the protocol, c and v, need to be modified. We start with process c. Because messages sent from process v to process c can be corrupted into error messages, process c should be able to receive error messages. Thus, the following action should be added to process c.

```
rcv error from v  ->     skip
```

This action changes each occurrence of message corruption to an occurrence of message loss.

In order to detect and recover from message loss and reorder, process c should have the following timeout action:

```
timeout ~readyc /\ (#ch.c.v + #ch.v.c = 0)  ->
                    send money to v;
                    send selection to v
```

The guard of this action indicates that process c has previously sent money and selection messages to process v but some of the sent messages were lost before being received by v or they were received out of order by v. In either case, the protocol eventually reaches a state where variable readyc is false and the two channels between c and v are empty. When this happens, the timeout action becomes enabled for execution, and its execution causes process c to resend the two messages to process v.

Because of this timeout action, process c may end up sending too many money messages to process v. Therefore, process v should be modified, as discussed in

Section 2.1, to return all the extra money messages it receives from c. Moreover, process c should be modified to receive the returned money messages. Thus, the following action should be added to process c.

```
rcv money from v  ->    skip
```

The modified process c can now be defined as follows:

```
process c

var     readyc        :        boolean

begin
        readyc                -> send money to v;
                                 send selection to v;
                                 readyc := false
[]      rcv item from v  -> readyc := true
[]      rcv error from v -> skip
[]      timeout ~readyc /\ (#ch.c.v + #ch.v.c = 0)  ->
                                 send money to v;
                                 send selection to v
[]      rcv money from v -> skip
end
```

Process v is exactly as defined in Section 2.1 except that an action for receiving error messages is added to it. The modified process v is as follows:

```
process v

var     readyv        :        boolean

begin
        rcv money from c  ->
                    if  readyv  ->    send money to c
                    [] ~readyv  ->    readyv := true
                    fi

[]      rcv selection from c    ->
                    if  readyv  ->    send item to c;
                                      readyv := false

                    [] ~readyv  ->    skip
                    fi

[]      rcv error from c  ->      skip
end
```

To make the request–reply protocol in Section 2.2 error tolerant, both processes in the protocol, processes p and q, need to be modified while maintaining their symmetry. Therefore, we need only to discuss the modification to one process, process p.

Because messages sent from process q to process p can be corrupted into error messages, process p should be able to receive error messages. Thus, the following action should be added to process p:

rcv error from q —>   **skip**

This action changes every occurrence of message corruption to message loss.

In order to detect and recover from message loss, process p should have the following timeout action:

timeout ~readyp $\wedge$ (request#ch.p.q + reply#ch.q.p = 0) —>
                    send request **to** q

The guard of this action indicates that process p has previously sent a request message to process q but one of two errors has occurred. Either the request message was lost before being received by q or the request message was received by q but the resulting reply message from q was lost before being received by p. In either case, the protocol eventually reaches a state where variable readyp is false, the channel from p to q has no request message, and the channel from q to p has no reply message. When this happens, the timeout action is enabled for execution, and its execution causes p to resend a request message to q.

The modified process p can be defined as follows. (The modified process q is similar except that each occurrence of p is replaced by q and vice versa, and each occurrence of readyp is replaced by readyq.)

process p

var   readyp   :   **boolean**

begin
        readyp   —>   **send** request **to** q;
                                          readyp := **false**
☐   **rcv** request **from** q —>   **send** reply **to** q
☐   **rcv** reply **from** q   —>   readyp := **true**
☐   **rcv** error **from** q   —>   **skip**
☐   **timeout** ~readyp $\wedge$
                (request#ch.p.q + reply#ch.q.p = 0) —>
                                          send request **to** q
end

To make the Manchester encoding protocol in Section 2.3 error tolerant, the sender process s remains as defined in Section 2.3, while the receiver process r is modified. The modification is such that after transmission errors cease to occur, process r eventually starts to correctly identify the data bits in the received bit stream and store them in order in array rcvd. Note that process r may store some bits that are not data bits in array rcvd while error actions are being executed.

Because sent bits from process s to process r may be corrupted into error messages, r should be able to receive error messages. Thus, the following action should be added to process r.

```
rcv error from s  ->     str := ~str
```

The occurrence of bit corruption causes corrupted data bits not to be stored in array rcvd, but it does not affect the correct identification of subsequent data bits in the received bit stream and their correct storage in array rcvd. Similarly, the occurrence of bit reorder causes reordered data bits to be stored out of order in array rcvd or not to be stored in array rcvd altogether, but it does not affect the correct identification of subsequent data bits in the received bit stream and their correct storage in array rcvd.

In order to detect and recover from message loss, process r should not depend solely on variable str to identify the data bits in the received bit stream. Rather, process r should also apply the following criterion. If the last two bits received by process r are equal, then the last received bit cannot be a data bit. To apply this criterion, a new variable, named lastb, is added to process r.

The modified process r can be defined as follows:

```
process r

var    rcvd  :     array [integer] of 0..1,
       y     :     integer,
       str   :     boolean,
       lastb :     0..1

begin
       rcv zero from s             ->
             if   str /\ lastb=1 -> rcvd[y], y, str :=
                                         0, y+1, false
             [] ~str \/ lastb=0 -> str := true
             fi; lastb := 0

[]     rcv one from s             ->
             if   str /\ lastb=0 -> rcvd[y], y, str :=
                                         1, y+1, false
             [] ~str \/ lastb=1 -> str := true
             fi; lastb := 1
```

```
[]      rcv error from s              —>        str := ~str
end
```

Note that this protocol tolerates message loss under the reasonable assumption that array data in process s has infinitely many 0 bits and infinitely many 1 bits.

5.4 NORMAL TIMEOUT ACTIONS

From the above (vending machine and request–reply) protocol examples, it is clear that message loss can be detected and corrected using timeout actions. Because our discussion of timeout actions in Chapter 3 was sketchy, we discuss these actions in more detail next.

In Section 3.2, we stated that a timeout action in a process p is of the following form:

```
timeout <protocol predicate> —> <statement of p>
```

If the protocol predicate in the guard of a timeout action is chosen arbitrarily, then it may not be easy to implement this timeout action using a real-time clock. This point can be illustrated by the following example.

Consider a network of two symmetric processes $p[i: 0 .. 1]$ that circulate one token message. Because the token message can be lost during an execution of the protocol, each of the two processes has a timeout action that can detect token loss and generate and send a new token when a token loss is detected. Process $p[i]$ in this network can be defined as follows.

```
process p[i : 0..1]
begin
     rcv token from p[i +₂ 1] —> send token to p[i +₂ 1]
[]   timeout #ch. p[i].p[i +₂ 1] + #ch.p[i +₂ 1].p[i] = 0
                                —> send token to p[i +₂ 1]
end
```

Now consider a protocol state where the two channels between processes $p[0]$ and $p[1]$ are empty, indicating a token loss. At this state, both timeout actions in $p[0]$ and $p[1]$ are enabled for execution. However, executing any of these two actions disables the other action. In general, it is difficult to implement two actions in different processes such that these actions can both be enabled at the same time, and when either of these actions is executed, the other action is disabled. Implementing such actions is difficult because any implementation requires tight synchronization between the two processes in order to ensure that when both actions are enabled, at most one of them is executed.

The difficulty of implementing the timeout actions in the above protocol is caused by the fact that executing the two timeout actions in parallel causes the protocol to reach a state that cannot be reached by executing the two actions in sequence.

This problem can be solved by modifying the two timeout actions such that executing these actions in parallel causes the protocol to reach a state that can be reached by executing them in sequence, one after the other. In particular, process p[i] in the modified protocol can be defined as follows:

```
process p[i : 0..1]
begin
   rcv token from p[i +2 1] —> send token to p[i +2 1]
[] timeout (i = 0) /\
            (#ch. p[i].p[i +2 1] + #ch.p[i +2 1].p[i] = 0)
                              —> send token to p[i +2 1]
end
```

In this protocol, when a token is lost, only process p[0] times out and sends a new token. Process p[1] never times out.

It is clear from this example that some timeout actions are easier to implement than others. In the remainder of this section, we identify a class of timeout actions, called normal timeout actions, that are easy to implement. Then in Section 5.5, we discuss how to implement these actions using real-time clocks.

A normal timeout action in process p is one whose guard can be written in the following form:

```
timeout
        (local predicate of process p) /\
        (mp#ch.p.q ≤ kp) /\
        (mq#ch.q.r ≤ kq) /\
            ...
        (mv#ch.v.w ≤ kv)
```

where the following three conditions are satisfied:

i. kp, kq, . . . , kv are integers.
ii. mp are messages sent from process p to process q, mq are messages sent from process q to process r, . . . , mv are messages sent from process v to process w.
iii. Every two consecutive conjuncts of the form

```
(ms#ch.s.t ≤ ks) /\
(mt#ch.t.u ≤ kt)
```

in the timeout guard satisfy the following condition. In process t, the guard of each action that can send mt messages to process u is of the form **rcv** ms **from** s.

Next, we recall a number of timeout actions that were discussed earlier and show that each of them is normal. Consider the following timeout action, taken from process c in the error-tolerant version of the vending machine protocol in Section 5.3:

```
timeout
      ~readyc /\(#ch.c.v + #ch.v.c = 0)    ->
                                         send money to v;
                                         send selection to v
```

To show that this action is normal, observe that the guard of the action can be written as follows:

```
timeout
      ~readyc /\
      (ms#ch.c.v ≤ 0) /\
      (item#ch.v.c ≤ 0)
```

In this form, ~readyc is a local predicate of process c, and ms denotes any (money or selection) message that can be sent from process c to process v. It remains to show that the following consecutive conjuncts satisfy condition iii:

```
(ms#ch.c.v ≤ 0) /\
(item#ch.v.c ≤ 0)
```

This condition is satisfied because the guard of each action that can send item messages from process v to process c is of the form **rcv** selection **from** c.

As a second example, consider the following timeout action, taken from process p in the error-tolerant version of the request–reply protocol discussed in Section 5.3:

```
timeout
      ~readyp /\ (request#ch.p.q + reply#ch.q.p = 0) ->
                                         send request to q
```

To show that this action is normal, observe that the guard of this action can be written as follows:

```
timeout
      ~readyp /\
      (request#ch.p.q ≤ 0) /\
      (reply#ch.q.p ≤ 0)
```

In this guard, ~readyp is a local predicate of process p. It remains to show that the following consecutive conjuncts satisfy condition iii:

```
(request#ch.p.q ≤ 0) ∧
(reply#ch.q.p ≤ 0)
```

This condition is satisfied because the guard of each action that can send reply messages from process q to process p is of the form **rcv** request **from** p.

As a third example, consider the following timeout action taken from process p[i] in the original circulating token protocol discussed at the beginning of this section.

timeout $(\#ch.p[i].p[i +_2 1] + \#ch.p[i +_2 1].p[i] = 0)$

$\longrightarrow$ **send** token **to** $p[i +_2 1]$

The guard of this timeout action can be written as follows:

timeout   **true** ∧

         $(token\#ch.p[i].p[i +_2 1] ≤ 0)$ ∧

         $(token\#ch.p[i +_2 1].p[i] ≤ 0)$

The last two conjuncts in this guard do not satisfy condition iii in Section 5.4 because some action in process p[i] that sends token messages to process $p[i +_2 1]$ is a timeout action. Thus, this timeout action is not normal.

Now, consider the following timeout action taken from process p[i] in the modified circulating token protocol discussed at the beginning of this section:

timeout $(i = 1)$ ∧

    $(\#ch.p[i].p[i +_2 1] + \#ch.p[i +_2 1].p[i] = 0)$

$\longrightarrow$ **send** token **to** $p[i +_2 1]$

The guards of the timeout actions in processes p[0] and p[1] can be written, respectively, as follows:

timeout

     true ∧

     $(token\#ch.p[0].p[1] ≤ 0)$ ∧

     $(token\#ch.p[1].p[0] ≤ 0)$

timeout

     false

Clearly, the timeout action in process p[0] is normal and the timeout action in process p[1] can be deleted.

5.5 IMPLEMENTING NORMAL TIMEOUT ACTIONS

In this section, we discuss how to implement normal timeout actions using real-time clocks. Consider the following guard in a normal timeout action in some process p:

```
timeout
        (local predicate of process p) ∧
        (mp#ch.p.q ≤ kp) ∧
        (mq#ch.q.r ≤ kq)
```

The second and third conjuncts in this guard can be implemented using a real-time clock in process p. To discuss such an implementation, we adopt the following notation:

T   Current time measured by the clock in process p

TM.i   Time instant, measured by the clock in p, at which the ith from the last mp message was sent by p: If the ith from the last mp message has not yet been sent by p at time T, then TM.i is undefined at T

D.p.q   Maximum time period needed for an mp message to travel from process p to process q

D.q.r   Maximum time period for process q to execute an action, whose guard is **rcv** mp **from** p, possibly sending mq messages to process r and for the sent mq messages, if any, to travel from process q to process r

nq   Maximum number of mq messages sent by process q in an action, whose guard is **rcv** mp **from** p; for convenience assume that nq divides constant kq in the guard of the timeout action

Using this notation, the second conjunct in the guard of the timeout action can be implemented by the following real-time predicate:

```
(TM.(kp) is defined at T)   ∧
(T - TM.(kp)  >  D.p.q)
```

This predicate is called a real-time predicate because its value, true or false, at time T depends on the value of T.

Similarly, the third conjunct in the guard of the timeout action can be implemented by the following real-time predicate:

```
(TM.(kp + (kq/nq)) is defined at T)   ∧
(T - TM.(kp + (kq/nq))  >  D.p.q)
```

In this book, most timeout actions are normal. Thus, these timeout actions can be implemented using real-time clocks as discussed in this section.

5.6 TRANSMISSION ERRORS IN THE INTERNET

In this section, we discuss how message corruption, loss, and reorder can occur in the Internet. We start the discussion by describing error-free message transmission. Consider two processes p and q that reside in two far-away computers c and d in the

Internet. Process p resides on top of the IP process in computer c, and process q resides on top of the IP process in computer d. For process p to send a message mg to process q, the following steps are executed (an illustration of these steps is shown in Figure 5.5):

i. Process p sends message mg to the IP process in computer c.

ii. The IP process in c adds an IP header hd to message mg yielding an IP message of the form (hd, mg). The added header hd contains the IP address dst of computer d. The IP process in computer c uses address dst to determine the best neighboring router r for reaching computer d, then sends message (hd, mg) to the IP process of r.

iii. When the IP process of router r receives the (hd, mg) message, it uses the address dst in the header hd to determine the best neighboring router r′ for reaching computer d, and then sends the (hd, mg) message to the IP process of r′.

iv. Step iii is repeated several times until the (hd, mg) message reaches the IP process of the closest router r′ to computer d. When this happens, the IP process of r′ sends the (hd, mg) message to the IP process in computer d.

v. When the IP process of d receives the (hd, mg) message, it removes the header hd and forwards the remaining message mg to process q.

These steps describe a scenario where a message is transmitted without errors from process p in computer c to process q in computer d. Next, we describe how message corruption, loss, and reorder can disrupt such a scenario:

a. Message corruption can occur for natural reasons. While the (hd, mg) message is being transmitted between the IP processes of two adjacent computers, it is possible that some bits in the message or its header are changed (from 0 to 1 or from 1 to 0) due to natural noise such as heavy rains or thunderstorms.

b. Message loss can occur for three reasons: message corruption, congestion,

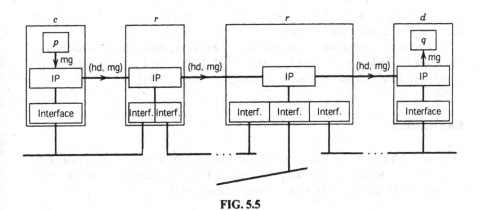

FIG. 5.5

and routing. First, if some bits in the header hd of message (hd, mg) are corrupted while the message is being transmitted to the IP process of a router, then the IP process of the router can detect the corruption and discards the message, causing a message loss. Second, if the IP process of a router receives the message while the router is busy routing other messages, a condition called congestion, then the router discards the message. Third, if the message is routed wrongly such that its time-to-live expires before it reaches its ultimate destination, then the message is discarded.

c. Message reorder can occur for two reasons: message loss and subsequent retransmission, and routing. These two causes of message reorder can be illustrated by two examples. First, consider a scenario where process p sends two messages, mg.0 followed by mg.1, to process q. Message mg.0 is lost (as discussed above) while message mg.1 is received by q. Later, process p detects the loss of message mg.0 and resends it to process q, causing q to receive mg.0 after mg.1. Second, consider a scenario where process p sends two messages, mg.0 followed by mg.1, to process q. The two messages are routed through different routes between p and q, and process q ends up receiving message mg.0 after message mg.1.

In summary, message corruption occurs due to natural noise; message loss occurs due to message corruption, congestion, and routing; and message reorder occurs due to message loss and subsequent retransmission and routing.

The above presentation concerning message transmission from process p to process q is full of details. These details can be abstracted away by stating that there is a "virtual" channel from process p to process q and that any message sent over this channel can be corrupted, lost, or reordered with other sent messages.

5.7 BIBLIOGRAPHICAL NOTES

The concept of error tolerance is discussed in Arora and Gouda [1993]. This concept is based on the theory of adaptive and stabilizing systems discussed in Gouda and Herman [1991], Schneider [1993], and Gouda [1995a]. Examples of adaptive and stabilizing network protocols are discussed in Arora et al. [1990], Gouda and Multari [1991], and Gouda [1995b].

The need for timeout actions in order to make network protocols error-tolerant is discussed in Fisher et al. [1985], Lynch et al. [1988], and Gouda and Multari [1991]. Abstract timeout actions are discussed in Gouda [1993].

EXERCISES

1 (Transmission Errors). What is the smallest number of transmission errors that can occur to change the content of a channel from < data(3, 31) ; data(4, 17) ; data(5, 1) ; data(6, 913) > to   < error ; data(6, 913) ; error >.

2   (Transmission Errors).What is the largest number of transmission errors that can occur to change the content of a channel from < data(3, 31) ; data(4, 17) ; data(5, 1) ; data(6, 913) > to < error ; data(6, 913) ; error >.

3   (Timeout Actions).   Consider a protocol that consists of the following two processes:

```
process p
var wait :     boolean
begin
    ~wait                --> send data to q; wait := true
[] rcv ack from q --> wait := false
[] timeout G         --> send data to q
end

process q
begin
    rcv data from p --> {store data} send ack to p
end
```

Assume that messages can be lost, but neither corrupted nor reordered, during transmission. Design the timeout guard G such that message loss cannot lead to data loss (but may lead to data duplication).

4   (State-Transition Diagram). Draw a state-transition diagram for the protocol in exercise 3. Use this state-transition diagram to argue that data cannot be lost in this protocol.

5   (Preventing Data Duplication). Although data cannot be lost in the protocol in exercise 3, data can be duplicated. Show a scenario of this protocol where some data are duplicated. Modify the protocol so that no data can be duplicated. (Hint: Modify the protocol by adding one bit to each data message.)

6   (State-Transition Diagram). Draw a state-transition diagram for the modified protocol in exercise 5. Use this state-transition diagram to argue that in this protocol data can neither be lost nor duplicated.

7   (Alternating-Bit Protocol). Consider a protocol that consists of the following two processes:

```
process p
var  bnow, b   :  boolean
begin
    true                      --> {resend current data msg}
                              S.0
[] rcv ack(b) from q --> {if this ack acknowledges}
```

```
                                          {current data message,  }
                                          {send next data message.}
                                          S.1
      end

      process q
      var cnow, c  : boolean
      begin
         rcv data(c) from p -> {if this is the next data}
                               {msg, store the message. }
                               S.2
      end
```

Assume that messages can be lost, but neither corrupted nor reordered, during transmission. Complete this protocol such that message loss cannot lead to data loss or data duplication.

8 (State-Transition Diagram). Draw a state-transition diagram for the protocol in exercise 7. Use this state-transition diagram to argue that data can neither be lost nor duplicated in this protocol.

9 (Protocol Comparison). The two protocols in exercises 5 and 7 perform the same task, namely that of transmitting data over a medium that can lose messages. Compare the two protocols in the following categories: use of timeout actions, the number of transmitted bits, and ease of implementation.

10 (Tolerating Message Corruption). Modify the protocol in exercise 5 such that it can tolerate message corruption.

11 (Tolerating Message Corruption). Modify the protocol in exercise 7 such that it can tolerate message corruption.

12 (Tolerating Message Reorder). Modify the protocol in exercise 5 such that it can tolerate message reorder.

13 (Tolerating Message Reorder). Modify the protocol in exercise 7 such that it can tolerate message reorder. (*Hint*: The protocol is modified by making the sequence numbers of data and ack messages to be of type integer rather than 0 and 1.)

14 (State-Transition Diagram). Draw a state-transition diagram for the protocol in exercise 13.

15 (Tolerating Message Duplication). Use the state-transition diagram in exercise 14 to argue that the protocol in exercise 13 can tolerate the possibility that any message in any channel in the protocol is duplicated a finite number of times in its channel.

16 (Error Recovery in a Ring Network). Consider a ring network with processes

p[i: 0 . . n − 1]. Each process p[i] receives messages only from its preceding process p[i −$_n$ 1] and sends messages only to its succeeding process p[i +$_n$ 1]. At each instant, there is exactly one message in all the channels in the network. The processes are defined, under the assumption that transmission errors cannot occur, as follows:

```
process p[0]
var      dst   :     1..n-1
begin
   rcv ack from p[n-1] -> dst := any;
                          send data(dst) to p[1]
end


process p[i : 1..n-1]
var      d    :     1..n-1
begin
   rcv data(d) from p[i-1] ->
      if  d = i -> {store data}
                    send ack to p[i +n 1]
      [] d ≠ i -> {ignore data}
                    send data(d) to p[i +n 1]
      fi
[] rcv ack from p[i-1] -> send ack to p[i +n 1]
end
```

Modify the processes such that the protocol can tolerate message corruption, loss, and reorder.

17 (Traffic Light System). Consider a protocol between two symmetrical processes that represent traffic lights at intersecting streets. Each process has exactly one local variable state that is declared as follows:

```
var    state  :    0..2
                   {state = 0 iff light is green}
                   {state = 1 iff light is yellow}
                   {state = 2 iff light is red}
```

When the variable state of either process has a value s, then that process sends st(s) messages to the other process. The protocol tolerates message loss and corruption and ensures that the two state variables never have the value 0 simultaneously. (*Hint:* Initially, one state variable has the value 0 and the other state variable has the value 2.)

18 (Traffic Light System). Draw a state-transition diagram for the protocol in exercise 17.

19   (State-Transition Diagram). Draw a state-transition diagram for the request–reply protocol in Section 2.2 under the assumption that message reorder can occur (but neither message loss nor message corruption can occur). Use this transition diagram to explain how does this protocol tolerate message reorder.

20   (Tolerating Errors in Data Messages). The following protocol is designed under the assumptions the messages cannot be corrupted, lost, or reordered:

```
process p
inp d    : array [integer] of integer,
var x    : integer,          {initially, x = 0}
    wait : boolean           {initially, wait = false}
begin
   ~wait                 ->   wait := true;
                              send data(d[x]) to q
 [] rcv ack from q       ->   wait, x := false, x+1
end


process q
var  e : array [integer] of integer,
     y : integer             {initially, y = 0}
begin
   rcv data(e[y]) from p -> y := y+1; send ack to p
end
```

Modify this protocol under the assumption that data messages can be corrupted, lost, or reordered, whereas ack messages cannot be corrupted, lost, or reordered.

21   (Tolerating Bit Loss). A process s has an input array named data whose elements are bits in the range 0 .. 1. Process s sends the bits of array data, one by one to another process r, which stores them in a variable array named rcvd. Assume that the sent messages carrying the bits of array data can be lost but no two consecutive messages can be lost. To overcome message loss, process s sends each bit of array data in two consecutive messages so that if one of these messages is lost, the other message is guaranteed to be received safely by process r. Design processes s and r.

22   (Tolerating Message Loss in Resource Allocation). Consider the following resource allocation protocol where users u[i: 0 .. n–1] compete for a single resource whose access is controlled by a controller c.

```
process u[i: 0 .. n-1]
var wait : boolean               {initially false}
begin
   ~ wait               -> wait := true; send rqst to c
 [] rcv grant from c -> wait := false; send rls to c
```

```
    []   rcv rjct from c  -> wait := false
    end

process c
const    n
var   avail  :  boolean              {initially true}
par   i      :  0..n-1
begin
    rcv rqst from u[i] ->
                     if  avail -> send grant to u[i]
                     [] ~avail -> send rjct to u[i]
                     fi; avail := false
    []       rcv rls from u[i] ->
                     avail := true
    end
```

Assuming that only grant and rjct messages can be lost, modify this protocol to ensure that it tolerates the loss of these messages as follows. If a grant or rjct message from process c to a process u[i] is lost, then u[i] times out and assigns its wait variable the value false. Moreover, if a grant message from c to u[i] is lost, then c times out and assigns its variable avail the value true.

23 (Tolerating Message Reorder). A process p that sends data messages to a process q is as follows:

```
process p
const     k
var       s     :     0..k-1
begin
    true    ->      send data(s) to q; s := s +_k 1
end
```

Each sent data message can be reordered with other messages in the channel from p to q before the message is received by q. Assume that neither message corruption nor loss can occur. Assume also that each sent message does not take part in more than r occurrences of message reorder. Recall that each occurrence of message reorder occurs between two adjacent messages in the channel from p to q.

a What is the relation between k and r so that process q can detect every occurrence of message reorder?

b Design process q such that it delivers the received messages in order.

24 (Error-Tolerant Voting). Consider a network that consists of a process array p[i: 0 .. n-1] and process c. The computation in this network proceeds in rounds. In each round, process c sends a rqst message to each process p[i] and then waits to receive a rply(b) message from each p[i], where b is either 0 or 1.

If in the xth round process c receives a rply(1) message from each p[i], then process c assigns a value 1 to element rslt[x] in its variable array rslt. If in the xth round process c receives a rply(0) message from at least one p[i], then process c assigns a value 0 to element rslt[x] in its variable array rslt. Design a process p[i] and process c in this network under the assumption that transmission errors, namely message corruption, loss, and reorder, can occur.

25 Two Circulating Tokens). It is required to design a network p[i: 0 . . n–1], where there are two channels between each p[i] and p[i +$_n$ 1]. Thus, the channels in the network form two unidirectional rings. The processes circulate exactly one token in each ring and can tolerate token loss. Process p[i] in this network is as follows:

```
process p[i : 0..n-1]
inp       N    :    set {i -n 1 ,  i +n 1}
par       j    :    N
begin
   rcv tkn from p[j]  ->   ...
[] timeout  ERR.j  ->...
end
```

Predicate ERR.j in process p[i] is defined as follows:

```
(j = i -n 1 /\
(For every k, 0 <= k < n, #ch.p[k].p[k -n 1] = 0)) \/
(j = i +n 1 /\
(For every k, 0 <= k < n, #ch.p[k]. p[k +n 1] = 0))
```

Complete the design of process p[i].

CHAPTER 6

CONNECTIONS

There are two types of communications in a network: connectionless and connection-oriented. In a connectionless communication, a process p can start sending data messages to another process q without obtaining a permission to do so from q. In this case, q can discard any data message that it receives from p. For example, q starts discarding messages when the number of messages received from p exceeds the number of available buffers to hold messages in q.

In a connection-oriented communication, before a process p can start sending data messages to another process q, p needs to obtain a permission from q to do so. For historical reasons, the fact that p has obtained a permission to send data messages to q is expressed by saying that p has established a connection to q. An established connection from p to q can later be "disconnected" by a request from p or from q. The message exchange for establishing and disconnecting connections between two processes is called a connection protocol. Connection protocols are the subject of this chapter.

The basic idea of a connection protocol is very simple. In order to establish a connection to q, process p sends a crqst message to q, then waits to receive either a crply message or a drply message from q. Receiving a crply message indicates that a connection from p to q has been established and that p can now send up to m data messages to q. Receiving a drply message indicates that no connection from p to q has been established, but p may try to establish a connection later.

Anytime after a connection has been established, the connection can be disconnected by p or by q as follows. Process p can disconnect the established connection by sending a drqst message to process q, then waiting to receive a drply message from q. Process q can disconnect the established connection by waiting to receive a (data or drqst) message from p, then sending back a drply message to p. In both cases, the connection is disconnected when process p receives a drply message from process q.

The five messages in this protocol have the following meanings:

crqst	A connection request from p to q
crply	A connection reply from q to p
data	A data message from p to q
drqst	A disconnection request from p to q
drply	A disconnection reply from q to p

Note that a drply message is used as a negative reply to a crqst message and as a positive reply to a drqst message.

Figure 6.1 shows the four main scenarios in a connection protocol. In the first scenario (Figure 6.1a), process p sends a crqst message to process q, which replies negatively with a drply message. In the other three scenarios, process q replies positively with a crply message to process p. These three scenarios differ in which process disconnects the established connection: process p (Figure 6.1b), process q (Figure 6.1c), or both p and q (Figure 6.1d). Note that in Figures 6.1c and 6.1d process q can still receive, data or drqst, messages after it has sent a drply message because process p has sent these messages before it has received the sent drply message.

Problems arise if message loss or reorder can occur during the execution of the protocol. Note that message corruption does not cause problems other than those caused by message loss. In fact, an action of the form **rcv error from** <other process> —> **skip** can be added to each of the two processes in the protocol so that each occurrence of message corruption is eventually transformed into an occurrence of message loss.

Message loss can cause the following problem. When process p sends a request (i.e., crqst or drqst) message, then p may wait indefinitely for a reply (i.e., crply or drply) message that never arrives because either the request or the reply is lost during transmission. This problem can be easily solved by making process p send and resend the request message many times until p receives a reply message.

Message reorder can cause a more serious problem. Consider the scenario where process p establishes a connection to process q and then sends some data messages followed by a drqst message to q. Although the drqst message is sent after all the data messages, a message reorder causes process q to receive the drqst message while some data message d is still in the channel from process p to process q. As a reply to the received drqst message, process q sends back a drply message to process p and the established connection is disconnected. Later process p sends a crqst message to process q, and another message reorder causes q to receive the crqst message while the old data message d remains in the channel from process p to process q. Process q sends back a crply message to process p, and a new connection is established from p to q. Process q now receives message d and thinks wrongly that d has been sent in the current connection and accepts it. In effect, a message

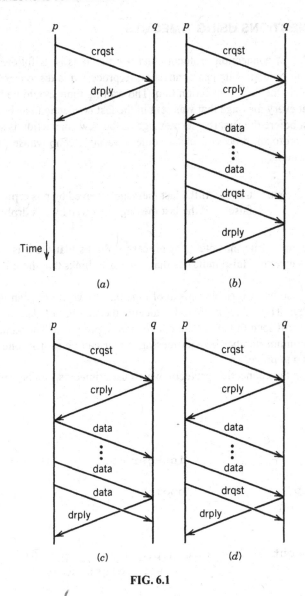

FIG. 6.1

that was sent in an earlier connection has been accepted in the current connection. This is clearly an erroneous behavior that should not be allowed.

There are two general techniques to deal with this problem: timeouts and connection identifiers. In Section 6.1, we discuss connection protocols that use timeouts, and in Section 6.2, we discuss connection protocols that use connection identifiers. Then in Section 6.3, we discuss protocols where each process can request to establish a connection to the other process in the protocol. Finally, we discuss the connection protocol in the Internet in Section 6.4.

6.1 CONNECTIONS USING TIMEOUTS

The main idea of connection protocols that use timeouts is as follows. Process p waits for some time after its last connection to process q is disconnected before it tries to establish the next connection to q. The waiting time should be long enough to ensure that every message that was sent in the last connection has been either received or lost before the first (crqst) message of the new connection is sent.

In such a protocol, process p has a boolean variable conp whose value has the following meaning.

$$conp = true \quad \text{if the last message received by p is crply}$$
$$false \quad \text{if the last message received by p is drply}$$

Informally, conp = true indicates that process p thinks that there is a connection from p to q and conp = false indicates that process p thinks that there is no connection from p to q.

Process p also has a variable cansnd of type 0 .. m, where m is an input of type positive integer. The value of cansnd indicates the number of data messages that process p can still send in the current connection to process q. The value of m indicates the maximum number of data messages that can be sent in one connection from process p to process q.

Process p in the connection protocol, which uses timeouts, can be defined as follows.

```
process p

inp    m                 :      integer              { m > 0 }

var    conp              :      boolean,
       cansnd            :      0..m

begin
       timeout ~conp /\ (#ch.p.q + #ch.q.p = 0)
                         -> send crqst to q

☐      rcv crply from q  -> conp, cansnd := true, m

☐      conp              ->
              if cansnd>0 -> send data to q;
                            cansnd := cansnd-1
                 ☐ true  -> send drqst to q;
                            cansnd := 0;
              fi
```

```
[]      rcv drply from q  -> conp := false
end
```

Process p has four actions. In the first action, when conp is false and the two channels between p and q are empty, indicating that every message sent in the last connection has been either received or lost, process p can send a crqst message to q. If the sent crqst message or its reply, whether crply or drply, is lost, this action becomes enabled one more time and another crqst message is sent, and so on.

In the second action, process p receives a crply message from process q and updates the value of conp to true and the value of cansnd to m.

In the third action, when conp is true and cansnd is larger than zero, process p can send a data message to q and decrement variable cansnd by one, or can send a drqst message to q and make variable cansnd equal 0. On the other hand, when conp is true and cansnd is zero, p can only send a drqst message to q.

In the fourth action, process p receives a drply message from process q and updates the value of conp to false.

Process q in this protocol is "passive." This means that process q does not send a message to process p unless it receives some message from p. In other words, every message that process q sends is a reply to some message that q has just received from p. Passive processes are nice because their presence in a protocol tends to make the protocol easier to understand.

Process q has only one boolean variable, conq. This variable is assigned the value true when q receives a crqst message and decides to accept the connection. It can be assigned the value false at any other time.

Process q in the connection protocol, which uses timeouts, can be defined as follows:

```
process q

var     conq            :       boolean

begin
        rcv crqst from p  ->
                if true       ->      conq := true;
                                      send crply to p
                   [] true    ->      conq := false;
                                      send drply to p
                fi

[]      conq            ->      conq := false

[]      rcv data from p   ->
                if ~conq      ->      {discard data msg}
                                      send drply to p
                   [] conq    ->      {store data msg} skip
```

```
            fi

□       rcv drqst from p   —>      conq := false;
                                   send drply to p
end
```

Process q has four actions. In the first action, q receives a crqst message from p and decides nondeterministically whether to assign variable conq the value true and send a crply message to p, or whether to assign variable conq the value false and send a drply message to p.

In the second action, process q detects that variable conq is true, and assigns it the value false.

In the third action, q receives a data message from p and decides, based on the current value of variable conq, whether to accept the data message or whether to discard the data message and send back a drply message to p. (The reason for discarding the data message in the second case is that previously q has disconnected the connection and no longer has reserved buffers to store the received data messages.)

In the fourth action, q receives a drqst message from p, then assigns variable conq the value false (it is possible that conq is false already), and sends a drply message to p.

The problem with this protocol is that process p cannot immediately establish a next connection to process q after removing the current connection. This problem does not occur in the connection protocol in the next section.

6.2 CONNECTIONS USING IDENTIFIERS

In this section, we discuss a connection protocol where connections are assigned unique identifiers. Before a process sends a message in a connection, it attaches the connection identifier to the message. When a process receives a message, it compares the attached connection identifier with the identifier of the current connection. If the two identifiers are equal, the process regards the received message as sent in the current connection and accepts the message. Otherwise, it regards the message as sent in a previous connection and discards the message.

The unique identifier of a connection is a pair (sp, sq), where sp is a sequence number selected by process p and sq is a sequence number selected by process q. Process p keeps track of sp and ensures that if a connection (sp', sq') is established after a connection (sp, sq), then sp' is larger than sp. Similarly, process q keeps track of sq and ensures that if a connection (sp', sq') is established after a connection (sp, sq), then sq' is larger than sq.

It is possible to design a connection protocol where each connection is uniquely identified by a single sequence number s. (Such a protocol is discussed in exercise 4 at the end of this chapter.) In this protocol, however, both p and q need to keep track of s so that they always agree on the current value of s. This requires both p and q to always remember s, even when there is no established connection from p to q. In our current protocol, where p keeps track of sp and q keeps track of sq, it is possible to make p forget sp and q forget sq when there is no established connection from p to q; this is discussed at the end of this section. Next, we describe one representative scenario of the current protocol.

Process p sends a crqst(sp) message to process q and then waits to receive a reply message from q. If the reply from q does not arrive at p for a long time, then p ends up sending several crqst(sp) messages to q. One of the sent crqst(sp) messages is finally received by process q, which decides to accept the request and sends a crply(sp, sq) message to process p. When p receives the crply(sp, sq) message, it sends a sequence of data(sp, sq) messages followed by a drqst(sp, sq) message to q. Then, p waits to receive a drply(sp, sq) message from q. If the drply(sp, sq) from q does not arrive at p for a long time, p ends up sending several drqst(sp, sq) messages to q. One of the sent drqst(sp, sq) messages is finally received by q, which sends back a drply(sp, sq) message to p and increments the value of its sq variable by 1. When p receives the drply(sp, sq) message, it increments the value of its sp variable by 1. Thus, connection (sp, sq) is terminated and the next connection will be identified by pair (sp + 1, sq + 1).

In this protocol, process p has six variables: conp, cansnd, sp, sq, x, and y. Variables conp and cansnd are as defined in the protocol in Section 6.1. Variables sp and sq store the identifier of the current connection, and variables x and y store the connection identifier in the last received message, whether crply or drply, from process q.

Process p in the connection protocol, which uses identifiers, can be defined as follows:

```
process p

inp    m              :      integer              { m > 0 }

var    conp           :      boolean,
       cansnd:               0..m,
       sp, sq         :      integer,
       x, y           :      integer

begin
       ~conp                          ->     send crqst(sp) to q

[]     rcv crply(x, y) from q  ->
               if ~conp /\ sp = x -> conp, cansnd, sq :=
                                          true, m, y
                   [] conp \/ sp ≠ x -> skip
               fi

[]     conp                            ->
```

```
        if cansnd > 0 -> send data(sp, sq) to q;
                             cansnd := cansnd-1
        [] true          -> send drqst(sp, sq) to q;
                             cansnd := 0
        fi

[]    rcv drply(x, y) from q  ->
        if sp = x    ->        conp, sp := false, sp + 1
        [] sp ≠ x    ->        skip
        fi
end
```

Process p has four actions. In the first action, when process p detects that its conp variable is false, it sends a crqst(sp) message to process q.

In the second action, when process p receives a crply(x, y) message, it checks the value of its variable conp and compares the value of its variable sp with x. If conp is false and sp equals to x (indicating that the received message is being received for the first time and that it belongs to the current connection), then process p accepts the message and updates its three variables conp, cansnd, and sq accordingly. Otherwise, process p discards the message.

The third and fourth actions are similar to the third and fourth actions, respectively, of process p in Section 6.1.

Process q in the connection protocol, which uses identifiers, can be defined as follows:

```
process q

var    conq        :        boolean,
       sq          :        integer,
       x, y        :        integer

begin
      rcv crqst(x) from p ->
          if true -> conq, y := true, sq;
                     send crply(x, y) to p
          [] true -> conq, sq, y := false, sq+1, sq;
                     send drply(x, y) to p
          fi

[]    conq                   -> conq, sq := false, sq+1

[]    rcv data(x, y) from p ->
          if sq ≠ y -> {discard data msg}
                       send drply(x, y) to p
          [] sq = y -> {store data msg} skip
```

```
                fi

[]      rcv drqst(x, y) from p  ->
            if sq ≠ y -> skip
            [] sq = y  -> conq, sq := false, sq+1
            fi; send drply(x, y) to p
end
```

This process q is the same as process q in Section 6.1 except for three modifications. First, process q now has three additional variables, sq, x, and y. Variable sq is the identifying sequence number of the current connection in process q, and variables x and y store the attached identifier of the last received message.

Second, when process q receives a data(x, y) or drqst(x, y) message from process p, q compares its identifier sq of the current connection with the identifier y in the received message. If sq is different from y (indicating that the received message belongs to a past connection), then process q replies by sending back a drply(x, y) message to process p. Otherwise, sq equals y (indicating that the received message belongs to the current connection). In this case, the received message is processed as in process q in Section 6.1.

Third, whenever variable conq is assigned the value false (indicating that q is rejecting or removing the current connection), variable sq is assigned the value sq + 1.

In this protocol, each of the two variables sp in process p and sq in process q is incremented by 1 before the establishment of each new connection. This protocol can be extended such that each of these variables is incremented by any value, rather than by 1, before the establishment of each new connection. Thus in the extended protocol, if a connection is identified by a pair (sp, sq), then the next connection is identified by a pair (sp', sq'), where sp < sp' and sq < sq'.

This extension suggests the following novel implementation of variables sp in process p and sq in process q. When there is no connection from p to q, process p can forget the current value of its variable sp and process q can forget the current value of its variable sq. When process p needs to establish a connection to process q, p copies the current value of its real-time clock into its variable sp, and q copies the current value of its real-time clock into its variable sq. These new values of variables sp and sq are guaranteed to be larger than their last values as required by the extended protocol.

6.3 FULL-DUPLEX AND HALF-DUPLEX CONNECTIONS

The connection protocols in the last two sections can be called simplex because they allow process p to establish connections to process q but do not allow q to establish connections to p. A connection protocol is called duplex if it allows each of the two processes to establish connections to the other process in the protocol. There are two types of duplex protocols: full-duplex and half-duplex. In a full-duplex protocol, the two processes can have connections to one another at the same time. In a half-duplex protocol, at most one process can have a connection to the other process at any given instant.

In this section, we discuss several duplex protocols between two processes r and s. The processes are called r and s, instead of p and q, because in designing processes r and s, we make use of processes p and q in Section 6.1. (Processes p and q in Section 6.2 can also be used in designing r and s.) In the remainder of this section, all references to processes p and q mean the processes in Section 6.1.

Because process r can establish a connection to process s, process r should behave like process p and process s should behave like process q. Similarly, because process s can establish a connection to process r, process s should behave like process p and process r should behave like process q. In summary, each of the two processes r and s should behave like the two processes p and q. This implies that processes r and s are symmetrical.

In order to make process r behave like processes p and q, process r is designed as follows. First, the variables of r consist of the variables of p and the variables of q. Second, the actions of r consist of the actions of p and the actions of q, with a slight modification discussed below. Note that in this protocol processes r and s can establish connections to one another at the same time, and so the protocol is full-duplex.

Process r in the full-duplex protocol can be defined as follows. (Process s in this protocol is identical to process r except that each occurrence of r is replaced by s and vice versa.)

```
process r

inp    m               :    integer                    { m > 0 }

var    conp, conq      :    boolean,
       cansnd          :    0..m

begin
       timeout
            ~conp ∧
            (crqst#ch.r.s + data#ch.r.s + drqst#ch.r.s
             + crply#ch.s.r + drply#ch.s.r = 0)
                            ->        send crqst to s

 []     rcv crply from s  ->      conp, cansnd := true, m

 []     conp               ->
            if cansnd>0 ->          send data to s;
                                    cansnd := cansnd-1
             [] true       ->       send drqst to s;
                                    cansnd := 0
            fi

 []     rcv drply from s  ->      conp := false
```

```
☐     rcv crqst from s    ->
                if true      ->          conq := true;
                                         send crply to s
                   ☐ true    ->          conq := false;
                                         send drply to s
                fi

☐     conq                  ->          conq := false

☐     rcv data from s       ->
                if ~conq     ->          {discard data msg}
                                         send drply to s
                   ☐ conq    ->          {store data msg} skip
                fi
☐     rcv drqst from s  ->               conq := false;
                                         send drply to s
end
```

The two variables conp and cansnd in process r correspond to the two variables of process p, while variable conq in process r corresponds to the variable of process q. The first four actions of process r correspond to the actions of process p, while the last four actions of process r correspond to the actions of process q.

Note that the guard of the first action in process r is slightly different from the guard of the corresponding first action in process p. Specifically, the guard of the first action in process r does not test whether the two channels between r and s are empty (as does the guard of the first action in process p). Instead, this guard tests that the two channels between r and s have no messages belonging to the connections from r to s. The number of messages, in the channels between r and s belonging to the connection from s to r are not tested.

The above protocol can be further generalized by allowing at most v full-duplex connections (instead of at most 1) to be established between processes r and s. This generalization can be achieved by assigning each full-duplex connection a unique identifier in the range $0 .. v - 1$. Also, each of the three variables in processes r and s, namely conp, conq, and cansnd, becomes an array of v elements. Thus, the element conp[c] denotes the value of conp for connection c, where c is the connection identifier in the range $0 .. v - 1$. Moreover, every messages sent in a connection is attached with the unique identifier of its connection.

Process r in the full-duplex, multiple-connection protocol can be defined as follows. (Process s in this protocol is identical to process r except that each occurrence of r is replaced by s and vice versa.)

```
process r

const v

inp    m              :         integer      { m > 0 }
```

```
var     conp, conq  :      array [0..v-1] of boolean,
        cansnd      :      array [0..v-1] of 0..m,

par   c             :      0..v-1

begin
        timeout
            ~conp[c] ∧
            (crqst(c)#ch.r.s + data(c)#ch.r.s +
            drqst(c)#ch.r.s + crply(c)#ch.s.r +
            drply(c)#ch.s.r = 0)
                            -> send crqst(c) to s
□   rcv crply(c) from s  -> conp[c], cansnd[c] :=
                            true, m

□   conp[c]               ->
        if cansnd[c]>0  -> send data(c) to s;
                           cansnd[c] := cansnd[c]-1
        □ true          -> send drqst(c) to s;
                           cansnd[c] := 0
        fi

□   rcv drply(c) from s  -> conp[c] := false

□   rcv crqst(c) from s  ->
        if true         -> conq[c] := true;
                           send crply(c) to s
        □ true          -> conq[c] := false;
                           send drply(c) to s
        fi

□   conq[c]              -> conq[c] := false

□   rcv data(c) from s   ->
        if ~conq[c]     -> { discard data msg }
                           send drply(c) to s
        □ conq[c]       -> { accept data msg } skip
        fi

□   rcv drqst(c) from s  -> conq[c] := false;
                           send drply(c) to s
end
```

This protocol can reach a state where a connection c is established from r to s and a connection c is established from s to r. At this state, the two processes r and s can exchange data messages over the full-duplex connection c. Next, we show how to modify this protocol such that at each instant, if connection c is established from r to s, then connection c is not established from s to r, and vice versa. The resulting protocol is a half-duplex, multiple-connection protocol.

In order to transform the above full-duplex protocol to a half-duplex one, process r is modified as follows. (Process s is modified similarly.)

i. A boolean variable array, named wait, is added to process r. Array wait has the following meaning:

```
wait[c] = true   iff   process r has not received a
                       drply(c) message after sending
                       the last crqst(c) message.
```

ii. The timeout action in process r is modified by adding ~conq[c] to its guard and adding wait[c] := **true** to its statement. The modified timeout action in process r is as follows:

```
timeout
~conp[c] ∧ ~conq[c] ∧
(crqst(c)#ch.r.s + data(c)#ch.r.s +
drqst(c)#ch.r.s + crply(c)#ch.s.r +
drply(c)#ch.s.r = 0)
          —> send crqst(c) to s; wait[c] := true
```

iii. The receive drply(c) action in process r is modified by adding wait[c] := **false** to its statement. The modified action is as follows:

```
rcv drply(c) from s —> conp[c], wait[c] :=
                              false, false
```

iv. The receive crqst(c) action in process r is modified by adding ~wait[c] as a guard in its selection statement. The modified action is as follows:

```
rcv crqst(c) from s —>
  if ~wait[c]          —> conq[c] := true;
                          send crply(c) to s
  [] true              —> conq[c] := false;
                          send drply(c) to s
  fi
```

Process r in the half-duplex, multiple-connection protocol can be defined as follows. (Process s in this protocol is identical to process r except that each occurrence of r is replaced by s and vice versa.)

```
process r
const v

inp    m                         : integer      { m > 0 }

var    conp, conq, wait : array [0..v-1] of boolean,
       cansnd            : array [0..v-1] of 0..m,
par    c                         : 0..v-1

begin
       timeout
               ~conp[c] ∧ ~conq[c] ∧
               (crqst(c)#ch.r.s + data(c)#ch.r.s +
               drqst(c)#ch.r.s + crply(c)#ch.s.r +
               drply(c)#ch.s.r = 0)
                          ->        send crqst(c) to s;
                                    wait[c] := true


 []    rcv crply(c) from s ->  conp[c], cansnd[c] :=
                                    true, m


 []    conp[c]                  ->
               if cansnd[c]>0 -> send data(c) to s;
                                    cansnd[c] := cansnd[c]-1
               [] true          -> send drqst(c) to s;
                                    cansnd[c] := 0
               fi


 []    rcv drply(c) from s ->  conp[c], wait[c] :=
                                    false, false


 []    rcv crqst(c) from s ->
               if ~wait[c]     ->  conq[c] := true;
                                    send crply(c) to s
                   [] true      ->  conq[c] := false;
                                    send drply(c) to s
               fi

 []    conq[c]                  ->  conq[c] := false


 []    rcv data(c) from s ->
               if ~conq[c]     ->  { discard data msg }
                                    send drply(c) to s
```

```
        □ conq[c]        ->     { accept data msg } skip
        fi
```

```
□     rcv drqst(c) from s  ->  conq[c] := false;
                                send drply(c) to s
end
```

6.4 CONNECTIONS IN THE INTERNET

There are two types of communications between application processes in the Internet: connection-oriented and connectionless. The protocol that provides connection-oriented communications between application processes is called transmission control protocol, or TCP for short. The protocol that provides connectionless communications between application processes is called user datagram protocol, or UDP for short. We discuss TCP in this section and UDP in Section 8.4.

Each computer c in the Internet has a TCP process that resides below the application processes and above the IP process in c. Moreover, each TCP process in computer c has a number of TCP ports that can be used in establishing and removing connections by the application processes in c.

Consider two application processes, process p in computer c and process q in computer d. For the two application processes p and q to exchange reliable streams of text, the following steps are executed.

i. First, process p requests from the TCP process in computer c to allocate TCP port i in c. Meanwhile, process q requests from the TCP process in computer d to allocate TCP port j in d.

ii. After TCP port i in c is allocated to process p and TCP port j in d is allocated to process q, process p requests from the TCP process in c to establish a connection between port i in c and port j in d. The requested connection can be identified by the four-tuple (c, i, d, j).

iii. After the (c, i, d, j) connection is established, the two processes p and q can start sending streams of text segments. Each text segment sent by process p to port i is first received by the TCP process in computer c, then forwarded to the TCP process in computer d (as discussed in Section 4.6). Then the TCP process in d delivers the text segment to port j to be received later by process q. Similarly, each text segment sent by process q is first received by the TCP process in computer d, then forwarded to the TCP process in computer c. Then the TCP process in c delivers the text segment to port i to be received later by process p.

iv. As discussed later in Section 9.4, the TCP processes in computers c and d ensure that every occurrence of a transmission error (i.e., message corruption, loss, or reorder) in either stream is detected and an appropriate recovery procedure is performed to recover from the error.

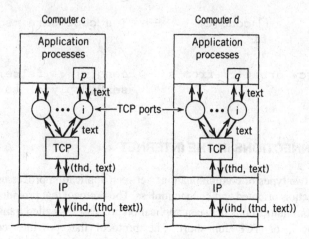

FIG. 6.2

v. After the two text streams between p and q are finished, the (c, i, d, j) connection is removed so that TCP port i in computer c and TCP port j in computer d can be released and become available for future connections.

Figure 6.2 shows the two text streams between processes p and q. In the direction from p to q, process p sends its text bytes via port i to the TCP process in computer c. The TCP process in c collects the sent bytes and adds a TCP header thd to them and sends the resulting TCP message (thd, text) to the IP process in c. The IP process in c adds an IP header ihd to the TCP message and forward the resulting IP message (ihd, (thd, text)) towards computer d. When the IP process in computer d receives the IP message (ihd, (thd, text)), it removes the IP header ihd and sends the resulting TCP message (thd, text) to the TCP process in d. The TCP process in d removes the TCP header thd and forwards the remaining text bytes to the TCP port j. Later, process q receives the text bytes from port j.

Next, we discuss steps ii and iii of the above procedure in more detail. In particular, we discuss how the TCP process in computer c establishes a (c, i, d, j) connection with the TCP process in computer d and how the established connection is later removed. For convenience, let tp and tq denote the TCP processes in computers c and d, respectively.

a. To request establishing the connection (c, i, d, j), process tp sends to process tq a synchronize message of the form syn(c, i, d, j, x), where x is the initial sequence number in the text stream to be sent from tp to tq over the connection (c, i, d, j). The value of x is chosen, by tp, based on the current value of the real-time clock in computer c.

b. When process tq receives the syn(c, i, d, j, x) message, it sends back to process tp an acknowledge-and-synchronize message of the form acksyn(c, i, d, j, x + 1, y). This message informs tp that tq has received the syn(c, i, d, j, x) message and is currently waiting to receive a data message with the sequence number x + 1. This message also informs tp that the initial sequence number in the text stream to be sent from tq to tp is y. The value of y is chosen, by tq, based on the current value of the real-time clock in computer d.

c.   When process tp receives the message acksyn(c, i, d, j, x+1, y), it sends back to process tq an acknowledge message of the form ack(c, i, d, j, y+1). This message informs tq that tp has received the acksyn(c, i, d, j, x+1, y) message and is currently waiting to receive a data message with the sequence number y+1.

d.   At this point, connection (c, i, d, j) has been established between tp and tq. Each of the two processes, tp and tq, can start sending data messages to the other process. Each data message sent by tp (or tq, respectively) is of the form dt(c, i, d, j, r, s), where r is the sequence number of the message and s is the sequence number of the next data message yet to be received by tp (or tq, respectively). The sequence number r of a dt(c, i, d, j, r, s) message sent by tp (or tq, respectively) equals x+B+1, where B is the total number of bytes in the text of all messages sent earlier by tp (or tq, respectively). The sequence numbers r and s in the data messages are used for detecting and recovering from any message loss or reorder, as discussed in Chapters 8 and 9.

e.   When tp finishes sending its data messages, it sends to tq a finish message of the form fin(c, i, d, j, r, s), where r equals x+B+1 and B is the total number of text bytes sent by tp in the connection. After sending the finish message, process tp waits to receive an acknowledge message of the form ack(c, i, d, j, r, s) where s equals x+B+2, to be sure that tq has received the finish message. Process tq does the same when it finishes sending its data messages.

f.   When both tp and tq send finish messages and receive the corresponding acknowledge messages, the connection (c, i, d, j) between tp and tq has been removed.

g.   After connection (c, i, d, j) has been established, it is possible for either process, tp or tq, to remove the connection abruptly by sending a reset message of the form rst(c, i, d, j) to the other process.

Each of the messages exchanged between processes tp and tq has 13 fields. The first 12 fields in a message constitute the message header and field 13, if any, is the message text. The 12 fields in a TCP header are as follows.

1. Source TCP port   16 bits
2. Destination TCP port   16 bits
3. Sequence number of the message   32 bits
4. Sequence number of next message to be received   32 bits
5. Length of the header   4 bits
6. To be determined later   6 bits
7. Message type bits   6 bits

8. Size of available buffer for receiving messages   16 bits
9. Checksum of the message   16 bits
10. Urgent pointer   16 bits
11. Other options, if any   x bits
12. Padding   y bits

Fields 1 and 2 contain the source and destination TCP ports of the message. Note that the IP addresses of the source and destination computers are not specified in any field in the message; rather, this information is passed separately, along with the message, between the TCP process and the IP process. Field 3 defines the sequence number of the message. Field 4 defines the sequence number of the next message to be received by the TCP process that sent the message. Field 5 defines the number of bits in the header divided by 32. (Note that the header has a variable length because of field 11.) Field 6 is reserved for future use.

Field 7 consists of six bits that determine the message type. These six bits are named synchronize, acknowledge, finish, reset, push, and urgent bits. If the synchronize bit is on, then the message is a synchronize message and field 3 contains the initial sequence number of the message stream. If the acknowledge bit is on, then the message is an acknowledge message and field 4 contains the sequence number of the next message to be received by the TCP process that sent the message. If both the synchronize and acknowledge bits are on, then the message is an acknowledge-and-synchronize message. If the finish or reset bit is on, then the message is a finish or reset message, respectively.

If the push bit is on, then the receiving TCP process should deliver all the text that it has accumulated so far (even if some intermediate text is missing). If the urgent bit is on, then the receiving TCP process should deliver the urgent text in this message as soon as it receives the message, possibly out of order with other received messages. If the urgent bit is on, then field 10 points at the end of the urgent text in the text field in the message.

Field 8 indicates the size of the available buffer to receive messages in the TCP process that sent the message. This field can limit the number of text bytes to be sent by the other TCP process. Field 9 has a checksum that can be used in detecting corruption that may occur in the message while the message is being transmitted. In Section 8.4, we discuss how this checksum is computed and used in detecting message corruption. Field 11 is optional, and field 12 is introduced to ensure that the number of bits in the message header is a multiple of 32.

6.5 BIBLIOGRAPHICAL NOTES

Connection Protocols are discussed in Cerf [1977] and Cerf and Postel [1978]. Overviews on connection protocols are given in Sunshine and Dalal [1978] and Watson [1980].

The TCP is discussed in Postel [1981c].

EXERCISES

1   (State-Transition Diagram of Connection Protocol). A possible initial state S
    for the connection protocol in Section 6.1 is defined as follows:

$$S = \sim conp \wedge cansnd=0 \wedge \sim conq \wedge ch.p.q=<> \wedge ch.q.p=<>$$
    This protocol can reach state S' defined as follows.

$$S' = conp \wedge cansnd=m \wedge conq \wedge ch.p.q=<> \wedge ch.q.p=<>$$

Sketch part of a state transition diagram for this protocol that includes five
states that the protocol can reach after state S and before S'. Show in your
sketch all the transitions that correspond to message loss and message reorder.

2   (Timeout Actions in Connection Protocol). Is the timeout action in Section 6.1
    normal? Explain your answer. (Recall that normal timeout actions are defined
    in Section 5.4.)

3   (Timeout Actions in Connection Protocol). Which timeout actions in Section
    6.3 are normal and which of them are not normal? Explain your answer. (Re-
    call that normal timeout actions are defined in Section 5.4.)

4   (Connections Using Identifiers). Show that both sequence numbers sp and sq
    are needed for the correctness of the connection protocol in Section 6.2. In par-
    ticular, give a scenario of a bad behavior of a protocol version where only sp is
    used; then give another scenario of a bad behavior of a protocol version where
    only sq is used.

5   (Connections Using Identifiers). Each connection in the protocol in Section
    6.2 is identified by a pair (sp, sq) of sequence numbers. It is required to design
    a protocol where each connection is uniquely identified by one sequence num-
    ber s. Both processes p and q start with the same connection identifier s.
    Process p sends a crqst(s) message to process q and then waits for a reply from
    q. Assume that the reply from q does not arrive at p for a long time. Thus,
    process p ends up sending several crqst(s) messages to process q. One of the
    sent crqst(s) messages is finally received by process q, which decides to accept
    the request and sends a crply(s) message to process p. When p receives the cr-
    ply(s) message, it sends a sequence of data(s) messages followed by a drqst(s)
    message to q. Then, p waits to receive a drply(s) message from q. If the dr-
    ply(s) from q does not arrive at p for a long time, p ends up sending several
    drqst(s) messages to q. One of the sent drqst(s) messages is finally received by
    q, which sends back a drply(s) message to p and increments the value of its s
    variable by 1. When p receives the drply(s) message, it increments the value of
    its s variable by 1. Thus, connection s is terminated and the next connection
    will be identified by s + 1. Processes p and q in this connection protocol can be
    defined as follows.

```
process p

inp     m             :       integer    { m > 0 }

var     conp          :       boolean,
        cansnd        :       0..m,
        sp, s         :       integer


begin
   timeout  ~conp    -> send crqst(sp) to q

[] rcv crply(s) from q         ->
        if   sp ≤ s ∧ ~conp -> conp, cansnd, sp
                                      := true, m, s
        []   sp > s ∨ conp  -> skip
        fi


[] conp                        ->
        if   cansnd > 0      -> send data(sp) to q;
                                cansnd := cansnd-1
        []   true            -> send drqst(sp) to q;
                                cansnd := 0
        fi

[] rcv drply(s) from q         ->
        if     sp ≤ s        -> conp, sp :=
                                false, s+1
        []     sp > s        -> skip
        fi
end

process q

var     conq          :       boolean,
        sq, s         :       integer

begin
   rcv crqst(s) from p  ->
        if sq > s -> send drply(sq-1) to p
        [] sq ≤ s -> conq, sq := false, s+1;
                     send drply(s) to p
        [] sq ≤ s -> conq, sq := true, s;
                     send crply(s) to p
        fi
```

```
☐ conq                          →      conq, sq := false, sq+1

☐ rcv data(s) from p     →
        if  sq > s →   {discard data msg}
                       send drply(sq-1) to p
            ☐  sq ≤ s →   {store data msg} sq := s
        fi

☐ rcv drqst(s) from p      →
        if  sq > s →   send drply(sq-1) to p
            ☐  sq ≤ s →   conq, sq := false, s+1;
                         send drply(s) to p
        fi
    end
```

Explain the role the sequence numbers play in the correctness of this protocol.

6 (Connections without Message Reorder). Simplify the connection protocol in Section 6.1 under the assumption that message reorder cannot occur.

7 (Connections without Message Reorder). Simplify the connection protocol in Section 6.2 under the assumption that message reorder cannot occur.

8 (Connections without Message Reorder). Simplify the duplex connection protocols in Section 6.3 under the assumption that message reorder cannot occur.

9 (Connections without Transmission Errors). Simplify the connection protocol in Section 6.1 under the assumption that transmission errors cannot occur.

10 (Connections without Transmission Errors). Simplify the connection protocol in Section 6.2 under the assumption that transmission errors cannot occur.

11 (Connections without Transmission Errors). Simplify the duplex connection protocols in Section 6.3 under the assumption that transmission errors cannot occur.

12 (Multiple Simplex Connections). Generalize the connection protocol in Section 6.1 to allow process p to simultaneously establish up to v connections to process q.

13 (Multiple Simplex Connections). Generalize the connection protocol in Section 6.2 to allow process p to simultaneously establish up to v connections to process q.

14 (Duplex Connections). The duplex connection protocols in Section 6.3 are based on the simplex connection protocol in Section 6.1. Design duplex connection protocols that are based on the simplex connection protocol in Section 6.2.

15 (Connections in a Star Network). A network consists of a process array p[i: 0 .. n − 1] and process q. Each process p[i] can establish a connection, using the timeout protocol in Section 6.1, to process q such that the following condition holds. At each instant, process q is involved in at most one connection. Design processes p[i: 0 .. n − 1] and q.

16 (Connections in a Star Network). Solve exercise 15 in the case where the connection protocol between each p[i] and q is similar to the connection protocol in Section 6.2.

17 (Connections in a Star Network). A network consists of a process array p[i: 0 .. n − 1] and process q. Each process p[i] can establish a connection, using the timeout protocol in Section 6.1, to process q such that the following condition holds. At each instant, process q is involved in at most v connections. Design processes p[i: 0 .. n − 1] and q.

18 (Connections in a Star Network). Solve exercise 17 in the case where the connection protocol between each p[i] and q is similar to the connection protocol in Section 6.2.

19 (Connections in a Fully Connected Network). Consider a fully connected network p[i: 0 .. n − 1], where there are two opposite-direction channels between any two processes in the network. Each process can try to establish a connection to any other process in the network such that no process can be involved in more than one connection at a time. Design a process in this network assuming that the connection protocol is similar to the one in Section 6.1.

20 (Connections in a Fully Connected Network). Solve exercise 19 in the case where the connection protocol is similar to the one in Section 6.2.

21 (Incorrect Connection Protocol). Give a scenario of the following connection protocol to show that the protocol is incorrect:

```
process p
inp        m                :      integer      { m > 0 }
var        conp             :      boolean,
           cansnd           :      0..m,
           sp               :      integer,
           x                :      integer
begin
    ~conp                              ->    send crqst(sp) to q
[] rcv crply(x) from q                 ->
        if  ~conp  /\  sp = x    ->
                        conp, cansnd := true, m
        []     conp  \/  sp ≠ x   -> skip
        fi
[] conp                             ->
        if cansnd > 0 -> send data(sp) to q;
```

```
                                              cansnd := cansnd-1
           []   true           ->  send drqst(sp) to q;
                                              cansnd := 0
              fi
  []  rcv drply(x) from q ->
      if    sp = x          ->        conp, sp := false, sp + 1
      []    sp ≠ x          ->        skip
      fi
  end


  process q
  var        conq           :        boolean,
             sq             :        integer,
             x              :        integer
  begin
     rcv crqst(x) from p       ->
            if true -> conq, sq := true, x;
                       send crply(x) to p
            [] true -> conq := false;
                       send drply(x) to p
            fi
  []  conq                              ->      conq := false
  []  rcv data(x) from p        ->
            if  sq ≠ x ->   {discard data msg}
                            send drply(x) to p
            []  sq = x ->   {store data msg} skip
            fi
  []  rcv drqst(x) from p       ->
            if  sq ≠ x ->  skip
            []  sq = x ->  conq := false
            fi; send drply(x) to p
     end
```

CHAPTER 7

DATA TRANSFER AND MULTIPLEXING

In the last chapter, we identified two types of communications: connectionless and connection-oriented. In a connectionless communication, a process p can send data messages to another process q without first establishing a connection to q. In a connection-oriented communication, p establishes a connection to q before it proceeds to send data messages to q. In either case, the stream of sent data messages from p to q is not a continuous autonomous stream. Rather, this stream is usually multiplexed with idleness periods and control characters. Moreover, this stream usually consists of multiple streams of data messages multiplexed with one another into one stream. Next, we explain why streams of data messages sometimes need to be multiplexed with idleness periods and control characters and why these streams consist of several streams multiplexed with one another.

If processes p and q are implemented in hardware, then process q is expected to receive one bit per time unit from process p. This necessitates that process p sends one bit per time unit to process q. When process p has no data bits to send to process q, process p still sends several bits that constitute an idleness period to process q. Thus, an idleness period, sent from p to q, informs q that p has not yet finished preparing the next data bit to send. Because preparing the next data bit may take an arbitrarily long time, an idleness period can be of an arbitrary length. When process q receives some bits and recognizes that they belong to an idleness period, q discards the bits, rather than storing them like data bits. A protocol for multiplexing and demultiplexing data bits with idleness periods is discussed in Section 7.1.

Before process p sends a sequence of data messages to process q, p usually inserts a number of control characters in each message and between messages. The inserted characters mark the different fields in a message and mark the boundaries between successive messages. For example, if a data message has three fields named header, body, and tail, then three control characters can be inserted into the message. The first character marks the beginning of the header field, the second character marks the beginning of the body field, and the third character marks the beginning of the tail field. When process q receives a character and recognizes that it is a control character, process q discards the character, rather than storing it like a data character. Two protocols for multiplexing and demultiplexing data and control characters are discussed in Section 7.2.

In general, the data messages sent from process p to process q are taken from different sources, for example, different arrays within process p. Moreover, these messages are expected to reach different destinations, for example, different arrays within process q. Thus, the single stream of data messages from process p to process q is in fact a collection of streams, with each stream having its own source and its own destination. When process q receives a data message from process p, it needs to deduce the constituent stream to which the message belongs in order to know where to store the message. Two protocols for multiplexing and demultiplexing several data streams are discussed in Section 7.3.

Our main objective in this chapter is to present the three types of multiplexing: multiplexing data with idleness, multiplexing data with control, and multiplexing data with data. Then in Section 7.4, we discuss how these three types of multiplexing are used in the Internet.

7.1 MULTIPLEXING DATA WITH IDLENESS

Consider the case where processes p and q and the channel from p to q are all implemented in hardware. In particular, the channel from p to q is implemented as a simple wire connecting p and q. In this case, process p sends bits over the channel by adjusting the voltage across the wire. For example, process p can send a 0 bit by making the voltage across the wire 5 V and can send a 1 bit by making the voltage across the wire 0 V. Process q periodically measures the voltage across the wire to determine whether p is sending a 0 bit or 1 bit during each period. When p has no data bits to send for some time, p makes the voltage across the wire 0 V and process q ends up receiving 1 bits during that time. Thus, the data messages and the idleness periods are sent from p to q as sequences of 0 and 1 bits.

We choose to define an idleness period as a sequence of k or more 1 bits, where k is an integer whose value is at least 2. The end of an idleness period and the start of the following data message is marked with one 0 bit called the starting flag. Similarly, the end of a data message and the beginning of the following idleness period is marked with one 0 bit, called the ending flag.

The starting and ending flags perform an important function. If the first bit in a data message is a 1 bit, then the starting flag serves as a delimiter that separates the 1 bits of the previous idleness period from the leading 1 bits, if any, of the data message. Similarly, the ending flag serves as a delimiter that separates the trailing 1 bits, if any, of the data message from the 1 bits of the next idleness period.

Defining an idleness period as a sequence of k or more 1 bits causes a problem. If a data message happens to have a sequence of k or more 1 bits, and if process p

sends these bits without modification, then process q will assume wrongly that
these bits constitute an idleness period rather than belonging to the data message.

To solve this problem, process p should be prevented from sending k or more
successive 1 bits in a data message. This is achieved by providing process p with a
variable x whose value is the number of successive 1 bits sent last by p. When p
sends a 1 bit, variable x is incremented by 1, and when p sends a 0 bit, variable x is
assigned the value zero. Now, if while sending the bits of a data message, the value
of variable x becomes $k - 1$, process p sends a 0 bit and makes the value of x zero.
This 0 bit is not a data bit. Rather, it is an additional bit inserted in the data stream
precisely to prevent p from sending k or more successive 1 bits in a data message.
When process q receives $k - 1$ successive 1 bits followed by a 0 bit, process q recognizes that the 0 bit is an inserted bit and discards it. This protocol is usually referred
to as the bit insertion protocol.

Process p in the bit insertion protocol can be defined as follows.

```
process p

const k                                    {k ≥ 2}

var     data    :       array [ integer ] of 0..1,
        i       :       integer,
        x       :       0..k               {initially, x = k}

begin
        true   ->  {send idleness bits}
                   if x = k ->     send bit(1) to q
                   ☐ x ≠ k ->
                   send bit(0) to q;
                   x := 0;
                   do x < k -> send bit(1) to q; x:= x+1
                   od
                   fi

☐       true   ->  {send a data bit}
                   if x = k-1 ∨ x = k ->
                       x := 0;  send bit(0) to q
                   ☐ x ≠ k-1 ∧ x ≠ k -> skip
                   fi;
                   send bit(data[i]) to q;
                   if data[i] = 0  -> x := 0
                   ☐ data[i] = 1  -> x := x+1
                   fi; i := i+1
end
```

There are two actions in process p. In the first action, process p sends idleness bits, and in the second, process p sends one data bit. Because process p can send idleness or data bits at any instant, the guards of these two actions are the predicate true.

In the first action, before sending any idleness bits, process p checks its x variable. If $x = k$, then p recognizes that the last k bits it has sent were all idleness bits, and so p sends one more 1 idleness bit while keeping $x = k$. On the other hand, if $x < k$, then p recognizes that the last bit it has sent was a data bit, and so it sends one 0 bit (the ending flag) followed by k 1 bits (the smallest idleness period); then p assigns its x variable the value k.

In the second action, before sending the next data bit, process p checks its x variable. If $x = k - 1$ (indicating that the last sent $(k - 1)$ 1 bits were all data bits) or $x = k$ (indicating that the last sent k bits were all idleness bits), then p sends a 0 bit. This sent bit is either an inserted bit (if $x = k - 1$) or a starting flag (if $x = k$). Process p then sends the ith data bit and updates its x variable depending on the value of the sent data bit. Finally, process p increments i by 1.

Process q in this protocol has five variables declared as follows:

```
var    rcvd  :      array [ integer ] of 0..1,
       j     :      integer,
       y, z  :      0..k,
       b     :      0..1
```

Array rcvd is used to store the received data bits from process p. Variable j is used to point at the element of array rcvd where the next received data bit is to be stored. Variables y and z are used to count the number of received 1 bits before and after, respectively, the last received 0 bit. Finally, variable b is used to hold the last received bit.

Variables y and z are needed so that process q can decide whether the last received 0 bit is a data bit. In particular, if $y < k - 1$ and $z < k$, then the last received 0 bit is a data bit. Otherwise, the last received 0 bit is one of the following: a starting flag (if $y = k$), an inserted flag (if $y = k - 1$), or an ending flag (if $z = k$).

Process q in the bit insertion protocol can be defined as follows:

```
process q

const k                                    {k ≥ 2}

var    rcvd  :      array [ integer ] of 0..1,
       j     :      integer,
       y, z  :      0..k,        {initially, y=0 and z=k}
       b     :      0..1

begin
       rcv bit(b) from p  ->
           if b = 1  ->        z := min(z+1, k)
```

MULTIPLEXING DATA WITH CONTROL

```
    []  b = 0 —>
            if y < k-1 /\ z < k —> rcvd[j], j := 0, j+1
            [] y ≥ k-1 \/ z ≥ k —> skip
            fi;
            y := z;
            if z < k —>
                do z > 0 —>
                        rcvd[j], j, z := 1, j+1, z-1
                od
            [] z ≥ k —> z := 0
            fi;
            { y, z := last z, 0 }
        fi
    end
```

Process q has only one action. In this action, q receives a bit b and checks its value. If b = 1, q recognizes that the z 1 bits following the last received 0 bit are still coming. In this case, q increments z by 1. If b = 0, q recognizes that the z 1 bits following the last received 0 bit have finished and q can now decide whether the last received 0 bit is a data bit, a starting flag, an inserted bit, or an ending flag. If the last received 0 bit is a data bit, then q stores it in array rcvd. Finally, q assigns variable y the value of variable z, stores z 1 bits in array rcvd, and assigns variable z the value 0.

7.2 MULTIPLEXING DATA WITH CONTROL

There are two common methods for multiplexing data and control characters in one character stream. The first method is called the character run method, and the second is called the character insertion method. Next, we discuss these two methods in order.

The first method for multiplexing data with control is based on the following concept of a character run. A run in a character stream is a maximal sequence of successive characters of the same type, either data or control. From this definition, each infinite character stream consists of a control run, followed by a data run, followed by a control run, followed by a data run, and so on.

In order to multiplex runs of different types into one stream, all runs of the same type in the stream are required to satisfy one of the following two conditions:

  i. Every run of the same type has the same predefined length, that is, the same number of characters.
  ii. Every run of the same type is preceded by a character whose value is the length of the run.

For example, consider a protocol for transferring data and control characters

from a process p to a process q. Each data character is in the range 0 . . r − 1, and
each control character is in the range 0 . . s − 1. Process p sends a control run, followed by a data run, followed by a control run, and so on. Each data run has at most
m characters, and each control run has exactly n characters. Each data run is preceded by a character that defines the length of (i.e., the number of characters in) the
data run. Note that the control runs in the character stream satisfy condition i above,
while the data runs satisfy condition ii above. The characters in the data runs are
taken from an array data in process p.

Process p in the character run protocol can be defined as:

```
process p

const m, n, r, s
            {m is the maximum length of a data run}
            {n is the fixed length of a control run}
            {range of each data character is 0..r-1}
            {range of each control character is 0..s-1}

var    data  :      array [integer] of 0..r-1,
       i     :      integer,        {index of data}
       c     :      0..s-1,         {control character}
       x     :      0..m,           {counter for data}
       y     :      0..n            {counter for control}

begin
       true  ->
           {send a control run of length n}
           c, y := any, n;
           do y > 0 -> send chc(c) to q; c, y := any, y-1
           od;

           {send length x of the next data run}
           x := any; send chc(x) to q;

           {send a data run of length x}
           do x > 0 -> send chc(data[i]) to q;
                       i, x := i+1, x-1
           od
end
```

Process p has one action where p first sends a control run of n characters, then
sends the length of a data run, and then sends the data run whose characters are tak-
en from array data.

Process q has an infinite array rcvd to store the received data characters from
process p. The received control characters are not stored. Process q also has a

boolean variable cntrl whose value is true iff the current run in the received stream
is a control run. It also has a variable len whose value is the number of characters
yet to be received in the current run.

Process q in the character run protocol can be defined as follows.

process q

const m, n, r, s   {as defined in p}

var   rcvd : **array [integer] of** 0..r-1,
        j   : **integer**,   {index of rcvd}
        cntrl : **boolean**,   {control run}
        len   : 0..max(m, n),   {length of run}
        d   : 0..max(m, r-1, s-1)   {rcvd character}

begin
        rcv chc(d) **from** p —>
            if   cntrl ∧ len > 0 —>
                                {d is control}
                                len := len-1
            [] cntrl ∧ len = 0 —>
                                {d is length}
                                cntrl, len := **false**, d
            [] ~cntrl ∧ len > 1 —>
                                {d is data}
                                rcvd[j], j, len :=
                                d, j+1, len-1
            [] ~cntrl ∧ len ≤ 1 —>
                                {d is data}
                                rcvd[j], j, cntrl, len :=
                                d, j+1, **true**, n
            fi
end

One problem of the character run protocol is that the length of a data or control
run is determined before sending any character in that run. This problem does not
occur in the second method for multiplexing data with control, which is based on
the concept of character insertion. In this method, to announce that a character c in a
stream is a control character, a special character s is inserted before c in the stream.
Character s itself cannot be a control character, but it can be a data character. In order to distinguish between a character s that precedes a control character and a data
character s, process p sends a special character s immediately before any data character s.

As an example, consider a protocol for transferring data and control characters
from a process p to a process q. Each data character is in the range 0 .. r − 1, and

each control character is in the range $0 .. s - 1$. In order that process q can correctly recognize the control characters (and not confuse them with the data characters), process p sends a character s immediately before every control character.

If $r > s$, then the special character s is also one of the data characters to be sent by p. In order that process q can distinguish between a character s that precedes a control character and a character s that is a data character, process p sends a character s immediately before any data character s. Therefore, when process q receives an s character for the first time, it recognizes that this s character is a special character and that the next character is either an s data character, or a control character in the range $0 .. s - 1$.

Process p in the character insertion protocol can be defined as follows:

```
process p

const r, s

var    data    :    array [integer] of 0..r-1,
       i       :    integer,            {index of data}
       c       :    0..s-1              {control character}

begin
       true   ->      {send one data character}
                      send chc( data[i] ) to q;
                      if data[i] = s -> send chc(s) to q
                      [] data[i] ≠ s -> skip
                      fi; i := i+1

[]     true   ->      {send one control character}
                      send chc(s) to q;
                      c := any;
                      send chc(c) to q
end
```

Process p has two actions. In the first action, process p sends the next data character, and if this data character happens to be s, process p sends a second s character. In the second action, process p first sends the special character s followed by a control character.

Process q in the character insertion protocol can be defined as follows:

```
process q

const r, s

var rcvd  : array [integer] of 0..r-1,  {rcvd data char}
    j     : integer,                     {index of rcvd}
```

```
        d       : 0..max(r-1, s),
        slast : boolean
begin
        rcv chc(d) from p —>
               if d ≠ s ∧ ~slast —> {d is data}
                                          rcvd[j], j := d, j+1
               [] d ≠ s ∧  slast —> {d is control}
                                          slast := false
               [] d = s ∧ ~slast —> {d is inserted}
                                          slast := true
               [] d = s ∧  slast —> {d is data}
                                          rcvd[j], j,  slast :=
                                          d, j+1, false
               fi
end
```

7.3 MULTIPLEXING DATA WITH DATA

Consider a protocol for transferring data characters from process p to process q. The data characters to be sent by process p are stored in n infinite arrays in p. These arrays are named data[0], data[1], . . . , data[n − 1]. Process q also has a set of infinite arrays, named rcvd[0], rcvd[1], . . . , rcvd[n − 1], such that the data characters in each data[i] array are to be transferred to array rcvd[i].

There are two methods for transferring the data characters from process p to process q such that q can decide to which rcvd array each received character belongs. These two methods are called asynchronous multiplexing and synchronous multiplexing. We discuss these two methods in some detail next.

In asynchronous multiplexing, data characters from different data arrays are sent in an arbitrary order. Each data character d, taken from a data[i] array, is sent along with the identifier i of its array in one message of the form asyn(i, d). When process q receives a message asyn(i, d), it recognizes that the data character d belongs to array rcvd[i]. The advantage of asynchronous multiplexing is its flexibility: data characters from different arrays can be sent in any order and with different frequencies. The disadvantage of asynchronous multiplexing is its efficiency: The identifier of the data array is sent with every data character in that array.

In synchronous multiplexing, data characters from different data arrays are sent according to a fixed order. When the turn of a data[i] array is reached, process p sends the next data character d from array data[i]. When process q receives a data character d from process p, it recognizes that d belongs to array rcvd[i] because q knows the order of data arrays according to which p sends the data characters.

It is possible that when the turn of a data[i] array is reached, process p decides not to send the next data character from that array and sends a null character instead. The function of the sent null character is to direct q to skip the current turn of array rcvd[i] to receive a data character. Each data or null character is sent in a message of the form syn(null, d), where null is a boolean value and d is a character in the range $0 .. r - 1$. If null = true, then d is a null character whose value is 0. If null = false, then d is a data character from the current data[i] array according to the fixed order.

The order of data arrays according to which process p sends syn messages to process q is defined in both p and q as follows:

```
var    order :       array [0..n-1] of boolean
```

This order can be changed arbitrarily by process p. When this happens, the new order is sent to process q so that both processes end up with the same new order before the sending of syn messages resumes according to the new order.

The data arrays in process p are defined as two arrays data and indx that are declared as follows.

```
var    data :       array [0..n-1, integer] of 0..r-1,
       indx :       array [0..n-1] of integer
```

Each indx[i] element points at the next data character to be sent from array data[i]. Thus, the next data character to be sent from data[i] is data[i, indx[i]].

Process p in the data multiplexing protocol can be defined as follows:

```
process p

const r, n

var    data :       array [0..n-1, integer] of 0..r-1,
       indx :       array [0..n-1] of integer,
                                    {index of data}
       i    :       0..n-1,         {index of indx)
       order :      array [0..n-1] of boolean,
       nxt  :       0..n-1,         {index of order}
       null :       boolean,
       d    :       0..r-1

begin
       true  ->      {send an asynchronous message}
                     i := any;
                     d, indx[i] :=
                     data[i, indx[i]], indx[i] + 1;
                     send asyn(i, d) to q
[]     order[nxt] ->
                     {send a synchronous message}
                     null, i := any, nxt
```

```
            if ~null -> d, indx[i] := data[i,
               indx[i]], indx[i] + 1
            [] null -> d := 0
            fi; send syn(null, d) to q;
            nxt := nxt +ₙ 1;
            do nxt≠n-1 ∧ ~order[nxt] ->
                          nxt := nxt +ₙ 1
            od

[]    true   ->    {send a new order message}
            order, nxt := any, 0;
            do nxt≠n-1 ∧ ~order[nxt] ->
                          nxt := nxt +ₙ 1
            od;
            send neword(order, nxt) to q
end
```

Process p has three actions. In the first action, p selects an arbitrary value for i in the range $0 .. n-1$, then sends an asyn(i, d) message to process q, where d is the next character in array data[i].

In the second action, process p sends a syn(null, d) message to process q where either null = true and d = 0 or null = false and d is the next data character from array data[nxt]. In either case, nxt is updated so that it points at the next element in array order whose value is true.

In the third action, process p updates array order and makes nxt point to the first element in array order whose value is true. Then process p sends copies of the new order and nxt to process q.

Process q of the data multiplexing protocol can be defined as follows:

```
process q

const r, n

var    rcvd  :    array [0..n-1, integer] of 0..r-1,
       indx  :    array [0..n-1] of integer,
                                  {index of rcvd}
       i     :    0..n-1,         {index of indx}
       order :    array [0..n-1] of boolean,
       nxt   :    0..n-1,
                                  {index of order}
       null  :    boolean,
       d     :    0..r-1

begin
       rcv asyn(i, d) from p ->
```

```
              rcvd[i, indx[i]], indx[i] := d, indx[i] + 1

[]     rcv syn(null, d) from p -->
              if  null --> skip
              [] ~null --> rcvd[nxt, indx[nxt]], indx[nxt]
                                :=  d, indx[nxt] + 1
              fi;
              i, nxt := nxt, nxt +_n 1;
              do nxt≠i /\ ~order[nxt] --> nxt := nxt +_n 1
              od

[]     rcv neword(order, nxt) from p --> skip
end
```

Process q has three actions. In each action, process q receives the message that is sent in the corresponding action in process p.

An important concept that is related to multiplexing data with data is encapsulation. For a process to multiplex multiple data streams into one, the process needs to encapsulate each character of each stream in a message that has a field for defining the stream to which the character belongs. Thus, each sent character d is encapsulated either in an asyn(i, d) message or in a syn(null, d) message. The receiving process receives each message, extracts from it the data character d, and forwards d to the intended destination array.

The concept of encapsulation applies not only to characters but to messages as well. For a process to multiplex multiple message streams into one stream, the process needs to encapsulate each message of each stream in a larger message that has a field for defining the stream to which the message belongs. As an example, consider a network where a process p receives data messages from the processes in a process array src[i: 0 .. n − 1]. Process p forwards the received data messages, in one message stream, to a process q, which in turn forwards them to the processes in a process array dst[i: 0 .. n − 1] such that a data message that is originated at a process src[i] is eventually delivered to process dst[i], for every i = 0, . . . , n − 1.

Processes p and q in the encapsulation protocol can be defined as follows:

```
process p
var    seq, txt    :          integer
par    i           :          0..n-1
begin
       rcv data(txt) from src[i] -->
              send encp(seq, i, txt) to q;
              seq := seq+1
end

process q
var    seq, txt    :          integer
```

```
par    i              :         0..n-1
begin
        rcv encp(seq, i, txt) from p  ->
               {use seq for recording purposes}
               send data(txt) to dst[i]
end
```

Note that each data(txt) message from process src[i] is encapsulated in a larger message of the form encp(seq, i, txt) as it is sent from process p to process q, then it is returned to its original form of data(txt) before it is forwarded to process dst[i].

7.4 DATA TRANSFER AND MULTIPLEXING IN THE INTERNET

In the last three sections, we presented three types of multiplexing: multiplexing data with idleness, multiplexing data with control, and multiplexing data with data. These different types of multiplexing are used in different protocol layers in the Internet. In this section, we discuss how and where each of these types of multiplexing are used in the Internet.

Multiplexing Data with Idleness

Multiplexing data with idleness is used in the lowest protocol layer in the Internet: the subnetwork layer. Consider an arrangement where several computers are connected to the same subnetwork in the Internet. These computers can exchange messages directly over the connecting subnetwork. When no computer is sending messages over the subnetwork, the subnetwork is idle and every computer connected to the subnetwork detects its idleness. When one computer is sending a message over the subnetwork, the subnetwork propagates the sent message to every computer connected to the subnetwork. Thus, every computer connected to the subnetwork should be able to distinguish between two situations: the situation when the subnetwork is idle and the situation when the subnetwork propagates a sent message. Depending on the type of subnetwork, different coding schemes are used to enable the connected computers to distinguish between these two situations.

As an example, consider the case where the connecting subnetwork is an Ethernet. In this case, idleness can be encoded as a continuous stream of three or more 0 bits, while the data bits of every sent message can be encoded using a Manchester code, similar to the one discussed in Section 2.3. In particular, each data 0 bit can be encoded as a sequence of two bits—a 1 bit followed by a 0 bit, and each data 1 bit can be encoded as a sequence of two bits: a 0 bit followed by a 1 bit. Thus, each computer connected to the Ethernet can distinguish between idleness and data propagation over the Ethernet.

As a second example, consider the case where the connecting subnetwork is a telephone line. In this case, idleness can be encoded as a continuous carrier signal that is not modulated in any way, while the data bits of every sent message are encoded by modulating the carrier signal to reflect the 0's and 1's of the data bits. Thus, each computer connected to the telephone line can distinguish between idleness and data propagation over the line.

Multiplexing Data with Control

The common method for performing multiplexing data with control in the Internet is the character run method, which is discussed in Section 7.2. This type of multiplexing is used in almost every protocol layer in the Internet.

For a process (for example, an IP process or a TCP process) to send a message, the process constructs the message as a control run followed by a data run. The control run in a message, called the message header, is usually of fixed length. However, in those cases where a message header has a variable length, the header has a control character that defines the length of the header. The data run in a message, called the message text, is usually of variable length, and the message header has a control character that defines the length of the text.

An Internet protocol that uses the character insertion method to multiplex data with control is the file transfer protocol, or FTP for short. This protocol is discussed in Section 22.4.

Multiplexing Data with Data

The common method for performing multiplexing data with data in the Internet is asynchronous multiplexing with encapsulation, discussed in Section 7.3. This type of multiplexing is used in three protocol layers in the Internet: IP (discussed in Section 4.6), TCP (discussed in Section 6.4), and UDP (to be discussed in Section 8.4).

When the TCP process in a computer c receives some text from one of its TCP ports, it encapsulates the text in a message with a TCP header and forwards the resulting TCP message to the IP process in c. Thus, multiple text streams from different TCP ports are multiplexed into one stream of TCP messages from the TCP process to the IP process in computer c. Similarly, multiple text streams from different UDP ports are multiplexed into one stream of UDP messages from the UDP process to the IP process in computer c.

When the IP process in computer c receives a TCP message or a UDP message, it encapsulates the received message in a larger message by adding to it an IP header. Then the IP process in c forwards the resulting IP message to the interface process of computer c. Thus, the two streams of TCP and UDP messages are multiplexed into one stream of IP messages from the IP process to the interface process in computer c.

In the opposite direction, the stream of IP messages that the IP process in computer c receives from the interface process in c is processed as follows. First, the IP header of each received message is removed, then the resulting message is forwarded to the TCP process or the UDP process in c, depending on whether the resulting message is a TCP message or a UDP message. Thus, the single stream of IP messages from the interface process to the IP process in c is demultiplexed into two streams: a stream of TCP messages to the TCP process in c and a stream of UDP messages to the UDP process in c.

When the TCP process in computer c receives a TCP message from the IP process in c, it removes the TCP header and forwards the remaining text to its destination TCP port. Thus, the single stream of TCP messages from the IP process in c to the TCP process in c is demultiplexed into several text streams, one for each TCP port in c. Similarly, the single stream of UDP messages from the IP process in c to the UDP process in c is demultiplexed into several streams, one for each UDP port in c.

7.5 BIBLIOGRAPHICAL NOTES

Multiplexing techniques are discussed in Tanenbaum [1980], Spragins et al. [1991], Halsall [1992], Saadawi et al. [1994], and Stallings [1994].

EXERCISES

1 (Simplified Multiplexing Data with Idleness). Simplify the sender process, process p, in the protocol for multiplexing data with idleness in Section 7.1 under the assumption that array data in process p does not have k consecutive 1 bits.

2 (Multiplexing Data with Idleness). Consider a protocol where process p sends data 0 and 1 bits multiplexed with idleness periods to process q, which stores the received data bits and disregards the idleness periods. Process p sends each 0 bit as a sequence of two messages—bit(0) followed by bit(1)—and sends each 1 bit as a sequence of two messages—bit(1) followed by bit(0). Process p sends each idleness period as a sequence of three or more bit(1) messages that ends with a bit(0) message as a starting flag. Design the two processes p and q in this protocol.

3 (Multiplexing Data with Idleness). Consider a protocol where process p sends data 0 and 1 bits multiplexed with idleness periods to process q which stores the received data bits and disregards the idleness periods. Process p sends each 0 bit as a bit(0) message and each 1 bit as a sequence of two messages: bit(1) followed by bit(0). Process p sends each idleness period as a sequence of two or more bit(1) messages that ends with a bit(0) message as a starting flag. Design the two processes p and q in this protocol.

4 (Multiplexing Data with Idleness). Consider a protocol where process p sends data 0 and 1 bits multiplexed with idleness periods to process q, which stores the received data bits and disregards the idleness periods. Process p sends each 0 bit as a bit(0) message and each data 1 bit as a sequence of two messages— bit(1) followed by bit(0). Process p sends each idleness period as a message se-

quence of the form bit(1); bit(1); (bit(1); bit(1))*. Design the two processes p and q in this protocol.

5 (Multiplexing Data with Idleness). The protocols in exercises 3 and 4 have two different patterns for idleness periods. Which of these two patterns is better? Explain your answer.

6 (Multiplexing Data with Idleness). Consider a protocol where process p sends data symbols, in the range 0 . . 2, multiplexed with idleness periods to process q, which stores the received data symbols and discards the idleness periods. Process p sends each symbol s as a sm(s) message, where s is in the range 0 . . 2. Assume that each data symbol 2 is followed by either a data symbol 0 or a data symbol 1. Define a message pattern for an idleness period and then design the two processes p and q in this protocol.

7 (Multiplexing Data with Idleness). It is required to design a protocol for transferring data symbols in the range 0 . . 2 from process p to process q. Array data in process p is declared as follows:

var   data   :   **array [integer] of** 0..2

At each instant, process p either sends a data symbol s as a message of the form sm(s) or an idleness period as a message sequence of the form sm(0); sm(1); sm(0); sm(1); . . . . Design processes p and q in this protocol.

8 (Multiplexing Data with Idleness). Consider a protocol consisting of two processes p and q. Process p has an infinite array of data bits that p sends to process q. At each instant, process p either sends data bits or sends idleness. To send data bits, p sends a 0 bit followed by the next k data bits, where k is a declared constant in processes p and q. To send idleness, p sends a 1 bit. Design processes p and q.

9 (Multiplexing Data with Idleness). Modify processes p and q in the protocol in exercise 8 to ensure that if some sent bits are lost, the synchronization between processes p and q is eventually restored.

10 (Multiplexing Data with Control). There is an implicit assumption in the character insertion protocol in Section 7.2 that data characters are sent more frequently than control characters. Modify this protocol under the assumption that control characters are sent more frequently than data characters.

11 (Multiplexing Data with Control). Simplify the character insertion protocol in Section 7.2 under the assumptions that $r \leq s$ and each character message sent from process p to process q is of the form chc(c), where c is in the range 0 . . s − 1.

12 (Multiplexing Data with Control). Design a new protocol for multiplexing data with control, similar to the protocol in Section 7.2, under the assumptions that

r = s and each character message sent from process p to process q is of the form chc(c), where c is in the range 0 .. r − 1.

13 (Multiplexing Data with Control). Process p has an input infinite array, named data, of 0 .. 1 elements. Process p sends the elements of array data one by one to process q, which stores them in an infinite array, named rcvd, of 0 .. 1 elements. Each 0 element is sent as a sequence of two messages: bit(1); bit(0). Similarly, each 1 element is sent as a sequence of two messages: bit(0); bit(1). Every now and then, process p sends a control signal to process q. There are three different types of control signals. Describe how to encode each of these control signals as a sequence of bit(0) and bit(1) messages. Design processes p and q of this protocol.

14 (Multiplexing Data with Idleness and Control). Consider a protocol where process p sends data blocks multiplexed with idleness periods and control blocks to process q, which stores the received data bits and disregards the idleness periods and control blocks. Process p sends each data block as a sequence of k + 1 messages: one bit(0) message followed by k messages of the form bit(d), where d is a data 0 or 1 bit. Process p sends each control block as a sequence of k + 1 messages: one bit(1) message followed by k messages of the form bit(c), where c is a control 0 or 1 bit. Assume that p sends at least one data block after each control block. Define a message pattern for an idleness period in this protocol such that the synchronization between p and q is eventually restored after it is lost due to some message loss. Design processes p and q in this protocol.

15 (Multiplexing Data with Data). Modify the protocol for multiplexing data with data in Section 7.3 to allow the sender process p to send the data characters from different data[i] arrays at different frequencies.

16 (Multiplexing). Consider a network that consists of two processes s and r. Process s has two input arrays data[0, integer] and data[1, integer] of 0- and 1 bits, and process r has two variable arrays rcvd[0, integer] and rcvd[1, integer] of 0- and 1 bits. The communication in this network proceeds in rounds. In each round, process s sends the bits of array data[i, integer], one by one, to process r, which stores them in the corresponding array rcvd[i, integer]. A round terminates when process s sends several bits to process r to inform it that s will change the sending array from data[i, integer] to data[i $+_2$ 1, integer] and so r should change the receiving array from rcvd[i, integer] to rcvd[i $+_2$ 1, integer]. Each sent message from process s to process r is of the form bit(b), where b is 0 or 1. There are no messages from r to s. Design processes s and r.

17 (Multiplexing). What types of multiplexing (multiplexing data with idleness, multiplexing data with control, or multiplexing data with data) are present in the network of exercise 16.

18 (Message Loss in the Bit Insertion Protocol). Consider the bit insertion proto-

col in Section 7.1. If some bit messages are lost after they are sent by p and before they are received by q, then the synchronization between p and q can be lost. Give a scenario of this protocol where the synchronization between p and q is lost due to some message loss.

19 (Tolerating Message Loss in the Bit Insertion Protocol). Consider the bit insertion protocol in Section 7.1. Explain how the synchronization between processes p and q in this protocol can be eventually restored after the synchronization is lost due to some message loss.

20 (Message Loss in the Character Insertion Protocol). Consider the character insertion protocol in Section 7.2. If some character messages are lost after they are sent by p and before they are received by q, then the synchronization between p and q can be lost. Give a scenario of this protocol where the synchronization between p and q is lost due to some message loss.

21 (Tolerating Message Loss in the Character Insertion Protocol). Consider the character insertion protocol in Section 7.2. Explain how the synchronization between processes p and q in this protocol is eventually restored after the synchronization is lost due to some message loss.

22 (Message Loss in the Data Multiplexing Protocol). Consider the data multiplexing protocol in Section 7.3. If some character messages are lost after they are sent by p and before they are received by q, then the synchronization between p and q can be lost. Give a scenario of this protocol where the synchronization between p and q is lost due to some message loss. *(Hint:* Loss of an asyn message does not lead to a loss of synchronization between p and q; however, loss of syn messages can lead to a loss of synchronization between p and q.)

23 (Tolerating Message Loss in the Data Multiplexing Protocol). Consider the data multiplexing protocol in Section 7.3. Explain how the synchronization between processes p and q in this protocol is eventually restored after the synchronization is lost due to some message loss.

24 (Simplified Multiplexing Data with Idleness). Simplify the protocol for multiplexing data with idleness in Section 7.1 under the assumption that every 1 bit is followed by a 0 bit in array data.

25 (Simplified Multiplexing Data with Idleness). It is required to design a multiplexing data with idleness protocol where a process p sends bit(0) and bit(1) messages to a process q. Process p sends each data 0 bit as bit(0); bit(0) and sends each data 1 bit as bit(1); bit(1). Design process p in this protocol.

26 (Multiplexing Data with Data). It is required to modify the multiplexing data with data protocol in Section 7.3 according to the following three conditions:

     a All data characters are sent, from process p to process q, based on synchronous multiplexing.

b To change array order, process p does not send neword messages to process q. Rather, process p sends add(i) or remove(i) messages, where i is in the range $0 .. n - 1$.

c After sending an add(i) message, data characters from array data[i] can be sent from p to q. After sending a remove(i) message, data characters from array data[i] cannot be sent from p to q.

Design process p in this protocol.

CHAPTER 8

ERROR DETECTION

As mentioned in Chapter 5, when a process p sends a sequence of messages to a process q, these messages may be subjected to three types of transmission errors: corruption, loss, and reorder. If a sent message is corrupted, lost, or reordered with other sent messages, then it is important that one of the two processes, p or q, detects the error occurrence and executes a corrective routine.

The corrective routine, executed by p or q, depends on the type of error that has occurred as follows. First, if process q detects that a received message has been corrupted, then process q discards the message, and so it transforms the occurrence of message corruption into an occurrence of message loss. Second, if process p detects that a sent message has been lost before it was received by process q, then p resends another copy of the message to q. Third, if process q recognizes that a message has been received out of order, then process q places the message in the right order with respect to other received messages before delivering the sequence of received messages. Note that this discussion suggests that process q detects message corruption and reorder, while process p detects message loss.

In this chapter, we discuss how process p or q detects each occurrence of transmission errors. In Section 8.1, we discuss how process q can detect message corruption. In Section 8.2, we discuss how process p can detect message loss, and in Section 8.3, we discuss how process q can detect message reorder. Finally in Section 8.4, we discuss how message corruption is detected in the Internet. Detection and recovery from message loss and reorder in the Internet are discussed in Section 9.4.

8.1 DETECTION OF MESSAGE CORRUPTION

Each sent message is a sequence of 0 and 1 bits. Sometimes, after a message is sent and before it is received, the values of some bits in the message are changed either from 0 to 1 or from 1 to 0. These bits are said to be corrupted during message transmission.

The probability of bit corruption is very small ranging from 10^{-6} to 10^{-9}. Therefore, only a very small number of sent messages ever suffer from bit corruption. Unfortunately, bit corruption is likely to occur in bursts. In other words, if a message has a corrupted bit, then this message is likely to have several adjacent corrupted bits. This observation suggests the following definition of a corruption burst in a message: The corruption burst in a message is the smallest number of consecutive bits that contain all the corrupted bits in that message. It follows from this definition that every message has exactly one corruption burst.

If the first and last bits of some message are corrupted, then the corruption burst of this message is the whole message, even if there is no other corrupted bits in the message. If all the corrupted bits in a message are adjacent, then the corruption burst of that message is those corrupted bits. If there are no corrupted bits in a message, then the corruption burst of the message is empty.

In the remainder of this section, we describe two corruption detection protocols. The first protocol uses parity bits, and the second uses checksums. We start by discussing the first protocol.

In the corruption detection protocol that uses parity bits, a process p sends a sequence of data blocks to a process q. Each sent block contains $m \times n$ data bits. (The wisdom of regarding the number of data bits in a block as a product of two integers will become apparent below.) Each block also contains n parity bits. When process q receives the data bits of a block, it computes the parity bits from the received data bits. It then compares the computed parity bits with the received parity bits in the block. If the two arrays of parity bits are equal, process q concludes that no bits are corrupted in the received data block and keeps the block. Otherwise, process q concludes that some bits are corrupted in the data block and discards the block.

If process q detects corruption in the received block, then indeed some bits in the block are corrupted. However, if process q detects no corruption in a block, then the block bits may or may not be corrupted. Nevertheless, as discussed below, process q is guaranteed to detect corruption in a data block if the length of the corruption burst in that block is larger than zero but not larger than n.

This corruption detection protocol is defined in terms of two constants m and n. If n is made large with respect to m, then large corruption bursts can be detected—an advantage. However, in this case, a large number of parity bits is needed in each block—a disadvantage. Therefore, some compromise is needed in choosing the values of m and n.

Now, we are ready to describe this corruption detection protocol in some detail. Because each block has $m \times n$ data bits, it is convenient to think of the data bits in a block as forming an m × n matrix. In this case, each data bit can be denoted by d.(i, j), where i is the row of the bit and j is the column of the bit in the matrix.

At the beginning, these data bits are in a one-dimensional array dp in process p. They are arranged linearly in array dp as follows.

```
d. (0,  0)    ; d. (0,  1)    ; ... d. (0,  n-1) ;
d. (1,  0)    ; d. (1,  1)    ; ... d. (1,  n-1) ;
...
d. (m-1, 0) ; d. (m-1, 1) ; ... d. (m-1, n-1)
```

In other words, the data bits are arranged linearly by row in array dp. They are also sent in that same order, that is, by row, from process p to process q.

Assume that n successive bits in the same block are corrupted while being transmitted from process p to process q. Because of the order in which the bits are sent, each corrupted bit is in a different column of the matrix. Therefore, if one parity bit is provided for each column, a bit corruption can be detected in each column in the matrix.

There are n parity bits in each block sent by process p: pp[0], pp[1], ..., pp[n − 1]. Each pp[j] is a parity bit for the data bits in column j: d.(0, j), d.(1, j), ..., and d.(m − 1, j). Thus, while these data bits are being sent by process p, the value of their parity bit pp[j] is computed by p. Finally, after all the data bits in the block are sent, process p sends the computed parity bits one by one.

Process p in the corruption detection protocol that uses parity bits can be defined as follows:

```
process p
const m, n
var    dp    : array [integer] of 0..1,   {data bits}
       pp    : array [0..n-1] of 0..1,   {parity bits}
       x     : integer,               {index of dp}
       i     : 0..m,                  {row of bit}
       j     : 0..n-1                 {column of bit}
begin
       true  ->    pp, i, j := 0, 0, 0;
                   do i ≠ m ->
                          send bit(dp[x]) to q;
                          pp[j], x, j :=
                              pp[j] +₂ dp[x], x+1, j +n 1;
                          if j≠0 -> skip
                          [] j = 0 -> i := i+1
                          fi
                   od; { i=m ∧ j=0 }
                   do j ≠ n-1 -> send bit(pp[j]) to q;
                               j := j+1
```

```
        od;
        send bit(pp[n-1]) to q
end
```

The data bits received by process q are stored in array dq even before checking whether some of them are corrupted. Therefore, array dq has two indices y and ye. Index y is the regular index that is updated whenever a data bit is added to array dq. Index ye is the external index that is to be read by the "outside world" to determine the extent of the data in array dq. As the data bits are received and added to array dq, index y is incremented while index ye remains constant. At the end of receiving a data block, if process q detects some corruption in the block, then q executes y := ye, thus discarding all the block bits from array dq. Otherwise, process q executes ye := y, thus keeping all the block bits in array dq and making them visible to the outside world.

Process q in the corruption detection protocol that uses parity bits can be defined as follows:

```
process q
const m, n

var   dq    :    array [integer] of 0..1, {data bits}
      pq    :    array [0..n-1] of 0..1, {parity bits}
      y, ye :    integer,            {indices of dq}
      i     :    0..m,               {row of bit}
      j     :    0..n-1,             {column of bit}
      crp   :    boolean,            {detect corruption}
      b     :    0..1
begin
      rcv bit(b) from p -->
          if i < m ∧ j < n-1 -->
                  dq[y], pq[j], y, j :=
                  b, pq[j] +₂ b, y+1, j+1
          ▯ i < m ∧ j = n-1 -->
                  dq[y], pq[j], y, i, j :=
                  b, q[j] +₂ b, y+1, i+1, 0
          ▯ i = m ∧ j < n-1 -->
                  if pq[j] = b --> skip
                  ▯ pq[j] ≠ b   --> crp := true
                  fi; j := j+1
          ▯ i = m ∧ j = n-1 -->
                  if pq[j] = b ∧ ~crp --> ye := y
                  ▯ pq[j] ≠ b ∨ crp   --> y := ye
                  fi;
                  pq, i, j, crp := 0, 0, 0, false
```

                    fi
end

Next, we describe a second protocol for detecting corruption. According to this protocol, each data block sent from process p to process q consists of m data bits followed by n check bits. This protocol is guaranteed to detect every corruption burst of length n or less. In this protocol, each of the two processes p and q has the same array of n + 1 input bits, called the generator array. Before process p sends a data block, p uses the m data bits in the block and its generator array to compute the n check bits in the block. When process q receives a block, it uses the m data bits in the block and its generator array to compute a new set of check bits. Process q then compares the computed check bits with the received check bits in the block. If they are equal, the received block is accepted. Otherwise, the received block is discarded.

The method for computing the n check bits in a block from the m data bits in the block and a generator array is as follows:

i. Define a polynomial D.x of order m + n − 1 as follows:

$$D.x = d_0 x^{m+n-1} + d_1 x^{m+n-2} + \ldots + d_{m+n-1} x^0$$

where d_0 is the first data bit in the block, d_1 is the second data bit in the block, and d_{m-1} is the last data bit in the block, and each of the remaining coefficients $d_m, \ldots, d_{m+n-1}$ is 0. Because each coefficient in D.x is binary, D.x is called a binary polynomial.

ii. Define a binary polynomial G.x of order n as follows:

$$G.x = g_0 x^n + g_1 x^{n-1} + \ldots + g_n x^0$$

where g_0 is the first bit in the generator array, g_1 is the second bit in the generator array, and g_n is the last bit in the generator array. We require that both g_0 and g_n are 1 bits.

iii. Performing the binary division of polynomial D.x by polynomial G.x yields a remainder R.x that is a binary polynomial of order n − 1 as follows:

$$R.x = r_0 x^{n-1} + r_1 x^{n-2} + \ldots + r_{n-1} x^0$$

The n coefficients in polynomial R.x are the computed check bits.

As an example, consider the case where m = 5, n = 2, the data bits in the block are <1; 1; 1; 0; 1>, and the generator array is <1; 0; 1>. In this case, the two polynomials D.x and G.x can be defined as follows:

$$D.x = 1x^6 + 1x^5 + 1x^4 + 0x^3 + 1x^2 + 0x^1 + 0x^0$$

$$G.x = 1x^2 + 0x^1 + 1x^0$$

The binary division D.x/G.x can be carried out as follows.

```
                  1 1 0 1 1
              101│1 1 1 0 1 0 0
                  1 0 1
                  ─────
                    1 0 0
                    1 0 1
                    ─────
                    0 1 1
                    0 0 0
                    ─────
                      1 1 0
                      1 0 1
                      ─────
                        1 1 0
                        1 0 1
                        ─────
          Remainder ─>   1 1
```

Thus the remainder R.x of D.x/G.x is the polynomial 1x + 1, and the check bits of the data block are <1; 1>. Process p attaches the computed check bits at the end of the data block and ends up sending the block <1; 1; 1; 0; 1; 1; 1>.

The generator arrays are declared as input arrays in processes p and q as follows:

```
inp   gp  :  array [0..n] of 0..1,   {generator of p}
inp   gq  :  array [0..n] of 0..1,   {generator of q}
```

These two arrays satisfy the following three conditions. First, gp[0] = 1. Second, gp[n] = 1. Third, for every j, $0 \le j \le n$, gp[j] = gq[j]. Note that these three conditions imply that gq[0] = gq[n] = 1.

Computing the check bits in process p is carried out in an array cp declared as follows:

```
var   cp  :  array [0..m+n-1] of 0..1,   {check bits of p}
```

Initially, the first m elements in array cp are the data bits in the block currently being sent, and the last n elements in array cp are zero. After computing the check bits, the computed check bits are in the last n elements in this array.

Process p in the corruption detection protocol that uses checksum can be defined as follows:

```
process p
const m,n            {m is # data bits in a data block}
                     {n is # check bits in a data block}
inp   gp   :         array [0..n] of 0..1,
                     {generator of p}
                     {gp[0] = gp[n] = 1, and}
                     {for every j, gp[j] = gq[j]}
```

```
var    dp    :        array [integer] of 0..1,
       cp    :        array [0..m+n-1] of 0..1,
       x     :        integer,                    {index of dp}
       i     :        0..m+n-1,
       j     :        0..n+1

begin
       true ->
                {initialize array cp}
                do i < m -> cp[i], i := dp[x+i], i+1 od;
                {i=m}
                do i > 0 -> cp[i], i := 0, i +m+n 1 od;
                {i=0}

                {send data and compute check bits in cp}
                do i < m ->
                        send bit(dp[x]) to q;
                        if cp[i] = 0 -> skip
                        [] cp[i] = 1 ->
                                j := 0;
                                do j ≤ n ->
                                        cp[i+j], j :=
                                        cp[i+j] +₂ gp[j], j+1
                                od
                        fi; { cp[i] = 0 because gn[0] = 1 }
                        x, i := x+1, i+1
                od;                    {i=m}

                {send check bits from array cp}
                do i > 0 -> send bit(cp[i]) to q;
                        i := i m+n 1
                od
                {i=0}
end
```

Computing the check bits in process q is carried out in an array cq declared as follows:

```
var   cq  :   array [0..m+n-1] of 0..1
```

Initially, the first m elements in array cq are the data bits in the block currently being received, and the last n elements in array cq are zero. After computing the check bits, the computed check bits are in the last n elements in this array.

Process q in the corruption detection protocol that uses checksum can be defined as follows:

```
process q
const m,n
inp    gq    :  array [0..n] of 0..1,
                   {generator of q}
                   {gq[0] = gq[n] = 1, and}
                   {for every j, gp[j] = gq[j]}

var    dq    :  array [integer] of 0..1,    {data bits}
       cq    :  array [0..m+n-1] of 0..1,   {check bits}
       y, ye :  integer,                  {indices of dq}
       i     :  0..m+n-1,
       j     :  0..n+1,
       crp   :  boolean,                   {initially false}
       b     :  0..1

begin
       rcv bit(b) from p —>
           if i < m-1 —>
                   {receive data bits}
                   dq[y], cq[i], y, i := b, b, y+1, i+1
           [] i = m-1 —>
                   {compute check bits in array cq}
                   dq[y], cq[i], y, i := b, b, y+1, 0;
                   do i < m —>
                       if cq[i] = 0 —> skip
                       [] cq[i] = 1 —>
                               j := 0;
                               do j ≤ n —>
                                   cq[i+j], j :=
                                       cq[i+j] +₂ gq[j], j+1
                               od
                       fi; i := i+1
                   od {i = m}
           [] i ≥ m —>
                   {compare computed and received checks}
                   if cq[i]=b —> skip
                   [] cq[i]≠b —> crp := true
                   fi;
                   cq[i], i := 0, i+ₘ₊ₙ 1;
                   if i≠0 —> skip
                   [] i=0 ∧  crp —>  y, crp := ye, false
                   [] i=0 ∧ ~crp —>  ye := y
                   fi
           fi
end
```

8.2 DETECTION OF MESSAGE LOSS

Three mechanisms are needed in order to allow process p to detect the loss of any data message that was sent earlier from process p to process q. These three mechanisms are unique identifiers, acknowledgments, and timeouts. First, each data message that is sent by process p has a unique identifier. Second, each data message that is received by process q is acknowledged promptly by q sending an acknowledgment message, identifying the received data message, to process p. Third, process p has a time-out capability to detect that the acknowledgment of a data message has not been received and in all probability will not be received in the future, indicating a message loss.

Note that if process p times out, then p is sure that a message was lost during its transmission. However, p cannot be sure whether the lost message is the data message from p to q or the acknowledgment message from q to p. Fortunately, there is only one thing that process p can do in either case: resend the data message to process q. Protocols for recovering from message loss are discussed in detail in Chapter 9.

8.3 DETECTION OF MESSAGE REORDER

As mentioned above, detection of message loss requires that each data message has a unique identifier. If the unique identifiers of consecutive data messages are consecutive integers, then process q can use these same identifiers to detect message reorder. In particular, process q keeps track of integer nr of the next data message to be received by process q.

Assume that process q receives a data message whose identifier is integer i. There are three cases to consider in this situation. First, $nr = i$, which indicates that no message reorder has occurred and that the received message is the expected one. Second, $nr > i$, which indicates that a message reorder has occurred and the received message is another copy of a message that was received earlier. Third, $nr < i$, which indicates that a message reorder has occurred and the received message has been received ahead of other messages that were sent earlier but have not yet been received. Protocols for recovering from message reorder are discussed in the next chapter.

8.4 ERROR DETECTION IN THE INTERNET

In this section, we discuss how message corruption is detected in the Internet; then in Section 9.4, we discuss how message loss and reorder are detected and corrected in the Internet. For simplicity, we focus our discussion in this section on how message corruption is detected in a hierarchy of three protocols. These protocols, from bottom to top, are the subnetwork protocol, the Internet protocol, or IP; and the user datagram protocol, or UDP. (Our discussion also applies to a similar hierarchy that involves TCP instead of UDP.)

Consider the case where two computers c and d are attached to subnetworks s and s', respectively, and let subnetworks s and s' be connected by a router r. For an application process in computer c to send a text segment to an application process in d, the following steps are executed:

i. The application process in c allocates some UDP port i in c and the application process in d allocates some UDP port j in d. Then the application process in c sends the text segment to UDP port i in c so that it can later be received by the UDP process in c.

ii. When the UDP process in computer c receives a text segment from its UDP port i, it attaches a UDP header uhd to the segment and forwards the resulting UDP message (uhd, text) to the IP process in c. As discussed below, the attached UDP header uhd identifies the two UDP ports i and j.

iii. When the IP process in computer c receives a UDP message (uhd, text) from the UDP process in c, it attaches an IP header ihd to the received message, then forwards the resulting IP message (ihd, (uhd, text)) to the interface process in c.

iv. When the interface process in computer c receives an IP message (ihd, (uhd, text)), it attaches an interface header fhd and interface tail ftl to the received message. It then sends the resulting interface message (fhd, (ihd, (uhd, text)), ftl) over subnetwork s to the interface process for s in router r.

v. When the interface process in router r receives an interface message (fhd, (ihd, (uhd, text)), ftl) over subnetwork s, it removes fhd and ftl from the message and sends the resulting IP message (ihd, (uhd, text)) to the IP process in router r. From ihd in the message, the IP process in r recognizes that the message should be sent over subnetwork s', and so it sends the IP message to the interface process for subnetwork s' in r.

vi. When the interface process for s' in r receives an IP message, it attaches an interface header fhd and interface tail ftl to the received message, then sends the resulting interface message (fhd, (ihd, (uhd, text)), ftl) over subnetwork s' to the interface process in computer d.

vii. When the interface process in d receives an interface message (fhd, (ihd, (uhd, text)), ftl) over subnetwork s', it removes both fhd and ftl from the message and sends the resulting IP message (ihd, (uhd, text)) to the IP process in d. The IP process in d removes ihd from the received message and forwards the resulting UDP message (uhd, text) to the UDP process in d. The UDP process in d removes uhd from the message and sends the remaining text to UDP port j in d so that it can be received later by the application process in d.

Figure 8.1 illustrates the steps of this procedure. This procedure describes the transmission of a text fragment through three protocols: the subnetwork protocol, IP, and UDP. Each of these protocols detects message corruption as follows. Before a process in some protocol sends a protocol message, it computes a checksum and

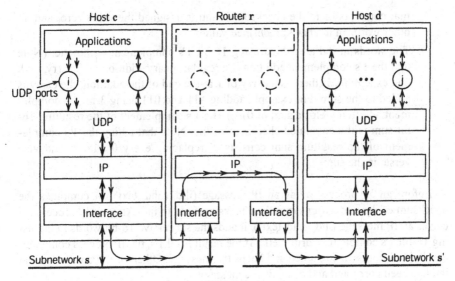

FIG. 8.1

includes it in the message. After a corresponding process in the same protocol receives the message, it computes a checksum and compares it with the checksum in the received message. If the two checksums are equal, the receiving process recognizes that the message is not corrupted and handles the message as discussed above. If the two checksums are unequal, the receiving process discards the message. Next, we describe in more detail how message corruption is detected in each of these three protocols.

In the subnetwork protocol, the checksum for an interface message (fhd, (ihd, (uhd, text)), ftl) is computed over the first four fields in the message, namely fhd, ihd, uhd, and text. The method for computing this checksum is similar to that in the second corruption detection protocol in Section 8.1.

Before an interface process sends an interface message (fhd, (ihd, (uhd, text)), ftl), it computes the checksum of the message and stores it in the last field, field ftl, of the message. After an interface process receives an interface message (fhd, (ihd, (uhd, text)), ftl), it computes the checksum of the message and compares it with the checksum in field ftl. If they are equal, the interface process concludes that the message has not been corrupted and keeps the message. Otherwise, it concludes that the message has been corrupted and discards the message.

In IP, the checksum for an IP message (ihd, (uhd, text)) is computed over the IP header ihd as follows.

i. As discussed in Section 3.4, the IP header ihd has a checksum field and the number of bits in ihd is a multiple of 32.

ii. The header ihd is divided into successive words of 16 bits each. The word that corresponds to the checksum in ihd is assigned the value zero, and all other words in ihd have predefined values.

iii. The words in ihd are added using 16-bit 1's complement arithmetic. (Note that the 1's complement addition is a regular binary addition with carry, with one exception: If there is a carry of 1 at the end of the addition, the carry is added to the sum. For example adding 111 and 011 using 3-bit 1's complement addition yields a sum of 011.) The 1's complement of the resulting 16-bit sum is the computed checksum of ihd. Note that taking the 1's complement of the resulting sum consists of replacing every 0 with 1, and vice versa, in the sum.

Before an IP process sends an IP message (ihd, (uhd, text)), it computes the checksum of ihd and assigns it to the checksum field in ihd. After an IP process receives an IP message (ihd, (uhd, text)), it adds the successive 16-bit words in ihd using 16-bit 1's complement arithmetic. If the result is all 1's, the IP process concludes that ihd has not been corrupted and keeps the message. Otherwise, it concludes that ihd has been corrupted and discards the message.

In UDP, the checksum for a UDP message (uhd, text) is computed over an augmented message that consists of three fields (phd, uhd, text), where phd is the pseudoheader of the message, uhd is the UDP header of the message, and text is the text in the message.

The pseudoheader of a (uhd, text) message consists of five fields:

1. IP address of message source   32 bits
2. IP address of message destination   32 bits
3. Padding   8 bits
4. Transport protocol of message (UDP)   8 bits
5. Length of the message   16 bits

Fields 1 and 2 contain the IP addresses of the source and destination computers of message (uhd, text). Field 3 is a padding of all 0 bits. Field 4 defines the transport protocol of message (uhd, text), which is of course UDP. Field 5 defines the length of message (uhd, text) measured as the number of bits in the message divided by 8.

The UDP header of a (uhd, text) message consists of four fields:

1. Source UDP port of message   16 bits
2. Destination UDP port of message   16 bits
3. Length of message   16 bits
4. Checksum of augmented message (phd, uhd, text)   16 bits

Fields 1 and 2 contain the source and destination UDP ports of message (uhd, text). Field 3 defines the length of message (uhd, text) measured as the number of bits in the message divided by 8. Field 4 contains the checksum of the augmented message (phd, uhd, text); this checksum is computed as follows:

i. The augmented message (phd, uhd, text) is divided into successive words of 16 bits each. This may necessitate adding some padding of 8 bits to the augmented message.

ii. The word that corresponds to the checksum in uhd is assigned the value zero, and all other words in phd, uhd, and text have predefined values.

iii. The words in the augmented message are added using 16-bit 1's complement arithmetic. The 1's complement of the resulting 16-bit sum is the computed checksum of the augmented message (phd, uhd, text).

Before a UDP process sends a UDP message (uhd, text), it computes the augmented message (phd, uhd, text) and then computes the checksum of the augmented message and assigns it to the checksum field in uhd. After a UDP process receives a UDP message (uhd, text), it computes the augmented message (phd, uhd, text) and then computes the checksum of the augmented message and compares it with the checksum field in uhd. If they are equal, the UDP process concludes that the (uhd, text) message has not been corrupted and keeps the message. Otherwise, it concludes that the message has been corrupted and discards it.

8.5 BIBLIOGRAPHICAL NOTES

Corruption detection codes and their relationship with corruption correction codes are discussed in Hamming [1950, 1986], Peterson and Brown [1961], and Sloane [1975]. The user datagram protocol, or UDP for short, is discussed in Postel [1980b].

EXERCISES

1 (Manchester Encoding). Simplify the corruption detection protocol that uses parity bits in Section 8.1. under the following assumptions. First, the data bits in array dp can be partitioned into pairs, where each pair consists of either a 0 bit followed by a 1 bit or a 1 bit followed by a 0 bit. Second, each sent block consists of an even number of data bits.

2 (Corruption Burst). What is the length of the longest corruption burst that can be detected by the corruption detection protocol that uses parity bits in Section 8.1. Assume that each sent block consists of $m \times n$ data bits.

3 (Corruption Burst). What is the maximum value of x such that the corruption detection protocol that uses parity bits in Section 8.1 can detect every corruption burst of length x. Assume that each sent block consists of $m \times n$ data bits.

4 (Corruption Burst). What is the maximum value of x such that the corruption detection protocol that uses parity bits in Section 8.1 can detect every corruption burst of length x or less. Assume that each sent block consists of $m \times n$ data bits.

5   (Corruption Burst). Consider the following data message consisting of 24 bits:

    < 1; 1; 0; 1; 0; 0; 0; 1; 0; 1; 1; 1;
    1; 0; 0; 1; 1; 1; 0; 0; 1; 0; 1; 0 >

    It is required to use the corruption detection protocol in Section 8.1 to compute
    parity bits for this message to ensure that every corruption burst of length 5 or
    less will be detected. What are the computed parity bits?

6   (Solid Corruption Burst). A corruption burst in a sent block is solid iff the cor-
    rupted bits in the block are consecutive. What is the length of the longest solid
    corruption burst that can be detected by the corruption detection protocol that
    uses parity bits in Section 8.1. Assume that each sent block consists of m × n
    data bits.

7   (Solid Corruption Burst). Solid corruption bursts are as defined in exercise 6.
    What is the maximum value of x such that the corruption detection protocol
    that uses parity bits in Section 8.1 can detect every solid corruption burst of
    length x.

8   (Solid Corruption Burst). Solid corruption bursts are as defined in exercise 6.
    What is the maximum value of x such that the corruption detection protocol
    that uses parity bits in Section 8.1 can detect every solid corruption burst of
    length x or less.

9   (Optimal Constants for Corruption Detection). A data message in the corrup-
    tion detection protocol that uses parity bits in Section 8.1 is defined in terms of
    two constants m and n. It is required to compute the optimal values of m and n
    given the following facts. Let b be the total number of data and parity bits in a
    data block, and let r be the maximum number of bits in a corruption burst.

If	$1 \le b < 100$	then	$r = 10$
If	$100 \le b < 200$	then	$r = 15$
If	$200 \le b < 300$	then	$r = 24$

    (*Hint:* The optimal values for m and n are those that minimize the ratio r/(m ×
    n), where r is the number of parity bits and m × n is the number of data bits in
    a data block.)

10 (Optimal Constants for Corruption Detection). Consider the corruption detec-
    tion protocol that uses parity bits in Section 8.1. Assume that the number r of
    data bits in a data block and the length n of the longest corruption burst that
    can occur in a data block satisfy the following relation.

    $$(30 \le r \le 1000) \wedge (n \le r/4 + 30)$$

    What are the best values for constants m and n in the corruption detection pro-
    tocol? Explain your answer.

11 (Optimal Constants for Corruption Detection). Consider the corruption detection protocol that uses parity bits in Section 8.1. This protocol can be used to detect corruption in the following two scenarios. In the first scenario, the protocol can be used to detect every corruption burst of length n or less in a data block consisting of m × n bits. In the second scenario, the protocol can be used to detect every corruption burst of length n/2 or less in two consecutive data blocks consisting of m × (n/2) bits each. (For convenience, assume that n is even.) Which of these two scenarios is better in terms of the number of parity bits used and the corruption that can be detected.

12 (Polynomial Division). Consider the corruption detection protocol that uses checksum in Section 8.1. If the data bits in a block are <1; 1; 1; 0; 0; 1; 0; 1; 0; 1; 1; 0; 1; 0; 0> and the generator bits are <1; 0; 0; 1>, what are the check bits that are computed in this protocol.

13 (Polynomial Division). Consider the corruption detection protocol that uses checksum in Section 8.1. If the data bits in a block are <1; 0; 0; 1> and the generator bits are <1; 1; 1; 0; 0; 1; 0; 1; 0; 1; 1; 0; 1; 0; 0>, what are the check bits that are computed in this protocol.

14 (Polynomial Division). The following code fragment is taken, with slight modifications, from process p in the corruption detection protocol that uses checksum in Section 8.1. In the first do statement, the data bits are copied into the subarray cp[0 .. m − 1]. In the second do statement, the rest of array cp, namely cp[m .. m + n − 1], is assigned zero elements. In the third do statement, the polynomial whose coefficients are in array cp are divided by the polynomial whose coefficients are in array gp, and the coefficients of the remainder polynomial are stored in cp[m .. m + n − 1].

```
{i=0}
do i < m -> cp[i], i := dp[x+i], i+1 od;        {i=m}
do i > 0 -> cp[i], i := 0, i +m+n 1 od;         {i=0}
do i < m ->
    if cp[i] = 0 -> skip
    [] cp[i] = 1 ->
          j := 0;
          do j ≤ n ->
                  cp[i+j], j := cp[i+j] +2 gp[j], j+1
          od
    fi; { cp[i] = 0 because gn[0] = 1 }
    i := i+1
od
```

Describe in detail how polynomial division is performed in the third do-statement.

15 (Detecting Message Loss). Consider a protocol where process p continuously sends data messages to process q and q records that it has received the ith message when it receives the ith message. The protocol can be defined as follows:

```
process p
begin
        true --> send data to q
end

process q
var     rcvd   :        array [integer] of boolean,
        i      :        integer
begin
        rcv data from p --> rcvd[i], i := true, i+1
end
```

Modify this protocol so that it can tolerate message loss, assuming that no more than x consecutive data messages can be lost. We are not interested in the trivial modification where each data message is attached an integer sequence number. Rather, we are interested in a modification where each data message is attached a sequence number in the range $0 .. r - 1$, where r is as small as possible.

16 (Detecting Message Reorder). Solve the same problem as before except that the modified protocol can tolerate message reorder, assuming that every data message can take part in at most y occurrences of message reorders.

17 (Detecting Message Loss and Reorder). Solve the same problem as before except that the modified protocol can tolerate both message loss and message reorder under the following two assumptions:

    a No more than x consecutive data messages can be lost.
    b Every data message can take part in at most y occurrences of message reorders.

18 (Detecting Message Reorder). Consider a protocol where a process p continuously sends blocks of three messages each to process q. The three messages in a block are as follows: first(integer), second(integer), and third(integer). Process p is defined as follows:

```
process p
var data   :    array [integer] of integer,
     i     :    integer
begin
     true   -->    send first(data[i]) to q; i := i+1;
                   send second(data[i]) to q; i := i+1;
                   send third(data[i]) to q; i := i+1
end
```

Design process q such that it receives the sent messages and stores their integer fields in an infinite array rcvd in order. Process q should tolerate message re-order, assuming that every message can take part in at most one occurrence of message reorder.

19 (Detecting Message Reorder). Solve the same problem as before except that every message can take part in at most two occurrences of message reorders.

20 (Detecting Message Reorder). Modify processes p and q in the above problem so that the protocol can tolerate message reorder, assuming that every message can take part in at most three occurrences of message reorder.

21 (Detecting Message Reorder). Solve the same problem as before except that every message can take part in at most four occurrences of message reorder.

CHAPTER 9

ERROR RECOVERY

In the last chapter, we discussed how processes p and q can detect transmission errors that occur during the transmission of data messages from process p to process q. We also discussed different corrective procedures that need to be executed when such errors are detected. In particular, we mentioned that corrupted messages are discarded, lost messages are resent, and reordered messages are rearranged into their right order before being delivered. In this chapter, we discuss a number of error recovery protocols that use these corrective procedures to ensure that the data messages sent by process p are delivered at process q without corruption or loss and in the right order.

There are two types of error recovery: forward and backward. In forward error recovery, the receiver of data messages does not send acknowledgment messages to the sender. Instead, the sender sends the data messages with a high degree of redundancy such that the receiver, by itself, can correct each occurrence of transmission errors. In backward error recovery, the receiver of data messages sends acknowledgment messages to the sender. The sender uses the received acknowledgments to identify and resend each message that has been corrupted or lost during transmission. In most cases, backward error recovery is more efficient than forward error recovery. However, in some cases, where transmission errors occur uniformly, forward error recovery is more efficient.

The rest of this chapter is organized as follows. In Section 9.1, we discuss techniques for forward error recovery. Then in Sections 9.2 through 9.5, we discuss techniques for backward error recovery. Finally in Section 9.6, we discuss error recovery techniques in the Internet.

9.1 FORWARD ERROR RECOVERY

Consider the case where a process p continuously sends data messages to process q. The sent data messages are provided with high degree of redundancy such that process q can recover from each occurrence of message corruption, loss, and reorder. Before we discuss the redundancy that needs to be added to the data messages (to enable q to recover from message corruption, loss, and reorder), we adopt the following three assumptions concerning message corruption, loss, and reorder:

i.   n-Bounded Corruption: The corruption burst in each data message from p to q consists of at most n bits. (Recall from Section 8.1 that the corruption burst in a data message is the smallest number of consecutive bits that contain all the corrupted bits in the data message.)

ii. n-Bounded Loss: In each sequence of 2n data messages sent from process p to process q, there are at most n consecutive messages that contain all the messages that are lost before they are received by q.

iii. n-Bounded Reorder: Each data message sent from process p to process q can interchange its position with adjacent messages, in the message sequence from p to q, no more than n times.

To enable process q to recover from any occurrence of n-bounded corruption, the following steps need to be executed by p and q:

1. Each data message sent from process p is of the form

$$\text{data(txt.0; chk.0; txt.1; chk.1)}$$

where:

;   is the concatenation operator

txt.0   is a copy of the message text

chk.0   is a checksum for detecting any corruption burst that consists of at most n bits, in txt.0

txt.1   is a second copy of the message text

chk.1   is a checksum for detecting any corruption burst that consists of at most n bits in txt.1

Note that because txt.0 and txt.1 are identical, chk.0 and chk.1 are identical. Note also that each chk.0 and chk.1 consists of n bits, as discussed in Section 8.1.

2. When process q receives a data(txt.0; chk.0; txt.1; chk.1) message from process p, q computes the checksum of txt.1 and then compares the computed checksum with chk.1. If the computed checksum is identical to chk.1, process q recognizes that txt.1 is not corrupted and accepts it as the message text.

3. If the computed checksum is different from chk.1, then q recognizes that the corruption burst (consisting of at most n bits) has occurred in the string chk.0; txt.1. This implies that txt.0 is not corrupted, and q accepts it as the message text.

To enable process q to recover from each occurrence of n-bounded loss, the following steps need to be executed by p and q:

1. Each data message from process p to process q is of the form data(i), where i is a sequence number in the range $0 .. 2n - 1$.

2. Process p sends two copies of each data message, but the two copies of a message are sent n messages apart. For example, p sends the first 2n messages in the following order (because p sends two copies of each message, p ends up sending 4n messages):

```
data(0) ; data(1)    ;    ...    ; data(n-1)         ;
data(0) ; data(1)    ;    ...    ; data(n-1)         ;
data(n) ; data(n+1)  ;    ...    ; data(2*n - 1)     ;
data(n) ; data(n+1)  ;    ...    ; data(2*n - 1)
```

3. Process q has a variable named exp to store the sequence number i of the next data(i) message expected by q. The value of variable exp ranges over $0, ..., 2n - 1$. When q receives a data(i) message, q compares the values of i and exp. If i and exp have different values, q discards the message. If i and exp have the same value, then q delivers the message and increments the value of exp by 1 mod 2n.

To enable process q to recover from each occurrence of n-bounded reorder, the following steps need to be executed by p and q:

1. Each data message from process p to process q is of the form data(i), where i is a sequence number in the range $0 .. 2n - 1$.

2. When process p sends a data(i) message followed by a data(i') message, then $i' = i + 1 \bmod 2n$.

3. Process q has a variable named exp to store the sequence number i of the next data(i) message expected by q. The value of variable exp ranges over $0 .. 2n - 1$. Process q also has a buffer that can store up to n data messages. When q receives a data(i) message, q compares the values of i and exp. If i and exp have different values, q adds the message to its buffer. If i and exp have the same value, then q delivers the message and increments the value of exp by 1 mod 2n. Then q searches its buffer for a data(i) message whose i equals the current value of exp. As long as q can find such a message, it removes the message from the buffer and delivers it, then increments the value of exp by 1 mod 2n and continues to search the buffer.

9.2 BACKWARD ERROR RECOVERY

In backward error recovery, a process p sends data messages to a process q that replies by sending back acknowledgment messages. Process p uses the received acknowledgments to identify and resend each corrupted or lost message. In general, backward error recovery protocols share the following three features:

  i.   Each sent data message is of the form data(i), where i is a sequence number of the message.

  ii. The receiving of data messages by process q is acknowledged by sending acknowledgment messages from process q to process p.

  iii. There is an upper bound on the number of data messages that process p can send without receiving acknowledgment for any of them.

For historical reasons, the upper bound in iii is called the window size, and the backward error recovery protocols are called sliding-window protocols.

Different sliding-window protocols differ in the form and meaning of their acknowledgment messages. In general, there are three types of acknowledgments: cumulative, individual, and block acknowledgments. We discuss each of these types next.

In a cumulative acknowledgment protocol, each data message is of the form data(i), and each acknowledgment message is of the form ack(j), where both i and j are integers. Process q sends an ack(j) message to acknowledge receiving the data messages: data(0), data(1), . . . , data $(j - 1)$. In other words, an ack(j) message acknowledges the reception of all data messages up to the data$(j - 1)$ message. Cumulative acknowledgment protocols are efficient because one ack message can be used to acknowledge receiving many data messages. However, these protocols require unbounded sequence numbers for their messages. Cumulative acknowledgment protocols are discussed in Section 9.3.

In an individual acknowledgment protocol, each data message is of the form data(i), and each acknowledgment message is of the form ack(j), where both i and j are in the range $0 . . r - 1$. Process q sends an ack(j) message to acknowledge receiving a data(j) message. Individual acknowledgment protocols are inefficient because one ack message can be used to acknowledge receiving exactly one data message. However, these protocols can employ bounded sequence numbers for their messages. Individual acknowledgment protocols are discussed in Section 9.4.

In a block acknowledgment protocol, each data message is of the form data(i), where i is in the range $0 . . r - 1$, and each acknowledgment message is of the form ack(j, k), where both j and k are in the range $0 . . r - 1$. Process q sends an ack(j, k) message to acknowledge receiving the data messages: data(j), data$(j +_r 1)$, . . . , data$(k -_r 1)$, data(k). Block acknowledgment protocols are efficient because one ack message can be used to acknowledge receiving many data messages. Moreover, these protocols can employ bounded sequence numbers for their messages. Block acknowledgment protocols are discussed in Section 9.5.

9.3 CUMULATIVE ACKNOWLEDGMENT

In a cumulative acknowledgment protocol, each data message that is sent from process p to process q has an integer sequence number. Reception of the data messages by process q is acknowledged by sending back ack messages from q to p. Each ack(j) message acknowledges that q has received the data messages data(0), data(1), ..., data(j − 1).

Process p has two integer variables na and ns defined as follows:

na   Sequence number of the next data message to be acknowledged in p

ns   Sequence number of the next data message to be sent by p

Therefore, every data(i) message, where i < na, has been sent by p and its acknowledgment has been received by p. Every data(i) message, where na ≤ i < ns, has been sent by p, but its acknowledgment has not yet been received by p. Every data(i) message, where ns ≤ i, has not been sent by p.

The relation between variables na and ns is defined as follows:

$$na \leq ns \leq na + w \tag{1}$$

Clearly, na ≤ ns holds because process p cannot receive acknowledgments for data messages it has not yet sent. Also, ns ≤ na + w holds because there is an upper bound, w, on the number of data messages that can be sent without receiving acknowledgments for any of them. Recall that w is a positive integer called the window size of the protocol.

Process q has one integer variable nr defined as follows:

nr   Sequence number of the next data message to be received by q

Therefore, if process q receives a data(i) message, where i < nr, then q recognizes that it has received and acknowledged an earlier copy of this message. On the other hand, if process q receives a data(i) message, where i ≤ nr, then q recognizes that this is a new message being received for the first time.

The relation between variables na, ns, and nr is defined as follows:

$$na \leq nr \leq ns \tag{2}$$

Clearly, na ≤ nr holds because process p cannot receive acknowledgments for data messages that process q has not yet received. Also, nr ≤ ns holds because process q cannot receive data messages that process p has not yet sent.

From (1) and (2) above, we end up with the following relation:

$$na \leq nr \leq ns \leq na + w \tag{3}$$

This relation is illustrated in Figure 9.1.

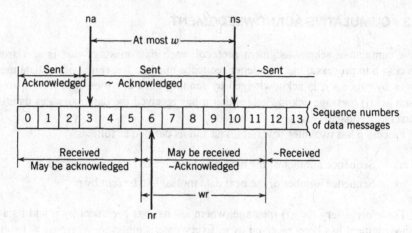

FIG. 9.1

Process p of the cumulative acknowledgment protocol can be defined as follows.

```
process p
const w
var    na, ns, i    :        integer
begin
       na+w > ns              ->      send data(ns) to q;
                                      ns := ns + 1
[]     rcv ack(i) from q ->            na := max(na,i)
[]     timeout t-guard    ->           send data(na) to q
[]     rcv error from q  ->            skip
end
```

Process p has four actions: one action for sending new data messages, one action for receiving ack messages, one timeout action for resending old data messages for which process p has not yet received acknowledgments, and one action for receiving corrupted messages. We discuss each of these actions in order.

In the first action, process p detects that it can still send another data message, that is, the sending window is still open. In this case, p sends the next data message with sequence number ns and increments ns by 1.

In the second action, process p receives an ack(i) message from process q. It then uses i to update na. Note that the ack messages can be received out of order by p. Thus, p may receive ack(j) and later receive ack(k), where j > k. Despite receiving the ack messages out of order, process p ensures that na is monotonically increased by updating variable na using the statement na := max(na, i).

In the third action, process p detects that the data(na) message or its acknowledgment has been lost, and so it resends this message. We delay discussing the guard of this action, the t-guard, until we discuss process q.

In the fourth action, process p receives a corrupted message and discards it, thus transforming an instance of message corruption to an instance of message loss.

Process q has an input wr whose value is the maximum number of data messages that process q can receive and store out of order. Because q does not need to store a data(j) message unless j ≥ nr, and because q cannot receive a data(j) message unless j < nr + w, it is reasonable to choose wr such that wr ≤ w. Constant wr is called the receiving window of the protocol.

Beside the integer variables nr and j, process q has the following variables:

```
var     rcvd   :      array [0..wr-1] of boolean,
        akn    :      boolean
```

An element rcvd[j mod wr] is true iff process q has already received the data(j) message from process p but has not yet delivered it because p is still waiting for the earlier data(nr) message. Variable akn is true iff process q has not yet acknowledged the last message it has received from process p.

Process q in the cumulative acknowledgment protocol can be defined as follows:

```
process q
const w
inp     wr     :      integer                      { 1 ≤ wr ≤ w }

var     nr, j  :      integer,
        rcvd   :      array [0..wr-1] of boolean,
        akn    :      boolean

begin
        rcv data(j) from p ->
                    if true                  ->      {busy q} skip
                    [] j < nr                ->      akn := true
                    [] nr ≤ j < nr+wr        ->
                        rcvd[j mod wr] := true;
                        do rcvd[nr mod wr] ->
                                 {deliver data(nr)}
                                 rcvd[nr mod wr], nr, akn :=
                                 false, nr+1, true
                        od
                    fi
[]      akn -> send ack(nr) to p; akn := false
[]      rcv error from p -> skip
end
```

Process q has three actions: one action for receiving a data message, one action for sending an ack message, and one action for receiving a corrupted message. We discuss each of these actions in turn.

In the first action, process q receives a data(j) message, then decides to perform one of the following activities:

i. Process q discards the message if q is busy or has no buffer to store the message. This is allowed because the protocol can recover from message loss, and discarding a message can be regarded as a form of message loss.

ii. Process q detects that j < nr, and so it recognizes that another copy of this message has been received earlier and that past acknowledgments of this message have been lost. In this case, process q does not store the message, but it sets akn to true so that it can acknowledge receiving the message one more time.

iii. Process q detects that nr ≤ j < nr + wr, where the receiving window wr is the maximum number of data messages that process q can store out of order. In this case, process q stores the message.

In the second action process q detects that variable akn is true, which indicates that an ack(nr) message needs to be sent from process q to process p. Thus, process q sends an ack(nr) message to process p and resets variable akn to false.

In the third action, process q receives a corrupted message and discards it, thus transforming an instance of message corruption to an instance of message loss.

To complete our description of this protocol, we now turn our attention to the timeout guard (t-guard) in process p. To be sure, process p can send data(na) messages at any frequency until it receives an ack message from process q. Therefore, we can choose the t-guard to be as follows:

$$\text{t-guard}_0 = na < ns \land (ack\#ch.q.p = 0)$$

Predicate t-guard$_0$ consists of two conjuncts. The first conjunct indicates that the data(na) message has been sent by p, but its acknowledgment has not yet been received by p. The second conjunct indicates that no acknowledgment is in the channel from q to p.

The problem of t-guard$_0$ is its inefficiency. Process p may end up sending many copies of the data(na) message even though the first message and its acknowledgment were not lost. A more efficient choice of the t-guard is one that allows process p to resend the data(na) message when and only when process p is certain that either the last data(na) message or its acknowledgment is lost. This t-guard can be defined as follows.

$$\text{t-guard}_1 = na < ns \land (\#ch.p.q + \#ch.q.p = 0) \land \sim akn$$

Predicate t-guard$_1$ indicates that the data(na) message has been sent, and its acknowledgment has not been received by p and that there are no more acknowledgments to be received by p until p sends a data message to q.

Correctness of the cumulative acknowledgment protocol is based on the fact that the sequence numbers of data messages are unbounded. It is straightforward to argue that this protocol cannot use bounded sequence numbers. Consider, for example a scenario in which process p sends two messages, data(3) then data(4), to process q. Process q first receives the data(3) message, assigns its variable nr the value 4, and then sends an ack(4) message to process p. Later, process q receives the data(4) message, assigns its variable nr the value 5, and then sends an ack(5) message to process p.

Because of a message reorder, process p receives the ack(5) message, which acknowledges both data(3) and data(4), while the ack(4) message remains in the channel from process q to process p. Because the sent data messages are acknowledged, process p continues to send new data messages to q and receive ack messages from q. If the protocol uses bounded sequence numbers, then eventually process p sends a new data(3) message to process q. It is possible in this case that this new data(3) message is lost, but process p receives the old ack(4) message and thinks that it is an acknowledgment for the lost data(3) message.

Two problems arise in this scenario. First, the data(3) message is lost and its loss is not detected. Second, the synchronization between na and nr is lost because na has just surpassed nr, violating relations (2) and (3) above.

In summary, a sliding-window protocol that uses bounded sequence numbers cannot be based on cumulative acknowledgment. In the next section, we discuss a sliding-window protocol that is based on individual acknowledgment. This protocol uses bounded sequence numbers.

9.4   INDIVIDUAL ACKNOWLEDGMENT

In the individual acknowledgment protocol, each data message from process p to process q has an identifier in the range $0 . . r - 1$. The reception of each data(i) message by process q is acknowledged by sending back an ack(i) message to process p.

As in the cumulative acknowledgment protocol in Section 9.3, the processes in the individual acknowledgment protocol have three variables na, ns, and nr. Variables na and ns are in process p, while variable nr is in process q. All three variables are in the range $0 . . r - 1$. They are defined as follows:

na   Sequence number of the next data message to be acknowledged in p

ns   Sequence number of the next data message to be sent by p

nr   Sequence number of the next data message to be received by q

The relation between the variables na, ns, and nr is similar to relation (3) in Section 9.3. However, this relation is stated differently because the values of these variables are now in the range $0 . . r - 1$. In particular, this relation can be defined as follows:

$$\text{within}(na, nr, ns) \land \text{within}(nr, ns, na +_r w) \tag{4}$$

Formally, within(x, y, z), where x, y, and z are in the range $0 .. r-1$, is defined as follows:

$$\text{within}(x, y, z) = (y = x \lor y = x +_r 1 \lor \ldots \lor y = z -_r 1 \lor y = z)$$
$$= (y -_r x \le z -_r x)$$

Informally, it is convenient to think of within(x, y, z) as $x \le y \le z$. Relation (4) is illustrated in Figure 9.2.

When process q receives a data(j) message from process p, process q needs to determine whether the received message is old (i.e., it is a copy of a message that was received earlier by q), or new (i.e., the message is being received for the first time by q). We choose a received data(j) to be old if within(nr $-_r$ w, j, nr $-_r$ 1) holds, and choose a received data(j) to be new if within(nr, j, nr $+_r$ w $-_r$ 1) holds.

In order that process q can distinguish between old and new messages, every sequence number j of a received data(j) message should indicate that either data(j) is not old or data(j) is not new. Therefore, the following relation should be satisfied at every instant

```
(For every j, 0 ≤ j < r,
      ~within(nr -_r w, j, nr -_r 1) ∨
      ~within(nr, j, nr +_r w -_r 1)
```

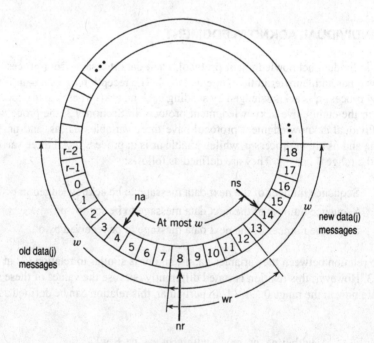

FIG. 9.2

This relation can be satisfied at each instant by choosing w and r such that $w \le r/2$.

Because the ack message can be received by process p out of order, process p needs an array, named ackd, to store the received ack messages until they can be processed in order. Array ackd is declared as follows.

var   ackd   :   **array** [0..r-1] **of boolean**

An element ackd[j] in this array is true iff process p has received an ack(j) message after p has sent the last data(j) message. Because na is the sequence number of the next data message to be acknowledged, ackd[na] is always false.

Process p in the individual acknowledgment protocol can be defined as follows:

```
process p
const w,r                    { 1 ≤ w ≤ r/2 }

var    na, ns, i   :     0..r-1,
       ackd        :     array [0..r-1] of boolean
par    k           :     0..r-1
begin
       na +r w ≠ ns         ->
                       send data(ns) to q; ns := ns +r 1
[]     rcv ack(i) from q ->
                       ackd[i] := true;
                       do ackd[na] -> ackd[na], na :=
                                      false, na +r 1
                       od
[]     timeout      bet(na, k, ns) ∧
                    ~ackd[k] ∧
                    (data(k)#ch.p.q + ack(k)#ch.q.p = 0)
                           ->     send data(k) to q
[]     rcv error from q  ->     skip
end
```

Process p has four actions. In the first action, process p detects that the sending window is still open and sends the next data message. In the second action, process p receives an ack message, stores it in array ackd, and updates na so that ackd[na] remains false. In the third action, process p resends the last data(k) message when three conjuncts are satisfied. The first conjunct is written in terms of a function bet(x, y, z), which for every x, y, and z in the range $0 .. r - 1$ is defined as follows:

$$\text{bet}(x, y, z) = (x \ne z) \wedge \text{within}(x, y, z -_r 1)$$

$$= (y -_r x < z -_r x)$$

The first conjunct bet(na, k, ns) indicates that a data(k) message was sent and its acknowledgment ack(k) may have not been received. The second conjunct indicates that indeed the ack(k) message was not received. The third conjunct indicates that the data(k) message and its acknowledgment ack(k) are not in the two channels between p and q. In the fourth action, process p receives a corrupted message and discards it.

In process q, the conditions for a received data(j) message to be old or new can be expressed in terms of function bet as follows:

$$\text{data(j) is old} = \text{bet}(nr -_r w, j, nr)$$

$$\text{data(j) is new} = \text{bet}(nr, j, nr +_r w)$$

Because new data messages may arrive out of order at process q, process q can only accept wr of them, where wr is the receiving window of the protocol, satisfying $1 \leq wr \leq w$. Thus, the condition for accepting new data messages can be expressed in terms of wr as follows:

$$\text{data(j) is accepted} = \text{bet}(nr, j, nr +_r wr)$$

Process q in the individual acknowledgment protocol can be defined as follows:

```
process q
const  w, r
inp    wr              :     integer      { 1 ≤ wr ≤ w ≤ r/2 }
var    nr, j           :     0..r-1,
       rcvd            :     array [0..wr-1] of boolean

begin
       rcv data(j) from p        ->
                 if true                          ->     skip
                 [] bet(nr -r w, j, nr)   ->
                       send ack(j) to p
                 [] bet(nr, j, nr +r wr)  ->
                       send ack(j) to p;
                       rcvd[j mod wr] := true;
                       do rcvd[nr mod wr] ->
                              {deliver data(nr)}
                              rcvd[nr mod wr], nr :=
                              false, nr +r 1
                       od
                 fi
       []    rcv error from p  ->     skip
end
```

Cumulative acknowledgment protocols have the advantage of allowing several data messages to be acknowledged by a single ack message. On the other hand, individual acknowledgment protocols have the advantage of using bounded sequence numbers. Both these advantages can be realized in block acknowledgment protocols, discussed in the next section.

9.5 BLOCK ACKNOWLEDGMENT

In the block acknowledgment protocol, each data message from process p to process q has an identifier in the range $0 .. r - 1$. Reception of the data messages by process q is acknowledged by sending back ack messages from q to p. Each ack message has two fields in the range $0 .. r - 1$. In particular, each ack(i, k) message acknowledges the reception of the data messages

$$\text{data(i) ; data(i} +_r \text{1) ; } \ldots \text{; data(k} -_r \text{1) ; data(k)}$$

Process p in the block acknowledgment protocol can be defined as follows:

```
process p
const w,r                   { 1 ≤ w ≤ r/2 }
var    na, ns, i, k:        0..r-1,
       ackd         :       array [0..r-1] of boolean

begin
       na +r w ≠ ns          ->
                       send data(ns) to q; ns := ns +r 1
[]     rcv ack(i, k) from q ->
                       do i ≠ k -> ackd[i], i := true, i +r 1
                       od;
                       ackd[k] := true;
                       do ackd[na] -> ackd[na], na :=
                                       false, na +r 1
                       od
[]     timeout        (na ≠ ns) /\
                      (data(na)#ch.p.q = 0) /\
                      (for every x, 0 ≤ x < r,
                             ack(na, x)#ch.q.p = 0) /\
                      (~akn \/ na ≠ nb)
                             ->    send data(na) to p
[]     rcv error from q  ->    skip
end
```

Process p in this protocol has similar variables to those of process p in the individual acknowledgment protocol in Section 9.4. Process p also has similar actions to those of process p in Section 9.4, with three exceptions. First, on receiving an ack(i, k) message from process q, process p assigns the following elements the value true.

$$\text{ackd}[i] \ ; \ \text{ackd}[i +_r 1] \ ; \ \ldots \ ; \ \text{ackd}[k -_r 1] \ ; \ \text{ackd}[k]$$

Then, process p increments variable na until ackd[na] is false. Second, the timeout action in process p resends the last data(na) message to process q. Third, the guard of this timeout action consists of the following four conjuncts:

  i. The first conjunct states that the last data(na) message has been sent but not yet acknowledged.
  ii. The second conjunct states that there is no data(na) message in the channel from process p to process q.
  iii. The third conjunct states that there is no ack message, acknowledgming the reception of the last data(na) message, in the channel from process q to process p.
  iv. The fourth conjunct states that process q has no ack messages to send (unless process p sends or resends some data message) or that future ack messages from q will not acknowledge the reception of the last data(na) message.

Process q of the block acknowledgment protocol can be defined as follows:

```
process q
const w,r
inp    wr          :      integer      { 1 ≤ wr ≤ w ≤ r/2 }
var    nb, nr, j   :      0..r-1,
       rcvd        :      array [0..wr-1] of boolean,
       akn         :      boolean

begin
       rcv data(j) from p        ->
                    if true                     ->     skip
                    ▯ bet(nr -r w, j, nr)       ->
                         send ack(j, j) to p
                    ▯ bet(nr, j, nr +r wr)      ->
                         rcvd[j mod wr] := true;
                         do rcvd[nr mod wr] ->
                              {deliver data(nr)}
                              rcvd[nr mod wr] := false;
                              akn, nr := true, nr +r 1
                    od
```

```
                        fi
☐    akn    ->      send ack(nb, nr -r 1) to p;
                        nb, akn := nr, false
☐    rcv error from p  ->      skip
end
```

This process q is very similar to process q of the cumulative acknowledgment protocol in Section 9.3 with one exception. Process q uses a new variable nb when it acknowledges the reception of new data messages. In particular, when a new data message is received, process q updates nr and assigns variable akn the value true. Later when akn is still true, process q sends an ack(nb, nr -r 1) message to process p, assigns variable nb the current value of nr, and assigns akn the value false.

9.6   ERROR RECOVERY IN THE INTERNET

The protocol that performs error recovery in the Internet is the transmission control protocol, or TCP. In Section 6.4, we presented an overview of TCP and discussed how TCP connections are established and removed. We also discussed how TCP processes exchange messages over established connections. In this section, we discuss how TCP processes detect and recover from message loss and reorder.

When two TCP processes exchange data messages, they recover from message loss and reorder using a protocol similar to the cumulative acknowledgment protocol in Section 9.3. The protocol used by the TCP processes, however, has four additional features that makes it more efficient:

    i. piggybacking acknowledgments in data messages,
   ii. controlling the sending of short data messages,
  iii. controlling the sending of acknowledgments, and
   iv. adjusting the timeout periods.

Next, we describe each of these four features in order.

Piggybacking Acknowledgments in Data Messages

If two TCP processes happen to be exchanging data messages, then these processes do not need to send acknowledgment messages to one another. Instead, each TCP process piggybacks its latest acknowledgment information in the data message that the process happens to be sending at the time. As discussed in Section 6.4, the header of any data message from a TCP process tp to a TCP process tq has the following two fields:

    1. sequence number of the data message (Field 3) and
    2. sequence number of the next data message expected by process tp (Field 4).

Field 3 contains the starting byte position of the message in the text stream from tp to tq. Field 4 contains the starting byte position of the next expected message by tp in the text stream from tq to tp.

Controlling the Sending of Short Data Messages

TCP processes do not send many data messages with little text in each of them. Consider the case where an application process p in computer c needs to send, via TCP, a stream of text segments to an application process q in another computer d. In this case, process p sends the text segments, one by one, to the TCP process tp in computer c; then process tp forwards these segments as TCP messages to the TCP process tq in computer d. When process tp receives a small text segment from process p, tp needs to decide whether to add a TCP header to the segment and send it as a TCP message right away or to wait to receive additional text segment(s) to be included with the previous segment in one TCP message. Process tp makes this decision according to the following three rules:

i. If process tp has already received an acknowledgment for every TCP data message that tp has sent earlier to tq, then tp adds a TCP header to the received segment and sends the resulting TCP message right away.

ii. If process tp has not received an acknowledgment for some TCP data message that tp has sent earlier to tq, then tp stores the received segment to be sent later.

iii. If the size of the stored segment(s) in tp equals the maximum size for a text in a TCP message, then tp adds a TCP header to the stored segments and sends the resulting TCP message.

The net effect of these three rules is to ensure that at any time at most one small TCP message can be in transit from process tp to process tq. These three rules are sometimes called Nagle's algorithm.

Controlling the Sending of Acknowledgments

When a TCP process tp receives a data message from another TCP process tq, tp does not send an acknowledgment message to tq right away. Rather, tp waits for some time before sending the acknowledgment. Process tp eventually sends the acknowledgment when any of the following events occurs:

i. Process tp sends a data message to tq. In this case, tp piggybacks the acknowledgment in the sent data message, as discussed above.

ii. Process tp receives a second data message from tq. In this case, tp sends one acknowledgment message for the two data messages to tq.

iii. Five hundred milliseconds have passed since tp has received the data message from tq without tp sending an acknowledgment to tq. In this case, tp sends an acknowledgment for the data message to tq.

Adjusting the Timeout Periods

While a TCP process tp sends data messages to another TCP process tq, tp keeps track of the round-trip delay between tp and tq by maintaining three local variables that have the following meanings:

avg   Average-round trip delay, in seconds, between the two TCP processes tp and tq

dev   Mean deviation of the round-trip delay, in seconds, between tp and tq

tout   Timeout period, in seconds, after which a data message is to be resent by process tp

The values of these three variables are updated according to the following three rules.

i. Initialization: Initially, tout is 6 seconds. Then if tp sends the first data message and receives an acknowledgment for it (without resending the message) after T seconds, tp computes avg, dev, and tout as follows:

$$avg := T + \tfrac{1}{2};$$

$$dev := avg/2;$$

$$tout := avg + (4 \times dev)$$

ii. Regular Update: If tp sends a later data message and receives an acknowledgment for it (without resending the message) after T seconds, tp updates avg, dev, and tout as follows:

$$avg := (\tfrac{7}{8} \times avg) + \tfrac{1}{8}T;$$

$$dev := (\tfrac{3}{4} \times dev) + \tfrac{1}{4}(|T - avg|);$$

$$tout := avg + (4 \times dev)$$

iii. Exponential Back-off: If tp sends a data message and does not receive an acknowledgment for it for a time period exceeding tout, then tp resends the data message, keeps variables avg and dev unchanged, but updates tout as follows:

$$tout := 2 \times tout$$

Note that if tp times out and resends a data message and later receives an acknowledgment for that message, then tp cannot decide which copy, the first or the second, of the data message is being acknowledged. In this case tp avoids the ambiguity by keeping the three variables avg, dev, and tout unchanged.

9.7   BIBLIOGRAPHICAL NOTES

A special class of the sliding-window protocols, called the alternating-bit protocol, is first discussed in Lynch [1968] and Bartlett et al. [1969]. The first sliding-window protocol is discussed in Cerf and Khan [1974]. Classifying the sliding-window protocols based on the types of their acknowledgments is discussed in Brown et al.[1989].

Verification of the alternating-bit protocol is discussed in Bochmann [1975], Hailpern [1985], and Gouda [1985]. Verification of the sliding-window protocols is discussed in Stenning [1976], Knuth [1981], Brown et al. [1989], Shankar [1989], Gouda [1992], and Shankar and Lee [1995].

A protocol that can adjust its degree of error recovery is discussed in Gong and Parulkar [1996].

EXERCISES

1   (Forward Recovery of Message Corruption). Design processes p and q in the protocol of forward recovery from message corruption discussed in Section 9.1.

2   (Forward Recovery of Message Loss). Design processes p and q in the protocol of forward recovery from message loss discussed in Section 9.1.

3   (Forward Recovery of Message Reorder). Design processes p and q in the protocol of forward recovery from message reorder discussed in Section 9.1.

4   (Forward Recovery of Message Corruption and Loss). Combine the two protocols in exercises 1 and 2 into one protocol.

5   (Forward Recovery of Message Corruption, Loss, and Reorder). Combine the two protocols in exercises 3 and 4 into one protocol.

6   (Exhibiting Data Transfer). It is required to modify the cumulative acknowledgement protocol in Section 9.3 as follows. The following two arrays are added to process p:

```
inp        txtp    :      array [integer] of integer
var        sent    :      array [0..w-1] of integer
```

Also, the following two variable arrays are added to process q:

```
var        txtq    :      array [integer] of integer,
           rcvt    :      array [0..wr-1] of integer
```

Each data message sent from process p has two fields of the form data(i, t), where i is the sequence number of the message as before and t is the message text. When data(i, t) is sent for the first time, its text t is taken from array txtp and is stored in array sent. If data(i, t) is resent, its text t is taken from array sent. The text t of a sent message data(i, t) remains in array sent until process p receives an acknowledgment for the message. When a data(i, t) message is received by process q, the message text t is stored in array rcvt. When this data(i, t) message is later delivered, its text t is copied from array rcvt into array txtq. Design the two processes p and q in the modified protocol.

7   (Exhibiting Data Transfer). Solve the same problem as before for the individual acknowledgment protocol in Section 9.4.

8   (Exhibiting Data Transfer). Solve the same problem as before for the block acknowledgment protocol in Section 9.5.

9   (Tolerating Message Reorder Only). Simplify the cumulative acknowledgment protocol in Section 9.3 under the following three assumptions. First, neither message corruption nor message loss can occur. Second, size of the receiving window wr equals size of the sending window w. Third, process q is not allowed to discard received data messages.

10   (Tolerating Message Reorder Only). Simplify the individual acknowledgment protocol in Section 9.4 under the same three assumptions in the above problem.

11   (Tolerating Message Reorder Only). Simplify the block acknowledgment protocol in Section 9.5 under the same three assumptions in the above problem.

12   (Tolerating Message Corruption and Loss Only). Simplify the cumulative acknowledgment protocol in Section 9.3 under the assumption that message reorder cannot occur. (*Hint:* In this case, the sequence numbers of data messages can be bounded in the range $0 \ .. \ r - 1$. What is the smallest possible value of r?)

13   (Tolerating Message Corruption and Loss Only). Simplify the individual acknowledgment protocol in Section 9.4 under the assumption that message reorder cannot occur.

14   (Tolerating Message Corruption and Loss Only). Simplify the block acknowledgment protocol in Section 9.5 under the assumption that message reorder cannot occur.

15   (Window Parameters). Consider an individual acknowledgment protocol. Assume that during execution, this protocol reaches a state S where na = 10 and ns = 4. Which of the following statements concerning the value of nr at state S is true, which of them is false, and which of them is inconclusive.

a   nr = 4
b   nr = 5
c   nr = 10

d   nr = 11

What is the smallest and largest possible value of w in this protocol?

16 (Alternating-Bit Protocol). Simplify the cumulative acknowledgment protocol in Section 9.3 in the case where w = 1.

17 (Alternating-Bit Protocol). Simplify the individual acknowledgment protocol in Section 9.4 in the case where w = 1.

18 (Alternating-Bit Protocol). Simplify the block acknowledgment protocol in Section 9.5 in the case where w = 1.

19 (Timeout Actions). Any of the following two timeout actions can be used in process p of the individual acknowledgment protocol in Section 9.4:

```
timeout  na≠ns ∧ bet(na, k, ns+ₙ1) ∧ ~ackd[k] ∧
         (data(k)#ch.p.q + ack(k)#ch.q.p = 0)—>
         send data(k) to p

timeout  na≠ns ∧ (#ch.p.q + #ch.q.p = 0)         —>
         i := na;
         do i≠ns —>
               if ~ackd[i] —> send data(i) to q
               ▯ ackd[i] —> skip
               fi; i := i +ᵣ 1
         od
```

Explain the advantage(s) of using any of these two actions over the other action.

20 (Error Recovery without Timeout Actions). Modify the cumulative acknowledgment protocol in Section 9.3 such that neither process p nor process q has any timeout action.

21 (Error Recovery without Timeout Actions). Modify the individual acknowledgment protocol in Section 9.4 such that neither process p nor process q has any timeout action. (*Hint:* The sequence numbers of the data messages need to be of type integer rather than of type range.)

22 (Negative Acknowledgments). Modify the cumulative acknowledgment protocol in Section 9.3 as follows. First, wr = 1. Second, if process q receives a data(j) message, where j > nr, then q discards the message and sends a negative acknowledgment message nack(j) to process p. Third, if process p receives a nack(j) message, it resends the data(j) message to process q.

23 (Negative Acknowledgments). Modify the individual acknowledgment protocol in Section 9.4 as follows. First, the sequence numbers of the data messages are of type integer rather than of type range. Second, wr = 1. Third, if process q receives a data(j) message, where j > nr, then q discards the message and sends a negative acknowledgment message nack(j) to process p. Fourth, if process p receives a nack(j) message, it resends the data(j) message to process q.

24 (Lossy Delivery of Data Messages). Modify the cumulative acknowledgment protocol in Section 9.3 as follows. First, wr = 1. Second, if process q receives a data(j) message, where j $\geq$ nr, then q delivers the received message, assigns nr the value j + 1, and may send an ack(j + 1) message to process p. Third, if process p receives a data(j) message, where j < nr, it discards the received message and may send an ack(nr) message to process p.

25 (Piggybacking of Acknowledgments). Consider a cumulative acknowledgment protocol where both processes p and q send data messages to one another. Each data message sent by p (or q) is of the form data(i, j), where i is the sequence number of the message and j is the sequence number of the next message to be received by p (or q, respectively). Thus, data messages carry acknowledgments as well. Note that both processes in this protocol are identical. Design process p in this protocol. (*Hint:* Process p has the following variables:

```
var      na, nr, ns, i, j   :      integer,
         akn                :      boolean              )
```

26 (Sequence of Sliding Windows). Consider a process array p[i: 0 .. n − 1]. Each process p[i], 0 < i < n − 1, receives data messages from p[i − 1] and sends back corresponding ack messages to p[i − 1]. It also forwards the received data messages to p[i + 1] and receives back ack messages from p[i + 1]. The exchange of data and ack messages between any two successive processes follows an individual acknowledgment protocol. Each process p[i], 0 < i < n − 1, has the following variables:

```
var   na, nr, ns, i   :   0..r-1,     {1≤w≤r/2}
      done            :   array [0..r-1] of boolean
```

Design processes p[i: 1, . . . , n − 2].

27 (Nagle's Algorithm). Modify the cumulative acknowledgment protocol in Section 9.3 as follows. Process p can send two types of data messages: regular and short. Each data message, whether regular or short, is of the form data(i), where i is the unique sequence number of the message. Process p does not send more than w data messages, whether regular or short, without receiving an acknowledgment message for any of them. Moreover, p does not send more than one short data message without receiving an acknowledgment message for all previous data messages.

28 (Nagle's Algorithm). Solve exercise 27 for the individual acknowledgment protocol in Section 9.4.

29   (Simplified Cumulative Acknowledgment Protocol). Simplify process q in the cumulative acknowledgment protocol in Section 9.3 under the assumption that array rcvd in q is an infinite array.

30   (Simplified Individual Acknowledgment Protocol). Simplify process q in the individual acknowledgment protocol in Section 9.4 under the assumption that array rcvd in q is an infinite array.

31   (Simplified block Acknowledgment Protocol). Simplify process q in the block acknowledgment protocol in Section 9.5 under the assumption that array rcvd in q is an infinite array.

32   (Simplified Cumulative Acknowledgment Protocol). Simplify the cumulative acknowledgment protocol in Section 9.3 under the following assumptions:

   a   All message transmissions are error free.

   b   Process q does not discard any received data message.

   c   The window mechanism is still used to control the flow of data messages.

   d   Data messages have no sequence numbers.

   e   Each ack message is of the form ack(i), where i is in the range 1 .. w, and w is the window size.

33   (Cumulative Acknowledgment Protocol without Retransmission). Redesign the cumulative acknowledgment protocol, in Section 9.3, under the following three assumptions:

   a   Sent messages can be corrupted or lost but not reordered.

   b   Process p sends each data message exactly once. (Thus, corrupted or lost messages are not retransmitted by p.) Rather, process q delivers the data messages it receives from p and ignores all corrupted or lost messages.

   c   The sliding-window mechanism is still used to ensure that process p never sends more than w data messages without receiving ack messages for any of them.

   (*Hint:* If process p sends w data messages and waits long enough to ensure that each of these messages has been lost or received by q and that each of the resulting ack messages, if any, has been lost or received by p, then process p times out and sends the next data message.)

CHAPTER 10

FLOW CONTROL

When a process p sends data messages to a process q, p needs to control the flow of data messages in an attempt to achieve a compromise between two conflicting concerns. On the one hand, process p tries to send to process q as many data messages as possible as fast as possible. On the other hand, process p tries not to send data messages faster than process q can handle them; otherwise, process q starts to discard the received data messages, as discussed in the last chapter.

To be sure, the sliding-window mechanism, which guarantees an upper bound on the number of data messages that process p can send without receiving ack messages for any of them, constitutes some form of flow control. Before the upper bound is reached, process p can send new data messages as fast as it can. After the upper bound is reached, process p cannot send any new data messages until it receives ack messages for some of the data message sent earlier.

Unfortunately, there are three problems that hinder the effectiveness of the window mechanism in controlling the flow of data messages:

i. The window size is constant. Therefore, process p cannot adapt the window size to changes in the current status of process q, from very busy to almost idle or from almost idle to very busy.

ii. In some situations, the window size is very large, and in those situations, the window mechanism is not effective in controlling the flow. (A special case of this situation is when the window size approaches infinity and the window mechanism is no longer present to control the flow of data messages from p to q.)

iii. In the window mechanism, an ack message performs two functions. First, it acknowledges that some data messages have been received correctly by process q. Second, it allows process p to send new data messages to process q. Thus, ack messages cannot be used to acknowledge the correct reception of some data messages without allowing process p to send new data messages to process q, even when process q is busy and cannot receive new data messages.

In this chapter, we discuss three new versions of the sliding-window protocol. In each version, one of the above problems is solved.

In Section 10.1, we discuss a version of the cumulative acknowledgment protocol where the window size is changed according to the following criteria. When process q becomes busy and discards a received data message, the window size is reduced to half of its value. When process q receives a specified number of consecutive data messages without discarding any of them, then the window size is incremented by 1.

In Section 10.2, we discuss a version of the individual acknowledgment window protocol where data messages are sent according to a sliding-window mechanism as well as to some specified rate. Thus, even if the window is open for sending data messages, no data message is sent, or resent, in violation of the specified rate.

In Section 10.3, we discuss a new sliding-window protocol where the window size equals the size of a circular buffer in the receiver process. Periodically, the receiver process sends a bit map describing the state of its circular buffer. The sender process receives these bit maps and deduces from them which data messages need to be resent and which data messages need not be resent. The sender process also determines from these bit maps the available store in the circular buffer and can compute the number of new data messages that it can send.

In Section 10.4, we describe some flow control features in the Internet.

10.1 WINDOW SIZE CONTROL

In this section, we describe how to modify the cumulative acknowledgment protocol in Section 9.3 such that the window size can be changed when a need arises. Similar modifications can be made to the individual acknowledgment protocol in Section 9.4 and to the block acknowledgment protocol in Section 9.5 to allow their window sizes to change over time.

In the modified protocol, the window size w is a variable whose value is in the range wmin . . wmax, where wmin and wmax are positive integers. The value of variable w is changed depending on the number of data messages that are sent correctly, without loss, from process p to process q. This is because most message losses are caused, not by transmission errors, but by process q discarding some data messages when the flow of messages becomes more than q can handle.

In the modified protocol, when a data message is ever resent from process p to process q, the window size w is reduced by a factor of 2 (provided that the new w is not smaller than wmin). On the other hand, if process p succeeds in sending cmax or more consecutive data messages to process q without having to resend any of them, then w is incremented by 1 (provided that the new w is not larger than wmax).

There is one more detail that we need to consider in this protocol. Assume, for example, that the protocol is in a state where na = 5 and ns = 9 when process p times out. This timeout causes p to reduce the window size w by a factor of 2 and to resend the data(5) message. Notice that each of the data messages data(6), data(7), and data(8) had been sent earlier, when w was still large, and so there is a good chance that some of these messages had been lost also. Therefore, process p should be designed such that when p later detects the loss of any of these messages, it does not reduce the window size w any further.

This can be accomplished as follows. Add two new integer variables, ra and rs, to process p. When p reduces the window size w and resends the data(5) message, p assigns the two variables ra and rs the values 6 and 9, respectively. In other words, variables ra and rs are assigned the values na+1 and ns, respectively. If later process p times out to resend the data(na) message, p first checks whether na satisfies the predicate (ra $\leq$ na $\land$ na < rs). If na satisfies this predicate, then p does not reduce the window size. If na does not satisfy this predicate, then p reduces the window size w by a factor of 2 and assigns variable rs the current value of ns. In either case, p assigns variable ra the current value of na+1 and resends the data(na) message.

Process p in the cumulative acknowledgment protocol with variable window size can be defined as follows:

```
process p

const wmin, wmax                        {wmin < wmax}

inp    cmax        :       integer      {cmax > 0}

var    na, ns, i   :       integer,
       w           :       wmin..wmax,
       c           :       integer,
       ra, rs      :       integer

begin
       na+w > ns              ->
                      send data(ns) to q; ns := ns+1
 []    rcv ack(i) from q ->
                      na, c := max(na,i), c + max(i-na, 0);
                      if c ≥ cmax -> w, c :=
                                     min(w+1,wmax), c-cmax
                      [] c < cmax -> skip
                      fi

 []    timeout      na<ns ∧ (#ch.p.q +#ch.q.p = 0) ∧ ~akn
                      ->
```

```
if    (ra ≤ na ∧ na < rs) -> skip
☐    ~(ra ≤ na ∧ na < rs) ->
       w, rs := max(w/2, wmin), ns
fi; ra, c := na+1, 0;
send data(na) to q

☐    rcv error from q ->    skip
end
```

The actions in this process p are similar to the actions in process p of the cumulative acknowledgment protocol in Section 9.3, with two exceptions. First, when this process p receives an ack(i) message, it increments a counter c by an amount equal to the number of data messages that are acknowledged by the ack(i) message. Thus, counter c counts the last consecutive data messages that are acknowledged without being resent. If c becomes bigger than cmax, then w is incremented by 1 and c is set to c − cmax. Second, before process p resends a data(na) message, it updates variables ra and c and may update variables w and rs as discussed earlier.

Process q of this protocol is identical to process q of the cumulative acknowledgment protocol in Section 9.3 with one exception. The requirement that wr ≤ w is now replaced by the requirement that wr ≤ wmax.

10.2 RATE CONTROL

In this section, we describe how to modify the individual acknowledgment protocol in Section 9.4 such that data messages are sent not only according to the window mechanism but also according to some specified rate. Similar modifications can be made to the cumulative acknowledgment protocol in Section 9.3 and the block acknowledgment protocol in Section 9.5.

In the modified protocol, when a data message is sent or resent from process p to process q, the number of data messages in the channel from p to q is less than a predefined value cap. This added restriction means that the number of data messages in the channel from p to q is never more than cap messages. In effect, this restriction implies that there is an upper bound on the rate at which process p sends data messages to process q.

Note that in the original protocol the number of data messages in the channel from process p to process q is never more than w. Therefore, the added restriction is meaningful only when cap < w.

Process p in the rate control protocol can be defined as follows:

process p

const w,r

inp   cap   :   **integer**   {0 < cap < w}

```
var    na, ns, i   :        0..r-1,
       ackd         :        array [0..r-1] of boolean,

par    k            :        0..r-1

begin
       timeout (na +r w ≠ns) ∧ (#ch.p.q < cap) ->
                   send data(ns) to q; ns := ns +r 1

[]     rcv ack(i) from q ->
                   ackd[i] := true;
                   do ackd[na] -> ackd[na], na :=
                                   false, na +r 1
             od

[]     timeout
                bet(na, k, ns) ∧ ~ackd[k] ∧
                (data(k)#ch.p.q + ack(k)#ch.q.p = 0) ∧
                (#ch.p.q < cap) ->
                   send data(k) to p

[]     rcv error from q ->      skip
end
```

This process p is similar to process p of the individual acknowledgment protocol in Section 9.4, with one exception. The conjunct (#ch.p.q < cap) is added to the guards of the first and third actions. Process q of this protocol is identical to process q of the individual acknowledgment protocol in Section 9.4.

This rate control protocol can be modified such that the value of cap is increased when p sends at least cmax consecutive data messages without errors, and the value of cap is decreased when a data message is resent due to some error.

10.3 CIRCULAR BUFFER CONTROL

The protocol that we consider in this section consists of two processes called receiver and sender. The receiver process q has a circular buffer where it stores the data messages that it has received from the sender process p until the messages are delivered to the host of the receiver.

Periodically, the receiver q sends the current state of its circular buffer to the sender p. On receiving a state message, p can decide which data messages have been lost during transmission and so need to be resent. It can also decide how many new data messages it can send to q. The state of the circular buffer consists of three components: (rcvd, qr, qt), where rcvd is a boolean map of the circular buffer and qr and qt are two pointers that always point to different locations of the circular buffer.

These two pointers divide the circular buffer into two nonempty regions: a "can-receive region" from qr to just before qt and a "cannot-receive region" from qt to just before qr. Process p can send and process q can receive data messages in the first region, but they cannot do so in the second region where old messages still reside waiting to be delivered to the host of the receiver.

Because qr and qt always point to different locations of the circular buffer, at least a third location is needed in order that one of these pointers can be incremented (in a circular fashion) without becoming equal to the other pointer. Thus, the number n of locations in the circular buffer is at least three; that is, $n \geq 3$.

Each sent message is given a sequence number in the range $0 .. n - 1$ to indicate the location in the circular buffer where the message is to be stored when it is received. Hence, even if data messages are received out of order, they still end up in the circular buffer in the same order in which they were sent.

When the sender p receives a state message that describes the state of the circular buffer, it can decide which data messages have been lost during earlier transmissions and so need to be resent. The rule for making this decision is simple. Process p keeps a variable count[k] for each data(k) message it sends. This variable counts the number of state messages that p has received after sending data(k) and from which p has concluded that data(k) has not been received by q. When count[k] equals a certain value m, then p concludes correctly that the sent data(k) message has been lost and so resends it and resets count[k] to 0.

Problems may also arise if m or more state messages can be present in the channel from q to p at the same instant. Consider the following scenario. Process p sends a new data(k) message and makes count[k] = 0 at an instant when there are m state messages in the channel from q to p. Shortly, process p receives all the state messages that were in the channel prior to sending data(k) and so detects in each of them that q has not yet received data(k). This causes count[k] to reach the value m and p to reach the wrong conclusion that the sent data(k) message has been lost and should be resent. To avoid such a scenario, the rate of sending state messages from q to p should ensure that at any instant at most $m - 1$ state messages can be in the channel from q to p. Therefore, $m \geq 2$.

Problems may arise if state messages are reordered (i.e., received in an order different from the one in which they were sent). Consider the following scenario. The sender p sends a data(k) message to the receiver, which receives it correctly and acknowledges its reception in two successive state messages. Process p receives the first state message and resumes sending new data messages without receiving the second state message. This second message can still be received later, after p receives any number of future state messages (because message reorder can occur). Because the sequence numbers of data messages are bounded, process p eventually returns to sequence number k and sends a new data(k) message. Suppose that this new data(k) message is lost but p receives the old state message that acknowledges the reception of a data(k) message by the receiver. In this case, p decides not to resend the lost data(k) message, causing a permanent message loss. Even if state messages are assigned bounded sequence numbers, a similar scenario can still lead to a permanent message loss.

In order to counter the effects of state message reorder, state messages are tagged with unbounded, monotonically increasing sequence numbers. Process p keeps track of the highest sequence number pk that it has received in a state message. When p receives a state message, it compares its sequence number with pk. If the sequence number is higher than pk, the message is processed as usual. Otherwise, the message is recognized as an old message and discarded.

So far, we have argued that some problems may arise during protocol execution if $n < 3$, $m < 2$, or more than $m - 1$ state messages can be present in the channel from q to p, or if data messages have no sequence numbers, or if state messages have bounded sequence numbers. This reasoning has necessitated that we make the following design decisions:

   i. $n \geq 3$.
  ii. $m \geq 2$.
 iii. At most $m - 1$ state messages are ever in the channel from q to p.
 iv. Data messages have sequence numbers in the range $0, \ldots, n - 1$.
  v. State messages have unbounded sequence numbers.

In describing this protocol in more detail, it is convenient to start with the receiver process q. Process q has the following variables:

```
var    rcvd        :      array [0..n-1] of boolean,
       qr, qt, j   :      0..n-1,
       qk          :      integer,
```

Array rcvd is used to record the current state of the circular buffer in q. Variables qr and qt are two pointers of array rcvd. They are defined as follows:

  qr Sequence number of the next data message to be received
  qt Sequence number of the next data message that cannot be received (there is an old data message in that position waiting to be delivered to the host of q)

Thus, qr and qt are never equal, and they divide the elements of array rcvd, as mentioned earlier, into two nonempty regions: can-receive region and cannot-receive region.

The can-receive region consists of those elements of array rcvd whose indices are in the set $\{qr, qr +_n 1, \ldots, qt -_n 1\}$. This region corresponds to the positions in the circular buffer where newly received data messages can be stored. The cannot-receive region consists of those elements of array rcvd whose indices are in the set $\{qt, qt +_n 1, \ldots, qr -_n 1\}$. This region corresponds to those positions in the circular buffer that are still occupied by old data messages, that is, by data messages that have been received earlier but have not yet been delivered to the host of process q. Thus the value of an element of array rcvd is as follows.

$$rcvd[k] = \begin{cases} \text{true} & \text{if} \quad bet(qr, k, qt) \text{ and } data(k) \text{ has been received} \\ \text{false} & \text{if} \quad bet(qr, k, qt) \text{ and } data(k) \text{ has not been received,} \\ & \quad\quad \text{or } bet(pt, k, pr) \end{cases}$$

Variable qk stores the sequence number of the last state message sent by q.

Process q has five actions: to send a state message, to receive a data message, to increment qr, to increment qt, and one action to receive an error message, if any. These five actions are described in detail next.

In the first action, process q sends a state message to p. Each state message contains the current state of the circular buffer as defined by array rcvd and the two variables qr and qt. Each state message also contains a unique sequence number qk:

```
timeout t-guard              ->
            qk := qk +1 ; send st(rcvd, qr, qt, qk) to p
```

We delay our discussion of the timeout predicate t-guard until after process p is discussed.

In the second action, process q receives a data(j) message from process p and updates the array element rcvd[j] to true:

```
rcv data(j) from p           ->        rcvd[j] := true
```

In the third action, process q recognizes that it has already received data(qr) and that $qr +_n 1 \neq qt$; it thus makes rcvd[qr] false and increments pr:

```
rcvd[qr] /\ qr +n 1 ≠ qt ->        rcvd[qr], qr :=
                                   false, qr +n 1
```

Note that this action cannot make qr equal qt.

In the fourth action of q, the data message in position qt in the circular buffer is delivered to the host of q and qt is incremented by 1:

```
qt +n 1 ≠ qr                 ->        qt := qt +n 1
```

Again this action cannot make pr equal pt.

In the last action of q, process q receives a corrupted error message from p and discards it:

```
rcv error from p             ->        skip
```

Process q in the circular buffer protocol can be defined as follows:

```
process q

const m, n                       {m ≥ 2 and n ≥ 3}

var   rcvd        :        array [0..n-1] of boolean,
      qr, qt, j   :        0..n-1,
      qk          :        integer
```

```
begin
        timeout t-guard              ->
                qk := qk +1 ; send st(rcvd, qr, qt, qk) to p
□       rcv data(j) from p           ->      rcvd[j] := true
□       rcvd[qr] ∧ qr +n 1 ≠ qt ->            rcvd[qr], qr :=
                                             false, qr +n 1
□       qt +n 1 ≠qr                  ->      qt := qt +n 1
□       rcv error from p             ->      skip
end
```

The variables in the sender process p are as follows.

```
var     ackd              :     array [0..n-1] of boolean,
        pr, pt, ps, i :     0..n-1,
        pk                :     integer,
        count             :     array [0..n-1] of 0..m-1,
        b                 :     array [0..n-1] of boolean,
        r, t              :     0..n-1,
        k                 :     integer
```

The four variables b, r, t, and k are used to store the fields of the last received state message. (Recall that q sends each state message with four fields: rcvd, qr, qt, and qk.) If the received sequence number k is bigger than pk, the highest received sequence number, then the values of b, r, t, and k are stored in variables ackd, pr, pt, and pk, respectively. Thus, array ackd is used to store the last received value of array rcvd. Similarly, variables pr and pt are used to store the last received values of variables qr and qt, respectively. It is convenient to interpret variables pr, pt, and ps as follows:

pr Sequence number of the next data message to be acknowledged
pt Sequence number of the next data message that cannot be sent (because the receiver q currently has no space to store it in the circular buffer)
ps Sequence number of the next data message to be sent

Therefore, bet(pr, ps, pt) always holds.

Array count is used in counting, for each sequence number k, the number of state messages that have been received by process p after it has sent the last data(k) message and before this last data(k) is acknowledged. Whenever count[k] reaches a specified value m, process p recognizes that the last sent data(k) message is lost and resends it.

Process p has three actions. In the first action, p receives one state message. If the message sequence number is at most pk, then the message is recognized as an old message and discarded. Otherwise, the message contents are used to update the variables ackd, pr, pt, and pk. Then, p updates array count and resends every data(i) message where bet(pr, i, ps) and count[i] = 0 and ~ackd[i]. (Recall that the value of

count[i] ranges from 0 to m − 1; thus count[i] reaching the value m can be detected
when count[i] = 0.)

```
rcv st(b, r, t, k) from q        ->
    if k > pk ->
            ackd, pr, pt, pk := b, r, t, k ;
            i := pr ;
            do i ≠ ps -_n 1 ->
                    count[i] := count[i] +_m 1;
                    if count[i] = 0 ∧ ~ackd[i] ->
                                        send data(i) to q
                    ⫿ count[i] ≠ 0 ∨ ackd[i] -> skip
                    fi; i := i +_n 1
            od
    ⫿ k ≤ pk -> skip
    fi
```

In the second action, process p recognizes that the sequence number ps can be
used to send the next data message, and so it attaches ps to a new data message and
sends the message to process q, and then resets count[ps] to 0 and increments ps.

```
ps +_n 1 ≠ pt              ->      send data(ps) to q;
                                   count[ps], ps := 0, ps +_n 1
```

In the third and last action, process p receives a corrupted error message from q
and discards it:

```
rcv error from q   ->      skip
```

Process p in the circular buffer protocol can be defined as follows:

```
process p

const m, n                          { m ≥ 2 and n ≥ 3 }

var     ackd                :       array [0..n-1] of boolean,
        pr, pt, ps, i :             0..n-1,
        pk                  :       integer,
        count               :       array [0..n-1] of 0..m-1,
        b                   :       array [0..n-1] of boolean,
        r, t                :       0..n-1,
        k                   :       integer

begin
        rcv st(b, r, t, k) from q        ->
                if k > pk ->
```

```
                    ackd, pr, pt, pk := b, r, t, k ;
                    i := pr ;
                    do i ≠ ps ·n 1 ->
                            count[i] := count[i] +ₘ 1;
                            if count[i] = 0 ∧ ~ackd[i] ->
                                            send data(i) to q
                            ▯ count[i] ≠ 0 ∨ ackd[i] ->
                                            skip
                            fi; i := i +ₙ 1
                    od
             ▯ k ≤ pk -> skip
             fi

▯      ps +ₙ 1 ≠pt                           ->
             send data(ps) to q;
             count[ps], ps := 0, ps +ₙ 1
▯      rcv error from q              ->        skip
end
```

We are now ready to define the t-guard predicate of the timeout action in process q. Each execution of the timeout action causes one state message to be sent from q to p. The time period between two successive executions of the timeout action should be large enough such that the following two conditions hold:

   i. The number of state messages in the channel from q to p never exceeds m − 1.

  ii. If process q sends a state message that when received by p causes a data(k) message to be resent by p, then the last data(k) message that p has sent is no longer in the channel from p to q (i.e., it has been lost) when the state message is sent.

To guarantee condition i, the timeout action should have the following guard (#ch.q.p < m−1). Because the timeout action sends one state message from q to p, this guard ensures that sending this message does not make the number of state messages in the channel from q to p exceed m − 1 (as required by condition i).

To guarantee condition ii, the timeout action should have the following guard:

```
(For every k in the range 0..n-1 :
        rcvd[k] ∨ count[k] + #ch.q.p < m-1 ∨
        data(k)#ch.p.q = 0
)
```

It follows that the guard of the timeout action is the conjunction of the above two guards. Thus, the timeout action can be written as follows:

```
timeout
    (#ch.q.p < m-1) /\
    (For every k in the range 0..n-1 :
        rcvd[k] \/ count[k] + #ch.q.p < m-1 \/
        data(k)#ch.p.q = 0
    )
                    ->      qk := qk+1;
                            send st(rcvd, qr, qt, qk) to p
```

10.4 FLOW CONTROL IN THE INTERNET

The protocol that performs flow control in the Internet is the transmission control protocol, or TCP. Recall that in Section 6.4, we presented an overview of TCP and discussed how TCP connections are established and removed and how data messages are sent over established connections. In Section 8.4, we discussed how TCP detects message corruption and discards corrupted messages. Then in Section 9.4, we discussed how TCP detects and recovers from message loss and reorder. In this section, we discuss the flow control features of TCP.

As discussed in Section 9.4, data messages are sent in TCP based on a sliding-window mechanism. The flow of data messages from one TCP process to another is controlled by periodically adjusting the window size in the sender. Consider two TCP processes tp and tq, and assume that process tp sends a stream of data messages to process tq. Let w denote the window size that process tp uses in sending its data messages to process tq. Periodically, process tp adjusts w to satisfy the following relation:

$$w := min(wrcv, wcong)$$

where wrcv is called the receiving window in process tq and wcong is called the congestion window between tp and tq. Next, we discuss how process tp periodically computes the two values wrcv and wcong.

From Section 6.4, each TCP message has a field, field 8, that indicates the available buffer (in bytes) for storing received data bytes in the TCP process that sent the message. Thus, field 8 in each (data or acknowledgment) message from process tq to process tp defines the available buffer in process tq for storing future received messages from tp. Therefore, wrcv is the value of field 8 in the latest message that process tp has received from tq.

When the TCP process tp times out to resend a data message, it recognizes that the earlier message has been lost during transmission (mostly due to congestion). So, process tp decreases the value of wcong to its smallest possible value wmin, which is the number of data bytes in one TCP message. From this point on, if tp sends a data message and receives its acknowledgment back without retransmission, tp increases the value of wcong by wmin. This continues until wcong becomes equal to half its value before it was decreased to wmin. From this point on, if tp sends wcong successive data messages and receives back their acknowledgments without retransmitting any of them, it increments wcong by wmin. This continues until wcong becomes equal a predefined maximum value.

In summary, a message loss causes wcong to be reduced to wmin. Then, wcong is incremented exponentially by doubling its value every time acknowledgments are received for wcong successive messages without retransmitting any of them. This continues until wcong reaches half of its value before the reduction. Then, wcong is incremented linearly by incrementing its value by wmin every time acknowledgments are received for wcong successive messages without retransmitting any of them. This continues until wcong reaches a predefined maximum value.

10.5 BIBLIOGRAPHICAL NOTES

Techniques for adjusting the window size in sliding window protocols are discussed in Bux and Grillo [1985], Jacobson [1988], Jain [1990], Hahne et al. [1991], and Kung and Chapman [1993]. Rate control is discussed in Clark et al. [1988]. Circular buffer control is discussed in Netravali et al. [1990], and Gouda et al. [1995]. Surveys on flow control are given in Khan and Growther [1972], Gerla and Kleinrock [1980], and Maxemchuck and El-Zarki [1990].

Adjusting the window size in the TCP is discussed in Jacobson [1988].

EXERCISES

1   (Window Size Control). Modify the individual acknowledgment protocol in Section 9.4 in the same way that the cumulative acknowledgment protocol is modified in Section 10.1, so that the size of its window can be changed over time.

2   (Window Size Control). Modify the block acknowledgment protocol in Section 9.5 in the same way that the cumulative acknowledgment protocol is modified in Section 10.1, so that the size of its window can be changed over time.

3   (Rate Control with Cumulative Acknowledgment). Modify the cumulative acknowledgment protocol in Section 9.3 in the same way that the individual acknowledgment protocol is modified in Section 10.2, so that there is a maximum rate, independent of the window size, at which data messages can be sent by process p.

4   (Rate Control with Block Acknowledgment). Modify the block acknowledgment protocol in Section 9.5 in the same way that the individual acknowledgment protocol is modified in Section 10.2, so that there is a maximum rate, independent of the window size, at which data messages can be sent by process p.

5   (Rate Control with Forward Recovery from Message Corruption). Modify the
protocol in exercise 1 of Chapter 9 such that the number of messages in the
channel from the sender process p to the receiver process q is never more than
an input integer cap.

6   (Rate Control with Forward Recovery from Message Loss). Modify the protocol in exercise 2 of Chapter 9 such that the number of messages in the channel
from the sender process p to the receiver process q is never more than an input
integer cap.

7   (Rate Control with Forward Recovery from Message Reorder). Modify the
protocol in exercise 3 of Chapter 9 such that the number of messages in the
channel from the sender process p to the receiver process q is never more than
an input integer cap.

8   (Variable Rate). Modify the rate control protocol in Section 10.2 to allow
process p to change the value of cap as follows. When process p detects that a
message was lost, p decreases the value of cap by a factor of 2. When process p
detects that cmax consecutive data messages have reached process q without
retransmission, p increases the value of cap by 1.

9   (Variable Rate). Modify the cumulative acknowledgment protocol with rate
control in exercise 3 such that the value of cap can be changed, during the protocol execution, as discussed in exercise 5.

10 (Receiver-Controlled Window). Modify the cumulative acknowledgment protocol in Section 9.3 as follows. Before the receiver process q sends an ack message to the sender process p, q chooses a value w from the range 0 . . wmax
and then includes it in the ack message to be sent. When process p receives an
ack message, it makes w in the received message its current window size.

11 (Receiver-Controlled Window). Modify the individual acknowledgment protocol in Section 9.4 as follows. Before the receiver process q sends an ack message to the sender process p, q chooses a value w from the range 0 . . wmax
and then includes it in the ack message to be sent. When process p receives an
ack message, it makes w in the received message its current window size.

12 (Receiver-Controlled Window). Modify the block acknowledgment protocol in
Section 9.5 as follows. Before the receiver process q sends an ack message to
the sender process p, q chooses a value w from the range 0 . . wmax and then
includes it in the ack message to be sent. When process p receives an ack message, it makes w in the received message its current window size.

13 (Receiver-Controlled Rate). Modify the cumulative acknowledgment protocol
in Section 9.3 as follows. Before the receiver process q sends an ack message
to the sender process p, q chooses a value cap from the range 0 . . cmax and
then includes it in the ack message to be sent. When process p receives an ack
message, it makes cap in the received message its current bound on the number
of data messages that can exist simultaneously in the channel from p to q.

14 (Receiver-Controlled Rate). Modify the individual acknowledgment protocol in Section 9.4 as follows. Before the receiver process q sends an ack message to the sender process p, q chooses a value cap from the range 0 . . cmax and then includes it in the ack message to be sent. When process p receives an ack message, it makes cap in the received message its current bound on the number of data messages that can exist simultaneously in the channel from p to q.

15 (Receiver-Controlled Rate). Modify the block acknowledgment protocol in Section 9.5 as follows. Before the receiver process q sends an ack message to the sender process p, q chooses a value cap from the range 0 . . cmax and then includes it in the ack message to be sent. When process p receives an ack message, it makes cap in the received message its current bound on the number of data messages that can exist simultaneously in the channel from p to q.

16 (Network-Controlled Window or Congestion Bit Protocol). Modify the individual acknowledgment protocol in Section 9.4 as follows:

a Add one process called net between the sender process p and the receiver process q. Process p sends all data messages to net, which forwards them to q, and process q sends all ack messages to net, which forwards them to p.

b Add a new boolean field c to each data and ack message. Field c is called the congestion bit.

c When p sends a data message to process net, field c in the message is false. When net receives the data message, it may assign field c the value true (indicating some congestion) before forwarding the data message to q.

d When q receives the data message and sends an ack message to process net, the c field in the ack message has the same value as the c field in the data message. When net receives the ack message, it may assign field c the value true (indicating congestion) before forwarding the ack message to p.

e If p receives an ack message with a true c field, and if p has not reduced the window size after receiving any of the last kmax acknowledgments, then p reduces the current window size by a factor of 2. On the other hand, if p receives cmax successive ack messages with false c fields and without timing out in the meantime to resend a data message, p increases the current window size by 1.

Design processes p, q, and net in this protocol protocol.

17 (Network-Controlled Window or Congestion Bit Protocol). Modify the cumulative acknowledgment protocol in Section 9.3 to include a congestion bit in each data and each ack message, as discussed in exercise 16.

18 (Network-Controlled Rate or Congestion Bit Protocol). Modify the rate control protocol in Section 10.2 to include a congestion bit in each data and each ack message as discussed in exercise 16 with one exception. If p receives an ack

message with a true c field, p reduces the current value of cap by a factor of 2. On the other hand, if p receives k successive ack messages with false c fields and without timing out in the meantime to resend a data message, p increases the current value of cap by 1.

19 (Reciever-Controlled Window). Consider the following protocol for controlling the flow between processes p and q under the assumption that the communication is error free:

```
process p
const    wmax
var  w   :        0..wmax    {initially, w = wmax}
begin
   w > 0                     -> send data to q; w := w-1
 ▯ rcv ack from q            ->  w := w+1
end


process q
begin
   rcv data from p   -> send ack to p
end
```

Modify this protocol such that process q can eventually dictate an upper bound wb on the value of w, where 1 ≤ wb ≤ wmax.

20 (Rate Control). Consider the following rate control protocol:

```
process p
const    n
inp      w    :        array [0..n-1] of integer
                               {for each i, w[i] > 0}
var      sent :        array [0..n-1] of integer
                               {initially 0}
par      i    :        0..n-1
begin
   timeout data(i)#ch.p.q < w[i] ->
                               send data(i) to q;
                               sent[i] := sent[i] + 1
end


process q
const    n
var      rcvd :        array [0..n-1] of integer,
                               {Initially 0}
         j    :        0..n-1
```

```
begin
   rcv data(j) from p  ->
                              rcvd[j] := rcvd[j] + 1
end
```

Assume that all message transmissions are error free and that the protocol starts at a state where the channel from p to q is empty. What is the relation between the values in array sent and those in array rcvd at each reachable state of the protocol? What is the maximum number of messages that can be in the channel from p to q at each reachable state of the protocol?

CHAPTER 11

MAINTAINING TOPOLOGY INFORMATION

So far, we have discussed protocols for reliably exchanging messages in binary networks, that is, in networks that consist of two processes and two opposite-direction channels between them. Starting from this chapter, we discuss protocols for exchanging messages in general networks. A general network is a network that consists of any number of processes and any number of channels such that the following restrictiaon is satisfied. For any two processes in the network, either there are no channels between the processes or there are exactly two opposite-direction channels between the processes. The reason for this restriction is that two opposite-direction channels are needed between any two processes so that the processes can reliably exchange data messages. For example, when one channel is used for sending data messages, the other channel is used for sending the corresponding acknowledgments, as discussed in Chapters 9 and 10.

Henceforth, we use the terms "network" and "general network" interchangeably, unless otherwise specified.

In this chapter, we define the concept of a network topology and discuss the local, global, and hierarchical topology information that can be maintained in each process in a network. We also discuss protocols for the network processes to keep their local, global, and hierarchical topology information current.

11.1 LOCAL AND GLOBAL TOPOLOGY INFORMATION

At each instant, each channel in a (general) network is either up or down. When a channel is up, then, as discussed in Chapter 5, any message sent via the channel is stored in the channel until the message is corrupted, lost, reordered with other messages in the channel, or received and removed from the channel. When a channel is down, the sequence of messages in the channel is always empty and any message sent via the channel is lost right away.

Two processes in a network are called neighbors iff there are two opposite-direction channels between them in the network.

When at least one of the channels between two neighboring processes is down for some time period, then neither process can reliably send messages to the other process during that period. Only when both channels between the two processes are up can the processes reliably exchange messages over the channels.

Two comments concerning channels being up or down are in order. First, an up channel becomes down for many reasons. For instance, a channel may become down as a result of some physical failure in the channel or in the process that receives from the channel. Also, a channel may become in effect down because the process that receives from that channel may decide that it is busy and start to discard every message it receives from the channel. Second, we assumed in our presentation that channels can become up or down but processes are always up. The reason for this assumption is economy of thought. A down process can still be included in our presentation by making all incoming and all outgoing channels of that process down. We are now ready to define the concept of a network topology.

The topology of a network at an instant t is a labeled undirected graph such that the following three conditions are satisfied:

i. There is one-to-one correspondence between the nodes in the graph and the processes in the network.

ii. There is an edge between two nodes in the graph iff the two corresponding processes are neighbors, that is, there are two opposite-direction channels between them in the network.

iii. Each edge in the graph is labeled either "up" or "down." An edge is labeled up iff the corresponding two opposite-direction channels are both up at t.

An example of a network topology at instant t_1 is shown in Figure 11.1. The net-

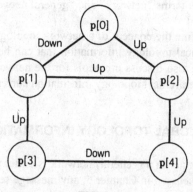

FIG. 11.1

work has five processes p[0 . . 4]. Process p[0] has two neighboring processes p[1] and p[2]. At instant t_1, at least one of the channels between p[0] and p[1] is down, while both channels between p[0] and p[2] are up. Thus at this instant, process p[0] cannot reliably exchange messages with its neighbor p[1], but it can reliably exchange messages with its neighbor p[2]. Assume that this network topology remains fixed for some time period after t_1, then it changes at instant t_2 to become as shown in Figure 11.2. In the new topology, the two channels between p[0] and p[1] are both up and at least one of the two channels between p[1] and p[3] is down. All other channels remain as they were during the time period from t_1 to t_2.

We adopt the following two assumptions concerning the change of topology of a network:

i. Topology Change Atomicity: The topology of a network remains fixed during any execution of any protocol action or error action in the network.

ii. Rare Occurrence of Topology Change: The topology of a network is changed a finite number of times along any, possibly infinite, execution of the network.

During any network execution, each process in the network can maintain some information concerning the current topology of the network. The maintained information is local or global. The local information maintained in process p[i] at any instant is the set containing each neighboring process p[g] such that the two channels between p[i] and p[g] are both up at that instant. The global information maintained in process p[i] at any instant is the topology of the network at that instant.

Because the topology of a network may change, the network processes need to exchange messages in order to detect any changes in the topology, when they occur, and reflect these changes in the information they maintain. These messages are exchanged according to some protocols for maintaining topology information. In Section 11.2, we present a protocol for maintaining local topology information. Then in Section 11.3, we present a protocol for maintaining global topology information.

Note that the local topology information maintained in each process is a part of

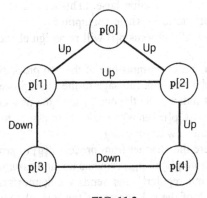

FIG. 11.2

the global topology information maintained in that process. Therefore, the protocol for maintaining global topology information in Section 11.3 is designed on the top of the protocol for maintaining local topology information in Section 11.2.

In Section 11.4, we introduce the concept of hierarchical topology information. Then in Section 11.5, we discuss protocols for maintaining this hierarchical information. These protocols consist of two parts: a protocol for maintaining local hierarchical information and a protocol for maintaining global hierarchical information.

11. 2 MAINTAINING LOCAL TOPOLOGY INFORMATION

Consider a network of n processes p[0 .. n − 1]. Each process p[i] has an input set N that contains the indices of all neighbors of p[i] in the network. Each p[i] also has an array "up" declared as follows:

```
var   up   :      array [N] of boolean
```

Process p[i] updates array up according to the following two rules. When p[i] detects that both channels between itself and one of its neighbors p[g] are up, process p[i] assigns the value true to element up[g]. When p[i] detects that at least one of the two channels between itself and one neighbor p[g] is down, process p[i] assigns the value false to the corresponding element up[g].

The protocol for p[i] to update element up[g] is straightforward. Both p[i] and p[g] circulate a chk message between them. When p[i] receives the chk message back from p[g], p[i] recognizes that the chk message has made a complete cycle from p[i] to p[g] and back to p[i]. This indicates that the two channels between p[i] and p[g] are up. In this case, p[i] assigns up[g] the value true and sends the chk message back to p[g].

On the other hand, p[i] may wait for a long time after it has sent the chk message to p[g] without receiving the chk message back. In this case, p[i] concludes that the chk message was lost due to at least one of the two channels between p[i] and p[g] being down and assigns up[g] the value false. (This conclusion may be incorrect: The message may be lost due to message corruption or loss in an up channel. If this is the case, then eventually process p[i] will re-assign element up[g] the value true.)

Loss of the chk message also prompts one of the two processes p[i] or p[g], but not both of them, to send a new chk message to the other process. We choose the process with the smallest index to be the one to send the new chk message. Thus, when the chk message is lost, p[i] sends the new chk message to p[g], provided i < g. Otherwise, p[g] sends the new chk message.

Consider the case where the channel from process p[g] to process p[i] becomes down while the channel from p[i] to p[g] remains up, and assume that i < g. In this case, process p[i] times out regularly and sends a chk message to process p[g]. Process p[g] receives each of the chk messages (because the channel from p[i] to p[g] is up) and returns it to process p[i], but the returned messages never reach p[i] (because the channel from p[g] to p[i] is down). Therefore, process p[i] correctly assigns its up[g] the value false, and process p[g] may wrongly assign its up[i] the value true.

This scenario is prevented by adding a bit to each chk message. The value of this bit is determined according to the following two rules. First, when a process times out and sends a chk message, the sent message is chk(0). Second, when a process receives a chk message and returns it, the returned message is chk(1). Therefore, when a process p[i] receives a chk(0) message from a neighbor p[g] it recognizes that this message was sent in a timeout action. In this case, p[i] assigns its up[g] the value false. On the other hand, when p[i] receives a chk(1) message from p[g], it recognizes that this message has made a complete cycle from p[i] to p[g] then to p[i]. In this case, p[i] assigns its up[g] the value true.

Process p[i] in the protocol for maintaining local topology information can be defined as follows:

```
process p[i : 0..n-1]

inp   N    :      set {g|p[g] is a neighbor of p[i]}

var   up   :      array [N] of boolean,
      b    :      0..1

par   g    :      N

begin
      rcv chk(b) from p[g]    —>
              send chk(1) to p[g];
              if b = 0    —>      up[g] := false
              []b = 1     —>      up[g] := true
              fi

[]    rcv error from p[g]         —>       skip

[]    timeout (#ch.p[i].p[g] + #ch.p[g].p[i] = 0) —>
              if i < g    —>      send chk(0) to p[g]
              [] i ≥ g    —>      skip
              fi; up[g] := false
end
```

Process p[i] has three actions. In the first action, p[i] receives a chk(b) message from a neighbor p[g] and then sends a chk(1) message to p[g]. Process p[i] then assigns a new value to its element up[g]. In particular, up[g] is assigned false if bit b in the received chk(b) message is 0, and it is assigned true otherwise

In the second action, process p[i] receives a corrupted message from a neighbor p[g] and discards it.

In the third action, p[i] detects that the two channels between p[i] and a neighbor p[g] are empty. In this case, p[i] sends a chk(0) message to p[g], provided that i < g, and assigns its element up[g] the value false.

11.3 MAINTAINING GLOBAL TOPOLOGY INFORMATION

As in the previous section, we consider a network of n processes p[0 .. n − 1]. Each process p[i] has an input set N that contains the indices of all neighbors of p[i]. Each p[i] also has an input array up declared as follows.

```
inp    up    :    array [N] of boolean
```

An element up[g] has the value true iff the two channels between process p[i] and its neighbor p[g] are both up.

The up arrays are declared as inputs in this network because the network processes do not update the values of these arrays. Rather, these arrays are kept current using a protocol for maintaining local topology information similar to the one discussed in the last section. This protocol, however, is outside the network discussed in this section.

Each process p[i] has a variable net declared as follows.

```
var    net    :    array [0..n-1,0..n-1] of boolean
```

Process p[i] updates array net according to the following two rules. When p[i] detects that any two processes p[j] and p[m] are neighbors and the two channels between them are up, p[i] assigns the value true to the two elements net[j, m] and net[m, j]. When p[i] detects that any two processes p[j] and p[m] are not neighbors or that they are neighbors but the two channels between them are not both up, p[i] assigns the value false to both net[j, m] and net[m, j].

To apply these two rules, each process p[i] periodically uses its up array to update the elements net[i, m] and net[m, i], for every m = 0, . . . , n − 1 in its net array. Also periodically, p[i] broadcasts the value of its up array to every other process in the network.

When p[i] receives the value of array up of a process p[j], p[i] uses the received value to update elements net[j, m] and net[m, j], for every m = 0, . . . , n − 1, in its net array. The periodic broadcast of the up arrays and the corresponding updating of the net arrays keep the net arrays current in all the processes.

Each process p[i] sends the value of its up array in a message of the form st(i, vp, t), where st is the message name, i is the index of process p[i], vp is an array of n boolean values representing array up in process p[i], and t is an integer called the time stamp of the message. Process p[i] sends a copy of the st(i, up, t) message to each of its neighbors. Later, when p[i] sends a copy of the next message to each of its neighbors, the time stamp of that next message is t + 1.

Each process p[i] has two variable arrays vp and ts, declared as follows:

```
var    vp    :    array [0..n-1] of boolean,
       ts    :    array [0..n-1] of integer
```

The value of element vp[j] is true iff p[j] is a neighbor of p[i] and the value of up[j] in process p[i] is true. The value of element ts[i] is the largest time stamp in a st message sent by p[i]. The value of element ts[j], where j is different from i, is the largest time stamp in a st(j, vp, t) message received by p[i]. When p[i] receives a st(j, vp, t) message from one of its neighbors p[g], process p[i] compares t with ts[j]. If t is less than or equal to ts[j], indicating that the message is old and may have been received earlier by p[i], then p[i] discards the message. If t is greater than ts[j] indicating that the message is new, then p[i] uses the received vp to update its net array, assigns ts[j] the value t, and forwards a copy of the message to every neighboring process other than p[g], where p[g] is the process from which p[i] received the message.

Each process p[i] uses a function NEXT that takes the set N of neighbors of p[i] and a neighbor g of p[i] and returns the next neighbor in set N after g. If g happens to be the last neighbor in set N, then NEXT returns the first neighbor in N.

Process p[i] in the protocol for maintaining global topology information can be defined as follows:

```
process p[i : 0..n-1]

inp    N     :    set { j|p[j] is a neighbor of p[i] },
       up    :    array [N] of boolean

var    net   :    array [0..n-1, 0..n-1] of boolean,
       vp    :    array [0..n-1] of boolean,
       ts    :    array [0..n-1] of integer,
       f, h  :    N,
       m     :    0..n,
       k     :    0..n-1,
       t     :    integer

par    g     :    N

begin
       true  ->
              ts[i], m := ts[i]+1, 0;
              do m<n ->
                     if (m in N ∧ up[m]) ->
                            net[m,i], net[i, m], vp[m]  :=
```

```
                         true, true, true
                  [] ~(m in N ∧ up[m]) ->
                         net[m,i], net[i, m], vp[m] :=
                         false, false, false
                  if; m := m +1
            od;
            h := NEXT(N,f);
            do h ≠ f ->
                  if up[h] ->
                         send st(i, vp, ts[i]) to p[h]
                  [] ~up[h] -> skip
                  fi; h := NEXT(N,h)
            od;
            if up[f] -> send st(i, vp, ts[i]) to p[f]
            [] ~up[f] -> skip
            fi

[]     rcv st(k, vp, t) from p[g]->
            if ts[k] ≥ t -> skip
            [] ts[k] < t ->
                  ts[k], m := t, 0;
                  do m<n ->
                         net[m,k], net[k,m], m :=
                         vp[m], vp[m], m+1
                  od;
                  h := NEXT(N, g);
                  do h ≠ g ->
                         if up[h] ->
                               send st(k, vp, t) to p[h]
                         [] ~up[h] -> skip
                         fi; h := NEXT(N,h)
                  od
            fi

[]     rcv error from p[g]        -> skip
end
```

Process p[i] has three actions. In the first action, process p[i] increments its time stamp ts[i] by 1, and uses its array up to update the elements net[m, i] and net[i, m], for every m in the range $0 .. n - 1$, and to compute array vp. Then, p[i] sends a st(i, vp, ts[i]) message to everyone of its up neighbors.

In the second action, p[i] receives a st(k, vp, t)message from a neighbor p[g] and uses the field t to check whether the received message is old. If the message is old, p[i] discards the message. If the message is new, p[i] uses the received array vp to update the elements net[m, k] and net[k, m], for every m in the range $0 .. n - 1$.

Then, p[i] forwards a copy of the message to every up neighbor of p[i], other than p[g].

In the third action, p[i] receives an error message from a neighbor p[g] and discards the message.

11.4   HIERARCHICAL TOPOLOGY INFORMATION

There are problems associated with maintaining local and global topology information in a network. On the one hand, with local topology information, each process in the network ends up knowing only the states of its immediate neighbors. This information can be inadequate for many applications. On the other hand, maintaining global topology information requires each process in the network to periodically broadcast its state messages to every other process in the network at a high cost.

This situation can be resolved by developing new types of topology information that are more informative than local topology information yet less expensive to maintain than global topology information. One such type of topology information is called hierarchical topology information.

To allow hierarchical topology information in a network, the processes in the network are partitioned into regions. Thus, each process in the network is identified with a pair (i, j),where i is the region to which the process belongs and j is the process identifier in region i. Without loss of generality, we assume that the network has r regions and each region has at most s processes. Thus, the network can be declared as a process array p[i: 0 .. r − 1, j: 0 .. s − 1].

Each region i in this network is connected in the following sense. For each two processes p and q in region i, there is a sequence of processes p.0, . . . , p.u in region i such that p is p.0, q is p.u, and for every k, $0 \le k < u$, p.k and p.(k +1) are neighbors.

The hierarchical topology information to be stored in every process in a region i is an undirected graph that has r + s nodes as follows.

  i. The nodes in the graph are labeled 0, 1, . . . , r + s − 1.
 ii. Each of the nodes 0, . . . , r − 1 represents a distinct region in the network.
iii. Each of the nodes r,. . . , r+ s − 1 represents a distinct process in region i.
 iv. There is an edge between two nodes y and z, where $0 \le y < r$ and $r \le z < r + s$, iff there are two up channels between a process in region y and the process represented by node z.
  v. There is an edge between distinct nodes y and z, where $r \le y < r + s$ and $r \le z < r + s$, iff there are two up channels between the two processes represented by nodes y and z.

As an example, Figure 11.3a shows the global topology of a network at time t.

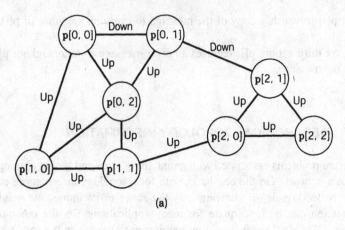

(a)

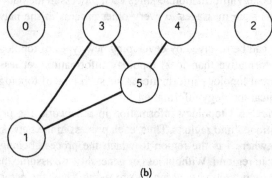

(b)

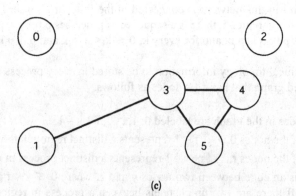

(c)

FIG. 11.3

The network has eight processes partitioned into three regions, and each region has at most three processes. Thus, r = 3 and s = 3 for this network.

In this network, the hierarchical topology information to be stored in every process in region 0 at time t is shown in Figure 11.3b. This graph has six nodes labeled 0 through 5. Nodes 0, 1, and 2 represent regions 0, 1, and 2, respectively.

Nodes 3, 4, and 5 represent the three processes p[0, 0], p[0, 1], and p[0, 2], respectively, in region 0. There is an edge between the node representing region 1 and the node representing process p[0, 0] because there are two up channels between some process in region 1 and process p[0, 0]. There is no edge between the node representing region 2 and any of the nodes representing processes p[0, 0], p[0, 1], and p[0, 2] because there are no up channels between any process in region 2 and any process in region 0.

The hierarchical topology information to be stored in every process in region 2 at time t is shown in Figure 11.3c, where nodes 3, 4, and 5 represent the three processes p[2, 0], p[2, 1], and p[2, 2], respectively. Note that the hierarchical topology information stored in every process in region 0 is different from the hierarchical topology information stored in every process in region 2.

11.5 MAINTAINING HIERARCHICAL TOPOLOGY INFORMATION

In order that the processes in a network $p[i : 0 .. r - 1, j: 0 .. s - 1]$ maintain hierarchical topology information, each process p[i, j] uses two protocols: a protocol for maintaining local topology information and a protocol for maintaining global topology information in region i. The use of these two protocols by process p[i, j] is discussed next.

First, each process p[i, j] uses a protocol for maintaining local topology information, similar to the one discussed in Section 11.2, to keep track of its up neighbors in the network. In particular, each process p[i, j] uses its input up array to maintain a variable array vp declared as follows:

var   vp   :   **array** [0..r+s-1] **of boolean**

The values in array vp are as follows:

For every y, $0 \leq y < r$,

vp[y] = true   iff   there are two up channels between process p[i, j] and
                          some process in region y.

For every z, $r \leq z < r + s$,

vp[z] = true   iff   there are two up channels between process p[i, j] and
                          process p[i, z − r].

Second, each process p[i, j] uses a protocol for maintaining global topology information, similar to the one discussed in Section 11.3, to broadcast its vp array to every other process in the same region i. Each process p[i, j] uses the received vp arrays from all processes in region i to update a variable array net whose value is the hierarchical topology information in process p[i, j].

Array net in process p[i, j] is declared as follows.

var   net   :   **array** [0..r+s-1, 0..r+s-1] **of boolean**

The values in this array are as follows:

For every y and z, where $0 \leq y < r$ and $r \leq z < r + s$,

net[y, z] = true   iff   there are two up channels between a process in re-
                              gion y and process p[i, z − r]

For every y and z, where $r \leq y < r + s$ and $0 \leq z < r$,

net[y, z] = true   iff   there are two up channels between process
                              p[i, y − r] and a process in region z.

For every y and z, where $r \leq y < r + s$ and $r \leq z \leq r + s$,

net[y, z] = true   iff   there are two up channels between the two
                              processes p[i, y − r] and p[i, z − r].

Process p[i, j] uses a function RGN that can be applied to the identifier ⟨i′, j′⟩ of
any process in the network to return the region i′ of that process.

Process p[i, j] in the protocol for maintaining hierarchical topology information
can be defined as follows. (Note that this p[i, j] is similar, with some modifications,
to p[i] in Section 11.3.)

```
process p[i : 0..r-1, j : 0..s-1]

inp   N    :   set { (i', j')|p[i', j'] is a
                   neighbor of p[i, j]},
      up   :   array [N] of boolean

var   net  :   array [0..r+s-1, 0..r+s-1] of boolean,
      vp   :   array [0..r+s-1] of boolean,
      ts   :   array [0..s-1] of integer,
      f, h :   N,
      m    :   0..r+s,
      k    :   0..s-1,
      t    :   integer

par   g    :   N

begin
      true  ->
            ts[j], m := ts[j]+1, 0;
            do m<r ->
```

```
            if (some f in N: RGN(f) = m ∧ up[f])
            --> net[m,j+r], net[j+r,m], vp[m] :=
               true, true, true
            ☐ ~(some f in N: RGN(f) = m ∧ up[f])
            --> net[m,j+r], net[j+r,m], vp[m] :=
               false, false, false
            if; m := m +1
        od; {m = r}
        do m<r+s -->
            if ( (i, m-r) in N ∧ up[i, m-r] ) -->
               net[m,j+r], net[j+r,m], vp[m] :=
               true, true, true
            ☐ ~( (i, m-r) in N ∧ up[i, m-r] ) -->
               net[m,j+r], net[j+r,m], vp[m] :=
               false, false, false
            if; m := m +1
        od;
        h := NEXT(N,f);
        do h ≠ f -->
            if (RGN(h) = i ∧ up[h]) -->
                   send st(i, vp, ts[i]) to p[h]
            ☐ ~(RGN(h) = i ∧ up[h]) --> skip
            fi; h := NEXT(N,h)
        od;
        if (RGN(f) = i ∧ up[f]) -->
                   send st(i, vp, ts[i]) to p[f]
        ☐ ~(RGN(f) = i ∧ up[f]) --> skip
        fi

☐    rcv st(k, vp,t) from p[g] -->
        if ts[k] ≥ t --> skip
        ☐ ts[k] < t -->
            ts[k], m := t, 0;
            do m<r+s -->
            net[m,k+r], net[k+r,m], m :=
            vp[m], vp[m], m+1
            od;
            h := NEXT(N,g);
            do h ≠ g -->
               if (RGN(h) = i ∧ up[h]) -->
                      send st(k, vp,t) to p[h]
               ☐ ~(RGN(h) = i ∧ up[h]) --> skip
               fi; h := NEXT(N,h)
            od
        fi
```

```
[]      rcv error from p[g]       -> skip
end
```

Process p[i, j] has three actions. In the first action, process p[i, j] increments its time stamp ts[j] by 1 and uses its array up to update the elements net[m, j + r] and net[j + r, m], for every m in the range $0 .. r + s - 1$ and to compute array vp. Then, p[i, j] sends a st(j, vp, ts[j]) message to everyone of its up neighbors in region i. Note that the first action has two if–fi statements. The first if–fi statement has a predicate (**some** f **in** N: RGN(f) = m $\land$ up[f]). The value of this predicate is true iff p[i, j] has a neighbor p[i′, j′], where i′ = m and the value of up[i′, j′] in process p[i, j] is true. The second if–fi statement has a predicate ((i, m − r) **in** N $\land$ up[i, m − r]). The value of this predicate is true iff p[i, j] has a neighbor p[i′, j′], where i′ = i, j′ = m − r, and the value of up[i′, j′] in process p[i, j] is true.

In the second action, p[i, j] receives a st(k, vp, t)message from a neighbor p[g] and uses the field t to check whether the received message is old. If the message is old, p[i, j] discards the message. If the message is new, p[i, j] uses the received array vp to update the elements net[m, k + r] and net[k + r, m], for every m in the range $0 .. r + s - 1$. Then, p[i] forwards a copy of the message to every up neighbor of p[i, j] in region i, other than p[g].

In the third action, p[i, j] receives an error message from a neighbor p[g] and discards the message.

This protocol is incomplete because the elements net[0 .. r − 1, 0 .. r − 1] in every process in the network are not updated to reflect changes in the network topology. To complete this protocol, one process in each region is selected as the "center" for that region. The center p[i, j] of a region i maintains a variable array gvp, declared as follows:

```
var    gvp   :    array [0..r-1] of boolean,
```

The value of gvp[m], $0 \le m < r$, in the center p[i, j] of region i is true iff there are two neighboring processes one in region i and the other in region m and the two channels between these neighbors are both up. Periodically, the center p[i, j] of region i uses its array net to update array gvp and broadcasts a copy of this array in a gst(i, gvp, t) message to every process in the network, where t is the time stamp of the message.

To keep track of the time stamps in the gst messages, each process p[i, j] in the network has an array gts, declared as follows:

```
var    gts   :    array [0..r-1] of integer
```

The value of element gts[k], where k is different from i, is the largest time stamp in a gst(k , gvp, t) message received by process p[i, j]. The value of element gts[i depends on whether or not p[i, j] is the center of region i. If p[i, j] is the center of region i, then gts[i] is the largest time stamp in a gst(i, gvp, t) message sent by process p[i, j]. If p[i, j] is not the center of region i, then gts[i] is the largest time stamp in a gst(i, gvp, t) message received by process p[i, j].

When a process p[i, j] receives a gst(k, gvp, t) message from one of its neighbors p[g], process p[i, j] compares t with gts[k]. If t is less than or equal to gts[k], indicating that the message is old and may have been received earlier by p[i, j], then p[i, j] discards the message. If t is greater than gts[k] indicating that the message is new, then p[i, j] uses array gvp in the message to update its net array, assigns gts[k] the value t, and forwards a copy of the message to every up neighbor other than p[g], where p[g].

11.6   MAINTAINING TOPOLOGY INFORMATION IN THE INTERNET

In the Internet, local topology information is maintained as part of address resolution, while hierarchical topology information is maintained as part of routing. In this section, we describe how local topology information is maintained in the Internet as part of address resolution. Then in Section 13.8, we describe how global topology information is maintained in the Internet as part of routing.

There are two protocols that maintain local topology information in the Internet. The first is called the address resolution protocol, or ARP for short, and the second is called the reverse address resolution protocol, or RARP for short. Next, we discuss these two protocols in order.

The function of ARP is to resolve IP addresses into hardware addresses, but first we need to explain why IP addresses need to be resolved into hardware addresses. Recall from Section 3.4 that each computer has at least one IP address that consists of three identifiers (n, s, c) , where n is the unique identifier of the network to which the computer belongs, s is the unique identifier of the subnetwork, in network n, to which the computer is attached, and c is the unique identifier of the computer in subnetwork (n, s).

Consider the case where two computers have the IP addresses (n, s, c) and (n, s, d). Clearly, these two computer are attached to the same subnetwork (n, s). Assume that the IP process in computer (n, s, c) needs to send an IP message mg to the IP process in computer (n, s, d). This can be accomplished by executing the following three steps:

  i.   The IP process in computer (n, s, c) sends the IP message mg to the interface process in computer (n, s, c) .

 ii.   The interface process in computer (n, s, c) sends message mg over subnetwork (n, s) to the interface process in compute r(n, s, d).

iii.   The interface process in computer (n, s, d) forwards the received message mg to the IP process in computer (n, s, d).

The question now is how to implement Step ii. This question has no straightforward answer because the interface process in a computer does not know the IP address of that computer. Rather, it is programmed in hardware to know only the hardware address of its computer. If message mg is sent over subnetwork (n, s) containing the IP address of computer (n, s, d) but not its hardware address, then, the interface process in computer (n, s, d) cannot realize that it should receive this message.

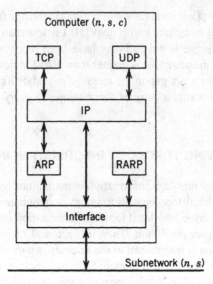

FIG. 11.4

One method to implement step ii is as follows. First the Interface process in computer (n, s, c) sends message mg in a broadcast mode over subnetwork (n, s). Second, the Interface process in every computer attached to subnetwork (n, s), including computer (n, s, d), receives a copy of mg and forwards it to the IP process in its computer. Third, each IP process compares the IP address in message mg with its own IP address and decides whether to keep the message (if the two addresses are equal) or discard it (if the two addresses are different). The problem of this method is its inefficiency: Most computers attached to subnetwork (n, s) have to receive, handle, and check every IP message sent over subnetwork (n, s) only to discover later that they should have ignored the message.

A more efficient method is used in the Internet to implement step ii. This method can be described as follows. Each computer in the Internet has a process called its ARP process, as shown in Figure 11.4. The ARP process in a computer knows both the IP address and the hardware address of its computer. The function of the ARP process in a computer (n, s, c) is to find out the hardware address of any computer (n, s, d) attached to the same subnetwork (n, s) as computer (n, s, c) .

The ARP process in a computer (n, s, c) can find out the hardware address of a computer (n, s, d) as follows:

a. The ARP process in computer (n, s, c) sends a rqst(h, n, s, d) message to the interface process in computer (n, s, c) , where h is the hardware address of computer (n, s, c) .

b. The interface process in computer (n, s, c) transmits the rqst(h, n, s, d) message in a broadcast mode over subnetwork (n, s). The interface process in every computer attached to subnetwork (n, s) receives a copy of the message and forwards it to the ARP process in its computer.

c. When an ARP process receives a rqst(h, n, s, d) message, it compares(n, s, d) with the IP address of its own computer. If they are different, then the ARP process discards the message. If they are equal, then the IP process adds the hardware address h' of its own computer to the message and returns the resulting rply(h, n, s, d, h') message to its interface process.

d. When an Interface process receives a rply(h, n, s, d, h') message from its ARP process, it forwards the message over subnetwork (n, s) to the interface process of computer h which in turn forwards the message to its ARP process.

e. When the ARP process of computer (n, s, c) receives the rply(h, n, s, d, h') message, it recognizes that the hardware address of computer (n, s, d) is h'.

Three comments concerning this procedure are in order. First, if the ARP process in computer (n, s, c) sends a rqst(h, n, s, d) message but does not receive back a rply(h, n, s, d, h') message, it assume that either the rqst message or the rply message is lost during transmission and resends the rqst(h, n, s, d) message. If the ARP process still does not receive back a rply(h, n, s, d, h') message, it concludes that the computer (n, s, d) is down and so it recommends that any IP message that needs to be sent to it should be discarded. This way, ARP also acts as a protocol for maintaining local topology information

Second, the above procedure can be refined by providing each ARP process with a cache. When an ARP process receives a rply(h, n, s, d, h') message, it stores the tuple (n, s, d, h') in its cache. Each stored tuple remains in the cache for a specified time period, then it is considered unreliable and is removed from the cache. Before an ARP process sends a rqst(h, n, s, d) message, it searches its cache for a tuple of the form (n, s, d, h'). If it finds such a tuple, it recognizes that there is no need for sending the rqst message because the ARP process already knows that the hardware address of computer (n, s, d) is h'. On the other hand, if the ARP process does not find such a tuple in its cache, it proceeds to send the rqst(h, n, s, d) message and then wait to receive a rply(h, n, s, d, h') message back.

Third, the above procedure can also be refined by adding the field (n, s, c) to the rqst message to become rqst(n, s, c, h, n, s, d). Recall that the ARP process of every computer attached to subnetwork (n, s) receives a copy of the rqst(n, s, c, h, n, s, d) message. When this happens, every ARP process can store the tuple (n, s, c, h) in its cache.

Now, we turn our attention to RARP. The function of RARP is to resolve hardware addresses into IP addresses. This is the reverse function of ARP (hence the name RARP). When a diskless computer (n, s, c) is turned on, the computer does not know its own IP address, namely (n, s, c) . It merely knows its hardware address h. To find out its IP address, each computer in the Internet has a process called its RARP process, as shown in Figure 11.4. The RARP process in a computer knows only the hardware address of that computer when the computer is first turned on. The function of the RARP process in a computer (n, s, c) is to find out the IP address of its computer given the hardware address h of its computer.

The RARP process in computer h can find out the IP address(n, s, c) of its computer as follows.

i. The RARP process in computer h sends an rrqst(h) message to its interface process, which forwards the message over subnetwork (n, s) in a broadcast mode.

ii. The interface process of each computer attached to subnetwork (n, s) receives a copy of the sent rrqst(h) message and forwards it to the RARP process in its computer. If the computer is not a RARP server, then its RARP process discards the rrqst(h) message. If the computer is a RARP server, then its RARP process has a tuple (h', n, s, d) for each computer h' attached to subnetwork (n, s). In this case, the RARP process sends an rrply(h, n, s, c) message to its Interface process, which forwards it over subnetwork (n, s) to computer h.

iii. When the Interface process of computer h receives an rrply(h, n, s, c) message, it forwards the message to the RARP process in its computer. From the received message, the RARP process concludes that the IP address of its computer is (n, s, c) .

If the RARP process in computer h sends an rrqst(h) message but does not receive back an rrply(h, n, s, c) message, it assumes that either the rrqst message or the rrply message is lost during transmission and resends the rrqst(h) message. If the RARP process still does not receive back an rrply(h, n, s, c) message, it concludes that the RARP server on subnetwork (n, s) is down and so reports its failure to obtain the IP address of its computer. This way, RARP also acts as a protocol for maintaining local topology information.

11.7 BIBLIOGRAPHICAL NOTES

The ARP is discussed in Plummer [1982]. Also see the bibliographical notes concerning routing in Chapter 13.

EXERCISES

1 (Request–Reply Protocol). Design a protocol for maintaining local topology information in a network p[i: 0 .. n − 1]. In this protocol, for a process p[i] to check whether or not a neighbor p[g] is up, p[i] sends a rqst message to p[g] and then waits until one of two events occurs. Either p[i] receives a rply message or p[i] times out, indicating that the rqst message or the rply message is lost, possibly because one of the two channels between p[i] and p[g] is down. In the former case, p[i] assigns its up[g] the value true, and in the latter case, p[i] assigns its up[g] the value false.

2 (Checking the Ability to Add). Modify the protocol for maintaining local topology information in Section 11.2 as follows. Each up[g] element in process p[i] is assigned the value true iff the two channels between p[i] and

p[g] are up and p[g] can correctly add two integers chosen by p[i]. This modification requires that each chk(b) message is replaced by a chk(b, x, y, sum) message. When process p[i] sends a chk(b, x, y, sum) message to process p[g], x and y are two integers chosen arbitrarily by p[i], and sum is the result of adding the two integers chosen arbitrarily by p[g] and sent to p[i] in the last chk message from p[g] to p[i].

3 (Checking the Ability to Add). Modify the request–reply protocol for maintaining local topology information in exercise 1 as discussed in exercise 2.

4 (Integer Up Arrays). Modify the protocol for maintaining local topology information in Section 11.2 such that array up in each process p[i] is declared as follows:

var   up   :   **array** [N] **of** 1..w

where N is the set of indices of neighbors of process p[i] and w is some constant. (Note that array up is no longer an array of boolean values.) In order to compute these up arrays, each process p[i] also has an input array cost declared as follows:

inp   cost :   **array** [N] **of** 1..w-1

Array up in each process p[i] is computed as follows:

up[g] = $\frac{1}{2}$ (cost[g] in p[i] + cost[i] in p[g])   if the two channels between p[i] and p[g] are up

     w   otherwise

5 (Integer Up Arrays). Modify the request–reply protocol for maintaining local topology information in exercise 1 as discussed in exercise 4.

6 (Integer Up Arrays). Modify the protocol for maintaining global topology information in Section 11.3 assuming, as suggested in exercises 4 and 5, that array up in each process p[i] is declared as follows:

inp   up   :   **array** [0..n-1] **of** 1..w

where n is the number of processes in the network and w is some constant.

7 (Integer Up Arrays). Modify the protocol for maintaining hierarchical topology information in Section 11.5 assuming, as suggested in exercises 5 and 6, that array up in each process p[i] is declared as follows:

inp   up   :   **array** [0..r+s-1] **of** 1..w

where r is the number of regions in the network, s is the number of processes per region, and w is some constant.

8 (Connections Assuming Local Topology Information). The connection proto-

col that uses timeouts in Section 6.1 is based on the assumption that the two channels between processes p and q are always up. It is required to modify this protocol such that each process takes advantage of an underlying protocol for maintaining local topology information. In particular, each process has a boolean input named up. The value of input up is true iff the two channels between the two processes are up. Design the two processes of the modified protocol.

9   (Connections Assuming Local Topology Information). Solve exercise 8 for the connection protocol that uses identifiers in Section 6.2.

10   (Unidirectional Ring Networks). Consider a uni-directional ring network $p[i: 0 .. n - 1]$, where there is one channel from each $p[i]$ to $p[i +_n 1]$. Each process in the network has a boolean variable up whose value is computed as follows:

```
up = true  iff  all channels in the network are up
```

Adapt the protocol for maintaining local topology information in Section 11.2 to this network such that each process in the network keeps the value of its up variable current.

11   (Unidirectional Ring Network). Adapt the request–reply protocol for maintaining local topology information in exercise 1 to the unidirectional ring network in exercise 10 such that each process in the network keeps the value of its up variable current.

12   (Ring Network). Consider a ring network $p[i : 0 .. n - 1]$, where each process $p[i]$ has exactly one left neighbor $p[i -_n 1]$ and one right neighbor $p[i +_n 1]$. Each process $p[i]$ has two variables left and right. Variable left stores the index x of the leftmost process, up to process $p[0]$, reachable from $p[i]$. Variable right stores the index of the rightmost process, up to process $p[0]$, reachable from $p[i]$. Each process $p[i]$ has the following two inputs:

```
inp    N    :    set {i -n 1, i +n 1},
       up   :    array [N] of boolean
```

The value of up[j] in $p[i]$ is true iff the two channels between $p[i]$ and $p[j]$ are both up. Design the processes in this ring network.

13   (Linear Network). In a network, there are two opposite-direction channels between processes p and q, and there are two opposite-direction channels between processes q and r. Periodically, process p sends a token message to process q, which forwards it to process r, which returns it to process q, which forwards it to process p. If the token returns to process p, p recognizes that all four channels in the network are up and assigns a boolean variable up the value true. If the token does not return to process p, p recognizes that one or more of the channels is down and assigns variable up the value false. Design processes p, q, and r in this protocol.

14 (Tree Network). Consider a network that consists of the processes: root, p[i: 0 .. m − 1], and q[i: 0 .. m − 1, j: 0 .. n − 1]. There are two opposite-direction channels between process root and each of the p[i] processes. Also, for each i, 0 ≤ i < m, there are two opposite-direction channels between process p[i] and each of the q[i, j] processes. Each p[i] process has a variable up whose value is true iff the two channels between p[i] and process root are up. Each q[i, j] process has a variable up whose value is true iff the two channels between q[i, j] and process p[i] are up and variable up in process p[i] is true. Adapt the protocol for maintaining local topology information in Section 11.2 to this network such that each process in the network keeps the value of its up variable current.

15 (Tree Network). Adapt the request–reply protocol for maintaining local topology information in exercise 1 to the tree network in exercise 14 such that each process in the network keeps the value of its up variable current.

16 (Star Network). Consider a network that consists of the processes p[i: 0 .. n − 1], sw, and q[i: 0 .. n − 1]. There are two opposite direction channels between process sw and each of the p[i] processes. Also, there are two opposite direction channels between process sw and each of the q[i] processes. Each p[i] process has a variable up whose value is true iff the two channels between p[i] and sw are up and the two channels between q[i] and sw are up. Similarly, each q[i] process has a variable up whose value is true iff the two channels between p[i] and sw are up and the two channels between q[i] and sw are up. Adapt the protocol for maintaining local topology information in Section 11.2 to this network such that each process in the network keeps the value of its up variable current.

17 (Star Network). Adapt the request–reply protocol for maintaining local topology information in exercise 1 to the star network in exercise 16 such that each process in the network keeps the value of its up variable current.

18 (Cost of Maintaining Global Topology Information). Consider a network that consists of n nodes and e edges. Derive an upper bound on the number of messages needed for one process to broadcast its up array to all the processes in the network, using the protocol for maintaining global topology information in Section 11.3, in each of the following cases.

   a   The topology has no cycles.
   b   The topology consists of one cycle.
   c   The topology is a general graph.

19 (Combined Protocol for Maintaining Local and Global Topology Information). Combine the protocol for maintaining local topology information in Section 11.2 with the protocol for maintaining global topology information in Section 11.3 into one protocol.

20 (Combined Protocol for Maintaining Local and Global Hierarchical Topology

Information). Combine the protocol for maintaining local hierarchical topology information in Section 11.5 with the protocol for maintaining global hierarchical topology information in Section 11.5 into one protocol.

21 (Local Load Estimation). In a network p[i: 0 .. n − 1], each process p[i] has a constant named lmax, an input named load, and a variable array named ld as follows:

```
const    lmax
inp      load   :      0..lmax
var      ld     :      array [N] of 0..lmax
```

where N is the set of indices of neighbors of process p[i]. Design process p[i] to maintain its variable array ld such that for each neighbor p[g] of p[i],

```
if the two channels between p[i] and p[g] are up,
then       ld[g] in p[i]       =       load in p[g],
else       ld[g] in p[i]       =       lmax
```

22 (Global Load Estimation). Modify the protocol in exercise 21 as follows. Array ld in process p[i] is declared as follows:

```
var      ld     :      array [0..n-1] of 0..lmax
```

The modified protocol should satisfy the following condition.

```
if there is an up path between any two processes p[i]
   and p[j] in the network,
```

```
then       ld[j] in p[i]       =       load in p[j], and
           ld[i] in p[j]       =       load in p[i],
else       ld[j] in p[i]       =       lmax, and
           ld[i] in p[j]       =       lmax
```

23 (Maintaining Global Topology Information in a Star Network). Simplify the protocol for maintaining global topology information in Section 11.3 to be used in a star network p[i : 0 .. n − 1], in which each pair of processes p[0] and p[j], where 1 ≤ j < n, are neighbors.

24 (Simplified Protocol for Maintaining Global Topology Information). Simplify the protocol for maintaining global topology information, discussed in Section 11.3, in the case where the network topology has no cycles and the message transmissions are error free.

25 (Simplified Global Topology Information). Consider a linear network p[i: 0 .. n − 1], where process p[0] has only one (right) neighbor, process p[n − 1] has only one (left) neighbor, and each middle process p[i], where 1 ≤ i < n − 1, has one left neighbor p[i − 1] and one right neighbor p[i + 1]. It is required to design a protocol for maintaining global topology information in this network. The global topology information to be maintained in each process p[i] consists of two variables named left and right, where left (or right) stores the index of the left-most (or right-most, respectively) process reachable from p[i]. The inputs, variables, and parameters of each middle process p[i: 1 .. n – 2] are defined as follows:

```
process p[i : 1..n - 2]
inp       N            :      set {i-1, i+1},
          up           :      array [N] of boolean
var       left, right  :      0..n-1,
          j            :      0..n-1
par       g            :      N
begin
          . . .
end
```

Design the actions of the middle process p[i: 1 .. n – 2].

26 (Simplified Global Topology Information). Consider a linear network p[i: 0 .. n – 1] where each process p[i], 0 < i < n – 1, has two neighbors p[i – 1] and p[i + 1], and p[0] has only one neighbor, p[1], and p[n – 1] has only one neighbor, p[n – 2]. The processes exchange only one msg chk(b), where b is boolean. This message can be lost, but not corrupted, when transmitted. Each process p[i] has a boolean variable up whose value is assigned the value true when all the channels in the network are up and is assigned false otherwise. Process p[i] can be defined as follows:

```
process p[i : 0..n-1]
inp       N      :      set {i-1 | i > 0} ∪
                               {i+1 | i < n-1}
var       up, b :      boolean,
          f      :      N
par       g      :      N
begin
          rcv chk(b) from p[g] —> S
□         timeout (i ≠ 0) ∧ (no chk(true) message in
                 any channel) —>
                               up := false
□         timeout (i = 0) ∧ (no message in any
                 channel) —>
                               up := false;
                               send chk(false) to p[1]
end
```

Define statement S.

CHAPTER 12

THE ABSTRACTION OF PERFECT CHANNEL

The discussion in Section 11.2 suggests that every process p[i] in a general network can have an input array up declared as follows:

```
inp    up    :        array [N] of boolean
```

In this declaration, N is the set of indices of the neighbors of process p[i].

Array up is declared as an input in process p[i] because the actions of p[i] do not modify its value. Rather, we assume the existence of an underlying protocol, similar to the one discussed in Section 11.2, that continuously updates the value of array up in order to ensure that this value satisfies the following property:

Immediate Detection: The value of any element up[g] in array up in process p[i] is true at any instant iff the two channels between processes p[i] and p[g] are both up at that instant.

To be exact, no underlying protocol, not even the one in Section 11.2, can ensure this strict property of immediate detection. In fact, regardless of the underlying protocol used to maintain array up, there will always be a nonzero delay between the time when the state of a channel is changed and the time when this change is reflected in the corresponding up arrays. Nevertheless, since changes in the state of a channel are rare, we assume that the values of up arrays in the network processes satisfy the immediate detection property.

In Section 11.1, we adopted two assumptions concerning the change of topology of a network: atomicity and rare occurrence. The atomicity assumption states that the topology of a network remains fixed during any action execution in the network. From this assumption and the immediate detection property, we conclude that the value of the up array in any process in a network remains fixed during any action execution in the network. The rare occurrence assumption states that the topology of a network changes a finite number of times along any, possibly infinite, execution of the network. From this assumption and the immediate detection property, we conclude that the value of the up array in any process in a network changes a finite number of times along any, possibly infinite, execution of the network.

It is mentioned in Chapter 11 that no pair of neighboring processes should exchange messages unless the two channels between the processes are up. Therefore, before a process p[i] sends a message to a neighbor p[g], p[i] should check, in the same action in which the message is to be sent, that element up[g] is true. Similarly, before process p[g] sends a message to p[i], it should check, in the same action in which the message is to be sent, that element up[i] is true. The direct exchange of messages between p[i] and p[g] can proceed as long as the two channels between p[i] and p[g] are up.

It is also mentioned in Chapter 11 that messages sent between two neighboring processes, when the two channels between the processes are up, can still be corrupted, lost, reordered, or discarded (if the messages are sent at a higher rate than the receiving process expects). Nevertheless, we assume the existence of some underlying protocols that ensure the following property.

Perfect Channel: Messages that are sent between two neighboring processes, when the two channels between the processes are up, are not corrupted, lost, reordered, or discarded.

The underlying protocols that can ensure this nice property are of three types: protocols for error detection (similar to those discussed in Chapter 8), protocols for error recovery (similar to those discussed in Chapter 9), and protocols for flow control (similar to those discussed in Chapter 10). Note that most of these protocols require two up channels between each pair of communicating processes. Fortunately, the existence of such channels is guaranteed by our requirement that processes check their up arrays before sending their messages.

Let us summarize here what we have achieved so far in this chapter. We started by assuming that each process in a general network has an input array up whose value satisfies the immediate detection property. Then, we required that no process p[i] sends a message to a neighboring process p[g] unless the corresponding element up[g] in process p[i] has the value true. Finally, we argued that if this requirement is satisfied, then we can assume that sent messages are not corrupted, lost, reordered, or discarded according to the perfect channel property.

12.1 USING THE ABSTRACTION OF PERFECT CHANNEL

The objective of the abstraction of perfect channel is to simplify process definitions by deleting from these definitions all the details that deal with message corruption, loss, reorder, and discarding. Next, we give an example to illustrate how this abstraction can be used to simplify process definitions.

Consider a network that consists of two processes p and q. Process p sends data messages to process q, and q replies by sending back an ack message for each data message it receives from p. The two channels between p and q can lose sent messages; thus, p and q are designed to detect message loss and resend lost messages.

Each sent data message is of the form data(t, b), where t is the message text and b is the message sequence number in the range 0, ..., 1. Process p obtains the text of each message from an input, infinite array called text. The sequence number of the first data message is 0, and the sequence number of each subsequent data message is different from that of the previous message. (Hence, this protocol is called an alternating-bit protocol.)

After process p sends a data message to process q, p waits until one of two events occurs. Either p receives an ack message from q or p times out indicating that the data message or its ack message is lost. In the former case, p sends the next data message, and in the latter case, p resends the current data message.

Process p in this protocol can be defined as follows:

```
process p

inp    text          :       array [integer] of integer

var    x             :       integer,      {index of text}
       wait          :       boolean,
       b             :       0..1

begin
       ~wait                 ->
                             {send the next data msg}
                             wait, x, b := true, x+1, b+₂1;
                             send data(text[x], b) to q

[]     rcv ack from q    ->      wait := false

[]     timeout wait ∧ #ch.p.q + #ch.q.p = 0   ->
                             {resend the current data msg}
                             send data(text[x], b) to q
end
```

Process q has a boolean variable named bnxt that stores the sequence number of the next data message. When q receives a data(t, b) message, it compares the value of b with that of bnxt. If they are unequal, then process q concludes that the received data(t, b) message is another copy of the last received message, and so q discards the message. If they are equal, then q concludes that the data(t, b) message is the next message to be received, and so it stores the message. In either case, process q sends an ack message to process p acknowledging the reception of the data(t, b) message.

Process q in this protocol can be defined as follows.

```
process q

var    rcvd        :      array [integer] of integer,
       y           :      integer,        {index of rcvd}
       bnxt, b     :      0..1,
       t           :      integer

begin
       rcv data(t, b) from p —>
              if bnxt ≠ b —> skip
              [] bnxt = b —> rcvd[y], y, bnxt :=
                                   t, y+1, b+₂1
              fi; send ack to p
end
```

Before a process, p or q, sends a message to the other process, it should ensure that the two channels between p and q are up. This is achieved by adding a boolean input "up" to both p and q. According to the immediate detection property, each input "up" is true when and only when the two channels between p and q are up. Thus, before a process p or q sends a message to the other process, the process checks that its input "up" is true.

The modified processes p and q can be defined as follows:

```
process p

inp    up          :      boolean,
       text        :      array [integer] of integer

var    x           :      integer,        {index of text}
       wait        :      boolean,
       b           :      0..1

begin
       ~wait ∧ up          —>
                           {send the next data msg}
                           wait, x, b := true, x+1, b+₂1;
                           send data(text[x], b) to q

       []     rcv ack from q    —>    wait := false

       []     timeout wait ∧ #ch.p.q + #ch.q.p = 0 ∧ up —>
                           {resend the last data msg}
                           send data(text[x], b) to q

end
```

```
process q

inp   up              :       boolean

var   rcvd            :       array [integer] of integer,
      y               :       integer,      {index of rcvd}
      bnxt, b         :       0..1,
      t               :       integer

begin
      rcv data(t, b) from p ->
          if bnxt ≠ b   -> skip
          [] bnxt = b   -> rcvd[y], y, bnxt :=
                                t, y+1, b+₂1
          fi;
          if ~up ->skip
          []  up        ->    send ack to p
          fi
end
```

Now, we can adopt the abstraction of perfect channel to simplify the definitions of processes p and q by assuming the existence of protocols, underneath p and q, that perform error detection, error recovery, and flow control. Therefore, all the details for performing error detection, error recovery, and flow control can be removed from p and q. For example, the sequence numbers of data messages, the timeout action in process p, and the ack messages from q to p can all be deleted from the definition of p and q.

The abstract definitions of p and q can be as follows.

```
process p

inp   up              :       boolean,
      text            :       array [integer] of integer

var   x               :       integer      {index of text}

begin
      up              ->    x := x+1;
                            send data(text[x]) to q
end

process q

inp   up              :       boolean

var   rcvd            :       array [integer] of integer,
      y               :       integer      {index of rcvd}
```

begin
      rcv data(t) **from** p-->   rcvd[y], y := t, y+1
end

Note that only the details for transferring the data from p to q remain in the abstract definition of p and q.

In the next three chapters, we discuss a number of protocols where each process has an array up as defined above. Moreover, each process checks the appropriate element of its up array before sending a message to a neighboring process. Therefore, the processes in these protocols can be, and in fact are, designed under the assumption that sent messages are not corrupted, lost, reordered, or discarded.

12.2 ABSTRACTION OF PERFECT CHANNEL IN THE INTERNET

In the Internet, application processes that exchange messages via TCP can be designed according to the abstraction of perfect channel. For example, consider two application processes p and q that reside in computers c and d, respectively. As illustrated in Figure 12.1, process p resides on top of the TCP process tp in computer c, and process q resides on top of the TCP process tq in computer d. For process p to send two text segments tx.0 and then tx.1 to process q, the following steps are executed:

   i. Process p sends the two text segments tx.0 and then tx.1 to the TCP process tp in computer c.

  ii. Process tp adds a TCP header hd.i to each segment tx.i yielding a TCP message of the form (hd.i, tx.i), and then sends the two TCP messages (hd.0, tx.0) and then (hd.1, tx.1) to the TCP process tq in computer d.

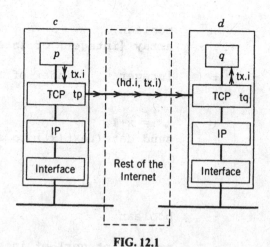

FIG. 12.1

iii. If any (hd.i, tx.i) message is corrupted (then discarded) or lost while being transmitted from process tp to process tq, tp eventually detects the resulting message loss and resends another copy of the (hd.i, tx.i) message to tq.

iv. If process tq receives message (hd.1, tx.1) before message (hd.0, tx.0), it detects message reorder and delivers the two text segments tx.0 and tx.1 to process q in the right order, that is, tx.0 followed by tx.1.

v. The final result is that the two text segments are delivered to process q in the same shape and the same order in which they were sent by process p.

This detailed description of message transmission from process p to process q can be abstracted in our notation by stating that there is a channel from p to q and that any sequence of messages sent over this channel will be received by q in the same shape and the same order in which the message sequence was sent by p.

12.3 BIBLIOGRAPHICAL NOTES

The abstraction of perfect channel is provided in the Internet by the TCP, which is discussed in Postel [1981c], Comer [1988], and Stevens [1994].

EXERCISES

1 (Connections Using the Perfect Channel Abstraction). Simplify the connection protocol in Section 6.1 using the abstraction of perfect channel. (*Hint:* Delete from the protocol definition in Section 6.1 all details that deal with message corruption, loss, reorder, or discarding. Keep only those details that deal with establishing and removing connections.)

2 (Connections Using the Perfect Channel Abstraction). Simplify the connection protocol in Section 6.2 using the abstraction of perfect channel.

3 (Connections Using the Perfect Channel Abstraction). Explain why the abstract protocol definitions that result from solving exercises 1 and 2 are similar.

4 (Multiplexing Using the Perfect Channel Abstraction). Explain why the perfect channel abstraction cannot be used to simplify the definitions of the three multiplexing protocols in Chapter 7.

5 (Corruption Detection Using the Perfect Channel Abstraction). Simplify the corruption detection protocol that uses parity bits in Section 8.1 using the abstraction of perfect channel.

6 (Corruption Detection Using the Perfect Channel Abstraction). Simplify the corruption detection protocol that uses checksums in Section 8.1 using the abstraction of perfect channel.

7 (Corruption Detection Using the Perfect Channel Abstraction). Explain why the abstract protocol definitions that result from solving exercises 5 and 6 are similar.

8 (Error Recovery Using the Perfect Channel Abstraction). Simplify the cumulative acknowledgment protocol in Section 9.3 using the abstraction of perfect channel.

9 (Flow Control Using the Perfect Channel Abstraction). Simplify the variable window size protocol in Section 10.1 using the abstraction of perfect channel.

CHAPTER 13

ROUTING

In a general network, a process p[i] may wish to send a data message to a far away process p[d], one that is not a neighbor of p[i]. In this case, process p[i] attaches the index d of the destination process to the data message then sends the data(d) message to a neighboring process p[g]. When process p[g] receives the data(d) message, it also forwards the message to a neighboring process p[h], and so on. Forwarding of the data(d) message continues until the message finally arrives at its destination process p[d].

The above scenario raises the following question. When a process p[i] needs to forward a data(d) message, to which of its neighbors should it forward the message? Routing is the task of determining the best neighbor to which a data(d) message is forwarded, given the ultimate destination d of the message.

Routing is usually performed by providing each process in the network with a table, called its routing table. The routing table of process p[i] lists for each possible ultimate destination d the best neighbor to which p[i] forwards every data(d) message.

There are three common problems associated with routing tables. First, a routing table has one entry for each possible ultimate destination in the network. Because each process is a possible ultimate destination, the number of entries in a routing table in a given network equals the number of processes in that network. Therefore, in a network with a large number of processes, routing tables are large.

The second problem of routing tables is that these tables need to be updated periodically to reflect any changes in the network topology. To update its routing table, each process may exchange additional messages with other processes in the network.

The third problem of routing tables is that they need to be updated whenever a "mobile" ultimate destination changes its location within the network. The mobility of ultimate destinations requires that each routing table in the network be augmented with extra information. It also requires that each process in the network exchange additional messages with other processes in the network.

In this chapter, we discuss six routing protocols that solve these three problems. In Section 13.1, we discuss a hierarchical routing protocol where the network processes are partitioned according to an artificial hierarchical structure with the sole purpose of reducing the number of entries in the routing tables. We also discuss an important variation of hierarchical routing called default routing.

In Section 13.2, we discuss a random routing protocol. In this protocol, routing tables are fixed and each table lists a set of possible neighbors for every ultimate destination. A message whose ultimate destination is d is routed to a neighbor selected at random from the set of possible neighbors associated with d.

In Section 13.3, we discuss a distributed routing protocol. In this protocol, each process periodically sends a copy of its routing table to every neighboring process. When a process receives the routing table of a neighboring process, it uses the received table to update its own routing table.

In Section 13.4, we discuss a backward learning protocol. In this protocol, each message carries additional information about the source process where the message is generated. When a process receives a message and before it routes the message to one of its neighbors, the process uses the additional information in the message to update its own routing table.

In Section 13.5, we discuss a source routing protocol where each process maintains a current copy of the network topology. When a message is generated at a process, the process uses its copy of the network topology to compute a route for the message from the process to the ultimate destination of the message. The computed route is attached to the message before it is sent out so that the message is routed at intermediate processes according to the attached route.

In Section 13.6, we introduce a procedure ROUTE that network processes can invoke to route their messages. This procedure acts as a black box that provides routing yet hides the details of how routing is performed. This procedure is used by the network processes in Section 13.7 and Chapters 14 and 15.

The routing protocols in Sections 13.1 to 13.5 can be used for routing messages to stationary tasks in network processes. In particular, any message, that is intended for some task in a process p[d] is routed to process p[d] because the task is permanently stationed in p[d]. In Section 13.7, we discuss how to extend the routing protocols in Sections 13.1 to 13.5 so that they can be used for routing messages to mobile tasks that may travel between processes.

Finally in Section 13.8, we discuss the routing protocols in the Internet.

13.1 HIERARCHICAL ROUTING

Consider a network where the processes are partitioned into m regions. The processes in each region are in turn partitioned into n districts. Each district has r processes.

In this network, each region i and each district j is connected in the following sense. For each of the two processes p and q in region i, there is a sequence of processes p.0, . . . , p.r such that p is p.0, q is p.r, and for every k, $0 \le k < r$, p.k and p.(k+1) are neighbors in region i. Similarly, for each two processes p and q in district j, there is a sequence of processes p.0, . . . , p.s such that p is p.0, q is p.s, and for every k, $0 \le k < s$, p.k and p.(k+1) are neighbors in district j.

Each process in this network can be uniquely identified by three identifiers i, j, and k. Identifier i indicates the region to which the process belongs. Identifier j indicates the district, in region i, to which the process belongs. Finally, identifier k indicates the process in district j in region i. Thus, the processes in the network constitute a process array with three indices as follows:

process p[i: 0..m-1, j: 0..n-1, k: 0..r-1]

In this network, when a data message is to be sent, the three identifiers (x, y, z) of its destination process are attached to the message before the message is sent. When a data(x, y, z) message arrives at a process, the process uses its routing table and the triple (x, y, z), which identifies the message destination, to determine the best neighbor to which the message is forwarded.

The routing table of each process p[i, j, k] consists of three arrays named rgn, dstr, and prs. Array rgn determines the best neighbor for reaching a destination process whose region is other than i. Array dstr determines the best neighbor for reaching a destination process whose region is i but whose district is other than j. Array prs determines the best neighbor for reaching a destination process whose region is i and whose district is j, but the process is other than p[i, j, k] itself.

The three arrays are declared in process p[i, j, k] as follows.

```
inp    rgn    :    array [0..m-1] of N,
       dstr   :    array [0..n-1] of N,
       prs    :    array [0..r-1] of N
```

In this declaration, N is an input set of triples (i', j', k') such that p[i', j', k'] is a neighbor of p[i, j, k].

When a data(x, y, z) message is received by process p[i, j, k], the triple (x, y, z) of the message destination is compared with the triple (i, j, k) of the receiving process. If x is different from i, then the message is forwarded to process p[rgn[x]]. If x = i but y is different from j, then the message is forwarded to p[dstr[y]]. If x = i and y = j but z is different from k, then the message is forwarded to p[prs[z]]. If x = i, y = j, and z = k, then the message has already arrived at its ultimate destination p[i, j, k]. Process p[i, j, k] in the hierarchical routing protocol can be defined as follows:

```
process  p  [i :   0..m-1,   {i is the process region}
             j :   0..n-1,   {j is the process district}
             k:    0..r-1    {k is the process}
            ]
```

```
inp   N     :     set {[i',j',k']|p[i',j',k'] is a
                       neighbor of p[i,j,k]},
      up    :     array [N] of boolean,
      rgn   :     array [0..m-1] of N,
      dstr  :     array [0..n-1] of N,
      prs   :     array [0..r-1] of N

var   x     :     0..m-1,
      y     :     0..n-1,
      z     :     0..r-1

par   g     :     N

begin
      true ->
              {generate a data(x, y, z) msg and route it}
              x, y, z := any, any, any;
              RTMSG

[]    rcv data(x,y,z) from p[g] ->
              {route the received data(x, y, z) msg}
              RTMSG
end
```

Process p[i, j, k] has two actions. In the first action, process p[i, j, k] generates a data message with an arbitrary ultimate destination (x, y, z) and routes the message to the best neighbor for reaching the ultimate destination. In the second action, process p[i, j, k] receives a data(x, y, z) message from a neighbor p[g], and then routes the received message to the best neighbor for reaching the ultimate destination.

Statement RTMSG, in the actions of the hierarchical routing protocol, is defined as follows:

```
if x≠i                    /\ up[rgn[x]] ->
                          send data(x,y,z) to p[rgn[x]]
[] x≠i                    /\ ~up[rgn[x]] ->
                          {nonreachable dest.} skip
[] x=i /\ y≠j             /\ up[dstr[y]] ->
                          send data(x,y,z) to p[dstr[y]]
[] x=i /\ y≠j             /\ ~up[dstr[y]] ->
                          {nonreachable dest.} skip
[] x=i /\ y=j /\ z≠k      /\ up[prs[z]] ->
                          send data(x,y,z) to p[prs[z]]
```

```
[]  x=i /\ y=j /\ z≠k        /\ ~up[prs[z]]  ->
                     {nonreachable dest.} skip
[]  x=i /\ y=j /\ z=k                       ->
                     {arrived at dest.} skip
fi
```

The advantage of hierarchical routing is that it yields small routing tables. In particular, the total number of entries in the three arrays rgn, dstr, and prs in one process is m + n + r. This is much less than m × n × r which is the total number of entries in a flat routing table. Next, we discuss an important variation of hierarchical routing called default routing.

In default routing, at least one process in each district is called a gateway of that district. The way a process p[i, j, k] routes a data(x, y, z) message depends on whether p[i, j, k] is a gateway of its own district, namely district (i, j). If p[i, j, k] is a gateway of district (i, j), then p[i, j, k] routes the message exactly as in hierarchical routing. If p[i, j, k] is not a gateway of district (i, j) and the ultimate destination (x, y, z) of the message is in another district, that is, x ≠ i or y ≠ j, then p[i, j, k] forwards the message toward a gateway of district (i, j) using its array prs. If p[i, j, k] is not a gateway of district (i, j) and the ultimate destination (x, y, z) of the message is in district (i, j), that is, x = i and y = j, then process p[i, j, k] forwards the message towards its ultimate destination using its array prs.

Not every process in a district can be a gateway for that district. Rather, each gateway of a district (i, j) should satisfy the following condition. If any process in district (i, j) has a neighbor in another district (i', j'), then each gateway of district (i, j) has a neighbor in district (i', j'). This condition guarantees that if a gateway receives a data message from within its district and if the ultimate destination of the message is outside the district, then the gateway can forward the message to a neighboring process outside the district. Note that this condition is trivially satisfied for a district if the district has only one gateway and each neighbor of each "interior" process in the district is in the district.

The main advantage of default routing is that each process that is not a gateway needs only to store array prs. Each gateway, however, needs to store all three arrays rgn, dstr, and prs.

A process p[i, j, k] in default routing is the same as process p[i, j, k] in hierarchical routing, except for two modifications. First, the following input is added to process p[i, j, k]:

```
inp  gtwy  :     0..r-1
```

Process p[i, j, gtwy] is a gateway of district (i, j), which is the same district of process p[i, j, k].

Second, statement RTMSG in process p[i, j, k] in hierarchical routing is replaced by statement RTMSG' in process p[i, j, k] in default routing, where RTMSG' is defined as follows.

```
if gtwy = k ->       RTMSG
[] gtwy ≠ k ->
        if (x≠i \/ y≠j) /\ up[prs[gtwy]] ->
                        send data(x, y, z) to p[prs[gtwy]]
        [] (x≠i \/ y≠j) /\ ~up[prs[gtwy]] ->
                        {nonreachable} skip
        [] (x=i /\ y=j) /\ z=k -> {arrived} skip
        [] (x=i /\ y=j) /\ z≠k /\ up[prs[z]] ->
                        send data(x,y,z) to p[prs[z]]
        [] (x=i /\ y=j) /\ z≠k /\ ~up[prs[z]] ->
                        {nonreachable} skip
        fi
fi
```

In this statement, RTMSG is as defined in hierarchical routing.

In our presentation of hierarchical and default routing, we assumed that the processes in a network are partitioned into a hierarchy of three layers: regions, districts, and processes. There is no magic to this particular number of layers. It is possible to partition the processes into a hierarchy of k layers for any value of k greater than 1.

13.2 RANDOM ROUTING

In random routing, each process p[i] has a routing table that lists for each ultimate destination d a set of neighbors to which p[i] can forward data(d) messages. To forward a message, process p[i] performs two steps. First, p[i] examines its routing table to determine, from the ultimate destination of the message, the set of neighbors to which the message can be forwarded. Second, p[i] randomly selects from this set one neighbor and forwards the message to that neighbor.

In this section, we discuss a random routing protocol where each routing table lists for each ultimate destination exactly two neighbors of p[i]. In particular, the routing table in process p[i] can be defined as follows:

```
inp    rtb    :      array [0..n-1, 0..1] of N
```

In this declaration, n is the number of processes in the network and N is the set of neighbors of p[i]. Any data(d) message in process p[i] is forwarded either to process p[rtb[d, 0]] or to process p[rtb[d, 1]]. The decision to forward data(d) to p[rtb[d, 0]] or p[rtb[d, 1]] is random.

To prevent any data message from being forwarded indefinitely without reaching its final destination (because of the randomness or because the final destination is nonreacheable), there is an upper bound on the number of hops that the message can make without reaching its final destination. Hence, each data message is of the form data(d, h), where d is the index of the ultimate destination of the message and h is the maximum number of hops that the message can make without reaching its final destination.

When a data message is generated, its field h is assigned an initial value. Each time the message is forwarded from one process to a neighboring process, its field h is decremented by 1. If field h ever becomes 0, without the message reaching its final destination, the message is discarded.

Process p[i] in the random routing protocol can be defined as follows:

```
process p[i : 0..n-1]

const hmax

inp    N      :     set { g |p[g] is a neighbor of p[i]},
       up     :     array [N] of boolean,
       rtb    :     array [0..n-1, 0..1] of N

var    x      :     0..1,          {random choice}
       d      :     0..n-1,        {ultimate destination}
       h      :     0..hmax        {# hops remaining}

par    g      :     N

begin
       true                         ->    d, h := any, any;
                                          RTMSG
[]     rcv data(d, h) from p[g] ->        RTMSG
end
```

Note that the two actions of process p[i] in the random routing protocol are similar to the two actions of process p[i] in the hierarchical routing protocol in Section 13.1.

Statement RTMSG, in the actions of the random routing protocol, is defined as follows:

```
if d=i         -> {arrived at dest.} skip
[] d≠i ∧ h=0   -> {nonreachable dest.} skip
[] d≠i ∧ h>0 ∧    (d in N ∧ up[d])    ->
                    send data(d, h-1) to p[d]
[] d≠i ∧ h=1 ∧ ~(d in N ∧ up[d])      ->
                    {nonreachable dest.} skip
[] d≠i ∧ h>1 ∧ ~(d in N ∧ up[d])      ->
       x := random;
       if up[rtb[d, x]]               ->
                    send data(d, h-1) to p[rtb[d, x]]
```

```
    [] ~up[rtb[d, x]] /\ up[rtb[d, 1-x]] ->
                 send data(d, h-1) to p[rtb[d, 1-x]]
    [] ~up[rtb[d, x]] /\ ~up[rtb[d, 1-x]] ->
                 {nonreachable dest.} skip
       fi
fi
```

To route a data(d, h) message, process p[i] performs the following.

   i. If d = i, then process p[i] itself is the ultimate destination of the message, and so it keeps the message.

  ii. If d ≠ i and h = 0, then the message has failed to reach its ultimate destination in the preassigned number of hops. In this case, p[i] discards the message.

 iii. If d ≠ i , h > 0, d is in N, and up[d] is true, then the ultimate destination of the message is an up neighbor of p[i]. In this case, p[i] forwards the message to that neighbor.

 iv. If d ≠ i, h = 1, d is not in N, and up[d] is false, then the message cannot reach its ultimate destination in the preassigned number of hops. In this case, p[i] discards the message.

  v. Otherwise, p[i] selects a random number x in the range 0 . . 1, and then checks whether up[rtb[d, x]] is true. If it is true, then p[i] forwards the message to neighbor p[rtb[d, x]]. If it is false but up[rtb[d, 1 − x]] is true, then p[i] forwards the message to neighbor p[rtb[d, 1 − x]]. If both up[rtb[d, x]] and up[rtb[d, 1 − x]] are false, then p[i] discards the message.

An extreme variation of random routing is called hot potato routing. In this variation, each process routes any data message to a random neighbor, other than the neighbor from which it has received the message. One advantage of hot potato routing is its simplicity: Processes do not not need routing tables to route data messages.

13.3 DISTRIBUTED ROUTING

In distributed routing, the routing table of each process p[i] consists of two arrays called rtb and cost. These arrays are declared as follows:

```
var    rtb    :        array [0..n-1] of N,
       cost   :        array [0..n-1] of 0..n
```

For each ultimate destination d, the entries of these arrays in process p[i] are defined as follows:

   rtb[d]   Best neighbor, of p[i], to which p[i] can forward a data(d) message whose ultimate destination is p[d].

cost[d]   Number of hops that a data(d) message makes after p[i], starting with
process p[rtb[d]], until the message reaches process p[d].

We adopt the convention that if cost[d] in p[i] equals n, then the ultimate destination process p[d] is not reachable from process p[i].

It follows from these definitions that some entries in arrays rtb and cost in
process p[i] have obvious values. In particular,

$$rtb[i] = any\ (don't\ care)\ value$$

$$cost[i] = 0$$

Also, for each neighbor p[g] of process p[i], where the two channels between p[i]
and p[g] are up,

$$rtb[g] = g$$

$$cost[g] = 1$$

The values of other entries in arrays rtb and cost may become obsolete due to
changes in the network topology. In order to keep the values of these entries current,
each process p[i] periodically sends a upd(c) message to each of its neighboring
processes, where c is the current cost array of process p[i].

When process p[i] receives an upd(c) message from a neighboring process p[g],
where c is the cost array of process p[g], process p[i] uses the received array to update every entry rtb[d] and cost[d] in its own arrays according to the following three
rules:

  i. If d = i, then cost[d] is assigned 0.
 ii. If d ≠ i and if one or more of the following conditions is true:
      a. rtb[d] = g
      b. cost[d] > c[d]+1
      c. ~up[rtb[d]]
      then rtb[d] is assigned g and cost[d] is assigned min(n, c[d]+1).
iii. Otherwise, rtb[d] and cost[d] remain unchanged.

Rule ii needs some explanation. If condition a (namely, rtb[d] = g) is true, then
cost[d] is assigned either n provided c[d] = n or c[d]+1 provided c[d] < n. If condition b (namely, cost[d] > c[d]+1) is true, then rtb[d] is assigned g and cost[d] is assigned c[d]+1. If condition c (namely, ~up[rtb[d]]) is true, then rtb[d] is assigned g
and cost[d] is assigned either n provided c[d] = n or c[d]+1 provided c[d] < n.

Assume that the distributed routing protocol starts executing at a state where the
entries in the routing table of every process p[i], other than those entries where the
ultimate destination is p[i] or a neighbor of p[i], are all wrong. Then, as the different

processes in the network start to exchange upd(c) messages and use the received upd(c) messages to update their routing tables, the entries of all routing tables start to "converge" to their correct values. Eventually, the entries in all routing tables in the network become correct. When this happens, the routing tables indicate a shortest path for every ultimate destination in the network.

Process p[i] in the distributed routing protocol can be defined as follows:

```
process p[i : 0..n-1]

inp     N               :       set { g | p[g] is a neighbor of
                                p[i] },
        up              :       array [N] of boolean

var     rtb             :       array [0..n-1] of N,
        cost, c         :       array [0..n-1] of 0..n,
        d               :       0..n-1,
        f, h            :       N,
        finish          :       boolean

par     g               :       N

begin
        true                            ->      d := any;
                                                RTMSG
[]      rcv data(d) from p[g]           ->      RTMSG

[]      true                            ->      SNDCOST

[]      rcv upd(c) from p[g]            ->      UPDRTB
end
```

Process p[i] has four actions. In the first action, process p[i] generates a data(d) message with an arbitrary ultimate destination d and then routes the message to a neighboring process based on its local routing arrays rtb and cost. In the second action, process p[i] receives a data(d) message from a neighbor p[g] and routes the message to a neighboring process based on the local routing arrays rtb and cost.

In the third action, process p[i] sends an upd(c) message, where c is a copy of its cost array, to every neighboring process. In the fourth action, p[i] receives an upd(c) message from a neighbor p[g] and updates its local routing arrays rtb and cost based on the received array c.

Statement RTMSG, in the first and second actions of the distributed routing protocol, is defined as follows:

```
if d=i       ->      {arrived} skip
```

```
[] d≠i ∧ (cost[d] < n ∧ up[rtb[d]]) —>
                        send data(d) to p[rtb[d]]
[] d≠i ∧ ~(cost[d] < n ∧ up[rtb[d]]) —>
                        {nonreachable} skip
fi
```

Statement SNDCOST, in the third action of the distributed routing protocol, is defined as follows:

```
f := NEXT(N, h);
do f ≠ h —>
        if up[f] —> send upd(cost) to p[f]
        [] ~up[f] —> skip
        fi; f := NEXT(N, f)
od;
if up[h] —> send upd(cost) to p[h]
[] ~up[h] —> skip
fi
```

Statement UPDRTB, in the fourth action of the distributed routing protocol, is defined as follows:

```
d, finish := 0, false;
do ~finish —>
        if (d=i)                 —>      cost[d] := 0

        [] (d≠i) ∧
           (rtb[d]=g ∨ cost[d]>c[d]+1 ∨ ~up[rtb[d]]) —>
                        rtb[d], cost[d] := g, min(n, c[d]+1)
        [] (d≠i) ∧
           ~(rtb[d]=g ∨ cost[d]>c[d]+1 ∨ ~up[rtb[d]]) —>
                        skip
        fi;
        if d < n-1 —> d := d+1
        [] d = n-1 —> finish := true
        fi
od
```

Distributed routing is both exact and expensive. On the one hand, distributed routing is exact because the routing tables are guaranteed to eventually point to a shortest route for every ultimate destination in the network. On the other hand, distributed routing is expensive because it requires that all neighboring processes exchange upd messages periodically.

In the next section, we discuss backward learning routing that is both approximate and inexpensive. It is approximate because there is no guarantee that any routing table will ever point to a shortest route for any destination. It is inexpensive because neighboring processes do not exchange any messages other than the data messages that they route. (These data messages, however, carry additional information that is used in updating the routing tables.)

13.4 BACKWARD LEARNING ROUTING

In backward learning routing, processes do not exchange messages other than the data messages that they route. However, the data messages carry additional information to be used in updating the routing tables. In particular, each data message is of the form data(src, h, dst), where:

src   Is the index of the source process of the message
h   Is the number of hops that the message has made so far
dst   Is the index of the destination process of the message

The routing table in each process p[i] consists of three arrays:

```
var    rtb        :        array [0..n-1] of N,
       cost       :        array [0..n-1] of 0..n-1,
       valid      :        array [0..n-1] of 0..vmax
```

These arrays in process p[i] have the following meanings for every ultimate destination dst in the range $0 .. n - 1$.

rtb[dst]   Best neighbor to which process p[i] can forward a data(src, h, dst) message.

cost[dst] The number of hops that a data(src, h, dst) message can make going from p[i] through the best neighbor p[rtb[dst]] until it reaches the ultimate destination p[dst].

valid[dst] Validity count for the entry cost[dst]. When p[i] updates cost[dst], valid[dst] is assigned its highest possible value vmax. Periodically, p[i] decrements the value of every valid[dst] by 1. If the value of some valid[dst] eventually becomes zero, then the current value of cost[dst] is no longer valid and cost[dst] is assigned its highest possible value $n - 1$.

When a process p[i] receives a data(src, h, dst) message from p[g], process p[i] uses dst and its routing array rtb to route the message. Process p[i] then uses src, h, and g to update its three arrays rtb, cost, and valid as follows. If p[i] detects that h is less than or equal cost[src], then p[i] recognizes that the received data message has traveled from p[src] to p[i] using a shorter or equal-length route than the route from p[i] to p[src] indicated in the routing table of p[i]. If so, p[i] replaces the route indicated in its routing table with the new route by assigning rtb[src], cost[src], and valid[src] the values g, h, and vmax, respectively. Process p[i] then decrements every valid[d] by 1, and assigns every cost[d], whose valid[d] is 0, the value n – 1.

Process p[i] in the backward learning routing protocol can be defined as follows:

```
process p[i : 0..n-1]

const hmax, vmax

inp    N          :  set {g|p[g] is a neighbor of p[i]},
       up         :  array [N] of boolean

var    rtb        :  array [0..n-1] of N,
       cost       :  array [0..n-1] of 0..n-1,
       valid      :  array [0..n-1] of 0..vmax,
       src, dst   :  0..n-1,
       h          :  0..hmax,    {#hops travelled}
       x, y       :  N,          {random neighbors}
       flag       :  boolean

par    g          :  N

begin
       true  ->    src, h, dst := i, 0, any; RTMSG
[]     rcv data(src, h, dst) from p[g] -> RTMSG; UPDRTB
[]     true  ->    UPDRTB'
end
```

Statement RTMSG, in the actions of the backward learning routing protocol, is defined as follows:

```
if dst=i               -> {arrived} skip
[] dst≠i ∧ h=hmax      -> {nonreachable} skip
[] dst≠i ∧ h<hmax ∧ (dst in N ∧ up[dst]) ->
       send data(src, h+1, dst) to p[dst]
[] dst≠i ∧ h=hmax-1 ∧ ~(dst in N ∧ up[dst])          ->
       {nonreachable} skip
[] dst≠i ∧ h<hmax-1 ∧ ~(dst in N ∧ up[dst])          ->
       if up[rtb[dst]] ->
             send data(src, h+1, dst) to p[rtb[dst]]
       [] ~up[rtb[dst]] ->
             x := random;
             y := NEXT(N, x);
             do ~up[y] ∧ y ≠ x -> y := NEXT(N, y) od;
```

```
            if up[y]      ->
                 send data(src, h+1, dst) to p[y];
                 rtb[dst], cost[dst], valid[dst] :=
                 y, n-1, 0
            [] ~up[y]      ->     {nonreachable} skip
            fi
       fi
fi
```

To route a data(src, h, dst) message, process p[i] performs the following.

   i. If dst = i, then process p[i] itself is the ultimate destination of the message, and so it keeps the message.

  ii. If dst ≠ i and h = hmax, then the message has failed to reach its ultimate destination in hmax hops. In this case, p[i] discards the message.

 iii. If dst ≠ i , h < hmax, dst is in N, and up[dst] is true, then the ultimate destination of the message is an up neighbor of p[i]. In this case, p[i] forwards the message to that neighbor.

 iv. If dst ≠ i, h = hmax-1, but dst is not in N or up[dst] is false, then the message cannot reach its ultimate destination in hmax hops. In this case, p[i] discards the message.

  v. Otherwise, p[i] checks whether the best neighbor for routing the message as indicating by array rtb is up. If so, p[i] forwards the message to that neighbor. If not, p[i] selects an up neighbor at random and forwards the message to it or discards the message if all neighbors of p[i] are down.

Statement UPDRTB in the second action of the backward learning routing protocol is defined as follows:

```
if cost[src] ≥ h ->
     rtb[src], cost[src], valid[src] := g, h, vmax
[] cost[src] < h -> skip
fi
```

Statement UPDRTB' in the third action of the backward learning routing protocol is defined as follows:

```
flag, dst := true, 0;
do flag ->   valid[dst] := max(0, valid[dst] - 1);
             if valid[dst] = 0 -> cost[dst] := n-1
             [] valid[dst] ≠ 0 -> skip
             fi;
             if dst < n-1 -> dst := dst + 1
             [] dst = n-1 -> flag := false
```

```
                        fi
od
```

13.5 SOURCE ROUTING

In this routing scheme, all processes have current and complete information about the network topology. Thus, when a data message is generated in a process, the process computes the best route to be traversed by the message to reach its ultimate destination. The computed route is attached to the message before it is sent out so that each process that receives the message can deduce to which neighboring process should the message be forwarded.

The global topology information stored in process p[i] is an input array "net" declared as follows.

inp   net   :   **array** [0..n-1, 0..n-1] **of boolean**

In this declaration, n is the number of processes in the network. The value of an element net[j, k] is true iff processes p[j] and p[k] are neighbors in the network and the two channels between them are up.

To compute a route from process p[i] to an ultimate destination process p[d], process p[i] has a procedure FINDRT defined as FINDRT(**in** net, i, d, **out** route). This procedure takes three inputs: the input array net in process p[i], index i of the source process p[i], and index d of the destination process p[d]. The procedure computes an array route with n + 1 elements whose value is defined as follows:

```
If    procedure FINDRT can compute a route:
      <p[i], p[g.1], p[g.2], ... , p[g.r], p[d] >,
      where
              r < n-1,
              p[g.1] is a neighbor of p[i],
              p[g.2] is a neighbor of p[g.1],
              ...
              p[d] is a neighbor of p[g.r]
then
      procedure FINDRT returns array route as follows:
              route[0]    = i,
              route[1]    = g.1,
              route[2]    = g.2,
              ...
              route[r]    = g.r,
              route[r+1] = d,
              route[r+2] = index of some process not a
```

                              neighbor of p[d]; for example
                              d.
else
        procedure FINDRT returns array route as follows:
              route[0] ≠ i

For a data message to be sent from one process p[i] to a neighboring process
p[g], the data message is provided with two fields as follows: data(route, x). Field
route stores, as defined above, the route to be traversed by the message. Field x
stores the position in array route that corresponds to the next process to receive the
message. In particular, when a data(route, x) message is sent from process p[i] to
process p[g], then route[x] = g.

Process p[i] in the source routing protocol can be defined as follows:

```
process p[i : 0..n-1]                      {n ≥ 2}

inp     N               : set {g|p[g] is a neighbor of p[i]},
        up              : array [N] of boolean,
        net             : array [0..n-1, 0..n-1] of boolean

var     route           : array [0..n] of 0..n-1,
        d               : 0..n-1,
        x               : 1..n-1

par     g               :       N

begin
        true  →
              d := any;
              FINDRT(in net, i, d, out route);
              if (route[0]≠i) →
                        {nonreachable dest} skip
              [] (route[0]=i) ∧ ~(route[1] in N) →
                        {arrived} skip
              [] (route[0]=i) ∧ (route[1] in N) ∧
                 ~up[route[1]] →
                        {nonreachable dest} skip
              [] (route[0]=i) ∧ (route[1] in N) ∧
                 up[route[1]] →
                        send data(route,1) to p[route[1]]
              fi
[]     rcv data(route,x) from p[g] →
              x := x+1;
              if ~(route[x] in N) →
                        {arrived} skip
```

```
        [] (route[x] in N) /\ ~up[route[x]] ->
                      {nonreachable} skip
        [] (route[x] in N) /\ up[route[x]] ->
                      send data(route,x) to p[route[x]]
      fi
end
```

Process p[i] has two actions. In the first action, p[i] generates a data message with an arbitrary destination d, computes the message route using procedure FIND-RT, and then routes the message according to the computed route. In the second action, p[i] receives a data message from a neighbor and then routes the message according to the route attached to the message.

In this protocol, if a process p[i] receives a data(route, x) message and detects that its neighbor p[route[x + 1]] is down, p[i] regards the message as nonreachable and discards it. This crude feature can be refined in two ways. First, p[i] can use array route in the received data message to compute the opposite route from p[route[x]] to p[route[0]]. Process p[i] can then send a down(i, route[x + 1]) message through this opposite route to inform each process on that route that at least one of the two channels between process p[i] and process p[route[x + 1]] is down. Second, p[i] can compute a new array route for the data message from p[i] to the ultimate destination of the message, then send the message according to this new route.

Procedure FINDRT used in the source routing protocol takes an undirected graph "net" and two nodes "i" and "d" in net and computes "route", a shortest path between nodes i and d in net. Procedure FINDRT is based on two ideas: partitioning the nodes in net into levels and defining a parent for each node in net. Level 0 consists of only one node, node i. Level 1 consists of every node whose shortest distance from node i is 1. In general, level x consists of every node whose shortest distance from node i is x, where $0 \leq x < n$.

Procedure FINDRT also computes a binary relation "parent" over the nodes in graph net as follows:

> Parent of node i = node i

For each node j, other than i,

> Parent of node j = node k such that k is a neighbor of j in net and level of
> k is one less than level of j

The computed relation parent defines a rooted spanning tree in graph net. In this tree, node i is the root, and the tree path between any node j and the root i is a shortest path between these two nodes in graph net.

Procedure FINDRT has three local arrays, named parent, dist, and done that have the following meanings for every node j in graph net:

parent[j]   Parent of node j

dist[j]   Shortest distance between j and i in net

done[j]   Is true iff parent[j] and dist[j] have already been computed

Procedure FINDRT in the source routing protocol is defined as follows:

```
procedure FINDRT(in net, i, d, out route)

local level     :     0..n,
      parent    :     array [0..n-1] of 0..n-1,
      dist      :     array [0..n-1] of 0..n-1,
      done      :     array [0..n-1] of boolean,
      j, k      :     0..n,
      r         :     0..n-1

begin
{Initialize array done to false}
j := 0; do j < n --> done[j], j := false, j+1 od;

{Define parent and dist of node i}
level, parent[i], dist[i], done[i] := 0, i, 0, true;

{Define parent and dist of every other node j}
level := 1;
do level < n -->
    j := 0;
    do j < n -->
            if done[j] -->
                    {Node j belongs to a previous level}
                    skip
            [] ~done[j] -->
                    {Node j belongs to current level?}
                    k := 0;
                    do k < n -->
                        if (done[k] /\ dist[k]=level-1 /\
                            net[j,k]) -->
                                parent[j], dist[j] :=
                                k, level;
                                done[j], k := true, n
                        [] ~(done[k] /\ dist[k]=level-1 /\
                            net[j,k]) --> k := k+1
                        fi
                    od
            fi; j := j+1
```

```
        od; level := level+1
od;

{Compute route}
if ~done[d] —>
        {There is no path between i and d}
        route[0] := i +ₙ 1
☐ done[d] —>
        {There is a path between i and d}
        r := dist[d];
        route[r], route[r+1] := d, d;
        do route[r] ≠ i —> route[r-1], r :=
                                parent[route[r]], r-1
        od
fi
end
```

13.6 ROUTING AS A BLACK BOX

So far in this chapter, each process p[i] has two inputs declared as follows.

```
inp  N   :  set { g |p[g] is a neighbor of p[i]},
     up  :  array [N] of boolean
```

Starting from the next section, we combine these two inputs into one input, declared as follows.

```
inp  N   :  set { g |p[g] is an up neighbor of p[i]}
```

In this declaration, a neighbor p[g] is an up neighbor of p[i] iff the two channels between p[i] and p[g] are both up.

This new set N in process p[i] may change over time by some underlying protocol that keeps track of the up neighbors of process p[i]. (One such protocol is discussed in Section 11.2.) We assume that the changes in N satisfy the two requirements of fault atomicity and rare occurrence, discussed in Section 11.1. In particular, we assume that N does not change during any action execution in the network and that N changes a finite number of times along any, possibly infinite, execution of the network.

Note that this set N in process p[i] can be used in defining enumerated and array variables in process p[i]. For example, an enumerated variable f can be declared as follows:

```
var  f    :      N
```

In this case, any change in N, that causes the current value of f to become outside N is accompanied by an implicit assignment of an arbitrary value from the new N to variable f.

Also starting from the next section, we assume that each process p[i] has a procedure called ROUTE that takes one input and returns one output as follows: ROUTE(in d, out f). The input of procedure ROUTE in process p[i] is index d of any process in the network other than p[i]. The output of ROUTE is index f of the best up neighbor, to which process p[i] can forward any message whose ultimate destination is p[d].

The different routing schemes discussed in this chapter can be regarded as different ways to implement the ROUTE procedures in network processes. Nevertheless, by assuming that network processes have ROUTE procedures, the specific details of how routing tables are structured and maintained are no longer needed in process definitions. In other words, the ROUTE procedure acts as a black box that provides routing yet hides the details of how routing is performed.

Note that the routing schemes discussed in this chapter can sometimes return an answer "destination d is nonreachable" for some destination d. Nevertheless, we assume for simplicity that no ROUTE procedure can return such an answer. As mentioned above, a ROUTE procedure always returns the most appropriate up neighbor g for every ultimate destination d.

In the next section and the next two chapters, network processes use ROUTE procedures to route their messages.

13.7 MOBILE ROUTING

A process in a network can have a number of tasks, and each task has a "home" process. There are two types of tasks: stationary and mobile. Stationary tasks remain in their home processes indefinitely, while mobile tasks can travel away from their home processes and visit other processes in the network. The routing protocols that we discussed so far in this chapter can be used for routing data messages to stationary tasks. Because stationary tasks remain in their home processes indefinitely, it is sufficient to route any data message, intended for some stationary task, to the home process of that task. In this section, we discuss how to augment each of the routing protocols in this chapter such that the augmented protocol can be used in routing data messages to mobile tasks.

Consider a network that consists of n processes p[i: 0 .. n − 1]. Each process p[i] is the home process for m mobile tasks with identifiers in the range 0 .. m − 1. Each task in the network is uniquely identified with a pair (d, tsk), where d is the index of the home process of the task and tsk is the unique identifier of the task in its home process p[d].

Because the tasks are mobile, they can travel between different processes in the network. Each process p[i] has an input boolean array called here that identifies all the tasks that are currently in process p[i]:

here[d, tsk] = true   iff   task (d, tsk) is currently in process p[i]

When a task (d, tsk) travels away from its home process p[d], the current process of the task is reported periodically to p[d], and process p[d] stores the information in a local array named prs:

prs[tsk] = e   iff   task (d, tsk) is currently in process p[e]

When a process generates a data(d, tsk) message, intended for task (d, tsk), the message is sent to the home process p[d] of task (d, tsk). When the message reaches p[d], array here in process p[d] is used to check whether task (d, tsk) is currently in process p[d]. If so, the message is delivered to the task. If not, process p[d] modifies the message to become of the form fwd(d, tsk, prs[tsk]), and the modified message is forwarded to process p[prs[tsk]]. When the fwd(d, tsk, prs[tsk]) message reaches p[prs[tsk]], array here in p[prs[tsk]] is used to check whether task (d, tsk) is currently in process p[prs[tsk]]. If so, the message is delivered to the task. If not, which indicates that the task has traveled to yet another process, the message is discarded.

Periodically, each process p[i] sends an upd(d, tsk, i) message to a process p[d] for every task (d, tsk) that is currently in p[i]. When process p[d] receives an upd(d, tsk, i) message, it assigns prs[tsk] the value i.

Process p[i] in the mobile routing protocol can be defined as follows:

```
proccess p[i : 0..n-1]

const m          {m is #tasks per process}

inp   N      :   set {g|p[g] is an up neighbor of p[i]},
      here   :   array [0..n-1, 0..m-1] of boolean

var   prs    :   array [0..m-1] of 0..n-1,
      d, e   :   0..n-1,
      tsk    :   0..m-1,
      f      :   N,
      flag   :   boolean

par   g      :   N
begin
      true   ->
               d, tsk := any, any;
               RTMSG

[]    rcv data(d, tsk) from p[g]      ->
               RTMSG
```

```
[]      rcv fwd(d, tsk, e) from p[g] ->
            if here[d, tsk] -> {arrived} skip
            [] ~here[d, tsk] /\ e = i ->
                        {nonreachable} skip
            [] ~here[d, tsk] /\ e ≠ i ->
                        ROUTE(in e, out f);
                        send fwd(d, tsk, e) to p[f]
            fi


[]      true -> SNDUPD


[]      rcv upd(d, tsk, e) from p[g] ->
            if d = i -> {arrived} prs[tsk] := e
            [] d ≠ i -> ROUTE(in d, out f);
                        send upd(d, tsk, e) to p[f]
            fi
end
```

Process p[i] has five actions. In the first action, p[i] generates a data message intended for task(d, tsk), and routes it to that task. In the second action, process p[i] receives a data(d, tsk) message, intended for task(d, tsk), and routes it to that task. In the third action, process p[i] receives a fwd(d, tsk, e) message and checks whether e = i. If so, then p[i] either delivers the message to task(d, tsk) provided that the task is in p[i] or discards the message otherwise. If e ≠ i, then p[i] routes the fwd(d, tsk, e) message to process p[e]. In the fourth action, p[i] sends an upd(d, tsk, i) message for each task(d, tsk) that is currently located at p[i] but d ≠ i. In the fifth action, process p[i] receives an upd(d, tsk, e) message and checks whether d = i. If so, then prs[tsk] is assigned the value e. Otherwise, p[i] routes the upd(d, tsk, e) message to p[d].

Statement RTMSG, in the first two actions of the mobile routing protocol, is defined as follows:

```
if here[d, tsk]                         -> {arrived} skip
[] ~here[d, tsk] /\ d ≠ i       ->
                ROUTE(in d, out f);
                send data(d, tsk) to p[f]
  ~here[d, tsk] /\ d = i ->
                e := prs[tsk];
                if e = i -> {nonreachable} skip
                [] e ≠ i ->
                        ROUTE(in e, out f);
                        send fwd(d, tsk, e) to p[f]
                fi
fi
```

In this statement, process p[i] routes a data(d, tsk) message. First, p[i] checks whether task(d, tsk) is in p[i]. If so, the message is delivered to the task. Otherwise, p[i] checks whether or not d = i. If d ≠ i, then p[i] is not the home process of task(d, tsk) and the generated data message is routed to the home process p[d] of task(d, tsk). If d = i, then p[i] is the home process of task(d, tsk) and the generated data message is changed to a fwd message and is routed to process p[prs[tsk]].

Statement SNDUPD in the fourth action of the mobile routing protocol can be defined as follows.

```
flag, d := true, 0;
do flag ->
      tsk := 0;
      do flag ->
            if ~here[d, tsk]          -> skip
            [] here[d, tsk] /\ d = i  -> prs[tsk] := i
            [] here[d, tsk] /\ d ≠ i  ->
                              ROUTE(in d, out f);
                              send upd(d, tsk, i) to p[f]
            fi;
            if tsk < m-1 -> tsk := tsk+1
            [] tsk = m-1 -> flag := false
            fi
      od;
      if d < n-1  ->      flag, d := true, d+1
      [] d = n-1  ->      skip
      fi
od
```

In this protocol, messages are routed using the ROUTE procedures discussed in Section 13.6. Recall that these procedures can be implemented using any of the routing protocols in Sections 13.1 through 13.5. Therefore, the net effect of our mobile routing protocol is to augment any of these protocols so that the resulting protocol can be used for routing data messages to mobile, instead of stationary, tasks.

13.8   ROUTING IN THE INTERNET

As mentioned in Sections 2.4 and 3.4, the Internet is organized into two levels: subnetworks and networks. In particular, each computer in the Internet is attached to at least one subnetwork, and subnetworks are grouped into networks. For the sake of routing, two more levels are added to this organization: autonomous systems and backbones. An autonomous system consists of one or more networks and all the computers and subnetworks that belong to these networks. A backbone is a collection of special routers that know every computer in the Internet.

It follows from this discussion that routing in the Internet is carried out at four different levels:

   i.   routing within a subnetwork,
  ii.   routing within an autonomous system,
 iii.   routing across autonomous systems, and
  iv.   routing within a backbone.

Next, we describe how routing is carried out at each of these four levels.

Routing within a Subnetwork

When the IP process in a computer c gets an IP message mg to route, it executes the following three steps:

   i.   The IP process in c extracts from the IP header of message mg the IP address
        of the message destination d.
  ii.   Then, the IP process in c checks whether or not c and d are connected to the
        same subnetwork. This is done by checking whether the two bit strings (IP.c
        AND M.c) and (IP.d AND M.c) are equal, where IP.c and IP.d are the IP ad-
        dresses of computers c and d, respectively, and M.c is the subnetwork mask
        of computer c. If these two bit strings are equal, then computers c and d are
        connected to the same subnetwork. Otherwise, c and d are not connected to
        the same subnetwork.
 iii.   If computers c and d are connected to the same subnetwork, then the IP
        process in c sends message mg directly to the IP process in computer d. If c
        and d are not connected to the same subnetwork, then the next step of the IP
        process in c depends on whether c is a host or a router. If c is a host, then the
        IP process in c sends message mg to the IP process of a predefined router,
        called the default router, on the same subnetwork as c. If c is a router, then
        the IP process in c looks up its routing table to determine the next router r to
        which message mg is to be forwarded. In this case, both c and r are connect-
        ed to the same subnetwork, and the IP process in c sends message mg direct-
        ly to the IP process in r.

Next, we discuss the structure and use of routing tables in routers as we discuss routing within autonomous systems.

Routing within an Autonomous System

Consider an autonomous system S and let r be any router in S. The IP process in r knows the following items:

   a.   the IP address and mask of every subnetwork in S,
   b.   a routing table that defines, for any subnetwork s in S, the best neighboring

router for reaching s starting from r, and

c. a routing table that defines, for any network t outside S, the best neighboring router for reaching t starting from r. Clearly, this routing table does not have an explicit entry for every network outside S (as there are so many of them). Rather, this routing table has explicit entries for networks that are located near S, and it has one entry for a default network. Any network outside S that does not have an explicit entry in the routing table is treated as the default network.

For convenience, we refer to the routing tables in b and c above as routing table B and routing table C, respectively.

When the IP process in router r receives a message whose destination has the IP address adr, the IP process in r determines whether or not the message destination is in S as follows:

i. If there is a subnetwork s in S satisfying the condition (IP.s = adr AND M.s), where IP.s and M.s are the IP address and mask of subnetwork s, respectively, then the message destination is connected to subnetwork s in S.

ii. If there is no such subnetwork s in S, then the message destination is outside S.

In case i, the IP process in r forwards the message to the best neighboring router for reaching subnetwork s, as indicated by routing table B in r. In case ii, the IP process in r forwards the message to the best neighboring router for reaching the network of the message destination, as indicated by routing table C in r. (Recall that the network of the message destination can be computed from the IP address of the message destination adr.)

So far, we have not discussed how the routing tables B and C are maintained or kept current. We delay discussing the maintenance of the C routing tables until we discuss routing across autonomous systems. In general, there are two methods for maintaining the B routing tables in an autonomous system: the distance vector method and the link state method. We discuss these two methods in some detail next.

In the distance vector method, each router periodically sends a copy of its B routing table to each neighboring router in the autonomous system. When a router receives the B routing table of a neighbor, it uses the received table to update its own routing table, as discussed in the distributed routing protocol in Section 13.3.

In the link state method, each router keeps track of the state (up or down) of each neighboring router. Periodically, every router broadcasts a list of its up neighbors to every router in the autonomous system. From these received lists, each router in the autonomous system can construct the topology of the autonomous system, as discussed in the protocol for maintaining global topology information in Section 11.3. The constructed topology of the autonomous system in each router can be used to construct the B routing table in that router.

A protocol for updating the B routing tables in an autonomous system based on the distance vector method is called the routing information protocol, or RIP for short. A protocol for updating the B routing tables in an autonomous system based on the link state method is called the open shortest path first protocol, or OSPF for short. Next, we briefly discuss RIP and OSPF in order.

In the case of RIP, each router in an autonomous system has a RIP process that operates on top of the UDP process in that router. Every 30 seconds, the RIP process in each router sends a response message to the RIP process in every neighboring router in the autonomous system. A response message that is sent by the RIP process in a router r contains pairs of the form (subnetwork.i, distance.i), where subnetwork.i is the IP address of some subnetwork in the autonomous system and distance.i is the smallest number of hops for reaching subnetwork.i from router r. The value of distance.i is in the range $1, \ldots, 16$. This value satisfies the following three conditions:

distance.i = 1   Indicates that subnetwork.i is connected to router r

distance.i < 16   Indicates that subnetwork.i is reachable from router r

distance.i = 16   Indicates that subnetwork.i is not reachable from router r

Because of this last condition, RIP cannot be used in an autonomous system where the smallest number of hops between any two routers is at least 16.

In case of OSPF, each router in an autonomous system has an OSPF process that operates on top of the IP process in that router. The routers in the autonomous system are partitioned into one primary area (also called backbone area) and zero or more secondary areas. Each router in the primary area is called a primary router and each router in a secondary area is called a secondary router. At least one router in each secondary area is connected to a primary router. Such a router is called a doorway for the secondary area.

The OSPF process in each primary router maintains a list of all subnetworks in the autonomous system. It also maintains the identity of the primary router that is closest to each subnetwork in the autonomous system. The OSPF process in each router in each (primary or secondary) area maintains the topology information of its area and the identity of the area doorways (if the area is secondary).

In order to route a message from a router r in some secondary area to a (host attached to a) subnetwork s in another secondary area within the same autonomous system, the following steps are executed:

  i. Router r recognizes that subnetwork s belongs to a different area and thus r forwards the message toward a doorway dr of its own area.

 ii. Doorway dr forwards the message to the primary router pr connected to it.

iii. The primary router pr forwards the message toward the primary router pr' that is closest to subnetwork s.

 iv. The primary router pr' forwards the message to a doorway dr' of the secondary area where subnetwork s is located.

  v. Doorway dr' forwards the message toward subnetwork s.

Routing across Autonomous Systems

Each autonomous system has one or more routers, called gateways, that are directly connected to other routers outside the autonomous system. These other routers are either gateways of neighboring autonomous systems or backbone routers. A gateway g in an autonomous system S exchanges routing information with the following routers:

a. every other gateway inside S,

b. every gateway outside S that is directly connected to g, and

c. every backbone router outside S that is directly connected to g.

Routers that exchange routing information with a gateway g are called the siblings of g. A protocol for exchanging routing information between sibling routers is called the border gateway protocol, or BGP for short.

Each gateway g has a BGP process that operates on top of the TCP process in g. Periodically, the BGP process in g, henceforth named process bg, exchanges routing information with the BGP process in every sibling of g. The exchanged routing information enables process bg to do the following:

i. Process bg maintains a list of all nearby networks, where a network is nearby if it is outside the autonomous system of g and it is reachable from g without going through any backbone router.

ii. Process bg maintains for each nearby network t a sequence of gateways for reaching t starting from g. In particular, for each nearby network t, process bg maintains a sequence $g.0; g.1; \ldots; g.k$ of gateways such that the following three conditions hold: $g.0$ is g, each two consecutive gateways $g.i$; $g.(i+1)$ in the sequence are siblings, and $g.k$ is a gateway for the autonomous system that has network t.

iii. Process bg maintains a sequence of gateways for reaching a backbone router starting from g.

Now, consider all the gateways of an autonomous system S. These gateways are siblings, and so each of them has the same set of nearby networks outside system S. For each nearby network t outside S, the gateways of S agree on which of them is the S-border for reaching network t. They also agree on which of them is the S-border for reaching the backbone.

Based on these agreements, each gateway g of S can construct its C routing table, mentioned above, as follows. For each nearby network, the C routing table of g directs each message whose ultimate destination is in network t toward the S-border for reaching t. For each other network t' outside S, the C routing table of g directs each message whose ultimate destination is in network t' toward the S-border for reaching the backbone.

Periodically, the C routing tables in the gateways of system S are propagated to the routers inside S so that each of them can update its own C routing table accordingly. Note that propagation of the C routing tables inside S can be achieved using either the distance vector method or the link state method mentioned above.

Routing within a Backbone

A backbone is a set of routers, called backbone routers, where each router B maintains the following information:

 i. Router B maintains a list of all networks in the Internet.
 ii. For every network t in the Internet, B maintains the identity of the backbone router, possibly B itself, that is closest to t.
 iii. For every network t whose closest backbone router is B, B maintains the identity of a gateway g such that B is directly connected to g and network t is reachable from g.

Note that the information in i and ii is maintained using a backbone routing protocol, whereas the information in iii is maintained using BGP mentioned above.

When a backbone router B receives a message to route from a gateway g that is directly connected to B, the following steps are executed:

 a. Router B examines the message destination (in the message IP header) to deduce network t where the message destination is located. Then, B forwards the message to the backbone router B' that is closest to t.
 b. Router B' determines the identity of a gateway g' such that B' is directly connected to g' and network t is reachable from g'. Then, B' forwards the message to gateway g'.
 c. The message is routed through the autonomous system that has gateway g'. Then, it is routed through several adjacent autonomous systems until it finally arrives at the autonomous system that has network t.

13.9 BIBLIOGRAPHICAL NOTES

Hierarchical routing is discussed in Kleinrock and Kamoun [1977, 1980] and Kamoun and Kleinrock [1979]. Random routing is discussed in Prosser [1962a,b]. Hot Potato routing and Backward learning routing are discussed in Baran [1962]. Distributed routing is discussed in Bellman [1957] and Ford and Fulkerson [1962]. Source routing, based on the shortest path algorithm in Dijkstra [1957], is discussed in Sunshine [1977]. Mobile routing is discussed in Perkins [1993] and Teraoka et al. [1993]. Reducing the time to route a message by adding information in the message header is discussed in Chandranmenon and Varghese [1996].

Surveys on routing protocols can be found in Schwartz and Stern [1980], Schwartz [1987], Maxemchuck and El-Zarki [1990], Bertsekas and Gallager [1992], Perlman [1993], and Steenstrup [1995].

Routing protocols in the ARPANET/Internet are discussed in McQuillan, Richer, and Rosen [1980], Rosen [1980], Khana and Zinky [1989], and Huitema [1995].

EXERCISES

1 (Hierarchical Routing Tables). Consider a network that has the following processes:

p[0, 0, 0], p[0, 0, 1], p[0, 0, 2]
p[0, 1, 0], p[0, 1, 1]
p[1, 0, 0], p[1, 0, 1], p[1, 0, 2]
p[1, 1, 0], p[1, 1, 1], p[1, 1, 2]

In this network, the following process pairs are neighbors:

(p[0, 0, 0], p[0, 0, 1])   (p[0, 0, 1], p[0, 0, 2])
(p[0, 0, 2], p[0, 0, 0])   (p[0, 0, 1], p[0, 1, 0])
(p[0, 0, 2], p[0, 1, 1])   (p[0, 1, 0], p[0, 1, 1])
(p[0, 1, 1], p[1, 0, 1])   (p[0, 1, 1], p[1, 1, 1])
(p[1, 0, 0], p[1, 0, 1])   (p[1, 0, 1], p[1, 0, 2])
(p[1, 0, 2], p[1, 0, 0])   (p[1, 0, 0], p[0, 0, 0])
(p[1, 0, 0], p[1, 1, 2])   (p[1, 0, 2], p[1, 1, 0])
(p[1, 1, 0], p[1, 1, 1])   (p[1, 1, 1], p[1, 1, 2])
(p[1, 1, 2], p[1, 1, 0])

Describe the hierarchical routing tables in each of the following processes: p[0, 1, 1], p[1, 0, 2], and p[1, 1, 1].

2 (Hierarchical Routing Tables). Solve exercise 1 when the number of layers in the network is reduced from three to two such that the name of each p[i, j, k] process becomes p[i, k'].

3 (Hierarchical Routing without Going Backward). Modify the hierarchical routing protocol in Section 13.1 such that when a process p[i, j, k] receives a data message from a process p[i', j', k'], p[i, j, k] does not forward that data message back to p[i', j', k'].

4 (Default Routing Tables). Consider a network that is partitioned into two districts. This network has the following processes:

p[0, 0], p[0, 1], p[0, 2], p[0, 3]
p[1, 0], p[1, 1], p[1, 2], p[1, 3], p[1, 4]

In this network, the following process pairs are neighbors:

(p[0, 0], p[0, 1])   (p[0, 1], p[0, 2])
(p[0, 2], p[0, 3])   (p[0, 3], p[0, 0])
(p[0, 2], p[1, 0])   (p[1, 0], p[1, 1])
(p[1, 1], p[1, 2])   (p[1, 1], p[1, 3])
(p[1, 1], p[1, 4])   (p[1, 2], p[1, 3])
(p[1, 3], p[1, 4])   (p[1, 4], p[1, 4])

Describe the default routing table(s) in each of the following processes: p[0, 0], p[0, 2], p[1, 0], and p[1, 3].

5   (Default Routing Tables). Consider a network p[i: $0 .. m - 1$, j: $0 .. n - 1$]. The processes p[i, 0], where $0 \le i < m$, are connected by a cycle such that each process p[i, 0] has two neighbors p[i $-_m$ 1, 0] and p[i $+_m$ 1, 0]. Also, the processes in each region i are connected by a cycle such that each process p[i, j] has two neighbors p[i, j $-_n$ 1] and p[i, j $+_n$ 1]. Assume that routing in this network is achieved using default routing. Define the routing table(s) in each process in the network.

6   (Default Routing Tables). Solve exercise 5 when the processes p[i, n − 1] where $0 \le i < m$, are also connected by a cycle such that each process p[i, n − 1] has two neighbors p[i $-_m$ 1, n − 1] and p[i $+_m$ 1, n − 1].

7   (Combined Hierarchical and Random Routing). Modify the hierarchical routing protocol in Section 13.1 as follows. If a process p[i, j, k] receives a data(x, y, z) message and detects that the best neighbor (as determined by the routing tables in p[i, j, k]) to forward the data(x, y, z) message to is down, then p[i, j, k] selects one of its up neighbors at random and forwards the data(x, y, z) message to it. In the modified protocol each data message carries the number of hops that the message can still make before being discarded for failing to reach its ultimate destination within a predefined number of hops.

8   (Combined Hierarchical and Random Routing). Modify the hierarchical routing protocol in Section 13.1 such that each routing table in a process p[i, j, k] lists for each ultimate destination exactly two neighbors of p[i, j, k]. In particular, the routing table in p[i, j, k] consists of the following three arrays.

```
inp       rgn    :       array [0..m-1, 0..1] of N,
          dstr   :       array [0..n-1, 0..1] of N,
          prs    :       array [0..r-1, 0..1] of N
```

When process p[i, j, k] receives a data(x, y, z) message, p[i, j, k] searches its three routing arrays for two neighbors that correspond to the ultimate destination (x, y, z). Then, process p[i, j, k] selects one of those neighbors at random and forwards the data message to that neighbor.

9   (Combined Hierarchical and Random Routing). Assume that the routing protocol in exercise 8 is used to route the data messages in the network in exercise 1.

Describe the routing tables in each of the following processes in that network: p[0, 1, 1], p[1, 0, 2], and p[1, 1, 1].

10 (Random Routing with Biased Probabilities). In the random routing protocol in Section 13.2, there are two neighbors rtb[d, 0] and rtb[d, 1] for each ultimate destination d such that a data(d, h) message is forwarded with equal probability to either of these two neighbors. Modify this protocol such that a data(d, h) message is forwarded with probability $2/3$ to neighbor rtb[d, 0], and is forwarded with probability $1/3$ to neighbor rtb[d, 1].

11 (Random Routing with Many Choices). Modify the random routing protocol in Section 13.2 to allow v neighbors rtb[d, 0], rtb[d, 1], . . . , rtb[d, v − 1] for each ultimate destination d such that a data(d, h) message is forwarded with equal probability to each of these neighbors.

12 (Random Routing without Going Backward). Modify the random routing protocol in Section 13.2 to ensure that a data message is never routed to the neighboring process from which it has just arrived.

13 (Hot Potato Routing).Design a routing protocol where each data(d, h) message received by a process p[i] is forwarded to a random up neighbor of p[i] other than the one form that process p[i] has received the data(d, h) message.

14 (Distributed Routing in Linear Networks). Consider a linear network where each process, except two, has two neighbors. The two exceptional processes are the left-most and right-most processes, and each of them has one neighbor. Simplify the distributed routing protocol in Section 13.3 to be used in this network.

15 (Distributed Routing in Star Networks). It is required to simplify the distributed routing protocol in Section 13.3 to be used in a star network p[i: 0 . . n − 1], in which each pair of processes p[0] and p[j], where $1 \leq j < n$, are neighbors. Note that in this network, the upd(c) messages are sent only from process p[0] to every process p[j], where $1 \leq j < n$. Design process p[i: 1 . . n − 1] in this network.

16 (Distributed Routing with Different Costs). The distributed routing protocol in Section 13.3 is based on the assumption that the cost of transmitting a data message from its source to its destination is measured by the number of hops that the message makes from the source to the destination. Modify this protocol assuming that each process p[i] has an input array cst, instead of its up array. Array cst in process p[i] is declared as follows.

```
inp        cst    :        array [N] of 1..cmax
```

In this declaration, N is the set of indices of the neighbors of process p[i], cmax is a constant, and for every g in N, cst[g] is the cost of transmitting a data message from process p[i] to neighbor p[g]. If cst[g] = cmax in p[i], then process p[i] should not try to send any data message to neighbor p[g].

17 (Distributed Routing with Second-Best Neighbors). In the distributed routing protocol in Section 13.3, the routing table indicates the best neighbor rtb[d] for each ultimate destination d. Modify this protocol such that the routing table indicates the second-best neighbor stb[d] as well as the best neighbor rtb[d] for each ultimate destination d. A data(d) message is forwarded to the second best neighbor stb[d] only if the best neighbor ngh[d] is down. (Hint: The messages exchanged in the modified protocol are the same as those in the original protocol.)

18 (Distributed Routing with Hop Counts). Modify the distributed routing protocol in Section 13.3 to allow each message to carry a hop count as discussed in the random routing protocol in Section 13.2.

19 (Distributed Routing with Network Diameter). Modify the distributed routing protocol in Section 13.3 assuming that each process p[i] in the network has a constant named diam whose value is the network diameter. (Hint: The network diameter is the maximum number of hops between any two processes in the network.)

20 (Distributed Routing with Added Information). Modify the distributed routing protocol in Section 13.3 such that each process p[i] includes a copy of its rtb array in every udp message that p[i] sends to its neighbors. When a process p[g] receives an upd(r, c) message from a neighboring process p[i], where r and c are copies of arrays rtb and cost in p[i], process p[g] uses both r and c in updating its own rtb and cost.

21 (Anycast Routing). Modify the distributed routing protocol in Section 13.3 as follows. Each process p[i] has an input array adr, declared as follows:

inp   adr   :   array [n..r-1] of boolean

In this declaration, r is a constant larger than n, and adr[k] = true iff process p[i] has an additional address k, beside its primary address i. A process can have several additional addresses, and several processes can have the same additional address. If the ultimate destination of a data message is an additional address k, $n \leq k < r$, then the message is to be delivered to any process that has the additional address k, if such a process can be reached in the network.

22 (Combined Hierarchical and Distributed Routing). Design a routing protocol that combines both the hierarchical routing protocol in Section 13.1 and the distributed routing protocol in Section 13.3. In particular, each process p[i, j, k] in this protocol has a hierarchical routing table that consists of three arrays, as discussed in Section 13.1. However, each entry in the routing table is aug-

mented with a cost, as discussed in Section 13.3. Moreover, the routing tables
are updated as discussed in Section 13.3.

23   (General Backward Learning Routing). In the backward learning routing protocol in Section 13.4, each data message is of the form data(src, h, dst). When
a process p[i] receives a data(src, h, dst) message, p[i] determines wether or
not to update the src entry in its routing table, that is, whether or not to update
the elements rtb[src], cost[src], and valid[src]. Modify this protocol such that
each data message becomes of the form data(rt, h, dst), where rt is an array of
process indices. When a process p[i] receives a data(rt, h, dst) message, array rt
contains the indices of all processes that the message has gone through before
reaching p[i]. In this case, p[i] determines for each k, $0 \leq k < h$, whether or not
to update the rt[k] entry in its routing table, that is, whether or not to update the
elements rtb[rt[k]], cost[rt[k]], and valid[rt[k]].

24   (Source Routing with Retries). In the source routing protocol in Section 13.5,
if a process p[i] receives a data(route, x) message and detects that its neighbor
p[route[x + 1]] is down, p[i] regards the message as nonreachable and discards
it. Modify this protocol such that if p[i] receives a data(route, x) message and
detects that its neighbor p[route[x + 1]] is down, p[i] computes a new array
route for the data message from p[i] to the ultimate destination of the message,
and then sends the message according to this new route.

25   (Source Routing with Down Messages). In the source routing protocol in Section 13.5, if a process p[i] receives a data(route, x) message and detects that its
neighbor p[route[x + 1]] is down, p[i] regards the message as nonreachable and
discards it. Modify this protocol such that if p[i] receives a data(route, x) message and detects that its neighbor p[route[x + 1]] is down, then p[i] uses array
route in the received data message to compute the opposite route from
p[route[x]] to p[route[0]] and sends a down(i, route[x + 1]) message through
this opposite route to inform each process on that route that one of the two
channels between process p[i] and process p[route[x + 1]] is down.

26   (Source Routing with Acknowledgments). Modify the source routing protocol
in Section 13.5 as follows. When a data(route, x) message reaches its ultimate
destination, the ultimate destination sends an ack(rroute, y) message, where
rroute is an array that contains the same indices in array route but in the reverse
order. The ack(rroute, y) message is routed in the same manner as any data
message, and so it follows the reverse route of the data(route, x) message, until
it reaches the original source of the data message.

27   (Mobile Routing with Repeated Forwarding). In the mobile routing protocol in
Section 13.7, a data message is first routed to the home process of the destination task; then it is forwarded to process p, where the task currently resides.
The message is finally discarded if it reaches process p and the destination task
is no longer in p. Modify this protocol such that if a forwarded message reach-

es a process where the destination task has resided but has since left, the message is returned to the home process of the task so that it can be forwarded to the new process where the task resides. (Hint: The number of times a data message is forwarded to a process where the destination task has resided but has since left should be bounded by some constant.)

28   (Mobile Routing without Forwarding). Modify the mobile routing protocol in Section 13.7 such that when a data message is first routed to the home process of the destination task, the home process does not forward the message to process p[i,] where the task is currently residing. Rather, the home process returns the address i of process p[i] to the original source of the message and the source resends the message directly to p[i].

29   (Routing in a Ring Network). Consider a ring network where each process has two neighbors. Design a routing protocol for this network.

30   (Routing in a Linear Network). Consider a linear network where each process, other than the left-most and the right-most, has two neighbors: a left neighbor and a right neighbor. Design a routing protocol for this network.

31   (Routing in a Star Network). Consider a star network that consists of the $n + 1$ processes p[i: $0 \ldots n - 1$] and q. In this network, for each i, $0 \leq i < n$, the two processes p[i] and q are neighbors. Design a routing protocol for this network.

32   (Routing in a Tree Network). Consider a tree network p[i: $0, \ldots, n - 1$] whose topology has no cycles. Design a routing protocol for this network.

33   (Routing in a Torus Network). Consider a torus network p[i: $0 \ldots m - 1$, j: $0 \ldots n - 1$] where each two processes p[i, j] and p[i, j $+_n$ 1] are neighbors and each two processes p[i, j] and p[i $+_m$ 1, j] are neighbors. Design a routing protocol for this network.

34   (Routing in a Mesh Network). Consider a mesh network p[i: $0 \ldots m - 1$, j: $0 \ldots n - 1$] where for each j, j $< n - 1$, the two processes p[i, j] and p[i, j $+_n$ 1] are neighbors, and for each i, i $< m$-1, the two processes p[i, j] and p[i $+_m$ 1, j] are neighbors. Design a routing protocol for this network.

35   (Routing in a Two-Layered Network). Consider a network p[i: $0 \ldots m - 1$, j: $0 \ldots n - 1$]. For each i, the processes p[i, j] constitute a subnetwork whose topology is fully connected. For each j, the processes p[0, j] constitute a subnetwork whose topology is a ring. Design a routing protocol for this network.

36   (Routing in a Hypercube). Consider a hypercube network p[i: $0 \ldots (2^k - 1)$]. Assume that in this network, each process p[i] can execute a statement of the form b := BNRY(j) to compute the binary representation of any value j in the range $0, \ldots, (2^k - 1)$ and store the result in a bit array b declared as follows:

```
var      b      :      array [0..k-1] of 0..1
```

Note that in this network, any two processes p[i] and p[j] are neighbors iff BNRY(i) and BNRY(j) differ only in one bit. Design a routing protocol for this network.

37 (Acknowledging Message Discarding). Consider a routing protocol where each data message has two fields s and d, where s denotes the index of the message source and d is the index of message destination. This protocol can be defined as follows:

```
process p[i : 0..n-1]
inp   N     : set {g|p[g] is a neighbor of p[i]},
      up    : array [N] of boolean,
      rtb   : array [0..n-1] of N
var   s, d  : 0..n-1
par   g     : N
begin
        true        ->      s, d := i, any; RTMSG
[]   rcv data(s, d) from p[g]      ->        RTMSG
end
```

Statement RTMSG in this protocol is defined as follows.

```
if d = i                    ->   {arrived} skip
[]  d ≠ i ∧ ~up[rtb[d]] ->   {unreachable} skip
[]  d ≠ i ∧ up[rtb[d]]  ->
                            send data(s, d) to p[rtb[d]]
fi
```

Modify this protocol such that if a data(s, d) message is discarded by a process p[i], because the message destination is unreachable from p[i], p[i] generates an error-reporting err(i, s) and sends it toward the source process of the discarded message. Ensure that in the modified protocol discarding an error-reporting message, because its destination is unreachable, does not generate another error-reporitng message.

38 (Acknowledging Message Discarding). Extend the protocol in exercise 37 as follows. Each data and error-reporting message has a third field h whose value is the maximum number of remaining hops that can be made by the message. When a message makes one hop, the value of its h field is decremented by 1. If a process p[i] receives a message whose h = 1 and detects that the ultimate destination of the message is not a neighbor of p[i], then p[i] discards the message. If the discarded message is a data message, then p[i] also generates an error-reporting message and sends it toward the source process of the discarded data message.

39 (Routing Cache). Consider the following routing protocol.

```
process p[i : 0..n-1]
inp N    :        set {g|p[g] is a neighbor of p[i]},
    up   :        array [N] of boolean,
    rtb  :        array [0..n-1] of N
var d    :        0..n-1
par g    :        N
begin
            true                        ->      d := i; RTMSG
[]          rcv data(d) from p[g]       ->      RTMSG
end
```

Statement RTMSG in this protocol is defined as follows.

```
if d = i                           ->      {arrived} skip
[] d ≠ i ∧ ~up[rtb[d]]             ->      {unreachable} skip
[] d ≠ i ∧ up[rtb[d]]             ->
                             send data(d) to p[rtb[d]]
fi
```

Modify this routing protocol as follows:

a   Each process p[i] has a routing cache that consists of the following three
    variable arrays:

```
const       c        {cache size}
var         chc   :        array [0..c-1] of 0..n-1,
            crtb  :        array [0..c-1] of N,
            age   :        array [0..c-1] of integer
```

b   To route a data(d) message, process p[i] searches its chc array for an ele-
    ment chc[x] whose value equals d. If p[i] finds such an element, then
    p[i] sends the data(d) message to neighbor p[crtb[x]] provided that
    up[crtb[x]] is true.

c   If p[i] does not find such an element, then p[i] routes the data(d) mes-
    sage using its regular routing table rtb as before and then updates its
    three cache arrays chc, crtb, and age.

40   (Routing Cache). Modify the routing protocol in exercise 39 as follows. Each
    data message has a boolean field f whose value is assigned by the source
    process that generates the message as follows.

$$f = \begin{cases} \text{false} & \text{if the message does not belong to a message flow} \\ \text{true} & \text{if the message does belong to a message flow} \end{cases}$$

If f in a data message is false, then the message is routed using the regular routing table rtb in each process reached by the message. If f in a data message is true, then the message is routed using the routing cache (namely the three arrays chc, crtb, and age) as in the protocol of exercise 39.

41 (Wave Routing). Consider a routing protocol in a network p[i: 0 .. n − 1]. The routing table in each process p[i] consists of the following two arrays:

```
var        rtb     :       array {0..n-1} of N,
           seq     :       array [0..n-1] of integer
```

Each process p[i] periodically increments its element seq[i] by 1 then sends an upd(i, seq[i]) message to each of its up neighbors. When a process p[j] receives an upd(i, s) message from a neighbor p[g], it first checks whether i = j. If i = j, then p[j] discards the message. Otherwise, p[j] compares the sequence number s in the message with element seq[i] in p[j]. If s ≤ seq[i], process p[j] discards the message. Otherwise, p[j] updates its routing table as follows.

$$rtb[i], seq[i] := g, s$$

Then, process p[j] forwards the received upd(i, s) message to each of its up neighbors, other than p[g]. Define process p[i] in this protocol.

42 (Loose Source Routing). Consider a routing protocol in a network p[i: 0, . . . , n − 1]. In this protocol, each message is of the form data(dst, x), where dst is an array of the destinations to be visited by the message and x is the position in array dst of the next destination to be visited by the message. The two variables dst and x are declared as follows:

```
const   v
var     dst   :   array [0..v-1] of 0..n, {dst[0] ≠ n}
        x     :   0..v-1
```

When a process p[i] generates or receives a data(dst, x) message, where x = 0 when the message is generated, process p[i] routes the message as follows:

```
if dst[x] ≠ i  —>
   p[i] routes data(dst, x) towards p[dst[x]]
☐ dst[x] = i ∧ (x ≠ v-1 ∧ dst[x+1] ≠ n)        —>
   p[i] routes data(dst, x+1) towards p[dst[x+1]]
☐ dst[x] = i ∧ (x = v-1 ∨ dst[x+1] = n)         —>
   p[i] is the final destination of data(dst, x)
fi
```

Design process p[i] in this protocol. (Hint: Make use of black box routing, discussed in Section 13.6.)

43 (Distributed Routing in Ring Networks). Simplify the distributed routing protocol in Section 13.3 to be used in a ring network p[i: 0 .. n − 1], in which each process has a left neighbor and a right neighbor.

44 (Distributed Routing with Constant Reach). Modify the distributed routing protocol in Section 13.3 to ensure that no data message travels more than 15 hops from its source to its destination. Thus, if the smallest number of hops between any two processes in the network is 16 or more, then each of the two processes is considered unreachable from the other process.

45 (Source Routing to Anycast Addresses). It is required to modify the source routing protocol in Section 13.5 as follows. Each process p[i] has an input array adr, declared as follows:

inp adr :   **array** [0..n-1, n..r-1] **of boolean**

In this declaration, r is a constant larger than n, and adr[j, k] = true iff process p[j] has an additional address k beside its primary address j. The input adr arrays in all processes are identical. A process can have several additional addresses, and several processes can have the same additional address. If the ultimate destination of a data message is an additional address k, $n \leq k < r$, then the message is to be delivered to any process that has the additional address k if such a process can be reached in the network. Design procedure FINDRT in the modified protocol:

procedure FINDRT(**in** net, adr, i, d, **out** route)

where i is in the range 0 .. n − 1, and d is in the range 0 .. r − 1.

46 (Mobile Routing with Explicit Task Movement). It is required to modify the mobile routing protocol in Section 13.7 such that array here becomes a variable (rather than an input) and the movements of tasks between the network processes become explicit (rather than implicit). This modification can be accomplished by adding two actions to each process in the protocol: one action for sending a task and one action for receiving a task. Define these two additional actions.

CHAPTER 14

SWITCHING

In general, a switch is a device that forwards messages from a set of sources to a set of destinations. Such a device usually consists of a number of switching elements. A message from a source is first sent to a switching element and then it is forwarded from one switching element to the next until the message finally arrives at its destination. The function of a switch is to allow the sent messages to compete for, allocate, and then release switching elements as the messages travel from their sources to their destinations.

In a network of processes, a message is sent from its source process to an intermediate process. The intermediate process then forwards the message to a second intermediate process, and so on. This continues until the message finally arrives at its destination process. In that respect, a network of processes can be regarded as a switch where each process acts as a source, as a switching element, and as a destination. A process is a source for all the messages originated at it. It is a switching element for all the messages passing through it. It is a destination for all the messages destined to it.

The protocols used by messages to compete for, allocate, and then release intermediate processes, as the messages travel from their source processes to their destination processes, are called switching protocols. In other words, the function of a switching protocol is the allocation of local buffers and execution times of intermediate processes.

Switching protocols can be classified into two classes: circuit and datagram protocols. Circuit switching protocols are based on allocating all the needed resources beforehand, whereas datagram switching protocols are based on allocating each resource when needed. For example, the telephone system is based on circuit switching because all the resources needed for a call are allocated before the call starts. By comparison, the mail system is based on datagram switching because each resource needed to deliver a mail item is allocated only when needed.

Circuit switching protocols are useful for sending a relatively large number of data messages from a source process to destination process in a network. In this case, the cost of maintaining a circuit for a long time divided by the large number of data messages to be sent over the circuit yields a reasonable cost per message. By contrast, datagram switching protocols are useful for sending a small number of data messages from a source process to a destination process. In Section 14.1, we discuss circuit switching protocols, and in Section 14.2, we discuss datagram switching protocols.

The switching protocols discussed in Sections 14.1 and 14.2 are based on the assumption that the underlying network topology is fixed over time. In particular, the set of up neighbors of every process in the network is assumed to be fixed. In Section 14.3, we discuss how these protocols can be modified to tolerate changes in the network topology. Switching in the Internet is discussed in Section 14.4.

14.1 CIRCUIT SWITCHING

In a circuit switching protocol, before a source process sends a sequence of data messages to a destination process, the source process obtains a permission to do so. The permission is obtained from the destination process and from every intermediate process that is to be visited by the data messages in their way from the source process to the destination process. To obtain this permission, the source process sends a crqst message to the first intermediate process. When an intermediate process receives a crqst message, it either rejects the request and sends back a drply message or accepts the request and forwards the crqst message to the next intermediate or destination process. Next, we discuss each of these two outcomes in turn.
In the case of rejection, the crqst message is sent forward from one process to the next until it reaches a process that replies to the crqst message by sending back a drply message. The drply message follows the reverse path of the crqst message until it reaches the source process.

In the case of acceptance, the crqst message is sent forward from one process to the next until it reaches the destination process, which replies to it by sending back a crply message. The crply message follows the reverse path of the crqst message until it reaches the source process. When the source process receives the crply message, it starts to send a sequence of data messages, one after the other. Each data message follows the same path of the crqst message, until it arrives at the destination process. Finally, the source process sends a drqst message which follows the same path of the crqst message until it arrives at the destination process.

Figure 14.1 shows the message exchange in the circuit switching protocol. Note that an intermediate process either replies to a received crqst message with a drply message or forwards the crqst message to the next process. The destination process, on the other hand, replies to a crqst message with either a drply message or a crply message.

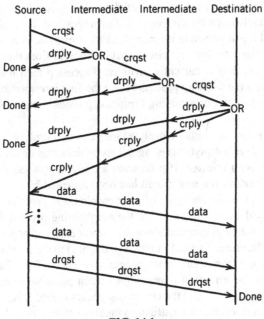

FIG. 14.1

The fact that a source process has sent a crqst message and later received a crply message can be expressed by saying that a "circuit" has been established from the source process to the destination process. It is instructive to think of the established circuit as a directed path that starts at the source process, passes through a sequence of intermediate processes, and ends at the destination process. Each process on that path, whether source, intermediate, or destination, is said to be involved in the established circuit.

A process that is involved in a circuit is required to perform certain tasks for that circuit. For instance, the process is required to receive all data messages that are sent along the circuit and forward them along the circuit. In order that a process can perform the required tasks for all the circuits in which it is involved, there is an upper bound v on the number of circuits in which the process can be involved at the same time. To keep track of the different circuits in which a process is involved at the same time, the process identifies each of the circuits with a unique identifier in the range $0 .. v - 1$. The circuit identifier in a process is local to that process. Thus, different processes involved in the same circuit may identify the circuit with different identifiers.

Next, we describe in more detail the activities of a process in establishing, using, and disconnecting a circuit. Because a process involved in a circuit can be a source process, an intermediate process, or a destination process for that circuit, our description consists of three parts. First, we describe the activities of a source process. Then, we describe the activities of an intermediate process. Finally, we describe the activities of a destination process.

For a process p to send a sequence of data messages to another process dst, process p first establishes a circuit from itself to process dst. To establish such a circuit, p waits until it is involved in no more than $v - 1$ circuits. When this happens, p chooses an identifier x for the new circuit that is different from the identifiers of all other circuits in which p is currently involved. Process p then invokes procedure ROUTE to choose a neighboring process f to be the first intermediate process in the circuit from p to dst. After determining f, process p sends a crqst(dst, x) message to process f.

Later process p receives either a drply(x) message or a crply(x, y) message from process f. If p receives a drply(x) message, it recognizes that its request to establish a new circuit has been rejected. If p receives a crply(x, y) message, it recognizes that its request to establish a new circuit has been accepted by every process along the circuit and that y is the identifier of the new circuit in process f. In this case, p sends a sequence of data(y) messages to the neighboring process f. Each of these data(y) messages will be forwarded along the circuit until it reaches the destination process dst. Finally, process p sends a message drqst(y) to the neighboring process f to remove the piece of the circuit from process p to process f. As the drqst message is forwarded along the circuit, it removes the circuit piece by piece until the drqst message reaches process dst and the circuit disappears completely.

When a process q receives a crqst(dst, x) message from a neighboring process f, where dst is different from q, process q recognizes that it is an intermediate process on a new circuit being established. Process q either rejects the circuit or accepts it. It rejects the circuit by sending back a drply(x) message to process f. Process q can accept the circuit only if it is currently involved in no more than v-1 circuits. It accepts the circuit as follows. First, q chooses an identifier y for the circuit that is different from the identifiers of all other circuits in which q is currently involved. Second, q invokes procedure ROUTE to select a neighboring process g to be the next process on the new circuit. Third, q sends a crqst(dst, y) message to process g, then waits to receive either a drply(y) message or a crply(y, z) message from process g. If q receives a drply(y) message from process g, process q recognizes that the circuit has been rejected and forwards a drply(x) message to process f. If q receives a crply(y, z) message from g, process q recognizes that the circuit has been accepted and sends a crply(x, y) message to process f. Later process q receives a sequence of data(y) messages from f and forwards them as data(z) messages to neighbor g. Finally, q receives a drqst(y) message from neighbor f, and then forwards a drqst(z) message to neighbor g indicating that the circuit has terminated.

After q receives a crply(y, z) message from g (indicating that the circuit has been established) and until q receives a drqst(y) from f (indicating that the circuit has been removed), process q maintains the five-tuple

$$(f, x; y; g, z)$$

In this tuple:

f   Identifies the process before q in the circuit
x   Is the circuit identifier in process f

y   Is the circuit identifier in process q
g   Is the process after q in the circuit
z   Is the circuit identifier in process g

When process dst receives a crqst(dst, x) message from a neighboring process g, process dst recognizes that it is the destination process for a new circuit being established. Process dst either rejects the circuit or accepts it. It rejects the circuit by sending back a drply(x) message to neighbor g. Process dst can accept the circuit only if dst is currently involved in no more than v − 1 circuits. It accepts the circuit as follows. First, dst chooses an identifier y for the circuit that is different from the identifiers of all other circuits in which dst is currently involved. Second, dst sends back a crply(x, y) message to neighbor g. Later process dst receives a sequence of data(y) messages from g. Then, finally, dst receives a drqst(y) message from neighbor g indicating that the circuit has terminated.

For convenience, Figure 14.2 shows a time chart for establishing, using, and disconnecting a circuit that involves a source process p, one intermediate processes g, and a destination process dst.

Consider a circuit switching protocol that consists of n processes p[i: 0..n − 1]. Each process p[i] has four variable arrays: ppr, npr, pid, and nid. Arrays ppr and npr in process p[i] are declared as follows.

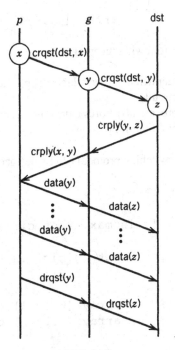

FIG. 14.2

```
var    ppr, npr    :      array [0..v-1] of NU{i}
```

Roughly, array ppr stores the previous process in the circuit and npr stores the next process in the circuit. Specifically, these arrays have the following meaning:

ppr[y] =   f   iff   p[f] precedes p[i] in circuit y of p[i]. (If ppr[y] = i, then
                               p[i] is the source process of the circuit.)
npr[y] =   g   iff   p[g] follows p[i] in circuit y of p[i]. (If npr[y] = i, then
                               p[i] is the destination process of the circuit.)

Arrays pid and nid are declared as follows.

```
var    pid, nid    :      array [0..v-1] of 0..v-1
```

Roughly, array pid stores the circuit identifier in the previous process in the circuit and nid stores the circuit identifier in the next process in the circuit. Specifically, these arrays have the following meanings:

pid[y] = x   iff   circuit y of p[i] is the same as circuit x in process p[ppr[y]].
nid[y] = z   iff   circuit y of p[i] is the same as circuit z in process p[npr[y]].

In addition to these four arrays, each process p[i] has two variable arrays named avail and str. These arrays are declared as follows.

```
var    avail, str :      array [0..v-1] of boolean
```

These two arrays have the following meaning:

avail[y] = true   iff   identifier y is available in p[i] to be assigned to a new
                          circuit.
str[y] = true   iff   process p[i] stores a data message to be forwarded, along
                          circuit y of p[i].

Process p[i] in the circuit switching protocol can be defined as follows.

```
process p[i : 0..n-1]

const v                {v is max. # of circuits in p[i]}

inp  N             :      set {g|p[g] is an up neighbor
                               of p[i]}

var    ppr, npr    :      array [0..v-1] of NU{i} ,
       pid, nid    :      array [0..v-1] of 0..v-1 ,
```

```
        avail, str  :      array [0..v-1] of boolean ,
        dst         :      0..n-1 ,
        f           :      N∪{i},
        x, y, z     :      0..v-1

par     g           :      N,
        w           :      0..v-1

begin
        avail[w] —>
              dst := any ;
              if dst = i  —>      skip
              ▯ dst - i  —>
                  ROUTE (in dst, out f);
                  avail[w], ppr[w], npr[w] := false, i, f;
                  send crqst(dst, w) to p[f]
              fi

▯       rcv crqst(dst,x) from p[g] —>
              if true —>   send drply(x) to p[g]
              ▯ true —>   y := 0;
                    do ~avail[y] ∧ y<v-1 —> y:= y+1
                    od;
                    if ~avail[y] —> send drply(x) to p[g]
                    ▯ avail[y] —>
                          avail[y] := false ;
                          if dst=i —>
                                  f := i;
                                  send crply(x, y) to p[g]
                          ▯ dst-i —>
                                  ROUTE(in dst, out f);
                                  send crqst(dst,y) to p[f]
                          fi;
                          ppr[y], npr[y], pid[y] :=
                          g, f, x
                    fi
              fi

▯       rcv drply(y) from p[g] —>
              f, x := ppr[y], pid[y];
              avail[y] := true;
              if f=i —>   skip
              ▯ f≠i —>   send drply(x) to p[f]
              fi
```

```
[]    rcv crply(y, z) from p[g] ->
            f, x, nid[y] := ppr[y], pid[y], z;
            if  f=i  ->   str[y] := true
            []  f≠i  ->   send crply(x, y) to p[f]
            fi


[]    ppr[w] = i ∧ str[w] ->
            if true ->   send data(nid[w]) to p[npr[w]]
            [] true ->   avail[w], str[w] :=
                         true, false;
                         send drqst(nid[w]) to p[npr[w]]
            fi


[]    rcv data(y) from p[g] ->
            f := npr[y];
            if f=i -> {arrived} skip
            [] f≠i ∧ ~str[y] -> {store data}
                                     str[y] := true
            [] f≠i ∧  str[y] -> {discard data} skip
            fi


[]    ppr[w] ≠ i ∧ str[w] ->
            str[w] := false ;
            send data(nid[w]) to p[npr[w]]


[]    rcv drqst(y) from p[g] ->
            avail[y], f, z := true, npr[y], nid[y];
            if f=i ->    str[y] := false
            [] f≠i ∧ ~str[y] ->
                 send drqst(z) to p[f]
            [] f≠i ∧  str[y] ->
                 str[y] := false;
                 send data(z) to p[f];
                 send drqst(z) to p[f]
            fi
end
```

Process p[i] has eight actions. In the first action, p[i] detects that it has an available circuit identifier w and starts the procedure for establishing a new circuit with identifier w.

In the second action, process p[i] receives a crqst for some circuit and either decides to reject the circuit (especially if p[i] is currently involved in v circuits) or accepts it. Process p[i] rejects the circuit by sending a drqst message backward along the circuit. It accepts the circuit either by sending a crply message backward along the circuit (if p[i] is the destination process for the circuit) or by sending a crqst message forward (if p[i] is not the destination process for the circuit).

In the third action, process p[i] receives a drply message along some circuit, disconnects its part of the circuit, and propagates the drply message backward along the circuit unless p[i] is the source process for the circuit.

In the fourth action, process p[i] receives a crply message along some circuit and propagates the message backward along the circuit unless p[i] is the source process for the circuit.

In the fifth action, process p[i] detects that some circuit for which p[i] is the source process, is established. In this case, p[i] sends either the next data message or a drqst message along the circuit.

In the sixth action, process p[i] receives a data message along some circuit. If p[i] is the destination process of that circuit, then the message is accepted. If p[i] is not the destination process of that circuit and p[i] currently stores a previous data message from the same circuit, then p[i] discards the received data message. Otherwise, p[i] stores the received data message.

In the seventh action, process p[i] detects that it is storing a data message that was received earlier along some circuit, and so it forwards the message along the same circuit.

In the eighth action process p[i] receives a drqst message along some circuit and disconnects its part of the circuit. Moreover, if p[i] is not the destination process for the circuit, then p[i] forwards the drqst message along the circuit behind any data message that happens to be stored in p[i] when the drqst message is received.

14.2 DATAGRAM SWITCHING

In a datagram switching protocol, a process p[i] sends a data message intended for a destination process p[d] in two steps. First, p[i] invokes procedure ROUTE to determine a neighboring process p[g] to which p[i] forwards the message. Second, p[i] attaches index d of the destination process to the data message and then sends the data(d) message to neighbor p[g]. Process p[g] repeats the same two steps and forwards the data(d) message to a neighbor p[h], and the cycle repeats. Forwarding of the data(d) message continues until the message finally arrives at its destination process p[d].

What makes this protocol a little complicated is the fact that each process has a limited number v of local buffers to hold the received data messages until they are forwarded to neighboring processes. Therefore, before process p[i] forwards a data(d) message to a neighbor p[g], p[i] asks for permission to do so by sending a rqst message to p[g]. After receiving the rqst message from p[i], process p[g] waits until it has an available buffer to hold the data message and then sends a prmt message to p[i]. When p[i] receives the prmt message from p[g], it sends the data(d) message to p[g].

The three messages rqst, prmt, and data(d) have fields whose values range over 0

.. v − 1. Thus, they are of the form rqst(x), prmt(x, y), and data(d, y), respectively, where x and y range over 0 .. v − 1. Process p[i] sends a rqst(x) message to p[g] asking for permission to send to p[g] the data message that is currently in buffer x of p[i]. Process p[g] replies with a prmt(x, y) message to p[i]. This message gives p[i] permission to send the data message in its buffer x to p[g] and promises that this message will be stored in buffer y of p[g]. As a result, process p[i] sends a data(d, y) message to p[g]. This message ends up in buffer y of process p[g].

Each process p[i] has three variable arrays: avail, dst, and rqstd. They are declared as follows.

```
var avail      :      array [0..v-1] of boolean ,
    dst        :      array [0..v-1] of 0..n-1 ,
    rqstd      :      array [N, 0..v-1] of boolean
```

In these declarations, N is the input set of up neighbors of process p[i]. As mentioned in Section 14.1, this protocol is designed under the assumption that the topology of the underlying network is fixed over time. Therefore, N is fixed over time. These arrays have the following meanings:

avail[x]   = true   iff   buffer x in p[i] is available for storing new data message

dst[x]   = the index of destination process for data message, if any, in buffer x of p[i]

rqstd[g, x] = true   iff   p[g] has sent rqst(x) message to p[i] and p[i] has not yet sent back prmt(x, y) to p[g].

Process p[i] in the datagram switching protocol can be defined as follows.

```
process p[i : 0..n-1]

const v                {v is # of buffers in p[i]}

inp  N     :      set {g|p[g] is an up neighbor of p[i]}
var  avail :      array [0..v-1] of boolean ,
     dst   :      array [0..v-1] of 0..n-1 ,
     rqstd :      array [N, 0..v-1] of boolean ,
     d     :      0..n-1 ,
     f     :      N ,
     x, y  :      0..v-1

par  g     :      N,
     z     :      0..v-1

begin
```

```
            avail[z]    ─>
                    d:= any;
                    if d=i ─>      skip
                    []  d-i ─>     avail[z], dst[z] := false, d;
                                   ROUTE(in d, out f);
                                   send rqst(z) to p[f]
                    fi
    []      rcv rqst(x) from p[g] ─>
                    y := 0;
                    do ~avail[y] ∧ y<v-1 ─> y := y+v1 od;
                    if ~avail[y] ─>    rqstd[g,x] := true
                    [] avail[y] ─>
                            avail[y] := false;
                            send prmt(x,y) to p[g]
                    fi

    []      rcv prmt(x,y) from p[g] ─>
                    send data(dst[x],y) to p [g];
                    SEARCH(in rqstd, out f,y);
                    if ~rqstd[f,y] ─> avail[x] := true
                    [] rqstd[f,y] ─>
                                rqstd[f,y] := false;
                                send prmt(y,x) to p[f]
                    fi

    []      rcv data(d,y) from p[g] ─>
                    if d=i ─>
                            {arrived}
                            SEARCH(in rqstd, out f,x);
                            if ~rqstd[f,x] ─> avail[y] := true
                            [] rqstd[f,x] ─>
                                    rqstd[f,x] := false;
                                    send prmt(x,y) to p[f]
                            fi
                    [] d≠i ─>
                            dst[y] := d;
                            ROUTE(in d, out f);
                            send rqst(y) to p[f]
                    fi
end
```

Process p[i] has four actions. In the first action, process p[i] detects that buffer z is available to hold a new data message. Thus, p[i] generates a new data message and stores it in buffer z and then stores the index of the message's destination process in dst[z]. Process p[i] then invokes procedure ROUTE to determine a neighbor p[f] to which the data message is to be forwarded. Finally, p[i] sends a rqst(z) message to neighbor p[f].

In the second action, p[i] receives a rqst(x) message from a neighbor p[g] and tries to find an available buffer. If p[i] does not find an available buffer, it records the request by making rqstd[g, x] true. If p[i] finds an available buffer y, it reserves the buffer by making avail[y] false and then sends a prmt(x, y) message to p[g].

In the third action, process p[i] receives a prmt(x, y) message from a neighbor p[g] and sends the corresponding data message to p[g]. Because buffer x in process p[i] has now become available, p[i] searches array rqstd for an earlier request. Procedure SEARCH returns a pair (f, y) such that rqstd[f, y] is false iff all elements of array rqstd are false. If no earlier request is found, avail[x] becomes true. If an earlier request is found (i.e., rqstd[f, y] = true), then rqstd[f, y] is made false and a prmt(y, x) is sent to p[f].

In the fourth action, p[i] receives a data(d, y) message from a neighbor p[g]. If the destination p[d] of that message is in fact p[i], then the data is delivered and buffer y in p[i] becomes available and so is treated as in the third action. Otherwise, the data message is stored in buffer y and procedure ROUTE is invoked to determine a neighbor p[f] to which the message can be forwarded. Then, p[i] sends a rqst(y) message to p[f].

14.3 SWITCHING IN NETWORKS WITH CHANGING TOPOLOGIES

The switching protocols in Sections 14.1 and 14.2 are assumed to execute under the severe assumption that the underlying network topology is fixed over time. In this section, we relax this assumption by showing how to modify these protocols so that their execution can tolerate changes in the network topology.

Changes in the topology of a network are represented by changes in the sets of up neighbors of some processes in the network. There are two types of changes that can occur to the sets of up neighbors: additions and deletions. Adding processes to some sets of up neighbors does not affect the correctness of the switching protocols discussed in Sections 14.1 and 14.2. Only deleting processes from sets of up neighbors can adversely affect the correctness of these protocols. We start by discussing the circuit switching protocol in Section 14.1.

Let <p.0; p.1; ... ; p.(k-1)> denote a circuit involving processes p.0 to p.(k-1). Process p.0 is the source process for the circuit, and process p.(k-1) is the destination process for the circuit. Assume that this circuit has been established according to the circuit switching protocol in Section 14.1. Therefore, when this circuit was being established, each process p.i, where i > 0, was an up neighbor of process p.(i-1). Assume that after the circuit was established, process p.2 ceased to be an up neighbor of process p.1. In this case, each of the processes p.2 to p.(k-1) waits indefinitely to receive data messages, which never arrive, along this circuit. Moreover, each of these processes continues to reserve one circuit identifier and one buffer for this circuit, which is no longer functional.

From this scenario, the circuit switching protocol in Section 14.1 needs to be modified to satisfy two additional requirements. First, each process in a circuit should be able to detect when a circuit is no longer functional. Second, each process in a circuit should be able to remove itself from that circuit.

The first requirement can be satisfied as follows. The source process of each circuit is modified to regularly send data messages forward along the circuit. (This necessitates that a source process sends "empty" data messages along its circuit when the process has no data messages to send.) Moreover, the destination process of each circuit is modified to regularly send ack messages backward along the circuit. When a process p[i] receives no data messages along a circuit for some time, p[i] recognizes that the circuit has been broken upstream. When a process p[i] receives no ack messages along a circuit for some time, p[i] recognizes that the circuit has been broken downstream. In either case, process p[i] decides to remove itself from the circuit.

The second requirement can be satisfied by allowing each process in a circuit to make its identifier of that circuit available for identifying any future circuit. Unfortunately, this solution causes another problem that can be illustrated by the following scenario.

Assume that process p[i] receives a crqst(d, x) message from a neighboring process p[f], accepts the circuit, and assigns it identifier y. Recognizing that this circuit needs to go from process p[i] to process p[g], process p[i] sends a crqst(d, y) message to process p[g]. Later, process p[i] detects prematurely that this circuit is no longer functional, and makes identifier y available for any future circuit. After a short time, process p[i] receives a crqst(d', x') message from another neighbor p[f'], accepts the circuit, and assigns it identifier y. Recognizing that this circuit also needs to go from process p[i] to process p[g], p[i] sends a crqst(d', y) message to process p[g]. Now, process p[i] receives a crply(y, z) message from process p[g] as a reply for the first circuit, which p[i] has discarded, and p[i] thinks wrongly that it is a reply for the second circuit, which p[i] still maintains.

This problem can be solved by making each process p[i] identify every circuit with a pair of numbers (x, c) instead of one number x, where:

x   Is in the range $0 .. v - 1$ as before
c   Is an integer that counts the number of circuits that were assigned identifier x by p[i] prior to the current circuit

Thus, the first time p[i] assigns identifier x to a circuit, it assigns the identifier (x, 0) to that circuit. The second time p[i] assigns identifier x to a circuit, it assigns the identifier (x, 1) to that circuit, and so on. It follows that messages of the forms crqst(dst, x), drply(x), crply(x, y), data(y), and drqst(y) are modified to become of the forms crqst(dst, x, c), drply(x, c), crply(x, c, y, d), data(y, d), and drqst(y, d), respectively.

In the above scenario, the first circuit is identified by (y, d) in p[i] and the second circuit is identified by (y, d + 1) in p[i]. Therefore, when process p[i] receives a crply message that belongs to the first circuit, the message is of the form crply(y, d, z, e) and p[i] correctly recognizes that the message belongs to the first circuit and discards it.

Similar modifications are needed for the datagram switching protocol in Section 14.2 to make it tolerate changes in the network topology. First, if a process p[i] sends a rqst(x) message to an up neighbor p[g] and, before it receives the corresponding prmt(x, y) message, it observes that p[g] is no longer an up neighbor, then p[i] discards the data message from its local buffer x making the buffer available for storing a future data message.

Second, each data message in a local buffer in a process p[i] is identified with a pair of numbers (x, c), instead of one number x, where:

x   Is in the range 0..v − 1 as before
c   Is an integer that counts the number of data messages that were stored in
    buffer x in process p[i] prior to the current message.

Thus, the first time p[i] stores a data message in its buffer x, the message is identified with (x, 0). The second time p[i] stores a data message in its buffer x, the message is identified with (x, 1), and so on.

Third, messages of the forms rqst(x), prmt(x, y), and data(dst, y) in the protocol are modified to become of the forms rqst(x, c), prmt(x, c, y, d), and data(dst, y, d), respectively.

14.4 SWITCHING IN THE INTERNET

The protocol that performs switching in the Internet is the Internet Protocol, or IP. The current version of IP (version 4) supports only datagram switching, whereas the next version of IP (version 6) is planned to support both circuit and datagram switching. In this section, we discuss how IP version 4 supports datagram switching and then discuss how IP version 6 supports both circuit and datagram switching.

Recall that IP version 4 is discussed in Sections 3.4 and 4.6. As discussed in Section 4.6, in order to send a message from a computer c to a computer d, the message is first encapsulated in an IP message and then is sent from the IP process in c to the IP process in an adjacent router r.0, one that is attached to a subnetwork to which c is attached. From there, the IP message is sent to the IP process in an adjacent router r.1, one that is attached to a subnetwork to which r.0 is attached, and so on. This continues until the IP message finally arrives at the IP process in the ultimate destination d. The IP process in d extracts the original message from the received IP message and delivers it.

The datagram switching protocol in the Internet is similar to the datagram switching protocol in Section 14.2 with one important exception. In the datagram switching protocol in Section 14.2, before a process sends a data message to an adjacent process, the sending process ensures that the adjacent process will have no more than v messages when it receives a message. In the datagram switching protocol in the Internet, an IP process can send a message to an adjacent IP process at any time without ensuring an upper bound on the number of messages in the adjacent IP process. Thus, an IP process may end up receiving more messages than it can handle, and so it may discard some of the received messages.

In effect, the datagram switching protocol in Section 14.2 is based on the assumption that the probability of many messages being in a process at the same time is relatively large, a pessimistic view. Thus, this possibility should be prevented. On the other hand, the datagram switching protocol in the Internet is based on the assumption that the probability of many messages being in a process at the same time is relatively small, an optimistic view. Thus, this possibility should be ignored. The datagram switching protocol in Section 14.2 is referred to as a pessimistic protocol, and the datagram switching protocol in the Internet is referred to as an optimistic protocol.

Note that the communication between any two TCP ports proceeds by first establishing a full-duplex connection between the two ports and then sending reliable streams of text segments over the established connection. Such a communication gives the illusion that a two-way circuit, as discussed in Section 14.1, has been established between the two ports. This illusion, however, is false. As discussed in Section 6.4, the communications between any two TCP ports is carried out via IP, using datagram switching, and without establishing any circuits.

In order to support both circuit and datagram switching, IP version 6 is currently being planned along with a new protocol called the resource reservation protocol, or RSVP for short. In the future, each computer in the Internet will have an RSVP process that is placed on top of the IP version 6 process in that computer. (IP version 6 is discussed in detail in Section 25.6. In this section, however, we mention some features of this protocol that are related to circuit and datagram switching.) In the remainder of this section, we refer to an IP version 6 process as an IP6 process.

To establish a circuit whose source computer is c and whose destination computer is d, the following steps are executed:

i. The RSVP process in the destination computer d sends a request message whose ultimate destination is the RSVP process in the source computer c. This request message specifies a label for the flow of data messages to be sent from computer c to computer d via the established circuit. It also specifies the needed resources for handling and forwarding these data messages. (Note that this request message is similar to the crqst message of the circuit switching protocol in Section 14.1 with one exception: This request message is generated by the destination of the circuit whereas the crqst message is generated by the source of the circuit.)

ii. The request message makes several hops after it is sent by the RSVP process in the computer d. The message first goes from the RSVP process in computer d to the RSVP process in a router r.0 adjacent to d, then to the RSVP process in a router r.1 adjacent to r.0, and so on. This continues until the message finally arrives at the RSVP process in computer c.

iii. If the RSVP process of a router r receives a request message, it determines whether r has the needed resources for handling and forwarding the expected data messages along the requested circuit. If r has the needed resources, the RSVP process in r requests from the IP6 process in r to allocate the resources for the circuit and then it forwards the request message to the RSVP process in the next computer (after r) along the circuit. If r does not have the needed resources, the RSVP process in r sends a reject message backward to the RSVP process in the previous computer (before r) along the circuit.

iv. If the RSVP process of a router r receives a reject message for the circuit, it requests from the IP6 process in r to release the allocated resources for the circuit and then it forwards the reject message to the RSVP process in the previous computer (before r) along the circuit.

v. If the request message arrives at the RSVP process in computer c, the RSVP process in c can either send back a reject message to reject the circuit or start sending data messages along the established circuit.

vi. As long as the circuit is established, the RSVP process in computer d periodically sends request messages for that circuit. These periodic messages cause the above steps to be executed periodically and the established circuit to be reaffirmed periodically.

vii. If the RSVP process in an intermediate router r does not receive a request message for the established circuit for a long period of time, it requests from the IP6 process in r to release the allocated resources for the circuit.

It remains now to discuss how the IP6 process in a router handles and forwards data messages that the router receives along established circuits. The IP6 process in a router consists of two parts—a classifier and a scheduler—that share several message buffers. Next, we describe the activities of the classifier and scheduler in a router as the router handles and forwards data messages.

When the IP6 process in a router r receives an IP6 (data) message, the classifier examines three fields in the message header to identify the circuit to which the message belongs, if any. These three fields are the IP address of the original source of the message, the IP address of the ultimate destination of the message, and the flow label of the message. (As discussed in Section 25.6, each IP6 message has a header that contains a field whose value is either zero, indicating that the message does not belong to any circuit, or a positive integer n, indicating that the message belongs to a circuit whose flow label is n.) Based on the identified circuit of the message, the classifier determines the buffer where the message is to be stored until the scheduler decides to send it out. Note that message buffers are of different priorities, and the priority of a buffer determines the frequency at which messages in that buffer are sent out. If an IP6 process receives a message that does not belong to any circuit or belongs to a circuit that is not registered in the IP6 process, then the classifier stores this message in the lowest priority buffer.

When the RSVP process in router r requests from the IP6 process in r to allocate the needed resources for a circuit, the IP6 process in r registers the circuit identifier (consisting of the IP addresses of the source and destination and the flow label of the circuit) and determines (based on the requested resources) the buffer where the data messages of that circuit are to be stored.

At a later time, when the RSVP process in router r requests from the IP6 process in r to release the allocated resources for this circuit, the IP6 process in r discards the circuit registration. If a data message that belongs to this circuit later arrives at router r, the classifier at r detects that the circuit of this message is not registered, and so it stores the message in the lowest priority buffer.

14.5 BIBLIOGRAPHICAL NOTES

Circuit switching is discussed in Beeforth et al. [1972]. Datagram switching is discussed in Baran [1962], Kleinrock [1964], Roberts [1973], Cerf and Khan [1974], Khan [1977, 1979], Pouzin [1977], and Fraser [1983]. A comparison between circuit switching and datagram switching is given in Pouzin [1976]. Virtual cutthrough switching, which combines both circuit switching and datagram switching, is discussed in Kermani and Kleinrock [1979]; see exercise 32 below.

EXERCISES

1   (Physical Circuits). In the circuit switching protocol in Section 14.1, no process can be involved in more than v circuits. Simplify this protocol in the case where $v = 1$.

2   (Physical Circuits in Ring Networks). Simplify the protocol in exercise 1 when the network topology is a cycle, that is, for each i, $0 \le i < n$, the two processes $p[i]$ and $p[i+_n 1]$ are neighbors.

3   (Physical Circuits in Linear Networks). Simplify the protocol in exercise 1 in the case where the network topology is a line, that is, for each i, $0 \le i < n - 1$, the two processes $p[i]$ and $p[i+_n 1]$ are neighbors.

4   (Livelocks in Circuit Switching). Consider the protocol in exercise 3. Give an infinite scenario of this protocol, where process $p[0]$ repeatedly tries to establish a circuit with process $p[n - 1]$ and process $p[n - 1]$ repeatedly tries to establish a circuit with process $p[0]$ but no circuit is ever established between $p[0]$ and $p[n - 1]$. (This phenomenon is called a livelock. Note that the probability of a livelock occurring is small when v is large.)

5   (Dynamic Buffer Allocation). In the circuit switching protocol in Section 14.1, each circuit is assigned one buffer (to hold a data message) in each process involved in that circuit. The assigned buffers remain assigned to that circuit until the circuit is removed. Modify this protocol such that the buffers in a process are assigned dynamically to the circuits in which the process is presently involved based on the evolving needs of these circuits.

6   (Dynamic Buffer Allocation). Modify the protocol in exercise 5 such that the number of buffers to hold data messages in a process is not necessarily equal to v, the maximum number of circuits in which the process can be involved.

7   (Transmission Errors over Circuits). In the circuit switching protocol, we as-
    sumed that the abstraction of virtual neighborhood of Chapter 12 holds. Can a
    data message sent over a circuit still be corrupted? Can it be lost? Can a se-
    quence of data messages sent over a circuit be reordered?

8   (Error Recovery over Circuits). Modify the circuit switching protocol in Sec-
    tion 14.1 as follows:

    a   Each data message sent by the source of a circuit is of the form data(x, s),
        where x is the identifier of the circuit in the source and s is a unique integer
        sequence number of the data message.
    b   When the destination of the circuit receives a data(y, s) message over the
        circuit, it sends back an ack(y, s) message over the circuit.
    c   Only when the source receives an ack(x, s) message over the circuit does it
        send the next message of the form data(x, s + 1).
    d   If the source waits long enough for an ack(x, s) message that does not ar-
        rive, the source recognizes that either the data message or its ack message
        is lost. In this case, the source resends the data(x, s) message over the cir-
        cuit and the cycle repeats.

9   (Alternating Bit Protocols over Circuits). Modify the protocol in exercise 8
    such that the sequence numbers of data and ack messages are of type 0 . . 1 in-
    stead of being integers.

10 (Cumulative Acknowledgment Protocols over Circuits). The protocol in exer-
    cise 8 provides error recovery using a sliding-window mechanism where the
    window size is 1. Modify this protocol such that error recovery is provided us-
    ing a cumulative acknowledgment mechanism, similar to that in Section 9.3,
    where the widow size is any integer w.

11 (Individual Acknowledgment Protocols over Circuits). Modify the protocol in
    exercise 8 such that error recovery is provided using an individual acknowl-
    edgment mechanism, similar to that in Section 9.4, where the widow size is
    any integer w.

12 (Block Acknowledgment Protocols over Circuits). Modify the protocol in exer-
    cise 8 such that error recovery is provided using a block acknowledgment
    mechanism, similar to that in Section 9.5, where the widow size is any integer
    w.

13 (Circuit Switching with Variable Number of Circuits). Modify the circuit
    switching protocol in Section 14.1 such that v, the maximum number of cir-
    cuits in which a process can be involved, is an input (rather than a constant) for
    every process in the protocol.

14 (Circuit Switching in Networks with Changing Topologies). In Section 14.3,
    we briefly discussed how to modify the circuit switching protocol in Section
    14.1 so that the protocol can be used in networks with changing topologies.
    Design this protocol.

15 (Destination-Initiated Circuits). Design a circuit switching protocol in a network p[i: 0 .. n − 1], where circuits are initiated by their destination processes. In particular, to establish a circuit from a source process p[s] to a destination process p[d], process p[d] sends a crqst message whose ultimate destination is process p[s]. If any process p[i] along the circuit receives the crqst message, process p[i] either sends backward a drply message rejecting the circuit or sends forward the crqst message accepting the circuit. If the source process p[s] receives the crqst message and accepts the circuit, it sends a crply message followed by data messages along the circuit. Anytime after receiving the crply message, process p[d] can remove the established circuit by sending a drqst message along the circuit to p[s] and then receiving back a drply message from p[s]. For convenience, assume that the network topology remains fixed.

16 (Destination-Initiated Circuits). Solve exercise 15 under the assumption that network topology can change over time.

17 (Circuit Switching with Flow Control). Modify the circuit switching protocol in Section 14.1 as follows. When a process forwards a data message to the next process in a circuit, it sends an ack message to the previous process in the (same) circuit. No process sends a next data message to the next process in a circuit until it receives an ack message for the previous data message from the next process in the circuit. Compare this modified protocol with the original protocol in Section 14.1.

18 (Persistent Circuit Switching). Modify the circuit switching protocol in Section 14.1 such that when a process rejects a circuit, the preceding process in the circuit tries to establish the circuit through a different route.

19 (Full-Duplex Circuit Switching). Modify the circuit switching protocol in Section 14.1 such that once a circuit has been established, data messages can be sent in both directions of the circuit.

20 (Circuit Switching in a Star Network). Simplify the circuit switching protocol in Section 14.1 for a star network p[i: 0 .. n − 1], where p[0] is a neighbor of every other process, and every other process has only one neighbor, namely p[0]. Assume that neither the source nor the destination of each circuit is process p[0].

21 (Circuit Switching in a Star Network). Modify the protocol in exercise 20 to ensure that the protocol tolerates changes in the network topology.

22 (Datagram Switching in a Star Network). Simplify the datagram switching protocol in Section 14.2 for a star network p[i: 0 .. n − 1], where p[0] is a neighbor of every other process and every other process has only one neighbor, namely p[0]. Assume that neither the source nor the destination of each message is process p[0].

23 (Datagram Switching in a Star Network). Modify the protocol in exercise 22 to ensure that the protocol tolerates changes in the network topology.

24 (Fair Search in Datagram Switching). Define procedure SEARCH(**in** rqstd, **out** f, x) in the datagram switching protocol in Section 14.2. Ensure that this procedure is fair such that each request in array rqstd is eventually granted.

25 (Priorities in Datagram Switching). Modify the datagram switching protocol in Section 14.2 as follows. Each data message has a field pr whose value is in the range 0 . . prmax. Field pr in a data message indicates the message priority. When a data message is generated, its pr is assigned an arbitrary value in the range 0 . . prmax. The value of pr in the message remains fixed until the message arrives at its ultimate destination. When a process has an available buffer, it grants the buffer to a message whose pr is the maximum value among all the data messages waiting for a buffer in that process. (*Hint:* Each rqst message in the protocol also has a field pr whose value is the same as that of field pr in the corresponding data message.)

26 (Hop Counts in Datagram Switching). Modify the datagram switching protocol in Section 14.2 as follows. Each data message has a field h whose value is in the range 0 . . hmax. Field h in a data message indicates the number of hops made by the message so far. When a data message is generated, its h field is assigned a 0 value. When the data message is sent from a process to a neighboring process, the value of h is incremented by 1. When it is clear that the value of h will become hmax without the message reaching its ultimate destination, the message is discarded.

27 (Hop Counts as Priorities in Datagram Switching). Modify the datagram switching protocol in exercise 26 as follows. When a process has an available buffer, it grants the buffer to a message whose h is the maximum value among all the data messages waiting for a buffer in that process. (*Hint:* Each rqst message in the protocol also has a field hp whose value is the same as that of field pr in the corresponding data message.)

28 (Datagram Switching in Networks with Changing Topologies). In Section 14.3, we briefly discussed how to modify the datagram switching protocol in Section 14.1 so that the protocol can be used in networks with changing topologies. Design this protocol.

29 (Optimistic Datagram Switching). In the datagram switching protocol in Section 14.2, a process does not send a data message to a neighboring process until it is sure that the neighboring process has an available buffer to store the message. Modify this protocol such that data messages are transmitted between neighboring processes using an optimistic, instead of a pessimistic, method. According to this optimistic method, each process sends its data messages to neighboring processes without being sure that these processes have available buffers to store the received messages. If a neighboring process receives a data message and detects that it has no buffer to store it, the process discards the message. (Note that the circuit switching protocol in Section 14.1 uses the same optimistic method in transmitting data messages between neighboring processes.)

30 (Pessimistic versus Optimistic Datagram Switching). The datagram switching protocol in Section 14.2 is a pessimistic protocol, whereas the protocol in exercise 29 is an optimistic one. Compare the advantages and disadvantages of these two protocols.

31 (Optimistic Datagram Switching with Priorities). Modify the optimistic datagram switching protocol in exercise 29 as follows. Each data message has a field pr whose value is in the range 0 . . pmax. Field pr in a data message indicates the message priority. When a data message is generated, its pr is assigned an arbitrary value from the range 0 . . pmax. The value of pr in the message remains fixed until the message arrives at its ultimate destination. When a process is ready to forward a data message in one of its buffers to a neighboring process, it forwards the data message with the highest priority among those waiting in the buffers.

32 (Cut-Through Switching). Modify the datagram switching protocol in Section 14.2 as follows:

   a   Each process p[i] has a first-in, first-out buffer bff[g] for storing received data messages before forwarding them to the up neighbor p[g] of p[i].

   b   When process p[i] receives a data(d) message, p[i] determines to which up neighbor p[g] should message data(d) be forwarded. Then p[i] decides to do one of the following: forward the data(d) message directly to neighbor p[g] only if buffer bff[g] is empty, store the data(d) message at the tail of buffer bff[g] only if there is a place for the message in bff[g], or discard the data(d) message if buffer bff[g] is full.

   c   If buffer bff[g] in process p[i] has some message(s), then p[i] removes the head message from buffer bff[g] and forwards it to the up neighbor p[g].

33 (Fake Circuits). Consider a protocol that combines both circuit and datagram switching as follows. Only the source p[s] and destination p[d] of a circuit are aware of the circuit. All other processes in the network treat the exchanged messages as datagrams. Each message in this protocol is of the form mg(t, x, src, dst), where:

   a   t is of type 0 . . 4, and indicates the type of message mg as follows:

        $t = 0$ message mg is crqst
        $t = 1$ message mg is drply
        $t = 2$ message mg is crply
        $t = 3$ message mg is data
        $t = 4$ message mg is drqst

   b   x is a unique identifier, in the range $0 . . v - 1$, of the circuit in the source process p[s]; and

   c   src and dst are the original source and ultimate destination of the message, respectively, where

$$\text{src, dst} = s, d \quad \text{if } t = 0, 3, 4$$

$$\text{src, dst} = d, s \quad \text{if } t = 1, 2$$

Process p[s] first sends an mg(0, x, s, d) to an appropriate up neighbor p[g]. Process p[g] treats the message as a datagram and forwards it to an appropriate up neighbor p[h], and so on. This continues until the mg(0, x, s, d) message arrives at its ultimate destination p[d]. Then, process p[d] prepares a reply message, either mg(1, x, d, s) or mg(2, x, d, s), and forwards it to an appropriate up neighbor, and so on. If p[s] receives an mg(2, x, d, s) message, it starts to send mg(3, x, s, d) messages and then sends an mg(4, x, s, d) message. Design this protocol under the following assumptions:

a Each process in the network has a procedure ROUTE for routing any message.

b Whenever a process receives a message that needs to be routed, the process forwards the message right away.

c Each process in the network can be involved, as a source or destination, in no more than v circuits.

34 (Circuit Switching in Linear Networks). It is required to simplify the circuit switching protocol in Section 14.1 as follows. First, network p[i: 0 .. n − 1] is linear, where each process p[i], 0 < i < n − 1, has two neighbors, namely p[i − 1] and p[i + 1], and each of the processes p[0] and p[n − 1] has only one neighbor. Second, each process p[i] can establish a circuit to a process p[j] provided that i < j.

35 (Worm-Hole Switching). Consider a network p[i: 0 .. n − 1] where all channels are always up. In this network, every data is sent as a sequence of messages, called a worm. Each worm consists of a head(d) message, followed by one or more (but no more than r) data messages, followed by a tail message, where p[d] is the ultimate destination of the data messages in the worm. When a process p[i] receives a head(d) message of a worm wm, p[i] uses its procedure ROUTE to compute a neighbor p[g] to which wm is to be routed. If the computed neighbor p[g] is currently being used by p[i] in routing another worm, then p[i] removes worm wm from the network and discards it. Each process p[i] has the following constants, input, variables, and parameter:

```
process    p[i : 0..n-1]
const      r
inp        N              :    set { g | p[g] is a
                                      neighbor of p[i] }
var        avail, rmv :         array [N] of boolean,
           rt             :    array [N] of NU{i}
           d              :    0..n-1,
           x              :    0..r-1
par        g              :    N
```

Design the actions of process pi].

36 (Worm-Hole Switching with Changing Topology). Solve exercise 35 under the assumption that the network topology can change over time.

CHAPTER 15

CONGESTION CONTROL

For simplicity sake, we have ignored an important feature of the switching protocols that we discussed in Chapter 14. When a data message is generated, an integer called the "time-to-live" is attached to the message. The time-to-live of a data message is decremented as the message travels from one process to the next. In particular, before a process p[i] sends a data message to one of its neighbors, p[i] subtracts from the time-to-live of the message the time period the message has spent in p[i]. If a data message spends in a process p[i] a time period larger than its current time-to-live, the message is discarded from p[i] and the buffer that the message has occupied in p[i] becomes available for another message. This time-to-live feature is intended as a safe guard to prevent any message from occupying a buffer for an indefinite period of time.

In summary, switching protocols may discard data messages if there are many messages being transmitted in the network at the same time and messages are forced to spend longer times in the buffers they occupy. This phenomenon of discarding messages when many of them are being transmitted at the same time is called congestion.

To explain the phenomenon of congestion, we need to discuss the relationship between two parameters: rate R at which messages are generated at the processes in a network and rate S at which messages arrive at their destination processes in the network. Clearly, R is always larger than or equal to S. The difference between these two parameters, R − S, is the rate at which messages are discarded from the network. As mentioned above, a message is discarded from a network if the message reaches a process that has no available buffers (in case of optimistic data transmission) or if the message fails to reach its destination process within its assigned time-to-live (in case of pessimistic data transmission).

275

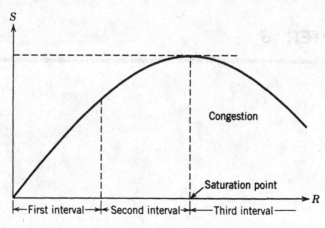

FIG. 15.1

The relation between R and S is illustrated in Figure 15.1. In this figure, the values of R can be partitioned into three intervals. In the first interval, R has a small value and S equals R. Thus in this interval, any increase in R causes an equal increase in S.

In the second interval, R has a medium value but S is less than R. In this interval, any increase in R still causes an increase in S, but the increase in S is less than the corresponding increase in R. In fact, the increase in S becomes less and less as R becomes larger and larger. The second interval ends at a point where any increase in R causes no increase in S. We refer to the value of R at this point as the saturation point of the network.

In the third interval, R has a large value and any increase in R causes a decrease in S. In fact, the corresponding decrease in S becomes larger and larger as R becomes larger and larger. The network is said to suffer from congestion in this interval.

Based on this discussion, we define congestion in a network as an increase in R, beyond the saturation point of the network, causing a decrease in S, where R is the rate at which messages are generated in the network processes and S is the rate at which messages arrive at their destination processes in the network.

Note that this definition of congestion applies to a region in a network as well as to the whole network. In the case of a network region, R is the combined rate of message generation in the region and message entry from the rest of the network into the region. Also, S is the combined rate of message arrival at their destination processes in the region and message leaving the region and going to the rest of the network.

Congestion can be prevented by ensuring that R is always less than the network saturation point. Unfortunately, this method of congestion prevention is sometimes hard to achieve in practice because it requires a central controller for the network. The central controller is a process that closely monitors the rates of message generation at different processes in the network and periodically computes R. When the computed R approaches the network saturation point, the central controller requests that some processes reduce their rates of message generation.

In the absence of a network central controller, we have to contend with a less ambitious goal than congestion prevention, namely congestion control. In this chapter, we discuss a number of methods for controlling congestion. In Section 15.1, we discuss methods for controlling congestion in networks that use circuit switching. In Section 15.2, we discuss methods for controlling congestion in networks that use datagram switching. Then in Section 15.3, we discuss a method for preventing deadlocks, an extreme symptom of congestion, in datagram networks. Finally in Section 15.4, we discuss congestion control in the Internet.

15.1 CONGESTION CONTROL IN CIRCUIT NETWORKS

The circuit switching protocol discussed in Section 14.1 already employs some form of congestion control. In particular, each process in this protocol cannot be involved in more than v circuits at the same time. This restriction is intended to limit the total number of circuits that can be established in the network at any one time.

Unfortunately, this protocol still has two sources of congestion:

i. *Lack of Admission Control:* The protocol does not limit the rate at which data messages can be generated and sent along an established circuit. In fact, once a process succeeds in establishing a circuit, the process can generate and send data messages along that circuit at a very high rate. This can cause congestion in all the processes involved in the circuit.

ii. *Lack of Process Scheduling:* The protocol does not set or dictate the rates at which each process serves the circuits in which the process is involved. Thus, a process that is involved in several circuits can arbitrarily serve some circuits at a high rate and serve the other circuits at a low rate. If the source of a circuit sends data messages along the circuit at a high rate and if the circuit is served at a low rate by one or more processes in the circuit, then these processes in the circuit become congested.

Next, we discuss methods for performing admission control and process scheduling in circuit switching networks. Note that admission control can be performed by using any of the sliding-window protocols in Chapter 9 or by using any of the flow control techniques in Chapter 10.

A method of admission control in circuits is as follows. When a circuit is established from a source process p[i] to a destination process p[d], p[i] sends data messages along the circuit to p[d] and p[d] sends back an acknowledgment for every data message it receives along the circuit. The sent acknowledgments travel backward along the circuit until they arrive at the source process p[i]. The source process p[i] does not send more than w data messages without receiving an acknowledgment for any of them, where w is a constant called the window size. Thus, the flow rate of data messages from process p[i] to process p[d] depends on the chosen value of w. Recall that the value of w can be made to change over time, as discussed in Section 10.1.

A second method of admission control in circuits is called leaky buckets. In this method, each process p[i] has a variable bucket[x] for each circuit x in which p[i] is the source process. Process p[i] uses variable bucket[x] to ensure that the flow rate (in bits per second) of data messages over circuit x is never more than a predefined value rt.x. Process p[i] uses variables bucket[x] as follows.

i. When circuit x is first established, process p[i] executes the following statement.

```
bucket [x]  := 0
```

ii. When process p[i] has a data message mg to send over circuit x, p[i] executes the following statements:

```
bucket [x]  := bucket [x] + min (T*rt.x , bmax);
if bucket [x] ≥ len —>
        {p [i] sends mg over circuit x}
        bucket [x] := bucket [x] · len
[] bucket [x] < len —>
        {p [i] does not send mg}
        skip
fi
```

where the variables are defined as follows:

T   Elapsed time (in seconds) since variable bucket[x] has been updated last .

rt.x   Maximum flow rate (in bits per second) for sending data messages over circuit x

bmax   Maximum length (in bits) of a data message to be sent over cicuit x by process p[i]

len   Length (in bits) of the data message mg

A method of process scheduling ensures that if a process p[i] is involved in a circuit x, then p[i] serves this circuit at a predefined rate of at least rt.x bits per second. To realize this method, the circuit switching protocol in Section 14.1 is extended as follows:

i. Each crqst message now has three fields: crqst(dst, x, rt.x), where rt.x is the flow rate (in bits per second) to be guaranteed for circuit x.

ii. When a process p[i] needs to establish a new circuit x with a guaranteed rate rt.x to a process p[dst] and recognizes that this circuit is to be forwarded first to a neighboring process p[g], p[i] checks whether the sum of rates of all circuits that go from p[i] to p[g], including the new circuit, is less than the physical channel capacity from p[i] to p[g]. If so, p[i] accepts the new circuit and sends a crqst(dst, x, rt.x) message to process p[g]. If not, p[i] rejects the new circuit.

iii. When a process p[i] receives a crqst(dst, x, rt.x) message and recognizes that this new circuit is to be forwarded to a neighboring process p[g], p[i] checks whether the sum of rates of all circuits that go from p[i] to p[g], including the new circuit, is less than the physical channel capacity from p[i] to p[g]. If so, p[i] accepts the new circuit and forwards a crqst(dst, y , rt.y) message to process p[g], where rt.x = rt.y. If not, p[i] rejects the new circuit.

iv. For each circuit x in which process p[i] is involved, p[i] maintains a deadline dl.x. The meaning of dl.x is as follows: If process p[i] has a data message that it has received, but has not yet sent, over circuit x, then dl.x is the deadline for sending this message. If p[i] has no such data message, then dl.x is the deadline for sending the last data message that p[i] has sent over circuit x. Specifically, p[i] maintains dl.x as follows:

  a. When circuit x is first established, process p[i] assigns dl.x the value zero.

  b. When process p[i] receives a data message over circuit x and it does not have the last received data message over x, p[i] executes the statement

```
dl.x : = max(dl.x, current time) + (len/rt.x)
```

  where the current time is measured from the instant circuit x is established, len is the number of bits in the received data message, and rt.x is the guaranteed rate for circuit x.

  c. When process p[i] sends a data message over circuit x and it has the next data message to be sent over circuit x, p[i] executes the statement

```
dl.x := dl.x + (len/rt.x)
```

  where len is the number of bits in the next data message to be sent by p[i] over circuit x, and rt.x is the guaranteed rate for circuit x.

v. When process p[i] has a chance to forward a data message to a neighboring process p[g], p[i] considers every circuit j that satisfies the following two conditions: Circuit j goes from p[i] to p[g], and p[i] has received but not yet sent a data message over circuit j. From all theses circuits, p[i] selects a circuit j whose deadline dl.j is the smallest and forwards a data message over that circuit to process p[g].

15.2 CONGESTION CONTROL IN DATAGRAM NETWORKS

The main reason for congestion in a datagram network can be regarded as an accident where many data messages are generated at different processes in the network within a short period of time. Most buffers in these processes become full, and each message in these buffers is forced to wait in its buffer until its time-to-live expires and the message is discarded.

One method for controlling congestion in datagram networks is called admission control. In this method, when a process recognizes that most of its buffers are full (a sign of possible congestion), the process generates control messages and sends them to nearby processes asking them to reduce the rates at which they generate data messages. One problem of this method is that when congestion starts to occur, many control messages can be generated, pushing the network further and further toward congestion. Therefore, this method needs to be used with care.

In an efficient variation of this method, each data message is of the form data(src, b, dst), where:

src　Is the index of the original source of the message
b　　Is a boolean field whose use is explained below
dst　Is the index of the ultimate destination of the message

If a process p[i] receives a data(src, false, dst) message when most of the buffers in p[i] are full, process p[i] generates a control message and sends it to the source process p[src] of the message, asking p[src] to reduce its rate of generating data messages. Then, process p[i] forwards the data message as data(src, true, dst). Because the boolean field b of this message has become true, this message can no longer cause control messages to be generated later. In effect, every sent data message can cause the generation of at most one control message. Field b is called a congestion bit and the protocol is called the congestion bit protocol.

Another method for controlling congestion in datagram networks is called isarithmic control. According to this method, an upper bound is imposed on the total number of data messages that can be in the network at any instant.

An upper bound on the number of data messages in the network can be achieved as follows. First, the network is provided with a fixed number of token messages. Initially, the token messages reside at different processes, but they can travel freely between processes in the network. Second, in order that a data message is generated at some process, the process must have at least one token message (as well as one available buffer to store the message after it is generated). When a data message is generated at a process, the number of token messages that reside in that process is reduced by 1. Third, when a data message finally arrives at its destination process, the number of token messages that reside in the destination process is increased by 1.

The net effect of these three rules is that the total number of token and data messages that can be in the network at any given instant is fixed. Therefore, the number of data messages that can exist in the network at any instant can never exceed the number of token messages that exist in the network initially.

Note that datagram switching without isarithmic control already imposes an upper bound on the number of data messages that can exist in a network. In particular, the number of data messages that can exist in a datagram network never exceeds n × v, where n is the number of processes in the network and v is the number of buffers per process. This upper bound, however, is very high. If the number of data messages in the network becomes n × v, the buffers in all processes in the network become full and the movements of data messages between different processes become impossible. Therefore, the function of isarithmic control is to make the upper bound on the number of data messages in the network a small fraction of n × v. Thus with isarithmic control, a large number of buffers in the network are available at any given time, and the data messages that exist in the network at that time can travel with minimal delay through these available buffers to their destination processes.

Note also that according to the method of isarithmic control, a process can not generate a new data message unless the process has at least one token message. Therefore, it is important in this method that "unused" token messages travel freely between network processes so that a process that needs to generate a new data message eventually receives a token message and is enabled to generate and send its data message.

Process p[i] in the isarithmic control protocol can be defined as follows:

```
process p[i : 0..n-1]

const v            {# of buffers in p[i]}

inp    N      :    set {g|p[g] is an up neighbor of p[i]},
       tmax   :    integer
                   {max. # of tokens in p[i]}

var    avail  :    array [0..v-1] of boolean ,
       dst    :    array [0..v-1] of 0..n-1 ,
       rqstd  :    array [N, 0..v-1] of boolean ,
       d      :    0..n-1 ,
       f      :    N ,
       x, y   :    0..v-1,
       tkn    :    0..tmax

par    g      :    N,
       z      :    0..v-1

begin
       avail[z] ∧ tkn > 0 ->
              d:= any;
              if d=i ->    skip
              [] d≠i ->
```

```
                                    avail[z], dst[z] := false, d;
                                    ROUTE(in d, out f);
                                    send rqst(z) to p[f];
                                    tkn := tkn-1
                        fi

[] rcv rqst(x) from p[g] ->      y := 0;
                        do ~avail[y] /\ y<v-1 -> y := y+1 od;
                        if ~avail[y] -> rqstd[g,x] := true
                        [] avail[y] ->
                                    avail[y] := false;
                                    send prmt(x,y) to p[g]
                        fi

[] rcv prmt(x,y) from p[g] ->
                        send data(dst[x],y) to p[g];
                        SEARCH(in rqstd, out f,y);
                        if ~rqstd[f,y] ->
                                    avail[x] := true
                        [] rqstd[f,y] ->
                                    rqstd[f,y] := false;
                                    send prmt(y,x) to p[f]
                        fi

[] rcv data(d,y) from p[g] ->
                        if d=i ->
                                    {arrived}
                                    SEARCH(in rqstd, out f,x);
                                    if ~rqstd[f,x] -> avail[y] := true
                                    [] rqstd[f,x] ->
                                            rqstd[f,x] := false;
                                            send prmt(x,y) to p[f]
                                    fi;
                                    if tkn = tmax ->
                                            f := random; send token to p[f]
                                    [] tkn < tmax ->    tkn := tkn+1
                                    fi
                        [] d≠i ->
                                    dst[y] := d;
                                    ROUTE(in d, out f)
                                    send rqst(y) to p[f]
                        fi

[] tkn > 0   ->
                        f, tkn := random, tkn-1; send token to p[f]
```

```
[] rcv token from p[g] —>
              if tkn = tmax —>   f := random;
                                 send token to p[f]
              [] tkn < tmax —>   tkn := tkn+1
              fi
end
```

This process p[i] is similar to the process of the datagram switching protocol in Section 14.2, but there are five differences between these processes:

i. This p[i] has a new variable "tkn" that counts the number of token messages that reside in the process. Variable tkn has an upper value tmax that is an input of process p[i].

ii. The guard of the first action of this p[i] has a new conjunct tkn > 0 to guarantee that process p[i] does not generate a new data message unless it has at least one token message. The statement of this action is also modified to decrement tkn by 1 when a new data message is generated and sent out.

iii. The fourth action in this p[i] has a new if–fi statement that causes process p[i] to generate a token message when it receives a data message and recognizes that p[i] is the ultimate destination for that message. The generated token message is either sent to a random neighboring process (if p[i] already has tmax token messages) or kept in p[i] (if p[i] has less than tmax tokens).

iv. The fifth action in this p[i] is new. In this action, p[i] sends one of its token messages, if any, to an arbitrary neighboring process.

v. The sixth action in this p[i] is also new. In this action, p[i] receives a token message and, depending on the value of variable tkn, decides either to forward the message to a random neighboring process or to keep it.

The above isarithmic control protocol can be made more sophisticated as follows. A network is partitioned into regions. Each region in the network is provided with a different type of token. The tokens in a region travel at random within the region but never leave the region. For a data message to enter a region, as it travels from its source to its destination, one of the tokens in that region is consumed. For a data message to leave a region, as it travels from its source to its destination, one of the tokens in that region is generated.

As an example, consider a network with the following properties:

i. A token message in this network is either black or white.

ii. A pair of channels between any two processes in the network are either black or white. Black channels are connected; that is, for any two black channels, there is a directed path of all black channels from one of the two channels to the other channel. Similarly, white channels are connected.

iii. A process in the network is black (or white, respectively) if some channels incident at the process are black (or white, respectively). A process that is both black and white is gray.

iv. Initially, each black token is at a black or gray process, and each white token is at a white or gray process. Black tokens can be sent only over black channels, and white tokens can be sent only over white channels.

v. A data message that is generated by consuming a black (or white, respectively) token is called a black (or white, respectively) data message. Black data messages can be sent only over black channels, and white data messages can be sent only over white channels.

vi. A black data message can become white in a gray process by the process consuming one white token and generating one black token. Similarly, a white data message can become black in a gray process.

In this example, the network is partitioned into two regions, black and white, that have disjoint channels. The black region consists of all black channels and all black and gray processes, and the white region consists of all white channels and all white and gray processes. It can be shown that the total number of tokens and data messages remains fixed in each of the two regions.

15.3 DEADLOCK PREVENTION IN DATAGRAM NETWORKS

Consider a region in a datagram network. This region is said to be deadlocked iff the following two conditions are satisfied. First, the buffers in every process in the region are full of data messages. Second, every data message in every process in the region needs to be sent to another process in the same region.

When a region in a network becomes deadlocked, every data message in every process in the region cannot be sent to the next process in the region. In effect, every data message is "stuck" in its place until it is discarded from the network after its time-to-live expires. Clearly, when a deadlock occurs, many of the messages involved in the deadlock end up being discarded from the network. Therefore, we need to prevent the occurrence of deadlocks.

One method to prevent deadlocks is based on the assumption that there is an upper bound s on the number of "hops" that a data message can make as it travels from its source process to its destination process. In other words, a data message can visit at most s+1 processes from the time it is generated until it arrives at its destination. This assumption is not hard to satisfy. If a data message makes s hops yet reaches a process other than its destination process, the message is discarded and the buffer it occupies in the process becomes available to store another data message.

Under this assumption, the method for preventing deadlocks consists of the following four rules:

i. Each process in the network has s + 1 buffers, named buffer 0 to buffer s.

ii. A data message is generated in a process only if buffer 0 of that process is available. The generated data message is stored in buffer 0 of the process.

iii. A data message in buffer k , k < s, of some process is sent to a neighboring process only if buffer (k + 1) of that neighboring process is available. The sent data message is stored in buffer k + 1 of the neighboring process.

iv. A data message in buffer s of some process has already made s hops. There are two possibilities in this case. Either the message is already at its destination process or the message could not reach its destination in s hops. In either case, the message is removed from buffer s of the process (and stored or discarded) and buffer s is made available to store another message.

It is straightforward to argue that these four rules prevent the occurrence of deadlocks. Assume that all the buffers in the network are full of data messages. We exhibit a scenario that makes all the buffers empty without any data message being discarded due to the expiration of its time-to-live. First, each data message in an s buffer can be removed because either it is already at its destination process or it has failed to reach its destination process in s hops. Thus, all the s buffers in the network become empty. Second, each data message in an s − 1 buffer can be moved to an s buffer (because all s buffers are now empty), where it can be removed. Thus, all the s and s − 1 buffers become empty. These activities can be repeated until all the buffers in the network are empty.

Process p[i] in the deadlock prevention protocol can be defined as follows:

```
process  p[i : 0..n-1]
const s          {max. # hops traveled by a data msg.}

inp    N     :   set {g|p[g] is an up neighbor of p[i]}

var    avail :   array [0..s] of boolean ,
       dst   :   array [0..s] of 0..n-1 ,
       rqstd :   array [N, 0..s] of boolean ,
       d     :   0..n-1 ,
       f     :   N ,
       x     :   1..s

par    g     :   N

begin
       avail[0] —>
              d:= any;
              if d=i —>      skip
              [] d≠i —>      avail[0], dst[0] := false, d;
```

```
                    ROUTE(in d, out f);
                    send rqst(1) to p[f];
          fi

[] rcv rqst(x) from p[g] ->
              if ~avail[x] -> rqstd[g,x] := true
              [] avail[x]  -> avail[x] := false;
                             send prmt(x) to p[g]
              fi

[] rcv prmt(x) from p[g] ->
          send data(dst[x-1],x) to p[g];
          SEARCH(in rqstd, x-1, out f);
          if ~rqstd[f,x-1] -> avail[x-1] := true
          [] rqstd[f,x-1]  -> rqstd[f,x-1] := false;
                             send prmt(x-1) to p[f]
          fi

[] rcv data(d,x) from p[g] ->
          if (d = i) \/ (x = s) ->
              {arrived or cannot reach dest.}
              SEARCH(in rqstd, x, out f);
              if ~rqstd[f,x] -> avail[x] := true
              [] rqstd[f,x]  ->
                      rqstd[f,x] := false;
                      send prmt(x) to p[f]
              fi;
          [] (d ≠ i) /\ (x < s) ->
              dst[x] := d;
              ROUTE(in d, out f)
              send rqst(x+1) to p[f]
          fi
end
```

Process p[i] has four actions. In the first action, p[i] detects that its own buffer 0 is available and generates a data message and stores it in that buffer. Then p[i] selects, based on the message destination, a neighboring process p[f] and sends a rqst(1) message to it (requesting a permit to forward the data message in its buffer 0 to buffer 1 of process p[f]).

In the second action, p[i] receives a rqst(x) message from a neighbor p[g] and checks whether its buffer x is available. If buffer x is not available, p[i] records the fact that p[g] has requested buffer x in array rqstd. If buffer x is available, then p[i] sends a prmt(x) message to p[g].

In the third action, p[i] receives a prmt(x) message from a neighbor p[g] then forwards the data message in its buffer $(x - 1)$ to $p[g]$. Then, $p[i]$ searches array rqstd to check whether some neighboring process has previously requested the now available buffer $x - 1$. If such a neighbor is found, $p[i]$ sends a prmt$(x - 1)$ message to that neighbor.

In the fourth action, $p[i]$ receives a data(d, x) message from a neighbor $p[g]$ then checks whether the message has arrived at its final destination or has traveled s hops. If so, $p[i]$ assigns buffer x to another message. If not, $p[i]$ stores the received data message in buffer x and sends a rqst$(x + 1)$ message to the neighboring process where the message needs to go next.

Procedure SEARCH, which is used in the third and fourth actions, is defined as follow:

```
procedure SEARCH(in rqstd, x, out f)

local g     :      N

begin
      g := random;
      f := NEXT(N, g);
      do f≠g ∧ ~rqstd[f, x] —> f := NEXT(N, f) od
end
```

There is another way to explain why the above protocol prevents deadlocks. Consider a directed graph where each node u corresponds to a distinct buffer B.u in the network. In this graph, there is a directed edge from a node u to a node w iff it is possible that a data message in buffer B.u can be sent to buffer B.w. In other words, there is a directed edge from the node corresponding to a buffer x in a process $p[i]$ to each node that corresponds to a buffer $x + 1$ in a neighboring process of $p[i]$. Clearly, this graph describes all possible movements of data messages in the network. Fortunately, this graph has no directed cycles. This means that each data message can move from a buffer in a process to another buffer in a neighboring process and can never be involved in a circular waiting of a deadlock state.

It is possible to modify the above protocol while maintaining the absence of directed cycles in the corresponding buffer graph to ensure that deadlocks cannot arise in the modified protocol. For example, the above protocol can be modified (in fact relaxed) in two ways. First, a data message generated in a process can be stored in any buffer in that process. However, if the message is generated in a buffer x, then this message can make no more than $s-x$ hops in the network (before it reaches its final destination or is discarded). Second, a data message in a buffer x in a process can move to any buffer y in a neighboring process, provided that $x < y$. However, if the message is moved to a buffer y, then this message can still make no more than s $- y$ hops in the network (before it reaches its final destination or is discarded). Note that the first modification does not change the buffer graph, and the second modification, although it adds many directed edges to the buffer graph, keeps the graph acyclic. Therefore, deadlocks cannot arise in the modified protocol.

15.4 CONGESTION CONTROL IN THE INTERNET

The protocol that performs congestion control in the Internet is called the internet control message protocol, or ICMP for short. This protocol consists of one process, called the ICMP process in each computer, whether a host or router, in the Internet. The ICMP process in a computer is placed above the IP process in that computer.

When the IP process in a router r receives an IP message mg and decides (for reasons explained below) to discard the message, the ICMP process in router r prepares an ICMP message mg' stating that message mg has been discarded and citing the reason for discarding it. Then the ICMP process in router r sends message mg' to the IP process in r which adds an IP header to mg' transforming it into an IP message mg''. The destination of message mg'' is the IP process in computer c where the discarded message mg has originated.

When the IP process in computer c receives the IP message mg'', it extracts from mg'' the ICMP message mg' and forwards it to the ICMP process in c. Thus, computer c becomes aware that its IP message mg has been discarded by router r and becomes aware of the reason for discarding this message.

There are four reasons for the IP process in a router r to discard an IP message mg:

   i. Router r detects that the time-to-live of message mg has expired, when mg arrives at r.
   ii. Router r detects some inconsistencies in the fields of message mg, when mg arrives at r.
   iii. Router r is busy routing other messages than mg.
   iv. Router r thinks, whether correctly or wrongly, that the ultimate destination of message mg is unreachable from r.

Reason i can be caused by erroneous routing that makes message mg travel in a loop until its time-to-live expires. Reason iii can be caused by a congestion occurrence in router r.

When a computer c becomes aware that some of its IP messages that were destined to a specific destination have been discarded by some congested router (reason iii above), computer c should reduce the rate at which its IP messages are sent to that destination.

From the above discussion, an ICMP message is sent from a router r to a computer c when any IP message that originated at computer c is discarded by router r. However, there are other circumstances when ICMP messages can be sent. For example, if a computer c needs to check whether another computer d is reachable from c, the ICMP process in c sends an echo request message to the ICMP process in d which replies by sending back an echo reply message.

As a second example, if a computer c needs to get the real time of another computer d, the ICMP process in c sends a timestamp request message to the ICMP process in d. The timestamp request message contains the real time t.1 at which the request is sent by computer c. The ICMP process in computer d replies by sending back a timestamp reply message to the ICMP process in computer c. The time stamp reply message contains three values: t.1, the real-time t.2 at which the request is received by computer d, and the real-time t.3 at which the reply is sent by computer d. The ICMP process in computer c uses the three received values t.1, t.2, and t.3, and the real time t.4 at which the reply is received by computer c to compute the real-time at computer d and the round-trip delay between computers c and d.

The first three fields of each ICMP message are the same for all ICMP messages. These three fields are as follows:

1. Type of the message   8 bits
2. Code of the message   8 bits
3. Checksum of the message   16 bits

Field 1 indicates the type of the ICMP message as follows.

$$
\text{Type} = \begin{cases}
11 & \text{if time-to-live of message expires} \\
12 & \text{if message fields are inconsistent} \\
4 & \text{if some router is busy to route the message} \\
3 & \text{if message destination is unreachable} \\
0 & \text{if message is an echo request} \\
8 & \text{if message is an echo reply} \\
13 & \text{if message is a time stamp request} \\
14 & \text{if message is a times tamp reply}
\end{cases}
$$

Field 2 specifies some extra information related to the type of message. For example, the code for an ICMP message of type 3 (indicating an unreachable destination) specifies the reason for the destination being unreachable. Example values for code in this case are as follows.

$$
\text{Code} = \begin{cases}
0 & \text{if network is unreachable} \\
1 & \text{if host is unreachable} \\
2 & \text{if protocol is unreachable} \\
3 & \text{if port is unreachable}
\end{cases}
$$

Field 3 contains a checksum for the ICMP message. This checksum is computed over the whole message in the same way as the checksum in the IP header is computed over the IP header.

Each ICMP message has other fields that depend on the type of the message. For example, each ICMP message that is sent when an IP message is discarded has a fourth field that contains the IP header along with the first 64 bits of the discarded message. Also, each ICMP message of type echo request or echo reply has two extra fields of 16 bits each that contain an identifier and a sequence number. The function of these two fields is to match each echo reply message with its request message.

Also each ICMP message of type timestamp request or timestamp reply has three extra fields of 32 bits each. The functions of these three fields is to store the three values t.1, t.2, and t.3, discussed above.

15.5 BIBLIOGRAPHICAL NOTES

Admission control in circuit networks using the leaky-bucket mechanism is discussed in Turner [1986]. Process scheduling in circuit networks is discussed in Demers et al. [1989], Zhang [1991], Golestani [1994], Zhang and Ferrari [1994], Cobb et al. [1996], Shreedhar and Varghese [1996], and Lam and Xie [1997]. Surveys on congestion control in circuit networks are presented in Partridge [1994], Tantawy [1994], Peterson and Davie [1996], and Keshav [1997].

Congestion control in datagram networks is discussed in Ramakrishna and Jain [1990] and Floyd and Jacobson [1993]. Isarithmic control in datagram networks is presented in. Deadlock prevention in datagram networks is discussed in Merlin and Schweitzer [1980a, b], Gunther [1981], and Brachman and Chanson [1989].

The ICMP is discussed in Postel [1981b].

EXERCISES

1   (Congestion Control in Circuit Networks Using Rate Control). Design a circuit switching protocol with rate control, where at any instant no more than cap data messages can be in transit along any circuit.

2   (Congestion Control in Physical Circuits Using Rate Control). Simplify the protocol in exercise 1 under the assumption that each process can be involved in at most one circuit at a time.

3   (Congestion Control by Agreeing on the Flow Rate). Modify the protocol in exercise 1 such that the value of cap for a circuit is negotiated during the establishment phase of the circuit.

4   (Congestion Control by Adjusting the Flow Rate). Modify the protocol in exercise 3 such that the value cap of a circuit is renegotiated periodically by all the processes in the circuit.

5   (Congestion Control by Adjusting the Flow Rate). Modify the circuit switching protocol in exercise 1 as follows. If a process p[i] receives a data(x) message over a circuit and it has no available buffer to store the message, process p[i] sends a nack(x) message backward over the circuit. The nack message is transmitted backward from one process to the next until it reaches the source of the circuit. When the circuit source receives a nack(y) message, it reduces the value of cap by a factor of 2. If the circuit source succeeds in sending cmax successive data messages without receiving one nack message, the value of cap is increased by 1.

6   (Congestion Control by Adjusting the Window Size). Modify the circuit protocol in Section 14.1 such that the source and destination of each circuit use a cumulative acknowledgment protocol with variable window size, similar to the
one in Section 10.1, in controlling the flow of data messages from the source to
the destination along the circuit.

7   (Congestion Bits). At the beginning of Section 15.2, we discussed briefly the
congestion bit protocol for controlling congestion in datagram networks. Design
this protocol.

8   (Isarithmic Control with Biased Randomness). In the isarithmic control protocol
in Section 15.2, unused token messages travel at random between the different
processes in the network. This means that each process has the same chance of
getting token messages as every other process in the network. Modify this protocol such that one predefined process has a better chance of getting token messages than any other process in the network.

9   (Isarithmic Control with Biased Randomness). Explain how the modified protocol in exercise 8 can be used to give process p[0] in the following network a
better chance of getting token messages than any other process in the network.
In this network, there are four processes p[i: 0 . . 3] and the following process
pairs are neighbors:

$$\{p[0], p[1]\}, \{p[0], p[2]\}, \{p[1], p[2]\}, \{p[1], p[3]\}, \{p[2], p[3]\}$$

10   (Isarithmic Control in Multiple Regions). At the end of Section 15.2, we discussed an isarithmic control protocol with two types of tokens, black and
white. Design this protocol.

11   (Isarithmic Control over Optimistic Datagram Switching). Modify the isarithmic control protocol in Section 15.2 such that data transmission is optimistic
rather than pessimistic.

12   (Deadlock Prevention with Hopping). At the end of Section 15.3, we briefly
discussed two modifications of the deadlock prevention protocol. Design the
modified protocol.

13   (Deadlock Prevention in a Linear Network). Consider a linear network where
each process, other than the leftmost and the rightmost, has two neighbors: a
left neighbor and a right neighbor. Simplify the deadlock prevention protocol
in Section 15.3 for this network. (Hint: Each process has two buffers.)

14   (Deadlock Prevention in a Unidirectional Ring Network). Consider a unidirectional ring network where each process has two neighbors, a left neighbor and
a right neighbor. Moreover, each process receives only from its left neighbor
and sends only to its right neighbor. Simplify the deadlock prevention protocol
in Section 15.3 for this network. (Hint: Each process has two buffers.)

15   (Deadlock Prevention in a Ring Network). Consider a ring network where each process has two neighbors. Simplify the deadlock prevention protocol in Section 15.3 for this network. (Hint: Each process has four buffers.)

16 (Deadlock Prevention in a Ring Network). Consider a datagram ring network p[i: 0 . . 9], where each process p[i] has two neighbors p[i $-_{10}$ 1] and p[i $+_{10}$ 1]. There are four buffers in each process for storing travelled data messages, and the travel of data messages is designed to ensure that deadlocks do not occur. Draw a buffer graph that describes all possible movements of data messages in this network.

17 (Deadlock Prevention in a Star Network). Consider a star network that consists of the n + 1 processes p[i: 0 . . n − 1] and q. In this network, for each i, $0 \le i <$ n, the two processes p[i] and q are neighbors. Simplify the deadlock prevention protocol in Section 15.3 for this network. (Hint: Each process p[i] has two buffers, and process q has one buffer.)

18 (Deadlock Prevention in a Tree Network). Consider a tree network p[i: 0 . . n − 1] whose topology has no cycles. Simplify the deadlock prevention protocol in Section 15.3 for this network. (Hint: Each process, other than the root, has two buffers. The root process has one buffer.)

19 (Deadlock Prevention in a Network). Consider a network p[i: 0 . . 4] where there is a channel from p[0] to p[1], and from p[1] to p[2], p[2] to p[0], and there are two channels between p[1] and p[3] and between p[4] and p[2] . Assume that each process p[i] has two buffers. Draw a buffer graph for this network that makes datagram switching deadlock free.

20 (Congestion Reporting). The processes in a process array p[i: 0 . . n − 1] exchange data messages of the form msg(0, src, dst), where p[src] is the message source and p[dst] is the message destination. When a process p[i] receives a msg(0, src, dst) message, it either routes the message using its ROUTE procedure or discards the message (due to congestion) and generates a congestion-reporting message msg(1, i, src) whose source is p[i] and whose destination is p[src]. When a process p[i] receives an msg(1, src, dst), it either routes the message using its ROUTE procedure or discards the message without generating a congestion reporting message. Design process p[i] in this protocol.

21 (Reorder-Tolerant Rate Control). In the following protocol, process p sends data messages to process q using rate control as a mean for controlling the flow from p to q. This protocol is designed under the assumption that transmission errors cannot occur:

```
process p
inp       cap    :       integer      {cap > 0}
var       txt    :       array [integer] of boolean,
          i      :       integer      {index of txt}

begin
```

```
    timeout (#ch.p.q < cap) ->
                send data(txt[i]) to q; i := i+1
end

process q
var      txt   :      array [integer] of boolean,
         j     :      integer      {index of txt}
begin
    rcv data(txt[j]) from p ->    j := j+1
end
```

Modify this protocol under the following five conditions:

a   The constant cap equals 2.

b   Message corruption and loss cannot occur.

c   Message reorder can occur; however, no data message can be reordered
with more than r adjacent messages for some constant r, $r \geq 1$.

d   Data messages can have bounded sequence numbers.

e   Message text is written in array txt in process q in order.

CHAPTER 16

THE ABSTRACTION OF VIRTUAL NEIGHBORHOOD

In the last three chapters, we discussed how routing, switching, and congestion control enable a process to send and receive messages from a "far-away" process as if the two processes are neighbors. As discussed in these chapters, the activities of routing, switching, and congestion control can cause sent data messages from a source process to be lost or reordered before they reach their destination process. For example, a sent message can be discarded by an intermediate process because the routing table of that process indicates that the message destination is unreachable or because the time-to-live of the message has expired.

To overcome the possibility of message loss and reorder, pairs of source and destination processes employ some error recovery mechanisms similar to those discussed in Chapter 9. For convenience, we refer to the error recovery between source and destination processes as end-to-end error recovery.

Next, we present an abstraction in which the details of routing, switching, congestion control, and end-to-end error recovery become invisible, yet their effects of enabling far away processes to exchange messages reliably remain visible. This abstraction, which we call the abstraction of virtual neighborhood, is intended to simplify subsequent discussion by hiding the specifics of routing, switching, congestion control, and end-to-end error recovery in process definitions.

The abstraction of virtual neighborhood consists of the following three axioms:

i. Virtual Neighbors: Each two processes in a network are virtual neighbors.

ii. Virtual Channels: There are two opposite-direction virtual channels between any two virtual neighbors in a network. These virtual channels are always up, and so they satisfy the axiom of a perfect channel in Chapter 12.

iii. Virtual Sending and Receiving: For a process p to send a message m to a virtual neighbor q, process p executes the send statement **send** m **to** q. Executing this send statement consists of placing the sent message m in the virtual channel from p to q where it remains unaltered until it arrives at the head of the channel. Finally, process q receives message m by executing the receive statement **rcv** m **from** p.

These three axioms suggest the following definition of the virtual topology of a network. The virtual topology of a network is a fully connected undirected graph where each node corresponds to a distinct process in the network. As an example, Figure 16.1a shows the topology of a network. In this topology, some channels are up and some are down, but there are up routes between any two processes in the network. Thus, the virtual topology for that network is the fully connected undirected graph in Figure 16.1b. Even if the network topology changes over time, for example to become as shown in Figure 16.1c, the virtual topology of the network remains as shown in Figure 16.1b.

Clearly, if many channels in a network become down, the network can be partitioned into unconnected parts. In this case, the abstraction of virtual neighborhood is no longer valid. Nevertheless, because the probability of this occurrence is relatively small, we regard the abstraction of virtual neighborhood as always valid.

16.1 USING THE ABSTRACTION OF VIRTUAL NEIGHBORHOOD

If the processes in a network are defined assuming the three axioms of the virtual neighborhood abstraction, then the resulting process definitions do not need to include any details concerning routing, switching, congestion control, and end-to-end error recovery. Thus, process definitions are kept simple and concise. In summary, the objective of the virtual neighborhood abstraction is to simplify process definitions.

As an example, the abstraction of virtual neighborhood can be used to simplify the definition of a message transfer protocol to become as follows:

```
process p[i : 0..n-1]

inp   N    :    set { g | 0 ≤ g < n   ∧   g ≠ i }

var   d    :    N

par   g    :    N

begin
      true                  ->
                  {generate a data msg and send it}
                  d := any; send data to p[d]
```

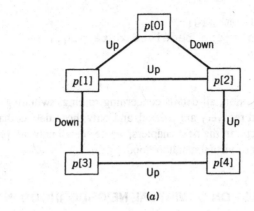

(a)

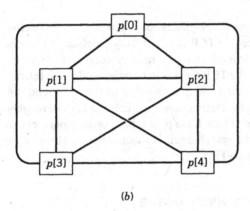

(b)

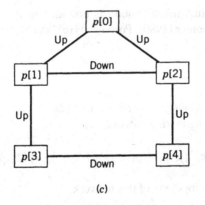

(c)

FIG. 16.1

```
[]      rcv data from p[g]—>
            {store the received data msg.}
        skip
end
```

In this abstract definition, all details concerning routing, switching, congestion control, and end-to-end recovery are deleted, and only those details that deal with message transfer are kept. In the next chapters, we define all network processes assuming this abstraction of virtual neighborhood.

16.2   THE ABSTRACTION OF VIRTUAL NEIGHBORHOOD IN THE INTERNET

The abstraction of virtual neighborhood is provided in the Internet by the transmission control protocol, or TCP for short. Any (application) process p on top of the TCP process in a computer c can reliably communicate with any (application) process q on top of the TCP process in a computer d in the Internet. In this case, the communication primitives in p are roughly of the form **send** <msg> **to** q and **rcv** <msg> **from** q, and the communication primitives in q are roughly of the form **send** <msg> **to** p and **rcv** <msg> **from** p. In other words, p and q communicate as if they are neighbors and the two channels between them are always up and satisfy the axiom of a perfect channel in Chapter 12.

16. 3   BIBLIOGRAPHICAL NOTES

The abstraction of virtual neighborhood is provided in the Internet by the TCP which is discussed in Comer [1980], Postel [1981c], and Stevens [1994].

EXERCISES

1   (Virtual Topology). Consider a network that consists of the five processes p[i: 0 .. 4], where the neighboring processes are

{p[0], p[1]}, {p[0], p[2]},{p[1], p[2]}, {p[1], p[3]}, {p[2], p[4]}, {p[3], p[4]}

Describe the virtual topology of this network.

2   (Virtual Topology). Describe the virtual topology for a network p[i: 0 .. m − 1, j: 0 .. n − 1}.

3   (Validity of the Virtual Neighborhood Abstraction). The virtual neighborhood abstraction is based on the implicit assumption that each process in a network is

always connected with up channels to the rest of the network. Consider the network in exercise 1, and assume that the probability that a channel is down is 10^{-4}. Calculate the probability that the virtual neighborhood abstraction is not valid for this network.

4   (Validity of the Virtual Neighborhood Abstraction). Calculate the probability that the virtual neighborhood abstraction is not valid for a general ring network p[i: 0 .. n − 1], where each process p[i] has two neighbors $p[i -_n 1]$ and $p[i +_n 1]$. Assume that the probability that a channel is down is 10^{-3}.

5   (Using the Virtual Neighborhood Abstraction to Simplify Process Definitions). Consider a network that consists of (2n) + 2 processes: p[i: 0 .. n − 1], r, s, q[j: 0 .. n − 1]. In this network, the p processes send data messages to process r which sends them to process s. Process s forwards the messages to the q processes such that each data message that originates at a process p[i] ends up at process q[i]. The processes are defined as follows:

```
process   r
const     n
var       i    :        0..n-1
begin
    rcv data from p[i]->
            send data to s; i := i +n 1
[]  timeout #ch.p[i].r = 0  ->
            send empty to s; i := i +n 1
end

process   s
const     n
var       j    :        0..n-1
begin
    rcv data from r    ->
            send data to q[j]; j := j +n 1
[]  rcv empty from r  ->    j := j +n 1
end

process p[i : 0..n-1]
begin
    true                 ->    {produce a new data msg}
                               send data to r
end

process q[j :   0..n-1]
begin
    rcv data from s    ->    {consume rcvd data msg}
```

skip

end

Simplify the definitions of processes p[i: 0 .. n − 1] and q[j: 0 .. n − 1] using the abstraction of virtual neighborhood.

CHAPTER 17

NAMING AND NAME RESOLUTION

As discussed earlier, any process p[i] in a network can send data messages to any other process p[d] in the network. The only requirement for p[i] to send data messages to p[d] is that p[i] knows the index d of the destination process. Because our routing and switching protocols are based on process indices, it is reasonable to refer to the index of a process as the "address" of that process.

Indices or addresses are usually assigned to processes based on their physical locations rather than on their logical relationships. For example, in hierarchical routing, the index of a process indicates the region, district, and identity of the process. Because indices are not assigned based on logical relationships, two logically related processes that exchange many messages may be assigned two completely unrelated indices because the processes are located at far apart locations.

A process p[i] that needs to send data messages to a process p[d] may not know the address d of p[d]. Instead, p[i] knows some identifying "name" of process p[d]. Because these identifying names are assigned to the processes to reflect the logical relationships between them, it is more likely that p[i] knows some name of p[d] rather than its address d. Therefore, process p[i] needs to use the name it knows of process p[d] to get its address d before it can start sending data messages to p[d]. The protocol for a process to get the address of another process using some name of that other process is called a name resolution protocol.

In this chapter, we discuss a class of name resolution protocols where names are hierarchical. First, hierarchical names are presented in Section 17.1. Then, a protocol for resolving hierarchical names is discussed in Section 17.2. This protocol is made more efficient by supplying each process with a name cache in Section 17.3. Naming and name resolution in the Internet are discussed in section 17.4.

17.1 HIERARCHICAL NAMES

A name hierarchy is a labeled, acyclic, and directed graph. Nodes that have no incoming edges in this graph are called roots. Each node in the graph is labeled with a string of characters called its primitive name. Primitive names in the graph satisfy the following two conditions. First, primitive names of any two roots are distinct. Second, primitive names of any two nodes that immediately succeed a common node are distinct.

A name in a given name hierarchy is a sequence of m primitive names pnm.0; pnm.1; ... ; pnm.(m-1) such that there is a directed path of m nodes n.0; n,1; ... ; n.(m-1) in the name hierarchy where n.0 is a root and the primitive name of each node n.j is pnm.j. In this case, the name pnm.0; pnm.1; ... ; pnm.(m-1) is said to be a name of node n.(m-1) in the given name hierarchy.

From this definition, each node in a name hierarchy has one or more names. In particular, each node has as many names as the number of directed paths that start with a root and end at the node. Note that each root has only one name: its primitive name.

The processes in a network are said to be named according to a given name hierarchy iff there is a one-to-one correspondence between the processes in the network and the nodes in the name hierarchy.

Let p[i: 0 .. n − 1] be a network where processes are named according to a name hierarchy H. Thus, there is a one-to-one correspondence between the processes in network p and the nodes in H. This correspondence ensures that the roots, successor relation, primitive names, and names in H are all carried over to p. For example, a process in network p is a root iff the corresponding node in the name hierarchy H is a root. A process p[i] is a successor of a process p[j] in network p iff the node in H that corresponds to p[i] is a successor of the node in H that corresponds to p[j]. A process p[i] has a name nm iff the node in H that corresponds to p[i] has the name nm.

Each process p[i] in the network stores the addresses of all root processes and the addresses of all successor processes of p[i]. These addresses are stored in the following input arrays in process p[i]:

```
inp    root, succ  :       array [0..r-1] of 0..n
```

In this declaration, primitive names range over 0 .. r − 1. Let pnm be a primitive name. If root[pnm] < n, then process p[root[pnm]] is a root in the network and its primitive name is pnm. Otherwise, root[pnm] = n and the network has no root whose primitive name is pnm. Similarly, if succ[pnm] < n, then p[succ[pnm]] is a successor of p[i] and its primitive name is pnm. Otherwise, succ[pnm] = n and p[i] has no successor whose primitive name is pnm.

Figure 17.1 shows an example of a name hierarchy with 21 nodes. The string of characters written inside each node is the primitive name of that node. The hierarchy has only two roots with primitive names com and edu. Each node, other than the two nodes with primitive names gouda and anish, has one name. For example, the

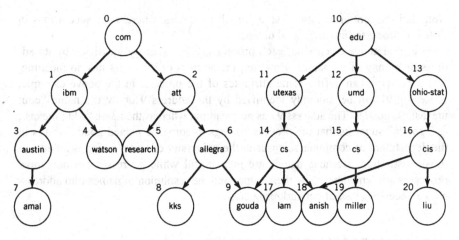

FIG. 17.1

node with primitive name ibm has the name "com; ibm." The node with the primitive name gouda has two names "edu; utexas; cs; gouda" and "com; att; allegra; gouda."

Let p[i: 0 . . 20] be a network where processes are named according to this name hierarchy. The correspondence between the processes in network p and the nodes in the name hierarchy is shown in Figure 17.1. In particular, a number i beside a node indicates that process p[i] corresponds to that node. Thus, process p[2] has the primitive name att. Also, p[2] has the name com; att. Process p[2] has two input arrays declared as follows:

inp   root, succ   :   **array** [P] **of** 0..21

where P is the set of all primitive names in the name hierarchy in Figure 17.1:

> P = {com, edu,
>   ibm, att, utexas, umd, ohio-state
>   austin, watson, research, allegra, cs, cis,
>   amal, kks, gouda, lam, anish, miller, liu}

The values of arrays root and succ in process p[2] are as follows:

$$
root[pnm] = \begin{cases} 0 & \text{if} \quad pnm = com \\ 10 & \text{if} \quad pnm = edu \\ 21 & \text{otherwise} \end{cases}
$$

$$
succ[pnm] = \begin{cases} 5 & \text{if} \quad pnm = research \\ 6 & \text{if} \quad pnm = allegra \\ 21 & \text{otherwise} \end{cases}
$$

Note that the root arrays are identical in all processes, whereas the succ arrays in different processes are in general distinct.

From the above discussion, each process can be uniquely identified by its address or by any of its names. However, the address of a process has no meaning, while its name can define some attributes of the process. In the above example, process p[9] can be uniquely identified by the address 9 or by the name "edu; utexas; cs; gouda." The address 9 has no meaning, whereas the name "edu ; utexas ; cs ; gouda" suggests that the process belongs to someone named gouda who is in the department of computer sciences at the university of texas, which is an educational institution. Because names are meaningful while addresses are not, most processes are remembered by their names and the resolution of names into addresses is a necessary task of network protocols.

17.2   NAME RESOLUTION

In this section, we discuss a name resolution protocol for a network p[i: 0 . . n − 1] where the processes are named according to some name hierarchy H. The correspondence between network p and the name hierarchy H is defined by the following input arrays in each process p[i] as discussed earlier:

```
inp    root, succ  :      array [0..r-1] of 0..n
```

For convenience, we assume that each two processes in network p are virtual neighbors. Thus, each process can send messages to and receive messages from every other process in the network.

In this name resolution protocol, processes generate arbitrary names and then proceed to resolve them. Resolving a name nm consists of determining whether nm is indeed a name of some process in the network and then computing the index d of process p[d] for which nm is a name.

In this protocol, a name nm is defined as an array of m elements, where m is the maximum number of primitive names in a name in the network. The value of each element in array nm ranges over 0 . . r, where r is the number of primitive names in the network. If the value of an element in nm is less than r, then this value corresponds to a primitive name. If the value of an element in nm equals r, then this value is a mere filler and the value of every succeeding element in nm should also equal r.

When a process p[i] generates a name nm, it checks whether the first primitive name nm[0] corresponds to a root process p[j]. If so, p[i] sends a message rslv(nm, 1, i) to the root process p[j]. Upon receiving this message, p[j] checks whether the second primitive name nm[1] corresponds to a successor process p[k] of p[j]. If so, p[j] sends a message rslv(nm, 2, i) to the successor p[k]. Upon receiving this message, p[k] checks whether the third primitive name nm[2] corresponds to a successor process, and so on.

This continues until one of two outcomes occur. First, the last primitive name in nm is reached and is recognized to correspond to some process p[d]. In this case, a message address(nm, d) is sent back to the first process p[i] announcing that nm is a name of process p[d]. Second, the current primitive name is recognized not to correspond to any successor of the current process. In this case, a message address(nm, n), where n is the number of processes in the network, is sent back to the first process p[i] announcing that nm is not a name of any process in the network.

Process p[i] in the name resolution protocol can be defined as follows:

```
process p[i: 0..n-1]

const r, m              {r is # of primitive names}
                        {m is maximum length of a name}

inp   N         :       set {g| (0 ≤ g < n)∧(g ≠ i)},
      root, succ :      array [0..r-1] of 0..n

var   nm        :       array [0..m-1] of 0..r,
      x         :       0..m-1,
      d, e      :       0..n

par   g         :       N

begin
      true  ->
              nm := any;
              CORRECT(in nm, out nm);
              if nm[0] = r ∨ root[nm[0]] = n ->
                      {nm is empty or nm[0] is not root}
                      skip
              ☐ nm[0] ≠ r ∨ root[nm[0]] ≠ n ∧
                (m=1 ∨ nm[1]=r) ->
                      d := root[nm[0]]
                      {d is the address of nm}
              ☐ nm[0] ≠ r ∧ root[nm[0]] ≠ n ∧
                (m>1 ∧ nm[1]≠r) ->
                      if root[nm[0]] ≠ i ->
                      send rslv(nm, 1, i) to p[root[nm[0]]]
                      ☐ root[nm[0]] = i ->
                         x, e := 1, i;
                         RESOLVE
                      fi
              fi

☐     rcv rslv(nm, x, e) from p[g]  ->  RESOLVE
```

```
[]      rcv address(nm, d) from p[g] ->
                if d = n -> {no address for nm} skip
                [] d ≠ n -> {d is the address of nm} skip
                fi
end
```

Process p[i] has three actions. In the first action, p[i] generates an arbitrary name nm, corrects its syntax if necessary, and then starts the resolution of nm. In the second action, process p[i] receives a rslv message from a process p[g]. This message contains some name that has been partially resolved, and so p[i] continues resolving the name. In the third action, process p[i] receives an address message from a process p[g]. This message announces the (positive or negative) result of resolving a name generated earlier by p[i].

Correcting the syntax of name nm is carried out in the first action by a procedure CORRECT defined below. In this procedure, the elements of array nm are checked one by one. If the value of an element of nm equals r, then the values of all subsequent elements of nm are made equal to r:

```
procedure CORRECT(in nm, out nm)

local y            :        0..m,
      found        :        boolean

begin
      y, found := 0, false;
      do y < m ->
            if  ~found ∧ nm[y] ≠ r   ->       skip
            []  ~found ∧ nm[y] = r   ->       found := true
            []   found               ->       nm[y] := r
            fi; y := y+1
      od
end
```

A step in the name resolution is carried out in the first and second actions by executing statement RESOLVE. This statement is defined as follows:

```
if   succ[nm[x]] = n ->
        {next primitive name is not successor of p[i]}
        if e = i -> {there is no address for nm} skip
        [] e ≠ i -> send address(nm, n) to p[e]
        fi
[] succ[nm[x]] ≠ n ∧ (x=m-1 ∨ nm[x+1]=r) ->
        {current primitive name is the last in nm}
        if e = i ->
              d := succ[nm[x]]
```

```
        {d is the address of nm}
    [] e ≠ i ->
        send address(nm, succ[nm[x]]) to p[e]
    fi
[] succ[nm[x]] ≠ n ∧ (x<m-1 ∧ nm[x+1]≠r) ->
        {current primitive name is not the last}
        send rslv(nm, x+1, e) to p[succ[nm[x]]]
fi
```

Different applications necessitate different extensions to this basic name resolution protocol. Four of these extensions are direct resolution, partial resolution, alias resolution, and name caches. The first three extensions are discussed briefly next, and the fourth extension is discussed in Section 17.3.

According to the above name resolution protocol, in order to resolve a name, the name has to visit as many processes as the number of elements (or primitive names) in the name. This situation can be helped by providing some chosen processes with a list of all the names and corresponding addresses of their descending processes. When a partially resolved name reaches one of those chosen processes, the name can be resolved completely by that process. This method is called direct resolution, and the processes provided with complete lists of names and addresses of their descendants are called name servers.

For example, consider a network whose processes are named according to the name hierarchy in Figure 17.1. In this network, the process whose primitive name is utexas can store the following list of names and corresponding addresses of its descendants:

edu; utexas; cs	:	14
edu; utexas; cs; gouda	:	9
edu; utexas; cs; lam	:	17
edu; utexas; cs; anish	:	18

When a name "edu; utexas; cs; gouda" reaches process utexas, the name is resolved directly to address 9 without having to be sent to other processes in the network. In this case, process utexas can be called a name server.

In some applications, generated names are not required to be completely resolved. Rather, they are required to be partially resolved up to a certain predetermined level. For example, consider a network whose processes are named according to the name hierarchy in Figure 17.1, and assume that each of the names "edu; utexas; cs; gouda," "edu; utexas; cs; lam," "edu; utexas; cs; anish," and is to be resolved up to level 3 only. In other words, each of these names is to be resolved as if it is "edu; utexas; cs." In this case, each of these names is resolved to address 14.

In some applications, each process generates some names much more frequently than other names. In these applications, each frequently generated name in a process can be identified by a unique primitive name, called its alias, in that process. For example, assume that the names "edu; utexas; cs; gouda," "edu; utexas;

cs; lam," and "edu; utexas; cs; anish" are frequently generated in some process p[i]. Then, these names can be given short hand aliases in process p[i] as follows:

edu; utexas; cs; gouda   Given the alias author
edu; utexas; cs; lam   Given the alias lam
edu; utexas; cs; anish   Given the alias friend

In this case, process p[i] keeps a table that defines for each alias the corresponding full name so that when an alias is generated in p[i], process p[i] replaces it by the full name before proceeding to resolve the full name to an address.

17.3 NAME CACHES

In practice, shortly after a process generates a name and resolves it into a process address (or index), the process generates the same name and, having forgotten about its recent resolution, proceeds to resolve it one more time. This situation can be avoided by providing each process in the network with a local name cache. In this cache, the process stores the last s names that have been resolved by the process and the corresponding addresses that have resulted from resolving these names. In this case, s is called the cache size.

When a process generates a name, the process first checks whether the name is in its local cache. If so, the address corresponding to the generated name can be found in the local cache. If not, the generated name is resolved using a protocol similar to the one discussed in Section 17.2. In this case, when the corresponding address, which resulted from resolving the name, is finally returned to the process that generated the name, both the name and its corresponding address are added to the local cache of the process, replacing the "oldest" entry in that cache.

In order to provide each process p[i] in the name resolution protocol in the last section with a local name cache, four modifications are needed in p[i]:

i. The following inputs and variables are added to process p[i].

```
inp    s      :      integer,    {cache size}
       amax   :      integer     {max age}

var  cch    :  array [0..s-1, 0..m-1] of 0..r,
     adr    :  array [0..s-1] of 0..n-1,
     age    :  array [0..s-1] of 0..amax,
     u      :  0..s,
     y      :  0..m,
     found  :  boolean
```

Array cch stores the last names resolved by p[i]. Array adr stores for each resolved name the address that resulted from resolving the name. Array age stores, for each resolved name, a measure of the time that has passed since this name has been resolved. When the time measure of an entry in the cache becomes amax, this entry is ignored.

ii. The first action in process p[i] is modified to become as follows.

```
true    ->
       nm := any;
       CORRECT(in nm, out nm);
       u, found := 0, false;
       do u<s /\ ~found ->
          y := 0;
          do y<m /\ nm[y] = cch[u, y] -> y := y+1 od;
          if y<m \/ age[u]=amax -> u := u+1
          [] y=m /\ age[u]<amax -> found := true
          fi
       od;
       if  found -> {adr[u] is address of nm} skip
       [] ~found ->
                {address of nm is not in cache} IFFI
       fi
```

In this action, statement IFFI denotes the if–fi statement in the first action in process p[i] in the protocol of the last section.

iii. Replace each occurrence of the comment {d is the address of nm} in process p[i] by the following statement:

```
u := 0;
do u<s /\ age[u]<amax -> u := u+1 od;
if  u<s ->
        y := 0;
        do y<m -> cch[u, y], y := nm[y], y+1 od;
        adr[u], age[u] := d, 0
[] u=s ->    skip
fi
```

iv. Add the following action to process p[i].

```
true    ->    u := 0;
              do u<s ->
                       age[u], u :=
```

$$\min(age[u]+1, amax), u+1$$
od

17.4 NAMING AND NAME RESOLUTION IN THE INTERNET

In the Internet, the database system that is used in resolving computer names into computer addresses and vice versa is called the Domain Name System, or DNS for short. This database is distributed over a large number of name servers throughout the Internet. There are three classes of name servers: local, organizational (or intermediate), and root. Before we discuss how name servers are used to resolve computer names into computer addresses and vice versa, we discuss the structure of computer names and addresses.

Each computer in the Internet has an address, called its IP address, and a name, called its domain name. As discussed in Section 2.4, the IP address of a computer is of the form x_0, x_1, x_2, x_3, where each x_i is in the range $0 .. 255$. The domain name of a computer is of the form $y_0, y_1, \ldots, y_{m-1}$, where each y_j is a string of one or more (up to 63) characters.

In Section 2.4, we discussed how a computer c is assigned its IP address x_0, x_1, x_2, x_3. In particular, we stated that this IP address is partitioned into three components: x_0, x_1 can be the first component, x_2 can be the second component, and x_3 can be the third component. In this case, the first component x_0, x_1 is assigned by the Network Information Center, or NIC for short, to uniquely identify the network where computer c resides. The second component x_2 is assigned by the administrator of network x_0, x_1 to uniquely identify the subnetwork to which computer c is attached in this network. The third component x_3 is assigned by the administrator of subnetwork x_2 in network x_0, x_1 to uniquely identify computer c in this subnetwork.

As mentioned above, the domain name of a computer c is of the form $y_0, y_1, \ldots, y_{m-1}$, where y_{m-1} indicates the type of organization to which computer c belongs as follows:

$$y_{m-1} = \begin{cases} edu & \text{if it is an educational organization} \\ com & \text{if it is a commercial organization} \\ gov & \text{if it is a governmental organization} \\ mil & \text{if it is a military organization} \\ net & \text{if it is a network organization} \\ org & \text{if it is any other organization} \\ int & \text{if it is an international organization} \\ <cc> & \text{if it is in a country indicated by the two-character code} \end{cases}$$

The component before last, y_{m-2}, in the domain name of computer c indicates the name of the organization to which c belongs. The last two components, y_{m-2}, y_{m-1}, in the domain name of computer c are assigned by the NIC to the organization to which c belongs. The remaining components in the domain name of c are assigned locally by the organization of c.

Associated with each application process in the Internet is a local name server. An application process sends a query to its local name server when it needs to resolve a domain name into an IP address or vice versa. If the local name server can resolve the query locally, it sends the resolution to the application process. Otherwise, the local name server forwards the query to one of the root name servers in the Internet. This implies that each local name server knows the IP address of the root name servers. (Currently there are eight root name servers in the Internet.)

When a root name server receives a query for resolving the domain name or the IP address of some computer c, it replies by sending back a list of IP addresses of some name servers in the organization to which computer c belongs. The root name server obtains this list by resolving the last two components y_{m-2}, y_{m-1} in the given domain name or by resolving the first integers (for example, x_0, x_1) that correspond to the network identifier in the given IP address.

When the local name server receives a list of IP addresses of some name servers in the organization of computer c, it forwards the query concerning computer c to one of the organization name servers in the received list. This query can later be forwarded recursively from one name server to another in the organization of computer c. Finally the local name server receives one of the following two responses:

i. A resolution of the given domain name or IP address of computer c or
ii. An error message "the given domain name or IP address cannot be resolved."

In case i, the local name server forwards the resolution to the application process that requested it. It also adds the resolution to its cache so that it can later carry out the same resolution locally. Any information added to the cache is usually kept for two days before it is considered invalid. In case ii, the local name server forwards the error message to the application process that initiated the resolution.

Each name server in an organization can resolve the domain names and IP addresses of hosts in a particular zone in the organization. A name server for a particular zone is duplicated into one primary name server and one or more secondary name servers. When a computer is added to a zone, both the domain name and IP address of the computer are added to the primary name server of the zone. Every three hours, each secondary name server queries the primary name server in the zone to check whether the data in the primary name server have changed in the last three hours. If so, the secondary name server updates its data to become identical to that of the primary name server.

17.5 BIBLIOGRAPHICAL NOTES

An overview of naming and its relationship to addressing is discussed in Shoch [1978]. The DNS of the Internet is discussed in Mockapetris [1987] and Mockapetris and Dunlap [1988].

EXERCISES

1   (Name Hierarchies with Cycles). A name hierarchy, as defined in Section 17.1, is an acyclic directed graph. Are there practical reasons to make name hierarchies have cycles? Explain your answer.

2   (Fat and Short Name Hierarchies). What are the advantages and disadvantages of making name hierarchies "fat" and "short."

3   (Thin and Long Name Hierarchies). What are the advantages and disadvantages of making name hierarchies "thin" and "long."

4   (Correspondence between Names and Addresses). It is mentioned in Section 17.1 that if the processes in a network p is named according to a name hierarchy H, then there is a one-to-one correspondence between the processes in p and the nodes in H. Can this one-to-one correspondence be replaced by a mapping from the processes in p to the nodes in H? Explain your answer.

5   (Nondeterministic Name Resolution). A name hierarchy, as defined in Section 17.1, satisfies two conditions. First, primitive names of the roots are distinct from one another. Second, primitive names of sibling nodes are distinct from one another. Discuss how the name resolution protocol in Section 17.2 is affected if these two conditions are dropped.

6   (Direct Name Resolution). Modify the name resolution protocol in Section 17.2 such that each root process in the network is a name server that can directly resolve every name that starts with the primitive name of that root.

7   (Partial Name Resolution). Modify the name resolution protocol in Section 17.2 such that when a process p[i] generates a name, it also generates the level up to which this name is to be resolved. The messages in the modified protocol are rslv(nm, x, lvl, i) and address(nm, lvl, h), where

   nm   Is the name to be resolved
   x   Is the level up to which nm has been resolved so far
   lvl Is the level up to which nm is to be resolved
   i   Is the address of the process that needs to resolve nm
   h   Is the address that results from resolving nm

8   (Partial Name Resolution). Modify the name resolution protocol in section 17.2 as follows. Each process p[i] has a boolean input named mask. When p[i] receives a rslv message, it checks the value of its mask. If the mask is true, p[i] does not resolve the name any further, that is, it resolves the name partially to its own address. If the mask is false, the resolution proceeds as before. Finally the originating process receives either address(nm, h, 0), indicating a partial resolution of the name, or address(nm, h, 1), indicating a complete resolution.

9   (Aliases). Modify the name resolution protocol in Section 17.2 to allow each

process p[i] to generate aliases and convert them to names using an input array in p[i] before proceeding to resolve these names into addresses.

10   (Group Names). Modify the name resolution protocol in Section 17.2 as follows. Each process p[i] has an input array gnm as follows:

inp gnm : **array** $[0..x\text{-}1, \ 0..y\text{-}1, \ 0..z\text{-}1]$ **of** $0..r$

An element gnm[j, k, l] is the lth primitive name in the kth name in the jth group in process p[i]. In the modified protocol, each process p[i] generates an arbitrary group name j in the range $0 .. x - 1$, then proceeds to resolve each of the y names in group j, namely gnm[j, 0, 0 .. z − 1], gnm[j, 1, 0 .. z − 1], . . . , and gnm[j, y − 1, 0 .. z − 1].

11   (Class Names). As discussed in Section 17.1, a name is defined as a sequence of primitive names. Now, define a class name as a sequence <x.0 ; x.1; ... ; x.(m-1)>, where each x.j is either a primitive name or the special symbol *. A class name in a name hierarchy H is the set of names in H that can be obtained by replacing each occurrence of the special symbol * in the class name by a primitive name in H. Thus, a class name in a name hierarchy H can be resolved into a set of addresses in any network whose processes are named according to H. Discuss how to modify the direct name resolution protocol in exercise 6 so that it can resolve class names.

12   (Name Caches). Modify the name resolution protocol with name caches, discussed in Section 17.3, as follows. When a process p[i] receives a rslv(nm, x, i) message, p[i] searches its own cache for the name nm before it tries to resolve that name any further.

13   (A Name Hierarchy for Organization X). Organization X consists of three divisions. Each division has five departments, each department has at most five groups, and each group has at most 15 employees. Design a name hierarchy for a network where there is a distinct process for each division, each department, each group, and each employee in organization X.

14   (Name Resolution for Organization X). Consider the network in exercise 13. Assume that a name resolution protocol, similar to the one in Section 17.2, is used in this network. Describe the contents of the two input arrays root and succ in each process in the network.

15   (Another Name Hierarchy for Organization X). Design a name hierarchy for a network where there is a distinct process for each division and each employee in organization X in exercise 13.

16   (Direct Name Resolution for Organization X). Design a direct name resolution protocol, similar to the one discussed in exercise 6, for the network in exercise 15.

CHAPTER 18

SECURITY

In order that two processes can securely exchange data messages in a network, the two processes need to perform some of the following five tasks.

i. *Authentication:* Initially, the two processes exchange several messages until each process is certain that it is communicating with the other process, rather than communicating with a third process pretending to be, that is, impersonating, that other process. During this initial exchange of messages, the two processes can end up with compatible security keys.

ii. *Privacy:* Each of the two processes uses its security key to encrypt any data message before sending it to the other process. It also uses its security key to decrypt any data message after receiving it from the other process. Thus, if an intermediate process eavesdrops on the communication between the two processes and gets a copy of every exchanged message, that process will not be able to understand the contents of these messages.

iii. *Integrity:* Before each of the two processes sends a message to the other process, the sending process uses its security key to compute an integrity check for the message and attaches it to the message. The function of the attached check is to allow the receiving process to prove to itself that the message, without any modification, was indeed sent by the other process.

iv. *Nonrepudiation:* Before each of the two processes sends a message to the other process, the sending process uses its security key to compute its digital signature for the message and attaches it to the message. The function of the attached signature is to allow the receiving process to prove to anyone that the message was indeed sent by the other process. Note that nonrepudiation implies integrity, but it is more expensive to achieve.

v. *Authorization:* If one of the two processes requests to access a resource protected by the other process, the second process checks whether the first process is authorized to access that resource. If so, the request is granted; otherwise it is rejected.

Protocols for performing these five tasks are called authentication, privacy, integrity, nonrepudiation, and authorization protocols, respectively. It is convenient to view authentication protocols as protocols for securely establishing connections between two processes in a network. Privacy, integrity, and nonrepudiation protocols can be viewed as protocols for securely transferring data messages between two processes in a network. Authorization protocols can be viewed as protocols for securely allocating network resources.

The rest of this chapter is organized as follows. First, in Section 18.1, we define the concepts of security keys and nonces and identify the different types of security keys, namely asymmetric and symmetric keys. Then we present authentication protocols that use asymmetric and symmetric keys in Sections 18.2 and 18.3, respectively. We discuss privacy and integrity protocols in Section 18.4 and discuss nonrepudiation protocols in Section 18.5 and authorization protocols in Section 18.6. The use of message digests in authentication, integrity, and nonrepudiation protocols is discussed in Section 18.7. Finally, some security protocols in the Internet are discussed in Section 18.8.

18.1 SECURITY KEYS AND NONCES

In this chapter, we assume that each data item is an integer and vice versa. We also assume that each security key is an integer in the range $0 .. r - 1$. Thus, every key is also a data item.

We also assume the existence of an encryption function NCR and a decryption function DCR. Each of these two functions takes a key and a data item as arguments and produces a data item as a result. Let K be a key and d be a data item. Then, the data item NCR(K, d) is called the encryption of data item d using key K and the data item DCR(K, d) is called the decryption of data item d using key K.

A pair of keys (K, L) is called secure iff the following two conditions hold:

i. *Restoration:* For every data item d,

$$d = DCR(L, NCR(K, d)) \text{ and}$$

$$d = DCR(K, NCR(L, d))$$

ii. *Hiding:* For every key K' other than K and every key L' other than L, there is a data item d such that

$$d \neq DCR(L', NCR(K, d)) \text{ and}$$

$$d \neq DCR(K', NCR(L, d))$$

A secure key pair (K, L) is called asymmetric iff K $\neq$ L. A secure key pair (K, L) is called symmetric iff K = L. Next, we discuss how these types of key pairs can be used in networks.

Consider a network where an asymmetric key pair (K, L) is used. In this case, every process in the network knows key K and exactly one process in the network, say process p, knows key L. In this case, key K is called a public key for process p, key L is called a private key for p, and the pair (K, L) is called an asymmetric key pair for p.

Consider a network where a symmetric key pair (K, K) is used. In this case, exactly two processes in the network, say p and q, know key K. There are two cases to consider. First, process p is a special process called the network authentication center, and in this case K is called an individual key for process q. Second, both p and q are regular processes in the network, and in this case K is called a shared key between processes p and q.

In general, encryption (and decryption) using public and private keys is more computationally intensive than encryption (and decryption) using individual and shared keys.

Throughout this chapter, we adopt the following notation concerning keys.

B.p   Denotes the public key of process p
R.p   Denotes the private key of process p
I.p   Denotes the individual key of process p
S.{p, q} Denotes a shared key between processes p and q

We also use S to denote a shared key between processes p and q when the identities of p and q are clear from the context.

A nonce is an integer, and so each nonce is a data item. During the execution of a security protocol, each process in the protocol can generate a nonce by executing a function NNC. The sequence of nonces generated by a process satisfies the following two conditions:

i. Unpredictability: The value of a generated nonce cannot be deduced from the values of all previously generated nonces in the sequence.

ii. Nonrepetition: The value of a generated nonce is different from the values of all previously generated nonces in the sequence.

18.2 AUTHENTICATION USING ASYMMETRIC KEYS

In this section, we present an authentication protocol that uses public and private keys. Then, in the next section, we present authentication protocols that use symmetric (namely shared or individual) keys.

Consider a network that consists of two processes p and q. In order that process p authenticates process q, p first generates a random nonce, and sends it to q. When process q receives nonce n from process p, q encrypts n using its private key R.q and sends the encrypted nonce, denoted R.q<n>, to process p. When process p receives the encrypted nonce from q, it decrypts it using the public key B.q for process q. (Recall that every process in the network knows the public key B.q, but only process q knows the private key R.q.) Process p then checks whether the final n equals the original n. If they are equal, then the authentication of q by p is successful, and the process claiming to be process q is indeed process q. If they are unequal, then the authentication of q by p has failed.

This simple protocol can be represented succinctly as follows:

```
p -> q : n
q -> p : R.q<n>,
```

The correctness of this protocol is straightforward. When p receives a message encrypted using R.q, it recognizes that q must have sent this message. Moreover, because the content of the message is the original nonce that p has selected at random and sent to q, p recognizes that q must have received that nonce prior to sending R.q<n>, .

Next, we discuss how to extend this protocol such that process q can send a key S to process p. Key S is to be shared between p and q. It can be used by each of the two processes to encrypt its data messages before sending them to the other process, which then uses S to decrypt the received messages.

Process q sends key S to process p by including it in the message from q to p. However, the message from q to p can not simply be R.q<n; S>, where n; S denotes the data item resulting from concatenating the two data items n and S. This is because the public key B.q of process q, which is known to every process in the network, can be used to decrypt this message. Thus, there is a danger of key S becoming known to a process other than p or q. This danger can be avoided by making the message from q to p as follows: R.q<B.p<n; S>>. In this case, only process p can use its private key R.p to decrypt B.p<n; S>, and so only process p can know key S. The extended protocol can be represented by the following sequence of steps:

```
p -> q : n
q -> p : R.q<B.p<n; S>
```

In this protocol, process p authenticates process q, but q does not authenticate p. In order to make process q authenticate process p, the protocol needs to be modified as follows. First, process q generates a random nonce m and attaches it to the message from q to p. Second, when process p receives this message, it decrypts its content to get S and then uses S to encrypt nonce m and sends the encrypted nonce S<m> to process q. The resulting protocol can be represented as follows:

```
p -> q : n
q -> p : R.q<B.p<n; S> , m
p -> q : S<m>
```

In this protocol, the first message from p to q is called a challenge, the second message from q to p is called a response, and the third message from p to q is called a second response. Next, we discuss how to define processes p and q in order to realize this protocol.

Process p has three variables: st, key, and nc. These three variables have the following meanings:

$$st \quad = \begin{cases} 0 & \text{if there is no authentication between p and q} \\ 1 & \text{if authentication procedure has started} \\ 3 & \text{if authentication has completed between p and q} \end{cases}$$

key = key S received by p during authentication

nc = nonce n generated by p to authenticate q

Process p has three actions. In the first action, p detects that st = 0 and so it makes st = 1, generates n and stores it in variable nc, and sends a chlng(n) message to process q.

In the second action, process p receives a rspn(R.q<B.p<n; S>>, m) message from process q, decrypts the message contents, and checks whether the received n equals nc. If n ≠ nc, process p discards the message. If n = nc, the authentication of q by p is successful. In this case, p makes st = 3, stores the received S in variable key, and sends an srspn(S<m>) message to process q.

The third action is a timeout action. In this action, process p observes the erroneous situation where st = 1 and the two channels between p and q are empty. This indicates that the process claiming to be q may in fact be other than q. In this case, process p resets st to 0.

Similarly, process q has three variables: st, key, and nc. These three variables have the following meanings:

$$st \quad = \begin{cases} 0 & \text{if there is no authentication between p and q} \\ 2 & \text{if authentication procedure has started} \\ 3 & \text{if authentication has completed between p and q} \end{cases}$$

key = key S generated by q during authentication

nc = nonce m generated by q to authenticate p

Process q has three actions. In the first action, q receives a chlng(n) message from p, makes st = 2, selects at random a key S and generates a nonce m, stores S in variable key and m in variable nc and then sends a rspn(R.q<B.p<n; S>, m) message to p.

In the second action, process q receives an srspn(S<m>) message from p, decrypts the message content, and checks whether the received m equals nc. If m ≠ nc, the message is discarded. If m = nc, the authentication of p by q is successful. In this case, process q makes st = 3.

The third action is a timeout action. In this action, process q observes the erroneous situation where st = 2 and the two channels between p and q are empty. This indicates that the process claiming to be p may in fact be other than p. In this case, process q resets st to 0.

So far, our presentation of this authentication protocol has been restricted to a network of two processes p and q. Next, we extend this protocol to a general network of processes p[i: 0 .. n − 1], where each process p[i] can act as p or as q with any other process p[g]. Thus, each process p[i] in this network has the following three variables for each other process p[g]: st[g], key[g], nc[g].

It is possible in this case that p[i] acting as p tries to initiate authentication with neighbor p[g], while p[g] also acting as p tries to initiate authentication with p[i]. When this happens, then the process with the smaller index between p[i] and p[g] ends up acting as p and the other process ends up acting as q.

Process p[i] in the authentication protocol that uses asymmetric keys, can be defined as follows:

```
process p[i: 0..n-1]

const r         {r-1 is the largest value for a key}

inp   N     :   set {g|0 ≤ g < n ∧ g ≠ i},
      rk    :   0..r-1,           {private key of p[i]}
      bk    :   array [N] of 0..r-1  {public keys}

var   st    :   array [N] of 0..3,
      key   :   array [N] of 0..r-1,
      nc    :   array [N] of integer,
      c, d, e : integer

par   g     :   N

begin
      st[g] = 0 ∨ st[g] = 3 ->
          st[g], nc[g] := 1, NNC;
          send chlng(nc[g]) to p[g]

□     rcv chlng(c) from p[g] ->
```

```
        if st[g] = 1 ∧ g ≥ i -> skip
        ▯ st[g] ≠ 1 ∨ g < i ->
               st[g], key[g], nc[g] := 2, random, NNC;
               c := NCR(rk, NCR(bk[g], (c; key[g])));
               send rspn(c, nc[g]) to p[g]
        fi

▯    rcv rspn(c, d) from p[g] ->
        (c, e) := DCR(rk, DCR(bk[g], c));
        if st[g] ≠ 1 ∨ c ≠ nc[g] ->
               {auth. fails} skip
        ▯ st[g] = 1 ∧ c = nc[g] ->
               st[g], key[g] := 3, e;
               d := NCR(key[g], d);
               send srspn(d) to p[g]
        fi

▯    rcv srspn(c) from p[g] ->
          c := DCR(key[g], c);
          if st[g] ≠ 2 ∨ c ≠ nc[g] ->
               {auth. fails} skip
          ▯ st[g] = 2 ∧ c = nc[g] ->
               st[g] := 3
          fi

▯    timeout  (st[g] = 1 ∨ st[g] =2) ∧
             (#ch.p[i].p[g] +#ch.p[g].p[i] = 0) ->
          st[g] := 0
end
```

Process p[i] has five actions. The first, third, and fifth actions of p[i] correspond to the actions of p. Similarly, the second, fourth, and fifth actions of p[i] correspond to the actions of process q.

The first action of p[i] is a parameterized action. In this action, process p[i] ends the authentication, if any, between itself and another process p[g]. Then, p[i] initiates a new authentication between itself and process p[g].

In the second action, the notation NCR(bk[g], (c; key[g])) means that the two data items c and key[g] are concatenated into a single data item which is then encrypted using the public key bk[g].

In the third action, the statement (c, e) := DCR(rk, c) means that the data item c on the right-hand side has been constructed by concatenating two data items into one, then encrypting the result using the public key of process p[i]. Thus, when c is decrypted using the private key of process p[i], the result is the two original data items.

18.3 AUTHENTICATION USING SYMMETRIC KEYS

In this section, we consider authentication protocols that use symmetric keys. There are two cases to consider. In the first case, each process pair in the network has a shared key. In the second case, each process in the network has an individual key that is known only to the process and the authentication center of the network. Next, we discuss an authentication protocol that uses shared keys and then discuss an authentication protocol that uses individual keys.

Consider a network consisting of two processes p and q that share a key S. We develop an authentication protocol between p and q in four stages. In each stage, we present a version of the protocol and point out some problem of this version and then discusses how to modify the protocol version to solve the problem. At the end, we achieve a correct and complete version of the protocol.

The first version of the protocol can be defined as follows:

```
p -> q : n
q -> p : S<n>,
```

This protocol version consists of two steps. In the first step, process p generates a random nonce n and sends it to process q. In the second step, process q encrypts the received nonce using the shared key S and sends the encrypted nonce S<n> to p. When p receives S<n> , it decrypts it using S and compares the result with the original n. If they are equal, the authentication of q by p is successful; otherwise, the authentication has failed.

One problem of this protocol is that an adversary can utilize this protocol to deceive process p into authenticating process q without q ever receiving or sending a single message. Consider, for example, the following scenario. The adversary intercepts message n after it is sent by p and before it is received by q. Then the adversary pretends to be process q trying to authenticate process p and sends a message n to process p. As dictated by the protocol, process p sends a message S<n> to process q. The adversary intercepts this message and places it in the channel from process q to process p. Process p receives this message, assumes that it is a reply to its original message to process q, and so authenticates q.

To prevent such a scenario, the second message in the protocol is modified to include the identity of its sender. The second version of the protocol is defined as follows:

```
p -> q : n
q -> p : S<n; q>
```

This protocol version needs to be modified to make processes p and q agree on another shared key S'. (Key S' can be used later in encrypting and decrypting the data messages exchanged between p and q, while key S is used solely for authenticating p and q.) The modification consists of making process q select key S' at random and include it in the message to process p. The third version of the protocol is defined as follows.

```
p -> q : n
q -> p : S<n; q; S'>
```

This protocol version needs to be extended to allow process q to authenticate process p. The extension consists of two steps. First, process q generates a random nonce m and includes it in the message to process p. Second, process p replies by sending back the encryption of nonce m using the new shared key S'. The fourth (and final) version of the protocol is defined as follows:

```
p -> q : n
q -> p : S<n; q; S'> , m
p -> q : S'<m>
```

We now turn our attention to an authentication protocol where each process p has an individual key I.p that is known only to p and to a special process called the authentication center ac. As we did in the previous protocol, we develop this authentication protocol in six stages.

The first version of the protocol can be defined as follows:

```
p  -> q  : n
q  -> ac : I.q<n>, p
ac -> p  : I.p<n>, q
```

This protocol version consists of three steps. In the first step, process p generates a random nonce n and sends it to process q. In the second step, q encrypts n using its individual key I.q and sends the encrypted nonce along with the identity of process p to the authentication center ac. In the third step, the authorization center ac decrypts n using I.q, encrypts n using I.p and then sends the encrypted nonce along with the identity of process q to p. When p receives I.p<n>, it decrypts n and compares it with the original n. If they are equal, the authentication of q by p is successful.

One problem of this protocol version is that an adversary can deceive process p into authenticating process q without q ever receiving or sending a single message. Consider, for example, the following scenario. The adversary intercepts message n after it is sent by p and before it is received by q. The adversary then pretends to be a third process r trying to authenticate p and sends a message n to p. As dictated by the protocol, process p sends a message (I.p<n>, r) to process ac. The adversary intercepts this message, modifies it slightly to become (I.p<n>, q), and places the modified message in the channel from process ac to process p. Process p receives this message and assumes wrongly that it is a reply to its request message to authenticate process q, and the authentication of q by p succeeds erroneously.

To prevent this scenario, the second message in the protocol is modified to become I.q<n; p> so that it cannot be easily manipulated by any adversary. The second version of the protocol is defined as follows:

```
p  —> q  : n
q  —> ac : I.q<n; p>
ac —> p  : I.p<n>, q
```

Consider the following scenario. An adversary intercepts message n after it is sent by p and before it is received by q. The adversary then pretends to be a third process r that process p is trying to authenticate and sends a message (I.r<n; p>) to process ac. As dictated by the protocol, process ac sends a message (I.p<n>, r) to process p. The adversary intercepts this message, modifies it slightly to become (I.p<n>, q), and places the modified message in the channel from process ac to process p. Process p receives this message and assumes wrongly that it is a reply to its request message to authenticate process q. The authentication of q by p succeeds without q receiving or sending a single message.

To prevent this scenario, the third message in the protocol is modified to become I.p<n; q> so that it cannot be easily manipulated by any adversary. The third version of the protocol is defined as follows.

```
p  —> q  : n
q  —> ac : I.q<n; p>
ac —> p  : I.p<n; q>
```

The second and third messages in this protocol have the same structure. This fact can be exploited by an adversary as illustrated by the following scenario. The adversary intercepts message n after it is sent by p and before it is received by q. The adversary then places message n in the channel from process q to process p, as if q is trying to authenticate p. As dictated by the protocol, process p sends a message I.p<n; q> to process ac. The adversary intercepts this message and places it in the channel from process ac to process p. Process p receives this message and assumes wrongly that it is a reply to its request message to authenticate process q. The authentication of q by p succeeds without q receiving or sending a single message.

To avoid this scenario, the second and third messages in the protocol need to have different structures. This can be accomplished by requiring the authentication center ac to generate a key S at random and insert it in the third message before sending this message to process p. The fourth version of this protocol can be defined as follows:

```
p  —> q  : n
q  —> ac : I.q<n; p>
ac —> p  : I.p<n; q; S>
```

Key S, generated by the authentication center ac, needs to be delivered to process q in the same secure way as it is delivered to process p. Therefore, process q generates a nonce m at random and sends it in its message to process ac. Then, process ac adds a field I.q<m; p; S> in its message to process p. Process p then forwards this field to process q. The fifth version of the protocol is as follows:

```
p  -> q  : n
q  -> ac : I.q<n; p> , m
ac -> p  : I.p<n; q; S> , I.q<m; p; S>
p  -> q  : I.q<m; p; S>
```

In this protocol, process p authenticates process q but q does not authenticate p. In order that q can authenticate p, nonce m, generated at random by q, is added to the message from process ac to process p. Then p includes a field S<m> in its last message to process q. The sixth (and last) version of the protocol is as follows.

```
p  -> q  : n
q  -> ac : I.q<n; p> , m
ac -> p  : I.p<n; q; S> , I.q<m; p; S> , m
p  -> q  : I.q<m; p; S> , S<m>
```

In this protocol, the first message, from p to q, is called a challenge. The second message, from q to ac, is called a second challenge. The third message, from ac to p, is called a response. The fourth message, from p to q, is called a second response.

To realize this protocol in a network consisting of the processes p[i: 0 . . n − 1] and ac, where process ac is the authentication center in the network, we adopt similar constants, inputs, and variables as those used in the authentication protocol in Section 18.2.

Process p[i: 0 . . n − 1] in the authentication protocol, that uses individual keys, can be defined as follows.

```
process p[i: 0..n - 1]

const r              {r-1 is the largest value for a key}

inp  N          :  set { g |0 ≤ g < n ∧ g ≠ i},
     ik         :  0..r-1, {individual key of p[i]}

var  st         :  array [N] of 0..3,
     key        :  array [N] of 0..r-1,
     nc         :  array [N] of 0..s-1,
     c, d, e, f :  integer,
     x          :  0..n-11
```

```
par    g      : N

begin
       st[g] = 0 ∨ st[g] = 3 →
              st[g], nc[g] := 1, NNC;
              send chlng(nc[g]) to p[g]


☐      rcv chlng(c) from p[g] →
              if st[g] = 1 ∧ g ≥ i → skip
              ☐ st[g] ≠ 1 ∨ g < i →
                     st[g], nc[g] := 2, NNC;
                     c := NCR(ik, (c; g));
                     send schlng(c, nc[g]) to ac
              fi

☐      rcv rspn(c, d, e) from ac →
              (c, x, f) := DCR(ik, c);
              if st[x] ≠ 1 ∨ c ≠ nc[x] → skip
              ☐ st[x] = 1 ∧ c = nc[x] →
                     st[x], key[x] := 3, f;
                     e := NCR(key[x], e);
                     send srspn(d, e) to p[x]
              fi

☐      rcv srspn(c, d) from p[g] →
              (c, x, f) := DCR(ik, c);
              d := DCR(f, d);
              if st[g] ≠ 2 ∨ c≠nc[g] ∨ c≠d ∨ x≠g → skip
              ☐ st[g] = 2 ∧ c=nc[g] ∧ c=d ∧ x=g →
                     st[g], key[g] := 3, f
              fi

☐ timeout
       (st[g] = 1 ∨ st[g] = 2) ∧
       (#ch.p[i].p[g] + #ch.p[g].ac + #ch.ac.p[i] = 0)
              → st[g] := 0
end
```

The authentication center ac can be defined as follows.

process ac

const r

inp   ik   :   **array** [0..n-1] **of** 0..r-1

```
                    {ik[i] in ac = ik in p[i] }

var    key       :    0..r-1,
       c, d, e   :    integer,
       x         :    0..n-1
par    g         :    0..n-1

begin
       rcv schlng(c, d) from p[g] ->
              (c, x) := DCR(ik[g], c);
              key := random;
              e := NCR(ik[x], (c; g; key));
              c := NCR(ik[g], (d; x; key));
              send rspn(e, c, d) to p[x]
end
```

18.4   PRIVACY AND INTEGRITY

In principle, privacy and integrity can be achieved using asymmetric or symmetric key pairs. In practice, however, using asymmetric key pairs in achieving these goals is more computationally intensive than using symmetric key pairs. Therefore, most privacy and integrity protocols use symmetric, in fact shared, keys. In this section, we discuss some of these protocols.

Consider a network that consists of two processes p and q and assume that p and q have a shared key S. (Note that S could have been generated during the mutual authentication phase between p and q, as discussed in Sections 18.2 and 18.3.) For p to send a data message to q and ensure that no adversary can understand this message, p encrypts the data message using the shared key S before sending the message to q. Thus, the protocol for achieving privacy can be defined as follows:

```
p -> q : S<data>
```

In order that p can send a data message to q and ensure that no adversary can modify the message before it is received by q, p attaches to the message some checksum of the message after it is encrypted using the shared key S. Thus, the protocol for achieving integrity can be defined as follows:

```
p -> q : data, CHKSM(S<data>)
```

To achieve both privacy and integrity, process p attaches to the data message some checksum of the message and then encrypts the resulting message using the shared key S and sends the encrypted message to q. Thus, the protocol for achieving both privacy and integrity can be defined as follows:

```
p -> q : S<data; CHKSM(data)>
```

To achieve privacy and integrity in a network p[i: 0 .. n − 1], each process p[i] has a shared key sk[g] with every other process p[g] in the network. Process p[i] uses sk[g] in encrypting each data message before sending it to p[g] and in decrypting any data message after receiving it from p[g]. Note that p[g] has an identical key, sk[i], that p[g] uses in encrypting each data message before sending it to p[i] and in decrypting each data message after receiving it from p[i].

Using the same key in encrypting and decrypting a large number of data messages between p[i] and p[g] may invite an adversary to try to deduce that key. Therefore, to encrypt a data message, p[i] first generates a random nonce nc, computes a new key from sk[g] and nc and then uses this new key in encrypting the data message.

The action in process p[i] for sending a data message to p[g] is as follows:

```
true    ->
                nc, d := NNC, GETDATA;
                key, chk := NEWKEY(sk[g], nc), CHKSM(d);
                e := NCR(key, (d; chk));
                send data(nc, e) to p[g]
```

In this action, d is the data item to be sent to p[g], chk is a checksum of the data item d, and e is the encryption of d and chk using the key NEWKEY(sk[g], nc).

When process p[g] receives a data(nc, e) message from p[i], p[g] uses its key sk[i] and the received nc to compute a new key NEWKEY(sk[i], nc). Then p[g] uses this new key to decrypt e and recover both d and chk. Process p[g] then checks whether CHKSM(d) equals chk. If so, p[g] concludes that the message was indeed sent by p[i] and stores the message; otherwise p[g] discards the message.

The action in process p[i] for receiving a data message from p[g] is as follows:

```
rcv data(nc, e) from p[g]        ->
                key := NEWKEY(sk[g], nc);
                (d, chk) := DCR(key, e);
                if CHKSM(d) = chk -> {store d} skip
                [] CHKSM(d) ≠ chk -> {discard d} skip
                fi
```

Process p[i] in the privacy and integrity protocol can be defined as follows:

```
process p[i: 0..n-1]

const r

inp    N           :       set {g|0 ≤ g < n ∧ g ≠ i},
       sk          :       array [N] of 0..r-1
                           {shared keys:          }
```

```
                                        {sk[g] in p[i] = sk[i] in p[g]}

var    key         :        0..r-1,       {new key}
       nc          :        integer,      {random nonce}
       d, chk, e   :        integer       {data and checksum}

par    g           :        N

begin
       true    ->
                   nc, d := NNC, GETDATA;
                   key, chk := NEWKEY(sk[g], nc), CHKSM(d);
                   e := NCR(key, (d; chk));
                   send data(nc, e) to p[g]

       rcv data(nc, e) from p[g]          ->
                   key := NEWKEY(sk[g], nc);
                   (d, chk) := DCR(key, e);
                   if CHKSM(d) = chk -> {store d} skip
                   [] CHKSM(d) != chk -> {discard d} skip
                   fi
end
```

18.5 NONREPUDIATION

Consider a network that consists of two processes p and q. In order that p can send a data message to q and provide q with a proof that p has indeed sent this message, p attaches to the message an encryption of the message using its private key R.p. An encryption of a message using the private key R.p of a process p is called a digital signature of the message by process p. Process q can use the digital signature attached to a received message to prove that p has indeed sent the message. Thus, the protocol for achieving nonrepudiation can be defined as follows:

p -> q : data, R.p<data>

Note that this protocol also achieves integrity.

To achieve both privacy and nonrepudiation, p attaches to the data message its digital signature of the message and then encrypts the resulting message using the shared key S between p and q. Thus, the protocol for achieving both privacy and nonrepudiation can be defined as follows:

p -> q : S<data, R.p<data>

Note that this protocol is similar to the protocol for achieving both privacy and integrity in Section 18.4 with one exception. The term CHKSM(data) in the earlier protocol is replaced by the term R.p<data> in the current protocol. Therefore, the network p[i: 0 .. n − 1] for achieving privacy and integrity in Section 18.4 can be modified slightly to achieve nonrepudiation as well.

18.6 AUTHORIZATION

Every process in a network should be prevented from accessing any network resource that the process is not authorized to access. This can be accomplished as follows. First, every network resource is protected by some process in the network. Second, every process maintains an authorization table that lists the processes that are authorized to access resources protected by the process. Third, before a process can access a network resource, it sends a request message to the process that protects the resource. The protecting process checks its authorization table to determine whether to grant the request or reject it.

Next, we discuss how to augment network p[i: 0 , . . . , n − 1] in Section 18.4 with an authorization protocol. The augmentation consists of the following five steps:

i. Add two constants v and w to each process p[i] in the network

    const v, w

    Constant v is the number of network resources protected by one process. Constant w is the number of access modes of a resource. For example, a file resource can have the access modes read, write, append, remove, and duplicate. In this case, w = 5.

ii. The authorization table in each process p[i] is declared as follows:

    inp athr : **array** [N, 0..v-1, 0..w-1] **of boolean**

    where athr[g, x, y] is true iff the virtual neighbor p[g] of p[i] is authorized to access resource x (protected by p[i]) using access mode y.

iii. Each data message sent from a process p[i] to a virtual neighbor p[g] in the augmented protocol is as follows:

    $$data(nc, e)$$

    where

    e   equals NCR(key, (t; x; y; d; chk));
    key   equals NEWKEY(sk[g], nc);
    sk[g] is the key in p[i] shared between p[i] and p[g];
    nc   is a random nonce;

t   is the message type defined as t = 0 if the message is a request, t = 1
         if the message is a grant, t = 2 if the message is a rejection;

x   is the requested resource;

y   is the requested access mode

d   is some text in the message

chk   equals CHKSM(t; x; y; d)

iv. The first action in process p[i] is modified to become as follows.

```
true ->
        nc, t, x, y, d := NNC, 0, any, any, any;
        key, chk := NEWKEY(sk[g], nc),
        CHKSM(t; x; y; d);
        e := NCR(key, (t; x; y; d; chk));
        send data(nc, e) to p[g]
```

v. The second action in process p[i] is modified to become as follows.

```
rcv data(nc, e) from p[g] ->
  key := NEWKEY(sk[g], nc);
  (t, x, y, d, chk) := DCR(key, e);
  if CHKSM(t; x; y; d) ≠ chk ->
                {discard msg} skip
  [] CHKSM(t; x; y; d) = chk ∧ t ≠ 0 ->
                {msg is grant or reject} skip
  [] CHKSM(t; x; y; d) = chk ∧ t = 0 ∧
    athr[g, x, y] ->
                nc, t, d := NNC, 1, any;
                key := NEWKEY(sk[g], nc);
                chk := CHKSM(t; x; y; d);
                e := NCR(key, (t; x; y; d; chk));
                send data(nc, e) to p[g];
  [] CHKSM(t; x; y; d) = chk ∧ t = 0 ∧
    ~athr[g, x, y] ->
                nc, t, d := NNC, 2, any;
                key := NEWKEY(sk[g], nc);
                chk := CHKSM(t; x; y; d);
                e := NCR(key, (t; x; y; d; chk));
                send data(nc, e) to p[g];
  fi
```

In summary, for a process p[i] to request and be granted a resource protected by
a process p[j], the four tasks of authentication, privacy, integrity, and authorization
are needed. First, p[j] needs to authenticate p[i]. Second, both privacy and integrity
need to be provided for every message exchanged between p[i] and p[j]. Third, p[j]
needs to check whether p[i] is authorized to access the requested resource.

18.7 MESSAGE DIGEST

It is possible to reduce the cost of authentication, integrity, and nonrepudiation by using message digest. A message digest MD is a function that computes for any data item d (of type integer), a data item MD(d) in the range $0, \ldots, k-1$ such that the following condition is satisfied:

> *Finger Printing:* There is no efficient algorithm that computes, for any MD(d), a data item d' such that MD(d) = MD(d'). Thus, MD(d) is a finger print of data item d.

Because of this condition, a message digest function MD can be known to every process in a network. Yet, when one process in the network computes MD(d), for some data item d, and another process in the network gets a copy of the computed MD(d), that other process cannot deduce d. Next, we discuss how the processes in a network can use a well-known message digest function MD in making authentication, integrity, and nonrepudiation protocols more efficient.

For a process p to authenticate another process q, p generates a random nonce n and sends it to q. Process q sends back the result MD(S; n; q) of applying function MD to the concatenation of a shared key S between p and q, the nonce n, and the identity of the sender q. This authentication protocol can be defined as follows:

```
p -> q : n
q -> p : MD(S; n; q)
```

This protocol is more efficient than an authentication protocol that does not use MD because MD(S; n; q) has a fixed length of $(\log_2 k)$ bits, whereas S<n; q> can have any number of bits.

For a process p to provide integrity for a data message sent to q, p attaches to the message the result MD(S; data) of applying function MD to the concatenation of the shared key S between p and q and the data message. This integrity protocol can be defined as follows.

```
p -> q : data, MD(S; data)
```

This protocol is more efficient than an integrity protocol that does not use MD, because MD(S; data) is easier to compute than CHKSM(S<data>).

For a process p to provide nonrepudiation for a data message sent to q, p attaches to the message the result R.p<MD(data)> of encrypting MD(data) using the private key R.p of process p. This nonrepudiation protocol can be defined as follows:

```
p -> q : data, R.p<MD.(data)>
```

This protocol is more efficient than a nonrepudiation protocol that does not use MD because R.p<MD(data)> is easier to compute than R.p<data>.

18.8   SECURITY IN THE INTERNET

Four of the five security measures discussed in this chapter, namely authentication, privacy, integrity, and authorization are implemented or proposed to be implemented in the Internet protocol, or IP for short. (The fifth security measure, nonrepudiation, can be implemented, if needed for some application, in the application protocol itself.) In this section, we first discuss how authorization is implemented in IP using firewalls and then discuss how authentication, privacy, and integrity are proposed to be implemented in IP using the simple key management in IP, or SKIP for short.

Authorization in IP

A firewall for an organization is the "augmented" IP process in a router placed at a point where the hosts, routers, and subnetworks belonging to the organization are connected to the rest of the Internet. This IP process is augmented with a predicate, called a message filter, that specifies those IP messages that are authorized to get into the organization. The function of a firewall for an organization is to use its message filter to detect received but unauthorized IP messages and prevent them from getting into the organization.

When a firewall receives an IP message from the outside, it checks whether the message satisfies its message filter. If so, the firewall accepts the message and proceeds to handle it in the usual way. Otherwise, the firewall discards the message.

A message filter specifies the set of conditions that need to be satisfied by any IP message for the message to be accepted by the firewall. These conditions involve the following six attributes of the IP message.

1. subnetwork from which the message is received,
2. IP address of the source of the message,
3. IP address of the destination of the message,
4. transport protocol of the message,
5. source port of the message, and
6. destination port of the message.

Note that attributes 2, 3, and 4 can be determined by the firewall from fields 11, 12, and 9, respectively, in the IP header of the message. Also, attributes 5 and 6 can be determined by the firewall from fields 1 and 2 in the transport header (whether a UDP header or a TCP header) in the message.

Unfortunately, firewalls alone are not sufficient to protect an organization. For example, if several computers in the organization are allowed to receive messages from the outside, and if at least one of these computers has some software that can take an encapsulated message, remove the encapsulation, and process the internal message, then each host, router, and subnetwork in the organization can be attacked from the outside. This situation can be avoided by enforcing the following three rules:

i.   The message filter in a firewall for an organization ensures that any message from the outside is accepted only if the message's destination is a specific IP address inside the organization. This IP address belongs to a host, called the bastion host of that firewall.

ii. Both the firewall and its bastion host are attached to the same subnetwork so that accepted messages from outside the organization can go directly from the firewall to the bastion host without passing through any other computer in the organization.

iii. The software on the bastion host is verified and guaranteed to have no back-doors or bypasses. Thus, if a message from outside the organization is received by the bastion host, then this message cannot harm the hosts, routers, or subnetworks inside the organization.

Following these three rules, two steps are needed to transfer a file from outside the organization to a host h inside the organization. First, the file is transferred from outside the organization to a bastion host of the organization. Second, the file is transferred from the bastion host to host h.

In general, an organization has multiple firewalls, one for each connection between the network of the organization and the rest of the Internet. Associated with each firewall are a message filter and a bastion host. In this case, the message filters of different firewalls need to be equally strict, and the software in each bastion host needs to be equally secure.

Authentication, Privacy, and Integrity in IP

There is a newly proposed protocol for providing authentication and privacy for any IP message. This protocol is called simple key management for IP, or SKIP for short. Next, we describe how the SKIP protocol can be used to provide authentication and privacy for IP messages.

When the IP process in a computer c wants to send a secure IP message whose ultimate destination is the IP process in a computer d, the IP process in c first computes a regular version of the message and sends it to the SKIP process in c. The SKIP process in c computes a secure version of the IP message and sends it out. The secure IP message is treated as a regular IP message by the IP process of every computer it visits before reaching computer d. When the secure IP message finally reaches computer d, it is forwarded to the SKIP process in d to check whether or not it is a legitimate message. If it is found to be legitimate, the SKIP process in d extracts the original IP message and forwards it to the IP process in d. Otherwise, the SKIP process in d discards the message.

As mentioned in Section 3.4, an IP message consists of two parts: an IP header and unencrypted text. By contrast, a secure IP message consists of the following four parts:

1. an IP header,
2. a SKIP header,
3. an authentication header, and
4. encrypted text

It remains now to discuss how a SKIP process computes the SKIP header, the authentication header, and the encrypted text for a secure IP message. We first need to present the three assumptions upon which the SKIP protocol was designed:

i. Each computer c in the Internet has a public key B.c (that is known, or can be known, to every computer in the Internet) and a private key R.c (that is known only to c).

ii. Each computer in the Internet knows the same key construction function F. Function F takes as inputs the private key of a computer c and the public key of another computer d and then computes a key S.c.d as follows:

$$S.c.d = F.(R.c, B.d)$$

Function F is required to satisfy the following symmetry condition for every pair of computers c and d in the Internet:

$$S.c.d = S.d.c$$

Only computer c can use F to compute S.c.d, and only computer d can use F to compute S.d.c. However, because S.c.d = S.d.c, the two keys S.c.d and S.d.c can be considered a shared key between the two computers c and d.

iii. Each computer in the Internet knows the same message digest function MD.

The SKIP process in computer c computes the SKIP header for a secure IP message, whose destination is computer d, as follows:

i. Compute the current time T in hours.

ii. Compute a current key CK as follows:

    CK := (MD(S.c.d ; T ; 1) ; MD(S.c.d ; T ; 0))

where ";" is the string concatenation operator, MD is the message digest function, S.c.d is the shared key between computers c and d, T is the current time in hours, 1 is a byte whose value is 1, and 0 is a byte whose value is 0.

iii. Select an encryption key EK at random.

iv. Use the current key CK to encrypt the encryption key EK as follows: CK<EK>.

v. The two main fields in the SKIP header are T, CK<EK>.

The SKIP process in computer c computes the authentication header for a secure IP message, whose destination is computer d, as follows:

   i. Compute an authentication key AK as follows:

$$AK := (MD(EK ; 3) ; MD(EK ; 1))$$

       where EK is the encryption key discussed earlier, 3 is a byte whose value is 3, and 1 is a byte whose value is 1.

  ii. Compute a string s that consists of the concatenation of the following four componenets in the secure IP message:

     a. the IP header (with every field that may change its value during the message transmission from computer c to computer d being assigned the value 0),

     b. the SKIP header,

     c. the authentication header (with its main field being assigned the value 0), and

     d. the encrypted text (discussed below).

 iii. The main field in the authentication header is $MD(AK; s; AK)$.

The SKIP process in computer c computes the encrypted text for a secure IP message, whose destination is computer d, as follows:

   i. Compute a privacy key pk as follows:

$$PK := (MD(EK ; 2) ; MD(EK ; 0))$$

       where EK is the encryption key discussed earlier, 2 is a byte whose value is 2, and 0 is a byte whose value is 0.

  ii. Encrypt the text in the original IP message using the privacy key PK discussed earlier as PK<text>.

Next, we discuss how the SKIP process in computer d can determine whether a received secure IP message is legitimate. When the SKIP process in d receives a secure IP message, it extracts from the message the following items: the two main fields T_c and $CK_c<EK_c>$ of the SKIP header, the main field $MD.(AK_c; s_c; AK_c)$ of the authentication header, and the encrypted text $PK_c<text_c>$. (Note that we use subscript c to identify each item computed by the SKIP process in computer c.) Then, the SKIP process in computer d, henceforth called process kd, executes the following steps:

   i. Process kd first compares T_c with its own current time T_d in hours. If $T_c \neq T_d$ and $T_c \neq T_d - 1$, then process kd considers the received IP message illegitimate and discards it. Otherwise, process kd considers the received IP message legitimate and proceeds to the next step.

ii. Process kd uses T_c and its version S.d.c of the shared key between c and d to compute the current key CK_d. It then uses CK_d to decrypt the received $CK_c<EK_c>$ and obtain the encryption key EK_d. Using EK_d, process kd proceeds to compute the authentication key AK_d and the privacy key PK_d.

iii. Then process kd computes string s_d from the received message, and computes $MD(AK_d; s_d; AK_d)$ and then compares the result with the received $MD(AK_c; s_c; AK_c)$. If they are unequal, process kd considers the received IP message illegitimate and discards it. Otherwise, it considers the received IP message legitimate and proceeds to the next step.

iv. Finally, process kd uses the computed privacy key PK_d to decrypt the received $PK_c<text_c>$ and obtain q. It then delivers the IP header and $text_d$ to the IP process in computer d.

18.9 BIBLIOGRAPHICAL NOTES

A theory of secrecy in communication systems is discussed in Shanon [1949]. Public and private keys and their use in authentication and privacy are discussed in Diffie and Hellman [1976, 1979]. A survey on symmetric and asymmetric encryption is given in Simmons [1979]. Authentication protocols are discussed in Needham and Schroeder [1978] and Steiner et al. [1988]. Authentication using passwords is discussed in Morris and Thompson [1979]. Privacy and integrity protocols are discussed in Schneier [1994] and Zimmermann [1995]. Digital signatures and their use in nonrepudiation protocols are discussed in Rivest et al. [1978], Saltzer [1978], and Steves et al. [1997]. The current message digest in the Internet, MD 5, is presented in Rivest [1992]. The SKIP is discussed in Aziz et al. [1995].

Formal verification of authentication protocols is discussed in Burrows et al. [1990] and Woo and Lam [1992].

EXERCISES

1   (Authentication Using Public and Private Keys). The authentication protocol that uses public and private keys in Section 18.2 is designed starting with the following construct.

```
p -> q   :      n
q -> p   :      R.q<n>
```

Starting with the following construct, design another authentication protocol that uses public and private keys.

```
p -> q   :        B.q<n>,
q -> p   :        n
```

2 (Authentication Using Public Keys). Is it possible to design an authentication protocol that uses public and private keys with the constraint that the encryption in every sent message is done using a public key? Explain your answer.

3 (Authentication Using Private Keys). Is it possible to design an authentication protocol that uses public and private keys with the constraint that the encryption in every sent message is done using a private key? Explain your answer.

4 (Incorrect Authentication Protocol). In the following authentication protocol, process p is supposed to authenticate process q and to get a shared key S generated by q:

```
p -> q   :        n
q -> p   :        B.p<R.q<n;  S>>
```

Exhibit a scenario of this protocol, involving activities of process p, process q, and an adversary process, where process p ends up authenticating process q even though the adversary process gets a copy of key S.

5 (Loose Authentication Protocol). In the following authentication protocol, process p is supposed to authenticate process q and to get a shared key S generated by q:

```
p -> q   :        n
q -> p   :        R.q<n;  B.p<S>>
```

Exhibit a scenario of this protocol, involving activities of process p, process q, and an adversary process, where process p ends up authenticating process q even though process q has not sent the message R.q<n; B.p<S>>.

6 (Correctness of Authentication Protocols). In each of the following two authentication protocols, process p is supposed to authenticate process q and to get a shared key S generated by q:

```
p -> q   :        R.p<n>,
q -> p   :        B.p<R.q<n;  S>>


p -> q   :        R.p<n; p>
q -> p   :        B.p<R.q<n;  S>>
```

Which of these two protocols, if any, is correct, and which, if any, is incorrect. Explain your answer.

7 (Loose Authentication Protocol). In the following authentication protocol,

each of the two processes p and q is supposed to authenticate the other process, and process p is supposed to get a shared key S generated by q:

```
p -> q  :     n
q -> p  :     R.q<B.p<n>> , R.q<B.p<S>> , m
p -> q  :     S<m>
```

Exhibit a scenario of this protocol, involving activities of process p, process q, and an adversary process, where process p ends up authenticating process q even though process q has not sent the message
R.q < B.p<n>> , R.q < B.p<S>> , m.

8   (Incorrect Authentication Protocol). In the following authentication protocol, each of the two processes p and q is supposed to authenticate the other process, and process p is supposed to get a shared key S generated by q:

```
p -> q  :     n
q -> p  :     B.p<R.q<n; S>> , m
p -> q  :     S<m>
```

Exhibit a scenario of this protocol, involving activities of process p, process q, and an adversary process, where the authentication is completed successfully even though the adversary process gets a copy of key S.

9   (Incorrect Authentication Protocol). In the following authentication protocol, each of the two processes p and q is supposed to authenticate the other process, and process p is supposed to get a shared key S generated by q:

```
p -> q  :     n
q -> p  :     R.q<n>, , B.p<S> , m
p -> q  :     S<m>
```

Exhibit a scenario of this protocol, involving activities of process p, process q, and an adversary process, where the authentication is completed successfully even though the adversary process gets a copy of key S.

10 (Correctness of an Authentication Protocol). In the following authentication protocol, each of the two processes p and q is supposed to authenticate the other process, and process p is supposed to get a shared key S generated by q:

```
p -> q  :     n
q -> p  :     R.q<B.p<n; S>
p -> q  :     S<S>
```

Is this protocol correct? Explain your answer.

11   (Correctness of Authentication Protocols). In the following two authentication
     protocols, each of the two processes p and q is supposed to authenticate the
     other process, and process p is supposed to get a shared key S generated by q:

```
p  ->  q    :        B.q<n>,
q  ->  p    :        B.p<n; m; S>
p  ->  q    :        B.q<m>

p  ->  q    :        B.q<n>,
q  ->  p    :        B.p<n; S>
p  ->  q    :        B.q<S>
```

     Which of these protocols, if any, is correct, and which, if any, is incorrect? Ex-
     plain your answer.

12   (Correctness of Authentication Protocols). Consider the following authentica-
     tion protocol that uses public and private keys that allow process p to authenti-
     cate process q and get a shared key S generated by q:

```
p  ->  q    :        R.p<B.q<n>>
q  ->  p    :        R.q<B.p<n; S>>
```

     Is this protocol loose? Is it incorrect? Explain your answer. (This protocol is
     loose if an adversary can cause process p to authenticate q even though q has
     not sent the message R.q<B.p<n; S>>.)

13   (Mutual Authentication). The authentication protocols between processes p
     and q in Sections 18.2 and 18.3 have the undesirable property that an adversary
     can cause the authentication to succeed in one direction and fail in the other di-
     rection. (For example, p succeeds in authenticating q but q fails in authenticat-
     ing p.) Is it possible to modify these protocols such that either the authentica-
     tion succeeds in both directions or fails in both directions. Explain your
     answer.

14   (Authentication Using One Message). Consider the following three authentica-
     tion protocols. In each protocol, process p sends one message to convince
     process q to authenticate p and to pass to q a shared key S to be used later be-
     tween processes p and q:

```
p  ->  q    :        B.q<p; n; R.p<n; S>>
p  ->  q    :        B.q<p; n; q; R.p<n; q; S>>
p  ->  q    :        B.q<p; t; q; R.p<t; q; S>>
```

     In the first two protocols, n is a random nonce generated by process p. In the
     third protocol, t is the real-time at process p when p sends the message to q.
     Because we assume that the two real time clocks at p and q are synchronized, t

is also the real time at process q when p sends the message to q. Which of these protocols, if any, is incorrect? Which of them, if any, is loose? Which of them, if any, is correct? Explain your answers. (Any of these protocols is incorrect if an adversary can send a message to a process q and convince it that it is a process p and moreover the adversary can get the shared key S. Any of these protocols is loose if an adversary can send a message to a process q and convince it that it is a process p but the adversary cannot get the shared key S. Any of these protocols is correct if no adversary can send a message to a process q and convince it that it is a process p.)

15 (Using an Authentication Center). The authentication protocol in Section 18.2 does not have an authentication center, like the protocol in Section 18.3. This is because we assumed that each process knows the public key of every process in the network. It is required to modify this protocol assuming that every process may or may not know the public key of any other process. However, the network has an authentication center ac that knows the public key of every process, and every process knows the public key of ac. Design this protocol for a network of three processes p, q, and ac.

16 (Using an Authentication Center). Extend the authentication protocol in exercise 15 to a general network that consists of n processes p[i: 0 .. n − 1] and an authentication center ac.

17 (Multiple Authentication Centers). Consider a network that consists of four processes p, q, ac, and ad. Process p has an individual key I.p that is known only to the authentication center ac, whereas process q has an individual key I.q that is known only to the authentication center ad. Assume that process ac has public and private keys B.c and R.c and process ad has public and private keys B.d and R.d. Design an authentication protocol between processes p and q.

18 (Multiple Authentication Centers). Solve exercise 17 in the case where the authentication centers ac and ad do not have public and private keys but they do have a shared key S.

19 (Multiple Authentication Centers). Extend the protocol in exercise 17 to a network that consists of processes p[i: 0 .. m − 1, j: 0 .. n − 1] and authentication centers ac[i: 0 .. m − 1]. Mutual authentication between any two processes p[i, j] and p[i, j'], where j ≠ j', can be carried out using only one authentication center ac[i]. Mutual authentication between any two processes p[i, j] and p[i', j'], where i ≠ i', can be carried out using two authentication centers ac[i] and ac[i'].

20 (Multiple Authentication Centers). Extend the protocol in exercise 18 to a network that consists of processes p[i: 0 .. m − 1, j: 0 .. n − 1] and authentication centers ac[i: 0 .. m − 1]. Mutual authentication between any two processes p[i, j] and p[i, j'], where j ≠ j', can be carried out using only one authentication center ac[i]. Mutual authentication between any two processes p[i, j] and

p[i´, j´], where i ≠ i´, can be carried out using two authentication centers ac[i] and ac[i´].

21 (Detecting Message Generation and Corruption). Explain how the data encryption protocol in Section 18.4 can detect, in the stream of received data messages, those illegitimate messages that are generated by an adversary. Also, explain how this protocol can detect message corruption.

22 (Tolerating Message Reorder). Modify the data encryption protocol in Section 18.4 so that it can tolerate message reorder.

23 (Tolerating Message Loss). Modify the data encryption protocol in Section 18.4 so that it can tolerate message loss.

24 (Tolerating Message Loss and Reorder). Modify the data encryption protocol in Section 18.4 so that it can tolerate message loss and message reorder.

25 (Integrity protocols). The following five protocols are intended to provide integrity for a data message sent from process p to process q:

```
p -> q    :        data, S<data>
p -> q    :        data, CHKSM(data)
p -> q    :        data, S<CHKSM(data)>
p -> q    :        data, CHKSM(S<data>)
p -> q    :        data, CHKSM(S; data)
```

In these protocols, S is a shared key between p and q and CHKSM is a function for computing a checksum for any data. Order these protocols (into the best, the second best, the third best, the fourth best, and the fifth best) based on the following criteria: correctness, number of sent bits, and difficulty of computation. Explain your answer in concise English.

26 (Privacy and Integrity Using Message Digest). The security protocol in Section 18.4 achieves both privacy and integrity. Make this protocol more efficient assuming that every process p[i: 0 .. n − 1] knows a message digest function MD.

27 (Achieving Privacy and Nonrepudiation). The security protocol in Section 18.4 achieves both privacy and integrity. Modify this protocol, as discussed in Section 18.5, to make the protocol achieve both privacy and nonrepudiation.

28 (Privacy and Nonrepudiation Using Message Digest). Make the protocol in exercise 27 more efficient assuming that every process p[i: 0 .. n − 1] knows a message digest function MD.

29 (Authentication and Integrity Using Message Digest). Consider the following authentication protocol.

```
p -> q    :        n
```

```
q -> p    :       MD(S; n)
```

In this protocol, n is a nonce generated at random by p, MD is a message digest function, and S is a shared key between processes p and q. The function of this protocol is to allow process p to authenticate process q. Modify this protocol, without increasing the number of exchanged messages, to allow process q to send some data to process p and to provide integrity for that data.

30 (Integrity Using Message Digest). Consider the following three protocols that provide integrity for a data message sent from process p to process q:

```
p -> q    :       data, MD(S; data)

p -> q    :       data, MD(S; data; p)

p -> q    :       n
q -> p    :       data, MD(S; data; p; n)
```

In these protocols, MD is a message digest function, S is a shared key between p and q, and n is a nonce generated at random by process p. Compare the effectiveness and cost of these three protocols.

31 (Secret Voting). Consider a network that consists of two processes p and q. The computation in this network is an infinite sequence of rounds. In each round, process p sends a vote request message to process q and then receives a vote message from q. Each vote has one of two meanings: yes or no. Process p has a private key rp and a public key bp, and process q has a private key rq and a public key bq. Design this protocol to prevent an adversary from manipulating the votes cast by q or from figuring out how q voted. The adversary can perform each of the following actions a finite number of times (during any infinite execution of the protocol): Remove a message from a channel. Copy a message from a channel. Replace a message in a channel with a message that it has copied earlier.

CHAPTER 19

DATA COMPRESSION

Before a process sends a sequence of data messages to one of its virtual neighbors, the process tries to reduce the number of bits in each message. Reducing, or compressing, the number of bits in sent messages is useful because short messages can be handled (i.e., sent, propagated, and received) in less time, and they can be stored in less storage than long messages. Moreover, if two or more consecutive messages in the message sequence become short enough, then these messages can be grouped together into one message, thus reducing the number of messages that need to be sent.

After a compressed message is received, the receiving process can decompress the message and restore it to its original form. The protocol for compressing data messages before sending them and decompressing messages after receiving them is called a data compression protocol.

In general, methods for compressing and decompressing data messages can be divided into two classes: inter-message methods and intra-message methods. We discuss these two classes of methods next.

Inter-message methods for data compression can be applied when the data messages to be sent have "close" contents. In this case, data compression can be achieved as follows. Only a small fraction of the messages are sent in full; these messages are called reference messages. For each other message, only the "difference" between the content of this message and the content of the last reference message is sent. Because the contents of consecutive messages are close, the difference between the contents of two consecutive messages is much less than the content of one full message. The specifics of inter-message methods depend on how to define closeness of message contents and how to compute the difference between two message contents. These issues are application dependent, and so inter-message methods are not discussed further in this chapter. Nevertheless, several problems are devoted to these methods at the end of this chapter.

In intra-message compression, each symbol in a message is encoded using a codeword of bits such that the total number of bits that encode the message is kept as small as possible. Consider a message that has 2^k distinct symbols. Thus in a straightforward encoding, each symbol can be encoded using k bits, and the message can be encoded using k × m bits, where m is the total number of symbols in the message. Intra-message compression can be used to encode this message using less than k × m bits.

There are three basic approaches to intra-message compression. They are as follows.

i. Occurrence Frequency Compression: Instead of encoding each symbol using k bits, each frequently occurring symbol is encoded using less than k bits, and each rarely occurring symbol is encoded using more than k bits. The net effect is that the message is encoded using less than k × m bits. This form of encoding is called occurrence frequency compression. A well-known method of occurrence frequency compression is Huffman compression, and it is discussed in detail in Sections 19.1 through 19.3.

ii. Context-Sensitive Compression: Instead of encoding each symbol using k bits, each symbol is encoded using r bits, where r > k. After assigning different codewords (of r bits each) to distinct symbols, there are $(2^r - 2^k)$ codewords left unassigned. Each of these codewords can be used to encode a sequence of symbols that occurs frequently in the message. Thus, a frequent sequence of s symbols can be encoded using one codeword of r bits, which is usually less than the k × s bits needed to encode this same sequence using straightforward encoding. This form of encoding is called context-sensitive compression. Three methods of context-sensitive compression are discussed in Section 19.4.

iii. Lossy Compression: Instead of encoding each symbol using k bits, each symbol is encoded using r bits, where r < k. On the positive side, the message is encoded using r × m bits (which is less than the k × m bits used in a straightforward encoding). On the negative side, two or more distinct symbols can be encoded using the same codeword. Thus, encoding a message and then decoding it may not yield the same exact message. This form of encoding is called lossy compression. A method of lossy compression is discussed in Section 19.5.

19.1 HUFFMAN CODING

Consider a data message that needs to be compressed before being sent. Let s.0, . . . , s.(n-1) denote the n distinct symbols in the message. In this message, if the number of occurrences of a symbol s.i is larger than the number of occurrences of another symbol s.j, then it is beneficial to use a smaller number of bits to encode s.i than that to encode s.j (instead of using the same number of bits to encode both s.i and s.j). In general, the number of bits used to encode a symbol s.i should be inversely proportional to the number of occurrences of s.i in the data messages.

The following procedure, called HUFFMAN, takes as an input the number of occurrences occr[i] of every symbol s.i in the data message and then computes for every i an integer rank[i] whose binary representation is the codeword for s.i:

```
procedure
    HUFFMAN (in    occr : array [0..n-1] of integer,
             out   rank : array [0..n-1] of integer)

local pre, post :
            set { (x, c) |
            x is a subset of {0, 1, ..., n-1} and
            c is the sum of occr[i] for every i in x
                        }

begin

i.     pre    :=    { ({i}, occr[i]) | 0 ≤ i < n }
       post   :=    the empty set

ii.    do pre has two or more elements →
               find two elements (x', c') and (x'', c'') in
               set pre such that c' and c'' are the two
               smallest c values in pre; then
               pre := (pre - {(x', c'), (x'', c'')}) ∪
                       {(x'∪x'', c'+c'')}
               post := post ∪ {(x', c'), (x'', c'')}
       od

iii.   Remove the last element ({0, ..., n-1}, occr[0]+
       ... +occr[n-1]) from set pre and add it to set
       post.

iv.    For each element (x, c) in set post, define a
       codeword w.(x, c) as follows.
           w.({0, ..., n-1}, occr[0]+ ... +occr[n-1]) :=
               empty bit string;
           do w.(x'∪x'', c'+c'') is defined ∧
              w.(x', c') is undefined ∧
              w.(x'', c'') is undefined →
                      w.(x', c') := (0 ; w.(x'∪x'', c'+c'') )
                      w.(x'', c'') := (1 ; w.(x'∪x'', c'+c'') )
           od
       Note that ";" is the concatenation operator over
       bit strings.
```

v.   For every i, 0 ≤ i < n, add a left most 1-bit to
        every w.({i}, occr[i]), then define rank[i] as
        follows.
          rank[i] := the integer whose binary
                        representation is w.({i}, occr[i])
end

For each i, $0 \leq i < n$, the codeword w.({i}, occr[i]) that results from step iv in procedure HUFFMAN is called a Huffman codeword of symbol s.i.

As an example of applying procedure HUFFMAN, consider a message whose distinct symbols are s.0 to s.5. Assume that the number of occurrences of each of these symbols in the message is as follows:

$$occr[0] = 50, \qquad occr[1] = 15, \qquad occr[2] = 10,$$
$$occr[3] = 5, \qquad occr[4] = 10, \qquad occr[5] = 10$$

After applying step i in procedure HUFFMAN, the local sets pre and post are as follows:

```
pre = {        ({0}, 50) , ({1}, 15) , ({2}, 10) ,
               ({3}, 5) , ({4}, 10) ,  ({5}, 10)
       }
post = the empty set
```

After applying steps ii and iii in procedure HUFFMAN, the sets pre and post are as follows:

```
pre = the empty set
post = {       ({0}, 50) , ({1}, 15) , ({2}, 10) ,
               ({3}, 5) , ({4}, 10) ,  ({5}, 10) ,
               ({2, 3}, 15) ,
               ({4, 5}, 20) ,
               ({1, 2, 3}, 30) ,
               ({1, 2, 3, 4, 5}, 50) ,
               ({0, 1, 2, 3, 4, 5}, 100)
        }
```

The elements in set post can be arranged in a binary directed tree as shown in Figure 19.1. This tree describes how the elements are combined as they are moved from set pre to set post. For instance, the two elements ({2}, 10) and ({3}, 5) are combined into a single element ({2, 3}, 15) as they are moved from pre to post. Also, the two elements ({1}, 15) and ({2, 3}, 15) are combined into the element ({1, 2, 3}, 30) as they are moved from pre to post.

Applying step iv, each element in set post is assigned a Huffman codeword as follows.

```
w.({0, 1, 2, 3, 4, 5}, 100) = empty bit string

w.({0}, 50)                  = 0

w.({1, 2, 3, 4, 5}, 50)      = 1

w.({1, 2, 3}, 30)            = 0 ; 1

w.({4, 5}, 20)              = 1 ; 1

w.({1}, 15)                = 0 ; 0 ; 1

w.({2, 3}, 15)             = 1 ; 0 ; 1

w.({2}, 10)               = 0 ; 1 ; 0 ; 1

w.({3}, 5)                = 1 ; 1 ; 0 ; 1

w.({4}, 10)               = 0 ; 1 ; 1

w.({5}, 10)               = 1 ; 1 ; 1
```

The Huffman codewords for the six symbols s.0 to s.5 are as follows:

```
w.({0}, 50) = 0

w.({1}, 15) = 0 ; 0 ; 1
```

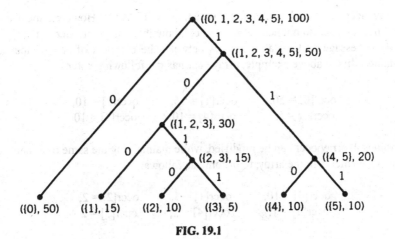

FIG. 19.1

```
w.({2}, 10) = 0 ; 1 ; 0 ; 1

w.({3}, 5)  = 1 ; 1 ; 0 ; 1

w.({4}, 10) = 0 ; 1 ; 1

w.({5}, 10) = 1 ; 1 ; 1
```

Therefore, to send a symbol s.0, a process needs only to send a single 0 bit. To send a symbol s.1, a process needs to send three bits: one 1 bit followed by two 0 bits.

Procedure HUFFMAN then proceeds to compute an integer representation for the Huffman codewords as follows. First, add a 1 bit to the left of each codeword. Second, compute the integer representation, called rank, for each codeword. The reason for adding a 1 bit to the left of each codeword before computing its rank is to ensure that the leftmost 0 bits in any original codeword, if any, do not disappear as we compute the rank of the codeword. For our example, the computed ranks are as follows:

```
rank[0] = 2

rank[1] = 9

rank[2] = 21

rank[3] = 29

rank[4] = 11

rank[5] = 15
```

Array occr is needed as input to procedure HUFFMAN. However, the values stored in array occr do not need to be the actual numbers of occurrences of symbols in a data message as long as the ratios between the numbers of occurrences are maintained. In the above example, array occr has the following values:

$$occr[0] = 50, \quad occr[1] = 15, \quad occr[2] = 10,$$
$$occr[3] = 5, \quad\; occr[4] = 10, \quad occr[5] = 10$$

The values in array occr can be modified, while maintaining the same ratio between every two elements in the array, to become as follows:

$$occr[0] = 10, \quad occr[1] = 3, \quad occr[2] = 2,$$
$$occr[3] = 1, \quad\;\; occr[4] = 2, \quad occr[5] = 2$$

Computing array rank based on this modified occr array yields the same value of rank as before.

The smallest possible value for a rank is 2, thanks to the 1 bit added to the left of every codeword. What is the largest possible value for a rank? The codewords correspond to the leaves of a binary directed tree that has n leaves; see, for instance, Figure 19.1. The number of bits in each codeword equals the number of edges in the directed path from the corresponding leaf to the root of the tree. A directed path from a leaf to the root, in a tree that has n leaves, has at most n-1 edges. Thus, a Huffman codeword has at most $n - 1$ bits. After adding a 1 bit to the left of each codeword, each codeword has at most n bits. Therefore, the largest possible value for a rank is $2^n - 1$.

The declaration of array rank in procedure HUFFMAN can now be modified to become as follows.

```
out    rank  :      array [0..n-1] of 2..2ⁿ-1
```

19.2 STATIC HUFFMAN COMPRESSION

Consider a network where a process p sends an infinite sequence of data units to a virtual neighbor q. The symbols to be sent are stored in an infinite array, named data, in process p. Array data is declared in p as follows:

```
var    data  :      array [integer] of 0..n-1
```

Thus, each data symbol is in the range $0 .. n - 1$.

The ranks of different symbols are provided as an input to both p and q as follows.

```
inp    rank  :      array [0..n-1] of 2..2ⁿ-1
```

Therefore, the following equality holds for every i, $0 \le i < n$:

$$\text{rank}[i] \text{ in process } p \ = \ \text{rank}[i] \text{ in process } q$$

Process p in the static Huffman compression protocol can be defined as follows:

```
process p

const n

inp    rank  :      array [0..n-1] of 2..2ⁿ-1
                    {rank[i] in p = rank[i] in q}
```

```
var    data   :        array [integer] of 0..n-1,
       xp     :        integer,              {index of data}
       rp     :        1..2ⁿ-1,
       bp     :        0..1

begin
       true  ->        rp := rank[data[xp]];
                       do rp ≠ 1 ->
                               bp, rp := rp mod 2, rp div 2;
                               send bit(bp) to q
                       od;
                       xp := xp + 1
end
```

Process p has only one action. In this action, process p first computes the rank of the next symbol in array data. Second, p computes the binary representation of rp and sends it bit by bit to process q starting with the rightmost bit. Note that the leftmost (1) bit is not sent because this bit is not part of the Huffman codeword.

Process q of the static Huffman compression protocol can be defined as follows:

```
process q

const n

inp    rank   :        array [0..n-1] of 2..2ⁿ-1
                       {rank[i] in p = rank[i] in q}

var    rcvd   :        array [integer] of 0..n-1,
       xq     :        integer,     {index of rcvd}
       rq     :        0..2ⁿ-1,     {initially, 0}
       pwr    :        1..2(n-1),   {initially, 1}
       bq     :        0..1,
       j      :        0..n-1

begin
       rcv bit(bq) from p ->
          rq, pwr, j :=
          (bq * pwr) + rq, (2 * pwr), 0;
          do rank[j] ≠ (rq + pwr) ∧ j ≠ n-1 ->
             j := j+1
          od;
          if rank[j] ≠ (rq + pwr) -> skip
          [] rank[j] = (rq + pwr) ->
             rcvd[xq], xq, rq, pwr :=
```

```
                    j, xq+1, 0, 1
        fi
end
```

Process q has only one action. In this action, q receives a bit bq from p and uses it to update rank rq of the symbol currently being received from p. Process q then compares the updated (rq + pwr) with the elements of array rank one by one. If there is no match, process q recognizes that (rq + pwr) is not yet a rank of a data symbol and waits for the next bit from p. If there is a match, that is, rq + pwr = rank[j], then q stores symbol j in the current element of array rcvd and resets rq and pwr to their initial values of 0 and 1, respectively.

19.3 DYNAMIC HUFFMAN COMPRESSION

The above protocol is called a static compression protocol because the value of array rank is fixed. In this section, we describe how to modify this protocol to allow rank to be updated periodically during any execution of the protocol. The modified protocol is called a dynamic Huffman compression protocol.

In the modified protocol, as process p sends the encoding of symbols in array data to process q, p keeps track of the number of occurrences of each symbol. In other words, p keeps array occr current. Periodically, process p calls procedure HUFFMAN, discussed in Section 19.1, to compute a new value for array rank and then sends this new value to process q.

The modified protocol can be obtained from the above protocol as follows.

i. Remove the input arrays rank from processes p and q.

ii. Add the following constant and variables to process p.

```
const   rmax
var     occr  :      array [0..n-1] of 0..rmax,
        rank  :      array [0..n-1] of 2..2ⁿ-1,
        r     :      0..rmax
```

iii. Replace the last statement in the action of process p by the following statement.

```
xp, i := xp+1, data[xp];
occr[i], r := occr[i]+1, r+1;
if r < rmax  ->     skip
[] r = rmax  ->     HUFFMAN(in occr, out rank);
                    send new(rank) to q;
                    occr, r := 0, 0
fi
```

iv. Add the following variable to process q.

var   rank   :   **array** $[0..n-1]$ **of** $2..2^n-1$

v. Add the following action to process q.

rcv new(rank) **from** p $\rightarrow$ **skip**

19.4   CONTEXT-SENSITIVE COMPRESSION

As discussed earlier, Huffman compression is based on the occurrence frequency of individual symbols in a message but does not take into account the occurrence frequency of symbol combinations in the message. Thus, Huffman compression can be regarded as a context-free compression. There are other compression methods that are context sensitive. As it happens, context-sensitive compression is more efficient than context-free compression, especially in compressing digital images and text.

In this section, we discuss three methods of context-sensitive compression: run length compression, differential compression, and dictionary-based compression. The first two methods are useful in compressing digital images, and the third method is useful in compressing text.

Run length compression can be used in compressing a data message where each symbol is likely to be followed by a similar symbol. For example, if each symbol in a message indicates the color of a pixel in some image, and if adjacent symbols in the message correspond to adjacent pixels in the image, then it is likely that the message consists of contiguous runs of the same symbol.

Each run of a symbol s.i is either short or long. A run of symbol s.i is short if the number of symbols in the run is at most r.i, where r.i is the smallest power of 2 that is greater than or equal to the median number of symbols in a run of symbol s.i. A run of symbol s.i is long if the number of symbols in the run is more than r.i. Next, we describe how to represent short and long runs of a symbol s.i.

A short run of a symbol s.i can be represented by a pair (s.i, k.i), where k.i is the number of symbols in the short run minus 1. Thus, the value of k.i is in the range $0..r.i-1$, where r.i is the smallest power of 2 that is greater than or equal the median number of symbols in a run of symbol s.i.

A long run of symbol s.i can be represented by a sequence of one or more pairs of the form (s.i, r.i − 1) followed by a pair of the form (s.i, k.i), where k.i is in the range $0..r.i-1$. In other words, a long run of symbol s.i can be represented as follows:

```
(s.i, r.i - 1); . . . . ; (s.i, ri - 1); (s.i, k.i)
```

Each of the pairs in this sequence can be encoded as a codeword of $(\log_2 n + \log_2 r.i)$ bits, where n is the number of distinct symbols and r.i is the median number of symbols in a run of symbol s.i.

As an example, consider a message that has four distinct symbols s.0, s.1, s.2, and s.3. In this message, let r.i denote the median number of symbols in a run of symbol s.i. The value of each r.i is as follows:

$$r.0 = 4 \quad \text{s.0 symbols}$$

$$r.1 = 5 \quad \text{s.1 symbols}$$

$$r.2 = 2 \quad \text{s.2 symbols}$$

$$r.3 = 1 \quad \text{s.3 symbols}$$

Because there are four symbols, each symbol s.i can be encoded using two bits: s.0 can be encoded as "0; 0," where ; is the concatenation operator of bit strings; s.1 can be encoded as "0; 1"; s.2 can be encoded as "1; 0"; and s.3 can be encoded as "1; 1." A short run of a symbol s.i is represented by a pair (s.i, k.i). Because the value of each k.i is in the range $0 .. (r.i - 1)$, each k.i can be encoded using the following number of bits:

k.0   Can be encoded using two bits
k.1   Can be encoded using three bits
k.2   Can be encoded using one bit
k.3   Can be encoded using zero bit

According to this encoding, a run of four s.0 symbols can be encoded by the bit pattern 0; 0; 1; 1, where 0; 0 encodes symbol s.0 and 1; 1 encodes the number (four) of s.0 symbols in the run minus 1. Similarly, a run of one s.0 symbol can be encoded by the bit pattern 0; 0; 0; 0. Also, a run of seven s.0 symbols can be encoded by the bit pattern 0; 0; 1; 1; 0; 0; 1; 0, where 0; 0; 1; 1 encodes a run of four s.0 symbols and "0; 0; 1; 0" encodes a run of three s.0 symbols.

As mentioned above, run length compression can be used in compressing a data message where each symbol s.i is likely to be followed by a similar symbol s.i. By contrast, differential compression can be used in compressing a data message where each symbol s.i is likely to be followed by symbols from a small set of symbols called FOLLOW(s.i).

As an example of differential compression, consider a message that contains n distinct symbols s.0 . . s.(n-1). Assume that for each symbol s.i, the set FOLLOW(s.i) is defined as

```
FOLLOW(s.i) = {s.i, s.(i+1)}
```

A differential compression of this message can be as follows. Each symbol s.i can be encoded using $1 + \log_2 n$ bits, where the leftmost bit is zero and the remaining ($\log_2 n$) bits have a distinct combination that indicates symbol s.i. If the symbols that occur after a symbol s.i in the message are in the set FOLLOW(s.i), then each of them can be encoded using two bits as follows:

s.i   Can be encoded using "1; 0"

s.(i+1)   Can be encoded using "1; 1"

For instance, consider the following message consisting of nine symbols:

s.2; s.2; s.3; s.3; s.4; s.5; s.4; s.5; s.5

The symbols in this message can be encoded using the following patterns of bits:

0; <combination for s.2>	Encod first s.2
1; 0	Encod second s.2
1; 1	Encod first s.3
1; 1	Encod second s.3
0; <combination for s.4>	Encod first s.4
1; 1	Encod first s.5
1; 0	Encod second s.4
1; 1	Encod second s.5
1; 1	Encod third s.5

This pattern consists of $2 \log_2 n + 16$ bits. It is shorter than a pattern consisting of $9 \log_2 n$ bits that results if straightforward encoding is used. The two-bit encoding of each symbol s.j in the set FOLLOW(s.i) is called a difference encoding between s.i and s.j. Hence this method is called differential encoding.

In dictionary-based compression, if each data message has at most n distinct symbols, then each symbol is encoded using r bits, where r is larger than $\log_2 n$. Therefore, after assigning each symbol to a distinct codeword, the remaining $2^r - n$ codewords are assigned to sequences of symbols, called words, that occur frequently in the messages. Thus, a frequent word is not encoded as a sequence of codewords corresponding to the symbols in the word. Rather, it is encoded as one assigned codeword, regardless of the number of symbols in it.

The mapping between frequent words and their assigned codewords is called a dictionary. Both the sender and receiver of data messages need to have identical dictionaries. The sender uses its dictionary to replace each word by the corresponding codeword in each sent message, and the receiver uses its dictionary to replace each codeword by the corresponding word in each received message.

The two dictionaries in the sender and receiver can be changed while data messages are being sent from the sender to the receiver. This can be accomplished as follows. The sender keeps track of the frequency occurrence of different words in sent messages. If the sender observes that some word w in its dictionary occurs less frequently than another word w' that is not in the dictionary, the sender replaces w by w' in its dictionary and requests from the receiver to replace w by w' in its dictionary. Thus, the two dictionaries in the sender and receiver remain identical. This technique is similar to the one discussed in dynamic Huffman compression in Section 19.3.

19.5 LOSSY COMPRESSION

Each compression protocol discussed so far can be regarded as "lossless" in the following sense. If a sender encodes a data message before sending it (according to some compression protocol), and if a receiver decodes the message after receiving it (according to the same protocol), the receiver ends up with the original message. In other words, no data are lost from a message by encoding it and later decoding it.

It is possible to design a lossy compression protocol that is more efficient than any lossless compression protocol. As an example, consider the case where a data message contains the following m × n distinct symbols:

```
s.(0, 0), s.(0, 1),     ...        , s.(0, n-1)
s.(1, 0), s.(1, 1),     ...        , s.(1, n-1)
...
s.(m-1, 0), s.(m-1, 1), ...    , s.(m-1, n-1)
```

Each symbol s.(i, j) defines the color and shade of a pixel in a digital image, where i determines the shade of the pixel and j determines the color of the pixel. (For example, s.(0,0) defines a light yellow pixel, s.(1, 0) defines a slightly dark yellow pixel, s.(m-1, 0) defines a very dark yellow pixel, and so on.)

If in some situation the shades of pixels are deemed unimportant, then each of the symbols s.(0, j), s.(1, j), ..., s.(m-1, j) can be encoded using the same codeword. In this situation, each symbol can be encoded using a codeword that consists of $\log_2$ n bits only, instead of the $\log_2$ m + $\log_2$ n bits needed for a straightforward encoding.

Similarly, if in another situation the colors of pixels are deemed unimportant, then each of the symbols s.(i, 0), s.(i, 1), . . . , s.(i, n − 1) can be encoded using the same codeword. In this situation, each symbol can be encoded using a codeword that consists of $\log_2$ m bits only (instead of the $\log_2$ m + $\log_2$ n bits needed for a straightforward encoding).

19.6 DATA COMPRESSION IN THE INTERNET

In the Internet, data compression is performed primarily in the application layer. Thus, the standard methods for performing data compression are application dependent. For example, a standard method for compressing digital images is called the Joint Photographic Expert Group method, or JPEG method for short. Also, a standard method for compressing video is called the Moving Pictures Expert Group method, or MPEG method for short.

19.7 BIBLIOGRAPHICAL NOTES

Huffman compression is discussed in Huffman [1952]. Dictionary-based compression is discussed in Ziv and Limpel [1977, 1979], and Welch [1984]. An overview of data compression is presented in Nelson [1992].

The JPEG standard is described in Wallace [1991]. The MPEG standard is discussed in Le Gall [1991].

EXERCISES

1 (Intermessage Compression). Process p has an input array, named data, whose elements are in the range $0 \ldots r - 1$. Process p needs to send the values in array data, one by one, to process q which stores them in an array named rcvd. The elements of array data satisfy the following condition: For almost every i, $|data[i] - data[i + 1]| < s$, where $s << r$. Process p can send each data[i] element in any one of the following three messages:

val(data[i])   if $i = 0 \vee | data[i] - data[i - 1] | \geq s$
pos(data[i] – data[i – 1])   if $i > 0 \wedge 0 \leq data[i] - data[i - 1] < s$
neg(data[i] – data[i – 1])   if $i > 0 \wedge 0 \leq data[i - 1] - data[i] < s$

Design processes p and q.

2 (Inter-message Compression with Periodic Refresh). Modify the protocol in exercise 1 such that process p sends at least one val(data[i]) message in every m consecutive messages that p sends to q for some constant m.

3 (Another Inter-message Compression). Process p has an input array, named data, whose elements are in the range $0 \ldots 1$. Process p needs to send the bits in array data, three bits at a time, to process q, which stores the received bits in an array named rcvd. The elements of array data satisfy the following condition: For almost every i,

$$data[3i] = data[3i + 3]$$

$$data[3i + 1] = data[3i + 4]$$

$$data[3i + 2] = data[3i + 5]$$

Design processes p and q.

4   (Efficiency of Inter-message Compression). Consider the protocol in exercise 1 and assume that every sent message is encoded as a sequence of binary bits. Also, assume that the phrase "for almost every i" means "for about 90% of the i's." Estimate the compression efficiency of this protocol.

5   (Efficiency of Inter-message Compression). Consider the protocol in exercise 3 and assume that the phrase "for almost every i" means "for about 85% of the i's." Estimate the compression efficiency of this protocol.

6   (Inappropriate Inter-message Compression). Assume that the protocol in exercise 1 is used in a situation where the elements of array data satisfy the opposite condition: For every i, where $i > 0$, $|data[i] - data[i-1]| \leq s$. Estimate the inefficiency of using this protocol in this situation.

7   (Rank Computation). Consider a message sequence that has seven distinct symbols. Assume that the number of occurrences of each symbol in the message sequence is as follows:

occr[0] = 704,   occr[1] = 12375,   occr[2] = 532,
occr[3] = 10,   occr[4] = 0,   occr[5] = 704,
occr[6] = 3412

Apply procedure HUFFMAN in Section 19.1 to compute the rank for each of these symbols.

8   (Rank Computation). Consider a message sequence that has eight distinct symbols. Assume that the number of occurrences of each symbol in the message sequence is as follows:

occr[0] = 100,   occr[1] = 211,   occr[2] = 0,   occr[3] = 0,
occr[4] = 0,   occr[5] = 0,   occr[6] = 32,   occr[7] = 157

Apply procedure HUFFMAN in Section 19.1 to compute the rank for each of these symbols.

9   (Static Huffman Compression). Modify process p in the static compression protocol in Section 19.2 as follows. Instead of array rank, process p has two input arrays code and length that store the Huffman codeword for each symbol:

```
inp  code      :    array [0..n-1, 0..n-1] of 0..1,
     length    :    array [0..n-1] of 0..n-1
```

These two arrays are defined such that for every i, where $i \leq length[k]$, code[k, i] is the ith bit in the codeword for the first kth symbol.

10 (Static Huffman Compression). Modify process q in the static compression

protocol in Section 19.2 as follows. Array rank in process q is sorted and each element in this array is tested at most once while q receives the bits that belong to the same codeword.

11   (Resynchronization in Static Huffman Compression). It is required to modify the static compression protocol in Section 19.2 by introducing a special codeword that can be recognized anywhere in the sent bit stream from p to q. This codeword does not correspond to any encoded symbol. Rather, it is sent periodically by the sender p so that the receiver q can resynchronize with p after some bit loss or corruption. Redesign procedure HUFFMAN in Section 19.1 to generate this special codeword along with the ranks of data symbols.

12   (Resynchronization in Dynamic Huffman Compression). Describe how to encode the message new(rank), in the dynamic compression protocol in Section 19.3, as a sequence of 0 and 1 bits.

13   (Run Length Compression). Design the sender and receiver processes for the run length compression example discussed in Section 19.4, where each message has four distinct symbols s.0, s.1, s.2, and s.3.

14   (Run Length Compression). Design a protocol where a process p has an infinite input array, named data, of 0 and 1 bits. Process p sends its data bits to a receiver process q that stores them in an infinite array, named rcvd, of 0 and 1 bits. Each message sent from p to q is of the form bit(b), where b is in the range 0 . . 1. The sent data bits are compressed using a run length compression under the following assumption. In array data, the median number of of symbols in a 0 run is r bits, and the median number of symbols in a 1 run is s bits, where r and s are powers of 2 that are declared as constants in processes p and q.

15   (Run Length Compression). Solve exercise 14 in the special case where s = 1.

16   (Dynamic Run Length Compression). Modify the run length protocol in exercise 15 such that the sender process keeps track of the median number of 0 bits between any two successive 1 bits and then modifies the value of r accordingly and informs the receiver process of the new value of r, Note that in the modified protocol, r is a variable and not a constant.

17   (Efficiency of Run Length Compression). In run length compression, the short and long runs of a symbol s.i are defined as follows:

Short :   (s.i, k.i)
Long: (s.i, r.i -1) ; . . . ; (s.i, r.i - 1) ; (s.i, k.i)

where k.i is in the range 0 . . r.i − 1 and r.i is the smallest power of 2 that is greater than or equal the median number of symbols in a run of symbol s.i. Give an example where the efficiency of run length compression can be increased by defining r.i differently.

18 (Differential Compression). Design the sender and receiver processes for the differential compression example discussed in Section 19.4, where each message has n distinct symbols s.0 .. s.(n − 1).

19 (Lossy Compression). Design the sender and receiver processes for the lossy compression example discussed in Section 19.5, where each message has m × n distinct symbols.

CHAPTER 20

BROADCAST AND MULTICAST

Our discussion so far has centered on one-to-one protocols, that is, protocols for sending messages from one source process to one destination process. In this chapter, we extend the discussion to include broadcast protocols, that is, protocols for sending messages from one source process to every other process in its network. There is in fact a third type of protocol, called multicast protocol, for sending messages from one source process to some (but not necessarily all) of the other processes in the network. Though multicast protocols are more general than broadcast protocols, they in fact can be derived in a straightforward manner from broadcast protocols. Therefore, we will not discuss them any further in this chapter except for several exercises at the end of the chapter.

Some broadcast protocols are designed under the assumption that each process can exchange messages only with its neighbors (rather than with its virtual neighbors) in the network. Such protocols are called low-level. Other broadcast protocols are designed under the assumption that each process can exchange messages with its virtual neighbors (which constitute all other processes) in the network. Such protocols are called high-level.

Low-level protocols operate on top of some data transfer and flow control protocols that guarantee that each process can exchange messages effectively with its neighboring processes in the network. By contrast, high-level protocols operate on top of some routing and switching protocols that guarantee that each process can exchange messages effectively with every process in the network. The fact that routing and switching protocols operate on top of data transfer and flow control protocols should explain the names low-level and high-level.

In a low-level protocol, in order that a source process can broadcast a sequence of data messages to all other processes in the network, the process maintains a spanning tree whose nodes are all the processes in the network. The source process is the root of the tree; it has no parent process and zero or more child processes. Every other process has exactly one parent process and zero or more child processes in the tree. The parent and child processes of a process are all neighbors of that process. The source process starts to send its data messages, one by one, to each of its child processes. When a process receives a data message from its parent process, it keeps one copy of the message and sends a copy of the message to each of its child processes. In other words, the data messages "flow" from the tree root (i.e., the source process) along the tree paths to every node in the tree (i.e., to every process in the network). A protocol for maintaining spanning trees is discussed in Section 20.1. Then, a low-level protocol for broadcasting data messages over the maintained trees is presented in Section 20.2.

In a high-level protocol, when a source process needs to broadcast a sequence of data messages to all other processes in the network, the process sends the messages, one by one, to every other process in the network. When each of these processes receives a data message, it replies with an acknowledgment message to the source process. The exchange of data and acknowledgment messages follows a window protocol similar to the one discussed in Section 9.4. This high-level broadcast protocol is discussed in more detail in Section 20.3.

20.1 MAINTAINING SPANNING TREES

In order that a process p[s] establish a spanning tree whose root is p[s] itself, process p[s] sends a message trqst(s, q), where q is a sequence number identifying the tree being established, to every neighboring process of p[s]. When a process p[i] receives a trqst(s, q) message for the first time from one of its neighboring processes p[g], p[i] recognizes that p[g] is its parent in tree q and forwards a copy of the trqst(s, q) message to each one of its neighboring processes other than p[g].

Later, process p[i] receives some reply message from every neighboring process other than p[g]. The reply is either an ack(s) message or a trqst(s, q) message. If p[i] receives an ack(s) message from a neighboring process p[h], p[i] recognizes that p[h] has received a trqst(s, q) message for the first time from p[i] and has become a child of p[i] in tree q. If p[i] receives a trqst(s, q) message from a neighboring process p[h], p[i] recognizes that p[h] has received a trqst(s, q) message for the first time from a process other than p[i] and has become a child of that other process in tree q.

When p[i] receives a reply message from every neighboring process, other than its parent p[g], p[i] sends an ack(s) message to its parent p[g]. When the source process p[s] receives a reply message from every neighboring process, p[s] recognizes that tree q has been established and that each process in the network knows its parent and child processes in the established tree.

Sometime after tree q is established, process p[s] initiates a new spanning tree, whose sequence number is q + 1, in place of tree q. This is done because some channels in tree q may have become down since the tree has been established, breaking the tree into unconnected fragments. By establishing a new tree, only up channels are included in the new tree. Process p[s] initiates the new tree by sending a trqst(s, q + 1) message to each of its neighboring processes, and the protocol proceeds as discussed above to establish tree q + 1. Some time after tree q + 1 is established, process p[s] initiates a new spanning tree, whose sequence number is q + 2, in place of tree q + 1, and so on.

There is another circumstance for establishing a new spanning tree. Assume that while tree q is being established, some trqst(s, q) or ack(s) message is lost after it is sent by some process and before it is received by another process. This causes the source process p[s] to never receive a reply message for every trqst(s, q) message it has sent to a neighboring process. Thus, tree q is never established. Process p[s] waits for the missing replies for some time then recognizes that some failure, such as a transmission error or a channel failure, has occurred and the missing replies will never arrive. This recognition causes process p[s] to initiate a new tree by sending a trqst(s, q + 1) message to each of its neighboring processes and the establishment of tree q +1 proceeds as discussed above.

To take part in the establishment of successive spanning trees whose root is process p[s], each process p[i] needs the following four variables:

lastq[s]   Stores the sequence number q in the last trqst(s, q) message received by process p[i]

prnt[s]   Stores the index of the neighboring process that is the parent of p[i] in the current tree whose root is process p[s]

chld[s, g] Has the value true iff the neighboring process p[g] is a child of p[i] in the current tree whose root is process p[s]

nrpl[s]   Stores the number of reply (i.e., trqst and ack) messages that p[i] needs to receive before it can send an ack message to its parent in the current tree whose root is p[s]

Each process p[s] in the network initiates successive spanning trees whose roots are p[s]. Therefore, the four variables lastqs, prnts, chlds, h, and nrpls in each process p[i] are elements of four variable arrays declared in p[i] as follows:

```
var    lastq :            array [0..n-1] of integer,
       prnt  :            array [0..n-1] of N,
       chld  :            array [0..n-1, N] of boolean,
       nrpl  :            array [0..n-1] of 0..r
```

In these declarations, n is the number of processes in the network, N is the set of indices of every neighbor p[g] such that the two channels between p[g] and p[i] are up, and r is the number of elements in set N.

Process p[i] in the spanning tree protocol can be defined as follows:

```
process p[i: 0..n-1]

inp   N    :  set {g|p[g] is an up neighbor of p[i]}
      r    :  integer  { # elements in N }

var   lastq :  array [0..n-1] of integer,
      prnt  :  array [0..n-1] of N,
      chld  :  array [0..n-1, N] of boolean,
      nrpl  :  array [0..n-1] of 0..r,
      s     :  0..n-1,
      q     :  integer,
      f, h  :  N

par   g     :  N

begin
      timeout
              (nrpl[i] = 0) \/
              (no trqst(i, lastq[i]) and no ack(i)
              message in any channel)
                      ->
              lastq[i], nrpl[i] := lastq[i]+1, r;
              send trqst(i, lastq[i]) to p[f];
              h := NEXT(N, f);
              do h ≠ f -> send trqst(i, lastq[i]) to p[h];
                      h := NEXT(N, h)
              od

[]    rcv trqst(s, q) from p[g]       ->
              chld[s, g] := false;
              if lastq[s] < q /\ r = 1 ->
                  lastq[s], prnt[s] := q, g;
                  send ack(s) to p[g]

              [] lastq[s] < q /\ r > 1 ->
                  lastq[s], prnt[s], nrpl[s] := q, g, r-1;
                  h := NEXT(N, g);
                  do h ≠ g ->       send trqst(s, q) to p[h];
                          h := NEXT(N, h)
                  od

              [] lastq[s] ≥ q ->
                  nrpl[s] := nrpl[s] - 1;
                  if nrpl[s] ≠ 0 \/ s = i -> skip
                  [] nrpl[s] = 0 /\ s ≠ i ->
```

```
                              send ack(s) to p[prnt[s]]
              fi
         fi

[]    rcv ack(s) from p[g] -->
                     chld[s, g], nrpl[s] := true, nrpl[s]
                     - 1;
                     if nrpl[s] ≠ 0 ∨ s = i --> skip
                     [] nrpl[s] = 0 ∧ s ≠ i --> send
                            ack(s) to p[prnt[s]]
              fi
end
```

Process $p[i]$ has three actions. In the first action, $p[i]$ initiates a new spanning tree by sending a trqst message to each of its neighboring processes. The guard for this action consists of two disjuncts. The first disjunct ($nrpl[i] = 0$) indicates that the last spanning tree initiated by process $p[i]$ has been established some time ago. The second disjunct indicates that if the last spanning tree initiated by $p[i]$ has not been established due to some failure, then every trqst or ack message that was sent earlier has been either received or lost.

In the second action, process $p[i]$ receives a trqst(s, q) message from a neighboring process $p[g]$. There are two main cases to consider in this situation. In the first case, $lastq[s] < q$, indicating that this is the first time that $p[i]$ has received a trqst(s, q) message, and so $p[g]$ is the parent of $p[i]$ in tree q being established by $p[s]$. In this case, if process $p[i]$ has no neighboring process other than $p[g]$, then $p[i]$ returns an ack(s) message to $p[g]$. Otherwise, $p[i]$ forwards a copy of the trqst(s, q) message to every neighboring process except $p[g]$. In the second case, $last[q] \geq q$, indicating that $p[i]$ has received a trqst(s, q) message before and that this copy of the message serves as a negative reply to the trqst(s, q) message that $p[i]$ has forwarded earlier to $p[g]$. In this case, $p[i]$ decrements its $nrpl[s]$ by one. If the resulting $nrpl[s]$ equals zero and s is different from i, then $p[i]$ sends an ack(s) message to its parent process $p[prnt[s]]$.

In the third action, process $p[i]$ receives an ack(s) message from a neighboring process $p[g]$. This message indicates that $p[g]$ has become a child of process $p[i]$ in the new tree being established by $p[s]$. Thus, $p[i]$ makes chld[s, g] true, decrements nrpls by one, and if the resulting nrpls equals zero and s is different from i, then $p[i]$ sends an ack(s) message to its parent process p[prnts].

20.2 LOW-LEVEL BROADCAST

The above protocol for initiating successive spanning trees by each process $p[i]$ can be augmented to allow $p[i]$ to broadcast data messages over its established trees. This is done by modifying each process $p[i]$ in the above protocol as follows:

i. The guard of the timeout action in p[i] is modified to become as follows:

```
timeout
      (nrpl[i] = 0 and no data(i) message in any
      channel) ∨
      (no trqst(i, lastq[i]), no ack(i), and no
      data(i) message in any channel)
```

ii. The following two actions are added to p[i]:

```
[] nrpl[i] = 0  ->
   if  chld[i,f]  -> send data(i) to p[f]
   [] ~chld[i,f]  -> skip
   fi; h := NEXT(N, f);
   do h ≠ f ->
            if chld[i,h]  -> send data(i) to p[h]
            [] ~chld[i,h]  -> skip
            fi; h := NEXT(N, h);
   od

[] rcv data(s) from p[g]  ->
      h := NEXT(N, g)
      do h ≠ g ->
            if chld[s, h]  -> send data(s) to p[h]
            [] ~chld[s, h]  -> skip
            fi; h := NEXT(N, h)
      od
```

The modified guard of the first timeout action in process p[i] causes p[i] not to initiate a new spanning tree until every data(i) message that was sent over the previous tree has been either received or lost.

The first added action allows process p[i], when its last tree is established, to send a data message to each one of its child processes. The second added action allows p[i], when it receives a data message from its parent process, to forward a copy of the message to each one of its child processes.

In this version of the protocol, the reception of data messages is not acknowledged. Therefore, this protocol is useful in applications where data messages are sent at a high rate and there is no time for the sender to wait for acknowledgments. This protocol is also useful in applications where the probability of message loss is very small or where some message loss can be tolerated by the application. For applications other than these, this protocol can be augmented so that data messages can be acknowledged as follows.

When a sent data message goes down the tree and reaches a tree leaf (i.e., reaches a process that has no child processes), the leaf process sends back an ack message to its parent process. When a process, other than the root, receives an ack message from each of its child processes, the process sends an ack message to its parent process. When the root process receives an ack message from each of its child processes, it recognizes that the data message has reached every process in the network and starts to broadcast the next data message.

If the root process waits for a long time without receiving an ack message from one or more of its child processes, it recognizes that some data or ack message has been lost and starts to broadcast the last data message once again. Therefore, a process in the network may receive the same data message a number of times. When a process receives a data message for the first time, the process keeps one copy of the message and forwards a copy of the message to each of its child processes. When a process receives the same data message later, the process does not keep a copy of the message but still forwards a copy of the message to each of its child processes.

Therefore, when a process receives a data message, the process should be able to determine whether or not it has received this message before. This is accomplished by attaching a bit b to each data message. When the root process p[s] broadcasts a data message for the first time, bit b in the message has a value different from its value in the last data message broadcasted by p[s]. Later, if p[s] rebroadcasts the same data message, bit b in the message has the same value as in the original message, which was broadcasted by p[s] earlier.

Every process stores the value of bit b in the last data message broadcasted by process p[s] for every s. When a process receives a data message, it compares the value of bit b in the message with the stored value of bit b. If the two values are different, the process concludes that the received message is new (i.e., has not been received before) and stores the message. Otherwise, the process concludes that the received message is a copy of a message that has been received earlier and discards the message.

20.3   HIGH-LEVEL BROADCAST

As mentioned earlier, a high-level broadcast protocol is to operate on top of routing and switching protocols in a network of processes. Thus, this protocol is designed under the assumption that a process can send messages to every other process in its network. In this protocol, a process p[i] broadcasts a data message by sending a copy of the message to every other process in the network. Each process acknowledges the receipt of the data message by sending back an ack message to p[i]. The exchange of data and ack messages between p[i] and the other processes in the network can follow any of the window protocols in Chapter 9. In this section, we discuss a high-level broadcast protocol where the exchange of data and ack messages between p[i] and the other processes follows the individual acknowledgment protocol in Section 9.4.

In this broadcast protocol, each process p[i] broadcasts data messages to all other processes and receives ack messages from all other processes. Thus, each process

p[i] acts as both a data sender p and a data receiver q in the individual acknowledgment protocol in Section 9.4. Recall that processes p and q in the individual acknowledgment protocol have three actions and one action, respectively. Thus, each
process p[i] in the broadcast protocol has four actions: three actions that correspond
to the actions of p and one action that corresponds to the action of q.

Because the transmission of data and ack messages follows a window protocol
with individual acknowledgment, each data and ack message has a sequence number in the range $0 . . r - 1$, where $1 \leq w < r/2$ and w is the window size. Recall that
the window size w is the maximum number of data messages that a process can
send without receiving acknowledgment for any of them.

To enforce this window protocol, each process p[i] has the following variables.
(recall that in the individual acknowledgment protocol, process p has three variables, ns, na, and ackd, while process q has two variables, nr and rcvd):

```
var    ns     :      0..r-1,
       na     :      array [0..n-1] of 0..r-1,
       ackd   :      array [0..n-1, 0..r-1] of boolean,
       nr     :      array [0..n-1] of 0..r-1,
       rcvd   :      array [0..n-1, 0..r-1] of boolean,
       dlvr   :      array [0..n-1] of integer
```

Variable ns stores the sequence number of the next data message to be sent (i.e.,
broadcasted) by p[i]. Element na[g] stores the sequence number of the next ack
message to be received by p[i] from p[g]. Element ackd[g, m]is true iff p[i] has received ack(m) from p[g] but has not yet received some earlier ack message from
p[g].

Similarly, element nr[g] stores the sequence number of the next data message to
be received by p[i] from p[g]. Element rcvd[g, m]is true iff p[i] has received
data(m) from p[g] but has not yet received an earlier data message from p[g]. Element dlvr[g] stores the number of data messages that have been received from
process p[g] and delivered by process p[i].

Process p[i] in the high-level broadcast protocol can be defined as follows.
```
process p[i : 0..n-1]

const w, r              {0 < w ≤ r/2}

inp   N    :      set { g | 0 ≤ g < n ∧ g ≠ i }

var   ns   :      0..r-1,
      na   :      array [0..n-1] of 0..r-1,
      ackd :      array [0..n-1, 0..r-1] of boolean,
      nr   :      array [0..n-1] of 0..r-1,
      rcvd :      array [0..n-1, 0..r-1] of boolean,
      dlvr :      array [0..n-1] of integer,
```

```
        x      :      0..n

par     g      :      N,
        m      :      0..r-1

begin
        (For every c, 0 ≤ c < n, ns ≠ na[c] +_r w) —>
            x := 0;
            do x < n —>
                if x = i —> skip
                [] x ≠ i —> send data(ns) to
                                         p[x]
                fi; x := x + 1
            od; ns := ns +_r 1

[]    rcv ack(m) from p[g] —>
            ackd[g, m] := true;
            do ackd[g, na[g]] —>
             ackd[g, na[g]], na[g] := false, na[g] +^r 1
            od

[]    timeout
            (There is c, 0 ≤ c < n ∧ c ≠ i,
                        bet(na[c], m, ns) ∧ ~ackd[c, m]
            ) ∧
            (For every c, 0 ≤ c < n ∧ c ≠ i,
                        data(m)#ch.p[i].p[c] +
                        ack(m)#ch.p[c].p[i] = 0
            )
                            —>
            x := 0;
            do x < n —>
                if ~(bet(na[x], m, ns) ∧ ~ackd[x, m] ∧
                    x ≠ i) —> skip
                [] (bet(na[x], m, ns) ∧ ~ackd[x, m] ∧
                    x ≠ i) —> send data(m) to p[x]
                fi; x := x + 1
            od

[]    rcv data(m) from p[g] —>
            send ack(m) to p[g];
            if  bet(nr[g] -r w, m, nr[g] ) —>
                {msg is from past} skip
            [] ~bet(nr[g] -r w, m, nr[g] ) —>
                {msg is expected }
```

```
                rcvd[g, m]  := true;
                do rcvd[g, nr[g]]  —>
                   {deliver data(nr[g]) msg from p[g]}
                   rcvd[g, nr[g]]  := false;
                   nr[g], dlvr[g]  :=
                   nr[g] +r 1, dlvr[g] + 1
                od
         fi
   end
```

Process p[i] has four actions. The first three actions correspond to the actions of p in the individual acknowledgment protocol, while the fourth action corresponds to the action of process q in the same protocol. In the first action, process p[i] detects that each window from p[i] to every other process in the network is "open." In this case, p[i] broadcasts the next data message to every other process in the network.

In the second action, process p[i] receives an ack message from another process p[g], then updates its array ackd[g, . . .] and element na[g] accordingly.

In the third action, process p[i] detects that it has not yet received an ack(m) message from some processes and that there is no data(m) or ack(m) message in any channel in the network. In this case, p[i] re-sends the last data(m) message to every process from which p[i] has not yet received an ack(m) message. Recall that predicate bet(x, y, z), where x, y, and z range over $0 . . r - 1$, is defined as follows.

$$\text{bet}(x, y, z) = \text{true} \quad \text{iff} \quad (x \neq z) \wedge (x = y \vee x +_r 1 = y \vee \ldots \vee z -_r 1 = y)$$

In the fourth action, process p[i] receives a data(m) message from another process p[g], and sends back an ack(m) message to p[g]. Process p[i] then updates its array rcvd[g, . . .] and the two elements nr[g] and dlvr[g].

20.4 ORDERED, PRECEDENCE, AND RECALL BROADCASTS

In the high-level broadcast protocol, data messages that are broadcasted by the same process are delivered by every process in the network in the same order in which these messages were broadcasted. However, data messages that are broadcasted by different processes may be delivered by different processes in different orders. For example, if a process broadcasts a message m and another process broadcasts a message m', then one process may deliver these messages as m followed by m', while another process may deliver the messages as m' followed by m.

In some situations, it is required that all processes in the network deliver all messages in exactly the same order. Thus, in the above example, if a process delivers the two messages as m followed by m', then every other process in the network should deliver these messages as m followed by m'. A high-level broadcast protocol that satisfies this requirement is called an ordered broadcast protocol.

The high-level broadcast protocol in Section 20.3 can be strengthened to become an ordered broadcast protocol as follows:

i. In order to distinguish between the data messages broadcasted by the same process, the sequence numbers of messages are made integers instead of being in the range $0 \ldots r - 1$. Thus, constant r is removed from the process definition, and every $0 \ldots r - 1$ range is replaced by integer in the process definition. Moreover, every $+_r$ operation is replaced by $+$, and every bet(x, y, z) predicate is replaced by the predicate $(x \le y \land y < z)$ in the process definition.

ii. The kth data message, data(k), broadcasted by a process p[i] can now be uniquely identified by the pair (k, i).

iii. One process in the network is designated to be the network leader, and each other process is designated to be a follower.

iv. The network leader delivers the received data messages as discussed in Section 20.3. The leader also delivers every data message it broadcasts when the message is broadcasted. The leader keeps a list that contains the unique identifier of each delivered message and the order in which the message is delivered. This list is broadcasted as a sequence of messages, called order messages, to every other process (i.e., every follower) in the network.

v. Each follower process delivers every data message that it has received or broadcasted according to the order described in the order messages from the network leader.

In some situations, ordered broadcast is too strong and costly to be used, and high-level broadcast is too weak. Most of these situations require a new type of broadcast, called precedence broadcast. In order to define this type of broadcast, we need to define what it means for a broadcast message to precede another broadcast message.

A message m precedes another message m' iff m' is broadcasted by a process after that process has delivered m.

A precedence broadcast is a high-level broadcast where if a message m precedes a message m' then every process in the network delivers m before m'.

The high-level broadcast protocol in Section 20.3 can be strengthened to become a precedence broadcast protocol as follows:

i. In order to distinguish between the data messages broadcasted by the same process, the sequence numbers of messages are made integers instead of being in the range $0 \ldots r - 1$. Thus, constant r is removed from the process definition, and every $0 \ldots r - 1$ range is replaced by integer in the process definition. Moreover, every $+_r$ operation is replaced by $+$, and every bet(x, y, z) predicate is replaced by the predicate $(x \le y \land y < z)$ in the process definition.

    ii. The kth data message, data(k), broadcasted by a process p[i] can now be uniquely identified by the pair (k, i).

   iii. Before a process in the network broadcasts a message, the process attaches to the message the unique identifier of every message that the process has so far delivered from every process in the network. This attached set of message identifiers is called the precede set of the message. Then, the process broadcasts the message along with its precede set and also delivers the message.

   iv. When a process in the network receives a message, the process does not deliver the message until every message identified in the precede set of that message has been received and delivered.

Precedence broadcasts are based on the assumption that a message "depends" on every message that precedes it. Therefore, no message should be delivered until every message that precedes this message has been delivered. This assumption, however, is not true in many situations. Often a message depends only on a very small number of messages that preceded it. We can take advantage of this fact by introducing a new type of broadcast called recall broadcast. In order to define this type of broadcast, we need to define the recall set of a message.

Associated with each message m is a set of message identifiers out of those messages that precede m; this set is called the recall set of m.

A recall broadcast is a high-level broadcast where if a message m is identified in the recall set of a message m', then every process in the network delivers m before m'.

The high-level broadcast protocol in Section 20.3 can be strengthened to become a recall broadcast protocol in the same way it can be strengthened to become a precedence broadcast protocol. However, the recall set of any message to be broadcasted by a process p[i] is not automatically computed by p[i]. Rather, it is provided to p[i] in the same way that the text of the message is provided to p[i].

20. 5 A HIERARCHY OF BROADCAST PRIMITIVES

In this chapter, we have defined five types of broadcasts: ordered, precedence, recall, high-level, and low-level. As argued next, these five types of broadcasts form a hierarchy, in which ordered broadcast is the strongest and low-level broadcast is the weakest:

    i. In an ordered broadcast, every process delivers all messages in the same order. Assume that a message m is delivered before a message m'. Then m is delivered before m' in every process in the network including process p[i], which broadcasted m. Process p[i] must have broadcasted m before delivering it, and so before delivering m'. Therefore, m' cannot precede m, and the order in which messages are delivered is guaranteed to satisfy the precede relation between messages. In other words, an ordered broadcast is also a precedence broadcast.

ii. In a precedence broadcast, a process p[i] delivers a message m only after all messages identified in the precede set of m have been delivered. Because each message in the recall set of m precedes m, p[i] is guaranteed to deliver m after all messages identified in the recall set of m are delivered. Therefore, a precedence broadcast is also a recall broadcast.

iii. By definition, a recall broadcast is a high-level broadcast.

iv. In a high-level broadcast, messages that are broadcasted by the same process are delivered by every other process in the network in the same order in which the messages were broadcasted. Because a low-level broadcast does not have ack messages, and so does not guarantee any message delivery, a high-level broadcast is also a low-level broadcast.

Figure 20.1 illustrates this hierarchy of five types of broadcasts.

20.6 BROADCAST AND MULTICAST IN THE INTERNET

In the Internet, a group is a collection of application processes, in the same host or in different hosts, such that when a message is sent to the group, a copy of the message is sent to each process in the group. Each group has a unique IP address of class D. Figure 20.2 shows an IP address of class D. (IP addresses of classes A, B, and C are discussed in Section 2.4.)

IP addresses of class D range in value from 224.0.0.0 to 239.255.255.255. Some of these addresses are assigned to well-known permanent groups:

224.0.0.1   Assigned to the group of all hosts in any subnetwork where this address is mentioned

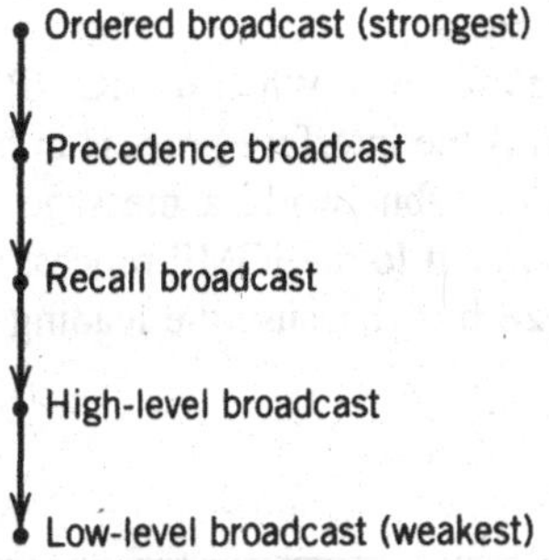

- Ordered broadcast (strongest)

- Precedence broadcast

- Recall broadcast

- High-level broadcast

- Low-level broadcast (weakest)

FIG. 20.1

224.0.0.2 Assigned to the group of all routers in any subnetwork where this address is mentioned

There are two complementary protocols that support groups in the Internet: the Internet group management protocol, or IGMP for short, and the core based tree protocol, or CBTP for short. The IGMP is used to support groups in one subnetwork, and CBTP is used to support groups across subnetworks. Next, we discuss how an application process can use IGMP and CBTP to join or quit a group or to send a message to (every member of) a group.

For the sake of discussing IGMP, it is sufficient to focus on one subnetwork in the Internet. Each host in this subnetwork has an IGMP process placed on top of the IP process in that host. One of the routers in this subnetwork, router r say, is designated to be the IGMP router for that subnetwork. Router r has an IGMP process for this subnetwork. The IGMP process in each host h in this subnetwork has the following three functions:

i. The IGMP process in host h keeps a list of every group that has one or more application processes in h. We refer to this list as the G-list of h.

ii. The IGMP process in h informs the interface process in h of each group in its G-list.

iii. The IGMP process in h informs the IGMP process in router r of each group in its G-list.

Function i is performed as follows. When an application process p in host h requests from the IGMP process in h to join a group gr, the IGMP process in h adds gr to its G-list (if it is not already there). Then, the IGMP process in h stores a record indicating that process p is a member of group gr so that when the IGMP process receives a data message intended for group gr, it forwards a copy of this message to process p. Later, when process p requests from the IGMP process in h to quit group gr, the IGMP process in h discards the record indicating that p is a member of gr. Moreover, if no other application process in h is a member of group gr, the IGMP process in h removes gr from its G-list and informs the interface process in h that it is no longer interested in messages intended for group gr.

Function ii is performed as follows. When the IGMP process in host h adds a group gr to its G-list, it informs the interface process in h of gr so that if the interface process encounters, on its subnetwork, a message intended for group gr, it copies the message and forwards it to the IGMP process in h. The effective IP address of a group consists of 28 bits (because the leading 4 bits 1110 in the IP ad-

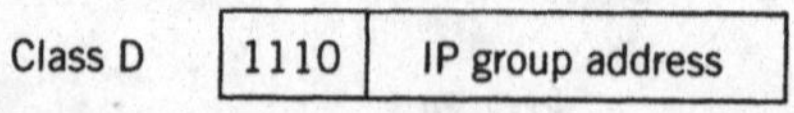

Class D	1110	IP group address

FIG. 20.2

dress are common to all groups). However, the hardware address of a group consists of 23 bits. Thus, the lowest order 23 bits from the effective IP address of a group constitute the hardware address of that group. Because of this address truncation, it is possible that the interface process in h copies a message from its subnetwork based on the hardware group address in the message and then forwards the message to the IGMP process in h, which then discovers from the IP group address in the message header that the message is not intended for any group in its G-list. When this happens, the IGMP process in h discards the message.

Function iii is performed as follows. When group gr is added to the G-list in the IGMP process in host h, the IGMP process in h sends a response(gr) message containing the IP group address gr to the IGMP process in router r. Moreover, the IGMP process in router r sends a query message every minute to the IGMP process in every host in the subnetwork. When the IGMP process in host h receives a query message, it sends back a response(gr) message for each group gr in its G-list. When the IGMP process in router r receives a response(gr) message, it adds gr to its G-list for the subnetwork. If the IGMP process in router r does not receive a response(gr) message after it sends several query messages, it removes gr from its G-list for the subnetwork.

Each IGMP message (whether a query or response) has the following five fields:

1. Version of IGMP   4 bits
2. Message type (query or response)   4 bits
3. Unused field (all zeros)   8 bits
4. Checksum of the message   16 bits
5. IP group address of the message   32 bits

Field 1 contains the version of the IGMP process that sent the message. (The current IGMP version is 1.) Field 2 specifies the message type: a value of 1 indicates that the message is a query and a value of 2 indicates that it is a response. Field 3 is currently unused, and its bits are all zeros. Field 4 contains a checksum computed over the message in the same way that the checksum in an IP message is computed over the message header. Field 5 contains an IP group address if the message is a response. Otherwise, it is an unused field and its bits are all zeros.

When the IGMP process in router r sends a query message, the IP process in r attaches to the message an IP header, where the message destination is 224.0.0.1 (which is the IP address of the group of all hosts in the subnetwork). Then the IP process in r forwards the resulting IP message to the interface process in r. The interface process in r attaches to the message an interface header where the message destination is 0.0.1 (which is the lowest 23 bits in the IP group address 224.0.0.1) and then sends the resulting interface message over the subnetwork.

When the IGMP process in host h sends a response(gr) message, the IP process in h attaches to the message an IP header where the message destination is the IP group address gr. Then the IP process in h forwards the resulting IP message to the interface process in h that attaches to the message an interface header, where the message destination is the lowest 23 bits in the IP address of group gr, and sends the resulting interface message over the subnetwork.

It follows from this discussion that when the IGMP process in a host h sends a response(gr) message, then the IGMP process in every host, whose G-list contains gr, receives a copy of the message. This fact can be exploited to minimize the number of response messages that are sent over the subnetwork as follows. When the IGMP process in router r sends a query message, the IGMP process in each host receives a copy of the query message and prepares to send a response(gr) message for each group gr in its G-list. However, the IGMP process in a host does not send all its response(gr) messages right away. Rather, for each gr in its G-list, it randomly selects a number t between 1 and 10 and decides to send its response(gr) message after t seconds from receiving the query message. If the IGMP process in a host h receives a response(gr) message before it sends its own response(gr) message, then the IGMP process in h decides not to send its own response(gr) message.

In summary, each IGMP designated router has a G-list for each subnetwork to which the router is attached. The G-list for a subnetwork contains every group in which an application process in some host on this subnetwork is a member.

If the G-lists of two or more IGMP-designated routers have the same group gr, then these routers need to be "connected" so that any message sent to group gr can be forwarded between these routers. Connecting such routers is the function of CBTP.

In CBTP, all the routers whose G-lists contain the same group gr are connected by a rooted tree, called the gr-tree. The root of each gr-tree is a predefined router, called the core of the gr-tree.

Each router in the Internet has a process, called the CBTP process, that performs the following four functions:

   i.   If a group gr appears in one of the G-lists of the router, then the CBTP process of the router makes the router join the gr-tree.

   ii. If the router joins a gr-tree, then the CBTP process of the router checks periodically whether the router is still in the gr-tree.

  iii. If the router is disconnected from a gr-tree, due to some failure, then the CBTP process of the router makes the router rejoin the gr-tree.

  iv. If the router receives a data(gr) message whose destination is group gr, then the CBTP process of the router determines how to route this message.

Function i is performed as follows. To join a gr-tree, the CBTP process of a router r sends a join request whose destination is the core of the gr-tree. The join request travels from the CBTP process of a router to the CBTP process of a neighboring router until it arrives at the CBTP process of a router r′ that is already in the gr-tree. (In the worst case, r′ is the core of the gr-tree.) The CBTP process of router r′ sends a join reply message whose destination is router r. The join reply follows backward the same path traveled forward by the join request. When the CBTP process in a router s receives the join reply from the CBTP process in a neighboring router s', router s joins the gr-tree and its parent in the gr-tree is s'. Finally, when the CBTP process in router r receives the join reply, r becomes in the gr-tree. If a router joins a gr-tree, then the CBTP process in that router maintains the identities of its parent and children, if any, in the gr-tree.

Function ii is performed as follows. To check that a router r is still in a gr-tree, the CBTP process of router r periodically sends an echo request message to the CBTP process of r's parent in the gr-tree and then waits to receive an echo reply from the CBTP process of that parent. As long as the CBTP process of router r succeeds in receiving an echo reply for each echo request it sends, it recognizes that router r is still in the gr-tree. If the CBTP process of router r fails to receive echo replies for several successive echo requests, it recognizes that router r is no longer in the gr-tree, due to some failure.

Function iii is performed as follows. To rejoin a gr-tree, the CBTP process of a router r sends a rejoin request whose destination is the core of the gr-tree. The rejoin request travels from the CBTP process of a router to the CBTP process of a neighboring router, until it arrives at the CBTP process of a router r' that is already in the gr-tree. The CBTP process of router r' forwards the rejoin request to its parent in the gr-tree, which also forwards it to its parent in the gr-tree, and so on. Eventually, the rejoin request arrives at the CBTP process of the core of the gr-tree that sends back a join reply whose destination is router r. The join reply follows backward the same path traveled forward by the rejoin request until it arrives at the CBTP process in router r and r becomes once again in the gr-tree.

Function iv is performed as follows. To route a data(gr) message, the CBTP process of a router r first checks whether r is in the gr-tree. If router r is in the gr-tree, the CBTP process of r forwards a copy of the data(gr) message to its parent and to each of its children in the gr-tree. It also sends a copy of the data(gr) message over any attached subnetwork where gr is in its G-list. If router r is not in the gr-tree, the CBTP process of router r routes the data(gr) message toward the core of the gr-tree.

In this presentation of CBTP, we assumed for simplicity that each gr-tree has only one core. In fact, each gr-tree has one primary core and several secondary cores. If the primary core fails or becomes disconnected from the rest of the gr-tree, then one of the secondary cores becomes the primary core.

20.7 BIBLIOGRAPHICAL NOTES

The use of multiple spanning trees to broadcast messages is discussed in Dalal and Metcalf [1978] and Deering et al. [1994]. The use of a single spanning tree to broadcast messages is discussed in Ballardie et al. [1993]. The use of a single adaptive spanning tree is discussed in Cobb and Gouda [1997a].

Ordered broadcast is discussed in Chang and Maxemchuck [1984]. Causal broadcast is discussed in Birman et al. [1991]. Recall broadcast is discussed in Abdel-Wahab and Gouda [1996]. Both causal broadcast and recall broadcast are based on the concept of message precedence discussed in Lamport [1978].

The IGMP is discussed in Deering and Cheriton [1990]. The CBTP is discussed in Ballardie et al [1993].

EXERCISES

1   (Cost of Maintaining Spanning Trees). Estimate how many messages need to be sent in a network in order to construct a spanning tree, according to the protocol in Section 20.1, in that network.

2   (Maintaining Spanning Trees without Transmission Errors). Simplify the spanning tree protocol in Section 20.1 under the following two assumptions. First, sent messages cannot be corrupted, lost, or reordered. Second, the network topology cannot change, at least while a spanning tree is being constructed.

3   (Low-Level Broadcast without Transmission Errors). Simplify the low-level broadcast protocol in Section 20.2 under the following two assumptions. First, sent messages cannot be corrupted, lost, or reordered. Second, the network topology cannot change, at least while a spanning tree is being constructed.

4   (Low-Level Broadcast with Individual Acknowledgments). Modify the low-level broadcast protocol in Section 20.2 such that every sent data message is acknowledged to the root process before the root process sends the next data message as discussed at the end of Section 20.2.

5   (High-Level Broadcast without Transmission Errors). Simplify the high-level broadcast protocol in Section 20.3 under the assumption that sent messages cannot be corrupted, lost, or reordered. Keep the sliding-window mechanism in the simplified protocol as a means for controlling the flow of data messages in the network.

6   (High-Level Broadcast without Transmission Errors and Flow Control). Simplify the high-level broadcast protocol in Section 20.3 under the following two assumptions. First, sent messages cannot be corrupted, lost, or reordered. Second, the flow of data messages does not need to be controlled. (Hint: The sliding-window mechanism is removed from the simplified protocol, and ack messages are not sent in it.)

7   (Ordered Broadcast). Modify the broadcast protocol in exercise 6 such that the broadcast is an ordered broadcast as discussed in Section 20.4.

8   (Precedence Broadcast). Modify the broadcast protocol in exercise 6 such that the broadcast is a precedence broadcast as discussed in Section 20.4.

9   (Recall Broadcast). Modify the broadcast protocol in exercise 6 such that the broadcast is a recall broadcast as discussed in Section 20.4.

10 (Maintaining Multicast Trees). Consider a network p[i: 0 . . n − 1] where each process p[i] has an input array "group", declared as follows:

inp   group   :   **array** $[0..n-1]$ **of boolean**

Design a protocol for maintaining multicast trees for this network such that each maintained tree with root p[i] is a minimal tree that contains every process where element group[i] has the value true.

11 (low-level Multicast). Consider the network in exercise 10. Design a low-level multicast protocol for this network such that each data message sent by a process p[i] is intended to be received by every process where element group[i] has the value true.

12 (High-level Multicast). Consider the network in exercise 10. Design a high-level multicast protocol for this network such that each data message sent by a process p[i] is intended to be received by every process where element group[i] has the value true.

13 (Broadcast in a Mesh Network). In a mesh network p[i: $0 .. m - 1$, j: $0 .. n - 1$], for each i, where $i < m - 1$, the two processes p[i, j] and p[i + 1, j] are neighbors, and for each j, where $j < n - 1$, the two processes p[i, j] and p[i, j + 1] are neighbors. Design a broadcast protocol for this network under the following two assumptions. First, sent messages cannot be corrupted, lost, or reordered. Second, all channels are always up.

14 (Broadcast in a Torus Network). In a torus network p[i: $0 .. m - 1$, j: $0 .. n - 1$], for each i and j, the two processes p[i, j] and p[i $+_m$ 1, j] are neighbors, and the two processes p[i, j] and p[i $+_n$ 1] are neighbors. Design a broadcast protocol for this network under the following two assumptions. First, sent messages cannot be corrupted, lost, or reordered. Second, all channels are always up.

15 (Broadcast in an Acyclic Network). The topology of an acyclic network is an acyclic graph. Design a broadcast protocol for this network under the following three assumptions. First, sent messages cannot be corrupted, lost, or reordered. Second, all channels are always up. Third, the flow of data messages does not need to be controlled.

16 (Error-Tolerant Broadcast in a Ring). Design a broadcast protocol in a ring network p[i: $0 .. n - 1$], where each process p[i] has exactly two neighbors p[i $-_n$ 1,] and p[i $+_n$ 1,]. Ensure that each broadcast message is delivered exactly once at each process under the assumption that there are at most one i where the two channels between p[i] and p[i $+_n$ 1] are down and all other channels in the ring are up.

CHAPTER 21

APPLICATION STRUCTURES

In the preceding chapters, we discussed how processes in a network can exchange messages effectively, efficiently, and securely. A net outcome of our discussion is that it is possible to design application programs as networks of processes that cooperate by exchanging messages in order to provide needed services. In this chapter, we discuss common features concerning the structure of these application programs. Then in the next chapter, we present examples of application programs that provide some important services such as echo, file transfer, and remote login.

The application programs we are interested in have three common features:

i. The processes in an application program are classified into clients and servers. Each client process is local to some user of the program, while each server process is local to some resources of the program (e.g., permanent files). The function of a client process is to receive commands from its local user and carry out these commands by accessing some resources of the program. The function of a server process is to ensure that the client processes access the local resources of the server according to a predefined set of rules.

ii. One method of communication between clients and servers in an application program is via special processes called sockets. Each application process, whether a client or a server, in an application program has a number of sockets. To send a message to an application process, the message is sent to a socket of that process. The socket receives the message and stores it in a local buffer until the application process is ready to receive it. Thus, the function of a socket is to protect its application process from being interrupted, whenever a message arrives, in order to receive and buffer the message.

iii. Another method of communciation between clients and servers in an application program is via remote procedures. In this case, each server is designed as a collection of procedures. Thus for a client to request a server to perform some function, the client first calls the procedure that corresponds to the required function in the server and then waits to receive the results of the call.

In this chapter, we discuss these three features of application programs in detail. Sockets are discussed in Section 21.1. Clients and servers that communicate via sockets are discussed in Section 21.2, and clients and servers that communicate by calling remote procedures are discussed in Section 21.3. Finally, application structures in the Internet are presented in Section 21.4.

21.1 SOCKETS

Consider an application program that consists of n processes p[i: 0 .. n − 1]. Associated with each application process p[i] are r processes named skt[i, 0], skt[i, 1], . . . , skt[i, r − 1]. These processes are called the sockets of process p[i]. For an application process p[j] to send a message to an application process p[i], p[j] sends the message to a socket skt[i, c] of p[i]. All messages sent to skt[i, c] are received and stored in an internal mailbox of skt[i, c].

When an application process p[i] is ready to receive the next message from its socket skt[i, c], it sends a nxt message to skt[i, c]. Process p[i] then waits to receive a message from skt[i, c] before sending another nxt message to skt[i, c]. Therefore, each process p[i] has a boolean array wait such that wait[c] is true iff p[i] has sent a nxt message to skt[i, c] but has not yet received the next message from skt[i, c].

An application process p[i] in the socket protocol can be defined as follows.

```
process p[i : 0..n-1]

const r, s              {r is the number of sockets for p[i]}
                        {s-1 is the max value of var. txt}

var    wait             :      array [0..r-1] of boolean,
       j                :      0..n-1,
       d                :      0..r-1,
       txt              :      0..s-1

par    c                :      0..r-1

begin
       true  ->
              j, d := any, any;
              if  j ≠ i  ->
```

```
            txt := any;
            send msg(txt) to skt[j, d]
     []  ~wait[d]    ->
            wait[d] := true;
            send nxt to skt[i, d]
     []  j = i /\ wait[d]->      skip
     fi
```

```
[]    rcv msg(txt) from skt[i, c] ->wait[c] := false
end
```

Process p[i] has two actions. In the first action, p[i] may send a message to a socket skt[j, d] of an arbitrary application process p[j], or send a nxt message to an arbitrary socket skt[i, d] of its own. In the second action, process p[i] receives a message from one of its own sockets, skt[i, c].

Process skt[i, c] has an infinite array mbox to store the text of every received message until the message is forwarded to p[i]. Array mbox has two pointers nr and ns. Pointer nr indicates the location where the next received message is to be stored. Pointer ns indicates the location where the next message to be sent to p[i] is stored. Note that $nr \geq ns$ and that mbox is empty whenever $nr = ns$.

Process skt[i, c] also has a boolean variable mrqst. When skt[i, c] receives a nxt message from p[i] and detects that its array mbox is empty, it assigns variable mrqst the value true. Later, when skt[i, c] receives a message and detects that mrqst is true, it forwards the message directly to p[i], instead of storing the message in mbox, and assigns mrqst the value false.

A socket process skt[i, c] in the socket protocol can be defined as follows:

```
process skt[i : 0..n-1, c : 0..r-1]

const s

var    mbox    :   array [integer] of 0..s-1,
       nr, ns  :   integer,
                   {indices of array mbox}
                   {nr is the next to receive}
                   {ns is the next to send}
       mrqst   :   boolean,
       txt     :   0..s-1

par    j       :   0..n-1

begin
       rcv msg(txt) from p[j]    ->
               if  mrqst  ->  mrqst := false;
                              send msg(txt) to p[i]
```

```
            ▯   ~mrqst   ->   mbox[nr], nr := txt, nr+1
            fi


▯     rcv nxt from p[i]            ->
            if  ns = nr -> mrqst := true
            ▯   ns    nr  -> send msg(mbox[ns]) to p[i];
                            ns := ns+1
            fi
end
```

21.2 CLIENTS AND SERVERS USING SOCKETS

The processes in application programs are classified into clients and servers. Each client process is local to some program user, and each server process is local to some program resources. A program user can ask its local client to perform some task. When this happens, the client starts to communicate with some server in the program. During the communication between the client and the server, the server may access its local resources. The communciation continues until the requested task is completed, and the client informs the user of its completion.

The communication between clients and servers can be carried out using sockets or using remote procedures. In this section, we discuss how the communication between clients and servers can be carried out using sockets. Then in the next section, we discuss how the communication between clients and servers can be carried out using remote procedures

The communication between a client and a server can proceed via two sockets, one belonging to the client and the other belonging to the server. Before the client starts to communicate with the server, the client reserves one of its available sockets for the communication and informs the server about that socket. Then the server reserves one of its available sockets for the communication and informs the client about that socket. From that point on, the communication between the client and the server proceeds via the two reserved sockets. When the communication is finished, the two reserved sockets are released and made available for future communications. The protocol for reserving and releasing sockets is discussed in more detail next.

Consider an application program with n processes p[i: 0 .. n – 1]. In this program, each of the processes p[i: 0 .. m – 1] is a client, and each of the other processes p[j: m .. n – 1] is a server. Each process p[i], whether a client or a server, has r socket processes skt[i, 0], skt[i, 1], . . . , skt[i, r – 1] . We start by discussing a client process and then discuss a server process. We end by discussing a socket process.

For a client process p[i] to start communicating with a server process p[j], p[i] reserves one of its available sockets skt[i, c] and sends a crqst(i, c) message to socket skt[j, 0] of p[j]. Socket skt[j, 0] is a well-known socket of server p[j]; it is reserved solely for receiving crqst messages from client processes. When p[j] receives a crqst(i, c) message from its skt[j, 0], it recognizes that client p[i] wants to communicate with p[j] and that it has reserved its socket skt[i, c] for the communication. In this case, p[j] reserves one of its available sockets skt[j, d], where d > 0, and sends a crply(d) message to skt[i, c]. When p[i] receives a crply(d) message from skt[i, c], which it has reserved earlier for communication with p[j], p[i] recognizes that p[j] has reserved skt[j, d] for the communication. From that point on, client p[i] sends its data messages to skt[j, d] and server p[j] sends its data messages to skt[i, c].

To terminate the communication, client p[i] sends a drqst message to skt[j, d]. When server p[j] receives a drqst message from skt[j, d], it sends a drply message to skt[i, c] and makes skt[j, d] available for future connections. When p[i] receives a drply message from skt[i, c], it makes skt[i, c] available for future connections.

The states of the sockets of a client p[i] are maintained in the following three arrays of p[i]:

```
var    con    :      array [0..r-1] of boolean,
       prs    :      array [0..r-1] of m..n-1,
       soc    :      array [0..r-1] of 1..r-1
```

For every c, where $0 \leq c < r$, con[c] = true implies that client p[i] is currently connected with server p[prs[c]] via the two sockets skt[i, c] and skt[prs[c], soc[c]]. Thus, p[i] can now send data and drqst messages to skt[prs[c], soc[c]] while server p[prs[c]] can send data and drply messages to skt[i, c].

Process p[i] also has an array wait declared as follows:

```
var    wait   :      array [0..r-1] of boolean
```

The value of wait[c] in p[i] becomes true when p[i] sends any of the following messages: a crqst(i, c) message to skt[prs[c], 0] or a drqst message to skt[prs[c], soc[c]]. While the value of wait[c] is true, p[i] cannot send any more messages to skt[prs[c], 0] or skt[prs[c], soc[c]]. The value of wait[c] becomes false when p[i] receives a reply for the last message it has sent.

A client process p[i] in the client and server protocol can be defined as follows:

```
process p[i : 0..m-1]             {Client}

const r, s            {r is # of sockets of p[i]}
                      {s-1 is the max value of var. txt}

var    con    :       array [0..r-1] of boolean,
       prs    :       array [0..r-1] of m..n-1,
       soc    :       array [0..r-1] of 1..r-1,
       wait   :       array [0..r-1] of boolean,
       e      :       0..r-1,
       txt    :       0..s-1

par    c      :       0..r-1
```

```
begin
      ~con[c]  ∧  ~wait[c]                    ->
            prs[c] := any;
            send crqst(i, c) to skt[prs[c], 0];
            send nxt to skt[i, c];
            wait[c] := true

□     rcv crply(e) from skt[i, c]   ->
            con[c], soc[c], wait[c] := true, e, false;
            send nxt to skt[i, c]

□     con[c]  ∧  ~wait[c]                    ->
            if true  ->
                  txt := any;
                  send data(txt) to skt[prs[c], soc[c]]
            □ true  ->  wait[c] := true;
                  send drqst to skt[prs[c], soc[c]]
            fi

□     rcv data(txt) from skt[i, c]   ->
            send nxt to skt[i, c]

□     rcv drply from skt[i, c]->
            con[c], wait[c] := false, false
end
```

As mentioned earlier, socket skt[j, 0] of a server p[j] is reserved for receiving crqst messages from all clients in the program. Every other socket of server p[j] can be used for receiving data and drqst messages from one client in the program. The states of these other sockets are maintained in the following three arrays in server p[j]:

```
var   con   :     array [1..r-1] of boolean,
      prs   :     array [1..r-1] of 0..m-1,
      soc   :     array [1..r-1] of 0..r-1
```

For every d, where $1 \leq d < r$, con[d] = true implies that skt[j, d] is currently reserved by server p[j] for receiving data and drqst messages from the client p[prs[d]] and that skt[prs[d], soc[d]] is reserved by p[prs[d]] for receiving data and drply messages from p[j].

A server process p[j] in the client and server protocol can be defined as follows:

```
process p[j : m..n-1]                        {Server}

const r, s             {r is # of sockets of p[j]}
```

```
                              {s-1 is the max value of var. txt}

var   con   :      array [1..r-1] of boolean,
      prs   :      array [1..r-1] of 0..m-1,
      soc   :      array [1..r-1] of 0..r-1,
      i     :      0..m-1,
      c, e  :      0..r-1,
      txt   :      0..s-1

par   d     :      0..r-1

begin
      rcv crqst(i, c) from skt[j, 0] ->
              {initially, mrqst = true in each skt[j, 0]}
              e := 1;
              do con[e]  /\ e < r-1 -> e := e + 1 od;
              if  con[e] ->       send drply to skt[i, c]
              [] ~con[e] ->
                           send crply(e) to skt[i, c];
                           send nxt to skt[j, e];
                           con[e], prs[e], soc[e] := true, i, c
              fi;
              send nxt to skt[j, 0]

[]    con[d] ->
              txt := any;
              send data(txt) to skt[prs[d], soc[d]]

[]    rcv data(txt) from skt[j, d]  ->
              send nxt to skt[j, d]

[]    rcv drqst from skt[j, d] ->
              send drply to skt[prs[d], soc[d]];
              con[d] := false
end
```

Server p[j] has four actions. In the first action, p[j] receives a crqst(i, c) message and then checks if one of its sockets is available. If a socket skt[j, e] is available, then p[j] sends a crply(e) message to skt[i, c], otherwise p[i] sends a drply message to skt[i, c]. In the second action, process p[i] detects that its socket skt[j, d] is connected and sends a data message to skt[prs[d], soc[d]]. In the third action, p[j] receives a data message from one of its own sockets, skt[j, d]. In the fourth action, server p[j] receives a drqst message from its socket skt[j, d], sends a drply message to skt[prs[d], soc[d]], and then makes its socket skt[j, d] available for future connections.

A socket process skt[i, c] has an infinite buffer to store every received message until its application process p[i], whether server or client, is ready to receive the message. This infinite buffer consists of the following four arrays:

```
var    mbox        :       array [integer] of 0..4,
       prs         :       array [integer] of 0..n-1,
       soc         :       array [integer] of 0..r-1,
       txt         :       array [integer] of 0..s-1
```

For every integer x, the values of mbox[x], prs[x], soc[x], and txt[x] depend on the xth message received by skt[i, c] according to the following rules:

If the xth received message is crqst(k, d), then

```
mbox [x] = 0, prs [x] = k,
soc [x] = d, txt [x] = <don't care>
```

If the xth received message is crply(d), then

```
mbox [x] = 1, prs [x] = <don't care>,
soc [x] = d, txt [x] = <don't care>
```

If the xth received message is data(t), then

```
mbox [x] = 2, prs [x] = <don't care>,
soc [x] = <don't care>, txt [x] = t
```

If the xth received message is drqst, then

```
mbox [x] = 3, prs [x] = <don't care>,
soc [x] = <don't care>, txt [x] = <don't care>
```

If the xth received message is drply, then

```
mbox [x] = 4, prs [x] = <don't care>,
soc [x] = <don't care>, txt [x] = <don't care>
```

A socket process also has three variables, nr, ns, and mrqst. These variables are used as discussed in Section 21.1.

A skt[i, c] process in the client and server protocol can be defined as follows:

```
process skt [i : 0..n-1, c : 0..r-1]

const s
```

```
var    mbox              :        array [integer] of 0..4,
                                  {0 indicates crqst}
                                  {1 indicates crply}
                                  {2 indicates data}
                                  {3indicates drqst}
                                  {4 indicates drply}
       prs               :        array [integer] of 0..n-1,
       soc               :        array [integer] of 0..r-1,
       txt               :        array [integer] of 0..s-1,
       nr, ns            :        integer, {indices of mbox}
       mrqst             :        boolean,
       k                 :        0..n-1,
       d, e              :        0..r-1,
       t                 :        0..s-1


par    j                 :        0..n-1


begin
       rcv crqst(k, d) from p[j] ->
            if  mrqst ->mrqst := false;
                          send crqst(k, d) to p[i]
            [] ~mrqst -> mbox[nr], prs[nr], soc[nr], nr
                          := 0, k, d, nr + 1
            fi


[]     rcv crply(d) from p[j]  ->
            if  mrqst -> mrqst := false;
                          send crply(d) to p[i]
            [] ~mrqst -> mbox[nr], soc[nr], nr :=
                          1, d, nr + 1
            fi
[]     rcv data(t) from p[j]    ->
            if mrqst ->  mrqst := false;
                          send data(t) to p[i]
            [] ~mrqst -> mbox[nr], text[nr], nr :=
                          2, t, nr + 1
            fi


[]     rcv drqst from p[j]       ->
            if mrqst -> mrqst := false;
                          send drqst to p[i]
            [] ~mrqst -> mbox[nr], nr := 3, nr +1
            fi
```

```
[]      rcv drply from p[j]        ->
            if  mrqst ->mrqst := false;
                            send drply to p[i]
            []  ~mrqst ->mbox[nr], nr := 4, nr + 1
            fi


[]      rcv nxt from p[i] ->
            if  nr = ns    ->
                mrqst := true
            []  nr ≠ ns  ∧  mbox[ns] = 0 ->
                send crqst(prs[ns], soc[ns]) to p[i];
                ns := ns + 1
            []  nr ≠ ns  ∧  mbox[ns] = 1 ->
                send crply(soc[ns]) to p[i];
                ns := ns + 1
            []  nr ≠ ns  ∧  mbox[ns] = 2 ->
                send data(txt[ns]) to p[i];
                ns := ns + 1
            []  nr ≠ ns  ∧  mbox[ns] = 3 ->
                send drqst to p[i];
                ns := ns + 1
            []  nr ≠ ns  ∧  mbox[ns] = 4 ->
                send drply to p[i];
                ns := ns + 1
            fi
end
```

21.3 CLIENTS AND SERVERS USING REMOTE PROCEDURES

It is possible to design a server as a collection of procedures. A client that needs such a server to perform a function calls the corresponding procedure in the server and then waits for the returned result. In this case, an application program merely consists of clients and procedures (that represent servers).

Consider an application program that consists of n clients $p[i: 0 .. n - 1]$ and m procedures $d[j: 0 .. m - 1]$. While a client $p[i]$ executes, it can call any procedure $d[j]$. When this happens, client $p[i]$ waits until the call is returned before it resumes execution. Each procedure is either local to or remote from each client. The protocol for calling a procedure $d[j]$ by and returning the call to a client $p[i]$ depends on whether $d[j]$ is local to or remote from $p[i]$.

Consider the case where a procedure $d[j]$ is local to a client $p[i]$. In this case, $p[i]$ can call $d[j]$ by sending one message that contains all arguments of the call to $d[j]$. After executing the procedure, all results of the call are returned in one message to $p[i]$. Note that when $d[j]$ is local to $p[i]$, $p[i]$ and $d[j]$ can exchange single messages with a lot of data because the exchanged messages can carry pointers to the data rather than the data itself.

Consider the case where a procedure d[j] is remote from a client p[i]. In this case, client p[i] can call procedure d[j] by sending a sequence of messages that contain the call arguments to d[j]. After executing the procedure, the results of the call are returned in a sequence of messages to p[i]. Note that when d[j] is remote from p[i], p[i] and d[j] cannot exchange messages with a lot of data. Rather, they exchange sequences of messages of moderate length.

It is beneficial to design the clients and procedures in an application program without taking into account the locality or remoteness relation between clients and procedures. This can be achieved by providing a process pstub[i] for each client p[i] and a process dstub[j] for every procedure d[j]. Process pstub[i] is local to p[i], and process dstub[j] is local to d[j]. The function of these processes is to hide from p[i] and d[j] whether they are local to or remote from one another.

In order to call a procedure d[j], a client p[i] merely sends a call(j) message to its pstub[i] process. Then, p[i] waits to receive a rtrn message from pstub[i] before resuming execution. At the other side, when procedure d[j] receives a call message from its dstub[j] process, it executes the procedure and then returns back a rtrn message to dstub[j]. Process pstub[i] communicates the call message to process dstub[j], and process dstub[j] communicates back the rtrn message to pstub[i].

Processes p[i] and d[j] in the remote procedure protocol can be defined as follows:

```
process p[i : 0..n-1]

const m

var    wait  :       boolean,
       j     :       0..m-1

begin
       ~wait    ->
                          wait, j := true, any;
                          send call(j) to pstub[i]
[]     rcv rtrn from pstub[i]    ->    wait := false
end

process d[j : 0..m-1]
begin
       rcv call from dstub[j]    ->
                          {execute procedure}
                          send rtrn to dstub[j]
end
```

Each process pstub[i] has an input array, named remote, whose value is defined as follows:

remote[j] = true   iff   d[j] is remote from p[i]

When process pstub[i] receives a call(j) message from its client p[i], pstub[i] checks the value of remote[j]. If remote[j] = false, then process pstub[i] sends a call message to process dstub[j] and then waits to receive back a rtrn message, which it then forwards to process p[i]. If remote[j] = true, then process pstub[i] sends a crqst message to dstub[j], and when it receives back a crply message, it sends a sequence of arg messages to dstub[j]. These arg messages contain the call arguments that need to be delivered to procedure d[j]. The end of the arg messages is signaled by a special arg message named last. The reply to the arg messages is a sequence of rslt messages from process dstub[j] to process pstub[i]. The end of the rslt messages is signaled by a special rslt message named last.

Process pstub[i] in the remote procedure protocol can be defined as follows:

```
process pstub [i : 0..n-1]

const m, ymax
        {ymax is max # of arg messages per remote call}

inp    remote:    array [0..m-1] of boolean

var    y      :    1..ymax

par    j      :    0..m-1

begin
       rcv call(j) from p[i]    ->
              if ~remote[j]      ->
                     send call to dstub[j]
              []   remote[j]     ->
                     send crqst to dstub[j]
              fi

[]    rcv rtrn from dstub[j]   ->    send rtrn to p[i]

[]    rcv crply from dstub[j] ->
              y := any;
              do y < 1 -> send arg to dstub[j]; y := y-1
              od;
              send last to dstub[j]

[]    rcv rslt from dstub[j]  ->
              {add rslt to previous rslts}
              skip
```

```
[]        rcv last from dstub[j]  ->
                    {add last to previous rslts}
                    send rtrn to p[i]
end
```

Process dstub[j] has an input array, named remote, whose value is defined as follows:

$$remote[j] = true \quad iff \quad p[i] \text{ is remote from } d[j]$$

Note that remote[j] in pstub[i] has the same value as remote[i] in dstub[j].

Process dstub[j] also has a boolean variable named con. If con = true, then dstub[j] is "connected" to pstub[caller], where caller stores the index i of the calling client p[i]. If con = false, then dstub[j] is not connected to any pstub[i] and the value of variable caller is irrelevant.

Process dstub[j] in the remote procedures protocol can be defined as follows:

```
process dstub[j : 0..m-1]

const n, zmax
        {zmax is max # of rslt messages per remote call}

inp    remote       :      array [0..n-1] of boolean

var    con          :      boolean,
       caller, k    :      0..n-1,
       wait         :      array [0..n-1] of boolean,
       z            :      1..zmax

par    i            :      0..n-1

begin
       rcv call from pstub[i]  ->
              if   con   ->   wait[i] := true
              []  ~con   ->   con, caller := true, i;
                              send call to d[j]
              fi

[]     rcv crqst from pstub[i]  ->
              if   con   ->   wait[i] := true
              []  ~con   ->   con, caller := true, i;
                              send crply to pstub[i]
              fi
```

```
[]      rcv arg from pstub[i]    ->
            {add arg to previous args} skip


[]      rcv last from pstub[i]   ->
            {add last to previous args}
            send call to d[j]


[]      rcv rtrn from d[j]       ->
            if ~remote[caller] ->
                send rtrn to pstub[caller]
            [] remote[caller] ->
                z := any;
                do z <1 -> send rslt to pstub[caller];
                    z := z-1
                od;
                send last to pstub[caller]
            fi;
            k := caller +n 1;
            do  k ≠ caller  /\  ~wait[k] -> k := k +n 1
            od;
            if ~wait[k] -> con := false
            []    wait[k]  /\  ~remote[k]    ->
                        wait[k], caller := false, k;
                        send call to d[j]
            []    wait[k] /\ remote[k] ->
                        wait[k], caller := false, k;
                        send crply to pstub[k]
            fi
end
```

21.4 APPLICATION STRUCTURES IN THE INTERNET

A typical application in the Internet is structured as a pair of communicating client
and server. The client and server communicate either via sockets or via remote procedures. Next, we describe how clients and servers in the Internet communicate via
sockets and then we describe how they communicate via remote procedures.

Clients and Servers Using Sockets in the Internet

Consider a client and server that communicate via sockets in the Internet. The client
and its socket reside in one computer and the server and its socket reside in another
computer. The client's socket and the server's socket are of the same type: They are
either datagram sockets or stream sockets. (There is a third type of socket, called a
raw socket, that we ignore in this presentation.)

First, consider the case where the two sockets of the client and server are data-gram sockets. In this case, each of the two sockets corresponds to a UDP port in its computer, and the client and server communicate by exchanging UDP messages be-tween the two UDP ports. Because UDP does not guarantee message delivery, sent messages between the client and server can be lost or reordered before they are re-ceived. Also in this case, the communication between the client and server tends to be a short-lived transaction, where the client sends a request message to the server and then the server replies by sending back a reply message to the client. Thus, the server itself deals with the message and does not need to fork out an agent process for communicating with the client over a long period of time. Such a server is called an iterative server.

Second, consider the case where the two sockets of the client and server are stream sockets. In this case, each of the two sockets corresponds to a TCP port in its computer, and the client and server communicate by exchanging reliable text streams between the two TCP ports. Also in this case, the communication between the client and server tends to be a long-lived session during which the client and server exchange several messages. Thus at the beginning of the session, the server forks out an agent process for communicating with the client over a long period of time. Such a server is called a concurrent server.

Each socket, whether a datagram or a stream socket, has an identifier and an ad-dress. The socket identifier is an integer that uniquely identifies the socket in its computer. The socket address defines the (UDP or TCP) port that corresponds to the socket. In particular, a socket address is a data structure that consists of the follow-ing four fields:

1. The socket family to which the socket belongs   16 bits
2. The port corresponding to the socket   16 bits
3. IP address of the computer where the port in 2 resides 32 bits
4. Unused   64 bits

Field 1 defines the socket family to which the socket belongs. For the Internet socket family, field 1 has the value AF_INET. (We ignore other socket families in this presentation.) Field 2 defines the port to which the socket belongs but does not indicate whether this port is a UDP port or a TCP port. This information is deter-mined from the type of socket when the socket is instantiated. Field 3 defines the IP address of the computer where the port in field 2 resides. Field 4 is currently un-used. The length of this socket address is 128 bits; however, the lengths of socket addresses from other socket families differ.

In what follows, we describe how a typical communication proceeds between a client and a server. We first discuss the case where the communication is carried out over datagram sockets and then we discuss the case where the communication is carried out over stream sockets.

A datagram communication between a client in computer c and a server in com-puter d proceeds in five steps:

i. The server executes the following two commands in computer d:

```
sskid  :=    socket (skfam, sktyp, skprt) ;
errb   :=    bind (sskid, sskadr, adrlen)
```

The first command allocates (to the server) a socket that belongs to the spec-ified socket family skfam and is of the specified type sktyp and uses the specified protocol skprt. If the allocated socket belongs to the Internet sock-et family and if it is of type datagram socket and uses the transport protocol UDP, then the values of skfam, sktyp, and skprt are as follows:

$$skfam = AF\_INET$$

$$sktyp = SOCK\_DGRAM$$

$$skprt = IPPROTO\_UDP$$

If executing the first command succeeds, then the resulting value of sskid is a nonnegative integer that identifies the allocated socket in computer d (of the server). Otherwise, the value of sskid is a negative integer that identifies the type of error that occurred when this command was executed.

The second command binds the allocated socket sskid to a predefined socket address sskadr that consists of adrlen bytes. Note that the first three fields in sskadr are defined as follows. Field 1 contains the value AF_INET, field 2 defines a UDP port, and field 3 defines the IP address of computer d where the server resides. If executing this command succeeds, then the re-sulting value of errb is zero. Otherwise, the resulting value of errb is a nega-tive integer that identifies the type of error that occurred when this com-mand was executed.

ii. Similarly, the client executes the following two commands:

```
cskid  :=    socket (skfam, sktyp, skprt) ;
errb   :=    bind (cskid, cskadr, adrlen)
```

where the values of skfam, sktyp, and skprt are as follows:

$$skfam = AF\_INET$$

$$sktyp = SOCK\_DGRAM$$

$$skprt = IPPROTO\_UDP$$

The first three fields in the socket address cskadr are defined as follows. Field 1 contains the value AF_INET, field 2 defines a UDP port, and field 3 defines the IP address of computer c where the client resides.

iii. After the server has allocated a socket sskid and has defined its address sskadr in computer d and the client has allocated a socket cskid and has defined its address cskadr in computer c, the client and server can start exchanging messages.

To send a message to the server in d, the client in c executes the following command:

```
errs := sendto (cskid, msg, msglen, toadr, adrlen)
```

where cskid is the identifier of the client's socket, msg is a pointer to where the message is stored in c, msglen is the number of bytes in the message, toadr is a socket address identical to the socket address sskadr of the server in d, and adrlen is the number of bytes in toadr. If executing this command succeeds, then the resulting value of errs is zero. Otherwise, the resulting value of errs is a negative integer that identifies the type of error that occurred when this command was executed.

If executing this command succeeds, then a copy of the message and a copy of the socket address cskadr along with the number of bytes in that socket address are sent to socket sskid of the server. The server receives the message by executing the following command:

```
errv := recvfrom (sskid, bff, bfflen, fromadr,
                  adrlen)
```

where sskid is the identifier of the server's socket, bff is a pointer to where the received message is to be stored, bfflen is the number of bytes to be stored from the received message, fromadr is a pointer to where the received socket address of the client is to be stored, and adrlen is a pointer to where the received number of bytes of the received socket address is to be stored. If executing this command succeeds, then the resulting value of errv is zero. Otherwise, the resulting value of errv is a negative integer that identifies the type of error that occurred when this command was executed.

Execution of a sendto command is nonblocking whereas execution of a recvfrom command is blocking as follows. When the client executes a sendto command, the client can resume execution without having to wait until the sent message arrives at the specified server's socket. On the other hand, when the server executes a recvfrom command, execution of the server blocks until the server receives a message from its specified socket.

iv. Similarly, for the server in computer d to send a message to the client in computer c, the server executes the following command:

```
errs := sendto (sskid, msg, msglen, toadr, adrlen)
```

For the client to receive a message from the server, the client executes the following command:

```
errv := recvfrom (cskid, bff, bfflen, fromadr,
                  adrlen)
```

v. When the server no longer needs to send or receive any more messages, it can close its allocated socket sskid by executing the following command:

```
errc := close (sskid)
```

Similarly, the client can close its allocated socket cskid by executing the following command:

```
errc := close (cskid)
```

Note that if a message is sent to a socket after that socket is closed, then the sent message is lost.

The stream communication between a client in computer c and a server in computer d can proceed as follows:

i. The server executes the following four commands in computer d:

```
sskid  :=    socket (skfam, sktyp, skprt) ;
errb   :=    bind (sskid, sskadr, adrlen) ;
errl   :=    listen (sskid, queue) ;
nskid  :=    accept (sskid, fromadr, adrlen)
```

The two commands socket and bind are as defined above except that the values of sktyp and skprt are defined as follows.

$$sktyp = SOCK\_STREAM$$

$$skprt = IPPROTO\_TCP$$

Also, field 2 in sskadr defines a TCP port.

The value of queue in the listen command specifies how many connection requests (from clients) for socket sskid can be queued by the server as they wait for the server to execute the accept command. Usually the value of queue is 5. If executing this command succeeds, then the resulting value of errl is zero. Otherwise, the resulting value of errl is a negative integer that identifies the type of error that occurred when this command was executed.

Executing the accept command proceeds as follows. First, the execution pauses until a connection request is received from the socket of some client, and the address of that socket is stored in fromadr and the address length of that socket is stored in adrlen. Second, a new socket is generated for the server. The identifier of the newly generated socket is nskid, and its address is identical to that of sskid. Third, a connection between the socket fromadr and the socket nskid is established. If executing this command succeeds, then the resulting value of nskid is a nonnegative integer that identifies the newly generated socket. Otherwise, the resulting value of nskid is a negative integer that identifies the type of error that occurred when this command was executed.

ii. The client executes the following two commands in computer c:

```
cskid   :=      socket (skfam, sktyp, skprt) ;
errn    :=      connect (cskid, toadr, adrlen)
```

The socket command is as defined above except that the values of sktyp and skprt are defined as follows:

$$sktyp = SOCK\_STREAM$$

$$skprt = IPPROTO\_TCP$$

Execution of the connect command proceeds as follows. First, a connection request for connecting the client's socket cskid with the server's socket, whose address is toadr and whose address length is adrlen, is sent to the server. Note that the socket address toadr is identical to the socket address sskadr in the server. Second, the server receives the connection request and executes the accept command to connect socket cskid in computer c with socket nskid in computer d. Third, an acceptance reply is sent from the server to the client to inform the client that the connection request has been accepted. If executing this command succeeds, then the resulting value of errn is zero. Otherwise, the resulting value of errn is a negative integer that identifies the type of error that occurred when this command was executed.

iii. After a connection is established between socket cskid in computer c and socket nskid in computer d, the client and server can start exchanging messages over the established connection.

For the client to send a message to the server, the client executes the following command:

```
errs   :=     send (cskid, msg, msglen)
```

where msg is a pointer to where the message is stored in computer c, and msglen is the number of bytes in the message. If executing this command succeeds, then the resulting value of errs is zero. Otherwise, the resulting value of errs is a negative integer that identifies the type of error that occurred when this command was executed.

For the server to receive a message from the client, the server executes the following command:

```
errv    :=    recv (nskid , bff , bfflen)
```

where bff is a pointer to where the received message is to be stored and bf-flen is the number of bytes to be stored from the received message. If executing this command succeeds, then the resulting value of errv is zero. Otherwise, the resulting value of errv is a negative integer that identifies the type of error that occurred when this command was executed.

Execution of the send command is nonblocking, whereas execution of the recv command is blocking.

iv. Similarly, for the server to send a message to the client, the server executes the following command:

```
errs    :=    send (nskid, msg, msglen)
```

For the client to receive a message from the server, the client executes the following command.

```
errv    :=    recv (cskid, bff, bfflen)
```

v. To close the established connection between the two sockets cskid in computer c and nskid in computer d, either the client executes the command

```
errc    :=    close (cskid)
```

or the server executes the command

```
errc    :=    close (nskid)
```

Clients and Servers Using Remote Procedures in the Internet

It is possible to design clients and servers that communicate by offering and calling remote procedures. In this case, each server offers several procedures, and each client can call any of the offered procedures and get back the results of executing the called procedure.

For a server to offer a procedure, it performs two steps. First, the server registers the procedure by executing the command:

```
sstate := registerrpc (srvr, vrsn, prcd, inmap, outmap)
```

where:

sstate   Stores the integer that results from executing the registerrpc command. If executing this command succeeds, then the resulting value of sstate is zero. Otherwise, the resulting value of sstate is a negative integer that identifies the type of error that occurred when this command was executed.

srvr   Is an integer that uniquely defines the server in its host computer.

vrsn   Is an integer that uniquely defines the version of the offered procedure.

prcd   Is an integer that uniquely defines the offered procedure in the server srvr.

inmap   Is a decoder that maps the actual parameters of the procedure call, after receiving them over the network, to a form suitable for processing by the called procedure. This decoder is written using the XDR programming language.

outmap   Is an encoder that maps the results of the procedure call, before sending them over the network, to a form suitable for sending over the network. This encoder is written using the XDR programming language.

Second, after the server registers all the procedures it wishes to offer, it goes to sleep by executing the command:

```
svc_run ( )
```

The execution of svc_run ( ) causes the server to go to sleep until a call arrives from a client for one of the procedures registered by the server. When such a call arrives, the server executes the called procedure and then sends the results of execution back to the calling client. The server then resumes its sleep.

A client can call any offered procedure by executing the command

```
cstate := callrpc (host, srvr, vrsn, prcd, inmap, in,
                   outmap, out)
```

where

cstate   Stores the integer that results from executing the callrpc command. If executing this command succeeds, then the resulting value of cstate is zero. Otherwise, the resulting value of cstate is a negative integer that identifies the type of error that occurred when this command was executed.

host   Is the IP address of the host where the server that offers the called procedure resides.

srvr   Is an integer that uniquely defines the server in its host computer.

vrsn   Is an integer that uniquely defines the version of the called procedure.

prcd   Is an integer that uniquely defines the called procedure in its server.

inmap   Is an encoder that maps the actual parameters of the procedure call, before sending them over the network, to a form suitable for sending over the network. This encoder is written using the XDR programming language.

in   Is a pointer that points to where the actual parameters of the procedure call are stored.

outmap   Is a decoder that maps the results of the procedure call, after receiving them over the network, to a form suitable for storing these results. This decoder is written using the XDR programming language.

out   Is a pointer that points to where the results of the procedure call are to be stored.

21.5 BIBLIOGRAPHICAL NOTES

Sockets and their use in designing client–server applications are discussed in Stevens [1990] and Comer and Stevens [1993]. Remote procedures and their use in designing client–server applications are discussed in Birrell and Nelson [1984] and Thekkath and Levy [1993].

EXERCISES

1   (Finite Store in Sockets). Modify the socket protocol in Section 21.1 such that array mbox in each socket process is finite. If a socket process receives a message when its mbox array is full, the socket process discards the message.

2   (Prompt Replies by Sockets). Modify the socket protocol in Section 21.1 such that if a socket process skt[i, c] receives a nxt message from its process p[i] when the mbox array in skt[i, c] is empty, process skt[i, c] returns a nomsg message to process p[i].

3   (Storing Sender Identities in Sockets). Modify the socket protocol in Section 21.1 such that each socket process stores the index of the sending process of each message that is received by the socket. Moreover, each process p[i] can send a nxt(j) message to any of its socket processes skt[i, c] asking it to send the next message that skt[i, c] has received from process p[j].

4   (Detecting Message Corruption in Sockets). Modify the socket protocol in Section 21.1 as follows. Each message sent from a process p[i] to a socket process skt[j, d] is of the form msg(txt, chk), where chk is a checksum computed by p[i] from txt as follows:

```
chk      := COMPCHK(txt)
```

When skt[j, d] receives msg(txt, chk), it checks whether the message has been corrupted during its transmission from p[i] to skt[j, d]. If so, skt[j, d] discards the message; otherwise skt[j, d] stores the message in its mbox array.

5   (Active and Idle Sockets). Modify the socket protocol in Section 21.1 as follows. Each socket process skt[i, c] has a boolean input named actv. Each process p[i] has an input array, named actv, declared as follows:

inp actv : **array** [0..r-1] **of boolean**

The value of input actv in a socket process skt[i, c] is the same as the value of element actv[c] in its process p[i]. If a process p[j] sends a message to a socket[i, c], whose input actv is false, then skt[i, c] discards the message. If a process p[j] sends a message to a socket process skt[i, c], whose input act is true, then skt[i, c] stores the message in its mbox array. Each process p[i] can expect to receive messages only from its active socket processes, and so it sends nxt messages only to each skt[i, c], whose input actv is true.

6   (Making Sockets Active and Idle). Modify the protocol in exercise 5 such that actv in each socket process skt[i, c] is a variable, rather than an input, and array actv in each process p[i] is a variable, rather than an input. A process p[i] can make any of its sockets active by sending a bind message to that socket and can make any of its sockets idle by sending a close message to that socket. Note that when a socket receives a bind message, it initializes its variables, making its mbox array empty.

7   (Limiting the Scopes of Sockets). Modify the protocol in exercise 6 such that each bind message is of the form bind(j) so that an activated socket stores messages sent by process p[j] and discards messages sent by other processes.

8   (Limiting the Scopes of Clients). Modify the client and server protocol in Section 21.2 such that at any instant each client can be connected at most once with any server.

9   (Limiting the Scope of Servers). Modify the client and server protocol in Section 21.2 such that each server has an integer input cmax and the server can be connected with at most cmax clients at each instant.

10   (Servers Acting as Clients). Modify the client and server protocol in Section 21.2 such that each server can pretend to be a client and communicate with other servers in the network.

11   (Active and Idle Sockets in the Client and Server Protocol). Modify the client and server protocol in Section 21.2 such that each client and each server keeps track of its active sockets and cycles only among those active sockets to receive messages from them.

12   (Making Sockets Active and Idle in the Client and Server Protocol). Modify the client and server protocol in Section 21.2 such that each client and each server uses a protocol similar to the one in exercise 6 to make its sockets active and idle. In particular, each client and each server sends a bind message to any of its sockets to make it active and sends a close message to any of its sockets

to make it idle. Note that when a socket receives a bind message, it initializes its variables, making its mbox array empty.

13 (Well-Known Socket Protocol). Design the following client and server protocol. Each client p[i: 0 .. m − 1] and each server p[j: m .. n − 1] has a well-known socket skt[i: 0 .. n − 1]. These well-known sockets are used only in establishing connections between clients and servers. The exchange of data, drqst, and drqst messages between a client and a server is carried out over other sockets skt[j: r .. s − 1] that can be requested from server p[m], whose sole purpose is to control the allocation of these sockets to clients and servers.

14 (Comparing Client and Server Protocols). Discuss the advantages and disadvantages of the client and server protocol in Section 21.2 with the protocol in exercise 13.

15 (Nested Procedure Calls) Modify the remote procedure protocol in Section 21.3 to allow procedures to call other procedures. Note that in this case each procedure has two stubs: one stub handles incoming calls and the other stub handles outgoing calls.

16 (Socket Sharing). Modify the socket protocol in Section 21.1 as follows. Processes are defined as p[i: 0 .. m − 1, j: 0 .. n − 1] and sockets are defined as skt[i: 0 .. m − 1, k: 0 .. r − 1]. A process p[i, j] can allocate any socket skt[i, k] by sending a bind message to it and later receiving an acpt message from it. The attempt to allocate skt[i, k] fails, if skt[i, k] is currently allocated to another process p[i, j′]. In this case, p[i, j] receives a rjct message as a reply to its bind message. Once p[i, j] allocates a socket skt[i, k], it can start receiving msg(txt) messages from it. A process p[i, j] can release any allocated socket skt[i, k] by sending a close message to it. If a process p[i′, j′] sends a msg(txt) message to a socket skt[i, k], the socket checks whether or not it is allocated to some process p[i, j]. If skt[i, k] is allocated, it stores msg(txt); otherwise, it discards the message.

CHAPTER 22

APPLICATIONS

In the last chapter, we discussed the common features of application programs. In particular, we stated that the processes in an application program are classified into clients and servers. Clients are local to the program users while servers are local to the program resources. We also explained how the communications between clients and servers proceed via sockets or via remote procedures.

In this chapter, we present several examples of application programs. To simplify our presentation, we make the following two assumptions concerning the application programs that we present:

  i. Each application program consists of multiple clients and only one server. (It is straightforward to extend the presentation to programs with multiple servers.)

  ii. The clients and server in each program communicate directly, rather than via sockets or via remote procedures. (It is straightforward to extend the presentation to programs where the clients and server communicate via sockets, as shown in Section 21.2, or via remote procedures, as shown in Section 21.3.)

The application programs we present in this chapter are as follows. In Section 22.1, we discuss an echo program where each client can send an arbitrary message to the server, which sends it back to the client. In Section 22.2, we discuss a file transfer program where files can be sent from each client to the server or vice versa. In Section 22.3, we discuss a remote login program where each client can log into the server. Finally in Section 21.4, we discuss some application programs in the Internet that perform echo, file transfer, and remote login.

22.1   ECHO

An echo program consists of an array of n client processes, named ecc[i: 0 .. n − 1], and one server process, named ecs. This program allows each process ecc[i] to send arbitrary bits to process ecs, which receives the bits and sends them back to ecc[i]. This service is useful in performing network diagnosis. In particular, when a client process ecc[i] receives back the bits that it has sent to process ecs, ecc[i] recognizes that server ecs is currently up.

Next, we describe the protocol between a client process ecc[i] and the server process ecs in some detail. Upon request from user[i], process ecc[i] sends an echo request erqst(b) message, where b is an arbitrary array of bits, to the server ecs. Process ecs replies by sending back an echo reply erply(b) message to process ecc[i]. If process ecc[i] receives an erply(b) message, it informs its user[i] that ecs has replied correctly. If ecc[i] receives an erply(c) message, where c ≠ b, it informs its user[i] that ecs has replied incorrectly. If ecc[i] does not receive the erply(b) message, it informs its user[i] that process ecs is not replying.

A client process ecc[i] in the echo protocol can be defined as follows:

```
process ecc[i : 0..n-1]

const m

var    wait  :        boolean,
       b, c  :        array [0..m-1] of 0..1
begin
       ~wait     ->
                 {local user[i] wants echo service from}
                 {a remote site whose echo server is ecs}
                 wait, b := true, any; send erqst(b) to ecs

[]     rcv erply(c) from ecs    ->
                 if b = c ->
                     skip
                     {"dest. replied correctly"}
                 [] b ≠ c ->
                     skip
                     {"dest. replied incorrectly"}
                 fi; wait := false

[]     timeout wait ∧
                 (#ch.ecc[i].ecs + #ch.ecs.ecc[i] = 0)   ->
                 {"dest. is not responding"}
                 wait := false
end
```

The server process ecs in the echo protocol can be defined as follows.

```
process ecs

const m, n

var    b     :        array [0..m-1] of 0..1

par    i     :        0..n-1

begin
      rcv erqst(b) from ecc[i]   ->
           send erply(b) to ecc[i]
end
```


22.2 FILE TRANSFER

A file transfer program consists of an array of n client processes, named ftc[i: 0 .. n − 1], and one server process, named fts. This program allows each process ftc[i] to exchange files with process fts. Next, we describe the protocol between a client process ftc[i] and the server process fts in some detail.

Upon request from user[i], process ftc[i] asks for the file transfer service by sending an ft message to process fts. Process fts replies to the ft message by sending a pwd message to process ftc[i], asking for the password of user[i]. Process ftc[i] gets the required password wrd from user[i] and sends it in a pass(wrd) message to process fts. Process fts uses the received password to check whether user[i] has an authorization to access the files of fts. If user[i] has no authorization, then fts sends back a rjct message to process ftc[i], and ftc[i] informs user[i] that its request to access the files of fts has been denied. If user[i] has an authorization, then fts sends back an acpt message to process ftc[i], and ftc[i] informs user[i] that its request has been granted.

When process ftc[i] receives an acpt message, it reaches a decision point and can send any of the following three messages:

i.   Process ftc[i] can send a write(fnm) message to process fts, asking to write file fnm in process fts. If this happens, process ftc[i] sends a sequence of sgmnt messages that constitute the segments of a new version of file fnm followed by an end-of-file eof message to process fts. Then, process ftc[i] waits to receive an end-of-transmission eot message from process fts before it returns to the decision point and the cycle repeats.

ii. Process ftc[i] can send a read(fnm) message to process fts, asking to read file fnm in process fts. If this happens, process ftc[i] receives a sequence of sgmnt messages that constitute the segments of file fnm followed by an eot message. When process ftc[i] receives the eot message, it returns to the decision point and the cycle repeats.

   iii. Process ftc[i] can send a quit message to process fts, asking to terminate the current session with fts. If this happens, process ftc[i] waits to receive a quit message from process fts before informing user[i] that the file transfer service has terminated.

Each eot message has a boolean field sccss. If sccss is true, then the preceding write or read operation has succeeded. Otherwise, sccss is false, and the preceding operation has failed.

A client process ftc[i] in the file transfer protocol can be defined as follows:

```
process ftc[i : 0..n-1]

const r, s

var    con, wait, actv    :    boolean,
       fnm                 :    0..r-1,
       wrd                 :    0..s-1,
       sccss               :    boolean

begin
       ~con  /\  ~wait     ->
              {user[i] wants to access files in}
              {a site whose server is fts}
              wait := true; send ft to fts

[]     rcv pwd from fts  ->
              {get password from user[i]; send it to fts}
              wrd := any; send pass(wrd) to fts

[]     rcv rjct from fts  ->
              {to user[i]: "access to files is denied"}
              wait := false

[]     rcv acpt from fts  ->
              {to user[i]: "access to files is granted"}
              con, wait := true, false

[]     con  /\  ~wait      ->
              fnm := any;
              if true  ->
                     {user[i] wants to write file fnm}
                     wait, actv := true, true;
```

```
                            send write(fnm) to fts
             []  true  ->
                            {user[i] wants to read file fnm}
                            wait := true;
                            send read(fnm) to fts
             []  true  ->
                            {user[i] wants to quit}
                            wait := true;
                            send quit to fts
        fi

[]     con /\ wait /\ actv  ->
             if true  -> {get next segment of file fnm}
                             send sgmnt to fts
             []  true  -> actv := false; send eof to fts
             fi

[]     rcv sgmnt from fts  ->
             {deliver received segment of file fnm}
             skip

[]     rcv eot(sccss) from fts  ->
             if sccss  -> {file transfer succeeded} skip
             []  ~sccss  -> {file transfer failed} skip
             fi; con, wait := true, false

[]     rcv quit from fts           ->
             {display "goodbye" to user[i]}
             con, wait := false, false
end
```

Process fts has the following five arrays:

```
inp   auth  :      array [0..n-1, 0..r-1] of boolean

var   fnm   :      array [0..n-1] of 0..r-1,
      lock  :      array [0..r-1] of 0..n,
      stw   :      array [0..n-1] of boolean,
      str   :      array [0..n-1] of boolean
```

These five arrays have the following meanings:

    auth[i, wrd] = true iff the password of user[i] is wrd and user[i] has an authorization to access, that is, read and write, the files protected by process fts.

fnm[i]   = file name mentioned in the last write or read message from process ftc[i].

lock[f]   = i, where $0 \le i < n$, if file f is locked to be written or read by user[i]. lock[f] = n if file f is unlocked.

stw[i]   = true iff user[i] has succeeded in locking file fnm[i] so that it can write the file.

str[i]   = true iff user[i] has succeeded in locking file fnm[i] so that it can read the file.

The server process fts in the file transfer protocol can be defined as follows:

```
process fts

const n, r, s

inp   auth :      array [0..n-1, 0..s-1] of boolean

var   fnm  :      array [0..n-1] of 0..r-1,
      lock :      array [0..r-1] of 0..n,
      stw  :      array [0..n-1] of boolean,
      str  :      array [0..n-1] of boolean,
      wrd  :      0..s-1

par   i    :      0..n-1

begin
      rcv ft from ftc[i]  ->
          send pwd to ftc[i]

[]    rcv pass(wrd) from ftc[i]  ->
          if ~auth[i, wrd] ->      send rjct to ftc[i]
          []  auth[i, wrd] ->      send acpt to ftc[i]
          fi

[]    rcv write(fnm[i]) from ftc[i] ->
          if lock[fnm[i]] != n       ->
                stw[i] := false
          [] lock[fnm[i]] = n        ->
                lock[fnm[i]], stw[i] := i, true
          fi

[]    rcv sgmnt from ftc[i]   ->
          if  stw[i] -> {append sgmnt to fnm[i]} skip
          []  ~stw[i] -> {discard rcvd sgmnt} skip
          fi
```

```
☐       rcv eof from ftc[i]   ->
            if    stw[i] -> lock[fnm[i]] := n
         ☐    ~stw[i] -> skip
            fi; send eot(stw[i]) to ftc[i]

☐       rcv read(fnm[i]) from ftc[i] ->
                if lock[fnm[i]] ≠ n       ->
                    send eot(false) to ftc[i]
             ☐  lock[fnm[i]] = n          ->
                    lock[fnm[i]], str[i] := i, true;
                    send sgmnt to ftc[i]
            fi

☐       str[i]    ->
                if true ->
                    {send next segment of fnm[i]}
                    send sgmnt to ftc[i]
             ☐  true  ->
                    {end of file fnm[i] is reached}
                    lock[fnm[i]], str[i] := n, false
                    send eot(true) to ftc[i]
            fi

☐       rcv quit from ftc[i]      ->
                send quit to ftc[i]
end
```

22.3 REMOTE LOGIN

A remote login program consists of an array of n client processes, named rlgc[i: 0 .. n – 1], and one server process, named rlgs. This program allows each process rlgc[i] to login the computer of process rlgs. Next, we describe the protocol between a client process rlgc[i] and the server process rlgs in some detail.

Upon request from user[i], process rlgc[i] asks for the remote login service by sending a login message to process rlgs. Process rlgs replies to the login message by sending a pwd message to process rlgc[i], asking for the password of user[i]. Process rlgc[i] gets the required password wrd from user[i] and sends it in a pass(wrd) message to process rlgs. Process rlgs uses the received password to check whether user[i] has an authorization to log into rlgs. If user[i] has no authorization, then rlgs sends back a rjct message to process rlgc[i], and rlgc[i] informs user[i] that its request to log into rlgs has been denied. If user[i] has an authorization, then rlgs sends back an acpt message to process rlgc[i], which informs user[i] that its request has been granted.

When process rlgc[i] receives an acpt message, it reaches a decision point and can forward any of the following messages from user[i] to process rlgs:

  i. Process rlgc[i] can forward a chr message to process rlgs. If this happens, process rlgc[i] returns to the decision point and the cycle repeats. Meanwhile process rlgs receives the chr message and sends it back to process rlgc[i], which displays it to user[i].

  ii. Process rlgc[i] can forward a rtrn message to process rlgs. If this happens, process rlgc[i] waits to receive a sequence of chr messages followed by a rtrn message from process rlgs. Process rlgc[i] displays each of the received chr messages to user[i] before returning to the decision point and the cycle repeats.

  iii. Process rlgc[i] can forward a logout message to process rlgs. If this happens, process rlgc[i] waits to receive a logout message from process rlgs before returning to its initial state.

Note that in this protocol every chr message, whether forwarded by rlgc[i] to rlgs or sent from rlgs to rlgc[i], is displayed to user[i].

A client process rlgc[i] in the remote login protocol can be defined as follows:

```
process rlgc[i : 0..n-1]

const r

var    con, wait   :     boolean,
       wrd         :     0..r-1

begin
       ~con ∧ ~wait            ->
           {local user[i] wants to log into a remote}
           {site whose remote login server is rlgs }
           wait := true; send login to rlgs

[]     rcv pwd from rlgs       ->
           {get password from user[i]; send it to rlgs}
           wrd := any; send pass(wrd) to rlgs

[]     rcv rjct from rlgs      ->
           {display "incorrect login" to user[i]}
           wait := false

[]     rcv acpt from rlgs      ->
           {display "correct login" to user[i]}
           con, wait := true, false

[]     con ∧ ~wait             ->
           if true -> {a data character from user[i]}
                    send chr to rlgs
           [] true -> {a return character from user[i]}
```

```
                       wait := true; send rtrn to rlgs
          [] true -> {a log out character from user[i]}
                       wait := true;
                       send logout to rlgs
          fi

[]   rcv chr from rlgs          ->
          {display received "chr" to user[i]}
          skip

[]   rcv rtrn from rlgs         ->
          wait := false

[]   rcv logout from rlgs       ->
          {display "log off" to user[i]}
          con, wait := false, false
end
```

The server process rlgs of the remote login protocol can be defined as follows:

```
process rlgs

const n, r

inp    auth  :      array [0..n-1, 0..r-1] of boolean

var    actv  :      array [0..n-1] of boolean,
       wrd   :      0..r-1

par    i     :      0..n-1

begin
       rcv login from rlgc[i]  ->
           send pwd to rlgc[i]

[]     rcv pass(wrd) from rlgc[i]  ->
           if ~auth[i, wrd] ->
               send rjct to rlgc[i]
           []  auth[i, wrd] ->
               {remote login user[i]}
               send acpt to rlgc[i]
           fi

[]     rcv chr from rlgc[i]       ->
           {add "chr" to previous "chrs" from rlgc[i]}
           send chr to rlgc[i]
```

```
[]    rcv rtrn from rlgc[i]   ->
              {it is now my turn to send characters}
              send chr to rlgc[i]; actv[i] := true


[]    actv[i]  ->
              if true  -> send chr to rlgc[i]
              []  true  -> actv[i] := false;
                           send rtrn to rlgc[i]
              fi


[]    rcv logout from rlgc[i]   ->
              {log out user[i]}
              send logout to rlgc[i]
end
```

22.4 APPLICATIONS IN THE INTERNET

In this section, we discuss some application protocols that perform echo, file transfer, and remote login in the Internet.

Echo in the Internet

In the Internet, two protocols that perform echo functions are the Packet Internet Groper, or Ping for short, and Trace Route (or Traceroute). Ping can be invoked in a host to check whether some other host is reachable from the first host. Traceroute can be invoked in a host to get a list of all routers that can be encountered by an IP message sent from this host to some other host. Next, we discuss these two protocols in some detail.

Each host in the Internet has a Ping process. When a user invokes the Ping process in a host c, the user identifies another host d in the invocation. This invocation prompts the Ping process in c to request from the ICMP process in c to send an ICMP echo request message intended for the ICMP process in host d. When the ICMP process in host d receives the ICMP echo request message, it replies by sending back an ICMP echo reply message intended for the ICMP process in host c. When the ICMP process in c receives the ICMP echo reply message, it informs the Ping process in c, which informs the user.

If the ICMP process in c does not receive the ICMP echo reply for some time, the Ping process informs the user of this fact. In this case, the user can conclude one of the following:

i. Either the ICMP echo request message or the ICMP echo reply message was lost during transmission and another invocation of Ping is in order.

ii. Host d is unreachable from host c.

iii. There is a security firewall between host c and host d that does not permit

ICMP messages to proceed, although electronic mail messages can still go through between the two hosts c and d.

Each of the ICMP echo request and reply messages has the following six fields:

1. Message type   8 bits
2. Message code   8 bits
3. Message checksum   16 bits
4. Unique identifier of current Ping invocation   16 bits
5. Message sequence number in current Ping invocation   16 bits
6. Optional data   x bits

Field 1 either has the value 0 if the message is an echo request or has the value 1 if the message is an echo reply. Field 2 is unused and has the value 0. The message checksum in field 3 is computed over all the ICMP message in the same way the checksum in the header of an IP message is computed over the message header (as discussed in Section 8.4).

We now turn our attention to Traceroute. Each host in the Internet has a Traceroute process. When a user invokes the Traceroute process in a host c, the user identifies another host d in the invocation. The invocation prompts the Traceroute process in host c to request from the UDP process in c to send a UDP message intended for the UDP port 30000 in host d. The Traceroute process in c also requests from the IP process in c to assign a value of 1 to the time-to-live field in the IP header attached to the sent UDP message. When the message reaches the first router r.1 on the route from c to d, router r.1 discards the message because its time-to-live has expired and sends an ICMP time-to-live expired message to host c. Host c receives the ICMP message and forwards it to its Traceroute process, which records that the first router on the route from c to d is r.1.

Then, the Traceroute process in c repeats the same procedure as before except that a value of 2 is assigned to the time-to-live field in the IP header attached to the sent UDP message. Eventually, host c receives an ICMP time-to-live expired from a router r.2 and forwards it to its Traceroute process, which records that the second router on the route from c to d is r.2. Then, the Traceroute process in c repeats the same procedure except that a value of 3 is assigned to the time-to-live field in the IP header attached to the sent UDP message, and so on.

Finally a sent UDP message from host c has a high enough value in the time-to-live field in its IP header that the message arrives at host d and is forwarded to UDP port 30000 in d, as specified in the UDP header of the message. Because usually there is no process waiting to receive from this port, the UDP process in host d sends an ICMP port unreachable message intended for host c. When host c receives an ICMP port unreachable message from host d, it forwards the message to its Traceroute process, which recognizes that it has completed tracing the route from c to d and prints the recorded route for the user.

File Transfer in the Internet

The application protocol for transferring files in the Internet is called the file transfer protocol, or FTP for short. For a user at a host c to transfer files between the file system of host c and the file system of another host d, the user communicates with an FTP client in c, and the FTP client in turn communicates with the FTP server in d, as shown in Figure 22.1.

The communication between the FTP client in c and the FTP server in d proceeds as follows. At the beginning, the FTP server opens a well-known TCP port, port 21, on host d. Then the FTP client, prompted by its user, connects to that port. The resulting connection is called a control connection. The communication between the FTP client and FTP server over the control connection consists of successive steps. In each step, the client sends one command to the server and then the server replies by sending one or more replies to the client. Each command is of the form

`<command type> <command parameters>`

Each reply is of the form

`<3-digit number> <English description>`

There are basically five types of replies. Each reply type has one of the following meanings:

1. The command has been accepted and the client should send the next command to proceed.
2. The command has been accepted and the client may send the next command.
3. The command has been accepted and the client should not send the next command until it receives the next reply.

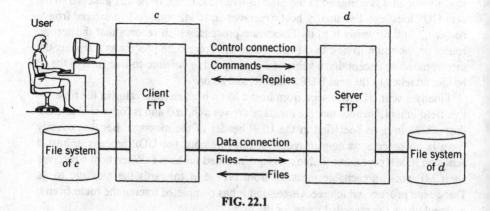

FIG. 22.1

4. The command has been rejected and the client may try it again later; the client may send the next command.

5. The command has been rejected and the client should not try it again; the client may send the next command.

The communications between the FTP client in host c and the FTP server in host d can be used in performing any of the following four functions:

   i. Allow the user, which is already logged in in host c, to log in host d (and so be able to request a file transfer between the two file systems of c and d).

  ii. Transfer a file from the file system of host c to the file system of host d, or vice versa.

 iii. List the files and directories in the file system of host d for the user in host c.

 iv. Terminate the current session between the FTP client and FTP server and close the control connection between them.

Function i can be performed in two steps:

Client sends to server: USER <user log-in name on d>.
Server sends to client: reply of type 1.
Client sends to server: PASS <user's password on d>.
Server sends to client: reply of type 2.

To perform function ii or iii, the FTP client first opens a TCP port and informs the FTP server of it. The FTP server then connects to that port, and the resulting connection is called a data connection. The required file or listing is transferred over the data connection and then the connection is closed. For example, transferring a file from the file system in d to the file system in c can be performed in two steps as follows:

Client sends to server: PORT <TCP port in host c>.
Server connects to specified port, establishing a data connection.
Server sends to client: reply of type 2.

Client sends to server: RETR <file name>.
Server sends to client: reply of type 3.
Server sends specified file over data connection.
Server sends to client: reply of type 2.
Server removes data connection.

Function iv can be performed in one step as follows:

Client sends to server: QUIT.

Server sends to client: reply of type 2.

Remote Login in the Internet

The main protocol that performs remote login in the Internet is called Telnet. Using Telnet, a user working on a terminal connected to a local computer c can log into a remote computer d as shown in Figure 22.2. In this case, all characters typed by the user on the terminal are sent to the Telnet client in computer c. The Telnet client in c modifies the received characters and then sends them to the Telnet server in computer d. The Telnet server in d modifies the received characters and then pretends to be a terminal of computer d and sends the modified characters to the operating system of d. The operating system in d replies to the received characters with some characters sent to the Telnet server in d. The Telnet server in d modifies the received characters and then sends them to the Telnet client in computer c. The Telnet client in c modifies the received characters and then forwards them to be printed on the user's terminal.

The reason that the received characters need to be modified at every stage before forwarding them is that the used terminal at computer c may be different from the terminals accepted by the operating system in computer d. Thus, the Telnet clients and servers in all computers recognize a standard terminal called the network virtual terminal, or NVT for short.

The Telnet client in computer c maps the characters from the user's terminal to the corresponding NVT characters before forwarding them to the Telnet server in computer d. It also maps the received characters from the Telnet server in computer d, which were sent as NVT characters, to the corresponding characters of the user's terminal before forwarding these characters to the user's terminal.

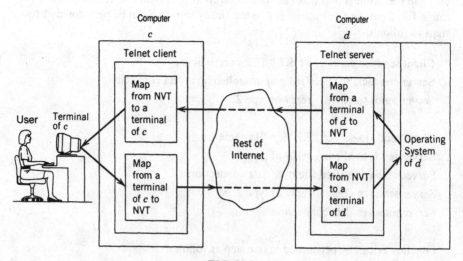

FIG. 22.2

Similarly, the Telnet server in computer d maps the received characters from the Telnet client in computer c to the corresponding characters of the terminals in computer d before forwarding them to the operating system of d. It also maps the received characters from the operating system in computer d to the corresponding NVT characters before forwarding them to the Telnet client in computer c.

Not all exchanged characters between the Telnet client in computer c and the Telnet server in computer d are generated by the user at c or by the operating system of d. In fact, some of the exchanged characters are commands intended to synchronize between the Telnet client at c and the Telnet server at d. Examples of these commands are as follows:

Suspend processing.

Abort processing.

Interrupt processing.

Go ahead.

Break.

Are you there?

Negotiate option.

The command characters are sent interleaved with the data characters (generated by the user at computer c or by the operating system of computer d). To distinguish between the command characters and the data characters in the same stream, each command character is preceded by a special character called the interpret-as-command character, or the IAC character for short. If a data character in the stream happens to be an IAC character, then another IAC character is inserted before it in the stream. (See the character insertion protocol in Section 7.2.)

There are four command characters for negotiating options between the Telnet client and the Telnet server: WILL, WONT, DO, and DONT. For example, the Telnet client can propose to adopt a certain option by sending the following three command characters to the Telnet server:

```
IAC ; WILL ; <option>
```

If the Telnet server accepts this proposal, it sends the following three command characters to the Telnet client:

```
IAC ; DO ; <option>
```

On the other hand, if the Telnet server rejects this proposal, it sends the following three characters to the Telnet client:

```
IAC ; DONT ; <option>
```

As another example, the Telnet client can propose that the Telnet server adopt a certain option by sending the following three command characters to the Telnet server:

```
IAC ; DO ; <option>
```

If the Telnet server accepts this proposal, it sends the following three command characters to the Telnet client:

```
IAC ; WILL ; <option>
```

On the other hand, if the Telnet server rejects this proposal, it sends the following three characters to the Telnet client:

```
IAC ; WONT ; <option>
```

Thus, the reply to WILL is either DO or DONT, and the reply to DO is either WILL or WONT. Also, the reply to WONT is DONT, and the reply to DONT is WONT.

22.5 BIBLIOGRAPHICAL NOTES

Definition of the network virtual terminal is given in Schicker and Duenki [1979]. Terminal protocols are discussed in Mangee et al. [1979] and Day [1980]. The FTP is discussed in Gien [1978].

EXERCISES

1 (Detecting Corruption and Loss in the Echo Protocol). Modify the echo protocol in Section 22.1 such that the last bit b[n − 1] in array b in message erqst(b) is an even parity bit for array b. When process ecc[i] receives an erply(b) message, it detects whether corruption has occurred by examining array b in the received message.

2 (Detecting Corruption and Loss in the Echo Protocol). Modify the echo protocol in exercise 1 such that a client process ecc[i] sends r rqst(b) messages for some integer input r. At the end of service, ecc[i] reports to its user[i] whether any of the expected r reply messages has been corrupted or lost.

3 (Detecting Corruption, Loss, and Reorder in the Echo Protocol). Modify the echo protocol in exercise 2 as follows. Each message sent by a client ecc[i] is of the form erqst(b, s), where b is an arbitrary bit array and s is a sequence number in the range 0 .. r − 1. At the end of service, ecc[i] reports to its user[i] whether any of the expected echoed replies has been corrupted, lost, or reordered.

4   (Detecting Corruption, Loss, and Reorder in the Echo Protocol). Modify the echo protocol in exercise 3 such that a client process ecc[i] can send any number, not exceeding an input rmax, of erqst(b, s) messages to ecs.

5   (Multiple Servers in the Echo Protocol). Modify the echo protocol in Section 22.1 to allow multiple servers ecs[j: $0 .. r - 1$].

6   (Explaining the File Transfer Protocol). Does the file transfer protocol in Section 22.2 allow concurrent reading or writing of the same file by different clients? Explain your answer.

7   (Concurrent Reading and Writing of Files). Modify the file transfer protocol in Section 22.2 as follows. If the server process fts receives a request to read or write a file fnm for a client while file fnm is being written by another client ftc[i], then fts stores the request until ftc[i] finishes with file fnm.

8   (Concurrent versus Sequential Access of Files). Compare the advantages and disadvantages of the protocol in exercise 7 versus those of the protocol in Section 22.2.

9   (Access Authorization of Files). Modify the file transfer protocol in Section 22.2 by adding the following access authorization array fauth to the server process fts:

inp fauth : **array** [0..n-1, 0..r-1] **of boolean**

where fauth[i, fnm] = true iff client ftc[i] is authorized to access, that is, read or write, file fnm.

10 (Access Authorization of Files). Modify the file transfer protocol in Section 22.2 by adding the following read and write authorization arrays to the server process fts:

inp rauth, wauth : **array** [0..n-1, 0..r-1] **of boolean**

where

$$\text{rauth}[i, f] = \text{true} \quad \text{iff} \quad \text{client ftc}[i] \text{ is authorized to read file } f$$
$$\text{wauth}[i, f] = \text{true} \quad \text{iff} \quad \text{client ftc}[i] \text{ is authorized to write file } f$$

11 (Encrypting the Password in the File Transfer Protocol). Modify the file transfer protocol in Section 22.2 such that the password wrd in the message pass(wrd) is encrypted in order to prevent an adversary from getting it.

12 (Authenticating Clients by the Server in the File Transfer Protocol). Consider the file transfer protocol in exercise 11. An adversary can obtain a copy of message pass(wrd) sent from a client ftc[i] to the server fts, where wrd is an encryption of the password of user[i]. Later, the adversary pretends to be ftc[i] and sends pwd(wrd) to fts, which convinces fts wrongly that the adversary is

indeed ftc[i]. Modify the protocol such that the server process authenticates each client when the client requests a service.

13 (Multiple Servers in the File Transfer Protocol). Modify the file transfer protocol in Section 22.2 to allow multiple servers fts[j: 0 . . r – 1].

14 (Encrypting the Password in the Remote Login Protocol). Modify the remote login protocol in section 22.3 such that the password wrd in the message pass(wrd) is encrypted in order to prevent an adversary from getting it.

15 (Authenticating Clients by the Server in the Remote Login Protocol). Consider the remote login protocol in exercise 14. An adversary can obtain a copy of message pass(wrd) sent from a client rlgc[i] to the server rlgs, where wrd is an encryption of the password of user[i]. Later, the adversary pretends to be rlgc[i] and sends pwd(wrd) to rlgs, which convinces rlgs wrongly that the adversary is indeed rlgc[i]. Modify the protocol such that the server process authenticates each client when the client requests a service.

16 (Multiple Servers in the Remote Login Protocol). Modify the remote login protocol in Section 22.3 to allow multiple servers rlgs[j: 0 . . r – 1].

17 (A Current Time Application). Design a current time application that consists of m clients ctc[i: 0 . . m – 1] and n servers cts[j: m . . n – 1]. Each server cts[j] has an input clock declared as follows:

```
const    r
inp      clock  :  0..r-1
```

Each user[i] can prompt its client ctc[i] to request the current time of any server cts[j]. When ctc[i] receives the current time of cts[j], it displays it to user[i].

18 (A Periodic Time Application). Design a periodic time application that consists of m clients ptc[i: 0 . . m – 1] and n servers pts[j: m . . n – 1]. Each server cts[j] has an input clock declared as follows.

```
const    r
inp      clock  :  0..r-1
```

Each user[i] can prompt its client ptc[i] to send a register message to any server pts[j]. When pts[i] receives a register message from ptc[i], pts[j] starts to periodically send its current time to ptc[i]. The periodic transmission of current times from pts[j] to ptc[i] continues until user[i] prompts ptc[i] to send a quit message to pts[j].

CHAPTER 23

RING NETWORKS

In a ring network, each process has exactly two neighboring processes; they are called its right and left neighbors. Also, each process has exactly one incoming channel and one outgoing channel. The incoming channel is from the left neighbor and the outgoing channel is to the right neighbor. Thus, a process can receive messages from its left neighbor only and can send messages to its right neighbor only. Figure 23.1 illustrates how processes and channels are arranged in a ring network. Note that a ring network is not a special case of a general network because there is only one channel between any pair of neighboring processes in a ring network.

Because each process in a ring network can send messages only to its right neighbor, the issue of message routing does not arise in ring networks.

We consider ring networks where the number of messages in the network remains fixed and where each message has the same number of bits. In such networks, each action in a process consists of receiving a message from the left neighbor of the process, updating the message fields and the process variables, then sending the updated message to the right neighbor of the process. Because the number of messages in the network remains fixed and because each message has the same number of bits, the issue of congestion control does not arise in ring networks.

From this discussion, it follows that only the issue of switching needs to be ad-

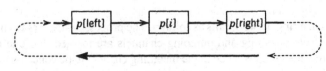

FIG. 23.1

dressed in ring networks. As it happens, the traditional switching methods, namely circuits and datagrams, do not take full advantage of the special topology of a ring network, and so these methods do not extend well to ring networks. Therefore, new switching methods are needed for ring networks. In fact, there are two common methods for performing switching in ring networks. Adopting either of these methods leads to a different type of ring networks. The two types of ring networks are presented in the next section.

23.1 TYPES OF RING NETWORKS

In this section, we consider two types of ring networks: slotted and token rings. The difference between these two types of rings is as follows. The processes in a slotted ring circulate several, relatively large, messages called slots, whereas the processes in a token ring circulate one small message called a byt message.

In a slotted ring, each slot message has four fields: a bit indicating whether the slot is empty or full, the index of the source process of the message, the index of the destination process of the message, and the sent data. By contrast, a byt message in a token ring has two small fields. The first field contains the type of the message. The second field contains one of the following items: index of some process, a small amount of text, or some control information.

In a slotted ring, a process p that needs to send data waits until it receives an empty slot message. Process p stores the data to be sent in the slot message along with its own index and the index of the destination process. It then marks the slot message full and sends it out. The slot message travels a complete cycle around the ring. Along the way, when the slot message reaches the destination process q, its data contents are copied into q. Finally, when the slot message returns to the source process p, process p marks the slot message empty and sends it out. This protocol is discussed in more detail in Section 23.2.

In a token ring, a process p that needs to send data waits until it receives a special byt message called token. There is at most one token message in the token ring. When process p receives the token message, it starts to send its data as a sequence of byt messages: one head message that contains the index of the destination process q, followed by a number of data messages, followed by one tail message. This sequence of byt messages travels a complete cycle around the ring. Along the way, when the sequence of byt messages reaches the destination process q, the data messages are copied into q. Finally, when the sequence of messages returns to the source process p, process p sends out the token message. This protocol is discussed in more detail in Section 23.3.

The ring networks discussed in this chapter are designed to tolerate two types of faults: process failures and message modifications. Next, we describe these two types of faults in order.

A process in a ring network fails as follows. The process disappears from the network and both its incoming and outgoing channels are merged into one channel. This causes the message sequence in the incoming channel to be concatenated at the tail of the message sequence in the outgoing channel, forming one message sequence.

A message in some channel in a ring network is modified as follows. The values of some fields in the message are changed, and the new value of each modified field is chosen arbitrarily from the domain of values of that field.

We adopt the following two assumptions concerning fault occurrence in a ring network:

i. *Fault Atomicity:* Faults, whether process failures or message modifications, cannot occur during any execution of any action in any process in the network.

ii. *Rare Occurrence of Faults:* Faults, whether process failures or message modifications, occur only a finite number of times along any, possibly infinite, execution of the network.

Because a process can fail either before an action is executed or after an action is executed but not in between, and because in each action a process receives one message and then sends one message, the number of messages in the network is guaranteed to remain fixed in the presence of process failures. Also, because message modification has no effect on the number of messages in the network, the number of messages in the network remains fixed in the presence of both types of faults.

The ring network protocols that we discuss in the next two sections tolerate faults in the following sense. After finitely many faults have occurred, rendering the protocol in a "bad" state, the protocol is guaranteed to converge to a "good" state within a finite time period, provided that no faults occur during that period.

23.2 SLOTTED RING NETWORKS

In this section, we present a protocol for slotted rings. The protocol is presented in two steps. First, we present a version of the protocol that cannot tolerate process failures or message modifications. Second, we show how to augment this version so that the resulting protocol can tolerate these types of faults.

In the first version of the protocol, a message has three fields: slot(full, src, dst). The first field full is a boolean value that indicates whether or not the slot message is carrying data. The second field src is the index of the source process of the data provided that full is true. The third field dst is the index of the destination process of the data provided that full is true. Note that there is no explicit data field in a slot message; nevertheless the fact of whether a slot message is carrying data can be deduced from value full in the slot.

When a process p[i] in a slotted ring receives a slot message from the left neighbor, it checks whether or not the message is empty, that is, not carrying data. If the received slot message is empty, p[i] can fill the message with data intended for some process p[d] in the ring. Process p[i] then updates the three fields of the slot message (full is assigned true, src is assigned i, and dst is assigned d) before forwarding the slot message to the right neighbor.

If the received slot message is carrying data whose source is p[i], then p[i] assigns false to the message field full and forwards the slot message to the right neighbor. If the received slot message is carrying data whose destination is p[i], then p[i] copies the data and forwards the slot message as is to the right neighbor. If the received slot message is carrying data whose source and destination are different from p[i], then p[i] forwards the slot message as is to the right neighbor.

Each process p[i] in the ring network has two inputs, left and right, that range over $0, \ldots, n-1$. Input left (or right) stores the index of the left (or right, respectively) neighbor of process p[i] in the network. Each process p[i] also has three variables named full, src, and dst. These variables are used to store the three fields of the received slot message.

Process p[i] in the slotted ring protocol can be defined as follows:

```
process p[i : 0..n-1]

inp    left, right :      0..n-1
                         {indices of neighbors of p[i]}

var    full         :     boolean,
       src, dst     :     0..n-1

begin
       rcv slot(full, src, dst) from p[left] ->
            if ~full     ->
                 dst := any;
                 if true -> skip
                 [] dst≠i -> full, src := true, i
                 fi
            [] full ∧ src = i    {dst ≠ i}   ->
                 full := false
            [] full ∧ src ≠ i ∧ dst = i   ->
                 {copy data} skip
            [] full ∧ src ≠ i ∧ dst ≠ i   ->
                 {ignore data} skip
            fi;
            send slot(full, src, dst) to p[right]
end
```

Process p[i] has only one action. In this action, p[i] receives one slot message from the left neighbor, updates the received slot message, and then forwards it to the right neighbor. The if–fi statement in this action has four branches. In the first branch, the received slot is not carrying data. In this case, p[i] may choose to fill the slot with data intended for process p[dst] before forwarding the slot. In the second branch, the received slot is carrying data whose source is p[i]. In this case, p[i] empties the slot before forwarding it. In the third branch, the received slot is carrying data intended for p[i]. In this case, p[i] copies the data and then forwards the slot as is. In the fourth branch, the received slot is carrying data whose source and destination are different from p[i]. In this case, p[i] forwards the slot as is.

This version of the protocol cannot tolerate process failures or message modifications. As illustrated next, the most harmful effect of these faults is to cause a number of slot messages to remain full indefinitely and never be emptied by any process in the network.

Consider a scenario where a process fills a slot message with data and then fails before it receives the slot message and marks it empty. Hence, the slot message remains full indefinitely and can never be used to carry new data. As a second example, consider a scenario where an empty slot message is modified and has become full. If the src field in this message stores the index of a process that has failed earlier, then the slot message will remain full indefinitely.

In order to counter these faults, the above version of the protocol is augmented so that a full slot message cannot remain full indefinitely. The protocol is augmented by making each process in the ring observe the slot messages one by one. Observing a slot message by process p[i] consists of the following steps. When p[i] receives the slot message, it checks whether or not the slot message is empty. If the observed slot message is empty, the checking is complete and process p[i] gets ready to observe the next slot message.

If the observed slot message is full, p[i] stores the value of the message field src in its lsrc variable and then waits to receive the slot message a second time. When p[i] receives the slot message a second time, it checks whether it is now empty. If the slot is empty, the observation of this slot message is complete and p[i] gets ready to observe the next slot message. If the slot is full and the value of its src field is different from the stored value of lsrc (implying that the slot message has been emptied and then filled by another process in the last cycle), then the observation of this slot message is complete and p[i] gets ready to observe the next slot message. If the slot is full and the value of its src field is the same as that of variable lsrc (indicating that the slot message has made a complete cycle without being emptied), then p[i] makes the slot message empty and gets ready to observe the next slot message.

In order to keep track of the slot message being observed, process p[i] has a variable obsrv whose value ranges over 0 . . r, where r is the fixed number of slot messages in the network. When p[i] receives a slot message, the value of obsrv is tested. If obsrv = 0, then the received slot is the one being observed in its first appearance at p[i]; in this case, obsrv is assigned the value r before sending the slot out. If obsrv > 1, then the received slot is not the one being observed and obsrv is decremented by 1 before sending the slot out. If obsrv = 1, then the received slot is the one being observed in its second appearance at p[i]; in this case, obsrv is assigned the value 0 before sending the slot out.

Process p[i] in the fault-tolerant slotted ring protocol can be defined as follows:

```
process p[i : 0..n-1]

const r                    {r is # of slots in ring}

inp   left, right :        0..n-1
                           {indices of neighbors of p[i]}

var   full        :        boolean,
      src, dst    :        0..n-1,
      lsrc        :        0..n-1,
      obsrv       :        0..r

begin
      rcv slot(full, src, dst) from p[left] ->
            { First, observe the slot }
            if obsrv > 1  ->   obsrv := obsrv-1
            [] obsrv = 1  ->   obsrv := 0;
                  if lsrc ≠ src  ->  skip
                  [] lsrc = src -> full := false
                  fi
            [] obsrv = 0  ->
                  if ~full -> skip
                  [] full -> obsrv, lsrc := r, src
                  fi
            fi;

            { Then, handle the slot as before }
            if ~full   ->dst := any;
                  if true -> skip
                  [] dst≠i -> full, src := true, i
                  fi
            [] full ∧ src = i  ->
                  full := false
            [] full ∧ src ≠ i ∧ dst = i  ->
                  {copy data} skip
            [] full ∧ src ≠ i ∧ dst ≠ i  ->
                  {ignore data} skip
            fi;
            send slot(full, src, dst) to p[right]
end
```

23.3 TOKEN RING NETWORKS

In this section, we present the token ring protocol in two steps. First, we present a
version of the protocol that is correct as long as process failures and message modi-

fications do not occur. Second, we discuss how to modify this protocol version to make it tolerate process failures and message modifications.

Consider a ring network p[i: 0 .. n − 1]. The processes in this ring circulate one message of the form byt(t, x), where t is the message type and x is an integer in the range 0 .. n − 1 whose value depends on the message type t. There are three types of messages: token, header, and data. For a token message, t = 0 and x is any (don't care) value. For a header message, t = 1 and x is the index d for a process p[d] that is the destination process for the data messages that follow the header message. For a data message, t = 2 and x is the message text.

Initially, the processes circulate a byt(0, x) token message. When a process p[i] needs to send a block of at most m data messages to another process p[d], p[i] receives the byt(0, x) token message and sends a byt(1, d) header message in its place. The function of the byt(1, d) header message is to inform process p[d] to store the text in each of the data messages that follow the header message. The byt(1, d) header message makes a complete cycle around the ring and then returns to process p[i], which then sends the first byt(2, text) data message in its place. Each byt(2, text) message sent by process p[i] makes a complete cycle around the ring, and its text is copied by process p[d] and stored, before the message returns to process p[i], which then sends the next byt(2, text) message in its place, and so on. When process p[i] sends the last byt(2, text) message and later receives it, it sends a byt(0, x) token message in its place, and the cycle repeats.

Each process p[i] in the ring has four variables named st, src, dst, and ndata. The value of variable st is in the range 0 .. 2, the two variables src and dst are boolean, and the value of variable ndata is in the range 0 .. m. These four variables in p[i] have the following meanings:

st = t	Iff the last message sent by process p[i] is of the form byt(t, x) for any x
src = true	Iff the sequence of messages that p[i] has sent since it has received the last byt(0, x) token message satisfies the regular expression byt(1, d); { byt(2, text) }*
dst = true	Iff the last sequence of messages received by p[i] satisfies the regular expression byt(1, i); { byt(2, text) }*
ndata	Is the number of data messages yet to be sent or received in the current block of data messages

Figure 23.2 shows a state-transition diagram that describes how the value of variable st in process p[i] is changed. In this diagram, each node has a label of the form st = t, and each directed edge has a label of the form t. A node with a label st = t corresponds to a state of process p[i] where the value of its variable st is t. A directed edge labeled t from a node st = s to a node st = t corresponds to a transition of process p[i], where p[i] sends a message byt(t, x) for some x and changes the value of its st variable from s to t.

Process p[i] in this protocol can be defined as follows:

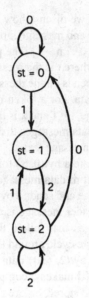

FIG. 23.2

```
process p[i : 0..n-1]

const m                    {max # data msgs in a block}

inp    left, right :       0..n-1
                           {indices of neighbors of p[i]}

var    t           :       0..2,
                           {t = 0: a token message}
                           {t = 1: a header message}
                           {t = 2: a data message}

       st          :       0..2,

       src, dst    :       boolean,
       ndata       :       0..m,
                           {# data msgs remaining in}
                           {current block}
       x           :       0..n-1

begin
       rcv byt(t, x) from p[left] ->
               UPDATE;
               send byt(t, x) to p[right]
end
```

Process p[i] has only one action. In this action, p[i] receives a byt(t, x) message from its left neighbor and updates t, x, and its four variables st, src, dst, and ndata and then sends a byt(t, x) message to its right neighbor. Statement UPDATE in this action is defined as follows:

```
if  t = 0    ->      {st ≠ 1  ∧  ~src}
       if true -> st := 0
       □ true. ->  x := any;
              if x = i  -> st := 0
              □ x ≠ i  -> t, st, src := 1, 1, true
              fi
       fi

□ t = 1  ∧  st ≠ 1  -> {~src}
       if x = i  -> dst := true
       □ x ≠ i  -> dst := false
       fi; st := 1

□ t = 1  ∧  st = 1  -> {src}
       t, st, ndata, x := 2, 2, m-1, any

□ t = 2  ∧  st = 1  -> {~src}
       if dst  -> {store data} skip
       □ ~dst  -> {ignore data} skip
       fi; st, ndata := 2, m-1

□ t = 2  ∧  st ≠ 1  ->
       {st = 2  ∧  (src ∨ ndata>0)}
       if src  ∧  ndata > 0 -> ndata, x := ndata-1, any
       □ src                -> t, st := 0, 0
       □ ~src  ∧  dst   ->
              {store data x} ndata := ndata-1
       □ ~src  ∧  ~dst  ->
              {ignore data x} ndata := ndata-1
       fi
fi
```

Statement UPDATE is an if–fi statement that consists of five branches. Each branch is selected for execution based on the type of the received message as follows:

   i. The first branch is selected for execution when the received message is a token message. Executing this branch involves either sending the received token message unchanged or sending a header message.

  ii. The second branch is selected for execution when the received message is a

header message and st ≠ 1. Executing this branch involves sending the received header message unchanged.

iii. The third branch is selected for execution when the received message is a
header message and st = 1. (This implies that the header message made a
complete cycle and returned to its originating process.) Executing this
branch involves sending a data message.

iv. The fourth branch is selected for execution when the received message is a
data message and st = 1. Executing this branch involves sending the received
data message unchanged.

v. The fifth branch is selected for execution when the received message is
a data message and st ≠ 1. (In this case, st = 2.) Executing this branch involves one of the following: sending another data message or a token message (if src is true) or sending the received data message unchanged (if src is
false).

Correctness of this protocol is based on the assumption that process failures and
message modifications cannot occur. Next, we discuss how to modify this protocol
to make it tolerate these two types of failures.

Process failures and message modifications cause processes to receive messages
unexpectedly. We illustrate this point with an example. Consider a scenario where a
process p[i] receives a token message and sends a header message in its place; then
p[i] fails before it receives back the header message. In this case, the sent header
message circulates around the ring, leaving the two variables st and src in every
process on the ring with the values 1 and false, respectively. Eventually, some
process p[j] receives the header message while its two variables st and src have the
values 1 and false, respectively. This situation contradicts the third branch in the
UPDATE statement in process p[j], which states that if p[j] receives a header message while its st variable has the value 1, then its src variable has the value true. In
other words, the header message arrives unexpectedly at process p[j].

To make this protocol tolerate process failures and message modifications, reset
messages of the form byt(3, x) are added to the protocol. These reset messages are
used as follows to reset the ring when a fault is detected:

i. When a process receives any message unexpectedly, the process assigns its
st variable the new value 3, assigns its src variable the value false, and sends
a byt(3, n − 1) reset message in place of the received message.

ii. When a process receives a byt(3, x) reset message, where x > 0, the process
assigns its st variable the new value 3, assigns its src variable the value false,
and sends a byt(3, x − 1) reset message.

iii. When a process receives a byt(3, 0) reset message (indicating that the reset
message has made at least one complete cycle around the ring), the process
assigns its st variable the value 0, assigns its src variable the value false, and
sends a byt(0, x) token message.

Figure 23.3 shows a state-transition diagram that describes how the value of variable st in a process is changed. This diagram is similar to the diagram in Figure 23.2 with some modifications. First, a new state labeled st = 3 is added to the diagram. Second, a new transition labeled 3 is added from each state to the new state st = 3. Third, two transitions are added from the state st = 3 to other states: One transition labeled 0 is added to the state st = 0 and the other transition labeled 1 is added to the state st = 1.

Process p[i] in the token ring protocol can be defined as follows:

```
process p[i : 0..n-1]

const m                     {max # data msgs in a block}

inp   left, right :         0..n-1
                            {indices of neighbors of p[i]}

var   t             :       0..3,
                            {t = 0: a token message}
                            {t = 1: a header message}
                            {t = 2: a data message}
                            {t = 3: a reset message}

      st            :       0..3,
```

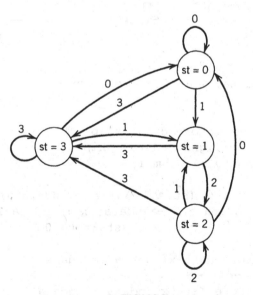

FIG. 23.3

```
        src, dst       :       boolean,
        ndata          :       0..m,
                               {# data msgs remaining}
                               {in current block}
        x              :       0..n-1

begin
        rcv byt(t, x) from p[left] ->
              UPDATE';
              send byt(t, x) to p[right]
end
```

This p[i] process is similar to the previous process except for two modifications. First, the new value 3 is added to the declarations of variables t and st. Second, statement UPDATE is replaced by statement UPDATE', defined as follows:

```
if   t = 0 /\ st ≠ 1 /\ ~src  ->
        if true ->  st := 0
        [] true ->  x := any;
                    if x = i  -> st := 0
                    [] x ≠ i  -> t, st, src := 1, 1, true
                    fi
        fi

[]  t = 1 /\  st ≠ 1 /\  ~src  ->
        if x = i  -> dst := true
        [] x ≠ i  -> dst := false
        fi; st := 1

[]  t = 1 /\ st = 1 /\ src  ->
        t, st, ndata, x := 2, 2, m-1, any

[]  t = 2 /\ st = 1 /\ ~src  ->
        if  dst  -> {store data} skip
        [] ~dst  -> {ignore data} skip
        fi; st, ndata := 2, m-1

[]  t = 2 /\ st ≠ 1 /\ (st = 2 /\ (src \/ ndata>0))  ->
        if src /\ ndata > 0 -> ndata, x := ndata-1, any
        []  src                  -> t, st := 0, 0
        [] ~src /\ dst           ->
               {store data x} ndata := ndata-1
        [] ~src /\ ~dst ->
               {ignore data x} ndata := ndata-1
        fi
```

```
□  (t = 0 ∧ (st = 1 ∨ src)) ∨
   (t = 1 ∧ (st = 1 ∨ src) ∧ (st ≠ 1 ∨ ~src)) ∨
   (t = 2 ∧ (st ≠ 1 ∨ src) ∧
   (st ≠ 2 ∨ (~src ∧ ndata = 0)))  ->
                            t, st, src, x :=
                            3, 3, false, n-1

□  t = 3 ∧ x > 0  ->       t, st, src, x :=
                           3, 3, false, x-1

□  t = 3 ∧ x = 0  ->       t, st, src := 0, 0, false
fi
```

Note that the first five branches in statement UPDATE' are similar to the five branches in statement UPDATE with one exception. Each of the predicates involving variable src, which appeared as comments in the branches of UPDATE, is added as part of the local predicate of its branch. This modification allows each process to detect, when it receives a message, whether or not the message has been received expectedly.

23.4 RING NETWORKS IN THE INTERNET

Many subnetworks in the Internet are token rings. Most token rings are based on the IEEE 802.5 standard for (untimed) token rings, but some are based on the Fiber Distributed Data Interface, or FDDI for short, standard for timed token rings. In this section, we discuss these two types of token rings in some detail.

(Untimed) Token Rings

Consider a subnetwork where the interface processes are connected by a token ring. In this ring, if no interface process needs to send a data message, the processes circulate a token message that consists of the following three fields:

1. Start delimiter   8 bits
2. Token, monitor, and priority bits 8 bits
3. End delimiter   8 bits

Field 1 is of the form JK0JK000, where J and K are nondata bits and 0 is a zero bit. For example, if a 0 data bit is represented by a high-voltage period followed by a low-voltage period and a 1 data bit is represented by a low-voltage period followed by a high-voltage period, then J can be represented by two successive high-voltage periods and K can be represented by two successive low-voltage periods.

Field 2 has eight bits named T, M, and six P bits. Bit T is 0 indicating that the message is a token message. Bit M is used by the ring's monitor as discussed below. The P bits are used only if the data messages to be sent have different priorities. If the data messages to be sent have the same priority, then the P bits are not used in this case.

Field 3 is of the form JK1JK11E where J and K are nondata bits (as in the start delimiter) and 1 is a 1 bit. Bit E is called an error bit, and it is set to 1 by any interface process that detects an error in the token message.

When an interface process fp needs to send a data message to an interface process fq, fp waits until it receives the token message then sends the data message instead of the token message to the next interface process in the ring. When an interface process, other than fq and fp, receives the data message, it forwards the data message unchanged to the next interface process in the ring. When the destination process fq receives the data message, it stores a copy of the message and still forwards the message to the next interface process in the ring. When the source process fp receives the data message, it removes the data message and sends a token message to the next interface process in the ring.

Each data message consists of the following nine fields:

1. Start delimiter   8 bits
2. Token, monitor, and priority bits   8 bits
3. Message type   8 bits
4. Hardware destination address   48 bits
5. Hardware source address   48 bits
6. Message text   x bits
7. Checksum of the message   16 bits
8. End delimiter   8 bits
9. Acknowledgment bits   8 bits

Fields 1, 2, and 8 in a data message are the same as fields 1, 2, and 3, respectively, in a token message, with one exception. Bit T in a data message is 1 indicating that the message is not a token message. Field 3 indicates the type of data message. Different types of data messages, namely "monitor is active" and "claim token" messages, are discussed below.

Fields 4 and 5 contain the hardware addresses of the source and destination, respectively, of the message. Fields 6 and 7 contain the message text and its checksum. Recall that in Section 8.4 we discussed how the message checksum is computed and used in detecting message corruption. Field 9 contains two acknowledgment bits A and C. Bit A is set by the destination interface process, when it forwards the message, to acknowledge that it has recognized its own hardware address in field 4 of the message. Bit C is also set by the destination interface process, when it forwards the message, to acknowledge that it has successfully copied the message.

One of the interface processes in the ring is called the monitor. An important function of the monitor is to detect the loss of the token message from the ring and to generate a new token message.

Another function of the monitor is to remove from the ring any data message whose source has become down after sending the data message but before removing the message from the ring. This function is achieved as follows. When a data message is first sent by its source interface process, the M bit in Field 2 of the message is set to 0. When the monitor receives the data message and checks that its M bit is 0, it sets the M bit to 1 and then forwards the message to the next interface process in the ring. If the monitor receives a data message and detects that its M bit is 1 (indicating that the message has made at least one cycle around the ring), the monitor removes the data message from the ring and sends a token message in its place.

Periodically, the monitor sends a message of type "monitor is active." If any interface process in the ring does not receive any "monitor is active" message for a long time (indicating that the monitor has become down), the interface process times out and sends a "claim token" message. Eventually, one of the up interface processes in the ring receives back its claim token message and becomes the new monitor and assumes the functions of the monitor.

Timed Token Ring

The ring network that supports a timed token is called an FDDI ring. The activities in an FDDI ring are similar to those in an (untimed) token ring except for the following features:

i.   *High Speed:* An FDDI ring can provide a transmission rate of 100 megabits per second, whereas a token ring can provide a transmission rate of 10 to 50 megabits per second.

ii. *Immediate Token Release:* When an interface process in an FDDI ring receives a token message, it sends zero or more data messages followed immediately by the token message. By contrast, an interface process in a token ring waits until it receives the data message it has sent before sending the token message.

iii. *Synchronous and Asynchronous Messages:* The interface processes in an FDDI ring can send two types of messages: synchronous and asynchronous. An interface process i in the ring is assigned a time period S.i for sending synchronous messages whenever process i receives the token. Process i can also send asynchronous messages, but only if it receives the token message earlier than expected, as discussed in iv and v below.

iv. *Target Token Rotation Time:* The token in the FDDI ring is expected to complete each cycle around the ring within a predefined time period called the target token rotation time, or TTRT for short. Thus,

$$\text{TTRT} \geq D + (\text{sum over } i, 0 \leq i < n, \text{ of } S.i)$$

where D is the token travel time over the ring, n is the number of processes in the ring, and S.i is the time period assigned to process i for sending synchronous messages. It is possible sometimes that the token rotation time exceeds the TTRT. When this happens, all the processes in the ring stop sending asynchronous messages until the token rotation time catches with the TTRT.

v. Token Holding Time: Each interface process i in an FDDI ring maintains three variables named trt, tht, and deficit, whose values are defined as follows:

trt   Last token rotation time, as observed by process i

tht   Maximum time period that process i can hold the token while sending asynchronous messages

deficit   Time by which the token rotation time, as observed by process i, exceeds the target token rotation time

When process i receives the token, it updates its three variables trt, tht, and deficit and sends synchronous and asynchronous messages and the token message according to the following pseudocode:

```
process i receives the token;
process i sends synchronous messages
for a time period less than or equal to S.i;
trt   :=      the time elapsed since process i
              sent the token last;
tht   :=      TTRT - (deficit + trt)
if tht ≥ 0 ->         process i sends asynchronous
                      messages for a time period less
                      than or equal to tht;
                      deficit := 0
[] tht < 0 ->         deficit := -tht
fi;
process i sends the token
```

The above token rotation algorithm provides two useful guarantees concerning the token rotation time. Let TTRT denote the target token rotation time and TRT.k the token rotation time in the kth cycle of the token and let n be a large number of consecutive token cycles. Then the above token rotation algorithm guarantees the following two relations:

1. For every k, $0 \leq k < n$, TRT.k $\leq$ 2*TTRT.
2. (Sum over k, $0 \leq k < n$, of TRT.k) $\leq$ n*TTRT.

23.5 BIBLIOGRAPHICAL NOTES

The slotted ring is discussed in Pierce [1972] and Hopper and Williamson [1987]. A refinement of the slotted ring, called the register insertion ring, is discussed in Liu [1978] and Liu et al. [1982].

The token ring is discussed in Farber and Larson [1972]. The IEEE standard for the token ring is presented in IEEE [1989]. A detailed overview of the token ring is presented in Sackett [1993]. The FDDI ring is discussed in Jain [1994].

An explanation of why ring networks are useful is given in Saltzer et al. [1983]. Overviews of ring networks are given in Tanenbaum [1980] and Saadawi et al. [1994].

EXERCISES

1 (Slotted Ring with Priorities). Modify the second slotted ring protocol in Section 23.2 such that process p[0] has twice as many chances to send data messages as any other process p[i: 1 .. n − 1] in the ring.

2 (Broadcast in Slotted Ring). Modify the second slotted ring protocol in Section 23.2 such that each process can send data messages that can be received by every other process in the ring.

2 (Multicast in Slotted Ring). Modify the second slotted ring protocol in Section 23.2 such that each process can send data messages that can be received by one or more other processes in the ring.

4 (Acknowledgments in Slotted Ring). Modify the second slotted ring protocol in Section 23.2 as follows. Each slot message has an additional boolean field named ack. When a process p[src] fills a slot, it makes field ack in the slot false. When the destination p[dst] of the slot receives the slot, it makes field ack in the slot true. When the slot returns to process p[src], p[src] checks field ack to deduce whether the destination p[dst] has received the slot.

5 (Fast Slotted Ring). Modify the first slotted ring protocol in Section 23.2 such that when the destination process of a slot receives the slot, it empties the slot. Assume that process failures and message modifications cannot occur.

6 (Fault-Tolerant Fast Slotted Ring). Modify the slotted ring protocol in exercise 5 to make it tolerate process failures and message modification.

7 (Fault-Detecting Slotted Ring). Modify the second slotted ring protocol in Section 23.2 as follows. Each slot message has four fields: slot(full, src, dst, count). The value of field count is in the range 0 .. n. In the modified protocol, processes that continue to fill slot messages can keep track of the number of up processes in the ring.

8 (Fault-Detecting Slotted Ring). Solve exercise 7 assuming that the value of field count is in the range 0 .. k, where k is an upper bound on the processes that can go down.

9 (Token Ring with Priorities). Modify the second token ring protocol in Section 23.3 such that process p[0] has twice as many chances to send data messages as any other process p[i: 1 .. n − 1] in the ring.

10   (Broadcast in Token Ring). Modify the second token ring protocol in Section 23.3 such that each process can send data messages that can be received by every other process in the ring.

11   (Multicast in Token Ring). Modify the second token ring protocol in Section 23.3 such that each process can send data messages that can be received by one or more other processes in the ring.

12   (Tail Messages in Token Ring). Modify the first token ring protocol in Section 23.3 as follows. Each data block consists of one header message, zero or more (at most m) data messages, and a tail message. Each tail message is of the form byt(4, x), where x is any (don't care) value in the range $0 .. n - 1$. Assume that process failures and message modifications cannot occur.

13   (Tail Messages in Fault-Tolerant Token Ring). Modify the token ring protocol in exercise 12 to make it tolerate process failures and message modifications.

14   (Checksums in Fault-Tolerant Token Ring). Modify the token ring protocol in exercise 13 such that each tail message in a data block is of the form byt(4, x), where x is the exclusive-or of all the y's in the byt(2, y) data messages in the data block. The destination of the data block uses x to determine whether or not the received data messages in the block have been corrupted during transmission.

15   (Register Insertion Ring). Design the following ring network p[i: $0 .. n - 1$]. When a process p[i] has no data block to send, p[i] acts as a repeater that receives messages from its left neighbor and sends them to its right neighbor, one by one. When p[i] has a data block to send, p[i] sends the data messages in the block in one action. After sending a data block, p[i] acts a repeater that receives messages from its left neighbor and sends them to its right neighbor, one by one. When p[i] receives the messages in the block that it has just sent, p[i] discards these messages. After discarding all messages in this block, p[i] can either send the next data block or act as a repeater, and so on.

16   (Fault-Tolerant Register Insertion Ring). Modify the register insertion ring in exercise 15 to make it tolerate process failures.

17   (Two Slotted Rings Connected by a Bridge). Let p[i: $0 .. m$] be a slotted ring, and p[i: $m .. n - 1$] be another slotted ring. These two rings have a common process p[m] that acts as a bridge between the two rings. For example, if p[m] receives a full slot message in the first ring p[i: $0 .. m$] and detects that this slot is intended for a process in the second ring p[i: $m .. n - 1$], then p[m] copies and stores the data from that slot. Later, when p[m] receives an empty slot in the second ring, it fills that slot with the stored data before sending it in the second ring. Design the processes p[i: $0 .. m - 1$], p[m], and p[i: $m + 1 .. n - 1$] in this network.

18   (Two Token Rings Connected by a Bridge). Let p[i: $0 .. m$] be a token ring and p[i: $m .. n - 1$] be another token ring. These two rings have a common process p[m] that acts as a bridge between the two rings. For example, if p[m] receives a data block in the first ring p[i: 0 . . m] and detects that this block is intended for a process in the second ring p[i: m . . n − 1], then p[m] copies and stores the data from that block. Later, when p[m] receives a token in the second ring, it sends the stored data as one block in the second ring. Design the processes in this network.

19 (Two Rings Connected by a Bridge). Let p[i: 0 . . m] be a slotted ring and p[i: m . . n − 1] be a token ring. These two rings have a common process p[m] that acts as a bridge between the two rings. Design the processes in this network.

CHAPTER 24

BROADCAST NETWORKS

Our presentation in previous chapters is based on networks where the basic communication primitive between network processes is one to one: One process sends a message to another process in the network. In this chapter, we discuss a new class of networks in which the basic communication primitive between processes is one to all: One process sends a message to every other process in the network. We refer to this class of networks as broadcast networks.

Informally, the execution of a broadcast network is an infinite sequence of successive network transitions. In each transition, one of the following occurs:

   i. No process sends a message.

  ii. Exactly one process sends a message.

 iii. Two or more processes send messages.

Next, we discuss these three types of transitions in more detail.

A network transition where no process in the network sends a message is called an idleness transition. In such a transition, each process in the network can detect that the current transition is an idleness transition and update its (local) variables.

A network transition where exactly one process in the network sends a message is called a broadcast transition. In such a transition, one process sends a message and updates its variables, while each other process can receive the sent message and update its variables.

Note that there are no channels between processes in broadcast networks. This is because each message that is sent in a transition is received, by every process that can receive that message, in the same transition. Thus, there is no need for channels to store sent messages until they are received.

A network transition where more than one process in the network sends a message is called a collision transition. In such a transition, two or more processes send messages and update their variables, while every process in the network, including the sending processes, can detect that the current transition is a collision transition and update its variables.

In summary, effective message transmission occurs only in broadcast transitions. Idleness transitions are usually used to tempt some or all processes in the network to start sending in the next transition. Collision transitions are usually used to convince some of the sending processes not to continue sending in the next transition in the hope that the next transition ends up being a broadcast transition.

The effectiveness of a broadcast network depends on how collision is handled in the network. In general, there are two methods to handle collision: prevention and resolution. Accordingly, there are two types of broadcast networks: collision prevention networks and collision resolution networks.

In collision prevention networks, collision cannot occur. Thus every transition in these networks is either an idleness transition or a broadcast transition. By contrast, collision can occur in collision resolution networks. However, each occurrence of collision is detected and later resolved by forcing the processes that sent their messages in the same transition, thus causing the collision, to resend their message in different transitions, one after the other.

The rest of this chapter is organized as follows. In Section 24.1, we discuss how to modify the syntax and semantics of our notation so that the modified notation can be used in defining broadcast networks. Then, we use the modified notation in discussing collision prevention networks in Section 24.2 and collision resolution networks in Section 24.3. Finally, we discuss broadcast networks in the Internet in Section 24.4.

24.1 BROADCAST PROCESSES

A process in a broadcast network is of the following form:

```
process <process name>

const <const name>, ... , <const name>
inp    <inp name> : <type>, ... , <inp name> : <type>
var    <var name> : <type>, ... , <var name> : <type>

begin
        <action>
[]      <action>
        ...
[]      <action>
end
```

As discussed in Section 3.2, the constants of a process are of type positive integer. Constants with identical names in different processes have identical values.

The inputs and variables of a process are of the following types: boolean, range, integer, enumerated, and array. The set type is not allowed. Boolean, range, integer, and array types are declared as discussed in Section 3.1. For convenience, enumerated inputs and enumerated variables are now declared by enumerating all their values. For example, a variable named degree whose value is low, middle, or high can be declared as follows:

```
var    degree:      {low, middle, high}
```

Each process has two reserved boolean inputs, named idleness and collision. Because idleness and collision are inputs, their values are not changed by the process actions. Rather, their values in any network transition depend on the type of the transition. In particular, the value of idleness (or collision) in a network transition is true iff the transition is an idleness (or collision, respectively) transition.

The actions of a process are of five types: sending, receiving, idleness detection, collision detection, and sending with collision detection. We discuss each of these action types in order.

A sending action of process p is of the form:

```
<local predicate of p> -> <local statement of p>;
                    send <message>
```

A local predicate of p is a boolean expression that involves the following: the constants, inputs, and variables of p; the six relations $=$, $\neq$, $<$, $\leq$, $>$, and $\geq$; and the three logical operators $\wedge$, $\vee$, and $\sim$.

A local statement of p is one of the following four statements: skip, assignment, sequential composition, and selection. These statements are as defined in Chapters 3 and 4. Notice that iteration statements are not allowed in the actions of broadcast processes. Notice also that the sending statement "send <message>" does not have the phrase "to <process name>." This is because each message is sent automatically to every process, other than the sending process, in the network.

A receiving action of process p is of the form

```
rcv <message> -> <local statement of p>
```

Notice that a receiving statement "rcv <message>" does not have a phrase "from <process name>." This is because each process can receive messages from any other process in its network.

Idleness detection and collision detection actions of process p are of the following forms:

```
idleness -> <local statement of p>
collision -> <local statement of p>
```

Note that **idleness** and **collision** are the two reserved boolean inputs of process p. The first action is executed in a network transition iff the transition is an idleness transition. The second action is executed in a network transition iff the transition is a collision transition.

A sending with collision detection action of process p is of the following form:

```
<local predicate of p>   ->
                <local statement of p>;
                send <message>;
                if  collision -> <local statement of p>
                []  ~collision -> <local statement of p>
                fi
```

In this action, after process p sends a message, it checks whether the sent message is transmitted without collision to every other process in the network or whether the sent message has collided with other messages that were sent by other processes in the same transition.

A state of a broadcast network is defined by one value for every constant, input, and variable in every process in the network.

A sending action (with or without collision detection) is said to be enabled at a network state S iff the guard (i.e., the local predicate) of this action is true at state S.

Starting from a network state S, at most one action is executed in each process, yielding the next state S'. According to the following three rules, the executed actions depend on the number of processes that have enabled sending actions at state S:

   i. If there is no process with enabled sending actions at state S, then starting from S, one idleness detection action is executed in every process that has such an action, yielding state S'.

   ii. If there is exactly one process with enabled sending actions at state S, then starting from S, one enabled sending action is executed in that process and a compatible receiving action is executed in every other process that has such an action, yielding state S'.

   iii. If there is more than one process with enabled sending actions at state S, then starting from S, an enabled sending action is executed in each of these processes and one collision detection action is executed in every other process that has such an action, yielding state S'.

Note that rule i corresponds to an idleness network transition, rule ii corresponds to a broadcast network transition, and rule iii corresponds to a collision network transition.

As an example, consider an array of three broadcast processes p[i: 0 . . 2]. each process has a boolean variable named active. When variable active in process p[i] is true, p[i] sends a data(dst) message, where dst is the index of the intended destination of the message.

One of two things occurs when a process p[i] sends a data(dst) message. Either no other process sends a message in the same transition and the transition ends up being a broadcast transition or another process sends a data(dst') message in this same transition and the transition ends up being a collision transition. In the first case, the sent data(dst) message is received and stored by process p[dst] and variable active in process p[i] becomes false. In the second case, the sent messages collide, and each of the sending processes detects the collision and assigns its active variable a random value: true or false. Thus, only some of these processes will attempt to send data messages in the next transition, and the cycle repeats.

This continues until variable active in every process in the network becomes false. In this case, the next transition is an idleness transition where each process assigns its variable active a nondeterministic value.

Process p[i] in this network can be defined as follows.

```
process p[i : 0..2]

var    active        :      boolean,
       dst           :      0..2

begin
       active       ->
              dst := any;
              if dst ≠ i -> skip
              [] dst = i -> dst := dst +3 1
              fi;
              send data(dst);
              if ~collision -> active := false
              []   collision -> active := random
              fi

[]     rcv data(dst)        ->
              if dst ≠ i -> {ignore data} skip
              [] dst = i -> {store data} skip
              fi

[]     idleness             ->       active := any
end
```

A state S of this network can be defined by the following set:

$$\{ i \mid \text{variable active in process p[i] is true at state S} \}$$

Therefore, there are eight distinct states of this network: the empty set { }, {0}, {1}, {2}, {0,1}, {0,2}, {1,2}, and {0, 1, 2}.

At state { }, variable active in every process in the network is false. Starting from this state each process executes its idleness detection action and its active variable is assigned a nondeterministic value. Thus, the network transition is an idleness transition, and the next state after state { } is any of the eight states of the network.

At a state {i}, where i = 0, 1, 2, variable active in process p[i] is true while variables active in the other two processes are false. Starting from state {i}, process p[i] executes its sending action and each of the other two processes executes its receiving action. Thus, the network transition is a broadcast transition, and the next state after a state {i} is state { }.

At state {0, 1, 2}, variable active in every process in the network is true. Starting from this state, each process executes its sending action and, detecting collision, assigns its active variable a random value. Thus, the network transition is a collision transition, and the next state after state {0, 1, 2} is any of the eight states of the network.

A state-transition diagram for this network is shown in Figure 24.1. Each node in this diagram corresponds to a network state. Each directed edge in this diagram corresponds to a network transition. An edge labeled I, B, or C corresponds to an idleness, broadcast, or collision transition, respectively.

24.2 COLLISION PREVENTION

In order to prevent collision in a broadcast network, the network should satisfy the following requirement. At each instant, no more than one process in the network can execute sending actions. There are two well-known protocols that satisfy this re-

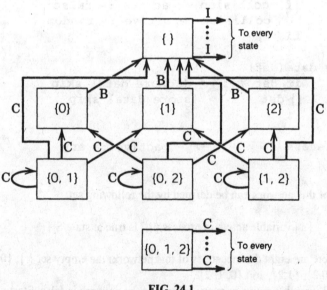

FIG. 24.1

quirement: the polling/selection protocol and the token bus protocol. In this section, we discuss these two protocols in order.

In the polling/selection protocol, one process is designated to be the primary process, and every other process in the network is designated to be a secondary process. Let p be the primary process, and let the process array s[i: 0 .. n − 1] be the secondary processes.

In this network, data messages are sent either from the primary process p to a secondary process s[i] or from a secondary process s[i] to the primary process p. Therefore, for a secondary process s[i] to send a data message to another secondary process s[j], process s[i] first sends the data message to process p. Then, process p forwards the message to process s[j].

The network execution proceeds in rounds, where each round consists of several network transitions depending on the round type. There are two types of rounds: polling and selection. In a polling round, a sequence of data messages is transmitted from a secondary process s[i] to the primary process p. In a selection round, a sequence of data messages is transmitted from the primary process p to a secondary process s[i]. At the beginning of each round, the primary process p decides whether this round is a polling round or a selection round.

In the first transition of a polling round, process p sends a poll(i) message, where i is the index of the secondary process selected by p to send data messages (to p) in this round. If process p detects idleness in the second transition, process p recognizes that process s[i] does not want to send data messages in this round and the round terminates. On the other hand, if process p receives a data message (from process s[i]) in the second transition, then p recognizes that s[i] will send data messages (to p) in this round. In this case, process s[i] continues to send data messages and process p continues to receive them until s[i] stops sending and p detects idleness and recognizes the termination of the current round.

In the first transition of a selection round, process p sends a slct(i) message, where i is the index of the secondary process selected by p to receive data messages from p. If process p detects idleness in the second transition of this round, then process p recognizes that process s[i] does not want to receive data messages in this round, and the round terminates. On the other hand, if process p receives an acpt message (from process s[i]) in the second transition, then p recognizes that s[i] will receive data messages (from p) in this round. In this case, p sends a sequence of data messages and then stops forcing an idleness transition that signals the termination of the current round.

The primary process p in the polling/selection protocol can be defined as follows:

```
process p

const n

var    sp     :      {nxtrnd, rcvdata, rcvacpt, snddata} ,
       dst    :      0..n-1
```

```
begin
        sp = nxtrnd  ->      sp, dst := rcvdata, any;
                             send poll(dst)

[]      sp = nxtrnd  ->      sp, dst := rcvacpt, any;
                             send slct(dst)

[]     rcv data      ->      {store data} skip

[]     rcv acpt      ->      sp := snddata

[]     sp = snddata ->
                             if true  -> skip
                             [] true  ->  sp := rcvacpt
                             fi; send data

[]      idleness     ->      if true  -> skip
                             [] true  ->  sp := nxtrnd
                             fi
end
```

Process p has six actions. In the first two actions, p decides nondeterministically whether the next round is a polling round or a selection round and starts the round. In the third action, process p receives a data message in a polling round. In the fourth and fifth actions, p receives an acpt message and sends a data message, respectively, in a selection round. In the sixth action, p detects idleness, which signals the end of the current round; then p decides nondeterministically whether or not to start the next round.

The secondary process $s[i]$ in the polling/selection protocol can be defined as follows:

```
process s[i : 0..n-1]

var  ss   :      {idle, snddata, sndacpt, rcvdata},
     k    :      0..n-1

begin
        rcv poll(k)  ->      if true -> ss := idle
                             [] k = i -> ss := snddata
                             fi

[]      ss = snddata->      if true -> skip
                            [] true -> ss := idle
                            fi; send data
```

```
☐      rcv slct(k) —>      if true —> ss := idle
                           ☐ k = i —> ss := sndacpt
                           fi


☐      ss = sndacpt—>      ss := rcvdata; send acpt


☐      rcv data      —>    if ss ≠ rcvdata —>
                              {ignore data} skip
                           ☐ ss = rcvdata —>
                              {store data} skip
                           fi


☐      idleness      —>    ss := idle
end
```

Collision is prevented in the polling/selection protocol because no process can send a message unless it has permission to do so from the primary process p and p ensures that at each instant no more than one process has such a permission.

Failures and subsequent repairs of secondary processes do not cripple this protocol because the primary process p can still communicate with the up secondary processes. However, failure of the primary process brings the protocol to a standstill because none of the secondary processes can act as a primary process. This problem is avoided in the next protocol, called the token bus protocol.

In the token bus protocol, the processes circulate a token in a fixed circular order, from each process p[i] to process $p[i +_n 1]$. When a process p[i] receives the token, p[i] can act as a primary process and send a sequence of data messages to any other process in the network before passing the token on to the next process $p[i +_n 1]$.

We present the token bus protocol in three stages. In the first stage, we present a version of the protocol where the token is circulated properly provided that no process fails while it has the token. In the second stage, we present a fault-tolerant version of the protocol where the token is circulated properly despite process failure. In the third stage, we present a full version of the protocol where the token is circulated properly and data messages are sent despite process failure.

In the first version of the protocol, when a process p[i] has the token, p[i] sends the token to process $p[i +_n 1]$. If process $p[i +_n 1]$ is up, then it receives the token in the same network transition and forwards it to $p[i +_n 2]$ in the next network transition. Thus, the next network transition is a broadcast transition. If process $p[i +_n 1]$ is not up, then the next network transition is an idleness transition. Therefore, if p[i] detects idleness in the next network transition, it recognizes that $p[i +_n 1]$ is not up and so it sends the token to $p[i +_n 2]$, and so on. Note that the correctness of this protocol version is based on the assumption that each process p[i] remains up as long as it has the token. Process p[i] in this protocol version can be defined as follows.

```
process p[i : 0..n-1]

var    st    :       {hastkn, wait, notkn},
       d, k  :       0..n-1        {initially, k = 1}

begin
       st = hastkn -->      st, d := wait, i +_n k;
                            send token(d)


[]     rcv token(d) -->     if d ≠ i --> st := notkn
                            [] d = i --> st, k := hastkn, 1
                            fi


[]     idleness      -->     if st = hastkn -->
                                    {impossible} skip
                            [] st = wait -->
                                    st, k := hastkn, k +_n 1
                            [] st = notkn --> skip
                            fi
end
```

In this protocol version, if a process fails while it has the token, the protocol reaches a deadlock state. Thus, we need to modify this protocol so that when this happens, exactly one of the up processes, namely the one with the largest index, eventually creates a new token.

An up process recognizes that the process that has the token has failed when it observes two successive idleness transitions. When an up process $p[i]$ recognizes that the process that has the token has failed, $p[i]$ sends a sequence of $i + 1$ bid messages and then checks the next network transition. If in the next transition $p[i]$ receives a bid message or detects a collision, $p[i]$ recognizes that another process $p[j]$, where $j > i$, is still sending bid messages. On the other hand, if in the next transition $p[i]$ detects idleness, $p[i]$ recognizes that it has the largest index among all up processes. In this case, process $p[i]$ creates a new token and sends it to process $p[i +_n 1]$ in the next network transition. Process $p[i]$ for this fault-tolerant protocol version can be defined as follows:

```
process p[i : 0..n-1]

var    st    :       {hastkn, wait, notkn, try, check},
       d, k  :       0..n-1,
       bd    :       0..n          {initially, k = 1}

begin
       st = hastkn -->      st, d := wait, i +_n k;
                            send token(d)
```

```
[]      rcv token(d)  ->      if d ≠ i -> st := notkn
                              [] d = i -> st, k := hastkn, 1
                              fi


[]      idleness       ->      if st = hastkn ->
                                      {impossible} skip
                              [] st = wait   ->
                                      st, k := hastkn, k +_n 1
                              [] st = notkn -> st := try
                              [] st = try   -> bd := i + 1
                              [] st = check ->
                                      st, k := hastkn, 1
                              fi


[]   st = try ∧ bd > 0 ->
                              if bd ≠ 1 ->
                                      {bd > 1} bd := bd - 1
                              [] bd = 1 -> st, bd := check, 0
                              fi; send bid


[]      rcv bid        ->      st := notkn


[]      collision      ->      st := notkn
end
```

In this protocol version, the token is guaranteed to circulate properly among the up processes but the up processes do not exchange data messages as they should. Therefore, we need to extend this protocol version to allow the process that has the token to send a sequence of data messages to any other process in this network. This extension consists of adding four new actions to each process $p[i]$. In the first added action, $p[i]$ detects that it has the token and sends a header(d) message. This message alerts process $p[d]$ to start receiving the subsequent data messages. In the second added action, process $p[i]$ sends a data message that is to be received by $p[d]$. In the third and fourth added actions, process $p[i]$ receives a header(d) message and a data message, respectively.

Process $p[i]$ in the token bus protocol can be defined as follows:

```
process p[i : 0..n-1]

var     st    :       {hastkn, wait, notkn, try, check,
                      snddata, rcvdata},
        d, k  :       0..n-1,
        bd    :       0..n           {initially, k = 1}

begin
```

```
          st = hastkn ->        st, d := wait, i +ₙ k;
                                send token(d)

[]    rcv token(d) ->           if d ≠ i -> st := notkn
                                [] d = i -> st, k := hastkn, 1
                                fi

[]    idleness      ->          if st = hastkn ->
                                       {impossible} skip
                                [] st = wait      ->
                                       st, k := hastkn, k +ₙ 1
                                [] st = notkn -> st := try
                                [] st = try   -> bd := i + 1
                                [] st = check ->
                                       st, k := hastkn, 1
                                [] st = snddata ->
                                       {impossible} skip
                                [] st = rcvdata -> st := try
                                fi

[]    st = try ∧ bd > 0 ->
                                if bd ≠ 1 ->
                                       {bd > 1} bd := bd - 1
                                [] bd = 1 -> st, bd := check, 0
                                fi; send bid

[]    rcv bid       ->          st := notkn

[]    collision     ->          st := notkn

[]    st = hastkn ->            st, d := snddata, any;
                                send header(d)

[]    st = snddata->            if true -> skip
                                [] true -> st := hastkn
                                fi; send data

[]    rcv header(d) ->          if d ≠ i -> st := notkn
                                [] d = i -> st := rcvdata
                                fi

[]    rcv data      ->          if st ≠ rcvdata ->
                                       {discard data} skip
                                [] st = rcvdata ->
                                       {store data} skip
```

```
                              fi
end
```

24.3 COLLISION RESOLUTION

In this section, we discuss two protocols in which collisions in broadcast networks can be detected and later resolved. The first protocol is called the Ethernet protocol, and the second is called the stack protocol. We start with the Ethernet protocol.

In the Ethernet protocol, each process p[i] has a variable named wait whose value is in the range 0 .. wmax. In each idleness or collision transition, process p[i] decrements the value of its variable wait by 1, provided that the current value of wait is positive. When the value of variable wait is 0 and process p[i] detects idleness in the current network transition, p[i] can start sending in the next network transition. First, process p[i] sends a header(d) message and then checks whether or not a collision has occurred. If no collision has occurred, then process p[i] sends a sequence of data messages intended for process p[d]. If a collision has occurred, p[i] assigns its variable wait a random value in the range 1 .. w − 1 and increases the value of w by a factor of 2 provided that w ≤ wmax and the cycle repeats.

Note that if subsequent trials to send the message also caused collision, then the value of w eventually becomes wmax and variable wait is assigned a random value in the range 1 .. wmax. This method of doubling the waiting period to resend a message, as more collisions arise, is called exponential back-off.

Process p[i] in the Ethernet protocol can be defined as follows:

```
process p[i : 0..n-1]

const wmin, wmax

var   st    :      {idle, try, snddata, rcvdata},
      d     :      0..n-1,
      w     :      wmin..wmax,
      wait  :      0..wmax

begin
      idleness      ->
                    {st = idle \/ st = rcvdata}
                    wait := max(0, wait-1);
                    if true     ->     st := idle
                    [] wait = 0 ->     st := try
                    fi

[]    st = try     ->
                    d := any; send header(d);
                    if  collision ->
```

```
                    st, wait := idle, random mod w;
                    w := min(2*w, wmax)
        [] ~collision       ->
                    st, w := snddata, wmin
        fi


[]    st = snddata->
                if true       -> st, wait := idle, random
                [] true       -> skip
                fi; send data


[]    rcv header(d) ->
                {st = idle}
                if d ≠ i       -> skip
                [] d = i       -> st := rcvdata
                fi


[]    rcv data      ->
                if st ≠ rcvdata -> {ignore data} skip
                [] st = rcvdata -> {store data} skip
                fi


[]    collision    ->      wait := max(0, wait-1)
end
```

The second collision resolution protocol that we discuss in this section is called the stack protocol. In this protocol, the processes are arranged in a stack. Each process p[i] keeps track of its own level in the stack and the bottom of the stack. A process whose level is 0 is at the top of the stack, and this process can start sending a sequence of data messages to any other process in the network. When a process (at the top of the stack) succeeds in sending without collision, the process joins the bottom of the stack by assigning its level the value of bottom.

A process p[i] can start sending in the next network transition in one of two occasions. In the first occasion, the current network transition is an idleness transition and the level of p[i] is 0. This occasion arises when the current bottom of the stack is 0; that is, the stack consists only of one level. In the second occasion, the current network transition is an idleness transition and the level of p[i] is 1. This occasion arises when the current level of every process in the network is at least 1.

A process p[i] starts sending by first sending a header(d) message (where d is the index of the intended destination process for the sequence of data messages to be sent next by p[i]) and then checking whether a collision has occurred. If no collision has occurred, then p[i] proceeds by sending a sequence of data messages.

If a collision has occurred, then each of the processes that have sent in this transition, causing the collision, flips a coin. If the result of the coin flip is a head, the process keeps its level 0 as before. If the result of the coin flip is a tail, the process makes its level 1. Each of the other processes detects that a collision has occurred and either increments its level by 1 (if its level is at least 1) or assigns its level the value 2 (if its level is 0). In the next transition, each process whose level is 0 sends a header(d) message and then checks whether a collision has occurred and the cycle repeats.

Notice that if the level of a process is positive, then the level is decreased by 1 in each idleness transition, and it is increased by 1 in each collision transition. On the other hand, if the level of a process is 0, then it remains 0 in each idleness transition, and it is increased by 2 in a collision transition.

Process $p[i]$ in the stack protocol can be defined as follows:

```
process p[i : 0..n-1]

var    st           :      {idle, try, snddata, rcvdata},
       level        :      integer,
       bottom       :      integer,
       d            :      0..n-1,
       coinhd       :      boolean

begin
       idleness      ->
              if level = 0->  {bottom = 0} st := idle
              [] level = 0 -> {bottom = 0} st := try
              [] level = 1 -> st, level := idle, bottom-1
              [] level = 1 -> st, level := try, 0
              [] level > 1 -> level := level-1
              fi; bottom := max(0, bottom-1)

[]     st = try        ->
              d := any; send header(d);
              if ~collision -> st := snddata
              []  collision ->
                     coinhd := random;  {flip a coin}
                     if  coinhd -> st, level := try, 0
                     [] ~coinhd -> st, level := idle, 1
                     fi; bottom := max(2, bottom+1)
              fi

[]     st = snddata->
              if true      -> skip
              [] true      -> st, level := idle, bottom
              fi; send data

[]     rcv header(d)  ->
              if d ≠ i     -> st := idle
```

```
          ▢ d = i        -> st := rcvdata
          fi

▢    rcv data  ->
          if st ≠ rcvdata   -> {ignore data} skip
          ▢ st = rcvdata    -> {store data} skip
          fi

▢    collision ->
          level, bottom :=
          max(2, level+1), max(2, bottom+1)
end
```

24.4 BROADCAST NETWORKS IN THE INTERNET

Many subnetworks in the Internet are broadcast networks that are based on two popular standards: the IEEE 802.3 standard for Ethernets and the IEEE 802.4 standard
for token buses. In this section, we summarize the main features of Ethernets and
token buses as described in these two standards. (Note that in the IEEE 802.3 standard, an Ethernet is referred to as a Carrier Sense Multiple Access with Collision
Detection, or CSMA/CD for short. Nevertheless, we keep the shorter name Ethernet
in this section.)

Ethernet

Consider two computers c and d that are attached to the same Ethernet. For the IP
process in computer c to send an IP message to the IP process in computer d, the
following three steps are executed. First, the IP process in computer c sends the IP
message to the interface process in c. Second, the interface process in c adds an in-
terface header and tail to the IP message and then sends the resulting interface message over the Ethernet. Third, the interface process in computer d receives the inter-
face message, removes the interface header and tail from it, and forwards the
resulting IP message to the IP process in computer d.

The interface process in computer c sends the interface message to the interface
process in computer d by executing the following steps:

   i. The interface process in computer c waits until the Ethernet is idle (i.e., until
       no interface process is sending over the Ethernet) and then sends the inter-
       face message and listens to the Ethernet for a time period 2T to detect
       whether some collision has occurred, where T is the maximum propagation
       delay over the Ethernet.
   ii. If the interface process in computer c does not detect any collision, it com-
       pletes sending the message.

iii. If the interface process in computer c detects a collision, it sends a jamming
signal over the Ethernet for a time period 2T to ensure that every interface
process that participated in the collision detects the collision. Then the interface process in computer c waits for some time period before it returns to
step i above and attempts to resend the message. The waiting time period is
2Tr, where r is a random integer in the range $0 . . 2^{min(k,10)} -1$, and k is the
number of times the message has been sent and collided in the past. Thus if a
message is collided in the first trial, then the interface process in c waits for
a random period 0 or 2T before trying to resend the message. If a message is
collided in the second trial, then the interface process in c waits for a random
period 0, 2T, 4T, or 6T before trying to resend the message. As mentioned in
Section 24.3, this potential doubling of the waiting time for resending a message after a collision is called exponential back-off.

Some explanations concerning steps i and iii are in order. In step i, we stated that
the interface process in computer c needs to send and listen for a time period 2T to
detect any collision. To see why such a time period is necessary, consider the following scenario involving two computers c and e at the two ends of an Ethernet. The
interface process in c starts to send a message at time 0 that arrives at computer e at
time T. Just before receiving this message, the interface process in computer e starts
to send another message that collides with the first message. The collision arrives at
computer c at time 2T. Thus, the interface process in computer c needs to send and
listen for a time period 2T, at least, in order to detect this collision.

The exponential back-off in step iii is intended to make the waiting time before
resending a message proportional to the number of messages that collided with this
message. For example, if only two messages collide, then each of these messages
ends up waiting for a random period taken from small range (e.g., 0 or 2T) before it
is resent. On the other hand, if 10 messages collide, then each of them ends up waiting for a random period taken from a large range (e.g., 0, 2T, . . . , 32T) before it is
resent.

The interface header (added to an IP message by the interface process in computer c and removed by the interface process in computer d before forwarding the message to the IP process in d) consists of the following five fields:

1. Preamble   56 bits
2. Start delimiter   8 bits
3. Hardware address of the source (c)   48 bits
4. Hardware address of the destination (d)   48 bits
5. Length of the IP message in bytes   16 bits

Field 1 allows the interface process in the destination computer d to synchronize
with the interface process in the source computer c. Field 2 consists of the bit pattern 10101011 that indicates the start of the Interface message. Fields 3 and 4 define the hardware addresses of the source and destination, respectively. Field 5 defines the number of bits in the IP message divided by 8.

The interface tail (added to an IP message by the interface process in computer c and removed by the interface process in computer d before forwarding the message to the IP process in d) consists of the following two fields:

1. Padding   x bits
2. checksum of the interface message   16 bits

Field 1 is an added padding to ensure that the total number of bits in the interface message equals the number of bits that can be sent by the interface process in computer c in 2T time units, where T is the maximum propagation delay over the Ethernet.

Field 2 contains a checksum for the interface message excluding the preamble and start delimiter. This is because the interface process in computer d may be out of synchronization with the interface process in computer c while it is receiving part of these two fields, and so it may not receive these two fields correctly. The method for computing this checksum is similar to the one in the corruption detection protocol that uses checksum in Section 8.2.

Token Bus

The token bus defined in the IEEE 802.4 standard is similar to the token bus protocol discussed in Section 24.2 except for the following three important differences:

i. In the token bus protocol in Section 24.2, all processes in the network participate in the virtual ring. In particular, each process p[i] always attempts to forward the token to $p[i +_n 1]$ first. If $p[i +_n 1]$ does not respond, then p[i] attempts to forward the token to $p[i +_n 2]$, and so on. This can be wasteful if process $p[i +_n 1]$ is down or does not need the token (to send data messages) for a long period of time. To overcome this problem, the token bus in the IEEE 802.4 standard allows processes to leave the virtual ring for long periods of time. When a process leaves the virtual ring, no process in the virtual ring will attempt to forward the token to it. The standard also allows processes that left the virtual ring to rejoin it at a later time.

ii. The token bus of the IEEE 802.4 standard allows data messages to have different priorities. The priority of a data message determines when the message is to be sent with respect to other messages. Consider a case where a process p[i] in the virtual ring needs to send a low-priority data message while another process p[j] needs to send a high-priority data message. In this case, when p[i] receives the token, it cannot send its data message. Rather, p[i] forwards the token so that p[j] can send its data message, then p[j] forwards the token to p[i] so that p[i] can send its data message afterward.

iii. The procedure for generating a new token message (when the current token message is lost) in the IEEE 802.4 standard is slightly more complicated, and also more efficient, than the procedure for generating a new token message in the token bus protocol in Section 24.2.

24.5   BIBLIOGRAPHICAL NOTES

Broadcast networks are discussed din Abramson [1970] and Metcalfe and Boggs [1976]. Polling/selection protocols are discussed in Hayes [1978, 1984]. The IEEE standard for the token bus protocol is discussed in IEEE [1990b]. The Ethernet protocol is discussed in Metcalfe and Boggs [1976]. The IEEE standard for the Ethernet protocol is discussed in IEEE [1990a]. Performance analysis of the Ethernet protocol is discussed in Lam [1980] and Tobagi [1980a]. The stack protocol is discussed in Capetanakis [1979a,b].

Overviews of broadcast (local-area) networks and protocols are given in Tobagi [1980b], Stallings [1993], and Saadawi et al. [1994].

EXERCISES

1   (Polling/Selection with Bounded Sending). Modify the polling/selection protocol discussed in Section 24.2 such that there is an upper bound kmax on the number of data messages that a process, primary or secondary, can send in one round.

2   (Polling/Selection with Priorities). Modify the polling/selection protocol discussed in Section 24.2 such that the secondary process s[0] has twice as many chances to send data messages as any other secondary process in the network.

3   (Polling/Selection with Dynamic Priorities). Modify the polling/selection protocol discussed in Section 24.2 such that if a secondary process s[i] sends data messages in a polling round; then the same secondary process s[i] is polled, with probability ½, to send data messages in the next polling round.

4   (Failure-Tolerant Polling/Selection). Modify the polling/selection protocol discussed in Section 24.2 such that if the primary process p fails, then eventually process s[0] acts as a primary process for the remaining secondary processes s[i: 1 .. n − 1].

5   (Token Bus with Bounded Sending). Modify the token bus protocol discussed in Section 24.2 such that there is an upper bound kmax on the number of data messages that a process can send when a process has the token.

6   (Token Bus with Priorities). Modify the token bus protocol discussed in Section 24.2 such that the process p[0] has twice as many chances to send data messages as any other process in the network.

7   (Collisions in the Token Bus). Although collisions can occur in the token bus protocol discussed in Section 24.2, this protocol is classified as a collision-preventing protocol. Describe the situations where collisions can occur in this protocol.

8   (Token Bus with Arbitrary Circular Order). Modify the token bus protocol discussed in Section 24.2 such that the token circulates around the processes

in an arbitrary order, not necessarily the order p[0]; p[1]; p[2]; . . . ; p[n − 1]; p[0]; . . . .

9   (Ethernet with Bounded Sending). Modify the Ethernet protocol discussed in Section 24.3 such that there is an upper bound kmax on the number of data messages that a process can send when it gets a chance to send data messages.

10   (Ethernet with Priorities). Modify the Ethernet protocol discussed in Section 24.3 such that process p[0] has twice as many chances to send data messages as any other process in the network.

11   (Waiting in Ethernet). For the Ethernet protocol in Section 24.3, explain why variable wait in a process p[i] is not decremented when another process p[j] sends a header or data message.

12   (Ethernet with Preferred Collision Resolution). Modify the Ethernet protocol discussed in Section 24.3 such that when a collision occurs, each process not involved in the collision assigns its wait variable the maximum value wmax. (This modification allows the processes involved in a collision to send their data messages before other processes can send their data messages.)

13   (Stack Protocol with Bounded Sending). Modify the stack protocol discussed in Section 24.3 such that there is an upper bound kmax on the number of data messages that a process can send when it gets a chance to send data messages.

14   (Stack Protocol with Priorities). Modify the stack protocol in Section 24.3 such that process p[0] has twice as many chances to send data messages as any other process in the network.

15   (Performance of the Stack Protocol). If x processes collided in the stack protocol in Section 24.3, then how many more collisions are needed for the colliding processes to send their data messages. Assume that each coin flip yields at least one process with a head and at least one process with a tail.

16   (Stack Protocol with Nonbinary Coins). Modify the stack protocol discussed in Section 24.3 as follows. Instead of a boolean variable coinhd, each process p[i] has a variable coin declared as follows:

```
const    cmax
var      coin  :      0..cmax-1
```

17   (Performance of the Stack Protocol with Nonbinary Coins). If x processes collided in the stack protocol in exercise 16, then how many more collisions are needed for the colliding processes to send their data messages.

CHAPTER 25

PROTOCOL LAYERS
AND HIERARCHIES

Starting from Chapter 6, we dedicated a chapter to discussing each of the different tasks of network protocols. For example, a chapter was dedicated to connections (Chapter 6), another chapter was dedicated to data transfer and multiplexing (Chapter 7), and so on. In each of these chapters, we presented several protocols for performing the task discussed in that chapter.

In order to design a network protocol that performs multiple tasks, several protocols, from different chapters, need to be combined together into a single protocol. For example, a protocol that performs both connections and data transfer can be designed by combining a protocol from Chapter 6 with a protocol from Chapter 7. The protocol from Chapter 6 performs connections, the protocol from Chapter 7 performs data transfer, and the combined protocol performs both connections and data transfer.

A common method for combining protocols is referred to as stacking. One protocol is stacked on top of another protocol, forming a protocol hierarchy. Each constituent protocol in a protocol hierarchy is called a protocol layer. Protocol layers and hierarchies are the subject of this chapter.

The rest of this chapter is organized as follows. In Section 25.1, we introduce the concept of a protocol layer and discuss how to convert a protocol into a protocol layer. We then give two examples where protocols are converted into protocol layers. In Section 25.2, we discuss how to convert a connection protocol (from Chapter 6) into a protocol layer, and in Section 25.3, we discuss how to convert an error recovery protocol (from Chapter 9) into a protocol layer. Then in Section 25.4, we discuss how to stack protocol layers into a protocol hierarchy and give an example of a protocol hierarchy. In Section 25.5, we discuss the protocol hierarchy in a typical computer network. Finally in Section 25.6, we present several updates that are currently being planned for the protocol hierarchy in the Internet.

25.1 PROTOCOLS VERSUS PROTOCOL LAYERS

In Chapter 3, we defined a protocol as a closed network of communicating processes. The requirement of a network to be closed means that each process in the network can communicate only with other processes in the network, but not with processes outside the network. This requirement is an abstraction intended to simplify our presentation by always focusing our attention on a single network and ignoring what lies outside that network.

A protocol layer, on the other hand, is an open network where each process communicates with some processes in the upper layer or with some processes in the lower layer. The communications between a process and the upper and lower processes are free from transmission errors. In other words, each sent message from a process to an upper or lower process is eventually received without being corrupted, lost, or reordered with other sent messages.

It is possible to convert any protocol into a protocol layer. The procedure for converting a protocol into a protocol layer can be described roughly as follows. First, replace each process in the protocol by a corresponding process in the protocol layer. Second, replace the direct communications between a process and other processes in the protocol with similar communications between the corresponding process in the protocol layer and some processes in the lower layer. Third, add communications between each process in the protocol layer and some processes in the upper layer.

As an example, consider a protocol that consists of two processes p and q, as shown in Figure 25.1a. This protocol can be converted into a protocol layer with

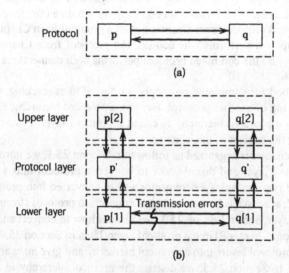

(a)

(b)

FIG. 25.1

two processes, named p' and q', as shown in Figure 25.1b. The direct communication between p and q in the original protocol is replaced in the protocol layer by communications between p' and a lower process p[1] and between q' and a lower process q[1]. Moreover, communications are added in the protocol layer between process p' and an upper process p[2] and between process q' and an upper process q[2].

Some protocol layers have no lower layers, and some have no upper layers. For example, the protocol layer consisting of processes p[1] and q[1] in Figure 25.1b has no lower layer, and p[1] and q[1] communicate directly over the two channels between them. Also, the protocol layer consisting of processes p[2] and q[2] in Figure 25.1b has no upper layer. As mentioned above, messages exchanged between a process and its upper and lower processes cannot be corrupted, lost, or reordered, whereas messages exchanged between processes in the same layer may be corrupted, lost, or reordered. Thus referring to Figure 25.1b, only the messages exchanged between p[1] and q[1] can be corrupted, lost, or reordered.

It is instructive to illustrate the procedure for converting protocols into protocol layers using some detailed examples. In Section 25.2, we discuss how to convert a connection protocol into a protocol layer. Then in Section 25.3, we discuss how to convert an error recovery protocol into a protocol layer.

25.2 A CONNECTION PROTOCOL LAYER

In this section, we discuss how to convert a connection protocol, similar to those in Chapter 6, into a protocol layer. Consider the following connection protocol between processes p and q:

```
process p

var    conp           :       boolean

begin
       timeout  ~conp  ∧  #ch.p.q + #ch.q.p = 0    ->
                                  send crqst to q

[]     rcv crply from q  ->    conp := true

[]     conp                ->    send drqst to q

[]     rcv drply from q  ->    conp := false
end

process q

var    conq           :       boolean
```

```
begin
      rcv crqst from p  ->
              if  true -> conq := true;  send crply to p
              []  true -> conq := false; send drply to p
              fi

[]    rcv drqst from p  ->       conq := false; send drply
                                            to p
end
```

This protocol is similar to the connection protocol in Section 6.1 except for two modifications. First, in this protocol, process p does not send data messages to process q after a connection from p to q has been established. As shown below, sending of data messages from p to q is performed in another layer. Second, in this protocol, process q does not remove an established connection until process p requests removal of the connection by sending a drqst message to q. The motivation for this second modification will become clear in Section 25.4.

This protocol can be converted into a protocol layer consisting of processes cp and cq that correspond to processes p and q, respectively. Process cp communicates with an upper process called sndr and with a lower multiplexer process called mp. Process sndr prompts process cp to establish a connection with process cq and later to remove the established connection. Process mp acts as an intermediate process between cp and cq. Thus, each message that cp needs to send to cq, cp sends to mp. Also, each message that cp needs to receive from cq, cp receives from mp. Processes sndr and mp are discussed in detail in Section 25.4. We now discuss process cp.

When process cp receives a crqst(val) message from process sndr, cp attempts to establish a connection with process cq and to pass the received value val to cq. If the attempt fails, process cp sends a drply message to process sndr and then waits to receive a next crqst(val) message from sndr, and the cycle repeats. If the attempt succeeds, process cp sends a crply message to process sndr and then waits to receive a drqst(val) message from sndr. When cp receives a drqst(val) message from process sndr, it removes the established connection with process cq and passes the received value val to cq. When the connection is removed, process cp sends a drply message to process sndr and then waits to receive a crqst(val) message from sndr, and the cycle repeats.

Process cp in the connection layer can be defined as follows:

process cp

```
var    conp        :     boolean,     {initially false}
       actv        :     boolean,     {initially false}
       val         :     integer

begin
       rcv crqst(val) from sndr->
```

```
                                    actv := true
 []      timeout
              ~conp ∧ actv ∧
              (no crqst, crply, drqst, or drpy messages
              in transit) ->      send crqst(val) to mp


 []      rcv crply from mp  ->    conp, actv := true, false


 []      rcv drqst(val) from sndr  ->   actv := true


 []      conp ∧ actv  ->   send drqst(val) to mp


 []      rcv drply from mp  ->
                                 conp, actv := false, false;
                                 send drply to sndr
end
```

Note that process cp is similar to process p in the above connection protocol except for the fact that cp communicates with the lower process mp instead of process cq and that cp also communicates with the upper process sndr.

Process cq communicates with an upper process called rcvr and with a lower multiplexer process called mq. Process rcvr determines whether process cq should accept or reject any connection with cp when cp requests to establish a connection. Process rcvr also prompts cq to remove the connection with cp when cp requests to remove the connection. Process mq acts as an intermediate process between cq and cp. Thus, each message that cq needs to send to cp, cq sends to mq. Also, each message that cq needs to receive from cp, cq receives from mq. Processes rcvr and mq are discussed in detail in Section 25.4.

Process cq in the connection layer can be defined as follows:

```
process cq

var    conq        :       boolean,
       wait        :       boolean,
       val         :       integer

begin
       rcv crqst(val) from mq  ->
              if   conq  ->   send crply to mq
              [] ~conq   ->   send crqst(val) to rcvr
              fi


 []    rcv crply from rcvr        ->     conq := true;
                                         send crply to mq
```

```
[]      rcv drqst(val) from mq  ->
            if  conq /\ ~wait  ->
                                    wait := true;
                                    send drqst(val) to rcvr
                []  conq /\ wait  ->       skip
                []  ~conq                -> send drply to mq
                fi


[]      rcv drply from rcvr         ->
                                    conq, wait := false, false;
                                    send drply to mq
end
```

Note that process cq is very similar to process q in the above connection protocol except for the fact that cq communicates with the lower process mq instead of process cp and that cq also communicates with the upper process rcvr.

25.3 AN ERROR RECOVERY PROTOCOL LAYER

In this section, we discuss a second example of converting a protocol into a protocol layer. In particular, we discuss how to convert an error recovery protocol, similar to those in Chapter 9, into a protocol layer. Consider the following error recovery protocol between processes p and q:

```
process p

const w

inp   txt        :      array [integer] of integer

var   na, ns, i  :      integer

begin
      na+w > ns  ->
                        send data(ns, txt[ns]) to q;
                        ns := ns + 1
[]    rcv ack(i) from q ->    na := max(na,i)
[]    timeout na < ns /\
            (data#ch.p.q + ack#ch.q.p = 0) /\
            ~akn ->
                        send data(na, txt[na]) to q
end
```

```
process q

const w

var     nr, j, t  :        integer,
        rcvd      :        array [0..w-1] of boolean,
        txt       :        array [integer] of integer,
        akn       :        boolean

begin
        rcv data(j, t) from p ->
                if j < nr   ->      akn := true
                [] j ≥ nr   ->
                        rcvd[j mod w], txt[j] := true, t;
                        do rcvd[nr mod w]   ->
                                rcvd[nr mod w] := false;
                                nr, akn := nr + 1, true
                        od
                fi

[]      akn  ->  send ack(nr) to p;  akn := false
end
```

This protocol is similar to the error recovery protocol in Section 9.3 except for three modifications. First, in this protocol, process p has an array txt from which p obtains the text of every data message it sends. Process q also has an array txt to store the text of every data message it receives. Second, in this protocol, input wr is replaced by the constant value w in process q. Third, the actions for receiving and discarding **error** messages are no longer in processes p and q because, as discussed in Section 25.4, error messages are received and discarded in a lower layer.

This protocol can be converted into a protocol layer consisting of processes dp and dq, which correspond to processes p and q, respectively. Process dp communicates with an upper process called sndr and with a lower multiplexer process called mp. Process sndr prompts dp to send data messages to dq and to receive ack messages from dq. Process mp acts as an intermediate process between dp and dq. Thus, each message that dp needs to send to dq, dp sends to mp. Also, each message that dp needs to receive from dq, dp receives from mp. Processes sndr and mp are discussed in detail in Section 25.4. We now discuss process dp.

When process dp receives a send request srqst(left, right) message from process sndr, dp attempts to send the data messages data(left, txt[left]), data(left + 1, txt[left + 1]), ..., data(right − 1, txt[right − 1]) to dq and to receive corresponding ack messages from dq. If this attempt succeeds, process dp waits until there are no data or ack messages in transit between dp and dq and then sends an srply(right) message to process sndr. At any instant, process dp can wait until there are no data or ack mes-

sages in transit between dp and dq and then can send an srply(na) message to
process sndr, thus aborting its attempt to send the data messages. After process dp
sends an srply message to sndr, it waits to receive the next srqst(left, right) message
from sndr, and the cycle repeats.

Process dp in the error recovery layer can be defined as follows:

```
process dp

const w

inp    text         :    array [integer] of integer

var    na, ns, i    :    integer,
       left, right  :    integer,
       actv         :    boolean

begin
       rcv srqst(left, right) from sndr  ->
                   na, ns, actv := left, left, true

[]     na+w > ns /\ ns < right /\ actv->
                   send data(ns, txt[ns]) to mp;
                   ns := ns + 1

[]     rcv ack(i) from mp  -> na := max(na, i)

[]     timeout
            actv /\
            no data or ack messages in transit /\
            ~akn
                   ->
            if na < ns  -> send data(na, txt[na]) to mp
            [] true     -> send srply(na) to sndr;
                           actv := false
            fi
end
```

Process dq communicates with an upper process called rcvr and with a lower
multiplexer process called mq. Process rcvr prompts dq to receive data messages
from process dp, store them in its txt array, and then send ack messages to dp.
Process mq acts as an intermediate process between dq and dp. Thus, each message
that dq needs to send to dp, dq sends to mq. Also, each message that dq needs to receive from dp, dq receives from mq. Processes rcvr and mq are discussed in detail in
Section 25.4. We now discuss process dq.

When process dq receives a receive request rrqst(left) message from process rcvr, it assigns its variable nr the value left and every element in its array rcvd the value false and then sends an rrply message to process rcvr. Process dq then waits to receive data messages from process dp, store them in its array txt, and send acknowledgments for all received messages.

Process dq in the error recovery layer can be defined as follows:

```
process dq

const w

var     nr, j, t      :        integer,
        rcvd          :        array [0..w-1] of boolean,
        txt           :        array [integer] of integer,
        akn           :        boolean,
        left          :        integer

begin
        rcv rrqst(left) from rcvr ->
                rcvd, nr := false, left;
                send rrply to rcvr

[]      rcv data(j, t) from mq ->
                if j < nr    ->    akn := true
                [] j ≥ nr    ->
                        rcvd[j mod w], txt[j] := true, t;
                        do rcvd[nr mod w]  ->
                                rcvd[nr mod w] := false;
                                nr, akn := nr + 1, true
                        od
                fi

[]      akn  -> send ack(nr) to mq; akn := false
end
```

25.4 A PROTOCOL HIERARCHY EXAMPLE

As mentioned earlier, protocol layers are stacked on top of one another, forming a protocol hierarchy. In this section, we make this point clear by discussing a particular protocol hierarchy that consists of five layers, including the two protocol layers (cp, cq) and (dp, dq) that we discussed in Sections 25.2 and 25.3, respectively. The five layers in this hierarchy are as follows:

>   Layer 5: (src, dst).
>   Layer 4: (sndr, rcvr).

Layer 3: (cp, cq).

Layer 2: (dp, dq).

Layer 1: (mp, mq).

These five layers are arranged in the protocol hierarchy as follows. Layer 5 is on top of layer 4, layer 4 is on top of layers 2 and 3, and layers 2 and 3 are on top of layer 1.

Figure 25.2 shows how the 10 processes in these five layers are arranged. Process src is on top of process sndr, process sndr is on top of processes cp and dp, and processes cp and dp are on top of process mp. Similarly, process dst is on top of process rcvr, process rcvr is on top of processes cq and dq, and processes cq and dq are on top of process mq. Because the lowest layer in the hierarchy is (mp, mq), the two processes in that layer, namely mp and mq, communicate directly with one another.

Referring to Figure 25.2, the five processes src, sndr, cp, dp, and mp reside in computer 1, while the other five processes dst, rcvr, cq, dq, and mq reside in computer 2. We refer to the five processes that reside in computer 1 as the protocol stack in computer 1 and refer to the five processes that reside in computer 2 as the protocol stack in computer 2.

Next, we show how the protocol hierarchy in Figure 25.2 can be used to transfer files from computer 1 to computer 2 over the connecting link that may corrupt or lose transmitted messages.

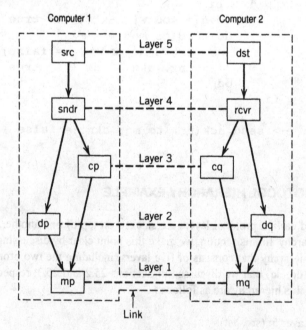

FIG. 25.2

The 10 processes in this protocol hierarchy perform the following tasks. Periodically, process src generates a file and asks process sndr to send it (to process dst). To send this file, process sndr first asks process cp to establish a connection with process cq. If the connection is established, then process sndr asks process dp to send the file as a sequence of data messages to process dq. When process dp finishes sending the data messages, it informs process sndr, which then asks process cp to remove the established connection with process cq and to inform process rcvr that the connection has been removed. Then, each of the two processes sndr and rcvr checks whether the whole file has been received by rcvr. If yes, then process rcvr delivers the file to process dst and process sndr informs process src that the file has been delivered to dst. If no, then process rcvr discards the partial file it has received and process sndr informs process src that the file has not been delivered to dst.

The two processes mp and mq act as multiplexers that continuously receive messages from each side and forward them to the other side. For example, process mp receives messages from cp and dp and forwards them to mq. Process mp also receives messages from mq and forwards each received message, depending on the message type, to either cp or cq.

There are two reasons for a file sent from process src not to be delivered to process dst. First, when process cp attempts to establish a connection with process cq, the connection may be rejected by cq because process dst is not yet ready to receive another file. In this case, process cp informs sndr that the connection has been rejected, and sndr informs process src that the file was not delivered to process dst. Second, when process dp attempts to send the file as a sequence of data messages to process dq, dp may decide at any instant to abort the task of sending the file. In this case, process dp informs process sndr, which in turn informs process rcvr, as part of removing the connection from cp to cq, to discard the partial file that has been stored in array txt of process dq. Finally, process sndr informs process src that the file was not delivered to process dst.

Processes src and dst in the file transfer layer, layer 5, can be defined as follows:

process src

```
var    left, right :      integer,
       wait, b      :      boolean
```

begin
```
    ~wait  ->
            {send a new file that exists in array text}
            {starting at left and ending at right}
            left, right := any, any;
            if left ≥ right -> skip
            [] left < right ->
                    wait := true;
                    send file(left, right) to sndr
            fi
```

```
[]       rcv rslt(b) from sndr  ->
                    {b is true iff file was delivered to dst}
                    wait := false
end

process dst

var    left, right :        integer

begin
         rcv file(left, right) from rcvr  ->
                 {copy the received file from array txt}
                 send ack to rcvr
end
```

Process src has two actions, one action for asking process sndr to send a file to process dst and another action for receiving from sndr the result of that request. The file to be sent is stored in array txt of process dp starting at location txt[left] and ending at location txt[right − 1], where left < right. Process dst has only one action for receiving a file from process rcvr and then sending an ack message to rcvr. The received file is to be stored in array txt of process dq starting at location txt[left] and ending at location txt[right − 1].

Process sndr in the session layer, layer 4, can be defined as follows:

```
process sndr

var    left, right :        integer,
       done        :        integer

begin
         rcv file(left, right) from src  ->
                 done := left; send crqst(left) to cp

[]       rcv crply from cp          ->
                 send srqst(left, right) to dp

[]       rcv srply(done) from dp  ->
                 if done = right  -> send drqst(right) to cp
                 [] done ≠ right  -> send drqst(left) to cp
                 fi

[]       rcv drply from cp         ->
                 if done = right  -> send rslt(true) to src
                 [] done ≠ right  -> send rslt(false) to src
                 fi
end
```

When process sndr receives a file(left, right) from process src, it sends a crqst(left) message to cp so that the value of left is communicated, via cp and cq, to rcvr. As a reply to the crqst message, process sndr receives either a drply message or a crply message. If sndr receives a drply message from cp, it recognizes that the request to establish a connection has been rejected. In this case, sndr sends a rslt(false) message to process src. If sndr receives a crply message from cp, it recognizes that a connection has been established. In this case, process sndr sends an srqst message to process dp and waits to receive an srply(done) from dp. If done = right, then process sndr recognizes that the file has been sent successfully to process rcvr, and so it sends a drqst(right) message to cp and waits to receive a drply message from cp before sending a rslt(true) message to process src. If done ≠ right, then process sndr recognizes that the attempt to send the file to process rcvr has failed, and so it sends a drqst(left) message to cp and waits to receive a drply message from cp before sending a rslt(false) to process src.

Process rcvr in the session layer, layer 4, can be defined as follows:

```
process rcvr

var     left, right :      integer,
        acpt        :      boolean       {initially true}

begin
        rcv crqst(left) from cq ->
                if   acpt -> send rrqst(left) to dq
                [] ~acpt -> send drply to cq
                fi

[]      rcv rrply from dq           ->       send crply to cq

[]      rcv drqst(right) from cq ->
                send drply to cq;
                if left < right      ->
                        acpt := false;
                        send file(left, right) to dst
                [] left ≥ right      ->       skip
                fi

[]      rcv ack from dst            ->       acpt := true
end
```

When process rcvr receives a crqst message from process cq, it decides, based on the current value of variable acpt, to reject or accept the connection. To reject the connection, process rcvr merely sends a drply message to process cq. To accept the connection, process rcvr first sends an rrqst(left) message to process dq and waits to receive an rrply message from dq before sending a crply message to process cq. If process rcvr accepts the connection, process dq starts to receive data messages from process dp and store them in its array txt, starting at location txt[left]. Finally, process rcvr receives a drqst(right) message from cq and decides based on the received value of right, whether the received file is complete and should be forwarded to process dst or is incomplete and should be discarded. If process rcvr forwards the file to process dst, it assigns variable acpt the value false and then waits to receive an ack message from dst before assigning acpt the value true again.

Processes dp and dq in the error recovery layer, layer 2, are as defined in Section 25.3, with one exception. The guard of the timeout action in process dp can now be stated formally as follows:

```
timeout
      actv ∧
      (data#ch.dp.mp + data#ch.mp.mq + data#ch.mq.dq +
      ack#ch.dq.mq + ack#ch.mq.mp + ack#ch.mp.dp = 0) ∧
      ~akn
```

Similarly, processes cp and cq in the connection layer, layer 3, are as defined in Section 25.2 with one exception. The guard of the timeout action in process cp can now be stated formally as follows:

```
timeout
      ~conp ∧ actv ∧
      (crqst#ch.cp.mp + crqst#ch.mp.mq + crqst#ch.mq.cq +
      crqst#ch.cq.rcvr + rrqst#ch.rcvr.dq +
      rrply#ch.dq.rcvr + crply#ch.rcvr.cq +
      crply#ch.cq.mq + crply#ch.mq.mp + crply#ch.mp.cp +
      drqst#ch.cp.mp + drqst#ch.mp.mq + drqst#ch.mq.cq +
      drqst#ch.cq.rcvr + drply#ch.rcvr.cq +
      drply#ch.cq.mq + drply#ch.mq.mp + drply#ch.mp.cp = 0
      )
```

Processes mp and mq in the multiplexing layer, layer 1, can be defined as follows:

```
process mp

var   v   :        integer

begin

      rcv crqst(v) from cp      ->      send crqst(v) to mq
   [] rcv crply from mq         ->      send crply to cp
   [] rcv drqst(v) from cp      ->      send drqst(v) to mq
   [] rcv drply from mq         ->      send drply to cp
   [] rcv data(v) from dp       ->      send data(v) to mq
```

```
    □    rcv ack from mq            ->      send ack to dp
    □    rcv error from mq          ->      skip
end


process mq


var    v      :         integer

begin
         rcv crqst(v) from mp       ->      send crqst(v) to cq
    □    rcv crply from cq          ->      send crply to mp
    □    rcv drqst(v) from mp       ->      send drqst(v) to cq
    □    rcv drply from cq          ->      send drply to mp
    □    rcv data(v) from mp        ->      send data(v) to dq
    □    rcv ack from dq            ->      send ack to mp
    □    rcv error from mp          ->      skip
    end
```

Process mp is a multiplexer that receives every message sent by cp or dp and forwards it to mq and receives every message sent by mq and either forwards it to cp or dp, depending on the message type, or discards the message if it is an error message. All crply and drply messages are forwarded to cp and all ack messages are forwarded to dp.

Similarly, process mq is a multiplexer that receives every message sent by cq or dq and forwards it to mp and receives every message sent by mp and either forwards it to cq or dq, depending on the message type, or discards the message if it is an error message. All crqst and drqst messages are forwarded to cq, and all data message are forwarded to dq.

25.5 PROTOCOL HIERARCHIES IN COMPUTER NETWORKS

In this section, we outline a possible protocol hierarchy in a computer network. A computer network can be represented by a connected and undirected graph with three types of nodes called subnetworks, routers, and hosts. Subnetworks are connected only to routers and hosts (but not to other subnetworks), and routers and hosts are connected only to subnetworks (but not to other routers or hosts). Each router is connected to at least two subnetworks, and each host is connected to exactly one subnetwork.

Figure 25.3 shows an example of a computer network with five subnetworks, three routers, and nine hosts. Note that each router is connected to at least two subnetworks, while each host is connected to exactly one subnetwork.

Each subnetwork in a computer network is implemented as a ring network (Chapter 23) or as a broadcast network (Chapter 24). Each router and host in a computer network is implemented as a computer. A subnetwork allows each computer

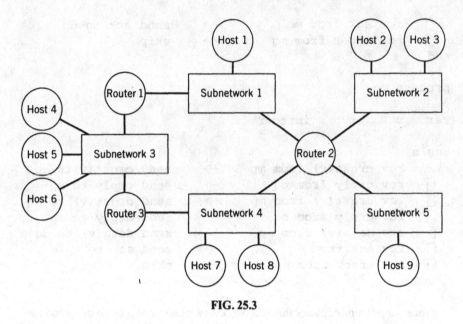

FIG. 25.3

(router or host) connected to it to directly send messages to every other computer (router or host) connected to it. For example, referring to Figure 25.3, router 1 can directly send messages to hosts 1 and 4 over subnetworks 1 and 3, respectively. In the remainder of this section we discuss possible protocol stacks for a router and for a host in a computer network.

Figure 25.4 shows a possible protocol stack for a router that is connected to three subnetworks. One of the subnetworks is a token ring (Section 23.3), and the other two are Ethernets (Section 24.3). The processes in this protocol stack are arranged into six layers:

Layer 1   Consists of three processes. Each is a part of a different subnetwork to which the router is connected. Each process in layer 1 receives messages from the process in layer 2 and then sends these messages over its subnetwork. It also receives messages over its subnetwork and sends them to the process in layer 2.

Layer 2   Consists of one process that detects message corruption. This process receives messages from the process in layer 3, computes a checksum for each of these messages, and sends each message appended with its checksum to a process in layer 1. This process also receives messages from a process in layer 1 and then checks whether the appended checksum in each message is correct. If so (indicating that the message transmission over the subnetwork was corruption free), the process sends the message to the process in layer 3. If not, the process discards the message.

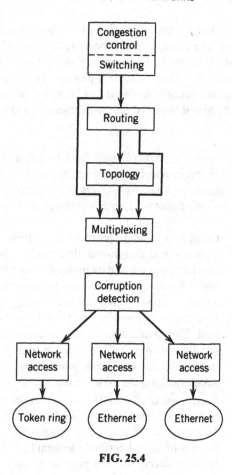

FIG. 25.4

Layer 3   Consists of a multiplexer processes. This process receives messages from a process in layer 4, 5, or 6 and then forwards these messages to the process in layer 2. It also receives messages from the process in layer 2 and sends each message to a process in layer 4, 5, or 6, depending on the message type.

Layer 4   Consists of one process that maintains the (local) topology of each subnetwork to which the router is connected. In particular, each process in layer 4 maintains the state, up or down, of each computer (whether router or host) in each subnetwork to which the router is connected. It also provides that information upon request to the routing process in layer 5.

Layer 5   Consists of a routing process. This process exchanges state messages (see, e.g., Section 13.3) with the routing processes in neighboring routers, in order to keep its routing table updated. It also provides, upon request, routing information to the switching process in layer 6.

Layer 6   Consists of a single process that performs both switching and congestion control. For example, this process receives a data message from a
subnetwork N via the multiplexer process in layer 3. Then, based on the
latest information from the routing process, the message is returned to
the multiplexer process so that it can be forwarded to another subnetwork N'. Note that N and N' are two subnetworks to which the router is
connected.

Figure 25.5 shows a possible protocol stack for a host that is connected to an
Ethernet. The processes in this protocol stack are arranged into 12 layers. The first 6
layers in this stack are similar to the above 6 layers of the protocol stack of a router.
The remaining layers, layers 7 through 12, in this protocol stack are as follows:

Layer 7   Consists of a single process that performs end-to-end error
recovery and end-to-end flow control. In particular, this
process sends every data message generated by a process in
layers 8 through 12. It resends the message until it receives
an ack, acknowledging that the message has been received,
from the corresponding process in layer 7 of the destination
host. This process also receives every data message destined to some process in layers 8 through 12, delivers the
message to its destination process, and sends back an ack
acknowledging the message reception.

Layers 8, 9, 10, 11   Each consists of a single process that performs its particular
task upon request from an application process in layer 12.
The process of layer 8 performs name resolution, the
process of layer 9 performs authentication and data encryption and decryption, the process of layer 10 performs data
compression and decompression, and the process of layer
11 performs message broadcast.

Layer 12   Consists of several application processes. Each application
process generates data messages that are sent via the
process in layer 7 to the application processes in other
hosts. It may also request that some process in layer 8, 9,
10, or 11 performs a task such as resolve a name or provide
data encryption or decryption.

25.6   THE NEXT INTERNET

There are two major changes that are currently taking place in the Internet. First, IP
addresses are being expanded from 4 bytes to 16 bytes each. Second, the current
version of the internet protocol, version 4, is being replaced by a new version, version 6. In this section, we discuss these two changes in some detail.

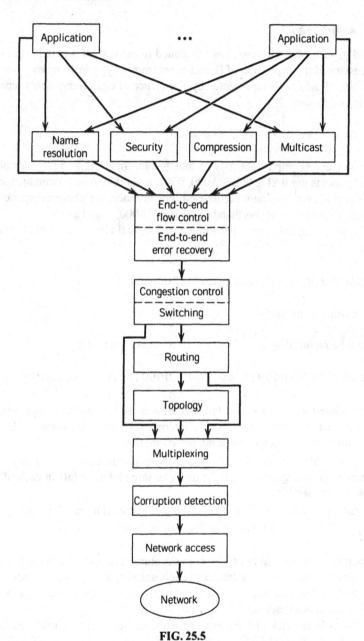

FIG. 25.5

New IP Addresses

The rapid growth of the Internet has threatened to exhaust all 4-byte IP addresses. This necessitated the expansion of IP addresses from 4 bytes to 16 bytes.

A 16-byte IP address is represented by a sequence of eight components separated by colons as follows:

```
<comp.0>:<comp.1>: ... :<comp.7>
```

Each component <comp.i> consists of four hexadecimal digits. Five examples of these components are 0A13, 00BF, A000, 0001, and 0000. As a shorthand, the leftmost zeros in each component are deleted. For instance, the above component examples can be rewritten in shorthand as A13, BF, A000, 1, and a space.

The 16-byte IP addresses are partitioned into several classes. Four of these classes are as follows:

    i. *Old IP Addresses:* Each 4-byte old IP address of the form

```
<comp>:<comp'>
```

    can be replaced by a 16-byte new IP address of the form

```
0000:0000:0000:0000:0000:0000:<comp>:<comp'>
```

    ii. *Provider-Based Addresses:* These addresses are assigned to companies, such as AT&T and MCI, that provide Internet services to customers. The three leftmost bits in each of these addresses are 010.

    iii. *Geographic-Based Addresses:* These addresses are assigned to organizations based on their geographic locations. The three leftmost bits in each of these addresses are 100.

    iv. *Multicast Addresses:* These addresses are assigned to multicast groups. The eight leftmost bits in each of these addresses are 11111111.

Although each of the old IP addresses is structured into a triple (network, subnetwork, computer), the new IP addresses are left unstructured. This is intended to allow providers and organizations that are assigned large blocks of addresses to structure their addresses as they see fit.

Unfortunately, the lack of a universal structure in the new IP addresses makes hierarchical routing more difficult. Recall that the universal structure of old IP addresses, namely (network, subnetwork, computer), encourages hierarchical routing of a message as follows. When the message is far away from its ultimate destination, that is, it has not yet reached the autonomous system of the destination, the message is routed based only on the network identity of the destination. When the message arrives at the autonomous system of its destination, the message is routed based only on the subnetwork identity of the destination. When the message arrives at the subnetwork of its destination, the message is routed only based on the computer identity of the destination.

To still support hierarchical routing in the absence of a universal structure in the new IP addresses, masks are added to the routing tables as follows:

i. A mask is a sequence of 128 bits partitioned into two intervals: a left interval whose bits are all 1-bits and a right interval whose bits are all 0 bits.

ii. Each routing table defines for every ultimate destination d the best neighbor B.d for reaching destination d and a mask M.d for destination d.

iii. To route a data message whose ultimate destination is h using some routing table, find in the routing table an ultimate destination d that satisfies the condition

$$d = (h \text{ AND } M.d)$$

Then send the message to neighbor B.d. If there are two or more destinations that satisfy this condition, then choose from these destinations the one destination d whose mask M.d has the most 1 bits and send the message to neighbor B.d.

This method of routing, where masks are used to support hierarchical routing, is called classless interdomain routing, or CIDR for short.

IP version 6

In order to support the new 16-bit IP addresses, a new version of IP, version 6, is designed. (IP version 4 is the current version of IP, and IP version 5 was a real-time prototype that was never deployed.) Beside supporting 16-bit addresses, IP version 6 has other advantage over version 4. For example, IP version 6 has features for speeding up the processing of IP messages and for supporting the authentication and privacy of IP messages.

Each IP version 6 message consists of one main header followed by zero or more extension headers followed by the message text. The main header of a message consists of the following eight fields:

1. IP version of the message source	4 bits
2. Priority of the message	4 bits
3. Flow label of the message	24 bits
4. Length of the message without the main header	16 bits
5. Type of the next extension header or transport protocol of the message	8 bits
6. Maximum number of remaining hops	8 bits
7. IP address of the message source	128 bits
8. IP address of the message destination	128 bits

Field 1 defines the IP version of the message source, which is 6. Field 2 defines the message priority in the range 0, . . . , 15. In the case of congestion, messages whose priorities are large numbers overtake messages whose priorities are small numbers. As a rule, priorities in the range 0, . . . , 7 are reserved for messages that have no real-time requirements (e.g., FTP messages), while priorities in the range 8, . . . , 15 are reserved for messages that have real-time requirements (e.g., audio and video messages).

Field 3 is still experimental. One possible use of this field is to define the circuit, if any, to which the message belongs, when the resource reservation protocol RSVP (discussed in Section 14.4) is deployed. In this case, if the value of field 3 in some message is zero, then the message does not belong to any circuit. On the other hand, if the value of field 3 is nonzero, then the message belongs to a circuit identified by the triple (message source, message destination, flow label of the message).

Field 4 contains the number of bytes in the message without its main header. Field 5 contains either the type of the extension header that follows the main header, if such a header exists, or the transport protocol of the message, if no extension header follows the main header. Each extension header has a field similar to field 5 of the main header. (The different types of extension headers are discussed below.)

Field 6 contains the maximum number of remaining hops for the message. Each time the message makes one hop, the value of field 6 in its main header is decremented by 1. If the value of this field becomes zero and the message has not yet reached its ultimate destination, the message is discarded. Fields 7 and 8 define the 16-byte IP addresses of the message source and destination, respectively.

The extension headers of an IP version 6 message, if any, are of several types. Examples of these types are hop-by-hop headers, routing headers, fragmentation headers, and authentication and encryption headers. These header types are discussed briefly next.

A hop-by-hop header of an IP message is examined by every router that receives the message while the message is being transmitted from its original source to its ultimate destination. One function of the hop-by-hop header is to define the number of bytes in the message when this number is larger than any that can be defined in field 4 in the main header of the message. Thus, IP version 6 messages can have very large number of bytes and so they can be used in (efficient) communications between supercomputers.

A routing header of an IP message defines a sequence of routers r.0; r.1; . . . ; r.(k-1) that the message should follow as it is transmitted from its original source to its ultimate destination. This header also has a sequence of bits b.1; . . . ; b.(k-1) that imply the following requirement. If any bit b.i equals 0, then the message should visit router r.i after, but not necessarily immediately after, it visits router r.(i-1). If any bit b.i equals 1, then the message should visit router r.i immediately after it visits router r.(i-1).

A fragmentation header of an IP message indicates that this message is in fact a fragment of a large message. This header also contains three values that can be used in assembling the large message from its fragments. These three values are a unique identifier of the large message, the position of this fragment in the large message, and a bit indicating whether this fragment is the last one in the large message. In IP version 6, only the source of a large message can fragment the message, and only the destination of the large message can assemble it after receiving all its fragments.

Authentication and encryption headers of an IP message are discussed in Section 18.8.

25.7 BIBLIOGRAPHICAL NOTES

Formal methods for constructing protocol hierarchies are discussed in Green [1986], Lam and Shankar [1994], and Liu [1996].

EXERCISES

1 (Connection Protocol Layer). The connection protocol layer (cp, cq) discussed in Section 25.2 acts as a medium for exchanging messages between the two processes sndr and rcvr in the upper layer. Describe the message exchange between sndr and rcvr via layer (cp, cq).

2 (Connection Protocol Layer without Message Reorder). Simplify the connection protocol layer (cp, cq) discussed in Section 25.2 under the assumption that the exchanged messages between cp and cq cannot be reordered.

3 (Connection Protocol Layer without Transmission Errors). Simplify the connection protocol layer (cp, cq) discussed in Section 25.2 under the assumption that the exchanged messages between processes cp and cq cannot be lost, corrupted, or reordered.

4 (Another Connection Protocol Layer). The connection protocol layer discussed in Section 25.2 is based on the connection protocol in Section 6.1. Design another connection protocol layer that is based on the connection protocol in Section 6.2.

5 (Another Connection Protocol Layer without Message Reorder). Simplify the connection protocol layer (cp, cq) in exercise 4 under the assumption that the exchanged messages between processes cp and cq cannot be reordered.

6 (Another Connection Protocol Layer without Transmission Errors). Simplify the protocol layer (cp, cq) discussed in exercise 4 under the assumption that the exchanged messages between processes cp and cq cannot be lost, corrupted, or reordered.

7 (Error Recovery Protocol Layer). The error recovery protocol layer (dp, dq) discussed in Section 25.3 acts as a medium for exchanging messages between the two processes sndr and rcvr in the upper layer. Describe the message exchange between sndr and rcvr via layer (dp, dq).

8 (Error Recovery Protocol Layer without Message Reorder). Simplify the error recovery protocol layer (dp, dq) discussed in Section 25.3 under the assumption that the exchanged messages between processes dp and dq cannot be reordered.

9 (Error Recovery Protocol Layer without Transmission Errors). Simplify the error recovery protocol layer (dp, dq) discussed in Section 25.3 under the assumption that the exchanged messages between processes dp and dq cannot be lost, corrupted, or reordered. (Note that in this case the window mechanism can still be used for flow control.)

10 (Another Error Recovery Protocol Layer). The error recovery protocol layer discussed in Section 25.2 is based on the error recovery protocol in Section 9.3. Design another connection protocol layer that is based on the error recovery protocol in Section 9.4.

11 (Another Error Recovery Protocol Layer without Message Reorder). Simplify the error recovery protocol layer (dp, dq) in exercise 10 under the assumption that the exchanged messages between processes dp and dq cannot be reordered.

12 (Another Error Recovery Protocol Layer without Transmission Errors). Simplify the protocol layer (dp, dq) discussed in exercise 10 under the assumption that the exchanged messages between processes dp' and dq' cannot be lost, corrupted, or reordered. (Note that in this case the window mechanism can still be used for flow control.)

13 (A Connection Protocol Layer with Many Processes). The connection protocol layer (cp, cq) in Section 25.2 consists of only two processes. It is required to generalize this protocol layer to one that has $2*n$ processes: (cp[i: $0 \ldots n-1$], cq[j: $0 \ldots n-1$]). Each process cp[i] has an upper process sndr[i] and a lower process mp[i]. Similarly, each process cq[j] has an upper process rcvr[j] and a lower process mq[j]. Each process cp[i] can try to establish a connection with any process cq[j]; however, each cq[j] can accept to establish a connection with at most one cp[i] at a time. Design this protocol layer.

14 (A Protocol Layer for Maintaining Local Topology Information). Convert the protocol p[i: $0 \ldots n-1$] for maintaining local topology information in Section 11.2 into a protocol layer (tp[i: $0 \ldots n-1$]). Each process tp[i] in this protocol layer has an upper routing process rp[i] but has no lower processes. Thus, each process in the protocol layer (tp[i: $0 \ldots n-1$]) communicates directly with its neighboring processes in that layer. Each process tp[i] exchanges a chk(b) message with each neighboring process tp[j] in the protocol layer. Every once in a while, process rp[i] sends a nxt message to process tp[i], which replies by sending back a new(v) message to process rp[i], where v is the current value of array up in process tp[i].

15 (A Protocol Hierarchy for Maintaining Local Topology Information). Consider a protocol hierarchy that consists of two layers: a layer for maintaining local topology information (tp[i: $0 \ldots n-1$]) and a multiplexing layer (mp[i: $0 \ldots n-1$]). Each process tp[i] has a lower process mp[i] but has no upper processes, and each mp[i] process has no lower processes. For a process tp[i] to send a chk(b) message to a neighboring process tp[j] in the same layer, tp[i] first sends a chk(b, j) message to its lower process mp[i], which forwards a chk(b) message to its neighboring process mp[j], which in turn forwards a chk(b, i) message to its upper process tp[j]. Design the two protocol layers (tp[i: $0 \ldots n-1$]) and (mp[i: $0 \ldots n-1$]) in this protocol hierarchy. Assume for simplicity that sent messages are not corrupted, lost, or reordered.

16 (A Protocol Stack). Consider the protocol hierarchy in exercise 13. Assume that for every i, where i ranges over $0 \ldots n-1$, processes cp[i] and cq[i] are assigned to computer i in a computer network. Draw the protocol stack in computer i.

17 (A Protocol Stack). Consider the protocol hierarchy in exercise 14. Assume that for every i, where i ranges over $0 \ldots n-1$, processes rp[i] and tp[i] are assigned to computer i in a computer network. Draw the protocol stack in computer i.

18 (A Protocol Stack). Consider the protocol hierarchy in exercise 15. Assume that for every i, where i ranges over $0 \ldots n-1$, processes tp[i] and mp[i] are assigned to computer i in a computer network. Draw the protocol stack in computer i.

19 (File Transfer Hierarchy). Consider the file transfer hierarchy discussed in Sections 25.2, 25.3, and 25.4. Explain why message corruption is handled in the multiplexing layer (layer 1) while message loss and reorder are handled in the connection layer (layer 3) and the error recovery layer (layer 4).

20 (File Transfer Hierarchy without Message Corruption). Simplify the file transfer hierarchy discussed in Sections 25.2, 25.3, and 25.4 under the assumption that message corruption cannot occur.

21 (File Transfer Hierarchy without Message Corruption and Loss). Simplify the file transfer hierarchy discussed in Sections 25.2, 25.3, and 25.4 under the assumption that message corruption and loss cannot occur.

22 (File Transfer Hierarchy without Transmission Errors). Simplify the file transfer hierarchy discussed in Sections 25.2, 25.3, and 25.5 under the assumption that transmission errors cannot occur.

23 (Bidirectional File Transfer Hierarchy). Modify the file transfer hierarchy discussed in Sections 25.2, 25.3, and 25.4 such that files can be transferred in both directions between computers 1 and 2. Assume that each of the two computers has only one multiplexer process m. (Hint: Each of the two computers has the following nine processes: src, dst, sndr, rcvr, cp, cq, dp, dq, and m.)

24   (A Protocol Stack for the Bidirectional File Transfer Hierarchy). Draw the protocol stack of computer 1 for the bidirectional file transfer hierarchy in exercise 23.

25   (File Transfer Hierarchy in a Fully Connected Computer Network). Modify the file transfer hierarchy discussed in exercise 23 such that each computer can transfer files to any other computer in a fully connected computer network. In this network, each computer i has the following nine processes: src[i], dst[i], sndr[i], rcvr[i], cp[i], cq[i], dp[i], dq[i], and m[i].

26   (A Routing Protocol Hierarchy). Consider a protocol hierarchy that consists of three layers: a routing layer (rp[i: 0 . . n − 1]), a layer for maintaining topology information (tp[i: 0 . . n − 1]), and a multiplexing (mp[i: 0 . . n − 1]). Each process rp[i] has two lower processes tp[i] and mp[i], but has no upper processes. Each process tp[i] has an upper process rp[i] and a lower process mp[i]. Each process mp[i] has two upper processes rp[i] and tp[i] but has no lower processes. Each process rp[i] can generate or receive data messages and route them according to the random routing protocol in Section 13.2. For a process rp[i] to send a data(d, h) message to a neighboring process rp[j], rp[i] first sends a data(d, h, j) message to its lower process mp[i], which forwards a data(d, h) message to its neighboring process mp[j], which forwards a data(d, h, i) message to its upper process rp[j]. Every once in a while, process rp[i] sends a nxt message to process tp[i], which replies by sending back a new(v) message to rp[i], where v is the current value of array up in process tp[i]. The exchange of messages between the tp[i] processes and the mp[i] processes is as defined in exercise 15. Design the three protocol layers in this protocol hierarchy.

BIBLIOGRAPHY

Abdel-Wahab, H., and M. G. Gouda [1996], "Systems of Recall Broadcast," *Information Sciences*, Vol. 90, Nos. 1–4, pp. 1–18.

Aho, A. V., A. T. Dahbura, D. Lee, and M. U. Uyar [1988], "An Optimization Technique for Protocol Conformance Test Generation Based on UIO Sequences and Rural Chiense Postman Tours," in *Proceedings of the International Workshop on Protocol Specification, Testing, and Verification*, North-Holland, Amsterdam.

Arora, A., and M. G. Gouda [1993], "Closure and Convergence: A Foundation for Fault-Tolerant Computing," *IEEE Transactions on Software Engineering*, Vol. 19, No. 3, pp. 1015–1027.

Arora, A., T. Herman, and M. G. Gouda [1990], "Composite Routing Protocols," in *Proceedings of the IEEE Symposium on Parallel and Distributed Processing*.

Aziz, A., T. Markson, and H. Prafullchandra [1995], "Simple Key Management for Internet Protocol (SKIP)," unpublished manuscript.

Ballardie, T., P. Frances, and J. Crowcroft [1993], "Core Based Trees: An Architecture for Scalable Inter Domain Multicast Routing," in *Proceedings of the ACM SIGCOMM Symposium*.

Baran, P. [1964], "On Distributed Communication Networks," *IEEE Transactions on Communications Systems*, Vol. CS-12, No. 3, pp. 1–9.

Bartlett, K. A., R. A. Scantlebury, and P. T. Wilkinson [1969], "A Note on Reliable Full-Duplex Transmissions over Half-Duplex Lines," *Communications of the ACM*, Vol. 12, No. 5, pp. 260–265.

Beeforth, T. H., R. L. Grimsdale, F. Halsall, and D. J. Woolons [1972], "Proposed Organization for Packet-Switched Data Communication Networks," *Proceedings of the IEE*, Vol. 119, No. 12, pp. 1677–1682.

Bellman, R. E. [1957], *Dynamic Programming*, Princeton University Press, Princeton, NJ.

491

Bertsekas, D., and R. Gallager [1992], *Data Networks*, 2nd ed. Prentice-Hall, Englewood Cliffs, NJ.

Birman, K., A. Schiper, and P. Stephenson [1991], "Lightweight Causal and Atomic Group Multicast," *ACM Transactions on Computer Systems*, Vol. 9, No. 3, pp. 272–314.

Birrell, A., and B. Nelson [1984], "Implementing Remote procdeure Calls," *ACM Transactions on Computer systems*, Vol. 2, No. 1, pp. 39–59.

Bochmann, G. V. [1975], "Proving the Correctness of Communication Protocols," in *Proceedings of the ACM SIGCOMM/SIGOPS Interprocess Communication Workshop*.

Bochmann, G. V., and J. Gecsei [1977], "A Unified Method for the Specification and Verification of Protocols," in *Proceedings of the IFIP Congress*, pp. 229–234.

Bochmann, G. V., and C. A. Sunshine [1980], "Formal Methods in Communication Protocol Design," *IEEE Transactions on Communications*, Vol. COM-28, No. 4, pp. 624–631.

Brachman, B. J., and S. T. Chanson [1988], "Fragmentation in Store-and-Forward Message Transfer," *IEEE Communications Magazine*, Vol. 26, No. 7, pp. 18–27.

Brachman, B. J., and S. T. Chanson [1989], "A Hierarchical Solution for Application Level Store-and-Forward Deadlock Prevention," *Proceedings of the ACM SIGCOMM Symposium*, pp. 25–32.

Brinksma, E. [1988], "On the Design of Extended Lotos," Ph.D. Thesis, University of Twente, The Netherlands.

Brown, G. M., M. G. Gouda, and R. E. Miller [1989], "Block Acknowledgments: Redesigning the Window Protocol," in *Proceedings of the ACM SIGCOMM Symposium*. Also, in *IEEE Transactions on Communications*, Vol. COM-39, No. 4, pp. 524–532, 1991.

Burrows, M., M. Abaddi, and R. M. Needham [1990], "A Logic of Authentication," *ACM Transactions on Computer Systems*, Vol. 8, No. 1, pp. 18–36.

Cerf, G. V. [1977], "Specification of the Internet Transmission Control Program, TCP (Version 2)," available from DARPA/IPTO.

Cerf, V. G., and R. E. Khan [1974], "A Protocol for Packet Network Intercommunication," *IEEE Transactions on Communications*, Vol. COM-22, No. 5, pp. 637–648.

Cerf, V. G., and J. B. Postel [1978], "Specification of the Internet Transmission Control Program, TCP (Version 3)," available from USC/ISI.

Chan, W. Y. L., S. T. Vuong, and M. R. Ito [1989], "An Improved Protocol Test Generation Procedure Based on UIOS," in *Proceedings of the ACM SIGCOMM Symposium*, pp. 283–289.

Chandranmenon, G. P., and G. Varghese [1996], "Trading Packet Headers for Packet Processing," *IEEE/ACM Transactions on Networking*, Vol. 4, No. 2, pp. 141–152.

Chandy, K. M., and J. Misra [1988], *Parallel Program Design: A Foundation*, Addison-Wesley, Reading, MA.

Chang, J. M., and N. F. Maxemchuck [1984], "Reliable Broadcast Protocols," *ACM Transactions on Computer Systems*, Vol. 2, No. 3, pp. 251–273.

Clark, D. D. [1988], "The Design Philosophy of the DARPA Intertnet Protocols," in *Proceedings of the ACM SIGCOMM Symposium*.

Clark, D. D., M. Lambert, and L. Zhang [1988], "NETBLT: A High Throughput Transport Protocol," *ACM Computer Communication Review*, Vol. 17, No. 5, pp. 353–359.

Clarke, E. M., E. A. Emerson, and A. P. Sistla [1986], "Automatic Verification of Finite State Concurrent Systems Using Temporal Logic Specifications," *ACM Transactions on Programming Languages and Systems*, Vol. 8, No. 2, pp. 244–263.

Cobb, J. A., and M. G. Gouda [1997a], "The Request-Reply Family of Group Routing Protocols," *IEEE Transactions on Computers*, Vol. 46, No. 2, pp. 659–672.

Cobb, J. A., and M. G. Gouda [1997b], "Flow Theory," *IEEE/ACM Transactions on Networking*, Vol. 5, No. 5.

Cobb, J. A., M. G. Gouda, and A. El-Nahas [1996], "Time Shift Scheduling: Fair Scheduling of Flows in High-Speed Networks," in *Proceedings of the IEEE International Conference on Network Protocols*, pp. 6–13.

Comer, D. E. [1988], *Internetworking with TCP/IP:* Vol. I: *Principles, Protocols, and Arhitecture*, Prentice-Hall, Englewood Cliffs, NJ.

Comer, D. E., and D. L. Stevens [1993], *Internetworking with TCP/IP:* Vol. III, *Client–Server Programming and Applications* (BSD Socket Version), Prentice-Hall, Englewood Cliffs, NJ.

Dalal, Y. K., and R. M. Metcalfe [1978], " Reverse Path Forwarding of Broadcast Packets," *Communications of the ACM*, Vol. 12, No. 12.

Danthine, A. A. S. [1980], "Protocol Representation with Finite-State Models," *IEEE Transactions on Communications*, Vol. COM-28, pp. 632–643.

Day, J. [1980], "Terminal Protocols," *IEEE Transactions on Communications*, Vol. COM-28, pp. 585–593.

Deering, S., and D. Cheriton [1990], "Multicast Routing in Datagram Networks and Extended LANs," *ACM Transactions on Computer Systems*, Vol. 8, No. 2.

Deering, S., D. Estrin, D. Farinacci, V. Jacobson, C. G. Liu, and L. Wei [1994], "An Architecture for Wide Area Multicast Routing," *Proceedings of the ACM SIGCOMM Symposium*, pp. 126–135.

Demers, A., S. Keshav, and S. Shenker [1989], "Analysis and Simulation of a Fair Queueing Algorithm," *Proceedings of the ACM SIGCOMM Symposium*, pp. 1–12.

Diffie, W., and M. E. Hellman [1976], "New Directions in Cryptography," *IEEE Transactions on Information Theory*, Vol. IT-22, pp. 646–654.

Diffie, W., and M. E. Hellman [1979],"Privacy and Authentication," *Proceedings of the IEEE*, Vol. 67, No. 3, pp. 397–427.

Dijkstra, E. W. [1959], " A Note on Two Problems in Connection with Graphs," *Numerical Mathematics*, Vol. 1, pp. 269–271.

Dijkstra, E. W. [1975], "Guarded Commands, Non-determinacy, and Formal Derivation of Programs," *Communications of the ACM*, Vol. 18, No. 8, pp. 453–457.

Dijkstra, E. W. [1976], *A Discipline of Programming*, Prentice-Hall, Englewood Cliffs, NJ.

Farber, D. J., and K. C. Larson [1972], "The System Architecture of the Distributed Computer System—The Communications System," paper presented at the Symposium on Computer Networks, Polytechnic Institute of Brooklyn.

Fisher, M. J., N. A. Lynch, and M. S. Paterson [1985], "Impossibility of Distributed Consensus with One Faulty Process," *Journal of the ACM*, Vol. 32. No. 2, pp. 374–382.

Floyd, S., and V. Jacobson [1993], "Random Early Detection Gateways for Congestion Avoidance," *IEEE/ACM Transactions on Networking*, Vol. 1, No. 4, pp. 397–413.

Ford, H., and D. R. Fulkerson [1962], *Flows in Networks*, Princeton University Press, Princeton, NJ.

Frances, N. [1986], *Fairness*, Springer-Verlag, New York.

Fraser, A. G. [1983], "Towards a Universal Data Transport System," *IEEE* Journal on Selected Areas in Communications, Vol. 1, No. 5, pp. 803–816.

Gerla, M., and L. Kleinrock [1980], "Flow Control: A Comparative Survey," *IEEE Transactions on Communications*, Vol. COM-28, No. 4, pp. 553–574.

Gien, M. [1978], "A File Transfer Protocol (FTP)," *Computer Networks*, Vol. 2, pp. 312–319.

Golestani, S. J. [1994], "A Self-Clocked Fair Queing Scheme for Broadband Applications," *Proceedings of IEEE INFOCOM*, pp. 636-646.

Gong, F., and G. Parulkar [1996], "An Application-Oriented Error Control Scheme for High-Speed Networks," *IEEE/ACM Transactions on Networking*, Vol. 4, No. 5, pp. 669–683.

Gouda, M. G. [1977], "Protocol Machines: Towards a Logical Theory of Communication Protocols," Ph.D. Thesis, Department of Computer Science, the University of Waterloo, Ontario, Canada.

Gouda, M. G. [1985], "On a Simple Protocol Whose Proof Isn't: The State Machine Approach," *IEEE Transactions on Communications*, Vol. COM-33, No. 4, pp. 380–382.

Gouda, M. G. [1992], "The Two-Dimensional Window Protocol," in *Proceedings of the International Symposium on Protocol Specification, Testing, and Verification, North-Holland, Amesterdam*, pp. 365–379.

Gouda, M. G. [1993], "Protocol Verification Made Simple," *Computer Networks and ISDN Systems*, Vol. 25, pp. 969–980.

Gouda, M. G. [1995a], "The Triumph and Tribulation of System Stabilization," in *Proceedings of the International Workshop on Distributed Algorithms, Lecture Notes in Computer Science*, Vo. 972, Springer-Verlag, Berlin.

Gouda, M. G. [1995b], "Stabilizing Client/Server Protocols without the Tears," in *Proceedings of the International Conference on Formal Description Techniques*.

Gouda, M. G., and T. Herman [1991], "Adaptive Programming," *IEEE Transactions on Software Engineering*, Vol. 17, No. 9, pp. 911–921.

Gouda, M. G., and N. Multari [1991], "Stabilizing Communication Protocols," *IEEE Transactions on Computers*, Vol. 40, No. 4, pp. 448–458.

Gouda, M. G., A. N. Netravali, and K. Sabnani [1995], "A Periodic State Exchange Protocol and Its Verification," *IEEE Transactions on Communications*, Vol. COM-43, No. 9, pp. 2475–2484.

Green, P. [1986], "Protocol Conversion," *IEEE Transactions on Communications*, Vol. COM-34, pp. 257–268.

Gries, D. [1981], *The Science of Programming*, Springer-Verlag, New York.

Gunther, K. D. [1981], "Prevention of Deadlocks in Packet-Switched Data Transport Systems," *IEEE Transactions on Communications*, Vol. COM-29, No. 4, pp. 512–524.

Hailpern, B. T. [1980], "Verifying Concurrent Processes Using Temporal Logic, Ph.D. Thesis, Stanford University, California. Published as *Lecture Notes in Computer Science*, Vol. 129, Springer-Verlag, Berlin, 1981.

Hailpern, B. T. [1985], "A Simple Protocol Whose Proof Isn't," *IEEE Transactions on Communications*, Vol. COM-33, No. 4, pp. 330–337.

Halsall, F. [1992], *Data Communications, Computer Networks, and Open Systems*. Addison-Wesley, Reading, MA.

Hamming, R. W. [1950], "Error Detecting and Error Correcting Codes," *Bell System Technical* Journal, Vol. 29, pp. 147–160.

Hamming, R. W. [1986], *Coding and Information Theory*, Prentice-Hall, Englewood Cliffs, NJ.

Hayes, J. F. [1978], "An Adaptive Technique for Local Distribution," *IEEE Transactions on Communications*, Vol. COM-26, No. 8, pp. 1178–1186.

Hayes, J. F. [1984], *Modelling and Analysis of Computer Communications Networks*, Plenum, New York.

Hoare, C. A. R. [1984], *Communicating Sequential Processes*, Prentice-Hall International, London.

Holzmann, G. J. [1979], "Coordination Problems in Multiprocessing Systems," Ph.D. Thesis, Delft University of Technology, The Netherlands.

Holzmann, G. J. [1982], "A Theory of Protocol Validation," *IEEE Transactions on Computers*, Vol. C-31, No. 8, pp. 730–738.

Holzmann, G. J. [1984], "The Pandora System—An Interactive System for the Design of Data Communication Protocols," *Computer Networks*, Vol. 8, No. 2, pp. 71–81.

Holzmann, G. J. [1988], "An Improved Protocol Reachability Analysis Technique," *Software Practice and Experience*, Vol. 18, No. 2, pp. 137–161.

Holzmann, G. J. [1991], *Design and Validation of Computer Protocols*, Prentice-Hall, Englewood Cliffs, NJ.

Hopper, A., and R. C. Williamson [1987], "Design and Use of an Integrated Cambridge Ring," in *Advances in Local Area Networks*, K. Kummerle, F. Tobagi, and J. Limb, Eds., IEEE Press, New York.

Huffamn, D. A. [1952], "A Method for the Construction of Mininmal Redundancy Codes," *Proceedings of the IRE*, Vol. 40, No. 9, pp. 1098–1101.

Huitema, C. [1995], *Routing in the Internet*, Prentice-Hall, Englewood Cliffs, NJ.

IEEE [1989], "Token Ring Access Method," IEEE 802.5, Institute of Electrical and Electronics Engineers, New York.

IEEE [1990], "Token Passing Bus Access Method and Physical Layer Specification," IEEE 802.4, Institute of Electrical and Electronics Engineers, New York.

Jacobson, V. [1988], "Congestion Avoidance and Control," *ACM Computer Communication Review*, Vol. 18, No. 4, pp. 314–329.

Jain, R. [1994], *FDDI Hanbook: High-Speed Networking Using Fiber and Other Media*, Addison-Wesley, Reading, MA.

Kamoun, F. [1976], "Design Considerations for Large Computer Communications Networks," Ph.D. Thesis, Computer Science Department, University of California at Los Angeles.

Karp, R. M., and R. E. Miller [1969], "Parallel Program Schemata," *Journal of Computer and System Sciences, Volume 3*, pp. 147–195.

Kaufman, C., R. Perlman, and M. Speciner [1995], *Network Security: Private Communication in a Public World*, Prentice-Hall, Englewood Cliffs, NJ.

Kermani, P., and Kleinrock, L. [1979], "Virtual Cut-Through: A New Computer Communication Switching Technique," *Computer Networks*, Vol. 3, pp. 267–286.

Keshav, S. [1997], *An Engineering Approach to Computer Networking: ATM Networks, the Internet, and the Telephone Network*, Addison-Wesley, Reading, MA.

Khan, R. E. [1977], "The Organization of Computer Resources into a Packet Radio Network," *IEEE Transactions on Communications*, Vol. COM-25, No. 1, pp. 169–178.

Khan, R. E. [1979], "The Introduction of Packet Satellite Communications," *Proceedings of the IEEE National Telecommunication Conference*, pp. 45.1.1–45.1.8.

Khanna, A., and J. Zinky [1989], "The Revised ARPANET Routing Metric," in *Proceedings of the ACM SIGCOMM Symposium.*

Kleinrock, L. [1964], *Communication Nets,* Dover, New York.

Kleinrock, L., and F. Kamoun [1977], "Hierarchical Routing for Large Networks," *Computer Networks,* Vol. 1, No. 3, pp. 155–174.

Kleinrock, L., and F. Kamoun [1980], "Optimal Clustering Structures for Hierarchical Topological Design of Large Computer Networks," *Networks,* Vol. 10, pp. 221–248.

Knuth, D. E. [1981], "Verification of Link Level Protocols," *BIT,* Vol. 21, pp. 31–36.

Kung, H. T., and A. Chapman [1993], "The Flow-Controlled Virtual Channels Proposal for ATM Networks," in *Proceedings of the IEEE International Conference on Network Protocols,* pp. 116–127.

Lam, S. S. [1980], "A Carrier Sense Multiple Access Protocol for Local Networks," *Computer Networks,* Vol. 4, No. 1.

Lam, S. S., and A. U. Shankar [1994], "A Theory of Interfaces and Modules I–Composition Theorem," *IEEE Transactions on Software Engineering,* Vol. 20, No. 1, pp. 55–71.

Lam, S. S., and G. G. Xie [1997], "Group Priority Scheduling," *IEEE/ACM Transactions on Networking,* Vol. 5, No. 2.

Lamport, L. [1978], "Time, Clocks, and the Ordering of Events in a Distributed System," *Communications of the ACM,* Vol. 21, No. 7, pp. 558–565.

Lampson, B., et al. [1992], "Authentication in Distributed Systems: Theory and Practice," *ACM Transactions on Computer Systems,* Vol. 10, No. 4, pp. 265 -310.

Lee, D., and M. Yannakakis [1994], "Testing Finite State Machines: Stste Identification and Verification," *IEEE Transactions on Computers,* Vol. 43, No. 4, pp. 306–320.

Lee, D., and M. Yannakakis [1996], "Principles and Methods of Testing Finite State Machines—A Survey," *Proceedings of the IEEE,* Vol. 84, No. 8, pp. 1090–1123.

Le Gall, D. [1991], "MPEG: A Video Compression Standard for Multimedia Applications," *Communications of the ACM,* Vol. 34, No. 1, pp. 46–58.

Liu, H., and R. E. Miller [1996], "Generalized Fair Reachability Analysis for Cyclic Protocol Validation," *IEEE Transactions on Networking,* Vol. 4, No. 2, pp. 192–204.

Liu, M. T. [1978], "Distributed Loop Computer Networks," in M. C. Yovits, Ed., *Advances in Computers,* Academic Press, New York, pp. 163–221.

Liu, M. T. [1989], "Protocol Engineering," in *Advances in Computers,* Vol. 28, pp. 75–195.

Liu, M. T. [1996], "Network Interconnection and Protocol Conversion," in *Advances in Computers,* Academic Press, Vol. 42, pp. 119–239.

Liu, M. T., W. Hilal, and B. H. Groomes [1982], "Performance Evaluation of Channel Access Protocols for Local Computer Networks," in *Proceedings of the COMPCON Fall Conference,* pp. 417–426.

Lundy, G. M., and R. E. Miller [1991], "Specification and Analysis of a Data Transfer Protocol Using Systems of Communicating Machines," *Distributed Computing,* Vol. 5, No. 3, pp. 145–157.

Lynch, N., Y. Mansour, and A. Fekete [1988], "The Data Link Layer: Two Impossibility Results," in *Proceedings of the ACM Symposium on Principles of Distributed Computing,* pp. 149–170.

Lynch, W. C. [1968], "Reliable Full-Duplex File Transmission over Half-Duplex Telephone Lines," *Communications of the ACM,* Vol. 18, No. 6, pp. 407–410.

Magnee, F., A. Endrizzi, and J. Day [1979], "Survey of Terminal Protocols," *Computer Networks*, Vol. 3, pp. 299–314.

Manna, Z., and A. Pnueli [1991], *The Temporal Logic of Reactive and Concurrent Systems*, Springer-Verlag, New York.

Maxemchuk, N. F., and M. El-Zarki [1990], "Routing and Flow Control in High Speed Wide Area Networks," *Proceedings of the IEEE*, Vol. 78, No. 1, pp. 204–221.

Maxemchuck, N. F., and K. Sabnani [1987], "Probabilistic Verification of Communication Protocols," in *Proceedings of the International Workshop on Protocol Specification, Testing, and Verification*, North-Holland, Amsterdam, pp. 307–320.

McGuire, T. M. [1994], "Implemeneting Abstract Protocols in C," M.A. Thesis, Department of Computer Sciences, the University of Texas at Austin. Also Technical Report TR 96–31, Department of Computer Sciences, University of Texas at Austin, 1996.

McQuillan, J. M., I. Richer, and E. C. Rosen [1980], "The New Routing Algorithm for the ARPANET," *IEEE Transactions on Communications*, Vol. 28, No. 5, pp. 253–261.

Merlin, P., and G. V. Bochmann [1983], "On the Construction of Submodule Specifications and Communication Protocols," *ACM Transactions on Programming Languages and Systems*, pp. 1–25.

Merlin, P. M., and P. J. Schweitzer [1980a], "Deadlock Avoidance—Store-and-Forward Deadlock," *IEEE Transactions on Communications*, Vol. COM-28, No. 3, pp. 343–354.

Merlin, P. M., and P. J. Schweitzer [1980b], "Deadlock Avoidance in Store-and-Forward Networks–Other Deadlock Types," *IEEE Transactions on Communications*, Vol. COM-28, No. 3, pp. 355–360.

Miller, R. E., and S. Paul [1994], "Structural Analysis of Protocol Specifications and Generation of Maximal Fault Coverage Conformance Test Sequences," *IEEE/ACM Transactions on Networking*, Vol. 2, No. 5, pp. 457–470.

Milner, R. [1980], *A Calculus for Communicating Systems, Lecture Notes in Computer Science*, Springer-Verlag, Berlin.

Mockapetris, P. [1987], Ed., "Domain Names—Implementation and Specification," RFC-035.

Mockapetris, P., and K. J. Dunlap [1988], "Development of the Domain Name System," in *Proceedings of the ACM SIGCOMM Symposium*.

Morris, R., and K. Thompson [1979], "Password Security: A Case Histroy," *Communications of the ACM*, Vol. 22, pp. 594–597.

Needham, R. M., and M. D. Schroeder [1978], "Using Encryption for Authentication in Large Networks of Computers," *Communications of the ACM, Vol 12, No. 12*, pp. 993–999.

Nelson, M. [1992], *The Data Compression Book*, M&T Books, San Mateo, CA.

Netravali, A. N., W. R. Roome, and K. Sabnani [1990], "Design and Implementation of a High-Speed Transport Protocol," *IEEE Transactions on Communications*, Vol. COM-38, No. 11.

Owicki, S., and D. Gries [1976], "An Axiomatic Proof Technique for Parallel Programs I," *Acta Informatica*, Vol. 6, No. 1, pp. 319–340.

Owicki, S., and L. Lamport [1982], "Proving Liveness Properties of Concurrent Programs," *ACM Transactions on Computer Systems and Languages*, Vol. 4, No. 3, pp. 455–495.

Partridge, C. [1994], *Gigabit Networking*, Addison-Wesley, Reading MA.

Perkins, C. [1993], "Providing Continuous Network Access to Mobile Hosts Using TCP/IP," *Computer Networks and ISDN Systems,* Vol. 26, pp. 357–370.

Perlman, R. [1984], "An Algorithm for Distributed Computation of a Spanning Tree," in *Proceedings of the Data Communication Symposium.*

Perlman, R. [1993], *Interconnections: Bridges and Routers,* Addison-Wesley, Reading, MA.

Peterson, L. L., and B. S. Davie [1996], Computer Networks: A Systems Approach, Morgan Kaufmann, San Francisco, CA.

Peterson, W. W., and D. T. Brown [1961], "Cyclic Codes for Error Detection," *Proceedings of the IRE,* Vol. 49, pp. 228–235.

Pierce, J. [1972], "How Far Can Data Loops Go?," *IEEE Transactions on Communications,* Vol. COM-20, No. 6, pp. 527–530.

Plummer, D. C., Ed. [1982], "An Ethernet Address Resolution Protocol," RFC 826.

Postel, J. B. [1980a], "Internetwork Protocol Approaches," *IEEE Transactions on Communications,* Vol. 28, No. 4, pp. 604–611.

Postel, J. B., Ed. [1980b], "User Datagram Protocol," RFC 768.

Postel, J. B., Ed. [1981a], "Internet Protocol," RFC 791.

Postel, J. B., Ed. [1981b], "Internet Control Message Protocol," RFC 792.

Postel, J. B., Ed. [1981c], "Transmission Control Protocol," RFC 793.

Prosser, R. T. [1962a], "Routing Procedures in Communication Networks—Part I," *IRE Transactions on Communication Systems,* Vol. 10, No. 12, pp. 322–329.

Prosser, R. T. [1962b], "Routing Procedures in Communication Networks—Part II," *IRE Transactions on Communication Systems,* Vol. 10, No. 12, pp. 329–335.

Ramakrishnan, K., and R. Jain [1990], "A Binary Feedback Scheme for Congestion Avoidance in Computer Networks with a Connectionless Network Layers," *ACM Transactions on Computer Systems,* Vol. 8, No. 2, pp. 158–181.

Rivest, R. L., Ed. [1992], "The MD5 Message Digest Algorithm," RFC 1320.

Rivest, R. L., A. Shamir, and L. Adleman [1978], "On a Method for Obtaining Digital Signatures and Public Key Cryptosystems," *Communications of the ACM,* Vol. 21, No. 2, pp. 120–126.

Roberts, L. [1972], "Extensions of Packet Communication Technology to a Hand Held Personal Terminal," in *Proceedings of the AFIPS Spring Joint Computer Conference.*

Rosen, E. C. [1980], "The Updating Protocol of ARPANET's New Routing Algorithm," *Computer Networks,* Vol. 4, pp. 11–19.

Saadawi, T. N., M. H. Ammar, and A. Elhakeem [1994], *Fundamentals of Telecommunication Networks,* Wiley, New York.

Sabnani, K., and A. Dahbura [1988], "A Protocol Test generation Procedure," *Computer Networks and ISDN Systems,* Vol. 15, pp. 285–297.

Sackett, G. C. [1993], *IBM's Token Ring Networking Handbook,* McGraw-Hill, New York.

Saltzer, J. H. [1978], "On Digital Signatures," *Operating System Review,* Vol. 12, pp. 12–14.

Saltzer, J. H. K. T. Pogran, and D. D. Clark [1983], "Why a Ring?" *Computer Networks,* Vol. 7, pp. 223–231.

Schicker, P., and A. Duenki [1978], "The Virtual Terminal Definition," *Computer Networks,* Vol. 2, pp. 429–441.

Schneier, B. [1994], *Applied Cryptography: Protocols, Algorithms, and Source Code in C,* Wiley, New York.

Schneider, M. [1993], "Self-Stabilization," *ACM Computing Surveys*, Vol. 25, No. 1.

Schwartz, M. [1987], *Telecommunication Networks: Protocols, Modelling, and Analysis*, Addison-Wesley, Reading, MA.

Schwartz, M., and T. E. Stern [1980], "Routing Techniques Used in Computer Communications Networks," *IEEE Transactions on Communications*, Vol. COM-28, No. 4, pp. 265–278.

Shankar, A. U. [1989], "Verified Data Transfer Protocols with Variable Control," *ACM Transactions on Computer Systems*, Vol. 7, No. 3, pp. 281–316.

Shankar, A. U., and D. Lee [1995]. "Mininmum Latency Transport Protocols with Modulo-N Incarnation Numbers," *IEEE/ACM Transactions on Networking*, Vol. 3, No. 3, pp. 255–268.

Shannon, C. [1949], "Communication Theory of Secrecy Systems," *Bell System Journal*, Vol. 28, pp. 379–423.

Shoch, J. F. [1978], "Internetwork Naming, Addressing, and Routing," in *Proceedings of the COMPCON Fall Conference*, pp. 72–79.

Shreedhar, M., and G. Varghese [1996], "Efficient Fair Queuing Using Deficit Round Robin," *IEEE/ACM Transactions on Networking*, Vol. 4, No. 3, pp. 375–385.

Sidhu, D., and T. Leung [1989], "Formal Methods for Protocol Testing: A Detailed Study," *IEEE Transactions on Software Engineering*, Vol. 15, No. 4, pp. 413–426.

Simmons, G. J. [1979], "Symmetric and Asymmetric Encryption," *ACM Computing Surveys*, Vol. 11, pp. 304–330.

Sloane, N. J. A. [1975], *A Short Course on Error Correcting Codes*, Springer-Verlag, Berlin.

Spragins, J. D., J. H. Hammond, and K. Pawlinkowski [1991], *Telecommunications, Protocols, and Design*, Addison-Wesley, Reading MA.

Stallings, W. [1993], *Local and Metropolitan Area Networks*, 4th ed., Macmillan, New York.

Stallings, W. [1994], *Data and Computer Communications*, 4th ed., Macmillan, New York.

Steenstrup, M. [1995], *Routing in Communication Networks*, Prentice-Hall, Englewood Cliffs, NJ.

Steiner, J. G., C. Neuman, and J. I. Schiller [1988], "Kerberos: An Authentication Service for Open Network Systems," in *Proceedings of USENIX Winter Conference*, pp. 191–202.

Stenning, N. V. [1976], "Data Transfer Protocol," *Computer Networks*, Vol. 1, pp. 99–110.

Stevens, W. R. [1990], *Unix Network Programming*, Prentice-Hall, Englewood Cliffs, NJ.

Stevens, W. R. [1994], *TCP/IP Illustrated*, Vol. I: *Tthe Protocols*, Prentice-Hall, Englewood Cliffs, NJ.

Steves, D. H., C. Edmondson-Yurkanan, and M. G. Gouda [1997], "Properties of Secure Transactions Protocols," *Computer Networks and ISDN Systems*, Vol. 29, 1997.

Sunshine, C. A. [1977], "Source Routing in Computer Networks," *ACM Computer Communications Review*, Vol. 7, No. 1, pp. 29–33.

Sunshine, C. A., and Y. Dalal [1978], "Connection Management in Transport Protocols," *Computer Networks*, Vol. 2, pp. 454–473.

Tanenbaum, A. S. [1981], *Computer Networks*, Prentice-Hall, Englewood Cliffs, NJ.

Tantawy, A., Ed. [1994], *High Performance Networks: Technology and Protocols*, Kluwer, Boston, Massachusetts.

Teraoka, F., Y. Yokte, Y., and M. Tokoro [1993], "Host Migration Transparency in IP Networks," *Computer Communication Reviews*, Vol. 23, pp. 45–65.

Thekkath, C. A., and H. M. Levy [1993], "Limits to Low-Latency Communication on High-Speed Network," *ACM Transactions on Computer Systems*, Vol. 11, No. 2, pp. 179–203.

Turner, J. [1986], "New Directions in Communications (or Which Way the Information Age?)," *IEEE Communications Magazine*, Vol. 25, No. 10, pp. 8–15.

Ural, H., and R. L. Probert [1986], "Step-Wise Validation of Communication Protocols and Services," *Computer Networks and ISDN Systems*, Vol. 11, No. 3, pp. 367–383.

Vissers, C., and L. Logrippo [1985], "The Importance of the Service Concept in the Design of Data Communication protocols," in *Proceedings of the International Workshop on Protocol Specification, Testing, and Verification*, North-Holland, Amsterdam, pp. 3–17.

Wallace, G. K. [1991], "The JPEG Still Picture Compression Standard," *Communications of the ACM*, Vol. 34, No. 1, pp. 30–44.

Walrand, J. [1991], *Communication Networks: A First Course*, Irwin, Boston, MA.

Watson, R. W. [1980], "Interprocess Communication: Interface and End-to-End (Transport) Protocol Design Issues," in *Distributed Systems: An Advanced Course*, Springer-Verlag, Berlin.

Welch, T. [1984], "A Technique for High Performance Data Compression," *IEEE Computer*, Vol. 17, No. 6, pp. 8–19.

West, C. H. [1986], "Protocol Validation by Random State Exploration," *Proceedings of the International Workshop on Protocol Specification, Testing, and Verification*, North-Holland, Amsterdam, pp. 233–242.

Wirth, N. [1971], "The Programming Language Pascal," *Acta Informatica, Volume 1*, pp. 35–63.

Woo, T. Y. C., and S. S. Lam [1992], "Authentication for Distributed Systems," *Computer*, Vol. 25, No. 1.

Zafiropulo, P., C. H. West, H. Rudin, D. D. Cowan, and D. Brand [1980], "Toward Analyzing and Synthesizing Protocols," *IEEE Transactions on Communications*, Vol. COM-28, No. 4, pp. 651–661.

Zhang, H. and D. Ferrari [1994], "Rate-Controlled Service Disciplines," *Journal of High-Speed Networking*, Vol. 3, No. 4, pp. 389–412.

Zhang, L. [1991], "Virtual Clock: A New Traffic Control Algorithm for Packet Switching Networks," *ACM Transactions on Computer Systems*, Vol. 9, No. 2, pp. 101–124.

Zimmermann, P. R. [1995], *The Official PGP User's Guide*, MIT Press, Cambridge, MA.

Ziv, J., and A Lempel [1977], "A Universal Algorithm for Sequential data Compression," *IEEE Transactions on Information Theory*, Vol. 23, No. 3, pp. 337–343.

Ziv, J., and A Lempel [1978], "Compression of Individual Sequences Via Variable-Rate Coding," *IEEE Transactions on Information Theory*, Vol. 24, No. 5, pp. 530–536.

INDEX FOR THE ABSTRACT PROTOCOL NOTATION

INDEX FOR
FUNDAMENTAL PROTOCOLS

INDEX FOR
INTERNET PROTOCOLS

Printed in the United States
By Bookmasters